THE
BATTLE
FILE

Sidney Shail

An Air-Britain Publication

Published in Great Britain by

Air-Britain (Historians) Ltd
12 Lonsdale Gardens, Tunbridge Wells, Kent

Sales Dept: 5 Bradley Road, Upper Norwood
London SE19 3NT

Correspondence to:

J.J.Halley, 5 Walnut Tree Road,
Shepperton, Middlesex, TW17 ORW
and not to the Tunbridge Wells address

ISBN 0 85130 225 4

Printed by
Hillman Printers (Frome) Ltd
Frome
Somerset

Cover painting by Alan Vernon

CONTENTS

INTRODUCTION

Derided by many as as an unfortunate failure because of its many defects, the Fairey Battle bomber was manufactured in large quantities and served in many capacities before and during World War Two. The Battle was originally designed as a single-engined light day bomber to a 1932 specification and it equipped seventeen squadrons of the Royal Air Force by 1939. It was obsolescent when it first saw war service in 1939 in its designed role as a day bomber and the Battle squadrons suffered crippling losses in the Battle of France in 1940. The Battle was slow and lacking in firepower and was undoubtedly an operational failure, some would say an operational disaster. However, in 1939 we had little else and there was no option but to use it when the need arose. Despite the Battle's appalling record in France, production continued until late 1940 and a total of over 2,000 were built. The vast majority of aircrews who fought in France were regular officers, NCOs and airmen who had joined the RAF in peacetime. They showed outstanding courage in the chaos and confusion of the war in France and a high proportion of them were killed or missing in action. The loss of these experienced and gallant crews was one which the RAF could ill afford as it expanded into its huge wartime size. The first RAF Victoria Crosses of World War II were awarded posthumously to two members of a Battle crew in an attack on bridges at Maastricht.

After the fall of France, during the 1940 invasion alarm, the Battle was used for a short time as a night bomber operating against the Channel invasion ports. Two Polish squadrons were introduced to operations on Battles during this period. Two squadrons were used for largely uneventful anti-invasion patrols along the coast of Northern Ireland and one squadron performed a similar function in Iceland. The South African Air Force used Battles in the campaign in East Africa, operating them successfully against the Italians in Somaliland and Ethiopia, despite the extremely unfavourable conditions of climate and terrain.

The Battle was a docile and ruggedly strong aeroplane and it was much used as a trainer in the Commonwealth Air Training Plan. Over 700 were sent to Canada and over 300 to Australia. A further 200 were sent to South Africa to be used in the separate Joint Air Training Scheme. After arrival in Canada, some Battles were fitted with gun turrets for gunnery training. Although a modified version of the Battle was produced with twin cockpit canopies, most had the single long canopy of the Battle bomber. Many Battles were also used as trainers in the UK. A target-towing version of the Battle was produced and was used for towing drogues for gunnery training both in this country and abroad.

Because of its general character and tough construction the Battle was particularly suitable for use as an engine test bed and several were used for this purpose. Some Battles were used by various RAF specialised units as general utility aircraft and others were used by operational squadrons as communications aircraft. Battles were sold and exported to several countries, including Greece and Belgium, where they operated against invading Axis forces.

Some members of the Air Staff and others foresaw the operational limitations of the Battle and expressed their misgivings before it went into full scale production. The Battle, however, was a key part of the Government's RAF Expansion Programmes and despite these reservations it went into quantity production and continued to be ordered long after it was known to be obsolete. Political expediency was in large measure, though not entirely, responsible for this. It helped to convince those politicians and members of the public who saw strength in numbers, regardless of performance, that something was being done about seeking parity with Germany in the air. The reactions of those who flew in the Battle varied from affection to outright hostility. Nearly sixty years after the Battle received its baptism of fire it still has its protagonists and its antagonists. The purpose of this book is to describe the life span of the Battle - its conception, its production, its operational career and its many non-operational uses.

K4303, the prototype Battle, at an early stage in its career, poses for the photographer. (Charles E Brown)

CHAPTER 1. SPECIFICATIONS AND TENDERS

Specification P.27/32

The Fairey Battle light bomber was conceived in 1932 when the Air Ministry decided that a new aircraft was needed to replace the Hawker Hart. There were many frustrations and delays between this decision being taken and the first flight of the prototype in 1936. The concept of the light day bomber as a tactical bombing and reconnaissance aircraft had been firmly established by the Royal Flying Corps in the First World War and had been continued by the Royal Air Force after it was formed in 1918. Despite the heavy losses of light bombers in the First World War, the Air Ministry still relied on this weapon as an essential part of its armoury. The specification for the Battle represented the updating of the light biplane day bomber to what were then advanced standards. In 1932 the perception of the multi-gun fighter with a very large margin of speed over hostile bombers was just beginning to take shape. The menace posed by such fighters to the lightly-armed day bomber was not foreseen and when it materialised, large scale production of the Battle was in full flow. The Battle's predecessor, the Hart, was a successful single-engined, two-seat biplane bomber which first flew in June 1928 and was in service with the RAF from 1930 to 1939. The advent of the cantilever-wing metal

monoplane, together with the much higher-powered engines which were becoming available, had made the old fabric-covered biplanes obsolete.

The Air Ministry decided that the new light bomber should be a single-engined monoplane with a crew of two and capable of carrying more bombs for a longer distance than the Hart. In August 1932, after initial discussions with manufacturers, the Director of Technical Development was asked to prepare a specification which included these basic requirements. In their initial design study, Fairey proposed a small single-engined monoplane bomber with a wingspan of 47 feet, a length of 38 feet and a crew of two. The engine would be Fairey's projected P12 Prince liquid-cooled engine. Bombs would be carried internally in the wing centre section and the undercarriage would be retractable. Towards the end of 1932, the Air Staff complained to the DTD about the delay in starting the preparation of the specification; this brought a promise that the work would be started immediately and the specification was agreed in April 1933.

Specification P.27/32 was contained in a 24-page document dated 12 April 1933. It called for a single-engined day bomber with the following main requirements:

(a) The bare weight of the aircraft (i.e. tare weight less the weight of fixed equipment) was not to exceed 6,300 lb.

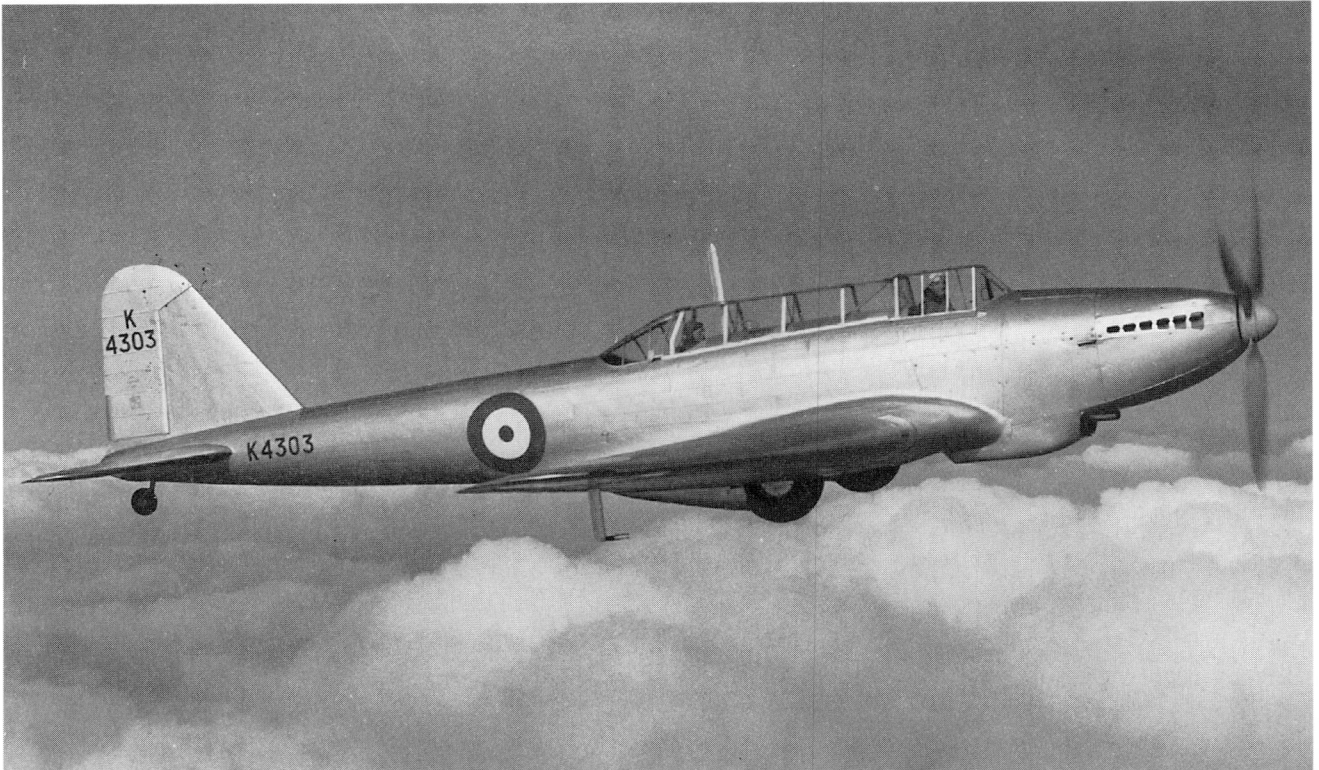

K4303 shows its sleek lines for the camera. The semi-retracted wheels were intended to protect the bottom of the fuselage in the event of a belly-landing. (via P Jarrett)

(b) The crew of two was to consist of a pilot and an observer, with their cockpits close enough together for written communications to be passed and, if possible, for conversation without voice pipes, though voice pipes were to be installed in any event. The observer was to perform the additional duties of Lewis gunner, W/T operator and bomb aimer. The crew positions were to be free from draughts and heating was to be provided by waste heat from the engine or cooling system. Both cockpits were to be properly shielded from the wind.

(c) Gun armament was to consist of a fixed Vickers or Lewis gun for the use of the pilot and a movable Lewis gun firing aft for the use of the observer. An early Air Ministry minute on Specification P.27/32 requirements described the fitting of a front gun as a "justifiable concession" for day bombers, commenting that it would rarely be used by aircraft flying in formation. It seems that without this somewhat reluctant assent, the Battle would have gone to war with only one machine gun. The observer's gun was to be situated aft of the pilot's cockpit and this cockpit was also to house the W/T and navigation equipment. A separate prone position was to be provided for the observer for use when he was acting as bomb aimer.

(d) The bomb load was to consist of any of the following, or any combination of them, up to 1,250 lb.

    eight 20-lb bombs
    eight 50-lb Low Capacity (LC) bombs
    eight 100-lb Anti Submarine (AS) bombs
    eight 112-lb Royal Laboratory (RL) bombs
    eight 120-lb General Purpose (GP) bombs
    four 250-lb. RL, GP or AS or Semi-Armour-Piercing (SAP) bombs

two 500-lb GP, AS or SAP bombs.

An amendment to the Specification stated the obvious requirement that the combination of bombs must be one for which the aircraft's bomb carriers were suitable.

(e) The engine was to be any suitably-rated British engine which had passed a 100-hour Service Type Test within one year of the Specification P.27/32 tenders being submitted. The airscrew could be either wood or metal.

(f) Fuel carried was to be sufficient for a range of 600 miles at 10,000 feet at normal rpm plus half-an-hour at maximum power at sea level. The fuel tanks were to be accommodated in the wings or fuselage.

(g) The maximum speed at 10,000 feet was to be not less than 195 mph, the service ceiling was to be not less than 22,000 feet and the landing speed was not to exceed 65 mph.

(h) Parts of the aircraft contributing to its strength in flight were to be of metal. Fabric could be used for mainplane and other coverings.

(i) The Specification also dealt with routine matters such as provision for testing by the Director of Technical Development, examination of the aircraft, test flights and maintenance.

Shortly after its issue the Air Ministry modified Specification P.27/32 to make it comparable with the B.9/32 Medium Bomber Specification. The B.9/32 Specification was for a very different aircraft. It resulted in the twin-engined Vickers Wellington and Handley Page Hampden bombers, and the issue of comparability complicated the P.27/32 project. The main amendment to Specification P.27/32 was for an increase in the aircraft's normal range and in its long range. The required normal range was increased to 720 miles at 15,000 feet and the maximum speed was to be not less than

The prototype Battle before it received RAF roundels

195 mph at 15,000 feet. The bomb load and range requirement was finally set at 1,000 lb for 1,000 miles. In all, 12 corrigenda to the original Specification P.27/32 were issued between October 1933 and May 1936.

When the definitive Specification P.27/32 was issued in 1933, it was obvious to Fairey that a larger aircraft than they had originally proposed would be needed. The Fairey management tried to convince the Air Ministry that a single engined aircraft to the P.27/32 Specification would be of inferior performance and they argued strongly for a twin-engined design. This would have given a higher speed and longer range. A Fairey General Arrangement drawing dated October 1933 shows a projected aircraft similar in shape to the Battle but with an orthodox twin-engined layout. The dimensions quoted were very like those of the Battle, the wingspan being two feet greater and the length one foot greater. The Air Ministry rejected this proposal and insisted on a single-engined aircraft in accordance with Specification P.27/32. Fairey's response was to submit several tender proposals covering single- and twin-engined types of aircraft, all to be powered by the Company's P12 Prince engines. The only Fairey tenders to receive consideration were those based on single-engined aircraft.

Tenders

There were many aircraft manufacturers in the UK in the 1930s and tenders to Specification P.27/32 were invited from twelve companies. The invitation was issued in June 1933 and the closing date for the receipt of tenders was 26 September 1933. Designs were submitted by eight manufacturers: Armstrong Whitworth, Boulton Paul, Bristol, Fairey,

Gloster, Hawker, Vickers and Westland.

Of these, all except Boulton Paul submitted tenders. The tenders for the prototype were analysed in November 1933, with details as follows:

Manufacturer	Price	Delivery	Proposed Engine
A Whitworth	£14,000	15-18months	A S Tiger
Bristol	£11,500	10 months	Bristol Perseus
Fairey (3 types)	£10,500	12 months	Fairey Prince
Gloster(2 types)	£15,400	12 months	A S Tiger
	£18,750	12 months	R-R PV (Merlin)
Hawker (2 types)	£ 7,000	12 months	R-R PV (Merlin)
	£ 6,600	12 months	Bristol Hydra
Vickers	£16,000	20 months	R-R Goshawk or Napier Dagger
Westland	£12,375	18 months	R-R Griffon

The table shows wide variations in the tender prices and a variety of proposed engines. The Armstrong Siddeley Tiger was a 14-cylinder radial engine of 1931 vintage and in its later developed form it powered the early Whitleys and the Ensigns; it was not a great success. The Bristol Perseus was a nine-cylinder sleeve-valve radial engine which was first run and tested during 1932. Though not very widely used, it was the engine selected by Blackburn for the Skua, Roc and Botha aircraft. The Fairey Prince was an in-line V12 liquid-cooled engine, as was the Rolls-Royce PV, which after a very troublesome development period became the superb and widely-used Merlin. The Bristol Hydra was a two-row 16-cylinder radial engine which was first flown in 1933 but was later abandoned as more advanced types came along. The Rolls-Royce Goshawk was a 12-cylinder in-line steam-cooled

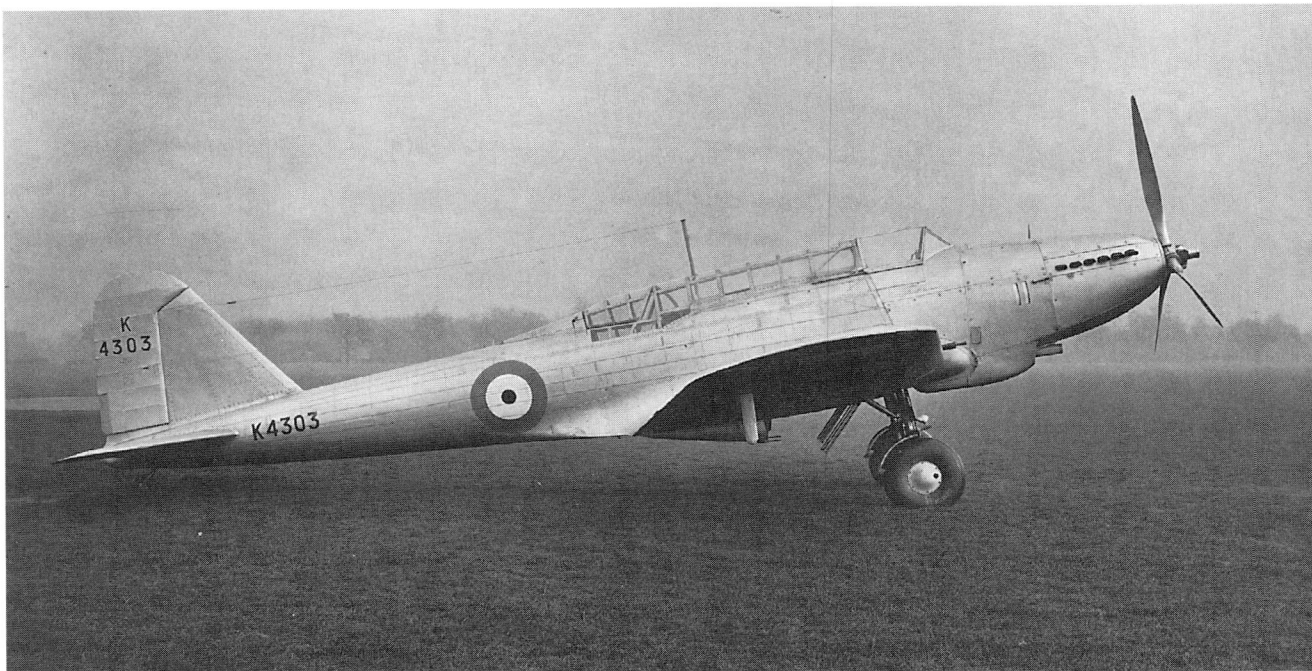

The spinner gave trouble at an early stage in the Battle's development and K4303 flew without one for most the time
(P Jarrett collection)

engine designed in 1928. It gave rise to considerable problems and did not go into quantity production. The Napier Dagger was a 24-cylinder air-cooled H-type engine which was not a very successful design; it powered the Hawker Hector and the ill-fated Handley Page Hereford. The Rolls-Royce Griffon was conceived as a development of the R-type racing engine used in the Schneider Trophy seaplanes of the early 1930s; it was not developed until the end of the 1930s, by which time Rolls-Royce had the experience of producing the Merlin to draw upon.

After consideration of the tenders, a Tender Design Conference was held in February 1934 and the recommended types were the second of the Fairey designs, the Fairey Type B, and the Armstrong Whitworth design, in that order. At this early stage, estimated performance for the Fairey Type B gave a top speed of 223 mph at 15,000 feet with a service ceiling of 25,000 feet, at a flying weight of 8,000 lb. Fairey had submitted tenders for three types of single-engined monoplanes. The Air Ministry was insistent on adhering to Specification P.27/32 and the Type B was the one which more nearly matched the specification. The conference considered possible engines for the P.27/32 aircraft and their order of preference was: Goshawk, Griffon, PV12, Prince, Dagger, Perseus, Tiger VI. Of these, all were at an early stage of development except the Goshawk. There was much discussion about engine developments by the Air Staff and others; in March 1934 the Chief of the Air Staff expressed concern that untried engines might hold up the building of the prototype. The Air Member for Supply and Research assured him that in the event of the Prince and Tiger VI engines failing, other engines could be substituted for them in the P.27/32 aircraft. On 11 June 1934, Contract 321541/34 was awarded to Fairey and Contract 321542/34 to Armstrong Whitworth for each to manufacture and supply one prototype single-engine day bombing low-wing monoplane to Specification P.27/32. The Fairey contract (for £11,060)

specified a 15-month delivery period, i.e. September 1935. Armstrong Whitworth were given slightly longer with an 18-month delivery period. Shortly after the contracts were awarded, the Deputy Chief of the Air Staff stressed the urgency of meeting delivery dates.

The Engine

Fairey's original intention had been to use their P12 Prince engine as a power plant for the P.27/32 project, but no development contract was awarded by the Air Ministry, who did not recognise Fairey as an engine contractor. By December 1934, a considerable amount of testing had been carried out on the Prince; in its normal version it had a maximum rating of 710 hp, and in its highly-supercharged version a maximum rating of 835 hp. A Prince was installed in a Fairey Fox II and this test-bed aircraft first flew in March 1935. These tests resulted in a proposal for a 16-cylinder version of the engine. The Air Ministry favoured the Rolls-Royce PV engine as the Battle's power plant; however, in April 1934, Fairey were given permission to instal the Prince P12 engine in the prototype. The contract specified the Prince engine for the prototype but the Air Ministry reserved the right to specify engines of a different type on further aircraft. In the event, the Prince was not ready in time and the prototype was powered by the Rolls-Royce PV12 Merlin.

The development of the Merlin was a long and troublesome process which started in the autumn of 1932 with the Rolls-Royce concept of a V12 liquid cooled engine of 27 litres capacity. The original intention was to build an inverted 60-degree V12 engine, but this was rejected in favour of an upright design. Two prototypes were built as private ventures and the first was run in October 1933. The Air Ministry was impressed by the new engine and financed its further development. The engine passed a type test in 1934; the international rating was 790 hp at 12,000 feet at 2,500 rpm.

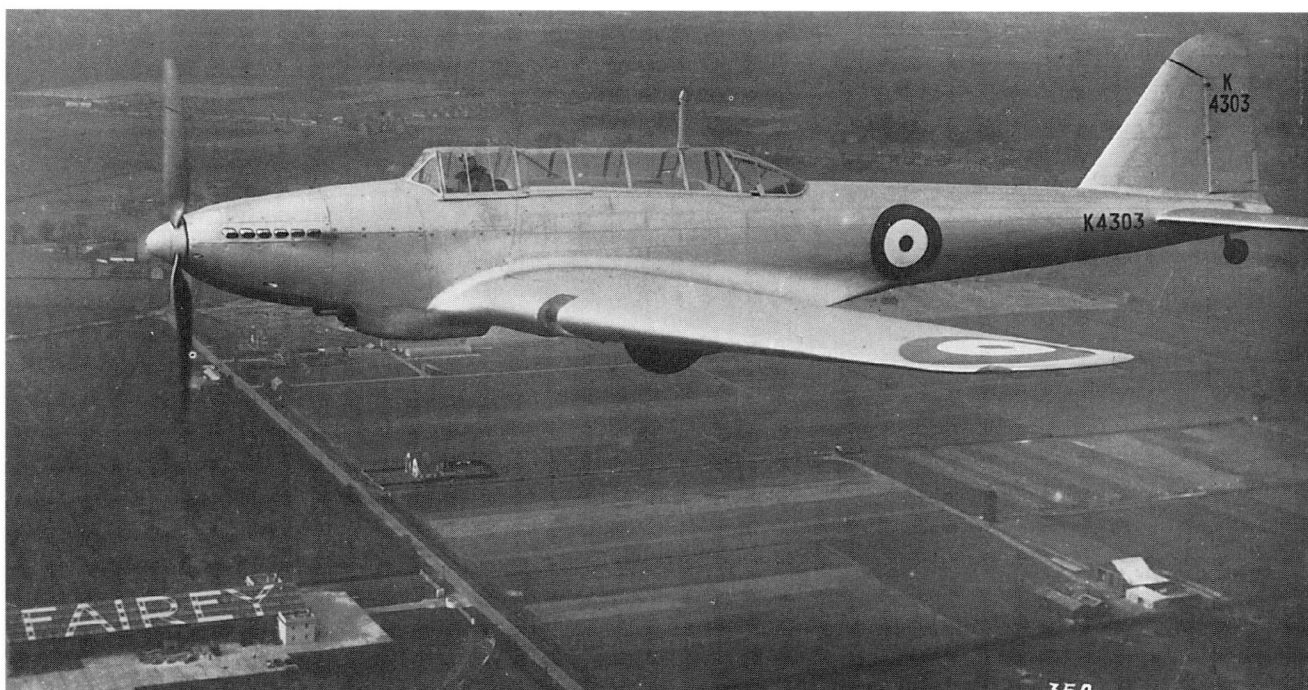

K4303 flies over the Fairey assembly hangar at Heath Row, which later became the London Airport central area fire station.
(Ray Sturtivant collection)

One of the PV12s was installed in a Hawker Hart for flight testing and first flew in February 1935, giving the Hart a high speed and a fast rate of climb. Design of the Merlin B engine with ramp cylinder heads was completed in late 1934 and it was tested in the following year. In the ramp-type cylinder head the inlet valve was inclined to the axis of the cylinder and the exhaust valve was parallel to the axis. This arrangement gave increased power on single-cylinder test sets but was of dubious effect when used in the 12-cylinder Merlin engine. The Merlin B had the cylinder block and crankcase in a single casting, but this caused problems and so the Merlin C with separate castings was designed. This engine was also tested in 1935. By now the Merlin had been chosen for the Hurricane, Spitfire and Battle, and the prototypes of the Hurricane and Spitfire first flew with Merlin C engines. The performance of the engine was not up to expectations and the ramp heads were prone to cracking; the Merlin C failed a 50-hour test in 1935. Modifications resulted in the E and F versions of the Merlin and an E type engine failed a 100-hour military test. Production of the Hurricane, Spitfire and Battle was being delayed by the uncertainties about the Merlin. The initial flight of the prototype Battle, K4303, finally took place on 10 March 1936 with a Merlin F driving a Fairey-Reed three-bladed fixed-pitch metal propeller with a spinner. The Merlin F still had ramp-type cylinder heads but these were discarded in the next version of the engine, the Merlin G, and replaced by conventional flat heads. The Merlin F was designated Merlin Mk. I and the G became the Merlin Mk. II. The Merlin II passed its type test in October 1936 and the Merlin I passed the test in November 1936. Most of the 180 production Merlin Is were sold to Fairey for use in the Battle, and these equipped the first 136 Battles produced. The Merlin I was not used in the Hurricane and Spitfire and the early versions of these fighters were powered with Merlin IIs. The Merlin I was internationally rated at 990 hp at 2,600 rpm at

12,250 feet, with a maximum rating of 1,025 hp at 3,000 rpm at 16,250 feet. The Merlin II, which was installed in some Fairey production Battles and in the early Austin production Battles, had an international rating of 950/990 hp at 2,600 rpm at 12,250 feet, with a maximum rating of 1,030 hp at 3,000 rpm at 16,250 feet. The weight of the Merlin I and II was 1,335 lb. An improved version of the Merlin, the Mk.III, was used in many Battles. The Mk.III engine had a standard shaft for use with a variable-pitch propeller and was fitted with a constant speed unit. Some Battles had Merlin IV engines, which had an improved cooling system, and some were equipped with Merlin Vs, which operated at higher boost pressures giving better performance at high altitudes.

Design Amendment

Wind tunnel tests of a 1/12th scale model of the proposed P.27/32 aircraft to supply design data were carried out by the Royal Aircraft Establishment. Various wings and flaps were tested and the drag of several features of the aircraft, notably the cockpits, the bomb cradle and the undercarriage were analysed. Modifications were made to the tail unit, resulting in a larger fin and rudder. In June 1934 the aircraft weight restrictions imposed by the Geneva Conference were abolished and in the autumn of that year Fairey's Chairman, Chief Designer and Chief Engineer visited the USA. The information gained about modern aircraft design during the American visit led to a request from Fairey for an extension of the delivery period to December 1935 so that the design could be amended. Substantial alterations were made to the design and these were agreed by the Air Ministry in January 1935. The main design modifications were a change from semi-cantilever to full-cantilever construction, provision for the bombs to be enclosed within the wings and the substitution of one long canopy for the two separate canopies

K4303 on the compass-swinging base demonstrates its clean lines. The pair of large landing lamps are prominent in the leading edge. (P Jarrett collection)

over the cockpits envisaged in the original design. This last change was to give improved airflow.

In informing Fairey of the acceptance of their modified design proposals, the Air Ministry stated that the acceptance was conditional upon delivery of the prototype by 31 December 1935 and that no increase in price would be admitted. Specification P.23/35 was issued in October 1935 to incorporate the amendments and to bring in some new requirements, the main one being the addition of a third member of the crew. It had originally been intended that the observer would act as air gunner, but the Air Ministry had now decided that a separate wireless operator/air gunner was required and so the third crew member was added, despite Fairey's objections that this would lead to an unacceptable increase in weight.

The sorry story of delays continued, snags in the development of the Merlin engine being mainly responsible, and the prototype made its first flight on 10 March 1936 from Fairey's Great West airfield, piloted by Chief Test Pilot Chris Staniland. Contractor's trials on the prototype were carried out between August and October 1936, by which time the Air Ministry was becoming impatient at the delays. Such was the pressure of the Expansion Programme that an order for 155 Battles had been given to Fairey in June 1935, some nine months before the prototype flew.

Further Battle Projects

Despite the Air Ministry's lack of interest in Fairey's proposals for a twin-engined Battle, design studies were carried out by Fairey in 1937 into a twin-engined fighter/bomber version. The engines considered were the Fairey P16 and the Merlin. Also studied were a P24-engined aircraft, (the P24 was a double version of the Prince P12 driving two contra-rotating airscrews), and a Sabre-engined Battle. In 1938 the Air Ministry was interested in acquiring a twin-engined fighter and Fairey were then asked to submit designs and costs for a twin- or double-engined fighter. The Ministry was also interested in possible conversions of Battles to take P24 or Sabre engines for use as cannon-armed fighters.

Interest in the twin-engine Battle project was discontinued when the Bristol Beaufighter became available, but tests were done with a P24 Battle and a Sabre Battle. Problems with the Sabre-engined machine gave it an inferior performance to the P24-engined version and the tests were concentrated on the latter. Test reports on the P24 Battle compared its performance very favourably against existing fighters. Only one Battle was re-engined with the P24 and, despite the good test reports it received, the Air Ministry did not proceed with the project.

FAIREY P27/32 — SCHEME 5

56'-0" SPAN

2'-8" WHEEL DIA.

17'-0" TRACK

43'-8" LENGTH TAIL UP

16'-0" HEIGHT TAIL UP

11'-6" AIRSCREW DIA.

19'-0" T/P SPAN

43'-0" LENGTH TAIL DOWN

12'-0" ROOT CHORD

THE FAIREY AVIATION CO LTD
HAYES   MIDDLESEX
TWIN-ENGINED DAY BOMBER
G.A. OF MACHINE – PRINCIPAL DIMENSIONS
OCTOBER 1933

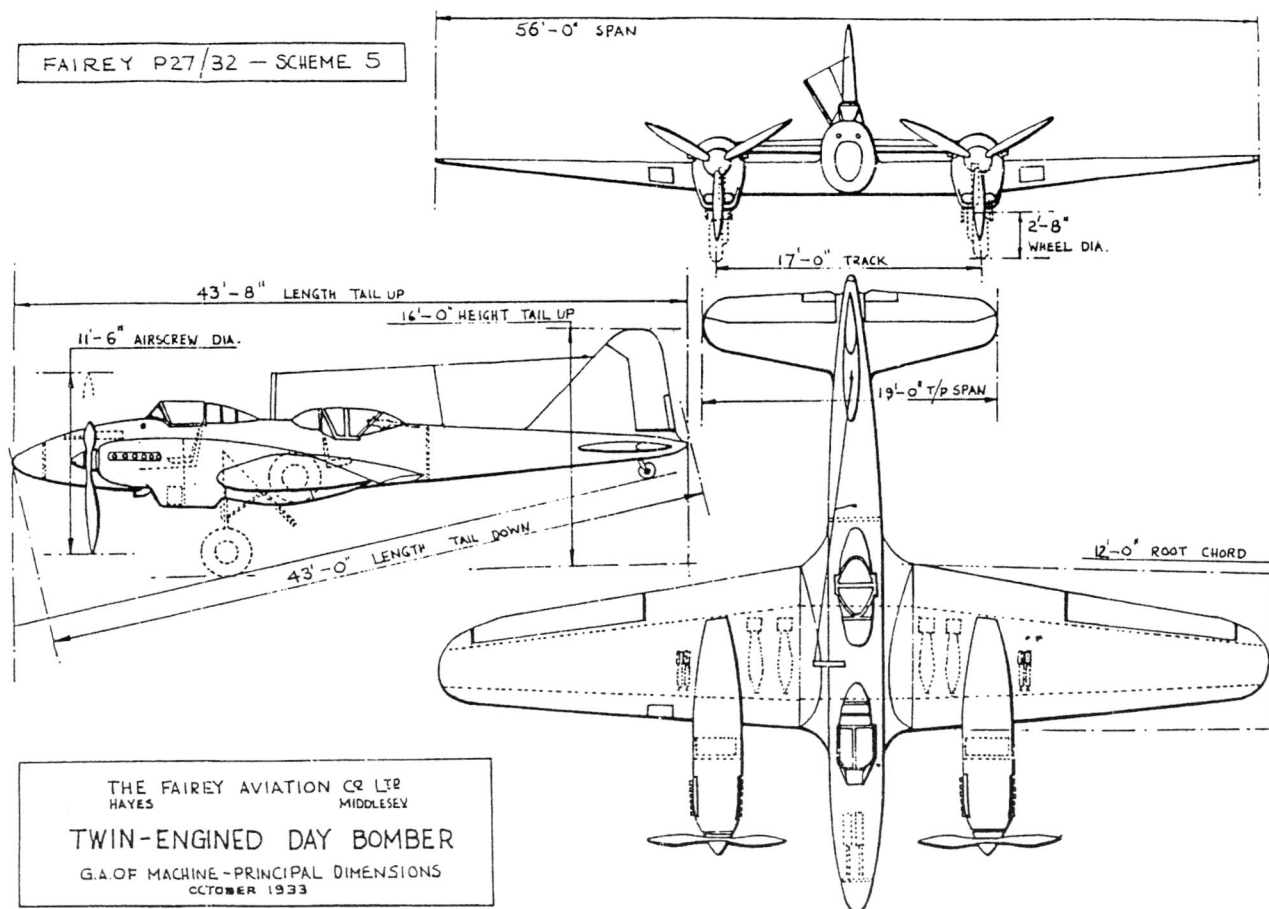

A twin-engined version of the Battle was proposed in October 1933 but was not accepted by the Air Ministry.

New types lined up at Northolt for inspection by a delegation of Members of Parliament included, front to back, the Wellesley, Battle, Blenheim, Venom and Hurricane. (Ray Sturtivant collection)

CHAPTER 2. THE BATTLE AND ITS COMPETITORS

The Aeroplane

The Battle was designed by Fairey's chief designer, the Belgian Marcel Lobelle. It was an all-metal cantilever low-wing monoplane of stressed skin construction and its smoothly elegant appearance was in marked contrast to its biplane predecessors. The Battle was designed for a crew of three; pilot, bomb aimer/observer and wireless operator/air gunner.

The prototype was built at Fairey's Hayes factory and was first displayed to the public at the RAF Display at Hendon in June 1936. The hydraulically-operated undercarriage retracted backwards into the wings and, when retracted, the wheels protruded visibly with fairings to their rear. This arrangement was preferred so that if a twin-engined version of the aircraft was approved by the Air Ministry the wheels would retract into the rear of the engine nacelles. The protruding wheels also gave some protection to the undersides of the aircraft in the event of a belly-landing.

The prototype, K4303, and most of the first production batch, were fitted with the Rolls-Royce Merlin I engine. Merlin II engines were installed in the last nineteen aircraft of this batch. The control surfaces were made of metal with a fabric covering. The oval section fuselage was in two parts; the section forward of the pilot's bulkhead was built of steel tubes and the rear section was of metal monocoque construction. This arrangement gave the facility to make

changes in the type of engine installed without making radical changes to the fuselage structure. The split flaps were metal-covered and there were no slots. The 1,000 lb bomb load was carried on racks in cells in the wings. The racks were supported by hydraulic jacks and were lowered for loading. The normal bomb load consisted of four 250-lb bombs, though the composition of the load could be varied. The bombs were lowered by the hydraulic jacks into the external position before release when dive bombing, in order to clear the fuselage. An additional bomb load of 500 lb could be carried externally if required. There were also smaller cells in each wing to accommodate flares. Electrical bomb releases were provided in the bomb aimer's and pilot's positions, the latter for use when dive bombing. The bomb aimer lay prone behind and below the pilot and there was a sliding panel in the floor of the fuselage, immediately behind the oil cooler, which was opened to give an aperture for bombing. The bomb sight was lowered through the opening for use. A .303-inch Browning machine gun, which the pilot fired with the aid of a ring-and-bead sight, was fitted in the starboard wing firing outside the arc of the airscrew. A moveable .303-inch Vickers 'K' machine gun was fitted in the rear cockpit. On most Battles this was on a Fairey high-speed mounting and the installation could be stowed away behind the rear cockpit in the fuselage fairing when not in use. Despite the vastly superior speed and armament of contemporary monoplane fighters, the Air Ministry obviously considered the gun

K4303 formates on the photographic aircraft and shows a remarkable resemblance at first glance to a Hurricane.
(P Jarrett collection)

armament of one fixed machine gun and one movable machine gun to be sufficient for the Battle. This had been a standard gun armament in the First World War but proved to be tragically inadequate in the Second.

The fuel was carried in two 106-gallon wing tanks together with an auxiliary wing tank holding 33 gallons and an auxiliary fuselage tank holding 55 gallons. There was some discussion about the tank in the fuselage. The C-in-C Bomber Command considered that it reduced the efficiency of the crew and was a fire hazard in crashes and he recommended that it be removed; the reduced range would not be a problem because it was assumed that the Battles would be operating from France. The Air Ministry wanted to keep the tank because it gave extra depth of penetration and more fuel would improve crew morale. The AASF settled the matter for its Battles on 18 September 1939 by issuing an instruction to remove all fuselage petrol tanks. Some original long-canopied Battles were fitted with a set of controls in the rear cockpit and were used as dual control trainers.

The Aeroplane and Armament Experimental Establishment at Martlesham Heath carried out preliminary flight tests of the prototype for a few days in July 1936, followed by a more comprehensive series of tests in October 1936, and the specified performance parameters were met. With the aircraft fully loaded at 10,450 lb, the top speed at 15,000 feet was 257 mph. The range at 200 mph with a 1,000-lb load was 980 miles at 14,500 feet with an endurance of 4.9 hours. The flying characteristics were generally good and A&AEE reported: "In general the aeroplane is simple and normal to fly, land and take-off, and should present no difficulties to the average service pilot."

The flying view was good except directly to the rear and the pilot's cockpit was "roomy and comfortable and not unduly noisy." With the cover open some glycol fumes entered the pilot's cockpit. The inter- communication system

was satisfactory. The bomb aiming position was heavily criticised as being dark, hot, draughty, in an unnatural position with little leg room and with oil and glycol fouling the bomb aimer's goggles. The field of view from the bomb aimer's position was satisfactory and the aircraft provided a good bombing platform. The bombs could be released either by the pilot (for dive bombing) or by the bomb aimer. The gunner's cockpit was said to be "adequately heated", with no great inconvenience suffered when operating in cold conditions. The free gun was securely locked in position when not in use but could easily be brought into action. The prototype had first flown with a Fairey-Reed three-blade fixed-pitch propeller, but this was replaced by a de Havilland three-blade variable-speed propeller and the rear canopy was modified before the Martlesham tests.

The first production Battle, K7558, and K7577 were used by A&AEE for assessment trials between July 1937 and mid-1938. The increased weight of the production Battle reduced the top speed at 15,000 feet to 238 mph. The lighting in the bomb aimer's position was now considered to be satisfactory and no fouling of goggles was reported during the tests. There was, however, still a lack of leg room and a chest rest was needed. In the pilot's cockpit the draught was uncomfortable, with a blast of hot or cold air. It was impossible to keep the cockpit at a reasonable temperature without frequent manipulation of the heating controls. Another test report on K7558 criticised the heavy rudder control but declared the pilot's cockpit comfortable and reasonably free from draughts! The view during approach was reasonably good and there was no tendency to swing during landing. The first Austin-built Battle, L4935, was tested by A&AEE at the end of 1938. It was adjudged to be very similar to a Fairey-built Battle and with a Merlin II engine had a top speed of 230 mph at 15,000 feet.

A report from the Royal Aircraft Establishment on

The prototype at the SBAC Display at Hatfield in 1936
(via Bruce Robertson)

handling tests carried out in May and June 1938, using K7558, contained the following conclusions:

(i) Take-off and landing were straightforward with an excellent view on approach.

(ii) The aircraft was longitudinally stable on the glide at all speeds except when near the stall with flaps down.

(iii) The fin area was adequate but the dihedral angle was too small.

(iv) The initial stall was gentle.

(v) The controls were fairly well harmonised at high speeds but the elevator was too light at low speeds.

The aircraft stalled at 64 mph with the flaps and undercarriage up and at 55 mph with the flaps and undercarriage down.

The Competitors

In competition with Fairey, Hawker's chief designer, Sydney Camm, produced a P.27/32 design for a low-wing monoplane with open cockpits, retractable undercarriage and one fixed machine gun and one movable machine gun. The bomb load was to be two 500-lb bombs carried in the fuselage and the projected engine was either the Rolls-Royce Merlin or the Bristol Hydra. Bristol also had a P.27/32 project, the Type 136, designed by Captain Frank Barnwell, utilising the Perseus engine. Both of these designs were abandoned when the contracts for prototypes were awarded to Armstrong Whitworth and Fairey.

Armstrong Whitworth fulfilled their P.27/32 prototype contract by producing the A.W.29, designed by John Lloyd. The A.W.29 project was considerably delayed because of work on the Whitley bomber and the Ensign air liner; the company's design and production departments did not have the facilities to work on all three of these projects simultaneously and priority was given to the Whitley and Ensign. Only one A.W.29 was produced (K4299) and this, piloted by C.K. Turner-Hughes, made its first flight on 6 December 1936 from Baginton, nine months after the prototype Battle first flew. By then the Battle had been ordered in quantity and there was little prospect of the Air Ministry awarding contracts to Armstrong Whitworth for the A.W.29, particularly in view of the company's commitment to the production of Whitleys and Ensigns. The A.W.29 was a single-engined mid-wing cantilever monoplane powered by a 920 hp Armstrong Siddeley Tiger VIII radial engine. A Hamilton Standard three-bladed, two-position propeller was fitted. Provision was made for a crew of two, a pilot and an observer/air gunner, who would also drop the bombs and operate the radio. The undercarriage was retractable backwards into the wings and the wheels protruded slightly in the retracted position. Construction was mainly of metal with some wing and control surfaces fabric covered. The bomb

load was 1,000 lb, made up of two 500-lb, four 250-lb, or eight 112-lb bombs, carried in compartments in the wing centre section. A fixed Vickers machine gun fired through the airscrew arc for the use of the pilot and there was a manually-operated gun turret to the rear of the pilot housing a Lewis machine gun. This cupola-type Armstrong Whitworth gun turret was foot-operated for rotation, and movement of the gun in the vertical plane was achieved by the gunner leaning forward or back. Though soon superseded by power-operated turrets, this turret was used operationally in early Ansons and Whitleys. No tested performance figures are available for the A.W.29 as the aircraft made a wheels-up forced landing shortly after its first flight and it was not repaired and did not fly again. There was a proposal that the aircraft be repaired and used as a test bed for the Armstrong Siddeley Deerhound engine, but this was dropped and the sole A.W.29 was scrapped. Its estimated performance figures were inferior to those of the Battle, its estimated maximum speed being 225 mph at 14,700 feet and its range 685 miles.

Table 1 shows comparative statistics for the Hawker Hart, Fairey Battle and Armstrong Whitworth A.W.29.

Table 1. Comparative Statistics

	Hawker Hart	*Fairey Battle*	*A.W. 29*
Wingspan	37 ft.3 in.	54 ft.	49 ft.
Length	29 ft.4 in.	42 ft.4 in.	43 ft.10 in.
Height	10 ft.5 in.	15 ft.6 in.	13 ft.3 in.
Wing Area	348 sq.ft.	422 sq.ft.	458 sq.ft.
Loaded Weight	4,635 lb	10,792 lb	9,000 lb*
Engine	525hp R-R	1,030hp R-R	920hp A.S.
	Kestrel 1B	Merlin	Tiger VIII
Maximum Speed	184 mph	257 mph	225 mph*
Crew	2	3	2
Service Ceiling	21,350 ft.	25,000 ft.	21,000 ft.*
Range	470 miles	1,000 miles	685 miles*
Bomb Load	500 lb	1,000 lb	1,000 lb*
Armament	1 fixed	1 fixed	1 fixed
(Machine guns)	1 movable	1 movable	1 movable
Initial A.M. Spec.	12/26	P.27/32	P.27/32
Prototype flew	June 1928	10 Mar 1936	6 Dec 1936
Into Service	1930	1937	----

* Estimated

Early Reservations

Even in the early days of the Battle project, senior RAF officers had expressed substantial reservations about its role as a light bomber. Before the prototype was completed, Sir Edgar Ludlow-Hewitt, then Deputy Chief of the Air Staff, had indicated his doubts about the Battle's capabilities. In December 1936, Sir Edward Ellington, then Chief of the Air Staff, had stated that no further orders for Battles should be placed. In November 1937, Sir Wilfrid Freeman, the Air Member for Research and Development, acknowledged that the Battle was a mistaken concept. Despite these strictures, Battles continued to be ordered and they were being manufactured until late 1940. The reasons for this were political rather than logical; the Expansion Plans called for sizeable quantities of aircraft and large scale production facilities for making Battles had been set up as a key part of those plans. It would have been politically inexpedient to have

The Battle prototype's wide-span flaps

Undercarriage with fairings removed and mud-flap

disrupted the plans by ceasing to produce the Battles, even after they became obsolescent, so production continued. The tragic consequences of these pre-war political decisions were seen in the very high losses of experienced aircrews in the Battle of France.

The later "stop gap" orders for the Battle were placed to keep together Fairey's skilled labour force so that they would be available to produce more advanced aircraft when these were ready to go into production. To place the Battle into context with its contemporaries, there is no doubt that when it was first designed it was a great advance on the RAF's then-current aircraft. It was good looking, fast by the standards of the early 1930s, had an impressive range and bomb load, but was still defensively-armed to First World War standards. By

the end of its long gestation period it had been overhauled by more modern types and the concept of the light day bomber was questionable because of the advent of the much faster well-armed monoplane fighters. The eight-gun Hurricane made its first flight on 6 November 1935, the Spitfire on 5 March 1936 and the Battle on 10 March 1936.

The prototype Battle was delayed by problems with the Mark I Rolls-Royce Merlin engine; the Mark II version of the same engine powered the early Hurricanes and Spitfires. Even the advocates of the belief that the bomber would always get through, of whom there were many in the 1930s, must have had grave doubts about the operational potential of the Battle when faced by contemporary fighters.

Rear view of the Battle prototype shows the gunner's blind spot caused by the fin and rudder.

The Battle prototype in a steep bank over Staines Reservoir. (P Jarrett collection)

Battles in production at the Heaton Chapel works. (via George Jenks)

CHAPTER 3. PRODUCTION AND DEVELOPMENT

Fairey Production

The initial order for 155 Battles to Specification P.23/35 was placed in June 1935, nine months before the prototype first flew. The order was conditional on a guarantee of a speed of at least 195 mph at 15,000 feet, a performance which was easily exceeded by the prototype. The first aircraft of this batch, K7558, was built at the Hayes factory and made its first flight from Fairey's Great West Aerodrome at Harmondsworth in April 1937. The remaining 154 aircraft of the first batch, K7559-K7712, were built at Fairey's new factory at Heaton Chapel, Stockport. The Stockport Battles were flight tested at Ringway Airport, Manchester. The first 136 aircraft were powered with the Merlin I engine, which, despite the delays in its development, was still not giving the required performance. The remaining nineteen aircraft of the first batch were equipped with the Merlin II. Fitting the Merlin II involved some change to the nose configuration and alterations to the engine controls. Some of these production models, including K7559, the first built at Stockport, were fitted with dual controls for pilot conversion training. The pilot under instruction sat in the normal pilot's cockpit at the front of the long canopy and the instructor sat in the rear cockpit at the back of the canopy, with an extremely poor view, particularly for landing.

Production Specification P.14/36 was issued in May 1936 and 500 Battles were ordered from Fairey. There were serious delays in production, mainly because of the late delivery of machine tools and the shortage of skilled labour. In 1937 Fairey's management, particularly in its lack of skill in production management, was heavily criticised at Government level. The initial contract for 155 Battles was due for completion in June 1937 but by December of that year only 84 had been delivered. The Air Ministry had informed Fairey's in March 1937 that Battles not expected to be delivered before 1 April 1939 would be cancelled. Later in the month, 189 aircraft out of the order for 500 were cancelled. The serial numbers allocated to the original order were K9176-K9675, of which K9487-K9675 were cancelled. In February 1938, the order for the cancelled 189 aircraft was reinstated to maintain the current level of aircraft production in 1938 and 1939. These were allotted serial numbers N2020-N2066, N2082-N2131, N2147-N2190 and N2211-N2258.

The gaps in the blocks of serial numbers were left deliberately in an attempt to confuse enemy intelligence about aircraft production levels. Sixteen Battles powered with Merlin III engines were built for the Belgian Air Force and were delivered in early 1938.

Because of slow deliveries by Austin, a decision was taken in September 1938 to order a further 200 Battles from

FAIREY "BATTLE"
Light Bomber

D.H. TWO POSITION VARIABLE PITCH AIRSCREW

ROLLS-ROYCE TWELVE CYLINDER SUPERCHARGED MERLIN ENGINE

STREAMLINE EXHAUST MANIFOLD

VENTURI FOR BLIND FLYING PANEL

GLYCOL HEADER TANK

HEADER TANK FOR AIRSCREW PITCH CONTROL

CARBURETTER AIR INTAKE

HAND STARTER CONNECTION

GLYCOL RADIATOR

FIXED OIL RADIATOR

BOMB SELECTOR PANEL FUSING AND FLARE SWITCHES

GUN SIGHTS

UNDERCARRIAGE EMERGENCY LOWERING HANDLE

AIRSCREW PITCH CONTROL

COCKPIT VENTILATOR

SEAT ADJUSTMENT LEVER

PILOT'S SLIDING HOOD

OIL TANK

PILOTS

CHARGING CONTROL PANEL

FUSE PANEL

STARBOARD PETROL TANK

VICKERS GUN IN WING

SWIVELLING LANDING LIGHT

AMMUNITION DRUMS

HINGED HOOD FOR GUNNER

GUNNER SEATED FOR WIRELESS OR NAVIGATION DUTIES

SEAT LOCKING LEVER

TRAILING AERIAL

THROTTLE

PILOT'S BOMB RELEASE SWITCH

COMPASS

HYDRAULIC SELECTOR LEVERS

BOMB & INSTRUMENT PANEL

PILOT'S PARACHUTE

COURSE SETTING BOMB SIGHT

LATERAL TRIM CONTROLS

UNDERCARRIAGE WARNING HOOTER

TAIL INCIDENCE INDICATOR

UPWARD RECOGNITION LIGHT

UNDERCARRIAGE HAND PUMP

DRIFT SIGHT HOLSTER

SPEED & COURSE CALCULATOR

AUTOMATIC PILOT'S

ALDIS LAMP

HAND DRIFT LIGHT

BOMB AIMER'S HATCH OPENING IN WIND

TAIL DRIFT LIGHT

BOMB RELEASE SWITCH

BOMB AIMER'S CUSHION

OXYGEN BOTTLES

SLIDING CHART TABLE

PLUNGEABLE PARACHUTE STOWAGE

OPENING IN CENTRE SECTION OF WING

GUNNER'S SWIVELLING & RISING SEAT

ACCUMULATORS

FIRST AID STOWAGE

HINGED HOOD

FIXED AERIAL

LEWIS GUN

TRANSMITTING & RECEIVING SET SLIDES BACK ON RAILS

CAMERA

DOWNWARD RECOGNITION LIGHT

LEAD IN

HYDRAULIC RAM LOWERING DOORS AND BOMBS

HINGED DOORS

UNDERCARRIAGE HYDRAULIC RAMS

MUDGUARD

SCRAPER

UNDERCARRIAGE FAIRING

RADIATOR COOLING CONTROL FLAP

SEMI-CANTILEVER UNDERCARRIAGE LEG

DOORS FOR LIGHT BOMBS LIGHT OR FLARES

FLIGHT

King George VI visiting Harwell in 1938. In the background are a Battle, Blenheim I, Wellesley, Whitley and Harrow.
(W Booth via P Jarrett)

Fairey. 150 were ordered in November 1938, serial numbers P2155-P2204, P2233-P2278, P2300-P2336 and P2353-P2369. The remaining 50 were ordered in December 1938 and were numbered P5228-P5252 and P5270-P5294. In December 1938 it was decided that a further 200 Battles should be ordered from Fairey to keep in being the production facility and labour force to be used in building Avro Manchester aircraft when these reached the production stage. The order was placed in February 1939 and the serial numbers of these aircraft were P6480-P6509, P6523-P6572, P6596-P6645, P6663-P6692, P6718-P6737 and P6750-P6769. The last 100 of this batch, starting with P6616, were built as Battle (T) trainers. Because of industrial difficulties, a further stop-gap order for 100 aircraft without engines was decided upon in April 1939 and the order was placed in September 1939. The serial numbers of these aircraft were R7356-R7385, R7399-R7448 and R7461-R7480, and they were all built as Battle (T)s.

Including the prototype, Fairey built 1,172 Battles. Many were sent directly to countries participating in the Commonwealth Air Training Plan and some were sent directly to other countries to fulfil export orders. All except the sixteen built for the Belgian Air Force were given RAF serial numbers.

Austin production

Discussions between the Air Ministry and Sir Herbert Austin in February 1936 resulted in an agreement for Austin to set up a Shadow Factory, in conjunction with Fairey, as part of the RAF expansion plans. The factory at Longbridge was intended to produce Battles in large numbers. It was hoped that the application of the motor industry's mass production techniques to the manufacture of aeroplanes would overcome bottlenecks in production. Experience proved this theory to be over-optimistic and production was slow in getting under way. The factory went into operation in 1938. Specification P.32/36, setting out the production standard for Austin-built Battles, was issued in August 1936 and at the same time 400 Battles and parts for a further 100 were ordered from Austin.

In February 1938, the Government acknowledged that the current Austin order should cover 500 Battles. The original intention had been to order 863 Battles from Austin, but the Air Ministry were now considering whether the remaining 363 aircraft should be Battles or Wellingtons; the RAF would certainly have preferred Wellingtons. This was ruled out because of potential production problems and it was decided to order Battles. The order for a further 363 Battles was placed with Austin in mid-1938. The total of 863 aircraft ordered were allocated the serial numbers L4935-L5797. The first three aircraft of this batch were non-standard because some of the equipment installed was not interchangeable. Fifty-nine were fitted with 1,030 h.p. Merlin II engines and the remainder with Merlin III engines. The first Austin-built Battle made its maiden flight in July 1938 and deliveries to squadrons started in October 1938. The last 200 aircraft, L5598-L5797, were built as Battle T.T. target tugs. Despite

Early production Battles were delivered to No.105 Squadron, here carrying the squadron's number before squadron codes were allocated. (P. Jarrett collection)

the initial enthusiasm of Austins and their optimistic forecasts, deliveries of their initial orders for 863 Battles were behind schedule. In April 1939 it was agreed to award a stop-gap order for 100 Battles and the order for 100 aircraft without engines was placed in June 1939. The serial numbers of this batch were R3922-R3971, R3990-R4019 and R4035-R4054. In October 1939 a further order for 300 Battles was placed, the first 100 to be target tugs. Only 66 aircraft of this order were built, the remaining 234 being cancelled. The serial numbers of the 66 built, all target tugs, were V1201-V1250 and V1265-V1280.

Austin built 1,029 Battles and, as with the Fairey production, many were sent directly to countries operating the Commonwealth Air Training Plan.

Production Summary

Altogether, 2,201 Battles were produced. The vast majority were the basic bomber version, several with dual controls for pilot conversion. 200 were built as trainers with two separate cockpit enclosures and 266 were built as target tugs. This takes no account of conversions and modifications made to machines after they went into service. Most Battles were fitted with Merlin II or III engines, but the first 136 had Merlin Is and some Battles were fitted with Merlin IV or Merlin V engines. Deliveries of the production Battle in the years it was being built were as follows:

	Fairey, Stockport	Austin	Total
1937	81	-	81
1938	352	28	380
1939	513	524	1,037
1940	218	480	698

The Fairey deliveries commenced in May 1937 and ended in November 1940. Those from Austin ran from October 1938 to October 1940. It was known that the Battle was obsolete as a bomber before 1939, yet over 1,700 of them were built in 1939/40. Whilst appreciating the political appetite for numbers of aircraft and the argument for maintaining the labour force, it seems wrong for production to have continued to such a late date. The tragic losses of Battles and their crews in France in 1940 demonstrated the magnitude of this error.

Stop-Gap Orders

During its expansion the RAF adhered, wherever possible, to the "doctrine of quality". This placed quality of aircraft as the paramount requirement rather than sheer numbers. Despite

A No.52 Squadron Battle, K7612, taxies out. Note the hinged roof of the gunner's cockpit which acted as a windscreen when the gun was in use. (P Jarrett collection)

this, it was sometimes necessary to issue stop-gap orders for obsolescent or even obsolete types, usually to keep a manufacturer's labour force together while awaiting the start of production of new types. Delays in the development and production of new and better aircraft exacerbated this process. The Battle was a prime example of this, several stop-gap orders being placed for it long after the RAF had decided that it was not suitable for operational use. Earlier in its life, the Battle was ordered in quantity in an effort to fulfil expansion programmes for which, at the time, nothing better was available. This at least mollified the politicians who were seeking numerical strength. The practice of awarding stop-gap orders applied to other aircraft manufacturers, but perhaps Fairey and the Battle is an extreme example. It is arguable whether or not other measures might have been taken to preserve the Fairey labour force and still discontinue production of the Battle earlier.

Modifications

Unlike some other types of aircraft, there was very little development of the Battle because it became obsolescent early in its production cycle. The Battle was originally designed with two cockpits, each with its own canopy, but the single long canopy was adopted to reduce drag. Several modifications were made to the prototype, K4303, after flight testing, the main ones being a revised rear canopy, an increase in the rudder area, kidney-type exhausts to replace

The Belgian Battles had a modified nose intake (M Evrard via D.Howley)

The twin-cockpit Battle Trainer

the original flush exhaust ports and a de Havilland variable-pitch propeller without spinner to replace the Fairey-Reed fixed-pitch propeller and spinner. The first 136 production Battles were fitted with the unsatisfactory Rolls-Royce Merlin I engine, which had been wisely rejected for the Hurricane as it failed to reach the required standards. Most production Battles were fitted with the much more satisfactory 1,030 hp Mk II Merlin engine or the Mk III Merlin engine. Some of the later Battles had Mk IV or Mk V Merlin engines. During the flying life of the Battles there were inevitably changes of engines and a different Mark of Merlin from that originally fitted was often installed. The sixteen Battles exported to Belgium had Mk III Merlin engines. They differed from the RAF Battles in having an extended radiator cowling and their camouflage colouring was applied more smoothly, allegedly giving them a higher top speed.

The bomb aimer's position was modified for greater comfort, but the unfortunate bomb aimer was still in a cramped and uneasy state. This was made worse when the bombing aperture was opened and he was assailed by heat and fumes from the adjacent oil cooler. Late in 1939 it was decided to instal a sheet of armour plate to protect the bomb aimer's prone position and another sheet to protect the gunner. There was no protection for the pilot. The lack of armour and self-sealing fuel tanks was a major operational disadvantage of the Battle and resulted in many casualties. Early encounters with Messerschmitt Bf 109s over France had made Battle crews painfully aware of how vulnerable they were to attack from below. In an attempt to protect the aircraft from such attacks, a mounting for a Vickers Gas Operated gun to fire through the bombing aperture was fitted

to AASF Battles, with dubious results. Some Battles were converted for gunnery training by the fitting of a Bristol Type I gun turret in the rear cockpit. This involved shortening the canopy and fairing it aft of the pilot's cockpit. Over 200 such conversions were made on Battles sent to Canada for use in the Commonwealth Air Training Plan by Canadian Car & Foundry. One of these aircraft, R7439, was re-engined with an 840 hp Wright Cyclone radial engine to test the feasibility of such an installation if the supply of Merlin engines was interrupted but a contract for such conversions by Fairchild was later cancelled. Some 104 Battles were converted to target tugs in Canada.

The Battle (T) Trainer

The Battle (T) Trainer was designed specifically as a training aircraft with two separate cockpits, each with its own canopy instead of the long glazed canopy of the bomber version of the aircraft. The bomb aimer's position was omitted and the rear cockpit, used by the instructor, had a full set of instruments and controls. The engine was a Rolls-Royce Merlin III with the maximum boost restricted. The prototype Trainer, P2277, was made by Fairey and tested by A&AEE at Boscombe Down in 1940 to determine its suitability as an intermediate training aircraft. Handling and diving trials led to the conclusion that "The aeroplane behaves exactly like a standard Battle". Aerobatic tests showed no hidden vices and the comment on the instructor's view from the rear cockpit was: "The view for landing is not good, but it should be possible for an instructor to correct a bad landing made by a pupil in the front seat". The Battle (T) entered service in

The Fairey P.4/34 was a cleaned-up version of the Battle for use as a fighter-bomber. This is the second prototype.
(Bruce Robertson)

1940. 200 production models were built by Fairey with serial numbers P6616-P6645, P6663-P6692, P6718-P6737, P6750-P6769, R7356-R7385, R7399-R7448 and R7461-R7480. Battle (T)s were used in the UK and in the Commonwealth Air Training Plan; their main virtue was the improved view from the rear cockpit as compared with the dual-control long-canopied version of the Battle.

The Battle T.T. Target Tug

The target tug version of the Battle was a standard Battle with much of the military equipment omitted and target-towing gear installed. The additional equipment consisted of a wind driven winch on the port side of the aircraft in front of the rear cockpit and a drogue container under the rear fuselage. Experiments with target-towing gear were carried out in 1939 in K7587. This aircraft was originally supplied by Fairey to Longbridge as a pattern for Austin production, was used for target-towing trials and ended its life in Canada. The prototype target tug was L5598 and this was tested by A&AEE at Boscombe Down in 1940. The test report stated that there was little difference in handling compared with the standard Battle. The main criticism was that the rear cockpit hood needed extra catches to stop it from blowing open. The Battle T.T. went into service in 1940. 266 Battle T.T.s were made, all by Austin, with serial numbers L5598-L5797, V1201-V1250 and V1265-V1280. This excludes standard Battles which were converted to target tugs.

Fairey P.4/34

Continuing their quest for a light day bomber, the Air Ministry issued Specification P.4/34 in 1934. The requirement was for a two-seat fast day bomber, capable of use for dive bombing, reconnaissance and as a fighter-bomber. The aircraft was to be single-engined with a normal bomb load of 500 lb and facility for carrying an overload of 500 lb. The minimum range was to be 600 miles and top speeds were to be not less than 235 mph at 5,000 feet and 255 mph at 15,000 feet. Both Fairey and Hawker built prototypes, the Hawker machine being accepted for production. This became the Henley and was used for target towing, the light bomber role having been superseded. The Fairey aircraft, designed by Lobelle, looked like a smaller, smoother version of the Battle and was much faster with a top speed of 284 mph. Its undercarriage retracted fully into the wings, unlike the partly exposed landing wheels of the Battle. Two prototypes were made and the first, K5099, made its first flight in January 1937. The machine gun armament was to have been the same as that of the Battle, one forward firing wing mounted gun and a movable gun in the rear cockpit. Light bombers were no longer in vogue but the Fleet Air Arm needed a two-seat fleet fighter and the P.4/34 was modified for carrier operation to Specification O.8/38. It was fitted with eight forward-firing wing mounted machine guns, the rear-firing gun was abandoned and it went into quantity production as the Fulmar fleet fighter.

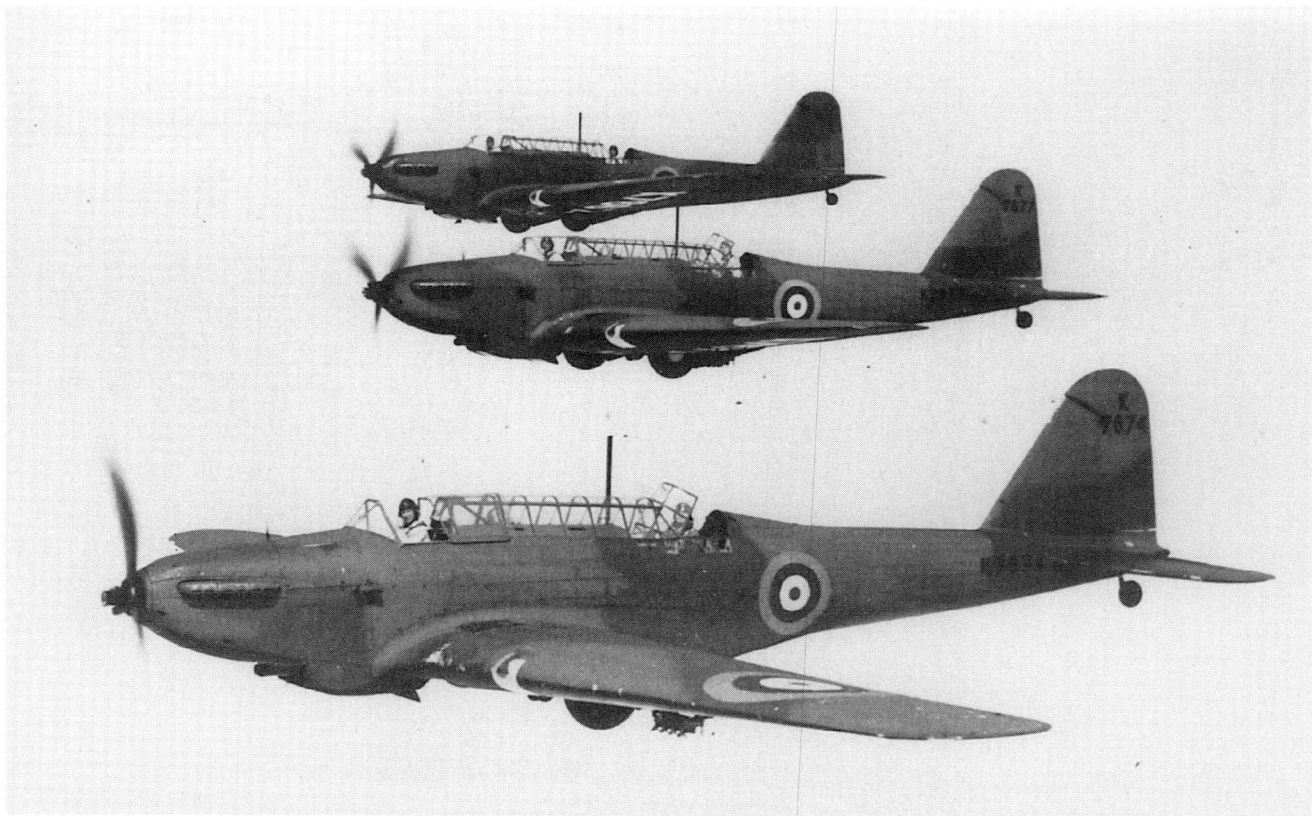

K7674, K7677 and K7662 with an anonymous No.12 Squadron early in 1938. (A. Thomas collection)

CHAPTER 4. EARLY RAF SERVICE

No.2 GROUP, BOMBER COMMAND

No.63 Squadron

The first Fairey Battles received by the RAF went to No.63 Squadron at Upwood in Cambridgeshire. A dual control aircraft, K7559, was delivered to the squadron on 20 May 1937, followed by a further three aircraft in June, four in July and four in August. Though powered with the suspect Mark I version of the Rolls-Royce Merlin, the Battles were favourably received by the squadron's aircrews. This is scarcely surprising as they were modern low-wing monoplanes replacing their old Hawker Audax biplanes, and they were almost 100 mph faster than the Audaxes. The squadron undertook intensive development trials with three of their Battles, K7562, K7563 and K7566. In August 1937 the squadron took part in air exercises to test the defences of London against air attack. The RAF used No.63 Squadron as its showpiece for the new Battle aircraft and in August 1937 Gaumont-British visited Upwood to take film for the making of "Under the Shadow of the Wing"; nine aircraft took part. A few days later a *Flight* photographer visited the squadron to take air-to-air pictures.

The British aircraft industry was active in export markets and during 1937 the squadron's Battles were inspected by representatives from Italy, Egypt, Belgium, China and Germany. Clearly the German Air Mission was not interested

in buying but in gathering information for future reference. Top ranking officers of the RAF wished to see their new bombers and the Battles were inspected by the Commander-in-Chief Bomber Command, Air Chief Marshal Sir E.R. Ludlow-Hewitt, and the Chief of the Air Staff, Marshal of the Royal Air Force Sir Edward Ellington. While these diversions continued, the squadron was engaged in normal training and working up on the new aircraft. Two flights of the squadron, eight aircraft in all, departed for a month of annual armament training at No.4 ATS, West Freugh, in October 1937. The remaining flight stayed behind at Upwood to continue the Battle development trials, which required 500 hours flying by each of the three aircraft taking part. The trials had not been completed by February 1938 and it was decided to give priority to finishing them. Where possible, each aircraft flew for three periods of three hours each day and the trials were completed in March 1938. In that month, night flying with the Battles started. Training continued through 1938 and the squadron took part in various defence exercises and demonstration flights. There were calibration flights for the Observer Corps and a visit by members of the Corps to the squadron, when passenger flights were given. During the Munich crisis in autumn 1938, the squadron made its preparations for mobilisation and was on precautionary standby. While taking part in a practice dawn raid on 25

K7561 of No.63 Squadron

K7602 of No.52 Squadron

November 1938, K7567 crashed into a wood at East Tisted, Hants., while trying to locate the Odiham flashing beacon. The pilot, P/O Ellis, was killed and his two crew were injured. In December 1938 the old Merlin I Battles were replaced by newer aircraft with Merlin II engines, and by February 1939 the squadron had its full strength of 21 Merlin II Battles. The Air Ministry decided in March 1939 that No.63 Squadron would become a non-mobilising training unit. Some of the more experienced Flying Officers and Pilot Officers would remain as instructors and the other aircrews would be posted to operational units. They would be replaced by Volunteer Reserve pilots and ex-FTS pupils, who would stay for periods of three to four months. Ten Ansons would be allocated to the squadron. There was an increased number of defence exercises in 1939 as war approached and in March the aircraft numbers and national markings were painted out and replaced by squadron code letters. A new establishment of 32 Merlin II Battles was declared in mid-1939. On 25 July 1939, Battle K9412 crashed and caught fire near Gayton in Norfolk while on a night cross-country flight. All three of the crew were killed. A Court of Inquiry was held but it failed to determine the cause of the crash.

Towards the end of August 1939, the various states of readiness were actioned, culminating in the general mobilisation of the RAF on 2 September and the declaration of war on 3 September. Shortly after this, the squadron moved to Abingdon and was transferred from No.2 Group to No.6 (Training) Group of Bomber Command as a Group Pool squadron. The function of the squadron was to train aircrews from Flying Training and Air Gunnery Schools up to operational standards so that they were available for operational squadrons when reinforcements were needed. Only ten days after the move to Abingdon, the squadron moved to Benson, exchanging aerodromes with the Whitleys from Benson, where the airfield was not suitable for use by the heavier aircraft. No.63 Squadron then settled down to its training role, with detachments at Squires Gate, Weston Zoyland and Penrhos. On 3 November 1939, Battle P2274 crashed into trees at Checkendon in the Chiltern Hills. The pilot was the sole occupant and was killed. He apparently lost sight of the leader while formation flying. The exceptionally severe winter weather interrupted training and the Battles were susceptible to tailwheel damage caused by bumping over ruts in the frozen airfield surface. In April 1940, the squadron was merged with No.52 Squadron and SHQ Benson to form No.12 OTU.

No.52 Squadron

Fairey Battles replaced the Squadron's Hawker Hinds in late 1937 at Upwood. The squadron's first Battle, K7599, was received on 9 November and re-equipment was completed by 14 December, with an establishment of 22 Battles. Early in 1938, two of the squadron's machines carried out trials with Dunlop de-icing equipment. The squadron's A Flight was detached to Northolt from March to July, 1938, to take part in Air Fighting Development Unit exercises with fighter squadrons. A mobilisation and dispersal test was carried out in May 1938 involving a move to the satellite airfield at Alconbury. In the same month, Battles from the squadron took part in the 1938 Empire Air Day displays and the aircraft were demonstrated to the visiting French Air Mission. In June 1938, B Flight took part in the opening ceremony at Ringway Airport, Manchester. The Combined Home Defence exercises took place in August 1938 and most of September was spent at No.8 ATS, Evanton, for armament training. In December a Battle piloted by F/O Murtens flew at its operational height for over seven hours, flying a distance of 945 miles. The squadron's Merlin I Battles were replaced by Merlin II machines in December 1938 and the old Battles went to Flying Training Schools.

In February 1939, the squadron was designated as a training unit for training air observers and VR pilots and ten Ansons were added to the aircraft strength. The first of the trainees joined the squadron on 1 April 1939. In May, the squadron again took part in Empire Air Day displays. The Empire Air Days were important events for the RAF, both to show the taxpayer how his money was increasing the strength of the force and as a recruiting medium. In late June, ten Battles were received from No.185 Squadron. During the summer of 1939, several exercises and trials were carried out by the squadron. In late August, it was put into a state of preparedness and six Battles were delivered to Benson and one to Harwell. On 1 September the squadron's 24 Battles and five Ansons were dispersed to the satellite airfield at Alconbury, five miles from Upwood.

On the outbreak of war on 3 September 1939, the squadron was transferred to No.6 (Training) Group of Bomber Command as a Group Pool squadron to provide reinforcements for the AASF in France. On 7 September the dispersed aircraft returned to Upwood and on 9 September the squadron moved to Abingdon, using Kidlington as a satellite airfield. A further move, to Benson, took place on 18

September. Towards the end of December it was decided that pilots, air observers and air gunners would do three weeks of elementary training with No.63 Squadron and three weeks of advanced training with No.52 Squadron, both squadrons being based at Benson. During the next few months there were a number of accidents in flying training; two deaths and some injuries resulted. In February 1940, the squadron was given the task of training 160 pilots from the AASF in gas spraying from the air on courses of two days duration. The squadron lost its identity when it was merged with Nos.63 and 207 Squadrons in April 1940 to form No.12 OTU.

K9176, K7709 and K9180 of No.35 Squadron. (via RCS)

No.35 Squadron

No. 35 Squadron started to convert from Wellesleys to Battles in April 1938, when it received a dual control Battle, K7695, at its Worthy Down base. On 20 April, the squadron moved to Cottesmore, where re-equipment with Battles was completed on 20 May with 16 aircraft on the unit strength.

Training on the new aircraft progressed steadily and two flights, each of nine aircraft, made a four-and-a-half-hour flight to appear at some of the 1938 Empire Air Day displays. On 20 June, K9179 force landed at Oulton Park in Cheshire and was damaged beyond repair. It became training airframe 1126M and was removed to the RAF College, eventually finishing its days with 215 Squadron of the ATC. On the following day the Battles were grounded briefly while Rolls-Royce engineers inspected the boost control valve needles. Night flying on the Battles started on 30 June. During the remainder of 1938 various exercises took place, including a long-distance formation cross-country flight by four aircraft lasting four-and-a-half hours, followed by a further flight by three aircraft of six-and-a-half hours duration in which a distance of 900 miles was flown. In October 1938, the squadron exchanged its Merlin II Battles for Merlin I Battles from No.226 Squadron. A composite flight of five aircraft from Nos.35 and 207 Squadrons was attached to No. 4 ATS, West Freugh, to train u/t wireless/operator air gunners in gunnery. The aircraft establishment was increased from 16 to 21 in October 1938 and five Merlin I Battles were received from No.150 Squadron. Merlin II Battles were received in late January and early February to replace the Merlin I aircraft. The squadron went to No.4 ATS for its annual armament training on 20 February 1939, but had to return to

Cottesmore on 1 March because the airfield at West Freugh was unserviceable. During night flying on 5 May 1939, K9469 crashed, killing the pilot and two passengers. The squadron was classified as a training squadron in July 1939 and two Ansons were received.

In August 1939 the squadron moved to Cranfield, followed by general mobilisation at the beginning of September. The aircraft establishment had been increased and eleven Merlin III Battles were received from Austin and five from other squadrons. On the outbreak of war it was confirmed that the squadron was to be a non-mobilising unit training aircrew to replace casualties in Nos.15 and 40 Squadrons, AASF. The squadron was transferred from No.2 Group to No.6 (Training) Group, Bomber Command, as a Group Pool squadron. By the end of September, the squadron had completed the training of all its u/t aircrew personnel, who were posted to Nos.63 and 98 Squadrons and was amalgamated with No.207 Squadron to form No. 1 Group Pool for training personnel for the AASF. In October 1939, the squadron was notified that it was to re-equip with Mk.IV Blenheims and the first Blenheims were received in the following month. There was a fatal accident on 29 October when K9472 crashed at Carew Cheriton and caught fire. All three crew were killed. Another Battle, K9473, force-landed near Bedford on 5 November. There were no injuries to the crew but the aircraft was a write-off. The squadron moved to Bassingbourn in December 1939. Battle L5183 force landed near Martlesham Heath on 10 December and was badly damaged. There were no injuries to the crew. The squadron had ceased to use its Battles by 1 February 1940.

K9200 of No.207 Squadron. (via PJ)

No.207 Squadron

No. 207 Squadron, based at Cottesmore, started to replace its Wellesleys with Merlin II Battles in April 1938 and the full complement of sixteen aircraft was on squadron charge by 26 May. Training on the Battles commenced and pilots reported no difficulty in the change of aircraft types. One aircraft from the squadron took part in Empire Air Day in May 1938 at Sealand and night flying in the Battles started in July. A new type of sparking plug was tested for the Air Ministry in July and October. Training continued in the remainder of 1938 and the squadron took part in the Home Defence Exercises in August. In October 1938, the squadron was disappointed when it had to exchange its Merlin II Battles for older Merlin I machines from No.105 Squadron, and some difficulties were found in keeping them serviceable. A detachment was sent to No.4 ATS at West Freugh in October to give training to air gunners. Intensive night flying to train pilots in cross-country night flights started in December 1938 and in that month the pilot of K7585 was killed when his aircraft hit a tree near the aerodrome and burst into flames during night flying. The unwelcome Merlin I Battles were exchanged for Merlin II models in January 1939 and the establishment of Battles was increased to twenty-one. Battle L4967 crashed near Swaffham in Norfolk on 23 March and its three crew were killed. The aircraft was damaged beyond repair. The squadron took part in several defence exercises in 1939 and nine aircraft were used in the May 1939 Empire Air Day displays. Two Ansons were received when the squadron was declared a training squadron in July 1939. Intensive armament training was undertaken at No.8 ATS, Evanton, in August and later in the month the squadron moved to Cranfield. When war was declared the squadron became a Group Pool squadron in No.6 (Training) Group, Bomber Command. Training continued and K9448 was lost on September 19 when it flew into a hillside at Winchcombe, near Cheltenham. The two crew were killed. The squadron moved to Cottesmore in December 1939 and in January 1940 a high level of unserviceability was reported because aircraft were awaiting spares. The unit moved to Cranfield early in April 1940, and later in the month to Benson, where it was merged with Nos.52 and 63 Squadrons in No.12 OTU.

K9202 of No.98 Squadron (A Thomas collection)

No.98 Squadron

The Hawker Hinds flown by No.98 Squadron were replaced by Merlin II Battles in mid 1938 at Hucknall. K9199 and K9201 were received on 27 May and the full establishment of 16 aircraft had been received by 17 June. Training on the Battles started and continued through the remainder of 1938 and 1939. In November 1938, the aircraft establishment of the squadron was increased to 21 and six new Battles were received. The squadron spent two weeks at No.5 ATS at Penrhos for annual armament training in January 1939. The first loss of a Battle occurred on 10 February, when K9216 crashed near Stow-on-the-Wold. A display for the 1939 Empire Air Day was given on 20 May. On mobilisation of the RAF on 1 September 1939, the squadron had 16 aircraft serviceable out of 21. There were 26 pilots, of whom 16 were fully trained; 14 observers, of whom only one was qualified and 22 wireless operator/air gunners of whom only three were fully trained. Together with the other No.2 Group Battle

squadrons, No.98 Squadron was transferred to No.6 (Training) Group, Bomber Command.

There followed a period of doubt about the squadron's future; it was allegedly disbanded, with its personnel posted to the AASF and Nos.35 and 207 Group Pool Squadrons. Then there were second thoughts and on 20 September 1939 the squadron was declared to be a reserve squadron. Training then continued with the squadron receiving aircrews from training at Group Pool squadrons prior to their posting to the AASF. Considerable doubt still existed as to the role of the squadron; in September the Operations Record Book refers to "lack of policy and organisation", and in November it is recorded that the squadron had been in a state of flux since the war started with constant postings in and out. No.6 Group were asked to define the policy to be adopted by the squadron. Three aircraft were detached to Weston Zoyland for gunnery training on 11 September, but these were recalled to Hucknall four days later. There were several movements of aircraft in and out of the squadron between September 1939 and the end of November. In September, two Battles were received from No.185 Squadron and six Battles were sent to Abingdon for armour plate to be fitted prior to their transfer to No.15 Squadron in France. There were two fatal accidents in late 1939; on 7 November, K9238 crashed at Stow-on-the-Wold, killing all three crew, and on 9 December there was another crash near Stow-on-the-Wold when K9467 flew into the ground in fog, seriously injuring the pilot and killing two crew. The new year opened badly when K9205 crashed while attempting a forced landing at Wilmington in Sussex on 2 January 1940. Between 2 and 11 March 1940, the squadron moved to Scampton. Information was received that the squadron would be moving to France in a non-operational capacity in April, where it would act as a training unit for the AASF and would hold a reserve of Battle aircrews. A move to Finningley was made on 20 March 1940 and the move to France, to Chateau Bougon, Nantes, took place on 16 April. The squadron took with it sixteen Battles, including one dual control aircraft; these were K9201, K9202, K9210, K9211, K9213, K9215, K9218, K9219, K9229, K9345, K9354, K9365, K9386, K9414, K9422 and K9452. While in France the squadron came under the direct control of AASF Headquarters.

Battles of No.52 Squadron at Harwell in 1938. (PJ)

K9176 'G', K9180 'X' and K9709 'O' of No.226 Squadron. (P Jarrett collection)

No.1 GROUP, BOMBER COMMAND

Squadrons and Locations

The squadrons of No.1 Group of Bomber Command started to re-equip with Battles in April 1937. The first squadron in the Group to operate Battles was No.105, followed by Nos.226, 88, 218, 12, 142, 15, 40, and 103 Squadrons. In August 1938, No.150 Squadron, which had been disbanded in 1919, was reformed with Battles. The ten squadrons of Battles in the Group were located in pairs at five RAF stations, each pair designated to form a wing in the AASF in the event of war. The squadrons and their bases on 1 September 1939 were:

105 and 226 Squadrons	Harwell
88 and 218 Squadrons	Boscombe Down
12 and 142 Squadrons	Bicester
15 and 40 Squadrons	Abingdon
103 and 150 Squadrons	Benson.

No.1 Group ceased to exist on 2 September 1939, when its squadrons went to France to form the bomber arm of the AASF. The Group AOC, Air Vice Marshal P.H.L. Playfair, also moved to France and assumed command of the AASF. The Group reformed in June 1940 with some of the surviving Battle squadrons which had been evacuated from France.

No.105 Squadron

Seventeen Merlin I Battles were received by the squadron at Harwell between 18 August and 22 December 1937. One became an instructional airframe in November, leaving 16 aircraft on strength on 31 December 1937. In October 1937 the squadron took part in a demonstration fly-past of new types of aircraft for visiting German staff officers. Press photographers from *The Aeroplane* came to take pictures of the Battles in November 1937 and in December the squadron held its annual training camp at Woodsford (later renamed Warmwell) in Dorset. Training on the Battles and exercises continued during 1938 and there were several visits to the squadron by the press and others. On 4 April, K7615 crashed at Harwell while the pilot was attempting a landing with a jammed undercarriage. The aircraft was not repairable and was broken up for parts shortly after the accident. The squadron spent three weeks at No.3 ATS at Sutton Bridge for its annual training camp in April. A display of formation flying and low level bombing was given at Hanworth Park airfield on Empire Air Day in May. Night flying with the Battles started in 1938 and on 21 July K7689 crashed at

K7578 of No.105 Squadron. (RCS collection)

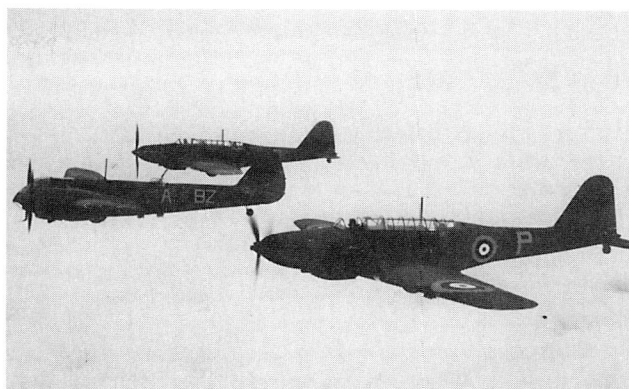

Two Battles of No.226 Squadron with a Blenheim of No.107

Lasham in Hampshire while engaged on AA searchlight co-operation. The pilot baled out but his two crew were killed. At the beginning of October 1938, the squadron held 19 Merlin I Battles.

It was decided that these should be exchanged for Merlin II machines in accordance with the policy of equipping the mobilising squadrons with aircraft with the later type of engine. Of the 19 Merlin I Battles, 16 went to No.207 Squadron and three to No.6 MU. Fifteen Merlin II Battles were received from No.207 Squadron and five from Fairey. During night flying on 8 November 1938, K9196 suffered engine failure near Harwell. Two crew parachuted safely and the pilot force-landed the aircraft, suffering concussion. The aircraft was a write-off and became a ground instructional machine. The squadron aircraft strength at the end of 1938 was 19 Merlin II Battles, with three Merlin I Battles awaiting disposal to No.6 MU. At the end of January 1939, the squadron went to No.4 ATS at West Freugh for annual training. While there, on 31 January, P/O D.G. O'Brien force landed K9340 on the beach at Sandhead after experiencing engine trouble. The aircraft was immersed by the tide and was a write-off. The squadron again provided aircraft for a display on Empire Air Day in May 1939. In July the squadron took part in the mass formation flight over France. At the end of August 1939, the squadron had 33 Battles on its strength. Mobilisation for war started on 26 August 1939 and was completed by 1 September.

On 2 September, the squadron moved to its war station at Reims in France. The advanced air party was flown out in the morning in Ensign aircraft and the advanced stores went by D.H.86. The advanced sea party left at noon and at 1430 sixteen Battles took off for Reims, where fifteen arrived at 1700. These were K9185, K9186, K9188-K9190, K9193-K9195, K9198, K9338, K9339, K9341, K9342, K9485 and K9486. The remaining Battle, K9197, piloted by Sgt B.F. Phillips, force-landed at Poix when a connecting rod broke through the engine sump. The aircraft was a write-off and was replaced by K9187 on the following day. The squadron aircraft which did not go to France were transferred to other units.

No.226 Squadron

The squadron re-equipped with 16 Merlin I Battles, replacing its Hawker Audaxes, between 14 October and 10 December

1937 at Harwell. An early loss occurred on 11 December 1937 when K7594 spun off a turn at low speed and height and crashed at Chesil Bank in Dorset. This happened while the crew were practising air-to-ground firing with the rear gun and the aircraft was damaged beyond repair. During the squadron's stay at No.4 ATS, West Freugh, for armament training, K7623 crashed and was badly damaged on 22 March 1938. It was struck off charge shortly afterwards. Training and other routine activities continued through 1938 and on 6 October K7589 crashed at Plynlimon and was damaged beyond repair. The Merlin I Battles were replaced by Merlin II machines and the aircraft strength was brought up to 21 in October and November 1938. Fourteen were received from No.35 Squadron and seven from Fairey. During 1939, particular attention was paid to training for low level attacks. There were two serious aircraft accidents in August 1939; K7711 crashed at Weatheroak Hill, Birmingham, on 5 August and K7706 crashed at Harwell on 17 August. More Battles were received and there were 31 on charge on 31 August. All preparations for war were completed by 1 September 1939 and the squadron's advance air party flew to Reims by civil aircraft the following morning. At 1400 on 2 September, fifteen Battles took off for Reims where they arrived two hours later. There should have been sixteen but one failed to start and this aircraft followed an hour later. The surplus Battles were sent to other units.

K7635 of No.88 Squadron at Boscombe Down.
(P Jarrett collection)

No.88 Squadron

Fifteen Merlin I Battles were received at Boscombe Down from Fairey between 17 December 1937 and 13 January 1938. A sixteenth, K7642, was on its delivery flight in bad weather when the pilot got lost and force-landed in a soft field. The aircraft skidded and dropped over a bank and was damaged beyond repair. A replacement, K7692, was received from Fairey on 1 April 1938. The squadron went to No.7 ATS at Acklington for its annual armament training in May 1938. Aircraft were sent to seven RAF stations to take part in the 1938 Empire Air Day displays on 29 May. On 18 June, K7637 crashed during a night landing at Boscombe Down and was badly damaged. It was not repairable and was designated as an instructional airframe. K7630 crashed at Norton Heath in Essex on 7 August, caught fire and was damaged beyond repair. The wireless operator baled out safely but the observer was killed when he jumped from too low a height. The pilot, F/Lt Gardiner, stayed with his aircraft and suffered burns. The squadron exchanged its Merlin I Battles for Merlin II machines in October 1938. Sixteen were received from No.106 Squadron and five were collected from Fairey at Ringway, bringing the aircraft strength up to twenty-one.

The 1939 annual armament training camp was at No.8 ATS at Evanton in April. While at Evanton, K9319 crashed as it was landing on 13 April. A display of formation flying and a demonstration of refuelling and rearming were given on Empire Air Day in May 1939. On 26 June, K9249 caught fire in the air, was abandoned by the crew and crashed at Netherhampton in Wiltshire. The pilot, P/O D.A.J. Foster, and the wireless operator parachuted safely but the observer was killed. In 1939 a further 15 Battles were taken on charge and a third flight was formed. On 2 September 1939, sixteen Battles flew from Boscombe Down to Auberive in France. They were K9242-K9245, K9247, K9248, K9250, K9316, K9318, K9321, K9322, K9348, K9349, K9351, K9352 and K9441. The remaining Battles were transferred to various units.

K7664 of No.218 Squadron. (P Jarrett collection)

No.218 Squadron

The initial complement of sixteen Merlin I Battles was received at Upper Heyford between 17 January and 11 February 1938. The squadron moved to Boscombe Down on 22 April 1938. On 18 May, K7661 crashed while landing at Boscombe Down and was damaged beyond repair. Visits were made to five RAF stations on Empire Air Day on 28

May to display the Battles on the ground. June 1938 was spent at No.4 ATS, West Freugh, for annual armament training. On 27 August, K7657 crashed when its under-carriage collapsed while landing at Boscombe Down. The aircraft was not repairable. Fifteen Merlin II Battles were received from No.185 Squadron in October 1938 to replace the old Merlin I aircraft and six new Merlin II Battles were collected from Fairey at Ringway, bringing the squadron strength of Merlin II aircraft to 21. While landing K9260 at Boscombe Down on 11 April 1939, the pilot overshot the airfield and crashed. Training on the Battles continued in 1939 and the squadron took part in Empire Air Day in May with demonstrations of formation flying and low level bombing. In June 1939, it was decided to form a third flight and eleven new Battles were collected from Austin in July. The squadron made two successful flights over France in July with the dual purpose of training and showing the flag. While taking part in a mock low level raid in the Home Defence Exercise on 11 August, K9328 hit an electricity pylon at Carlton, near Bedford, and crashed. The pilot and observer were killed and the wireless operator died later in hospital. The aircraft was a write-off. The squadron mobilised for war at the end of August 1939 and on 2 September 16 Battles took off from Boscombe Down at 1510 and flew to Auberive in France, where they landed at 1740. The aircraft were K9251, K9252, K9254-9256, K9273, K9323-K9327, K9329, K9353 and K9355-K9357. The remaining squadron aircraft were dispersed to other units.

No.12 Squadron

Between 11 February and 1 April 1938, the squadron's Hawker Hinds were replaced by sixteen Merlin I Battles. The Battles were flown from Fairey to the squadron's base at Andover. In 1938 and 1939, the squadron took part in a variety of exercises and practice flights, including fighter affiliation, mock raids, gunnery and bad weather flying. A month was spent at No.4 ATS, West Freugh for bombing and gunnery training in June/July 1938. The Operations Record Book contains the interesting comment ".....the results obtained were very good, indicating the aptitude of 'Battle' aircraft for dive bombing". The squadron participated in Home Defence Exercises in August 1938 and on 5 September K7691 crashed while landing at Andover. All but one of the squadron's Merlin I Battles were exchanged for Merlin II machines in autumn 1938, of which thirteen came from No.150 Squadron, three from Fairey and six from Austin. The squadron again visited No.4 ATS at West Freugh for annual armament training in February 1939. On the flight back to Andover, engine trouble forced K9287 to force-land near Grimley, Worcester. When attempting to fly the undamaged aircraft out of the field where it had landed, F/O P.H.M.S. Hunt took off but the engine failed at 150 feet and the aircraft crashed and was damaged beyond repair. The squadron moved from Andover to Bicester on 9 May 1939.

On Empire Air Day in May 1939, six aircraft gave a dive bombing demonstration at Upper Heyford and Ansty and another six demonstrated at Halton and Henlow. Eleven new Battles were received from Fairey in June 1939 to form a third flight for training new aircrew. Nine aircraft took part in a mass formation flight over France on 11 July 1939 and a flight was detached to Catterick for ten days in July to take part in intensive gas spraying exercises with the Army. Home Defence Exercises were held in early August and mobilisation

Battles of No.207 Squadron lined up at Cottesmore early in 1939. (ACM Sir Neil Wheeler)

to a war footing started on 23 August. On 2 September 1939 the squadron left Bicester for its war station at Berry-au-Bac, north west of Reims. The forward maintenance parties left by air and sea in the morning, the air party taking some of its stores by civil aircraft. Sixteen Battles and one Magister left Bicester at 1415 and arrived without incident at Berry-au-Bac at 1645. The remaining Battles were dispersed to MUs or other squadrons.

No.142 Squadron

The squadron's Hawker Hinds were replaced by Battles between 4 March and 23 April 1938 at Andover. Of the sixteen Battles received, eight were fitted with Merlin I engines and eight with Merlin IIs, a situation which led to servicing difficulties. During the rest of 1938, all of the Merlin I Battles were transferred to other squadrons and thirteen Merlin II machines were received. The whole of the squadron took part in Empire Air Day on 28 May 1938 with a varied programme, which included formation flying, flight drill, a set piece exercise and the dropping of a dummy parachutist. In June four aircraft were detached to No.4 ATS at West Freugh for five days for air gunnery training. Training continued in 1938 with live bombing and air to ground firing and mock raids were mounted during the Home Defence exercises in August. The squadron went to No.4 ATS at West Freugh for annual armament training in October. On 14 October, K7702 crashed while landing at West Freugh and was damaged beyond repair. There were

twenty Battles on the squadron strength at the end of 1938. Three aircraft were lost in crashes in the early part of 1939. On 28 January, K9335 crashed during a forced landing at Tarrant Keynestor in Dorset and on 1 March, K9334 crashed during a forced landing near Honiton in Devon. On 2 March, K9294 crashed on take off at Andover. The squadron moved to Bicester on 9 May 1939 and a few days later went to Leuchars for annual training. Thirteen aircraft took part and the training syllabus was completed with "average results". A further thirteen Battles were received in mid-1939. In July 1939, 'A' flight was detached to No.8 FTS at Montrose where it successfully carried out a gas spraying exercise in collaboration with Scottish Command. In the following month the squadron took part in the Home Defence exercises, flying from its satellite airfield at Weston-on-the-Green. The squadron flew to its war station at Berry-au-Bac on 2 September 1939. Sixteen Battles flew out without incident; these were K7696, K7697, K7700, K7701, K7703, K9184, K9259, K9292, K9293, K9333, K9337, L4936, L4937, N2087, N2088 and P2195. Essential maintenance staff were flown to France in an Ensign.

No.15 Squadron

A complement of twenty-one Merlin II Battles was received by the squadron between 13 June and 27 October 1938 at Abingdon. These replaced Hawker Hinds. Six Battles made simulated high and low level attacks in the Home Defence exercises in August 1938 and in October the squadron was

K9315 of No.40 Squadron after an undercarriage leg collapsed at West Freugh, 12 January 1939. (W Huntley via A Thomas)

one of three which made a series of tests to ascertain the war-loaded operational range of the Battle. Six of the squadron's aircraft flew in formation at various heights and speeds and remained in the air for four-and-a-half hours. No aircraft achieved a range of 1,000 miles. Night flying and practice bombing started in October 1938. The first serious accident occurred on 22 November 1938 when K9305 crashed during a forced landing at Steppingley in Bedfordshire. Air gunners from the squadron were sent to No.4 ATS at West Freugh in January 1939 for gunnery training and the results were said to be "very promising indeed". On 20 February 1939, L4939 crashed while taking off from Abingdon. March 1939 was a busy month with the squadron participating in a demonstration for Arab delegates at Northolt and a fly-past to welcome the French President on his arrival at Dover.

There was a tragic incident on 5 April 1939 when P/O Shennan was killed when he fell out of the rear cockpit of a Battle during low level bombing practice at Abingdon. It was decided that the pilot of the aircraft was in no way to blame. On 21 April, F/O P.G. Chapman force landed K9302 on the airfield at Abingdon when the engine failed at 700 feet after take-off. The observer and a passenger were slightly injured and the aircraft was damaged beyond repair. Dive bombing displays were given at Filton and Whitchurch on Empire Air Day on 20 May 1939. Twelve Merlin III Battles were received from Austin in July 1939 to form a third flight, which brought the squadron strength up to 32 Battles. On 25 July, nine aircraft took part in the mass flight over France and were airborne for five-and-a-half hours. The squadron moved

to its war station at Bétheniville in France on 2 September 1939. Civil aircraft carrying key ground personnel and stores left Abingdon at 1000 and sixteen Battles left in flights of four at ten-minute intervals, starting at 1100. All landed safely at Bétheniville and the Battles were refuelled and dispersed round the airfield boundary. The Battles which flew to France were K9224, K9226-K9228, K9233, K9300, K9301, K9303, K9311, K9359, K9457, K9479, L4938, L4940, L4980 and N2024. The remaining aircraft stayed at Abingdon for disposal to other units.

No.40 Squadron

The squadron received twenty-one Merlin II Battles at Abingdon, to replace its Hawker Hinds, between 30 June and 31 October 1938. Six aircraft took part in the October 1938 endurance trials with full war load, but recorded a range of only 859 miles. This was a much lower mileage than was attained by other squadrons taking part and was disregarded in assessing the results because the aircraft had flown at incorrect speeds during the tests. On 7 December 1938, K9241 crashed while attempting a forced landing near Cambridge. A composite unit was formed from Nos.15 and 40 Squadrons in January 1939 for three weeks and this went to No.4 ATS at West Freugh where the air gunners received gunnery training. During this detachment K9315 crashed while landing at West Freugh on 12 January and was damaged beyond repair. The annual training camp was held at No.8 ATS at Evanton in April 1939 and the squadron gave

Battle L4945 of No.150 Squadron at Benson in 1939. (P Jarrett collection)

demonstrations at Empire Air Day in May 1939. Another aircraft was written off when K9306 crashed into a reservoir at Naseby on 14 July. Nine aircraft flew in the cross-country flight over France on 25 July. Twelve new Merlin III Battles were received to form a third flight in July and August 1939. Between 1200 and 1300 on 2 September 1939, sixteen Battles took off to fly to the squadron's war station at Bétheniville, north-east of Reims. One aircraft, L4979, ditched in the English Channel en route and the other fifteen landed safely at Bétheniville. A replacement aircraft for L4979 was flown out from Abingdon on the following day. The squadron's remaining Battles were dispersed from Abingdon to other units.

No.103 Squadron

The squadron's Hawker Hinds were replaced by twenty-one Merlin II Battles between 18 July and 7 November 1938. Initially based at Usworth, near Sunderland, the squadron moved to Abingdon on 2 September 1938. While attempting a forced landing near Ditchling in Sussex on 19 October, K9261 hit trees and crashed. It was damaged beyond repair. A further move, to Benson, was made on 1 April 1939. Training on the Battles continued and the squadron held its annual armament training camp at No.6 ATS at Warmwell in May 1939. While there they took part in an Empire Air Day display. In July and August 1939, a further eighteen Battles were received to form a third flight. The squadron lost K9263 and K9373 when they collided over Nottingham on 6 August 1939. On 2 September 1939, the squadron moved to its war station in France. Sixteen Battles in three formations of six, four and six aircraft took off for Challerange at 1500 and all had landed safely by 1730. They were K9264-K9266, K9268-

K9271, K9295, K9299, K9372, K9374, K9404, K9409, K9411, K9456 and L4957. The Battles remaining in England were dispersed to various units, most of them to No.22 MU.

No.150 Squadron

No.150 Squadron was disbanded in 1919 and was re-formed at Boscombe Down in August 1938. Sixteen Merlin II Battles equipped the squadron and these were received from Fairey between 16 August and 1 September 1938. At the end of September, thirteen of the Merlin II Battles were transferred to No.12 Squadron in exchange for ten Merlin I Battles. Shortly after this, in November 1938, fourteen Merlin II Battles were received from the manufacturers and the Merlin I Battles were transferred to other units. On 7 February 1939, K9482 crashed during a forced landing near Aylesbury. A short armament course was held for two weeks at No.1 ATS, Catfoss, in February and March 1939. The squadron moved to Benson on 3 April 1939. On approach to Benson on 17 April 1939, K9381 crashed and was damaged beyond repair. On 4 July 1939, K9391 crashed into high ground in cloud at Two Bridges on Dartmoor and was struck off charge. Fourteen additional Battles were received in July and August 1939 to form a third flight. The squadron took part in Home Defence exercises in August and mobilisation for war started on 23 August. Fifteen Battles flew to the squadron's war station at Challerange on the afternoon of 2 September 1939. These were K9379, K9380, K9387, K9389, K9390, K9392, K9483, K9484, L4945-L4948, L5225, N2028 and N2093. The sixteenth aircraft, K9283, flew to Challerange on the next day after being delayed by a burst tyre. Most of the squadron's remaining Battles were transferred to No.22 MU.

K7639 of No.106 Squadron. (P Jarrett collection)

No.5 GROUP, BOMBER COMMAND

No.106 Squadron

The squadron started to replace its Hawker Hinds with Merlin II Battles on 11 July 1938 when it was based at Abingdon. On 1 September 1938, the squadron moved to Thornaby and on 26 September it moved to Grantham. By the end of September the squadron had received its full complement of sixteen Battles. In early October, the Merlin II Battles were exchanged for Merlin I machines from No.88 Squadron and the squadron returned to Thornaby on 14 October 1938. More Merlin I Battles were received in late 1938 and early 1939 to bring the squadron strength up to twenty-one. On 13 January 1939, K7631 crashed into the sea off South Shields and neither the bodies of the two crew nor the aircraft were recovered from the sea. It was assumed that the pilot lost control in cloud while flying in formation. Half of the squadron went to No.8 ATS at Evanton for three weeks in February 1939 for preliminary armament training in high level bombing and air-to-air firing. On 18 April 1939, K7563 bellylanded at Thornaby and on 29 June K7562 crashed near Thornaby. Both aircraft were badly damaged and were written off. In May 1939, the squadron started to convert to Handley Page Hampdens and sixteen Hampdens were received to replace the Battles, which were dispersed to other units, mainly training schools.

No.185 Squadron

The squadron's Hawker Hinds were replaced by sixteen Merlin II Battles between June and September 1938. Originally based at Abingdon, the squadron moved to Thornaby on 1 September 1938 and to Grantham on 27 September. In October and November 1938, the squadron's Merlin II Battles were replaced by Merlin I Battles. The squadron returned to Thornaby on 15 October 1938. On 11 November, K7664 hit a hut at Henlow and was struck off charge shortly afterwards. In January 1939, the squadron strength was brought up to twenty-one aircraft and in the same month re-equipment with Merlin II Battles started. By 15 February 1939, the squadron had received its full complement of twenty-one Merlin II Battles. The old Merlin I machines were sent to various units, most of them to No.1 AAS. On 13 March 1939, L4972 crashed at Thornaby and was damaged beyond repair. The squadron was affiliated to the town of West Hartlepool and on 15 April 1939, nine Battles visited Hartlepool's municipal airport to take part in the opening ceremony. In June 1939, Handley Page Hampdens replaced the Battles, most of which were sent to training units.

Battle K7659 of No.185 Squadron at Odiham in 1938.
(A Thomas collection)

Three Battles of No.12 Squadron in formation with four Hawk 75-C1s of Groupe de Chasse II/4. (P Jarrett collection)

CHAPTER 5. THE BATTLES GO TO FRANCE

Anglo-French Policy

Early in 1939, agreement had been reached with the French for the establishment of two separate RAF commands in France in the event of war. The Air Component of the Field Force was to consist of medium bomber, fighter and army co-operation squadrons and its main functions would be to provide reconnaissance facilities and air protection for the British army units in France. The Advanced Air Striking Force was to remain a part of Bomber Command, located in France so that the limited range of its light bombers would enable them to reach Germany or to take part in Continental operations if the Germans advanced from their western borders. It was to consist of light or medium bombers and some fighters.

The employment of the projected AASF was the subject of much debate between the British Air Staff and the French. The political instability of France in the 1930s had ensured that by 1939 the French air forces were equipped with a variety of obsolete aircraft, with very few modern types. Because of the poor state of its air defences and its proximity to German air bases, France was vulnerable to air attack by the Germans. Fearful of retaliation, the French would not agree to British bombers based on French airfields having a free hand to bomb Germany and they insisted that the AASF should be used to counter any German ground attack. Knowing the limitations of the aircraft available to them, grave doubts were expressed by the British Air Staff as to the possible effectiveness of such a course of action, but they reluctantly agreed to the French proposal to use the AASF bombers to attack German columns, communications and air bases.

The French had earmarked airfields in France for the use of the British air forces and in May 1939 1,000 tons of bombs and a supply of ammunition and pyrotechnics were sent to France. These munitions were stored at the French ammunition depot at Nogent l'Abbesse, 6 miles east of Reims, convenient for use at the airfields allocated to the AASF in that area. The bombs were 500-lb, 250-lb and 40-lb explosive types, together with a supply of incendiary bombs. The Chief of the Air Staff estimated that the availability of the bombs would enable the AASF first echelon to operate two days earlier than if the bombs had not been stored in France. The transfer of the bombs was made in the guise of a sale to the French and it was decided that the issue of paying rent for the storage space should be left in abeyance, unless the French pursued it.

Movement of Squadrons to France

There was an expectation, perfectly reasonable at the time, that if war broke out the Germans might mount an immediate attack on France. Because of the deteriorating political situation, the order for the mobilisation of the 1 Group squadrons and their preparation for the planned move to France was given on 24 August 1939. Two days later an

Bombing-up a Battle in the severe winter of 1939/40 in France. (IWM C.604)

advance party of officers went to France to set up a headquarters for the AASF at Chateau Polignac at Reims, and this was done by 1 September. On 2 September, the ten Battle squadrons of 1 Group flew to the Reims area where they became the Advanced Air Striking Force, and Air Vice Marshal P.H.L. Playfair, the former AOC of 1 Group, assumed command. The area had been selected because it was close to Germany. These ten squadrons formed the bomber arm of what was intended to be the first echelon of the Advanced Air Striking Force. In the event, the squadrons which would have formed the second echelon, from No. 2 Group, Bomber Command, were retained in England and the bomber strength of the AASF remained at ten squadrons. The main reason for this was that the French failed to provide ten satellite airfields as agreed in the original plans. In the absence of these satellites, the airfields intended to house the second echelon were used for dispersing the squadrons of the first echelon. The fighter arm of the AASF consisted of two squadrons of Hurricanes, Nos. 1 and 73, and these flew to France on 8/9 September 1939, initially as part of the Air Component but they were transferred to the AASF in October 1939. In all, 160 Battles were scheduled to leave England on the day before war was declared on Germany. The Battles started to fly out on the morning of 2 September, with 15 Squadron leaving first. This squadron began its departure at 1100 in flights of four aircraft at ten minute intervals. 40 Squadron left between 1200 and 1300 and the remaining squadrons followed during the afternoon. They crossed the English coast at Shoreham in Sussex then flew over the Channel to France and on to their designated airfields near Reims.

From Abingdon:	15 Squadron, 16 to Bétheniville.
	40 Squadron, 15 to Bétheniville.
	one ditched in the English Channel.
From Harwell:	226 Squadron, 16 to Reims.
	105 Squadron, 15 to Reims.
	one forced to land in France en route.
From Bicester:	12 Squadron, 16 to Berry-au-Bac.
	142 Squadron, 16 to Berry-au-Bac
From Benson	103 Squadron, 16 to Challerange.
	150 Squadron, 15 to Challerange.
	one was delayed until the following day.
From Boscombe	218 Squadron, 16 to Auberive.
Down:	88 Squadron, 16 to Auberive.

The No. 40 Squadron Battle which came down in the English Channel was L4979, piloted by F/Lt W.G. Moseby. The ditching was caused by engine trouble and occurred 15 miles north of Dieppe. The aircraft sank in two minutes, but the crew was rescued from the sea by a cross-Channel steamer. On arrival in England, F/Lt Moseby was admitted to hospital suffering from concussion; the other two members of the crew were uninjured. The No. 105 Squadron machine which failed to reach its destination was K9197, which suffered engine failure and force-landed near Poix. The aircraft was a write-off but none of the crew were injured. In addition to the aircraft and their crews, some essential maintenance staff

No.12 Squadron crews walk out to their aircraft in the snow at Berry-au-Bac. (IWM C 366)

and equipment were flown to France in a variety of civil aircraft. The majority of the squadrons' personnel, with their transport and equipment, followed some days later by sea and land. As well as the operational squadrons, various ancillary units necessary for the maintenance of the AASF were set up in September and October. The main ones were:

No. 1 Salvage Section, Reims
No. 2 Salvage Section, Mourmelon
No. 4 Air Stores Park, Ludes
No. 5 Air Stores Park, Puisieux
No. 6 Air Stores Park, Avize
Forward Air Ammunition Park, Nogent l'Abbesse
Railheads at Rilly, Germaine, Vertus
No. 1 Medical Receiving Station, Prosnes
No. 2 Medical Receiving Station, Mareuil-sur-Ay
No. 4 Casualty Clearing Station, Epernay.

The Air Stores Park at Puisieux was later moved to Verzenay because of the extremes of mud at Puisieux. The arrangements made by the French for the reception and accommodation of the AASF, which were supposed to have been agreed well in advance, revealed the inefficiency and incompetence of our ally. In many instances airfield installations were completely inadequate and the billeting and feeding of personnel were chaotic. Fortunately the weather was generally fine, so that those who perforce had to sleep in the open or in draughty barns were not assailed by cold or rain, uncomfortable though many undoubtedly were. The squadrons needed some time to settle in their new surroundings, but the process was made doubly difficult by the lack of co-operation, or sheer indifference, of the French services. Many hard-pressed squadron officers took matters into their own hands when it became obvious that little could be expected from the French. The movement of the Air Component, under the command of Air Vice Marshal C.H.B. Blount, took place over a longer period as it was keyed in with the BEF army movements to France.

Early Organisation

The command structure of the British air forces in France at the beginning of the war was cumbersome and would have been extremely difficult to work if France had been attacked while it was in being. The AASF was under the direct control of Bomber Command Headquarters in England, so that any requests from the French for operations were subject to confirmation by Bomber Command. There was little scope for direct action or initiative by the local commanders. The Air Component was under the control of Lord Gort, the C-in-C of the British Expeditionary Force. There was also a British Air Mission, led by Air Marshal A.S. Barratt, at the headquarters of General Vuillemin, the CinC of the French Air Forces, at Coulommiers. Its function was to liaise with the French in co-ordinating the activities of the Allied air forces. The AASF Battle squadrons were formed into five

The landing grounds used by the Advanced Air Striking Force in 1939-40 had few facilities and much of the accomodation on the airfield was in tents, as used here by No.12 Squadron's dispersal. (IWM C.357)

wings, each of two squadrons. The wings, their commanding officers and the locations of their headquarters were:

No.71 Wing
Nos.15 and 40 Sqns   G/C H.S.P. Walmsley   Bétheniville
No.72 Wing
Nos.105 and 226 Sqns   G/C H.S. Kerby   Reims
No.74 Wing
Nos.103 and 150 Sqns   G/C R.T. Leather   Challerange
No.75 Wing
Nos.88 and 218 Sqns   G/C A.H. Wann   Auberive
No.76 Wing
Nos. 12 and 142 Sqns   G/C H.S. Field   Berry-au-Bac

Initially the two squadrons of each wing were based together on the same airfield, but in order to give a better dispersal of aircraft, one squadron of each wing was moved to its satellite airfield on 12 September. The distribution of the Battle squadrons thus became:

No.71 Wing	No.40 Squadron	Bétheniville
	No.15 Squadron	Condé-Vraux
No.72 Wing	No.226 Squadron	Reims
	No.105 Squadron	Villeneuve-les-Vertus
No.74 Wing	No.103 Squadron	Challerange
	No.150 Squadron	Ecury-sur-Coole
No.75 Wing	No.218 Squadron	Auberive
	No.88 Squadron	Mourmelon-le-Grand

No.76 Wing	No.12 Squadron	Berry-au-Bac
	No.142 Squadron	Plivot.

The AASF set up an advanced headquarters at Chateau Fagnières, near Chalons, on 26 September 1939. In October 1939, No.75 Wing headquarters moved to St. Hilaire and in November No.74 Wing headquarters moved to Tours-sur-Marne. Before the end of September, No.142 Squadron moved back to Berry-au-Bac. In November, the French decided that they needed the airfield at Challerange and No.74 Wing headquarters and No.103 Squadron moved to Plivot. In February 1940, No.103 Squadron moved again, this time to Bétheniville. No.12 Squadron moved to Amifontaine in December 1939. The airfields allotted to the AASF bomber squadrons by the French needed a lot of work on them to make them properly operational and the number of airfields available would only accommodate ten squadrons. More aircraft would have led to a dangerous level of overcrowding and it was therefore decided not to send a second echelon of the AASF to France, but to retain the aircraft and operate them from England. In December 1939, two of the Battle squadrons returned to England to re-equip with Blenheim aircraft. This was supposed to be the first part of a phased replacement programme but no further AASF Battle squadrons were re-equipped. No.40 Squadron left France on 2 December for Wyton and was replaced at Bétheniville by No.139 Squadron, flying Blenheim IVs. No.15 Squadron left France on 9 December for Wyton,

A Battle of No.88 Squadron taxies to the airfield from its disperal at Berry-au-Bac

where it eventually assembled after most of the aircraft had landed at other airfields because of bad weather. No.114 Squadron, flying Blenheim IVs, replaced No.15 Squadron at Condé-Vraux.

Reform

The unsatisfactory command structure of the RAF in France was examined and a fundamental change was made to increase its efficiency. The change also gave the French their wish to have an officer of C-in-C status to be in overall command so that they could get immediate action if needed. Air Marshal A.S. Barratt was appointed C-in-C British Air Forces in France on 15 January 1940. He took over control of the AASF from Bomber Command and assumed control of the Air Component, though the latter was still subject to the operational control of Lord Gort. Air Marshal Barratt established the headquarters of BAFF at Coulommiers, with an advanced battle headquarters at Chauny, where the headquarters of the French Air Commander, Northern Zone, was located. Air Vice Marshals Playfair and Blount continued as AOCs of the AASF and Air Component respectively. Shortly after this change the five bomber wings were reorganised into three, Nos.72 and 74 Wings being disbanded. The constitution of the new wings, after some initial reshuffling, was:

No.71 Wing   G/C H.S. Field, with headquarters at Fagnières; Nos.105, 114, 139, and 150 Squadrons.

No.75 Wing   G/C A.H. Wann, with headquarters at St. Hilaire, Nos.88, 103 and 218 Squadrons.

No.76 Wing   G/C H.S. Kerby, with headquarters at Neufchatel, Nos.12, 142 and 226 Squadrons.

Potential Targets

The arguments with the French about targets for the British bomber force, which had started before the outbreak of hostilities, rumbled on through the first autumn and winter of the war. The French were still opposed to bombing targets in Germany because of their fears of retaliatory bombing of French cities, whereas the British wanted to use their heavy bombers in attacks on German targets. In the absence of agreement an unsatisfactory compromise was adopted. The medium bombers would be used for bombing enemy columns moving by road and rail and for bombing river crossings and other traffic concentrations. The heavy bombers would attack communications west of the Rhine and rail marshalling yards east of the Rhine. Cabinet approval would be needed before attacks on the Ruhr oil refineries could be made. All of this was only to come into effect if the Germans mounted an offensive. Such timidity on the part of the French High Command was typical of their half-hearted approach to the war and their apparent fear of doing anything which might provoke the enemy into a bombing offensive.

RAF Services in France

Much effort by the British went into airfield construction in France in the winter of 1939 and the spring of 1940, most of which was wasted because the new airfields were not ready for use when the German attack started in May 1940. In addition to the various headquarters and squadron organisations, it was necessary to set up many ancillary units to provide stores, transport, salvage, training and other utility facilities. In April 1940, No.98 Squadron moved from England to Nantes, where it came under the direct control of AASF headquarters. This was a non-operational reserve squadron used for the operational training of aircrews from the Group Pool squadrons before they were posted to first line squadrons in France. Also working under the auspices of the AASF was the curious "M" Balloon Unit. Its function was to release small balloons carrying propaganda leaflets towards Germany. The leaflets were released by the action of a burning fuse. After the German attack on 10 May there were many movements of AASF units; these are dealt with in the chapters relating to events after that date.

Training

In the first instance no arrangements had been made for organised training in France because it had been expected that the AASF would be in action soon after the declaration of war. Between September and the end of 1939, the AASF wings and squadrons had arranged training flights in formation flying, fighter affiliation, mock bombing and territory familiarisation on a local basis. From early 1940, AASF headquarters took control of training. The very strict methods of aircraft route controls and other procedures imposed by the French made effective flying training impossible, but when the British threatened to remove their units to the UK for training, some of the restrictions were removed. The AASF formed its No.1 ATS at La Salanque airfield near Perpignan and bombing, gunnery and night flying training were carried on there. Each of the eight AASF Battle squadrons visited Perpignan for training, some on two occasions. The very bad winter weather hampered the training effort but much good work was done. In addition, from November 1939, the AASF was allowed to use the bombing range at Moronvilliers for live bombing practice on two days per week. A smaller range at St. Hilaire was also used later, but this was only suitable for mock low flying attacks with practice bombs. French flying control constraints were still proving a hindrance to proper training but eventually agreement was reached to enable night flying, cross-country flying, low flying and cloud flying to be practised in certain areas. Various tactical exercises were carried out by the AASF squadrons, some without the use of aircraft, others simulating attacks on units of the British Expeditionary Force. There were several accidents to AASF Battles during training flights, most of which occurred in early 1940 after the training programme was intensified. The most serious of these are listed below.

No.88 Squadron
6.5.40: Aircraft crashed SE of Laval, near Le Mans during an endurance test. The pilot, Sgt N.F.F. Giddings, and his air gunner were killed and the observer was injured.

No.103 Squadron
1.3.40: L5236 crashed during a forced landing at Chandon, near Amboise. The pilot, F/O A.J. Carver and his two crew were injured. The aircraft was a write off.

27.3.40; P2256 crashed in a wood near the range at St Hilaire-le-Grand while on a low level night bombing exercise. The pilot, P/O J.P. Hinton, and his two crew were killed. The aircraft was burned out.

No.105 Squadron
17.12.39: K9185 force landed near Issoudon while low flying. The aircraft was a write-off but only the air gunner had minor injuries.
15.2.40: K9195 force-landed at Beausse. The aircraft was a write-off but there were no injuries to the crew.
20.2.40: K9193 force-landed on a beach near the bombing range at La Salanque while on a dive bombing exercise. The aircraft was a write-off.
26.3.40: L4980, piloted by P/O A.M. Edgar, crashed and burst into flames at Cheniers while on a night training flight. All three crew were killed.
31.3.40: P2250 crashed at Champigneul during a night AA co-operation flight. The pilot, F/Lt C.R. Mace, and his passenger were killed.

No.142 Squadron
8.4.40: N2088, piloted by F/O P.A.L. Farrell, crashed near Neufchatel during night flying. All three crew were killed and the aircraft was burned out.

No.150 Squadron
19.9.39: L5225 crashed and caught fire at Ecury-sur-Coole while on a local photographic flight. Two crew were killed and the pilot, P/O J.L. Calvert died later.
31.3.40: P2244 crashed near the range at St.Hilaire-le-Grand during a night low level bombing exercise in poor visibility. The pilot, F/O D. Devoto, and his two crew were killed.

No.218 Squadron
13.11.39. K9356 crashed at Auberive during dive bombing exercise. P/O R. Thynne and his two crew were killed.
12.1.40: K9357 force-landed at Pommiers and went through a hedge while on a practice attack on convoys. It was a total write-off.
23.1.40: K9329 collided with K9327 while landing. The pilot of K9329, F/O I.G. Richmond, was injured. Both aircraft were badly damaged and were abandoned when the aerodrome was evacuated in May 1940.
1.3.40: An aircraft crashed 40 miles north of Dijon while on a cross country flight. The pilot, F/O E.V. Hulbert, was injured and his two crew were killed.

No.226 Squadron
7.4.40: P2265 crashed during night flying. The pilot, P/O Dunn, parachuted successfully. His two crew were killed.

Land Operations before 10 May 1940

The Allies in France waited for the Germans to attack from September 1939 until 9 May 1940. On land there was some limited activity shortly after the declaration of war when, on 9 September 1939, French troops moved into the Saarland in an area sixteen miles long and five miles deep. The area had

A trio of No.226 Squadron formates over France in February 1940. (RCS collection)

already been evacuated by the Germans. This move merely straightened out two pockets of land in the frontier near the Warndt Forest. The French took possession of several villages which had been evacuated by their inhabitants and booby trapped, and some casualties were caused by the devices and by mines. No air support was deemed necessary. Some of the press (and others) were deluded into thinking that this was a full scale offensive by the French, but this was certainly not so. The French troops had orders to continue their advance only to the Siegfried Line outposts and not to provoke the enemy. In May 1939 the French had given an undertaking to the Poles that France would take offensive action "with the major part of her forces" on the fifteenth day after mobilisation. This token advance into the Saar was the French Commander in Chief's puny attempt to honour the undertaking. The scale of Gamelin's offensive was hardly likely to help the hard-pressed Poles, nor (more importantly) was it likely to arouse his German opponents into retaliation. When Poland collapsed, the French troops were withdrawn to the Maginot Line, an operation which was completed by 4 October 1939. Apart from this brief inglorious action, in which only nine divisions took part, the only land operations on the Western Front before 10 May 1940 were some patrolling and a limited amount of artillery firing.

P2177, LS-Y of No.15 Squadron. (Bruce Robertson Colln.)

A flight of Battles of No. 218 Squadron in France. (IWM C.449)

CHAPTER 6. OPERATIONS TO 9 MAY 1940

The "Phoney War"

Fighting on the Western Front had been expected to start immediately after the declaration of war, but this did not happen and the lull between September 1939 and May 1940 became known as the "Phoney War" period. The AASF aircrews arrived at their French airfields on 2 September 1939 and within a few days they had made local flights to get to know the areas near their bases. The Battles and their crews were then engaged on daylight reconnaissance flights until 30 September 1939. The purpose of these flights was twofold, to familiarise the aircrews with the front line area and to photograph much of this area. Starting on 8 September, the Battles operated on 20 of the next 23 days, though some of the operations were reconnaissances limited to a distance of 15 miles inside the French side of the border and some were aborted because of bad weather or technical faults. Nearly 300 sorties were completed and on the busiest day, 20 September, nine out of the ten Battle squadrons of the AASF made reconnaissance flights, 30 sorties in all. Most of these flights were made by sections of three aircraft but, starting on 20 September, at least one stronger flight of six aircraft was sent out each day into enemy territory for high level work. All of the squadrons took their turn in mounting the larger flights. German AA fire was met on several occasions, causing minor damage to aircraft, but it was not particularly lethal. The main weaknesses of the Battle, its

slow speed and its lack of armament, were demonstrated in the three clashes with Messerschmitt Bf 109s during the month. The fatal encounter of five aircraft from No.150 Squadron with Bf 109s on 30 September finally convinced the Air Officer Commanding AASF of the futility of sending unescorted Battles over enemy territory in daylight and the reconnaissance flights by Battles were immediately stopped.

Most of the Western Front daylight reconnaissance sorties up to 9 May were then flown by Blenheims. These flights were made by squadrons based in England or by Air Component squadrons based in France. Nos.114 and 139 Blenheim squadrons joined the AASF in December 1939 to replace Nos.15 and 40 Battle squadrons, but took little part in the reconnaissance work. The AASF Battle squadrons flew no further operations until March 1940, when night leaflet dropping/reconnaissance flights over the Rhine were started.

Referring to the September reconnaissance flights, the No.74 Wing Operations Record Book noted: "These patrols have established that the observer cannot assist much with the navigation when the air gunner is 'at ready', because there is not room for two people in the rear cockpit of a Battle and the observer can only see vertically downwards if he remains inside the fuselage. Thus navigation during operational flying must be the responsibility of the pilot. Similarly, oblique photography must be limited; it would clearly be disastrous to

A rare example of a named Battle, 'Old Faithful' belonged to No.226 Squadron. FOs Butler and Scholey pose in front.
(via J D Oughton)

remove the gunner from the rear cockpit over enemy territory in order to allow the observer to take hand-held photographs". Such remarks emphasise the difficulties caused to crews by the restricted working space in the Battle. The AASF Battle squadrons were unhappy about the vulnerability of their aircraft to fighter attack, particularly to attack from behind and below the aircraft. Several initiatives were taken to remedy this by the installation of a Vickers GO gun, firing below and to the rear of the aircraft. On 8 October 1939, No.105 Squadron mounted a gun on a bracket attached to the bombsight spigot in K9486. This was inspected by Air Chief Marshal Sir R. Brooke-Popham and Air Marshal Sir C.S. Burnett on 15 October and an operational trial was carried out four days later. No.150 Squadron had also been experimenting with a third gun to be operated by the air observer through the bombing aperture and had fitted a mock-up of the proposed installation to L4948. The gun could be fired both forward and to the rear, but when firing to the rear it had to be turned upside down and for use in this position it was fitted with a second set of sights. The installation was devised and fitted by one of the squadron's air observers, Sgt. H. Beddall. It was inspected by the ubiquitous Brooke-Popham and Burnett on 21 October and they were very interested in it. The aircraft was flown to Reims on 24 October, where Air Chief Marshal Sir E. Ludlow-Hewitt and Air Vice Marshal P.H.L. Playfair examined the gun mounting and were so impressed by it that the Bomber Command AOC-in-C ordered an aircraft to be flown to Fairey Aviation at Stockport to demonstrate the installation with a view to its adoption for RAF use. L4948 was flown to the Fairey factory on 26 October and immediate action must have been taken because six of the squadron's aircraft were fitted with a third gun by

30 October. While this was going on, No.142 Squadron had flown an aircraft to Fairey to demonstrate another installation of a third gun firing downwards and backwards through a hole cut in the bottom of the fuselage. The mounting had been designed by Group Captain R.M. Field, the Officer Commanding No.76 Wing, and the Wing Operations Record Book records that it was considered to be a great improvement on the mounting already being produced by Fairey. Tests were carried out by Fairey and it was decided that it would be dangerous to cut a hole in the aircraft fuselage to accommodate the gun installation. A critical note was struck by No.218 Squadron when F/Lt H.C. Daish and his crew tested a downward firing gun in K9323 on 25 October and tersely noted "It was found to be impracticable". The AASF Battle squadrons had their aircraft fitted with the third gun installation and no doubt it gave some reassurance to the crews that their defensive armament had been increased by 50%. An Air Ministry meeting on 1 November reported that 16 sets of Fairey-type mountings had been sent to France and a further 300 sets were on order. Trials on the mountings were carried out at A&AEE in November. The squadrons trained in firing from the installation during their visits to the Armament Training School at Perpignan. The third gun fitting was a hastily-adopted expedient and was not a great operational success. The use of a Vickers gun upside down and sighted through a mirror from a prone position could hardly be completely satisfactory. Some observers bent down and looked through their legs to fire the gun; No.103 Squadron noted that when firing astern the observer had to operate the gun "from an unnatural position". The third gun posed a hazard to the Aircraft's radiator when being fired; in March 1940, a design for a gunstop to prevent bullets from

hitting the radiator was submitted by No.226 Squadron and accepted by the AASF.

The winter of 1939/40 was the worst suffered in northern Europe for many years. For the officers and airmen of the AASF it was particularly harsh because of the primitive conditions in which many of them lived. Heavy falls of snow and freezing temperatures made flying from the grass airfields impossible on many days and the AASF ground crews had an extremely difficult job to maintain the aircraft in the open air. Various expedients were adopted to prevent the engines of the Battles from freezing, including tents containing paraffin heaters over the engines. Engines were started at intervals to keep the oil thin and this often had to be done manually because the batteries were often flat in the prevailing low temperatures. When the thaw came, the melting snow caused mud and slush which made taxying the Battles hazardous. Some squadrons had metal mesh laid on parts of their airfields, which made conditions slightly more tolerable. After a very bad month of February, signs of approaching spring were welcome after a winter when the weather proved to be a greater enemy than the Germans.

Before the outbreak of war the Air Ministry started to draw up a number of 'Western Air Plans', each plan setting out a course of air action which might be taken in the event of war. The last of these plans was W.A.16, and it envisaged the mining of German internal waterways. The rivers and canals in Germany were a vital means of communication and if their use could be made hazardous by mining much damage would be done to the transport system. The instigator of the scheme was Mr. Winston Churchill, then First Lord of the Admiralty, and he envisaged large quantities of the mines being laid in a sustained operation. After some unsuccessful designs had been tested, the final design, that of a 35-lb version, was submitted at the end of December 1939 and was accepted, after trials, in April 1940. The mines were called "W bombs" to mask their true purpose and a supply was taken to France, the "W" in the name indicating "Water". The waterways selected for mining were the Elbe, Weser and Rhine rivers and the Dortmund-Ems and Mittelland Canals. The Rhine operation was allocated to the AASF Battles and the other targets to Wellingtons and Whitleys of Bomber Command. At the same time as the aerial mining, it was intended that mines should be floated down the Rhine from French territory above Karlsruhe. The mining had been planned to start in the April 1940 moon period, about 18 April, but the French intervened to postpone it because of their fear of German retaliation if any warlike action was taken. The French said that they were improving their defensive measures against air attack and promised to give a firm date when mining could commence. This was unlikely to be before July 1940 and if the relative calm on the Western Front had continued one wonders whether the French would ever have agreed to the operations being carried out. The project was allegedly highly secret, but at least one war correspondent, Charles Gardner of the B.B.C., found out about it "after pledges of great secrecy". In the spring of 1940, the Battle crews carried out intensive night flying training and a mock 'river' was set up by using two lines of hurricane lamps on the bombing range at St. Hilaire for practising night approaches and attacks. In preparation for the mining operation, the AASF squadrons carried out night reconnaissance flights over stretches of the Rhine, Neckar and Main rivers during the moon periods of March and April 1940. Propaganda leaflets were dropped on these flights, but

this was done to disguise the main purpose, that of reconnaissance. Each of the three bomber Wings of the AASF was allocated a particular section of the rivers to reconnoitre; No.71 Wing had the southern section from Germersheim to Worms, No.75 Wing had the middle section from Worms to Linz and No.76 Wing had the northern section from Bingen to Bonn. The flights provided valuable experience to the aircrews in operational night flying. The Battles flew on these flights on eight nights in March and 23 sorties were completed and seven aborted. In April the action was concentrated into three nights, with 65 sorties completed and four aborted. During these operations one aircraft was lost to enemy action and one aircraft was abandoned when the crew were lost with an unserviceable radio. No W bombs were dropped by French-based Battles, but after the invasion of France some were launched from land into the Rhine at Strasbourg and in June and July 1940 some were dropped by Bomber Command aircraft and some by Fleet Air Arm aircraft.

During the period between September 1939 and May 1940 the AASF squadrons were called to readiness several times in anticipation of enemy attacks; all were false alarms until 9 May. On that day the warning of imminent German action was genuine and the Blitzkrieg on The Netherlands, Belgium, Luxembourg and France started on the following day.

No.12 Squadron

The squadron's first operational flight was a reconnaissance of an area five miles behind the Franco-German border on the afternoon of 17 September. The three Battles taking part were led by F/Lt J.R. Gillman and met no opposition. A similar mission on the following day was aborted and the three aircraft returned to base because of low cloud over the hills. On 20 September, F/Lt W. Simpson led three aircraft on a very low (100 - 300 feet) reconnaissance over the Siegfried Line and photographs of military installations were taken. The German anti-aircraft machine gunners succeeded in putting two bullet holes into a wing of one of the aircraft. F/Lt Simpson has recorded that many of the German troops waved at the aircraft as they passed overhead; he also admitted that he went beyond his orders, both in distance flown over enemy territory and in the height he flew at. On both 21 and 23 September, three aircraft attempted reconnaissance flights but were forced by low cloud to return to base. Three aircraft, with S/L R.W.G. Lywood leading, succeeded in carrying out a frontier reconnaissance on 22 September at a height of 3,000 feet with no opposition. On 25 September seven aircraft, led by F/Lt J.R. Gillman, set out to photograph a line overlap of the Saarbrücken area at 23,000 feet. One aircraft returned with engine trouble and one returned when the observer fainted from lack of oxygen. The remaining five aircraft failed to find their designated reconnaissance area and penetrated German air space as far as Speyer. Heavy flak was encountered over Karlsruhe and three aircraft were slightly damaged. On 27 September three aircraft made an unopposed reconnaissance of an area five miles behind the Maginot Line. The following day, the squadron CO, W/C A.G. Thackray, led three aircraft on a reconnaissance 15 miles on the French side of the border. A similar flight by three aircraft on 29 September was the squadron's last operational flight in 1939.

No.12 Squadron operated on three nights in March and

Marshal of the Royal Air Force Lord Trenchard on a visit to No. 12 Squadron in France. (IWM C 1208)

April 1940 on Rhine reconnaissance and leaflet dropping missions. Seven successful sorties were made and a further two were aborted. On the night of 24/25 March, F/O G.D. Clancy and his crew, flying in L5249, dropped leaflets on Andernach from 8,000 feet and reconnoitred the Rhine to Bingen at heights between 6,000 and 9,000 feet. Neither the river itself nor any shipping were seen because of mist in the river valley. F/Lt Simpson, in L5190, dropped leaflets on Koblenz from 9,000 feet and also carried out a reconnaissance of the Rhine to Bingen, flying at 3,000 feet. He had no difficulty in seeing the river but was unable to see industrial installations at Andernach. Both aircraft met heavy AA fire but reported it as being inaccurate. Almost a month later, on the night of 20/21 April, four aircraft operated:

P2243, F/Lt P.H.M.S. Hunt, dropped leaflets on Bonn from 10,000 feet and reconnoitred the west side of the Rhine from Bonn to Neuwied at 3/4,000 feet. The Rhine was clearly visible.

L5249, P/O B.G.F. Drinkwater, dropped leaflets on Andernach from 10,000 feet and reconnoitred the Rhine to Bingen at 8/10,000 feet.

P2204, F/O D.E. Garland, dropped leaflets on Koblenz and reconnoitred the east side of the Rhine valley.

L5227, Sgt Parkhurst, dropped leaflets on Lahnstein from 10,000 feet and reconnoitred the east side of the Rhine valley to Bingen at 800/6,000 feet. The river was visible with the cliffs obscured by shadows. There was a good deal of searchlight activity and some desultory inaccurate AA fire.

On the following night, 21/22 April, three aircraft set out on leaflet/reconnaissance sorties. P2332, F/O N.M. Thomas, returned early with W/T failure and P2204, P/O A.W. Matthews, returned with an oil leak. P2243, F/O E.R.D. Vaughan, dropped leaflets on Koblenz and carried out a reconnaissance of the Rhine valley to Bingen at heights of 4/10,000 feet. Five Messerschmitt Bf 110s were reported as being seen over Koblenz but they did not interfere. The AA fire encountered was again inaccurate and irregular. This concluded the squadron's operations until the Battle of France started. No operational losses were sustained by the squadron between their arrival in France in September 1939 and 9 May 1940.

No. 15 Squadron

After moving from Bétheniville to Condé-Vraux on 12 September, the squadron commenced operations on 17 September with a reconnaissance by three aircraft to within ten miles of the frontier. A similar mission by three aircraft on 20 September was abandoned because of low cloud east of Verdun. On 24 September six aircraft, led by F/Lt H.Y. Lawrence, set out at 0750 on a high level photo reconnaissance 15 miles into enemy territory in the Bottenbach - Hutschenhausen area. Cloud frustrated the photography and the flight returned via Zweibrücken. A photo reconnaissance of the frontier area between Walweistroff and St. Avold at 3,000 feet was carried out by

48

aircraft were made on 27 and 28 September. A photo reconnaissance flight 20 miles into enemy territory to photograph the Sierr - Schondorf - Osburg area was made by six aircraft led by F/Lt P.G. Chapman on 29 September. Flak was encountered but no damage was done. The squadron's last operation before leaving the AASF was a reconnaissance by three aircraft to within 15 miles of the frontier on 30 September. On 9 and 10 December, the squadron flew to Wyton in the UK for conversion to Blenheims. After re-equipping with Blenheim IVs, No.15 Squadron flew operationally from England with No.2 Group. No.114 Squadron, flying Blenheim IVs, joined the AASF to replace No.15 Squadron at Condé-Vraux.

No.40 Squadron

Flying from their Bétheniville base, No.40 Squadron's first operation was a reconnaissance to within three miles of the frontier in the Thionville - St. Avold - Bitche - Metz area on 17 September 1939. A photo reconnaissance of the same area was made by three aircraft on the following day. A reconnaissance flight by three aircraft on 19 September was aborted because of bad weather. Three aircraft carried out a photo reconnaissance of the Freudenberg - Merzig - Saarlautern area on 20 September. A high level photo reconnaissance flight over the Merzig - Losheim area by six aircraft led by F/Lt Wilson was made on the morning of 21 September. Fairly accurate AA fire was met east of Merzig and two aircraft were hit by shrapnel over Losheim, with little damage. On 22 and 23 September photo reconnaissances of the Sierck - St. Avold area were flown by three aircraft on each day. No flights were made on 24 September, when red, white and blue roundels were painted on the underside of the wings of all squadron aircraft as an aid to identification. There was a reconnaissance by three aircraft of the Thionville - St. Avold - Bitche area on 25 September. A photo reconnaissance of the Saarbrücken - Neunkirchen area at 23,000 feet was carried out on the morning of 26 September by six aircraft, led by the squadron CO, W/C E.C. Barlow. One aircraft was hit by shrapnel over Neunkirchen with no serious damage. The squadron's last operation on Battles was a photo reconnaissance by three aircraft in the Sierck - St. Avold area on 27 September. No.40 Squadron left Bétheniville for Wyton in the UK on 2 December 1939, where it re-equipped with Blenheim IVs, after which it operated from England with No.2 Group. It was replaced at Bétheniville by No.139 Squadron, flying Blenheim IVs.

No.88 Squadron

No.88 Squadron moved from Auberive to Mourmelon on 12 September 1939 and commenced operations on 20 September. On that day three aircraft left Mourmelon at 1000 for a reconnaissance flight in the Sarreguemines area. After coming under AA fire, probably French, the Battles were attacked by three Messerschmitt Bf 109s over Aachen. K9245, F/Sgt Page, was shot down in flames and K9242, F/O R.C. Graveley, had to make a forced landing with the pilot suffering from burns, the gunner dead and the observer severely injured. The observer died later in hospital. The leader of the three Battles, F/O L.H. Baker in K9243, returned safely. His observer, Sgt. Letchford, had fired at one of the attackers and claimed to have shot it down. This was hailed as the first enemy aircraft shot down by an allied aircraft in the war, but the Bf 109 was not, in fact, shot down. The first engagement of the AASF with enemy fighters thus resulted in the loss of two Battles out of three, the unfortunate No.88 Squadron being the victims. On 26 September, six aircraft, led by F/Lt A.J. Madge, carried out a photo and visual reconnaissance of enemy territory east of Saarbrücken at a height of 23,000 feet with an escort of eight French fighters. The aircraft were fired on by AA but no damage was done. The squadron flew no further operational flights until March 1940.

The first leaflet raid by an AASF Battle was made on the evening of 18 March 1940 by one aircraft, P2247, piloted by F/Lt A.J. Madge. 10/10 cloud was encountered and leaflets were dropped on Mannheim and Saarbrücken on ETA. Because of the cloud, the planned reconnaissance of the Rhine between Mainz and Worms could not be carried out effectively. On the night of 23/24 March, two aircraft were despatched on leaflet raids and reconnaissance flights. F/O D.L.R. Halliday in P2247 took leaflets to Oppenheim and reconnoitred the Rhine between Wiesbaden and Worms. On returning with an unserviceable radio, he was unable to locate his base and after more than five hours in the air the crew abandoned the aircraft and parachuted to safety at Pont-sur-Yonne. F/O J.A.F. MacLachlan in K9321 dropped leaflets on Bad Durkheim and carried out a reconnaissance of the Rhine and Neckar rivers in the Worms - Heidelberg area. Two aircraft took off for leaflet raids and reconnaissance on 25 March; one returned because of bad weather, the other returned because of W/T failure. The next operation was on 20/21 April when four aircraft dropped leaflets in the Mannheim and Frankfurt areas and carried out a Rhine river reconnaissance. The mission was completed successfully. In the period 3 September 1939 to 9 May 1940, the squadron lost three aircraft on operations.

No.103 Squadron

S/L J. Coverdale led the squadron's first operation from their base at Challerange on 17 September 1939. Three aircraft took off at 0855 and carried out a reconnaissance at 3,000 feet between Bouzonville and Lauterbourg along the Franco - German frontier, meeting no opposition. An attempted frontier reconnaissance on the morning of 19 September was abandoned when the three aircraft taking part got lost in bad weather and were fired on by AA between Saarlautern and Saarbrücken. On the afternoons of each of the three days 20, 21 and 22 September, three aircraft made further reconnaissance flights in the Bouzonville - Lauterbourg area. At 0940 on 23 September, six aircraft led by F/Lt C.E.R. Tait took off for a high level photo reconnaissance flight to Lebach in Germany. Flying at 24,500 feet, it was found that the rear Vickers K guns in the Battles would not fire in the intense cold. Over-oiling was suspected to be the cause, and this was proved to be the case when a test later in the day with dry guns gave satisfactory results. No photography was possible on this flight because of 10/10th cloud. K9456 returned to Challerange shortly after take-off with engine trouble. Uneventful frontier reconnaissance flights were made by three aircraft on both 25 and 26 September. Three aircraft led by F/Lt M.C. Wells took off at 1220 on 27 September for what was expected to be just another routine frontier reconnaissance flight between Bouzonville and the Rhine. Flying at 3,000 feet, the Battles were attacked by three

French Curtiss Hawk fighters over Bitche. After the British aircraft had fired recognition signals and descended to ground level, the French fighters discontinued the attack and made off. Shortly after this, three Bf 109s attacked the Battles. With a badly wounded observer in great pain and a damaged engine, F/Lt A.L. Vipan force-landed K9271 near Rohrbach with one wheel of his undercarriage still retracted. During the melée the air gunner in F/Lt Vipan's aircraft, A/C Summers, shot down a Bf 109. The observer, Sgt Vickers, was taken to hospital where he died on 7 October. The other two Battles, K9372 and K9265, returned to base undamaged. On 28 September, six aircraft were led by the squadron CO, W/C H.J. Gemmel, on a morning reconnaissance flight at 27,000 feet; nothing of note occurred. The squadron's last operation in 1939 was a reconnaissance by three aircraft which took off at 1005 on 30 September. L4957 returned early with engine trouble. The other two, led by S/L J. Coverdale, completed the flight. The squadron moved to Plivot on 28 November 1939 and to Bétheniville on 15 February 1940.

A night leaflet raid and reconnaissance to Koblenz was carried out by one aircraft, K9246 piloted by F/Lt C.E.R. Tait, on 20/21 March 1940. Searchlights were seen and there was light AA fire. On 24 March, two aircraft set out for a night reconnaissance and leaflet raid on Frankfurt. The observer in K9246 was taken ill and the aircraft returned. Sgt Perry, flying K9269, met searchlights and heavy AA fire and his aircraft was hit by splinters; he completed the flight. On the following night two aircraft dropped leaflets over Frankfurt, Hanau and Wiesbaden in very bad weather conditions which caused the aircraft from other squadrons taking part to abandon the operation. The intended reconnaissance could not be made because of the weather. On the night of 20/21 April, four aircraft reconnoitred the Frankfurt area and leaflets were dropped on Darmstadt and Frankfurt. Searchlights were active but no AA fire was encountered. The operation was repeated by six aircraft on the night of 22/23 April 1940. Searchlights were very active and there was light AA fire. The squadron lost one aircraft on operations between 3 September 1939 and 9 May 1940.

No.105 Squadron

No.105 Squadron commenced operations from Reims on 9 September 1939 when F/Lt C.R. Mace led three aircraft on a reconnaisance flight to within 15 miles of the Franco-German frontier. The operation was repeated on the following day, when the three aircraft taking part were led by the squadron CO, W/C D. Macfadyen. The squadron moved to Villeneuve-les-Vertus on 12 September. On each of the five days 17, 18, 20, 21 and 23 September, three aircraft made reconnaissance flights to within three miles of the frontier without meeting any opposition. On 24 September, six aircraft took off at 1500 for an unopposed photo reconnaissance at 20,000 feet in the Saarbrücken area. No photography was possible because of cloud. A further photo reconnaissance in the Saarbrücken area to Lebach was flown by six aircraft on 29 September. The flight was at 21,500 feet, but heavy AA fire led to the pilots taking evasive action and varying their height. Five out of the six Battles were hit by shell splinters but the photography was successful. Daylight reconnaissance flights by the AASF Battles were discontinued after 30 September and the squadron did not operate again until the following spring.

A single aircraft, K9342, piloted by S/L G.C.O. Key, took off from Villeneuve at 2350 on 20 March 1940 to fly a

Rhine reconnaissance and a leaflet raid on Mannheim. The reconnaissance was thwarted by 10/10th cloud over the Rhine, but the leaflets were dropped. On the night of 24/25 March, two of the squadron's aircraft reconnoitred parts of the rivers Rhine and Neckar and dropped leaflets on Worms and Darmstadt. Considerable searchlight activity was encountered. Rhine reconnaissances and leaflet raids were mounted on three consecutive nights in April, with leaflets dropped on Mannheim, Worms, Heidelberg and Speyer. On each of these nights, four aircraft operated and met many searchlights and some AA fire. The reconnaissances on 20/21 and 21/22 April were successful but those on 22/23 April were hindered by bad visibility. No aircraft were lost by the squadron on operations between 3 September 1939 and 9 May 1940.

No.142 Squadron

No.142 Squadron was based at Berry-au-Bac with No.12 Squadron except for a few days at Plivot from 12 to 16 September. The squadron's first operation, a reconnaissance to the frontier by three aircraft on 19 September, was abandoned because of low cloud and the aircraft returned to base. Three aircraft carried out daylight frontier reconnaissances on 20, 21, 22, 23, 25, 26 and 28 September. On 22 September, five aircraft, with a French fighter escort, reconnoitred to a depth of ten miles over the frontier to Homburg at 20,000 feet, meeting some AA fire. No photography was possible because of poor visibility. Seven aircraft made a photo reconnaissance flight 12 miles into enemy territory to Bettingen at 21,000 feet on 27 September. Again, poor visibility interfered with the photography and the flight met heavy and accurate AA fire over the Saar area. The squadron did not take part in the March 1940 leaflet raids and Rhine reconnaissance flights because it was at Perpignan for armament training during the moon period. There was only one operation during the April moon period, on 20 April, when eight aircraft set out for a leaflet raid and a reconnaissance of the Rhine in the Bonn/Bingen area. Many searchlights were active and there was heavy AA fire. F/Lt K.R. Rogers in P2194 crossed the frontier but then turned back with leaking coolant. Leaflets were dropped on Lahnstein, Koblenz, Andernach and Bonn. The Rhine reconnaissances were made from heights between 3,000 and 1,000 feet. The German blackout was reported to be good, but traffic on the Rhine was visible in the moonlight. The French blast furnaces at Thionville showed up and neutral Luxembourg was fully lit up. The squadron lost no aircraft on operations between September 1939 and 9 May 1940.

No.150 Squadron

No.150 Squadron flew its first operation from Challerange on 10 September when three aircraft led by S/L W.L.M. Macdonald carried out an afternoon reconnaissance in the border area. The squadron moved to Ecury-sur-Coole on the following day. The next operation was on 17 September, when three aircraft led by F/Lt A.E. Hyde-Parker made a border reconnaissance flight. Similar flights were attempted on 18 and 19 September but these were frustrated by low cloud and the aircraft returned to base. In better weather conditions, S/L Macdonald led three aircraft in a frontier reconnaissance flight on 20 September. On the following day, a similar flight of three aircraft was also led by S/L

Macdonald. The three aircraft which took off for an afternoon frontier reconnaissance on 23 September returned because of bad weather. On 25 September, six aircraft led by the squadron CO, W/C A. Hesketh, flew a morning high level photo reconnaissance in the area from Hornbach to three miles east of Rohrbach. The leading aircraft was hit by shrapnel over Zweibrücken. On the same morning, F/O F.M.C. Corelli led a flight of three aircraft on a low level frontier reconnaissance flight. On each of the next three days, three aircraft carried out frontier reconnaissances. An attempted frontier reconnaissance by three aircraft on 29 September was aborted because of poor visibility and the aircraft returned to base. September 30th was a black day for the squadron, when it suffered its first operational losses. At 1100, six aircraft left for a high level photo reconnaissance, planned to fly via Puttelanges to N.W. of Saarbrücken, then to N.W. of Neunkirchen, then to head south to Wittring before returning to base. P/O A.R. Gulley in L4954 lost contact with the flight after his engine started to give trouble and he turned back to base before crossing the frontier. At 1200, over Saarbrücken, the remaining five aircraft were fired on by AA then were attacked by fifteen Messerschmitt Bf 109s. Four of the Battles were shot down, most of them going down in flames. The aircraft and pilots were K9387, F/O F.M.C. Corelli, N2093, F/Lt A.E.Hyde-Parker, N2028, P/O M.A. Poulton and K9484, P/O J.R. Saunders. The surviving aircraft, K9283, piloted by the formation leader, S/L Macdonald, was badly shot up but returned to base. On landing, the aircraft swung round to port, caught fire when it came to rest and was burnt out. A claim was made for one Bf 109 shot down but this was not confirmed, though some of the German fighters were hit by fire from the Battles. Only S/L Macdonald emerged unscathed from this action, the casualty figures being five killed, one wounded, one burned, six injured or suffering from burns but landed by parachute and one prisoner of war. As a result of this action, the whole of S/L Macdonald's crew received decorations subsequently, the DFC for S/L Macdonald, the DFM for AC1 Murcar and the MBE for Sgt Gardiner. Later in the morning, three aircraft carried out a frontier reconnaissance. There was no further operational flying until March 1940.

The squadron's reconnaissance and leaflet dropping flights started on 22 March 1940 when F/O W.M. Blom in K9380 dropped leaflets on Koblenz and carried out a reconnaissance of the Rhine and Nahe rivers. The aircraft was recalled because of bad weather, but did not receive the signal. On the same night F/Lt A.E. Parker in P2182 was recalled from a similar sortie. On 24 March, K9379, piloted by F/O H.R.M. Beall, dropped leaflets on Speyer and reconnoitred the Rhine between Speyer and Mannheim, while F/Lt A.E. Parker in K9380 took leaflets to Mannheim and reconnoitred the Neckar river. Both aircraft were fired on by AA. Two aircraft set out for leaflet and reconnaissance missions on 25 March but both encountered bad weather. P2182, en route to Heidelberg, returned with engine trouble and K9380, bound for Mannheim, returned after W/T delays. The squadron operated on three nights during the April moon period, using four aircraft on each occasion. On 20/21 April the sorties were:

K9390, F/Lt A.E. Parker, leaflets to Worms, Rhine recce., Mannheim - Worms.

K9379, F/O H.R.M. Beall, leaflets to Mannheim, Neckar recce., Heidelberg - Mannheim.

K9369, F/O W.M. Blom, leaflets to Heidelberg, Rhine recce., Speyer - Mannheim.

K9417, Sgt Pay, leaflets to Speyer, Rhine recce., Germersheim - Speyer.

Four identical sorties were flown on the following night by K9380, Sgt Barker, K9369, F/O W.M. Blom, K9379, F/O H.R.M. Beall and K9390, F/Lt A.E. Parker respectively. The four sorties were flown on 22/23 April by P2336, F/O J. Ing, P2184, Sgt Beale, P2182, Sgt Pay, and K9380, Sgt White respectively. On this night there was a slight variation from the previous two nights; the aircraft which went to Mannheim, P2184, did the Speyer - Mannheim reconnaissance and the aircraft which went to Heidelberg, P2182, did the Heidelberg - Mannheim reconnaissance of the Neckar river. Five aircraft, including K9283, which burned after landing, were lost by the squadron in operations between September 1939 and 9 May 1940, all on 30 September 1939.

No.218 Squadron

Based at Auberive, the squadron sent out its first operational flight of three aircraft on a reconnaissance of the area Reims - Nancy - Bitche - Sierck on 10 September 1939. The squadron CO, W/C L.B. Duggan, led this flight. A similar reconnaissance, led by P/O Freeman, was flown on 15 September. A third aircraft was to have taken part but did not go because of bad weather. An afternoon reconnaissance over the frontier to Lauterbourg, led by F/Lt H.C. Daish, was made on 17 September. A high level photo reconnaissance to a depth of ten miles over the frontier was made by six aircraft on the afternoon of 20 September. A promised escort of French Morane fighters failed to materialise and the Battles flew over Breidenbach, Hoheinod, Waldfischbach and Roppeviller. Because of 10/10th cloud, the six aircraft landed at the Aero Club at Gray, 20 miles E.N.E. of Dijon, and stayed there the night. On 22 September, two frontier reconnaissances at 1,500 feet were flown by three aircraft each in the Thionville - Lauterbourg area. No photographs were taken because of poor visibility. The squadron's final operation before daylight reconnaissance by Battles was suspended was on 28 September, when F/Lt H.C. Daish led six aircraft on a high level unescorted reconnaissance at 23,000 feet to a depth of 20 miles into enemy territory. Photographs of the Bitche - Kaiserslautern - Wissembourg area were taken. P/O Freeman in K9355 returned early when his oxygen system failed.

Two aircraft, piloted by F/Lt Rogers and Sgt Dockrill, operated on 23/24 March 1940; one dropped leaflets on Koblenz and reconnoitred the Rhine from Boppard to Linz, and P2249 dropped leaflets on Mainz and did a Rhine reconnaissance from Boppard to Mainz. On the following night, F/O Shaw in P2192 dropped leaflets on Wiesbaden and P/O A.M. Imrie in P2201 took leaflets to Frankfurt; both aircraft carried out reconnaissances over the rivers Main and Rhine. Four aircraft took off on 20 April for a leaflet raid and Rhine reconnaissance between Worms and Mainz. Sgt Horner in L5237 returned shortly after take-off with W/T failure. P2201 was shot down at Kreilsheim; the pilot, P/O H.D. Wardle, was taken prisoner and his two crew members were killed. An announcement to this effect was made on Hamburg Radio and was later confirmed by the International Red Cross. L5235, F/O Newton, and P2192, F/Lt Drews, completed the flight. On 22/23 April, five aircraft dropped leaflets on Bad Kreuznach and Mainz and carried out Rhine reconnaissance. One aircraft of the six originally detailed for

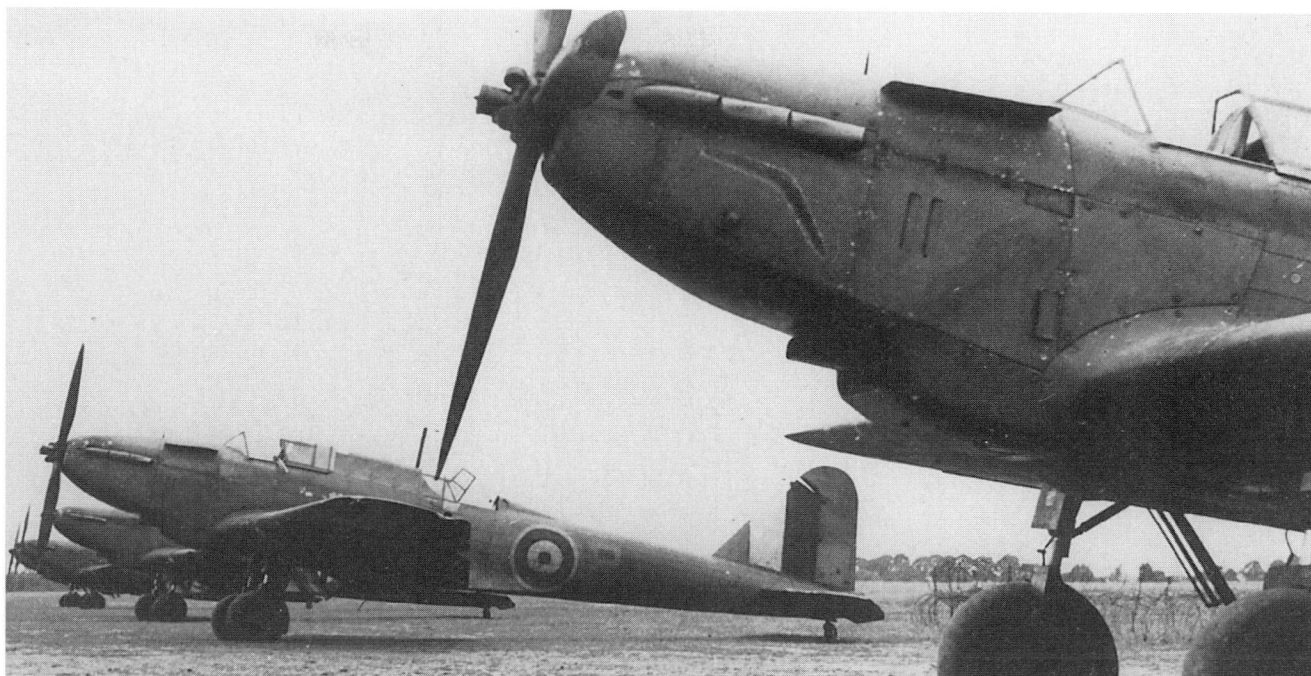

Battle L5420 of No.12 Squadron, in foreground, has a boomerang marking on the nose. Note the anti-dazzle plates fitted for night flying. (RCS collection)

the flight was unserviceable and could not operate. The squadron lost one Battle on operations between September 1939 and 9 May 1940.

No.226 Squadron

During September 1939, the squadron flew reconnaissance flights from its Reims base on ten days of the month. On each of the days 8 and 9 September, three aircraft carried out reconnaissance to within 15 miles of the frontier in the Thionville area. These uneventful flights were flown at 2,500-3,000 feet. Similar flights were attempted on 14 and 15 September but both were aborted. On 16 September, three aircraft, led by S/L C.E.S. Lockett, set out for a reconnaissance to within three miles of the frontier but returned because of bad weather over Verdun. On the following day, F/Lt B.R. Kerridge led three aircraft in a reconnaissance of the frontier area but bad weather forced them to land at Fère-Champenoise; they returned to Reims later. On 19 September, a morning line reconnaissance flight by three aircraft led by S/L Lockett, turned back at Metz because of poor visibility. A similar flight on the morning of 20 September met with more success when F/O Warren led three aircraft and photographed enemy territory. On 22 September six aircraft led by S/L Lockett carried out a photo reconnaissance from Breidenbach to Hohenoid. After a forced landing at St. Dizier, K9182 returned to base later. A reconnaissance of the Saarlautern - Merzig area was undertaken by six aircraft on 27 September. Heavy AA fire was met and two aircraft were hit but there were no casualties. Weather conditions were bad and four aircraft of this flight landed at Laon short of fuel. This reconnaissance completed the squadron's operations for 1939.

On 16 March 1940, L5247 piloted by F/Lt B.R. Kerridge took off for a leaflet raid on Mannheim but the flight was abandoned because the aircraft did not receive the necessary W/T signal to proceed. Two nights later the same aircraft with the same pilot succeeded in dropping leaflets in the Mannheim area, though the projected reconnaissance of the Rhine from Speyer to Karlsruhe was hampered by low cloud. Inaccurate AA fire accompanied searchlight activity. In an effort to stop the white parts of the RAF roundels from showing at night, the squadron covered them with lampblack mixed with water and washed the black covering off with Cameron in P2267 took leaflets to Mainz on 21 March, but reconnaissance was restricted by low cloud. On 24 March, F/Lt R.G. Hurst in P2267 carried out a Rhine reconnaissance between Andernach and Bingen and dropped leaflets on Lahnstein. Sgt Martin in P2180 took leaflets to Neuwied and also made a successful Rhine reconnaissance. Both aircraft encountered heavy searchlight and AA activity. On the night of 21/22 April, seven leaflet/reconnaissance sorties were made. Only six aircraft took part because P2255 flew twice in the operation. The individual sorties were:

P2255, Sgt Hopkin, leaflets to Bonn, reconnaissance Bonn - Neuwied.

P2254, Sgt Annan, leaflets and reconnaissance, Andernach - Bingen.

L5247, Sgt Moseley, leaflets to Bonn, reconnaissance Bonn - Neuwied.

K9354, S/L C.E.S.Lockett, leaflets to Koblenz, reconnaissance Koblenz - Bingen.

P2255, F/O R.W. Bungay,leaflets and reconnaisance.

K9183, P/O D.A.C. Crooks, leaflets to Koblenz, reconnaissance Koblenz - Bingen.

K9180, F/O F.O. Barrett leaflets to Lahnstein, reconnaissance Koblenz - Bingen.

A leaflet raid planned for 23 April was cancelled. No aircraft were lost by the squadron in their operations up to 9 May 1940.

German troops head for the countryside as Battles attack their column. (IWM C1737)

CHAPTER 7. THE BATTLE OF FRANCE (1)

AASF Operations

The "Report on the Advanced Air Striking Force in France", written shortly after the fall of France, described four phases of the operations of the AASF between 10 May 1940 and 18 June 1940. The AASF Battle squadrons were withdrawn to the UK at the end of the third phase. The four phases were:

    1. 10 May - 16 May. Bomber and fighter squadrons operated from the Reims area. Most of the bomber operations were by daylight.
    2. 17 May - 10 June. Bomber and fighter squadrons operated from Southern Champagne until early June, when their bases were moved to the Loire Basin. Advanced Landing Grounds in Southern Champagne continued to be used.
    3. 10 June - 15 June. Bomber and fighter squadrons operated mainly in the lower Seine and Somme areas. As this phase ended the bombers were withdrawn to England.
    4. 15 June - 18 June. The fighter squadrons operated from Nantes and Dinard to cover the evacuation of British forces from western French ports.

When the long awaited German attack on the Low Countries and France started on 10 May 1940, the AASF had ten bomber squadrons. Eight of these were equipped with

Fairey Battles and two with Bristol Blenheim IVs. There were also two squadrons of Hawker Hurricanes to provide fighter support. The German action started in the early hours of 10 May when Panzer divisions made a three-pronged attack. The main assault was through the Ardennes and Luxembourg towards Sedan; the other attacks were made into Belgium and The Netherlands, with back up commando attacks on key Dutch and Belgian bridges. A glider-borne attack was made on the Eban-Emael fortress in Belgium and paratroops were dropped to take bridges over the Meuse River and the Albert Canal and to take key points in The Hague. The *Luftwaffe* made extensive bombing attacks on airfields in Belgium, Holland and France. Early morning attacks were made on AASF aerodromes at Berry-au-Bac (No.142 Squadron), Bétheniville (No.103 Squadron), Mourmelon (No.88 Squadron) and Reims (No.226 Squadron). Little damage was done in these raids but in an evening attack on Mourmelon, three Battles and a training aircraft were set on fire and destroyed. At 0740 on 10 May, AASF Headquarters was informed that the Low Countries had been attacked and permission was given for fighters and reconnaissance aircraft to fly over those countries. Bombers were not permitted to do so. All AASF squadrons were ordered to put 50% of their aircraft on 30 minutes notice. After a morning of utter

L5540 'JN-C' of No.150 Squadron shot down by flak in Luxembourg on 10 May 1940. (A Thomas collection)

confusion in the French High Command, Air Marshal Barratt finally lost patience and ordered the AASF into action. Low flying attacks were made throughout the afternoon on German columns advancing through Luxembourg. All the Battle squadrons except No. 88 took part. They were met by devastating fire from light AA guns carried in lorries and machine guns mounted in motor cycle combinations and of the 32 aircraft which operated, thirteen were lost, two force-landed and all the others were damaged. The aircraft were using 250-lb bombs with 11-second delay fuses. Several hits on transport and on roads were claimed but many crews did not observe the results of the bombing. The Blenheims of Nos.114 and 139 Squadrons were not in action.

On 11 May, the Germans continued their attacks on the AASF airfields by making early morning raids on Mourmelon (No.88 Squadron), Condé (No.114 Squadron) and Ecury (No.150 Squadron). The attack on Condé was very successful; a petrol dump was set alight and several Blenheims of No.114 Squadron were destroyed and all the others were damaged. An early morning raid on the AASF Headquarters at Reims was reported, with little damage done, and there was also an attack on No.75 Wing Headquarters at St Hilaire-le-Grand. After the disastrous results of the previous day's operations, Air Marshal Barratt, seeking to limit his losses, ordered only eight Battle sorties on 11 May, again to attack enemy columns in Luxembourg. Seven out of the eight Battles failed to return and the eighth was damaged and force-landed away from its base. Out of 40 Battle sorties in two days, 20 aircraft were missing and all of the others were damaged, some beyond repair. This was a wholly unsustainable rate of losses, but the Battles were to be called upon for many more daylight operations with tragic losses of valuable crews.

By 12 May, the successful advances of the German armour were causing grave concern in the Allied High Command and the AASF bomber squadrons were ordered into action in an attempt to stem the flow. Throughout the day, attacks were made against vital bridges and against

transport and armoured columns. In a vain and heroic effort to destroy two bridges over the Albert Canal at Maastricht by No.12 Squadron, all five of the attacking Battles were shot down. Of the 23 Battles which operated during the day, eleven were missing. The AASF Blenheims also suffered grievously; No.139 Squadron sent nine aircraft to attack enemy columns and seven of these were shot down. In the evening, Air Marshal Barratt received a message from the Chief of the Air Staff expressing concern at the losses of medium bombers and saying that if they continued, effective operations would not be possible when the critical phase of the battle arrived. Barratt had done his best with his limited resources to meet the urgent demands of the French, who obviously regarded the situation as already critical, and the comments of the CAS did not help. Enemy attacks on the AASF bases continued during the day with two attacks on Reims and attacks on Auberive, Mourmelon, Berry-au-Bac and Bétheniville. No serious damage was done to the airfields.

On 13 May, the Germans continued their heavy pressure at Sedan and made crossings of the Meuse at several places. There was intense German air activity over the battle area but little from the Allied side. The AASF bombers, after their losses of the preceding three days, made only one raid. In response to a French request, seven Battles from No.226 Squadron operated in the Breda - Antwerp area. No AASF airfields were attacked during the day, though there was much enemy air activity in the vicinity of Bétheniville.

On 14 May, the situation in the land battle was so critical that virtually the whole of the AASF bomber force was sent into action in a desperate attempt to stop or to slow the flow of German columns across the Meuse. In the morning ten Battles bombed bridges near Sedan at the cost of one aircraft, which force-landed not far from its base. The bombing was not particularly effective. As the land situation deteriorated around Sedan, the decision was taken to concentrate the air offensive, both French and British, in this area. At 1340, the whole of the AASF bomber force was put on 30-minutes notice. During the course of the afternoon, all eight of the

Battle squadrons and the two Blenheim squadrons were committed to the action. Bombing attacks were made on bridges over the Meuse and on German columns between Sedan and Givonne. The Battles made 63 sorties and 36 of them were missing. In the eight sorties by the two Blenheim squadrons, five aircraft were missing. Some of the pontoon bridges were claimed as destroyed, others were damaged and damage was caused to permanent bridges. Hits were made on vehicles and on the road near Givonne. As was to be expected, the AA fire against the bombers was very intense and most of the casualties were caused by ground fire. The bomber force was also attacked by German fighters. British fighters were operating in the area but the enemy used considerable resources to defend his bridges and columns. More than half the bombers sent out on this black day were shot down. It is thought that little delay was caused to the German advance but the action was necessary to try to alleviate the grave situation of the Allied armies. During the day, Mourmelon was bombed three times with little damage and Auberive also received enemy attention.

After the devastating losses of the first five days of the Battle of France, the C-in-C, Air Marshal Barratt, decided on 15 May that Battles should not be used on daylight operations unless it was essential to do so. Night bombing in the same area would take place. A further problem was that the rapid German advance was now threatening the AASF airfields and orders were issued for the squadrons to move to the Southern Champagne area. During the day, Mourmelon, Bétheniville, Auberive and Berry-au-Bac were bombed. The airfield at Berry-au-Bac was cratered, but fit for daylight flying and a Battle and a tractor were destroyed at Auberive. In accordance with the C-in-C's orders, there were no daylight operations by the Battle squadrons but four of the squadrons sent nineteen aircraft on night attacks on columns and roads in the Monthermé area. Little damage was done in these raids and all the aircraft returned safely. Two of the eight Battle squadrons moved south on 15 May and the remainder moved on the following day. Also on 16 May, the AASF moved its headquarters to Troyes. No.75 Wing Headquarters moved to Méry-sur-Seine and No.76 Wing to Marigny-le-Chatel.

The operations in this first phase of the Battle of France proved conclusively that low level attacks by relatively slow lightly-armed aircraft on strongly defended targets, with little fighter support, were not feasible because of the excessive casualties suffered by the attackers. The Battle and Blenheim squadrons had sustained the highest level of losses of any RAF operations in World War II. During the whole of this phase, the UK-based Blenheims of No.2 Group were heavily engaged and Bomber Command heavy bombers operated at night.

No.12 Squadron

After an uneventful morning on 10 May, 12 Squadron at Amifontaine received orders at 1625 to send two half sections to attack an enemy column on the road between Luxembourg, Junglister and Echternach, in continuation of the AASF attacks begun earlier in the day. German transport had been streaming along this road since the early morning. Four Battles took off:
1650 P2243 F/Lt P.H.M.S.Hunt; L5249 P/O C.L. Hulse;
1705 L4949 F/Lt W. Simpson; L5190 P/O A.W. Matthews

They were met by intense AA fire and F/Lt Hunt did not reach the target, force-landing at Piennes, between Thionville

and Verdun, with control cables shot away. The other three aircraft made low level attacks on the target and some hits were thought to have been made. F/Lt Simpson nursed his badly-damaged Battle as far as Virton in Belgium, near the French border, and force-landed in flames. He suffered appalling burns and became one of Sir Archibald McIndoe's star patients after his repatriation by the Germans in 1941. His gunner was burnt about the hands, injuries sustained while rescuing the pilot from the burning aircraft. The observer returned to the squadron. All three were subsequently decorated, F/Lt Simpson being awarded the DFC, and the observer, Sgt Odell and the gunner, LAC Tomlinson, the DFM. F/Lt Simpson became a PoW when the Germans overran France. P/O Matthews was shot down in the target area; he and his two crew were taken prisoner, all wounded. P/O Hulse's was the only Battle to return to base, badly damaged and with a wounded observer. There was no flying by the squadron on 11 May.

At 0700 on 12 May, orders were received for six volunteer crews to bomb the Veldwezelt and Vroenhoven bridges over the Albert Canal near Maastricht. All of the squadron's crews volunteered so the next six crews on the duty roster were selected to carry out the operation. F/O T.F.S. Brereton was unable to take off because the radio in his Battle was unserviceable and on changing over to the spare aircraft this was also found to be unusable because of defective hydraulic gear on the bomb racks. This left five aircraft, with the first section of two led by F/O N.M. Thomas and the second section of three led by F/O D.E.Garland. Take off was shortly after 0815. The aircraft taking part were:
P2332 F/O N.M. Thomas; L5241 P/O T.D.H. Davy; P2204 F/O D.E. Garland; L5439 P/O I.A. McIntosh; L5227 Sgt F. Marland

The first section made a dive bombing attack on the Vroenhoven bridge. F/O Thomas was shot down and he and his crew were taken prisoner. P/O Davy bombed the already-damaged bridge but did not observe the results. His aircraft was attacked by a Bf 109 and badly damaged; the crew were ordered to bale out and did so. P/O Davy managed to fly his aircraft to friendly territory, where he crash-landed at St Germaincourt. His observer made his way back alone and the injured gunner was taken prisoner. The second section made a low level attack on the Veldwezelt bridge and were met by intense AA fire. The Germans had used their time to good effect in setting up a formidable ring of AA guns at the bridges. F/O Garland bombed and his badly-damaged Battle crashed close to the bridge; all the crew were killed. P/O McIntosh, his aircraft on fire, jettisoned his bombs and crash-landed. He and his crew were taken prisoner. Sgt Marland bombed and his badly-hit aircraft crashed, killing the whole crew. Some damage was done to the bridge, but it was not critical. F/O Garland and Sgt Gray, his observer, were awarded the Victoria Cross for this action. The gunner in this aircraft, LAC Reynolds, received no award. A fighter escort of ten Hurricanes had been provided for the raid but these had soon been fully engaged by the many German fighters operating in the area. There was no flying by the squadron on 13 May. Several air raid warnings were received but the airfield at Amifontaine was not attacked.

On 14 May, the squadron received the congratulations of the CAS on the Maastricht operation two days earlier. At 1530 five aircraft took off to attack a column on the road between Sedan and Givonne. They were:

'Q' of No.142 Squadron after being shot down by light flak near St.Lambert. (via David Vincent)

L4950 F/O E.R.D. Vaughan; L5538 P/O J.J. McElligott;
L5188 Sgt H.R.W. Winkler; L4952 F/O G.D. Clancy;
P5229 Sgt A.G. Johnson.

They were met by intense light AA and machine gun fire. P/O McElligot dive bombed the main road in Givonne and his was the only aircraft to return from the attack. F/O Vaughan's bombs were seen by McElligot to hit the main road in Givonne; he and his observer were killed and his air gunner was taken prisoner. Sgt Winkler and his crew became PoWs, F/O Clancy was taken prisoner and his two crew were killed and Sgt Johnson and his observer were killed and his air gunner taken prisoner.

On 15 May, the squadron received orders to make a night attack on columns at Monthermé. Six aircraft were sent to Reims, the base of No.226 Squadron, and five of them took off for Monthermé between 2315 and 0145. The sixth Battle, L4944, would not start and it was abandoned and destroyed the next day when Reims was evacuated. The aircraft taking part in the raid were:
P6597 S/L B.E. Lowe; K9377 F/Lt P.H.M.S. Hunt;
L5249 P/O C.L. Hulse; L5538 F/O T.F.S. Brereton
Serial not known P/O R.A.D. Meharey

Difficulty was experienced in bombing because of the darkness with no moon. The area was bombed and fires were started. There was light AA fire; all aircraft returned safely.

The squadron moved to Echimines on 16 May and reported five aircraft serviceable.

No.88 Squadron

The squadron's airfield at Mourmelon was bombed twice on 10 May. The first attack at 0535 damaged two aircraft, the second at 1840 by four Ju88s set three Battles and a training aircraft on fire and they were destroyed. The squadron was the only AASF Battle squadron which did not operate on 10 May. The airfield was again bombed at 0430 and at 1700 on 11 May, with little damage recorded. Shortly after 0900, four Battles set out to bomb enemy columns in Luxembourg. Three failed to return and the fourth did not bomb because of damage to its bomb release gear. The aircraft were:
P2251 F/Lt A.J. Madge; P2202 P/O A.W. Mungovan;
P2261 P/O B.I.M. Skidmore; serial not known P/O N.C.S. Riddell.

F/Lt Madge force-landed between Bastogne and Neufchâtel and he and his gunner were taken prisoner; the observer was killed. P/O Mungovan and P/O Skidmore were shot down by ground fire near St. Vith; P/O Mungovan and his crew were captured and P/O Skidmore and his crew were killed. P/O Riddell force-landed his damaged Battle at Vassincourt and he and his crew returned to Mourmelon by road.

On 12 May, an early morning bombing attack was made on Mourmelon, resulting in cratering of the airfield surface and damage to telephone lines and the HF/DF station. The airfield was still usable. The squadron did not operate on 12 or 13 May. Mourmelon was obviously a favourite target for the German bombers; it was attacked at 0630, 1300 and 1700 on 14 May but was not made unserviceable. At 1545 on 14 May, ten Battles set out on bombing raids, four to attack a bridge near Villers and six to attack a column on the road between Bouillon and Givonne. These raids were claimed to be successful. One aircraft, L5581, piloted by Sgt W.G. Ross was shot down. All three crew were killed. The *Luftwaffe* bombed Mourmelon at 0700 and 1230 on 15 May. Eight of the squadron's aircraft made a night attack on a wood north of Sedan. All bombs fell on the wood but little obvious damage was caused and the results were described as "not very satisfactory". All aircraft returned; one had W/T failure and remained airborne for eight hours, landing at 0630. There were two raids on Mourmelon on 16 May, a very heavy one at 0600 and another at 1740. On this day, the squadron moved to Les Grandes Chappelles. Battle L5233 was abandoned at Mourmelon.

No.103 Squadron

The day started on 10 May with a dawn air raid on the squadron's airfield at Bétheniville. There was no damage or casualties. Shortly before 1400, four Battles were despatched to bomb enemy columns in Luxembourg. Amid heavy AA fire the leader's aircraft bombed transport on the Bascharage - Dippach road, straddling the target. The bombs from the second aircraft appeared to undershoot the target. Two other aircraft were seen making a low level (150 feet) attack three miles east of Dippach; the results of their attack are not known because neither of these aircraft returned. The aircraft taking part were:
K9372 F/Lt M.C. Wells; K9270 Sgt C.H. Lowne;
K9264 P/O K.J. Drabble; serial not known: F/Lt J.A. Ingram

Three of these aircraft were shot down by the intense AA fire, the only one to return being that piloted by F/Lt Ingram. F/Lt Wells and his crew and Sgt Lowne and his crew became PoWs. P/O Drabble and his crew were killed. There were no operations on 11 May. The squadron was in action early on 12 May with a dawn attack by three aircraft on enemy columns; all returned safely. Shortly after 1240, three aircraft took off for Bouillon, where they successfully attacked a pontoon bridge. Enemy fighters were encountered but the three Battles returned safely. At 1630, a further section of three aircraft took off to bomb a mechanised column near Bouillon. The aircraft were:
L5512 F/O G.B. Morgan-Dean; P2193 P/O E.E. Morton;
serial not known: P/O V.A. Cunningham

P/O Cunningham attacked tanks near Bouillon in a shallow dive attack from 3,000 - 1,000 feet. He did not observe the results of his bombing. The other two aircraft were shot down and their crews, of two in each aircraft, killed. Bétheniville was attacked by He 111s during the day and two were claimed as shot down; little damage was done to the airfield. There were no operations on 13 May. At dawn a large number of enemy aircraft flew over Bétheniville and three were claimed as shot down by AA fire. Later in the morning Bétheniville village was heavily bombed.

On 14 May, eight aircraft took off shortly after 0500 to bomb three pontoon bridges over the Meuse between Neuvion and Douzy. There was heavy and accurate AA fire over the bridges and most of the Battles recorded near misses, only one bridge being claimed to have been hit. One aircraft was lost in this raid, P2191 piloted by Sgt C.D. Parry. Sgt Parry was wounded in the attack but flew his aircraft nearly back to

Bétheniville before force-landing. Later in the day, eight aircraft set out at 1530 to bomb bridges in the Sedan area. Encountering heavy AA fire in the target area and with enemy fighters operating in the vicinity, three Battles were lost in this attack. P/O V.A. Cunningham was hit by AA and he and his gunner were killed. F/O T.B. Fitzgerald was wounded and force-landed his aircraft, he and his gunner returning to Bétheniville on the following day. Sgt G. Beardsley was shot down but he and his gunner returned some days later. The road bordering the airfield at Bétheniville was choked by civilian refugees and retreating French and Belgian troops and there was looting by French soldiers. There was a good deal of bombing of the village by German aircraft. The airfield was bombed at 0730 on 15 May and bombs were dropped nearby at 1100 and 1200. At 1500, orders were received for the squadron to be at three hours notice to move. That night the officer's mess was barricaded as a precaution against looting or other action by the retreating French soldiers. At dawn on 16 May, the serviceable Battles and the No.501 Squadron Hurricanes took off for their new airfield at Rhèges. A Battle which crashed on take-off (L5234) and an unserviceable Battle (K9404) were abandoned at Bétheniville.

No.105 Squadron

Four Battles took off from Villeneuve at 1530 on 10 May to attack columns on the Echternach - Luxembourg road. Amid intense AA and small arms fire, columns on the west of Luxembourg were bombed. The aircraft took evasive action and the results of the bombing were not observed. The aircraft taking part were:
P2190 F/O R.N. Wall; P2200 P/O D.G. O'Brien;
K9188 Sgt Richardson; K9338 Sgt C. Bowles

P/O O'Brien was shot down and he and his crew became prisoners. The other three aircraft returned badly damaged and could not be repaired on the unit. The air gunners in K9188 and K9338 were wounded. After a quiet day on 11 May, the squadron bombed a bridge and a village full of German troops near Bouillon on the afternoon of 12 May. The aircraft were:
P2176 F/Lt H.C. Sammels; L5523 P/O D.C.F. Murray;
K9485 P/O T. Hurst

The Battles were met by intense heavy AA and small arms fire and P/O Hurst was shot down and crashed into a hillside near Bouillon; he and his two crew were killed. The remaining two aircraft returned to base badly damaged. The squadron did not operate on 13 May.

The following day, 14 May, was disastrous for No.105 Squadron. Out of eleven aircraft sent to attack bridges in the Sedan area, only four returned. The Battles, which took off at 1540, were:
L5230 F/Lt H.C. Sammels; K9342 P/O F.A.G. Lascelles;
L5250 P/O D.C.F. Murray; L5523 P/O H.E. White;
P2248 Sgt A.J.C. Eagles; L5200 Sgt K. Lord;
L5238 F/O R.N. Wall; L5585 F/O C.F. Gibson;
P2177 F/O P.D.E. Pitcairn; K9189 P/O F.H. Ridley;
K9186 Sgt L. Wilson

The results of the squadron's efforts are not recorded. In four of the aircraft shot down, L5523, L5239, K9189 and L5238, all of the crews were killed. F/O Gibson and his crew in L5585 were shot down and taken prisoner. The unfortunate F/O Gibson escaped and made his way to Allied lines, where he was shot and wounded by the French, who were, of course, unaware of his nationality when they sighted him. He was taken to a French hospital where he became a PoW when France capitulated. P/O Murray force-landed at Suippes in L5250 and returned to the unit with his crew after abandoning their damaged aircraft. P/O Lascelles was shot down, crashed near the frontier and returned to the squadron with his crew by car the following day. When the four surviving aircraft landed at Villeneuve, one was found to be damaged beyond repair and the remaining three were bombed-up immediately. A poignant note is struck in the squadron's Operations Record Book where it is noted "The squadron had given of its best". This was No.105 Squadron's last operation in France. On 15 May, it was ordered to move to Echimines, but much confusion and doubt surrounded the order. At 0830 on 16 May, the C-in-C of Bomber Command, Air Chief Marshal Sir E. Ludlow-Hewitt, arrived at Villeneuve and 'suggested' that the move was unnecessary. At 1030, No.71 Wing decided to evacuate non-operational personnel. At 1200, the whole squadron was instructed to move immediately. At the end of this very confused day, the squadron's three serviceable aircraft and most of their operational equipment were at Echimines, but there was still much other equipment at Villeneuve.

No.142 Squadron

No.142 Squadron was the first AASF bomber squadron to go into action on 10 May. Before this, however, their airfield at Berry-au-Bac was bombed twice in early morning raids. At 0435, six Heinkel He 111s bombed and machine gunned the aerodrome from 600 to 1,000 feet. Some damage was done to the aerodrome surface, two aircraft were slightly damaged but there were no casualties. The second attack came at 0600, when a single enemy aircraft dropped incendiary bombs from a high altitude, causing no damage or casualties. At 1200, eight Battles took off to attack enemy columns on the Luxembourg - Dippach road. P/O I.C. Chalmers in K9367 could not retract his undercarriage and returned to base. The remaining seven aircraft made low level attacks on their target, being heavily engaged by concentrations of light AA along the road. The aircraft taking part were:
L5517 F/O A.D.J. Martin; P2246 P/O W.H. Corbett;
L5242 F/O A.D. Gosman; L5231 F/O M.H. Roth;
L5578 P/O F.S. Laws; serials not known: Sgt A.N. Spear
and Sgt Heslop

F/O Roth was shot down and he and his crew became PoWs. P/O Laws and his crew were killed when their aircraft was shot down. Sgt Spear force-landed his badly-damaged aircraft at Colmey and he and his crew returned to Berry-au-Bac on the following day. P/O Corbett and his gunner were wounded and their observer killed. F/O Gosman's gunner was slightly wounded. The squadron did not operate on 11, 12 or 13 May. Enemy air activity was reported in the vicinity of Berry-au-Bac on 11 May but there was no damage to the airfield. Some hits were made in raids on the airfield on 12 May and in a raid at 0730, K9259 received a direct hit and was destroyed. There were two further enemy attacks on 13 May, when bombs fell in fields and a wood near the airfield.

On 14 May, the squadron was the first to take off in the afternoon attacks on the Sedan bridges. Eight aircraft took off at 1330 after being ordered to destroy bridges over the Meuse between Sedan and Mouzon, also to attack pontoon bridges and bridge building material. The aircraft were:
P2246 S/L J.F. Hobler; P2333 Sgt A.N. Spear;

L5517 F/Lt K.R. Rogers; K9333 P/O H.L. Oakley;
L5226 F/Lt W.B. Wight; K7696 P/O I.C. Chalmers;
K7700 F/O J. Reed; K9366 P/O W.D.K. Franklin

There was intense light AA fire from the ground and Bf 109s also attacked the Battles. The target was bombed and some hits on bridges were made. F/Lt Rogers was shot down and he and his crew were killed. S/L Hobler was shot down by Bf 109s over enemy-occupied territory and after destroying the aircraft he and his crew returned over the lines. S/L Hobler was burned in the crash and went to hospital. Sgt Spear was also shot down by Bf 109s and his two crew were killed. Spear baled out and landed behind enemy lines. Evading capture, he returned to the squadron and was later awarded the DFM. P/O Oakley force-landed at Ecly and he and his crew returned by road. Of the four Battles which returned to Berry-au-Bac, F/O Reed and P/O Franklin had been attacked by six Bf 109s and claimed one shot down.

On 15 May the squadron had six aircraft and crews standing by at half-an-hour's notice. At 1500, the airfield was bombed and the thirteen craters left by the raiding He 111s made it unserviceable for night flying. Five aircraft were flown to Reims for night bombing operations. Four of these operated and bombed woods near Monthermé which were thought to contain dumps of war materials. No results of this raid are recorded; the aircraft taking part were:
K7696 F/O J.M. Hewson; K9367 F/O Ricalton;
L5226 Sgt Tweed; serial not known: F/O A.D.J. Martin.

None was missing. There was a night standby at Berry-au-Bac in case the enemy attacked. The squadron moved to Faux-Villecerf on 16 May, abandoning several unserviceable Battles at Berry-au-Bac. These included K7700, K9259, K9366, L5440 and L5242.

No.150 Squadron

Four Battles took off from Ecury-sur-Coole at 1535 on 10 May to attack enemy columns on the Luxembourg - Echternach road. Seeing no columns there, the aircraft attacked a column on the Luxembourg - Grevenmacher road with bombs and machine guns. The results were not observed. The aircraft taking part were:
L5539 F/Lt E. Parker; L5540 F/O A.C. Roberts;
K9369 F/O W.M. Blom; K9390 Sgt R.A.deC. White.

K9390, L5540 and L5539 failed to return and K9369 was badly damaged and landed with both tyres punctured. Sgt White crash-landed near Gosselies and he and his crew returned to base by road on 13 May. F/Lt Parker was shot down by ground fire and was killed, his crew later being taken prisoner. F/O Roberts and his crew became PoWs. Ecury airfield was bombed at 0610 on 11 May and part of a wood, the armoury tent and the pyrotechnic store were set on fire. Battle P2334 was set on fire and it was destroyed when its bomb load exploded; P2335 was damaged. The squadron was not in action on 11 May. On 12 May, three aircraft made a successful attack on a mechanised column between Neufchateau and Bertrik. The aircraft were:
P2262 F/Lt R.A. Weeks; P2336 P/O I. Campbell-Irons;
P2184 Sgt S.E. Andrews

P/O Campbell-Irons sustained a direct hit from the intense AA fire put up by the Germans and his aircraft exploded and crashed in flames, killing all three of the crew. The other two aircraft returned safely, though P2184 was badly damaged. There were no operations on 13 May. The

squadron was in action early on 14 May; at 0735 two aircraft took off to attack pontoon bridges near Sedan. They were:
L5524 P/O A.R. Gulley; P2179 P/O S.R. Peacock-Edwards

The target was dive bombed amid a hail of light AA fire and both aircraft were damaged. A further two aircraft left at 0740 to bomb pontoon bridges west of Douzy:
L5457 Sgt R.G. Beale; K9483 P/O D.G. Long.

These aircraft also dive bombed their target. Though hits on the bridges were made, the results of the attacks were not observed. Joining in the afternoon attacks on the Meuse bridges at Sedan, four aircraft took off at 1524:
L4946 F/O J. Ing; K9483 P/O A.F. Posselt;
P2182 P/O J. Boon; P5232 Sgt G.T. Barker

All four were shot down and their crews killed, with the single exception of LAC A.K. Summerson, the gunner in Sgt Barker's aircraft. In a gallant effort to rescue his pilot from the burning aircraft, he was badly burned; unfortunately Sgt Barker was already dead before LAC Summerson pulled him clear. In great pain, LAC Summerson got back to the French lines and was taken to hospital, where he later became a PoW. The results of the raid are not known. The situation of the squadron at Ecury was now extremely hazardous with German raids on neighbouring targets and reported parachutists in the area and on 15 May a move was made to Pouan. The squadron did not operate on 15 or 16 May.

No.218 Squadron

At 1430 on 10 May, the squadron sent out four Battles to attack columns on the Dippach - Luxembourg road. Some hits were scored on a stationary column near Dippach. The four aircraft all returned to their base at Auberive, but all four had been damaged by AA fire. L5402 and three other aircraft took part in the attack. The squadron was again in action on 11 May when four Battles took off at 0930 to bomb enemy columns in Luxembourg. All four failed to return. The aircraft were:
K9325 F/O A.J. Hudson; P2249 P/O H.M. Murray;
P2326 F/O C.A.R. Crews; P2203 Sgt C.J.E. Dockrill

The crews of K9325, P2249 and P2326 were all taken prisoner, except for the gunner in P2326, who was killed. Sgt Dockrill and his crew in P2203 were killed. The next day, 12 May, started with an early morning enemy raid on Auberive but little damage was done. At 1630, three Battles took off to attack columns near Bouillon. They were:
K9353 Sgt J.B. Horner; P2183 P/O F.S. Bazalgette;
serial not known: P/O Anstey

Approaching the target at 1,000 feet, the leading aircraft piloted by Sgt Horner had its starboard wingtip shot away by AA fire; it crashed and burst into flames on the ground, the three crew being killed. The other two aircraft bombed the target in Bouillon, then P/O Bazalgette was shot down. He died after crashing but his two crew escaped to the Allied lines. P/O Anstey returned safely. There were no operations on 13 May.

The squadron suffered calamitous losses on 14 May. Eleven aircraft took off in the afternoon, seven to attack a column on the Bouillon - Givonne road and four to attack a bridge at Douzy. Ten were shot down. Precise details of the action are not available but included in the aircraft lost were:
L5232 P/O W.A.R. Harris two crew killed; P/O Harris wounded but returned to squadron.
L5235 P/O A.M. Imrie Gunner killed, P/O Imrie taken prisoner.

P2324 F/O D.A.J. Foster Pilot and gunner taken prisoner
P2360 P/O R.T.L. Buttery Pilot and gunner killed.
L5422 F/O J.F.R. Crane Pilot killed, gunner taken prisoner.

It is likely that the other five aircraft lost were K9251, K9273, L5192, P2189 and P2192. On the afternoon of 15 May, Auberive was bombed and a Battle was destroyed when its bomb load exploded after it was hit; a tractor was also destroyed. The squadron moved to Moscou Ferme on 15 May and on to St. Lucien Ferme, Rhèges, on 16 May. There were no operations on either of these two days.

No.226 Squadron

Reims airfield, the base of No.226 Squadron, was attacked by enemy bombers on the morning of 10 May. The bombing was from a height of 16,000 feet and 70 incendiary and 16 high explosive bombs were dropped. There were no casualties and no damage to aircraft. At 1700, four Battles were despatched to bomb columns near Luxembourg. Some hits on vehicles were claimed. The aircraft involved were:
K9330 Sgt G. Mc Loughlin; P2180 Sgt H.J. Barron;
K9183 F/O D.A. Cameron; L5247 F/Lt B.R. Kerridge

In the intense AA fire, F/Lt Kerridge was shot down in flames. F/O Cameron was also shot down and he and his crew were taken prisoner but F/O Cameron died of his wounds. Sgt Barron was wounded. There was enemy bombing in the vicinity of the airfield on 11 May but no damage was recorded. There were two enemy raids on Reims airfield on the morning of 12 May. At 0700, a bombing attack was made on the airfield and the neighbouring village by at least nine aircraft. Several HE bombs hit the airfield, leaving 15 craters. Three Do 17s attempted a low level attack at 0930 but they were repelled by the airfield defences. The squadron did not operate on this day. On the morning of following day, 13 May, many enemy aircraft were heard in the vicinity of the airfield and explosions were heard but the airfield was not attacked. On 13 May, No.226 Squadron was the only AASF bomber squadron to go into action. At 1020, seven Battles took off to stop or delay German tanks reported on the road between Breda and Antwerp. The aircraft were:
P2180 F/Lt R.G. Hurst; P2267 P/O D.A.C. Crooks;
L5418 Sgt G.G. Martin; L5438 F/O R.W. Bungay;
K9343 Sgt Groves; K9176 P/O D. Salway;
P2353 P/O W.M. Waddington

No tanks were found so an attempt was made to block the road. The first three aircraft led by F/Lt Hurst dive bombed a large red building to bring it down across the road at Boeimeer, south-west of Breda. The next three, led by F/O Bungay, bombed Rijsbergen village. P/O Waddington's aircraft was hit by AA fire on the outward journey and force-landed near Brussels, the pilot being slightly wounded. He and his crew rejoined the squadron on 17 May.

On 14 May, there were frequent air raid alarms at Reims and explosions were heard but no damage was done to the airfield. At 1525, six aircraft took off to bomb bridges near Sedan:
P2267 S/L C.E.S. Lockett; P2254 Sgt R.S. Annan;
K9345 F/Lt W.S. Butler; K9383 Sgt E.E. Hopkins;
K9343 Sgt H. Moseley; L5438 F/Sgt W.A. Dunn

The aircraft received the usual extremely intense AA fire. S/L Lockett was shot down and was taken prisoner; his two crew were killed. Sgt Annan was hit before reaching the target and his bomb release gear failed, forcing him to return.

German soldiers examine the wreck of a Battle of No.12 Squadron near Sedan. (P Jarrett collection)

F/Lt Butler dive bombed a bridge at Mouzon and saw one bomb hit the bridge; his aircraft was badly damaged by AA fire. Sgt Hopkins bombed but did not observe the results; his aircraft was also damaged and his gunner injured. Sgt Moseley and F/Sgt Dunn were shot down and the three crew of each aircraft were killed. The airfield again escaped damage on 15 May, though explosions were heard and two enemy aircraft were claimed as shot down by AA fire. Two aircraft from the squadron operated at night, bombing a road near Sedan, and both returned safely. On 16 May, the squadron was ordered to move to Faux-Villecerf. Stores at Reims were abandoned and seven unserviceable aircraft and two spare engines were destroyed. The aircraft destroyed were: K7707, K9180, K9330, K9383, L5418, P2180 and P2255. The squadron's two remaining serviceable aircraft were flown to Faux-Villecerf.

L5511 'PM-B' of No.103 Squadron abandoned in May 1940. (A Thomas collection)

L5512, 'PM-L' of No.103 Squadron crash-landed in France on 22 May 1940. The white in the roundels and fin flash has been blacked out for night operations. (P Jarrett collection)

CHAPTER 8. THE BATTLE OF FRANCE (2)

The second phase of AASF operations in France took place during the period 17 May - 10 June 1940, when the squadrons were based at airfields in southern Champagne. After the movements of units between 15 and 19 May, the AASF headquarters units and the Battle squadrons were in the following locations:

AASF Headquarters	Troyes
No.71 Wing Headquarters	Nantes
No.75 Wing Headquarters	Méry-sur-Seine
No.88 Squadron	Les Grandes Chappelles
No.103 Squadron	Rhèges (St Lucien Ferme)
No.150 Squadron	Pouan
No.218 Squadron	Rhèges (St Lucien Ferme)
No.76 Wing Headquarters	Marigny-le-Chatel
No.12 Squadron	Echimines
No.105 Squadron	Echimines
No.142 Squadron	Faux-Villecerf
No.226 Squadron	Faux-Villecerf

On 23 May, Nos.105 and 218 Squadrons were transferred to No.71 Wing and moved without their aircraft

or equipment to Nantes. The intention was to refit the two squadrons and to form No.71 Wing as a reserve Wing of the AASF. This was not done and the squadrons remained in a state of considerable uncertainty for the rest of their stay in France. The two severely depleted Blenheim squadrons of the AASF had also finished their operational flying in France and were sent to Nantes. The Battle squadrons did not operate on 17 and 18 May; they were salvaging equipment from their former airfields, completing their moves and settling in at the new bases. The squadrons also received urgently needed reinforcements of aircraft and aircrews. The rapid German advance continued and on 17 and 18 May the tasks of bombing and reconnaissance were carried out by Blenheim squadrons of No.2 Group operating from England and by Blenheims of the Air Component. They suffered very heavy losses.

On 19 May, with the enemy push towards the coast continuing and the BEF in grave danger of being cut off, it was decided that daylight bombing of the German columns was necessary. The No.2 Group Blenheim squadrons had lost so many aircraft and crews in the previous few days that they were rested to enable the surviving crews to recuperate and for damaged aircraft to be repaired. This left only the AASF Battles to attempt to stem the enemy advance. A force of 33 Battles escorted by fighters from No.67 Wing was sent on a mid-morning attack on columns in the battle area; six failed to return. The results of the raid were mixed, some bombs falling on troops and vehicles. On 20 May, with the No.2 Group Blenheims back in daylight action, the Battle squadrons switched to night operations. The only daylight action by the AASF was a photographic flight by an aircraft of No.142 Squadron in the Troyes area. Most of the Battle squadrons made night raids on 20/21 May, their targets being German communications and storage locations at Dinant, Givet, Fermoy, Monthermé, Montcornet, Mezières and Charleville. The Battles operated singly and some did not bomb because the targets were obscured by mist. Others bombed on ETA over the target. Little damage was caused by the raids though fires were reported from Givet and Monthermé. One aircraft failed to return. Orders for night attacks by 41 Battles were transmitted to the squadrons on 21 May, but these were cancelled at 2245 and the units were told to prepare for low level attacks on tanks in the Amiens - Abbeville - Arras area at dawn on the following day. The cancellation was too late for some squadrons and twelve aircraft had taken off for the night raids by the time it was received. Eleven of them bombed communications and storage targets; some hits were made and fires were started. Despite Air Marshal Barratt's very strong protests about the unsuitability of Battles for attacking tanks, higher authority insisted on the early morning attacks taking place. A total of fifteen aircraft took off shortly after dawn on 22 May to find and attack tanks in the Amiens - Abbeville - Arras area. The weather was bad, with visibility restricted by low cloud. Four aircraft returned because of the bad weather and one pilot was unable to locate the target and returned with his bombs. The remaining aircraft attacked the tanks and armoured fighting vehicles, but they were extremely difficult to identify and only one or two hits were claimed. At least three aircraft landed away from their home bases. This operation was a failure and there were no further daylight raids on 22 May. On the night of 22/23 May, twenty-six Battles were detailed to attack communications targets at Fumay, Revin, Conz and Bingen, and the revictualling yard at Florenville. Nine aircraft failed to find their targets in very bad weather with rain clouds and mist obscuring the ground and they returned with their bombs. The other aircraft bombed various targets with mixed results. In several instances bombs were dropped on ETA at the target and no results were observed because of the weather. Some hits were claimed, including hits on the revictualling yard at Florenville. The night's operations, hindered by the atrocious weather, were mainly ineffectual. On 23 May, with the British Expeditionary Force troops in retreat from Arras, Battles were sent out in the early evening to attack columns of armoured fighting vehicles, tanks and troop carriers on the Doullens - Amiens road. At least ten aircraft took part and in very poor weather conditions scored a number of hits on vehicles. No aircraft were missing. That night over thirty Battles were sent to attack road and rail communications at Fumay, Monthermé and Bingen, an ammunition dump near Charleville and the revictualling yard at Florenville. The weather was again bad and six aircraft failed to locate their targets and returned with their bombs. In the poor visibility it was difficult to ascertain the results of the bombing, but it was claimed that fires were started. One aircraft was missing and one crashed on landing. The ground

situation in France was now critical with the BEF cut off from the French and preparing for evacuation. The badly-mauled Battle squadrons carried on with their night operations with a welcome marked reduction in the casualty rate. On 24 May, it was decided that a maximum effort would be made that night by the AASF Battle squadrons. There were now only six squadrons of Battles making up the full bomber strength of the AASF and they all operated on the night of 24/25 May. Over thirty Battles attacked the revictualling yard at Florenville, the ammunition siding at Libramont and communications at Bouvignes, Givet and Fumay. Successful results were claimed, though some aircraft bombed on ETA. All aircraft returned safely. On the morning of 25 May, an enemy column was reported to be jammed on the road between Abbeville and Hesdin. Twelve Battles were sent out shortly after noon to attack the vehicles. No column was found and nine aircraft attacked isolated vehicles or groups of vehicles. One aircraft was missing, one returned with its bombs after the pilot could not find a target and one returned with engine trouble. The operation was described as "most unsatisfactory" by AASF headquarters.

Reports were now being made by the Wings that many aircraft were suffering mechanical failures which led to forced landings or early returns. Criticism was also made of the state of new aircraft arriving from the UK. Night bombing continued on 25/26 May with about thirty Battles taking part. Many aircraft did not bomb because of mechanical failures, including faulty bomb release gear. The targets were at Florenville, Libramont, Bouillon, Sedan, Givet and Nouzonville. AASF Intelligence reported that sixteen aircraft returned because of inability to find the targets or equipment failure. The aircraft which did bomb claimed a few hits, mainly on road or rail targets. One Battle was missing. At 0240 on 26 May the AASF headquarters received a message from the Air Ministry giving a "very suitable" target. This was Chateau Roumont, near Ochamps airfield, where twenty senior Luftwaffe officers were reputed to be attending a meeting. Twelve Battles were sent out to bomb the chateau, reaching the target shortly after 1000. Fighter escort was provided. The bombing was carried out from varying heights in driving rain and intense AA fire. Two hits on the chateau were claimed with other bombs falling around it; it is not known whether there was in fact a meeting at the chateau. Two aircraft were missing from this operation. The weather conditions on the night of 26/27 May were very bad and only four aircraft operated. The targets were in the Givet area but only one aircraft managed to locate its target and bomb it. Thirty-six Battles were detailed to attack airfields at St Hubert, Chimay and Ochamps and railway sidings at Recogne, Libramont, Nouzonville, Mezières and Chaource on the night of 27/28 May. Five of these did not attack for various reasons. Fires were started at St. Hubert and Ochamps airfields and five aircraft attacked the revictualling yard at Libramont, causing fierce fires. Hits were claimed on the railway line near Mezières and on a train in Mezières station. Despite heavy AA fire, all the aircraft returned safely. On 28 May, with the Dunkirk evacuation in full progress, twelve Battles were ordered to attack armoured columns advancing along the Doullens - Amiens road and the Albert - Amiens road. It had been intended to provide fighter cover but this did not materialise, which was not surprising in view of the heavy commitments of the fighter squadrons. Ten aircraft arrived in the target area but found only small groups of vehicles and troops. These were attacked, but the results were of little significance. One aircraft force-landed and was abandoned, the others returned safely. That night, 28/29 May, the weather conditions were so bad that No.76 Wing cancelled operations. Of the seventeen aircraft ordered to operate from No.75 Wing, seven did not take off or returned early and four had technical problems and aborted their sorties. Six aircraft reached the target area around Givet and Charleville; four bombed on ETA and the other two bombed a railway and lights at Conz. On the following night, 29/30 May, the weather was again bad and No.76 Wing cancelled operations. Nine Battles from No.75 Wing were detailed to attack Charleville and targets in the Trier area. One aircraft crashed on take-off and two returned early because of the bad weather. Four aircraft bombed Charleville on ETA and the others bombed targets near Trier. In the continuing bad weather, only five Battles were sent out on a night operation to bomb Conz on 30/31 May. Three of these returned early because of the weather, one force-landed and one pilot dropped his bombs from 2,500 feet "in the target area". On the morning of 31 May, a daylight attack was ordered to be flown by twelve Battles against enemy aircraft parked at Laon airfield and Laon Racecourse. There was 10/10th cloud over the target and none of the pilots located it; four returned with their bombs, one aircraft could not release its bombs because of faulty release gear, four bombed on ETA and the others bombed railway lines and AA batteries. The night of 31 May/1 June saw thirty-two Battles sent out to bomb targets at Libramont, Conz, Rudesheim, Givet, Mezières and Charleville. Twenty-five aircraft attacked, but many of these could not locate their targets visually and bombed on ETA. Some fires were started and all aircraft returned safely after encountering little AA fire. One aircraft force-landed on its return journey but returned to its base the next day.

As the relentless German advance and the evacuation from Dunkirk continued, the only daylight operation for the Battles on 1 June was a continuous patrol of one aircraft between Reims and Chalons to report any large formations of enemy aircraft. Two aircraft alternated on this work from 1320 to 1850. There were no night operations on 1/2 June. The AASF bases were again in jeopardy from the advancing enemy forces and orders were given on 2 June for the squadrons to move to the Vendôme area, but operations were to continue during the move. Echimines and Faux-Villecerf in the southern Champagne area were still to be used, but only as Advanced Landing Grounds for refuelling purposes. The weather was bad on 2 June and there were no daylight operations, but seventeen Battles were despatched to bomb Givet and Conz on the night of 2/3 June. Fires were started in Conz. Most of the AASF Battle squadrons were moving on 3 June and the only daylight activity for them on that day was a short-lived continuation of the Reims - Chalons patrol by one aircraft from 1230 to 1520. After the movements of units between 3 and 6 June, the AASF Headquarters units and the Battle squadrons were in the following locations:

AASF Headquarters	Muide, near Blois
No.71 Wing Headquarters	Nantes
No.105 Squadron	Nantes, not operational
No.218 Squadron	Nantes, not operational
No.75 Wing Headquarters	Chateau Rochaux, Freternal
No.88 Squadron	Moisy
No.103 Squadron	Herbouville
No.76 Wing Headquarters	Montoire
No.12 Squadron	Souge
No.142 Squadron	Villiers-Faux
No.150 Squadron	Houssay
No.226 Squadron	Faux-Villecerf

Night bombing continued on 3/4 June, but only five sorties were flown. The target was rail communications at Conz, but pilots had difficulty in locating it and four aircraft bombed lights and other possible targets in the Conz area. One aircraft failed to bomb because its bomb release gear would not work. On the following night, 4/5 June, nineteen Battles operated against communications in the Hirson and Givet areas. In poor visibility most of the aircraft bombed on ETA or bombed alternative targets when these were seen. Amid desultory AA fire, several fires were claimed to have been started but there were no major ones.

With their operations at Dunkirk completed, the German forces now concentrated their efforts in the Somme area. The AASF bombers made an evening attack on columns of tanks and armoured vehicles on the Péronne - Roye and Amiens - Montdidier roads. Eleven aircraft took part and most found and bombed tanks or vehicles. Those which failed to locate their targets bombed road junctions. All aircraft returned safely. On the night of 5/6 June, fourteen aircraft were detailed to attack convoys in the Guise - Rocroi - Givet area. Two became unserviceable en route to Echimines. A few convoys were found and bombed and Guise airfield was bombed, but in the poor visibility and in the glare from searchlights, results were not observed. Difficulties were reported from Echimines, which, although it was only an ALG for refuelling, was being used as a full operational station. On 6 June, nine Battles set out to attack convoys in the Roye area. Five aircraft bombed the Sancourt - Matigny road, diving from 8,000 feet to attack. No hits on vehicles were made but one bomb made a direct hit on the road. Three aircraft attacked Chaulmes and one returned with a defective air speed indicator. A flight of fighters acted as escort and many enemy aircraft were seen in the target area. The night flying programme was interfered with by enemy raids on Herbouville and Echimines on 6/7 June. Of twenty-four aircraft detailed to operate, only seventeen were able to take off for their targets. Attacks were made on the canal bridge at St. Valéry, various roads and motorised columns, Laon and Guise aerodrome. Mixed loads of HE and incendiary bombs were carried and fires were started in Laon. As usual with the night sorties, many crews did not observe the results of their efforts. No AA fire was reported and there was little search-light activity. The strain on the Battle aircrews was now in evidence, as is shown by a telephone message on 7 June from No.76 Wing to AASF headquarters which stated that the twelve aircraft required for night operations could not start off before 2200 as the crews were exhausted and needed rest. In the late afternoon of that day, twenty-two Battles were sent to attack columns south of the river Somme. Nineteen aircraft reached the battle area and sixteen were able to bomb various road and rail targets. There was intense AA fire and German fighters were active. Three Battles were missing from this raid and one Bf 109 was claimed as shot down and two Bf 109s and a Bf 110 were claimed as probables. Sixteen Battles were on night operations on 7/8 June, attacking communications targets and armoured columns. One aircraft was missing.

On the afternoon of 8 June, the Battles made 23 sorties against armoured and motorised columns and troop concentrations in the Abbeville - Longpré - Poix - Aumale area. Operating with a fighter escort, some convoys were bombed and the aircraft which did not find any vehicles attacked road and railway targets. Four aircraft were missing. The same night, 8/9 June, attacks were made by ten aircraft on road and rail communications at Trier and Laon. A further eleven aircraft attacked Somme crossings and exits from Amiens and Abbeville. There was little AA and searchlight activity and all aircraft returned safely. There were no daylight operations by the Battles on 9 June. Eighteen aircraft made sorties on the night of 9/10 June to attack bridges over the river Somme, communications in the Laon area, Trier aerodrome and the Forêt de Gobain. One aircraft was missing from these raids.

In addition to the operations of the AASF, the Blenheims of No.2 Group, operating from airfields in England, made daylight attacks on enemy columns and installations on nearly every day during the period 17 May - 10 June. They suffered extremely heavy losses in doing so. The heavy bombers of Bomber Command were active in night attacks on enemy communications and supplies. The blitzkrieg tactics of the German army, aided by overwhelming air superiority and effective AA defences, were very successful and the combined efforts of the AASF Battles, the No.2 Group Blenheims and the Bomber Command heavies had little more than nuisance value and had little effect on the speed of advance of the German armoured columns. The AASF made a considerable effort in their night bombing activities, but the difficulties of locating targets and the inaccuracies of bombing on ETA, coupled with equipment faults in the aircraft, gave very dubious results. The raids kept the German defences on the alert but achieved little material damage.

No.12 Squadron

After completing their move to Echimines, the squadron was in daylight action on the morning of 19 May, when six Battles took off to attack enemy troops in the forward area. The aircraft were:
K9377 F/O B.G.F. Drinkwater; L5249 Sgt W.H. Kellaway;
P5237 P/O R.A.D. Meharey; P6597 S/L B.E. Lowe;
L5538 P/O J.J. McElligott; N2178 F/O P.R. Barr

No movement of troops was found and the villages of Seraincourt and St. Fergau were bombed amid desultory AA fire. Bf 109s were encountered and two of the Battles were shot down. After bombing St Fergau village, P/O McElligot was attacked by six Bf 109s and crashed in a wood. His gunner claimed one Bf 109 shot down. P/O McElligot and his gunner were wounded and taken to a French hospital, where the pilot died. The observer returned to the squadron two days later. F/O Barr was shot down and he and his gunner were wounded. His observer was killed. On 20 May the squadron was ordered to send five aircraft on a night operation to bomb Mezières and Montcornet. The aircraft took off at intervals between 2315 and midnight and bombs were to be dropped singly at intervals or in salvo if suitable targets were found. The aircraft were:
K9377 F/Lt P.H.M.S. Hunt; L5249 P/O C.L. Hulse;
L5520 P/O P.C.D. Eaton; P6597 P/O C.N. McVeigh;
L5580 Sgt F. Field

All aircraft bombed but the results were not observed, except by F/Lt Hunt, who claimed to have bombed a road and rail junction at Mezières from 8,000 feet, blowing up a large railway building. Searchlights were active but AA fire was

desultory. The following awards were announced on 21 May:

DFC   F/Lt W. Simpson, P/O T.D.H. Davy.
DFM   Cpl R.T. Tomlinson, Sgt E.N. Odell, AC1 G.H. Patterson.

On 23 May, four aircraft were ordered to attack columns of 150 tanks on the Doullens - Arras road. The Battles, which took off shortly before 1900, were:
L5383 F/O T.F.S. Brereton; L5249 P/O T.D.H. Davy;
Serials not known: F/Lt B.G.F. Drinkwater and P/O P.C.D. Eaton

With a cloud bank from 3,000 to 8,000 feet, F/O Brereton and P/O Davy failed to find the target. The other two aircraft bombed but no results were observed. All returned safely though two landed at other airfields. Two aircraft set out to bomb the revictualling yard at Florenville and the town of Charleville on the night of 23/24 May. They were:
P6597 P/O C.N. McVeigh; L5415 Sgt G.R. Wheeldon;

With 10/10 cloud at 4,000 feet and ground mist, neither pilot located his target and they both returned with their bombs. The next night, 24/25 May, seven aircraft were sent to cause maximum disturbance to communications by bombing Givet, Bouvignes and Fumay. No bombs were to be brought back if the aircraft were over enemy territory. In the poor visibility which prevailed, five aircraft failed to find their targets and bombed on ETA. The other two aircraft bombed railway targets. Searchlights were active and there was moderate light AA fire. The aircraft were:
K9377 F/Lt P.H.M.S. Hunt; L5249 P/O T.D.H. Davy;
L5451 P/O J.S. Shorthouse; L5546 Sgt W.H. Kellaway;
L5520 P/O P.C.D. Eaton; P6597 P/O C.N. McVeigh;
L5415 Sgt G.R. Wheeldon

Two aircraft were sent out at 1130 on 25 May to attack an enemy column reported to be jammed in a defile on the road between Conchy and Hesdin. The aircraft were:
L5520 P/O R.A.D. Meharey; P2162 Sgt F. Field

Neither pilot saw any sign of a column; P/O Meharey dropped his bombs near a railway line and Sgt Field bombed some transport. AA fire was was intense but inaccurate. Night bombing continued on 25/26 May when three aircraft were despatched to bomb Givet and Nouzonville. They were:
L5546 P/O J.S. Shorthouse; L5451 F/O T.F.S. Brereton;
L5580 F/Lt B.G.F. Drinkwater.

F/Lt Drinkwater force-landed at Chappelle on the outward journey with engine trouble, returning to the squadron on the following day. The other two aircraft bombed on ETA because of bad visibility. On the night of 27/28 May, nine aircraft took off to bomb St. Hubert aerodrome, Ochampes aerodrome, Libramont railway installations and the revictualling yard at Florenville. They were:
N2150 F/Lt P.H.M.S. Hunt; L5249 P/O T.D.H. Davy;
L5324 Sgt W.H. Kellaway; P6597 P/O C.N. McVeigh;
L5424 P/O R.A.D. Meharey; L5383 P/O J.S. Shorthouse;
L5415 Sgt G.R. Wheeldon; L5520 P/O P.C.D. Eaton;
L5580 Sgt F. Field

Eight aircraft bombed on ETA because of bad visibility and Sgt Field had a near miss on a fire near a railway. There was much searchlight activity but the AA fire was moderate. On 31 May the squadron received orders for a morning attack by six aircraft on Laon airfield and Laon racecourse, where German aircraft were said to be parked. The Battles were to fly to the target in cloud and make a surprise attack when they

got there. The six aircraft, which took off at 1100, were:
L5324 Sgt W.H. Kellaway; L5451 Sgt J. Wilcox;
L5328 Sgt A. Preston; P2162 S/L B.E. Lowe;
L5420 F/Lt B.G.F. Drinkwater; L5520 P/O P.C.D. Eaton

Sgt Preston, F/Lt Drinkwater and one other bombed on ETA, S/L Lowe bombed a wood thought to contain AA batteries and the remaining aircraft returned without bombing. The poor results were caused by 10/10th cloud in the target area. Six of the squadron's aircraft were detailed to bomb Libramont railway junction on the night 31 May/1 June. The aircraft were:
L5580 Sgt F. Field; L5415 Sgt G.R. Wheeldon;
N2150 F/Lt P.H.M.S. Hunt; L5249 P/O T.D.H. Davy;
L5324 F/O T.F.S. Brereton; L5383 P/O J.S. Shorthouse

In the intense darkness all the pilots had difficulty in finding the target and all bombed on ETA. Sgt Field force-landed at Blois after being unable to get a D/F bearing and running short of fuel. He returned to Echimines the next day. On 3 June, the squadron moved to Souge but left twelve aircraft at Echimines ALG for operations. Nine aircraft took off from Echimines at varying times for a night attack on convoys at Hirson and on woods north of St Michel on 4/5 June. Those taking part were:
L5546 F/Lt P.H.M.S. Hunt; L5383 P/O J.S. Shorthouse;
L5458 F/O T.F.S. Brereton; N2150 P/O T.D.H. Davy;
L5568 Sgt W.H. Kellaway; P6597 P/O C.N. McVeigh;
L5420 F/Lt B.G.F. Drinkwater; L5520 P/O P.C.B. Eaton;
L5580 Sgt F. Field

Most of the aircraft bombed on ETA in poor visibility and so results were not observed, but some fires were started. P/O Shorthouse force-landed at Chaumont and returned the next day. P/O Eaton crash-landed at Faux-Villecerf, where his aircraft was abandoned. The pilot and crew were uninjured. On 5 June, three aircraft took off shortly before 2000 to attack convoys in the Poix and Neufchatel areas; they were:
L5546 F/Lt P.H.M.S. Hunt; L5568 P/O G.M. Hayton;
L5458 P/O J.F. McFie

A convoy of seven armoured vehicles was bombed near Neufchatel. F/Lt Hunt was attacked by six French Morane fighters near the target and he claimed two put out of action. P/O Hayton and P/O McFie force-landed at Faux-Villecerf but returned the next day. At 1700 on 7 June, nine aircraft left to attack tanks, armoured units and troops in the Poix area. The aircraft were:
L5415 Sgt G.R. Wheeldon; L5458 P/O J.F. McFie;
L5420 P/O C.N. McVeigh; P2162 Sgt F. Field;
L5237 P/O P.H. Blowfield; L5328 Sgt A. Preston;
L5249 Sgt J. Wilcox; L5451 P/O J.S. Shorthouse;
L5568 P/O G.M. Hayton

The Battles were attacked by Bf 109s and Sgt Field was shot down in flames. P/O McVeigh was attacked by six Bf 109s and possibly shot one down. Sgt Wheeldon sustained damage to his port wing, elevator and tailplane but managed to bring his aircraft back to base. Columns in the target area were bombed but no results are recorded. On 8 June, four aircraft took off at about noon to attack tanks and troops in the Abbeville - Longpré - Poix - Aumale area. They were:
L5580 S/L B.E. Lowe; L5458 P/O P.H. Blowfield;
L5546 F/O T.F.S. Brereton; N2150 P/O T.D.H. Davy

No large concentrations were seen but bombs were dropped on the head of a mechanised column near Avèsnes and other small columns were bombed. F/O Brereton was shot down by ground fire and became a PoW; his two crew

were killed. Two aircraft were on night operations on 8/9 June, one to attack the aerodrome at Trier and one to attack the exits from Laon. The aircraft were:
P6597 P/O C.N. McVeigh; L5396 Sgt E. Wheeldon

Neither pilot found his target because of low mist; P/O McVeigh bombed an AA battery north of Trier and Sgt Wheeldon bombed a searchlight concentration.

No.88 Squadron

The squadron operated from their new base at Les Grandes Chappelles on 19 May, when "all available aircraft" bombed targets at Hirson. No further details of this action are known except that one air gunner was wounded. The next operation was a night raid on 20/21 May, again with "all available aircraft". A night raid was made on Givet on 21/22 May. Five aircraft took part in an early morning attack on tanks in the Arras area on 22 May; the operation was not a success. The squadron was next in action in a night raid on 23/24 May, when P2356 piloted by P/O A.E. Wickham was missing. All three crew were killed. Another aircraft force-landed but was undamaged. On 24/25 May, the squadron took part in a night raid on the Frankfurt area. Three aircraft set out on 25 May before noon to attack a column on the Abbeville - Hesdin road. One returned early with engine trouble. The others failed to find the column. The squadron was on night operations on 25/26 May to attack targets north of Sedan. One aircraft hit a Crossley tender on take-off and there were minor accidents to three other aircraft. One aircraft was missing, L5467, piloted by P/O C.C.R. Anderson. All three aboard were killed. Four aircraft operated on the night of 26/27 May in appalling weather conditions with targets at Givet. Two returned early because of the weather and one failed to locate the target and returned with its bombs. One aircraft bombed Givet. The squadron was again on night operations on 27/28 May. The aircraft piloted by Sgt D. Haywood hit a tree on take-off and crashed. The pilot was unhurt but his two crew sustained slight injuries. On 28/29 May there was an abortive night operation against targets in the Givet area, the bad weather making things very difficult for the Battle crews. The squadron was again on night operations on 29/30 May, when the target was a petrol dump at Givet. One aircraft, P2313, piloted by F/O H.G. Evitt, crashed immediately after taking off and a bomb exploded, killing all three crew. Several sorties were cancelled because of the bad weather, but those who did fly dropped their bombs, mostly on ETA with dubious results. On the return journey two aircraft landed safely at other airfields, returning to Les Grandes Chappelles the next day. Seven aircraft took part in the night operations on 31 May/1 June. Their target was Givet, which was located and bombed.

On 1 June, the squadron maintained a patrol of one aircraft in the Reims - Chalons area to report on any large formations of enemy aircraft. Two Battles alternated on this between 1320 and 1850. On 3 June, the squadron moved to Moisy. There were no further operations until the night of 5/6 June, when five aircraft, flying from Echimines, took part in attacks on targets in the Guise area. Five aircraft took part in a late afternoon attack on 6 June, with enemy convoys as targets. Few vehicles were seen but the road was bombed in the Sancourt area. The squadron's base was bombed three times during the night and one aircraft was damaged. During night operations the squadron attacked targets in the St. Quentin area, using Echimines en route. On the following

The wreck of GS-P from No.105 Squadron is removed by rail to Germany. (A Thomas collection)

night, 7/8 June, attacks were made on targets in the St Valéry area, using Faux-Villecerf as an ALG. Four aircraft, using Echimines, left at noon to attack enemy columns in the Abbeville area. All returned safely, again via Echimines. The squadron operated on the night of 8/9 June but no details are available. Three aircraft attacked targets in the Abbeville area on the night of 9/10 June.

No.103 Squadron

The rear party of the squadron remained at Bétheniville until 20 May, salvaging equipment and destroying items which might be of value to the enemy. The rest of the squadron was settling in at its new base at Rhèges. The CO, W/C Dickens, appropriated three Hurricanes which had been left at Bétheniville and had them flown to Rhèges. He was ordered to return them to No.501 Squadron! On 19 May, the squadron sent six aircraft on a morning attack on troop concentrations in the Condé-sur-Seine area. All returned safely. The squadron had now abandoned its low level approach and attack tactics for daylight operations and were using a high approach at 8,000 feet then diving to 4,000 feet to attack. This was thought to reduce the casualty rate. Another ploy adopted was to send aircraft out singly instead of in sub-formations of three, to increase manoeuvrability. Five of the squadron's aircraft took part in a bombing raid on Fumay on the night of 20/21 May. The squadron took over all of No.218 Squadron's aircraft and equipment on 21 May because of the latter squadron's move to Nantes. Squadron aircraft strength was now 31 Battles. On 22 May, four aircraft made an early morning attack on tanks in the Amiens - Bernaville area without conspicuous success. The aircraft

piloted by Sgt W.R. Critch was damaged by AA fire and he force-landed; he and his crew returned to the squadron the next day. Five aircraft took part in night attacks in the Trier area on the night of 22/23 May; two force-landed and later returned to the squadron base. Four aircraft flew on night operations on 23/24 May and a further four aircraft made a night raid on Fumay on 24/25 May. On 25 May, three aircraft took off before noon to attack a column near Abbeville. It was not found but one Battle, piloted by Sgt G. Beardsley, was shot down. Sgt Beardsley and his gunner rejoined the squadron two days later; there was no observer aboard the aircraft. The squadron was on night operations on 25/26 May. Four aircraft led by F/O J.R. Havers took off at 1000 on 26 May to attack Chateau Roumont, near Libramont. Hits on the target were claimed and there was heavy AA fire. One aircraft was missing, L5514, piloted by F/Lt J.N. Leyden. He was taken prisoner and the other two crew were killed. One aircraft, L5515, crash-landed with a defective undercarriage and one aircraft was forced to land at Verdun. The squadron took part in night operations on 27/28 May. Six aircraft were detailed on 28 May for a late morning attack on armoured columns on roads leading to Amiens. One returned early with an unserviceable airspeed indicator and a glycol leak. Five reached the target area but only small groups of vehicles and isolated detachments of troops could be found. These were attacked, but they were not targets of any importance. L5515, piloted by F/O R.D. Max, was badly damaged by AA fire and he force-landed near Chalons, abandoning the aircraft. F/O Max and his observer were wounded. There was a night operation on 29/30 May when the squadron sent three aircraft to attack targets in the Trier area. One returned because of bad weather, the others bombed communications targets. One of these returned after landing at Sens because of a faulty D/F bearing. On the next night, 30/31 May, four aircraft took off to attack Conz. Two returned early because of the weather conditions, one force-landed and one reached the target area and released his bombs from 2,500 feet. This latter pilot radioed a bad weather report from the target area and any further operations that night were abandoned. The squadron was next in action in a night raid on 2/3 June on communications targets south of Trier. The squadron started its move to Herbouville in the early hours of 3 June, the aircraft following later. The surface of the airfield was incomplete, which added to the hazards faced by the crews of the aircraft. On 5 June, seven aircraft were sent to Echimines ALG for night operations and these attacked enemy convoys and Guise airfield. There was poor visibility and the results of the bombing were not observed. During this operation, P/O Harper's aircraft was hit by AA fire and he ordered his two crew to bale out. After they had done so, P/O Harper made a wheels-up landing on soft ground by the light of a parachute flare with little damage to the aircraft. All three escaped without injury. A daylight attack on the afternoon of 6 June was made on convoys in the Roye area. In the absence of vehicles as targets, roads were bombed. The enemy made three raids on the squadron's airfield at Herbouville on the night of 6/7 June. The squadron operated in the St. Quentin area on 6/7 June, working via Echimines. One aircraft force-landed but later was able to return to base. The enemy raided Echimines during night operations and 23 bombs hit the airfield, causing considerable chaos and badly damaging two aircraft. Using Faux-Villecerf as an ALG, the squadron raided targets in the St. Valéry area on the night of 7/8 June. On this occasion four incendiary bombs were carried in the cockpit of each aircraft for use over the target area. Six of the squadron's aircraft attacked columns in the Poix area on 8 June. The most notable feature of this operation was an attack by P/O G.W.Thorougood on a large number of Ju 87s which he saw bombing a village. He claimed one shot down, then was attacked by German fighters. His air gunner, P/O Webber, on his first operational flight, claimed to have shot down a Bf 109. The badly damaged Battle, P2315, crash-landed near Paris with the gunner wounded. Another of the squadron's Battles, N2253, was shot down on this raid and the pilot, Sgt G. Beardsley, and his crew were taken prisoner. Six aircraft operated on the night of 8/9 June over the battle area, but no details are available. A further six aircraft attacked targets in the Abbeville area on the following night, 9/10 June. The aircraft piloted by S/L H. Lee, L5246, suffered engine trouble and the crew abandoned it by parachute after being unable to locate their base.

No.105 Squadron

After its confused move to Echimines on 18 May, the squadron was ordered to move to Nantes. They entrained on 20 May and arrived at Nantes on 22 May. At Nantes they moved into a camp site in woods three miles from Bougenais. There they remained, without equipment or transport, for the rest of their stay in France.

No.142 Squadron

After their move to Faux-Villecerf, the squadron salvaged

equipment from Berry-au-Bac on 17 and 18 May. On 19 May, the three available aircraft were sent on a morning raid on enemy positions west of Laon; none returned. The aircraft were:

K7696 P/O H.H. Taylor; L5226 Sgt A.J. Godsell;
P5238 Sgt G.H. Ebert

P/O Taylor and his two crew were taken prisoner. Sgt Godsell and his observer were also taken prisoner but the gunner in this aircraft was killed. Sgt Ebert force-landed south of Epernay and he and his gunner returned to the squadron; his seriously wounded observer died. Some urgently needed reinforcements of Battles were received from Pouan, bringing the squadron strength of aircraft up to 25. On the morning of 20 May, P/O I.C. Chalmers made a photographic reconnaissance of the Troyes area in P2177. Four aircraft were detailed to take part in night operations on 20/21 May. One did not take off because its radio was unserviceable. As one of the others was being got ready for the raid a flare ignited and set the aircraft alight. The bomb load exploded and five ground crew were killed and an adjacent Battle was damaged by bomb splinters. The two remaining aircraft carried out the raid but no results are known.

The squadron stood by all day on 21 May. At 0500 on 22 May, six aircraft took off to attack tanks in the Amiens - Abbeville area. The weather was bad with low cloud and two were recalled by W/T. Two others returned because of the weather conditions. P/O B.W. Perriman in P2325 was unable to locate the target and returned with his bombs after refuelling at Rouen en route. The remaining aircraft, piloted by F/O A.D. Gosman, bombed tanks in the Amiens area then got lost and force-landed near Paris. F/O Gosman and his crew returned to the squadron the next day. Four aircraft were on night operations on 22/23 May. S/L W.B. Wight returned because of bad weather and Sgt Holliday, in P2359, failed to locate the target and returned with his bombs. P/O Edwards did not locate the target, got lost and force-landed north of Paris. He and his crew returned to the squadron by rail. P/O Sutton was the only pilot to find the target at Florenville and bomb it in the extremely bad weather conditions. The target was again Florenville on the night of 23/24 May, when four aircraft operated. The crews had great difficulty in finding Florenville in the poor weather conditions. P/O Ricalton in P2177 bombed an AA battery and Sgt Ebert bombed a searchlight battery. The results obtained by the other two crews are not known. Four aircraft attacked Givet, Dinant and Mezières on the night of 24/25 May. There was ground mist in the target area and hits on a road leading out of Givet were claimed. The following night, 25/26 May, saw six aircraft detailed for attacks on Givet and Dinant. One aircraft bombed Givet, one bombed Dinant and two bombed a convoy near Fumay. One aircraft returned early with its bombs after encountering lightning and one bombed Mezières after failing to find the primary target. On 26 May, six aircraft made a morning attack on Chateau Roumont. Five bombed from 2,000 feet, claiming one hit on the chateau and hits around the building. The sixth aircraft bombed a railway junction. All returned safely, though one aircraft force-landed at at its base with a defective undercarriage. The squadron joined in the night attack on St. Hubert aerodrome on 27/28 May. A fire already burning at the target was bombed. There were no further operations until four aircraft were sent to attack Bingen and Florenville on the night of 31 May/1 June. On the afternoon of 2 June, the operations tent was destroyed

Belgian Air Force Battles were also engaged in the initial phase of the German invasion but lost most of their aircraft in the first days. (via D Howley)

by fire and much operational equipment was lost, including flying helmets, parachutes and maps. On 3 June, one of the squadron's Battles went out to patrol the Reims - Chalons area at 1230 but was recalled at 1520. Also on that day, the squadron moved to Villiers-Faux, five miles west of Vendôme, where they had to borrow flying helmets from other squadrons because of the loss of their own. Five aircraft operated on the night of 3/4 June against railway targets in the Givet and Trier areas. One aircraft failed to release its bombs and the other four had great difficulty in finding the primary target and bombed various other targets. On 5 June, four aircraft made an evening attack on enemy convoys in the Roye area. The squadron completed its move to Villiers-Faux on 6 June. Two aircraft were on night operations on 7/8 June, one to bomb bridges near Abbeville and one to bomb St. Hubert aerodrome. The latter aircraft, piloted by P/O H.L. Oakley, got lost on the return journey and, with fuel running low, the crew parachuted to safety. The Battle crashed near Chateauneuf and the crew returned to the squadron the next morning. The night of 8/9 June saw three of the squadron's aircraft attacking the Forêt de Gobain, which was thought to contain troops, vehicles and war material. The attack was made from 6,000 feet and fires were started. On the return journey to Villiers-Faux, two of the aircraft came under heavy French AA fire despite their having fired recognition signals.

No.150 Squadron

From their new base at Pouan, the squadron sent six aircraft to take part in the morning attacks on enemy columns on 19 May. Their targets were concentrations of mechanised units north of the river Aisne. The aircraft were:

L5545 F/O H.R.McD. Beall; P5235 P/O D.E.T. Osment;
L5437 P/O D.G. Long; P2179 P/O Rafter;
L5541 S/L R.M. Bradley; L5583 F/O A.D. Frank

The results of the raid were not observed because of bad weather. S/L Bradley failed to find the target and bombed an AA battery. The Battles were met by heavy AA fire and P/O Osment failed to return. He and his two crew were taken prisoner. P/O Frank force-landed his aircraft at Sommesous airfield, where it was abandoned. On the night of 22/23 May, five aircraft set out to bomb communications targets on the Germany/Luxembourg border. They were:

L5524 P/O A.R. Gulley   P2327 Sgt R.G. Beale
L5543 Sgt S.E. Andrews   L5288 Sgt W.C. Pay
L5512 P/O S.R. Peacock-Edwards

P/O Peacock-Edwards and Sgt Pay returned because of bad weather. The other aircraft bombed but the results were not observed. On 23 May, four aircraft made an evening attack on armoured vehicles on the Doullens - Arras road. They were:
L5541 S/L R.M. Bradley; L5288 F/O J.E. Vernon;
L5106 F/O A.D. Frank; L5579 P/O C.H. Elliott

All four aircraft found and bombed targets. Eight aircraft set out to bomb Monthermé on the night of 23/24 May. They were:
L5510 F/O W.M. Blom; P6602 Sgt W.C. Pay;
L5524 P/O A.R. Gulley; P2327 P/O D.G. Long;
L5545 F/Lt H.R.McD. Beall; L5106 Sgt R.A.deC. White;
L5543 Sgt S.E. Andrews; L5437 Sgt R.G. Beale

Sgt Beale returned because of the weather conditions but the others continued. In very bad visibility it was not easy to find the target and some crews bombed on ETA. All seven bombed but no results were observed. F/Lt Beall's bombs were not fused and did not explode. On the following night, 24/25 May, eight aircraft were briefed to attack the railway centre of Libramont. They were:

P2179 P/O P. Edwards; L5437 Sgt S.E. Andrews;
L5545 F/Lt H.R.McD. Beall; L5106 Sgt R.A.deC. White;
L5510 F/O W.M. Blom; P6602 Sgt W.C. Pay;
P2327 P/O D.G. Long; P5524 P/O A.R. Gulley

P/O Long could not find the target and returned with his bombs. The other seven bombed railway targets. On the late morning of 25 May two aircraft took off to attack a column of armoured vehicles in the Abbeville area. They were:

L5112 F/Lt R.A. Weeks; L5237 P/O Rafter

F/Lt Weeks bombed the Abbeville - Hesdin road ahead of the vehicles; P/O Rafter bombed the road after mistaking white patches on the road for vehicles. There were night operations for eight of the squadron's aircraft on 25/26 May with Libramont as the target. The aircraft were:

L5437 Sgt R.G. Beale; P2327 P/O D.G. Long;
P2179 P/O S.R.Peacock-Edwards; L5524 P/O A.R. Gulley;
L5459 Sgt R.A.deC. White; P6602 Sgt W.C. Pay;
L5545 F/Lt H.R.McD. Beall; L5510 F/O W.M. Blom;

P/O Long returned with his bombs because of engine trouble. P/O Peacock-Edwards dropped unfused bombs and they did not explode. Five of the other aircraft bombed Charleville and one bombed a searchlight on ETA at the target. Two aircraft made a morning attack on Chateau Roumont on 26 May. They were:

L5459 F/O J.G. Vernon; P6602 P/O C.H. Elliott

F/O Vernon attacked from 3,000 feet and claimed hits on the chateau. On the way back he was attacked by four Bf 110s and successfully evaded them. Passing an airfield near Florenville, he saw an aircraft landing there and attacked it with his front gun, claiming hits on it. Eventually he had to land his badly-damaged aircraft near Avioth in the German lines, where he set it alight. Becoming separated from his crew, F/O Vernon reached the Maginot Line from where he returned to the squadron. His observer and gunner were taken prisoner. P/O Elliott bombed the target and returned via Verdun.

Eight aircraft operated on the night of 27/28 May:

L5106 Sgt R.A.deC. White; P6602 Sgt W.C. Pay;
L5545 F/Lt H.R.McD. Beall; L5510 F/O W.M. Blom;
L5524 P/O A.R. Gulley; P2327 P/O D.G. Long;
L5437 P/O S.R.Peacock-Edwards; L5543 Sgt S.E. Andrews

The main target was the railway at Nouzonville but bad visibility meant that several pilots could not identify it and they bombed searchlight batteries or other targets. Only two aircraft claimed to have bombed the target. Bad weather again interfered with the next operation on the night of 28/29 May, when four aircraft left to attack targets in the Charleville area. They were:

L5543 Sgt S.E. Andrews; L5524 P/O A.R. Gulley;
P2327 P/O S.R. Peacock-Edwards; L5437 Sgt R.G. Beale

Sgt Andrews and Sgt Beale returned because of bad weather. The other two pilots bombed targets in the designated area. In the now familiar poor weather, one aircraft operated on the night of 30/31 May:

L5543 Sgt S.E. Andrews

The weather was so bad that operations for the rest of the squadron were cancelled. Sgt Andrews got lost and landed at Mâcon. Eight aircraft took off to attack Charleville on the night of 31 May/1 June. They were:

L5510 F/O W.M. Blom; P6602 Sgt W.C. Pay;

L5545 F/Lt H.R.McD. Beall; L5437 Sgt R.G. Beale;
L5106 Sgt R.A.deC. White; P2327 P/O D.G. Long;
P2179 P/O S.R. Peacock-Edwards; L5524 P/O A.R. Gulley

P/O Long returned early with engine trouble; he did not drop his bombs. Sgt White was unable to locate the target and bombed a searchlight. P/O Peacock-Edwards dropped his bombs but they were not fused. The remaining five aircraft all bombed Charleville. Seven aircraft were on night operations on 2/3 June, when the targets were in the Givet/Mezières area. The aircraft were:

P2179 P/O S.R. Peacock-Edwards; L5437 Sgt R.G. Beale;
L5543 Sgt S.E. Andrews; L5510 F/O W.M. Blom;
P6602 Sgt W.C. Pay; L5106 Sgt R.A.deC. White;
L5545 F/Lt H.R.McD. Beall

Sgt Andrews returned early with engine trouble, the other six aircraft bombed in the target area. The squadron moved to Houssay on 3 June, nineteen aircraft flying to the new base. On 5 June, nine aircraft were flown to the forward base at Echimines for night operations. On 6/7 June, eight aircraft made a night attack on various targets in the Laon area. On the evening of 7 June six aircraft attacked columns in the Poix - Abbeville area. They were:

L5474 P/O C.H. Elliott; L5112 F/Lt R.A. Weeks;
L5237 P/O Rafter; L5579 F/O A.D. Frank;
L5288 F/O J.E. Vernon; serial not known: Sgt Popplestone

Convoys of vehicles and a road and rail junction were bombed. F/O Vernon was shot down and he and his crew were killed. Six aircraft were in night action on 7/8 June bombing communications targets in the battle area. The aircraft were:

L5545 F/Lt H.R. McD. Beall; L5106 Sgt R.A.deC. White;
L5237 P/O D.G. Long; L5524 P/O A.R. Gulley;
P2179 P/O S.R. Peacock-Edwards; P6602 F/O W.M. Blom

P/O Peacock-Edwards bombed a road and rail junction; no results were observed by the other five aircraft. On the afternoon of 8 June, three aircraft attacked columns near Hornoy:

K9323 Sgt Popplestone; L5237 P/O Rafter;
L5112 F/Lt R.A. Weeks.

F/Lt Weeks was shot down by ground fire and all three crew of the aircraft were killed. The other two aircraft bombed a convoy but did not observe the results. Seven aircraft attacked communications targets in the Laon area on the night of 8/9 June. The aircraft were:

L5545 F/Lt H.R. McD. Beall; L5106 F/O W.M. Blom;
P6602 Sgt W.C. Pay; L5543 Sgt S.E. Andrews;
L5524 P/O A.R. Gulley; L5437 Sgt R.G. Beale;
P2179 P/O S.R. Peacock-Edwards

The targets bombed were mainly roads, railways and vehicles. The aircraft operated from the ALG at Echimines. The squadron was again in night action on 9/10 June with targets at Trier aerodrome, Laon and Forêt de Gobain.

No.218 Squadron

The squadron sent aircraft on the morning attacks on enemy columns from their new base at Rhèges on 19 May and also on the night operation on 20/21 May. No details of these actions are available. On 21 May, the squadron's aircraft and equipment were handed over to No.103 Squadron and orders were received for all personnel to go to No.2 Base Area at Nantes. No.218 Squadron took no further part in operations in France and remained at Nantes until their evacuation to the UK.

No.226 Squadron

The squadron received much needed replacement aircraft at their new base at Faux-Villecerf on 17 May. On 19 May, two aircraft took off for a morning attack on enemy columns. They were:

K9176 Sgt N.N. Hoyle; P2254 P/O D.A.C. Crooks

Sgt Hoyle bombed a column of lorries north of Ecly and P/O Crooks bombed a wood near Hauteville. Both aircraft returned safely. Seven new aircraft were received from the U.K. on 20 May. The squadron's next operation was a night attack by six aircraft on Montcornet on 20/21 May. The aircraft were:

L5468 P/O D. Salway; P6601 F/Lt W.S. Butler
L5428 Sgt G.F. McLoughlin; P5234 F/O F.O. Barrett
P2335 F/O R.W. Bungay; K9176 Sgt R.S. Annan

Sgt Annan failed to return; he and his gunner were taken prisoner and the observer was killed. The other five Battles bombed the target and fires were observed. On the following night, 21/22 May, four aircraft took off between 2130 and 2215 to bomb Florenville. They were:

P6601 P/O Rae; L5234 S/L R.G. Hurst;
L5428 Sgt G.G. Martin; P2254 Sgt N.N. Hoyle

The first two pilots did not observe the results of their bombing, Sgt Martin saw his bombs burst near a burning building and Sgt Hoyle had a near miss on a river bridge near Carignan. The next night, 22/23 May, six aircraft were sent to attack various communications targets. They were:

P6601 F/O R.W. Bungay; P5234 F/O F.O. Barrett;
L5450 Sgt G.F. McLoughlin; P2254 F/O D.A.C. Crooks;
P2335 Sgt Groves; P2331 P/O D. Salway

Sgt McLoughlin returned with his bombs because of the rain. The other aircraft dropped their bombs, mainly on targets of opportunity, and all returned safely. In the evening of 23 May two aircraft bombed a convoy of armoured vehicles on the Arras/Doullens road. The aircraft were:

L5450 Sgt G.F. McLoughlin; L5468 Sgt N.N. Hoyle

Both aircraft returned safely, but Sgt McLoughlin landed at Auxerre. On 23/24 May the targets for night attacks were Florenville and Charleville. The six aircraft taking part were:

P6598 Sgt G.G. Martin; L5468 P/O Rae;
P6601 F/Lt W.S. Butler; L5460 F/O D.A.C. Crooks;
L5419 Sgt E.E. Hopkins; L5234 S/L R.G. Hurst

Sgt Hopkins returned early with his bombs because of bad weather. Sgt Martin could not find the target and returned with his bombs. The others all bombed but no results were observed because of the poor visibility. The following night, 24/25 May, six aircraft operated to make attacks on Sedan, Givet, Dinant and Charleville. They were:

P2254 Sgt G.F. McLoughlin; P6601 F/O R.W. Bungay;
L5468 P/O D. Salway; L5419 Sgt E.E. Hopkins;
P5234 F/Lt F.O. Barrett; P6598 Sgt N.N. Hoyle

All the aircraft bombed with some success and all returned safely, though F/Lt Barrett landed at Auxerre. On the morning of 25 May, two aircraft were sent to bomb armoured vehicles on the Abbeville - Hesdin road:

P2331 F/O Kercher; L5461 P/O Heywood

F/O Kercher narrowly missed the road and P/O Heywood dropped two bombs on vehicles then had the frustrating experience of his remaining two bombs hanging up. On the night of 25/26 May, seven aircraft were detailed for operations. They were:

L5234 S/L R.G. Hurst; P6601 F/Lt W.S. Butler;

P2254 F/O D.A.C. Crooks; P2161 P/O Rae;
L5461 P/O D. Salway; L5419 F/O R.W. Bungay
Serial not known: Sgt G.F. McLoughlin

This was a most unsuccessful night for the squadron. F/Lt Butler did not take off because of engine trouble. Engine problems made S/L Hurst and P/O Crooks return early and Sgt McLoughlin returned with a petrol leak. P/O Rae could not locate the target and returned with his bombs. P/O Salway bombed Nouzonville and F/O Bungay also bombed but did not observe the results. Six aircraft operated on the night of 27/28 May:

P6601 F/Lt W.S. Butler; P5234 S/L R.G. Hurst;
L5450 F/Lt F.O. Barrett; L5498 Sgt N.N. Hoyle;
K9351 Sgt E.E. Hopkins; P2331 P/O D. Salway

This was again an unproductive night for the squadron. F/Lt Butler returned early with engine trouble, F/Lt Barrett and Sgt Hoyle could not locate the target and bombed searchlights and Sgt Hopkins and P/O Salway bombed on ETA. Only S/L Hurst claimed to have bombed the target. Such were the difficulties of night bombing in poor visibility with the primitive equipment available to the crews in 1940. On 28 May, six aircraft took off to attack armoured columns on roads near Amiens. They were:

L5461 F/O R.W. Bungay; P2161 P/O Heywood;
P6598 Sgt G.G. Martin; L5428 F/O D.A.C. Crooks;
L5305 Sgt G.F. McLoughlin; L5419 P/O Rae

P/O Rae returned almost immediately with a perspex panel blown out of his aircraft. The other five found no major targets but attacked vehicles and troops with bombs and machine guns. All returned safely. The squadron's next operation was a daylight attack on enemy aircraft parked on Laon airfield and Laon racecourse on 31 May. Six Battles took off at 1030, they were:

L5419 F/Lt W.S. Butler; L5461 P/O Heywood;
L5468 P/O D. Salway; L5498 Sgt N.N. Hoyle;
L5035 F/Lt F.O. Barrett; serial not known: F/O Hollis

With 10/10th cloud in the area the target could not be located; F/O Hollis bombed on ETA, F/Lt Butler tried to do the same but his bombs did not release, P/O Heywood and P/O Salway returned with their bombs and Sgt Hoyle and F/Lt Barrett bombed alternative targets. On 31 May/1 June, the squadron sent six aircraft on a night attack on Conz. They were:

P2254 F/O D.A.C. Crooks; K9351 Sgt E.E. Hopkins;
L5460 Sgt G.F. McLoughlin; L5037 P/O Rae;
P6601 F/O R.W. Bungay; P6598 Sgt G.G. Martin

Sgt Martin returned shortly after take-off with his pilot's perspex panel blown out. P/O Crooks bombed Conz and machine gunned a train and Sgt Hopkins bombed lights in the target area. The other three aircraft bombed on ETA and did not observe the results. The squadron moved to Souge on 3 June. The squadron records for June were lost during the evacuation from France and therefore details of their operations in that month are sadly lacking. It is likely that up to ten aircraft took part in a night attack in the Hirson and Givet areas on 4/5 June. On 5 June, four of the squadron's aircraft took part in an evening attack on convoys in the Peronne area. Four aircraft attacked targets in the Laon area on the night of 6/7 June. Seven aircraft attacked columns in the Poix - Abbeville area in the evening of 7 June; one aircraft was missing. The squadron took part in the attacks on enemy columns in the Abbeville area on 8 June and also operated on the night of 8/9 June but no details are available.

The wreckage of Battles litter a scrapheap at the end of the Battle of France. ((A Thomas collection)

CHAPTER 9. THE BATTLE OF FRANCE (3)

The third and final phase of the AASF bomber operations in France, from 10 to 15 June 1940, was concerned mainly with attacking targets in the area of the lower Seine. The AASF headquarters was at Muides, near Blois, and the six remaining operational Battle squadrons operated from their bases near Vendôme. The advanced landing grounds at Echimines and Faux-Villecerf, which were now in the path of the advancing German army, were no longer needed and they were evacuated on 12 June. With the enemy approaching Paris and French resistance crumbling, the AASF Battles were called upon for daylight operations in a desperate attempt to slow the advance of the German armour.

On the morning of 10 June twelve Battles were sent to attack bridges over the Seine and enemy columns in the Vernon area. Most of the bridges were reported as already destroyed, including the bridge at Vernon, so the Battles dive bombed and machine gunned columns near Vernon and bombed convoys in the Forêt de Vernon in the face of intense AA fire. One aircraft, last seen being attacked by a Bf 109, was missing and one aircraft returned badly damaged after failing to reach the target. Later in the morning six aircraft attacked tanks and armoured vehicles in the Poix, Aumale and Abbeville areas; all returned safely. Two of the Seine bridges, at Vironwy and Pont-de-l'Arche, were reported to be still standing and a force of twelve Battles was sent out in the early evening to bomb them. The bridges were claimed to be destroyed and direct hits were scored on transport concentrations. All the Battles returned safely. Attacks on road and rail communications north of the Seine river and in the Meuse valley were ordered for the night of 10/11 June. It was a night of bad weather with low cloud and mist and several of the 24 Battles detailed for operations failed to take off or returned early and others failed to locate their targets.

Incendiary and HE bombs were dropped on armoured vehicles and troops in woods in the Vernon area and fires were started. All aircraft returned safely, one after a forced landing.

With French resistance to the German army crumbling, the AASF bombers had a busy time in the few days before their withdrawal from France. Their attacks on bridgeheads and enemy columns had little effect on the inevitable outcome of the battle, but Barratt persevered in his attempts to help the hapless French. On 11 June a dawn raid was made by twelve Battles on a pontoon bridge reported south west of Les Andelys. In ground mist, the few pilots who saw the river could not find the bridge. Nine of the aircraft attacked various alternative targets, two returned without bombing because of lack of suitable targets and one returned early with a sick pilot. Shortly after noon six aircraft were sent out to attack a bridge near Les Andelys; two bombed a girder bridge at St. Pierre, claiming a direct hit, and two bombed a pontoon bridge. One aircraft was missing from this operation, for which a fighter escort was provided. Later in the afternoon, sixteen sorties were made by the Battles against troop concentrations in the Forêt de Bizy. Again there was a fighter escort; one Battle was missing. The final daylight operation was mounted when six aircraft were sent with a fighter escort to attack tanks reported to be on the road between Etretat and Le Havre. This was largely a wasted effort as no tanks were seen and five aircraft returned with their bombs; the sixth bombed two armoured vehicles. The night attacks planned for 11/12 June were frustrated by very bad weather and most squadrons cancelled operations. Only three Battles are known to have taken off for Les Andelys and Vernon and of these only one aircraft bombed Les Andelys, the others returning because they could not locate their targets. The Battles mounted several operations on 12 June. At dawn nine aircraft were sent to Les Andelys to attack pontoon bridges. Only one crew found a bridge, at Vesillon, and bombed it. The remaining aircraft bombed roads and woods. At about 0830, a further twelve aircraft were sent to attack pontoon bridges over the Seine at Verberie and Pontpoint and some hits were made on the bridges. One aircraft was missing from this operation and another force-landed and was destroyed by its crew. A fighter escort had been provided. Later in the morning, four Battles attacked a bridge at Le Manoir which was being used by enemy columns; hits on the bridge and on troop concentrations were claimed. In mid-afternoon twelve aircraft were sent to bomb the bridge at Vesillon; seven of these bombed the target or other targets in the vicinity. Night operations were again hampered by bad weather on 12/13 June when fifteen Battles were detailed to attack troops at Pavilly and the approaches to Les Andelys, including the pontoon bridge there. Several aircraft did not take off because of malfunctions and others returned without finding their targets in the appalling weather conditions. Les Andelys and Vernon were bombed and one aircraft was missing. By 13 June, the French appeared to be accepting that their position was hopeless and in an attempt to boost their sagging morale the British Prime Minister, Winston Churchill, sent a message to the French Prime Minister and to the French C-in-C promising an increased effort by the RAF. Blenheims, heavy bombers and fighters operating from England would be available, together with the bombers, (six squadrons of Battles), and the fighters of the AASF. The tired Battle aircrews and their worn aircraft were again to be used in an impossible task - to check the German advance. Shortly after dawn on 13 June, six aircraft carried out an armed reconnaissance of the Vernon - Pacy - Evreux area. They had little to report and all returned safely. Later in the morning, ten aircraft set out to attack enemy columns. Five of these bombed convoys, railways and roads, four were missing and one returned early. Enemy fighters were very active against these raids. It was reported that 500 tanks were in the Forêt de Gault and the French requested that these be attacked. A force of 38 Battles was sent on this mission and HE bombs and incendiaries were seen to burst among tanks in the wood. Fires were started and armoured vehicles were machine gunned. Seven aircraft were missing from this operation.

The French armies were now disorganised and defeated, but the AASF carried on with its hopeless task on 14 June. Early in the morning, ten Battles were sent to attack enemy troops in the battle area near Evreux. The clouds were down to ground level, the targets could not be seen and the Battles returned without bombing. Because of the proximity of German troops, the headquarters of No.75 Wing and the ground echelons of Nos.88 and 103 Squadrons moved to Nantes. The aircraft of No.88 Squadron, which had flown the abortive early raid from their base at Moisy, returned to Houssay then, at noon, flew to Abingdon en route for Driffield, their time in France over. At 1125, four aircraft went out on an armed reconnaissance of the Louviers - Vernon - Pacy - Evreux area. They found much enemy transport on the roads near Evreux and woods and troops were bombed. In the afternoon, nine aircraft attacked targets on these roads. Further attacks on columns of vehicles and troop concentrations in the Evreux - Pacy area were made by twelve aircraft in the early evening. Five Battles were missing from the day's operations and one was badly damaged and written off after it returned to its base. The five squadrons of

Battles remaining in France were all in action on 15 June before returning to England. Shortly after dawn at least thirteen aircraft flew an armed reconnaissance into the battle area. Enemy columns in the Louviers - Vernon - Viry - Damville - Evreux area were attacked; one aircraft was missing. Later in the morning further sorties for reconnaissance and for attacks on enemy columns were made. During the day all of the Battles which were still serviceable were flown back to England and the operations of the AASF bombers in France were over. Several unserviceable aircraft were destroyed before the squadrons left. The ground echelons of the Battle squadrons were making their way towards embarkation ports for their return to England. The AASF operational training unit, No.98 Squadron, flew their aircraft from their base at Chateau Bougon, Nantes, to Gatwick on 15 June. The squadron's ground crews made their way to St. Nazaire, where they boarded SS *Lancastria*. The ship was sunk by bombing with the loss of at least 75 of No.98 Squadron's personnel. The Blenheims of No.2 Group operated in daylight throughout this third phase and the heavy bombers lent support at night.

About 230 Battles were lost in France between September 1939 and June 1940. This figure includes losses from all causes including enemy action, accidents and aircraft abandoned when airfields were evacuated. It is not possible to give an accurate figure of losses because many Battles disappeared from RAF records after the squadrons returned to England and these were presumed to have been lost in France. Far more serious than the loss of aircraft was the loss of so many trained aircrews in the Battle of France. The AASF Battle crews fought magnificently against a better armed and numerically superior enemy. Despite a dauntingly high rate of casualties they continued the fight until the situation became impossible, then the survivors returned to England to continue their war.

No.12 Squadron

Operating from their Souge base, six aircraft took off at 1130 on 10 June to attack tanks and armoured vehicles in the Poix, Aumale and Abbeville areas. All six bombed and the aircraft taking part were:
L5383 P/O J.S. Shorthouse; N2150 Sgt J. Wilcox;
L5451 P/O G.M. Hayton; L5420 P/O P.H. Blowfield;
L5396 P/O B. Willoughby; P5237 P/O J.F. McPhie
At dawn on 11 June, three aircraft set out to bomb a pontoon bridge south west of Les Andelys. The aircraft were:
P5237 P/O J.F. McPhie; L5580 Sgt E. Wheeldon;
L5568 P/O J.S. Shorthouse

P/O Shorthouse was taken ill and returned early with his bombs. The other two pilots failed to find the bridge and bombed the town and an AA battery. At 1805, six aircraft took off to attack tanks and vehicles reported to be on the road between Etretat and Le Havre. The aircraft were:
L5580 P/O B. Willoughby; L5249 F/O B.E. Moss;
L5531 P/O P.H. Blowfield; L5324 P/O G.M. Hayton;
L5396 P/O R.C.L. Parkhouse; L5568 Sgt J. Wilcox;

There was no sign of tanks and five aircraft saw nothing and brought their bombs home; Sgt Wilcox spotted two armoured vehicles and bombed them. All in all, a most frustrating day for the squadron. On the night of 12/13 June two aircraft set out to attack troops in the Pavilly area; they were:
L5420 F/Lt B.G.F. Drinkwater; P6597 P/O C.N. Mcveigh

72

Both aircraft returned before reaching the target area because the cloud base was down to ground level. Later in the night four aircraft were sent to attack the pontoon bridge at Les Andelys and the woods south of the town. The aircraft were:
P6597 P/O C.N. McVeigh; P5237 Sgt G.R. Wheeldon; L5249 F/Lt P.H.M.S. Hunt; L5383 P/O T.D. Davy

P/O McVeigh and Sgt Wheeldon found the bridge to be obscured by mist, so they bombed the town of Les Andelys. The other two aircraft returned to base because of the bad weather. On 13 June, six aircraft were briefed to attack tanks reported to be concealed in the Forêt de Gault. No tanks were seen but the wood was bombed from a high level. The Battles met intense and accurate AA fire and fighters were active in the area. The aircraft which took part were:
L5324 P/O J.S. Shorthouse; L5451 F/O B.E. Moss; L5580 P/O R.C.L. Parkhouse; L5396 Sgt G.R. Wheeldon; L5531 P/O J.F. McPhie; serial not known: P/O G.M. Hayton

P/O Parkhouse and P/O Mcphie were shot down and they and their crews were taken prisoner. P/O Shorthouse was also shot down and he and his gunner suffered burns; the observer was killed. Sgt Wheeldon was attacked by Bf 109s but managed to drive them off. In mid-afternoon on 14 June, three aircraft were sent to attack transport concentrations in woods near Evreux and the aerodrome at Le Coudray. They were:
L5396 P/O P.H. Blowfield; L5249 Sgt D.H. Preston; L5383 Sgt J. Wilcox

P/O Blowfield and Sgt Wilcox were shot down by enemy fighters. P/O Blowfield was shot while trying to evade capture, his observer managed to get back to England and his gunner was killed. Sgt Wilcox and his two crew were killed. Sgt Preston was unable to locate the target and returned with his bombs. In the evening of 14 June there was an air raid on the squadron's aerodrome and one aircraft was set on fire. Four aircraft were detailed for an attack on troops in the battle area Louviers - Vernon - Ivry - Damville - Evreux at 0900 on 15 June. Two of the aircraft were unable to start because of faults in equipment. The two aircraft which took off were:
P5237 P/O Rothwell; L5415 Sgt G.R. Wheeldon

Finding no enemy troops, P/O Rothwell bombed an aerodrome and a railway junction at Plessis-Grohan and Sgt Wheeldon bombed the Forêt d'Ivry. On their return the squadron was ordered to fly to England. Despite an enemy air attack on the airfield, eight Battles took off and flew to Abingdon then on to Finningley.

No.88 Squadron

The squadron, operating from Herbouville, took part in two actions on 10 June. At 1045, three aircraft took off to attack bridges and columns in the Vernon area and at 1645 a further three aircraft were sent to bomb the remaining two bridges and columns in the same area. All returned safely. Three of the squadron's aircraft took part in operations in the Abbeville area on the night of 10/11 June. P/O J.M. Talman force-landed but later returned to base. On 11 June, three aircraft took part in the dawn operation against a pontoon bridge near Les Andelys; the bridge was not found and alternative targets were attacked. In the late afternoon the squadron took part in the attack on troop concentrations in the Forêt de Bizy. One aircraft, L5519, piloted by P/O J.D.W. Gillam, was shot down. The squadron operated against pontoon bridges at Verberie and Pontpoint on the morning of

12 June and lost two aircraft; L5334 piloted by F/Lt A.L. Pitfield was shot down by AA fire and P/O J.M. Talman who bombed and machine gunned his target but his aircraft was badly damaged by AA fire. He force-landed at a French aerodrome at Mitry-Mory, set fire to his aircraft and he and his gunner rejoined the squadron four days later. In the afternoon, the target was the pontoon bridge at Vesillon and the results of the operation are not known; F/O F.W. Snell was taken ill and was forced to return early. On 13 June, an afternoon attack was made on the Forêt de Gault, where tanks were thought to be concealed. One Battle, piloted by Sgt Hayward, was shot down by Bf 109s. The two crew were both wounded and taken to hospital. Also on 13 June, the squadron received orders to move to Nantes. At dawn on 14 June "all available aircraft" from the squadron were detailed to attack troop concentrations near Evreux. In conditions where the cloud base was down to ground level the operation was aborted. The ground crews of the squadron had left Moisy for Nantes and the aircraft returned to Houssay. At noon, they left to fly to Abingdon, then on to Driffield. Their very active stay in France was over.

No.103 Squadron

Three aircraft, operating from Herbouville, took part in the morning attack on bridges and columns in the Vernon area on 10 June. P/O C.V. Thomas in P2328 was shot down and he and his gunner were killed. Sgt W.R. Crich, piloting K9409, had his aircraft severely damaged by ground fire and though he returned to base the Battle was damaged beyond repair. The remaining Battle, piloted by F/O D. Kelly, was attacked by a Hurricane on the outward journey and had to return to base damaged. Three aircraft from the squadron joined the early evening attack on two bridges and columns near Vernon without incident. Three aircraft took part in night operations in the Abbeville area on the night of 10/11 June. On 11 June, three aircraft went to attack a pontoon bridge near Les Andelys but did not find it and bombed alternative targets. A further operation against troop concentrations in the Forêt de Bizy was mounted in mid-afternoon. On 12 June, the squadron sent out six aircraft in the morning and six in the afternoon to bomb undemolished bridges over the Seine. Hits were claimed on the bridges and on other alternative targets. All aircraft returned safely. The squadron took part in the night operations on 12/13 June but no details are available except that one aircraft returned with a faulty magneto. On 13 June, the squadron made two raids during the day without loss. Orders were received to move to Nantes. At 0630 on 14 June, the squadron's air party, consisting of sixteen Battles and two Magisters, flew from Herbouville to Souge. In the evening, four aircraft attacked enemy columns in the Evreux - Pacy area. Two Battles were missing from this raid. Sgt Brumby crash-landed near Laval and he and his crew rejoined the squadron. P/O Hawkins and his sole crew member were taken prisoner. P/O Hawkins later escaped and returned to England. A low level attack on Souge by enemy aircraft resulted in several of the squadron's aircraft being hit and set on fire. The squadron's ground party left that night for Nantes. Three aircraft went out on an armed reconnaissance at 1000 on 15 June and all returned safely. At 1200, the squadron was ordered to fly its aircraft from Souge to Abingdon. A heavy enemy air attack was made on the airfield after most of the Battles had taken off; several aircraft on the ground were destroyed and there were casualties. There was a further enemy attack while the squadron CO, W/C T.C. Dickens, was making a final inspection of the airfield, destroying his aircraft in the process. After the departure of the enemy, W/C Dickens and two of his pilots flew in a damaged Battle to Nantes. Altogether nine Battles flew from Souge to Abingdon.

No.142 Squadron

On the morning of 10 June, six aircraft took off to attack bridges and columns in the Vernon area. A hit on a pontoon bridge under construction was claimed and, as other bridges appeared to have been destroyed, enemy troops and villages were attacked. Four of the squadron's aircraft were sent to attack armoured vehicles and troops in woods in the Vernon area on the night of 10/11 June. Three aircraft bombed with incendiaries and HE bombs and left fires burning. There was low cloud and mist in the target area and one aircraft overshot the target and returned without bombing. Six aircraft were sent to attack bridges in the Les Andelys and Le Manoir areas on 11 June; not all found the bridges and these bombed alternative targets. Heavy AA fire was encountered and P/O B.W. Peryman in L5200 was shot down and he and his two crew were taken prisoner. In the extremely bad weather on the night of 11/12 June, only one aircraft took off, bound for Vernon, but the pilot (S/L W.B. Wight) was forced by low cloud to return to base. On 12 June, a morning raid on a bridge at Le Manoir was made by four aircraft. Sgt A.N. Spear, flying L5252, claimed a direct hit on the bridge and P/O L.H. Child, flying P6600, also claimed a hit. Three aircraft set out for a night raid on Cisors on 12/13 June. In extremely poor visibility one aircraft bombed on ETA, one aborted and returned to base and the other, piloted by F/Lt A.D.J. Martin was missing. The crew of three were killed. At 0500 on 13 June, six aircraft took off for an armed reconnaissance in the Vernon - Pacy - Evreux areas. Nothing of note was seen and F/O Bilton bombed an AA battery and Sgt Tweed bombed woods. At 1045 three aircraft went out to raid enemy columns on the Pacy - Vernon - Rouen road. Bombs were dropped along the road after the aircraft approached the target at 4,000 feet in 7/10 cloud. F/Lt J.M. Hewson was shot down by Bf 109s. After landing his burning aircraft, F/Lt Hewson made his way to Villiers-Faux. His observer, who had parachuted, went to St. Malo and thence to England. The gunner was wounded and was taken prisoner. P/O K.R. Sutton was shot down and his observer and gunner were injured. P/O W.D.K. Franklin returned in a badly damaged machine with a wounded observer. At 1200, P/O L.H. Childe bombed an enemy convoy south of the river Seine. Later in the afternoon five aircraft were sent to bomb tanks reported to be refuelling in woods near Montmirail, in the Forêt de Gault. Sgt D.J. Holliday was missing from this raid and he and his two crew were taken prisoner. During the morning of 14 June, four aircraft flew an armed reconnaissance south of the river Seine. P/O L.H. Childe bombed roads and Sgt Tweed bombed troops in the target area. In the afternoon, three aircraft attacked Bf 109s at dispersal on Le Caudray aerodrome, near Evreux. These were piloted by P/O R.H. Edwards, Sgt A.N. Spear and Sgt G.H. Ebert. The squadron was ordered to move to Rennes and preparations to do so were made during the day. At dawn on 15 June, three aircraft flew an armed reconnaissance in the Evreux area. One aircraft bombed an AA battery. At 0500 the ground party left Villiers-Faux for Rennes. Three aircraft were destroyed

on the aerodrome and at 1300 the air party in thirteen Battles took off for England. One force-landed near Rennes, the other twelve flew to Waddington.

No.150 Squadron

Five aircraft took off to bomb armoured vehicles and troops in woods in the Vernon area on the night of 10/11 June. They were:

L5563 P/O D.G. Long; L5524 P/O A.R. Gulley;
L5543 Sgt S.E. Andrews; L5437 Sgt R.G. Beale;
L5510 F/O W.M. Blom

P/O Long and P/O Gulley returned because of the bad weather and the bombs failed to release in Sgt Andrews' aircraft. The other two aircraft bombed Vernon and its nearby woods. In the afternoon of 11 June six aircraft attacked troop concentrations in the Forêt de Bizy. They were:

L5541 S/L R.M. Bradley; L5593 F/O A.D. Frank;
L5524 P/O A.R. Gulley; L5237 P/O Rafter;
L5474 P/O C.H. Elliott; K9323 Sgt Popplestone

All the aircraft bombed the forest and returned safely. Six aircraft were detailed for a night attack on Les Andelys on 11/12 June, but in the very bad weather conditions prevailing only two took off. They were:

L5106 Sgt R.A.DeC. White   L5545 F/Lt H.R.McD. Beall

F/Lt Beall, in the only aircraft to attack that night, bombed the Forêt de Andelys. Sgt White abandoned his flight because of the weather and returned early. Four aircraft went to Les Andelys to attack a pontoon bridge at dawn on 12 June but could not find it. As alternative targets they bombed roads and woods. The aircraft were:

L5510 F/O W.M. Blom   P6602 Sgt W.C. Pay
L5524 P/O A.R. Gulley   L5543 Sgt S.E. Andrews

On the morning of 13 June six aircraft attacked enemy columns in the Vernon - Poix - Evreux area. They were:

L5106 F/Lt H.R.McD. Beall   P6602 Sgt W.C. Pay
L5514 Sgt R.A.DeC. White   L5563 F/O W.M. Blom
L5524 P/O A.R. Gulley   L5437 Sgt R.G. Beale.

P/O Gulley and Sgt Beale were shot down by Bf 109s. Sgt Beale and his two crew were killed; P/O Gulley was killed and his two crew were taken prisoner. In the evening six aircraft were sent to bomb tanks in the Forêt de Gault. They were:

K9323 Sgt Popplestone   L5543 Sgt S.E. Andrews
L5574 P/O C.H. Elliott   L5579 F/O A.D. Frank
P2179 P/O S.R. Peacock-Edwards L5591 S/L R.M. Bradley

Sgt Andrews and P/O Peacock-Edwards bombed tanks but did not observe the results. Sgt Popplestone could not locate the target and returned with his bombs. P/O Elliott and F/O Frank were attacked by Bf 109s, got lost and returned with their bombs, P/O Elliott in a badly damaged aircraft. S/L Bradley was shot down in flames by Bf 109s; he crash-landed his aircraft and he and his observer made their way to Nantes.

A German soldier guards a shot-down Battle of No.150 Squadron. (P. Jarrett collection)

The wounded gunner was taken to hospital. At 0930 on 14 June, the squadron was ordered to be ready to leave on six hours notice. At 1815, three aircraft took off to look for enemy movements in the Evreux - Pacy - Vernon area. The aircraft were:

L5106 Sgt R.A.DeC. White   P6602 Sgt W.C Pay
L5545 F/Lt H.R.McD. Beall

Sgt White bombed two lorries and F/Lt Beall bombed a wood, where he started fires. Sgt Pay bombed a convoy of vehicles, then was attacked by seven Bf 109s, which he evaded by coming down to ground level. On 15 June, ten aircraft took off soon after dawn to attack troop concentrations in the Louviers - Vernon - Viry - Damville - Evreux area. The aircraft were:

L5545 F/Lt H.R.McD. Beall   L5106 Sgt R.A.DeC. White
L5579 F/O A.D. Frank   P6602 Sgt W.C. Pay
L5593 P/O C.H. Elliott   L5541 P/O Benjamin
P2179 P/O S.R. Peacock-Edwards L5563 F/Lt W.M. Blom
L5237 P/O Rafter   P2327 P/O D.G. Long

P/O Benjamin was attacked by three Bf 109s and, after evading them, crash landed his badly damaged aircraft at La Ferte Vidame. His wounded gunner was put into a French ambulance, the aircraft was "sabotaged" and P/O Benjamin and his observer made their way to Nantes. On landing, the aircraft were refuelled preparatory to their leaving for England. The ground party had left for Nantes. At 1100, the air party in twelve Battles flew to Abingdon then on to Stradishall.

No.226 Squadron

The squadron took part in the daylight operations on 11 June but no details are available. One aircraft, P6598, piloted by Sgt G.P. McLoughlin, was shot down near Vernon. All three crew were killed. The squadron was in daylight action against bridges over the Seine on 12 June. During the actions of 13 June, the squadron lost one aircraft, P2161, piloted by Sgt E.E. Hopkins. The pilot survived but the observer and gunner were killed. The squadron attacked targets in the Evreux area on 14 June. One aircraft, P2335, was missing; its pilot, F/O K.N. Rea, was killed. The ground party left for Rennes on 15 June, followed by the air party, which flew to Thirsk.

After the fall of France, Polish crews formed new Battle squadrons in Britain. This photograph of a Polish gunner shows details of the Fairey rear gun mounting. (Bruce Robertson collection)

CHAPTER 10. ANTI-INVASION OPERATIONS

No.1 Group Bomber Command

On 18 June 1940, the Air Ministry decided that No.1 Group of Bomber Command should be reconstituted from four squadrons which had re-formed after returning from service with the AASF in France. The formation of Group Headquarters at Hucknall began on 24 June 1940 and the squadrons moved to their operational stations on 3 July. Nos. 12 and 142 Squadrons were based at Binbrook and Nos.103 and 150 Squadrons at Newton. It was reported on 5 July that the squadrons were available for operations in an emergency but that they were not fully operational. The Group then had, in total, 45 Battles and 55 crews available. Because of the threat of invasion, Binbrook and Newton were each ordered to have six aircraft standing by fully armed from one hour before dark until released the following morning. The Battles went into action on the night of 21/22 July when six aircraft from Newton were detailed to attack oil tanks at Rotterdam. For the rest of July, the targets for the Battles were aerodromes, aerodrome installations and aircraft on the ground. The results of these raids were disappointing. The squadrons based at Newton, Nos.103 and 150, did not operate

in August 1940 and the two Binbrook squadrons, Nos.12 and 142, were moved to Eastchurch where they were placed under the command of No.16 Group, Coastal Command, for operations and training. The attachment lasted from 7 August to 6 September 1940 and both squadrons were in action, mainly against invasion ports, during this period. Enemy bombing caused much damage to aircraft and airfield installations at Eastchurch and Nos.12 and 142 Squadrons returned to Binbrook and recommenced operations from there in mid-September 1940. The Newton squadrons restarted their operations on 7 September 1940. The efforts of the Battles, together with those of many other Bomber Command aircraft, were now concentrated on bombing shipping in the invasion ports. Two Polish bomber squadrons, Nos. 300 and 301, were formed at Bramcote in July 1940 and moved to Swinderby in August. This gave No.1 Group a strength of six Battle squadrons. The Polish squadrons joined in the bombing campaign against the invasion ports on 14 September 1940. Attacks on enemy shipping in the Channel ports by Battles continued into October 1940. The last Battle operation carried out by No.1 Group was an attack on shipping at Calais and Boulogne on 15/16 October 1940. Though they were most unsuitable for night bombing, the Battles made a contribution to Bomber Command's major effort against the German preparations for invasion of the UK.

Operations

A summary of the operations carried out by the No.1 Group Battles in 1940 follows. Most of these were night bombing attacks and many were made with a load of six 250-lb bombs instead of the normal load of four 250-lb bombs.

21/22 July

Three aircraft from No.103 Squadron and three from No.150 Squadron took off to bomb oil storage tanks at Rotterdam. Only one aircraft claimed to have bombed the primary target but no results were observed in the poor weather conditions. One other attempted to attack the target but the bombs overshot the storage tanks and it was claimed that they hit a nearby plant. Two aircraft bombed alternative targets and two turned back with equipment failures.

22/23 July

Aircraft on the ground and installations at Schiphol aerodrome were the target for three aircraft from No.103 Squadron and three from No.150 Squadron. Three aircraft attacked but were unable to observe the results. One attacked the aerodrome at Marienbach after failing to locate the main target and two turned back with faulty equipment.

23/24 July

Six aircraft were detailed for operations, three from No.12 Squadron and three from No.142 Squadron. None of the No.12 Squadron aircraft took off; two were involved in a taxying accident and one suffered radio failure. Two of the No.142 Squadron aircraft failed to locate the target in bad weather and one returned early with engine trouble.

25/26 July

Twelve Battles were briefed to attack Evère aerodrome, Brussels, and Hingene aerodrome, Antwerp. There were three from each of Nos.12, 142, 103 and 150 Squadrons. In the bad weather, only one aircraft (from No.150 Squadron) reached the target area but could not locate the targets and its bombs were jettisoned in the sea. Eight aircraft returned bacause of the weather, two returned early with technical problems and one did not take off because of W/T failure.

28/29 July

Six aircraft from No.142 Squadron were detailed to attack Evère aerodrome. One aircraft bombed but did not observe the results and one reached the the target area but could not locate the target. One aircraft returned early after losing its W/T aerial and one did not take off because of engine trouble. Two Battles were missing from the operation.

29/30 July

Waalhaven aerodrome was to have been the target for three aircraft from No.150 Squadron but the operation was aborted because of bad weather conditions.

31 July/1 August

Three of the six No.12 Squadron aircraft briefed to attack

Waalhaven aerodrome reached the target area but could not locate the target in low cloud conditions; they jettisoned their bombs in the sea. Two aircraft returned early with faulty equipment. One Battle was shot down by a friendly night fighter near Skegness on its outward journey. The comment was made in the No.1 Group Operations Record Book: "A culmination of many unsuccessful efforts as recorded last Month." The AOC decided to suspend operations during the no moon period.

The Newton Battle squadrons, Nos.103 and 150, did not operate in August. The Binbrook squadrons, Nos.12 and 142, were attached to No.16 Group, Coastal Command, from 7 August to 6 September and were based at Eastchurch. A summary of the Battle operations carried out while Nos.12 and 142 Squadrons were with Coastal Command follows:

17 August

An evening attack in daylight on shipping in Boulogne harbour was mounted by six aircraft from No.12 Squadron and six from No.142 Squadron. The Battles operated from Detling because Eastchurch was badly bomb-damaged. Eight aircraft bombed within the target area and one attempted two attacks but its bombs failed to release. Two aircraft returned early with faults and one aircraft failed to take off. On its return, damaged by AA fire, one Battle crashed on landing.

18 August

A dusk attack on E-boats in Boulogne harbour was ordered, with six aircraft from No.12 Squadron and six from No.142 Squadron. Seven aircraft bombed in the target area, three did not bomb because of technical failures, one failed to locate the target and one did not take off because of air compressor failure. There was intense AA fire over the target.

19/20 August

Five aircraft from No.12 Squadron and two from No.142 Squadron set out to attack shipping in Boulogne harbour. The target was obscured by cloud and only one aircraft is known to have bombed. Three aircraft returned with their bombs, two returned early with equipment faults and one was missing.

21 August

One aircraft from No.142 Squadron was sent on an evening attack on Boulogne harbour. The crew were unable to locate the target because of low cloud and returned with their bombs.

23 August

The only squadron to operate was No.142 and it made two raids on Boulogne harbour. In the early morning, five aircraft set out in poor visibility and four failed to locate the target. The remaining aircraft bombed the target but could not see the results in the bad weather conditions. In the evening a daylight attack by six aircraft was aimed at seaplanes and E-boats. In the face of intense AA fire, three Battles bombed the target but were unable to observe the results. One bombed a factory near Boulogne and two aircraft were missing.

24 August

At first light, a successful attack was made by one aircraft of No.12 Squadron on shipping in Boulogne harbour. Facing intense AA fire, P/O Tillett dived from 9,000 feet to 3,500 feet and bombed a mole where barges were moored.

25/26 August

A night attack on Le Crotoy aerodrome by three aircraft of No.142 Squadron was mounted. One bombed hangars without seeing the results and two failed to find the target and returned with their bombs.

26 August

In the afternoon, one aircraft from No.142 Squadron made a reconnaissance of the Calais area seeking minesweepers. Nine minesweepers were seen but they ran for harbour when the aircraft approached them.

27 August

Three aircraft from No.12 Squadron and one from No.142 Squadron took off to make an early morning attack on E-boats in Calais harbour. Two bombed the target, one did not attack because the target was obscured by clouds and one failed to locate the target. This last aircraft crashed on landing at Eastchurch.

29 August

One aircraft from No.12 Squadron set out at 1230 to bomb Mardyck aerodrome if sufficient cloud cover was available. With a clear sky over mid-Channel, the pilot turned back.

1/2 September

One aircraft from No.142 Squadron was sent to bomb shipping in Calais harbour. The pilot located the harbour but could not identify any shipping, so he dropped his bombs on the outer harbour.

The two squadrons at Eastchurch, Nos.12 and 142, survived several enemy raids while based there and several Battles were destroyed or damaged by bombing. They returned to Binbrook, again fully under the control of No.1 Group, on 6 September. The detachment had not been a success, with control of the squadrons partially under No.1 Group and partially under Coastal Command. Nos.103 and 150 Squadrons were still at Newton and resumed operations on 7 September. Two Polish Battle squadrons, Nos.300 and 301, based at Swinderby, commenced operations with No.1 Group in mid-September.

7 September

Six aircraft from No.103 Squadron and six from No.150 Squadron were briefed to make an evening attack on barges and shipping in Calais harbour. Eleven aircraft bombed in the target area but no results were observed because of very bad weather and intense AA fire. One aircraft failed to find the target and jettisoned its bombs in the sea.

9 September

Six aircraft, three from No.103 Squadron and three from No.150 Squadron, made an evening attack on barges and shipping in Calais harbour. The attack was claimed to have been successful. One aircraft from No.103 Squadron was shot down by AA fire. The crews reported much light AA fire but little heavy AA.

10/11 September

Three aircraft from No.103 Squadron and three from No.150 Squadron attacked barge concentrations in Boulogne harbour. Five aircraft bombed the target area but extensive cloud obscured the results. One aircraft failed to locate the target

and returned with its bombs.

11/12 September

Six aircraft, three from No.103 Squadron and three from No.150 Squadron, were detailed to attack barges and shipping in Boulogne harbour. In very bad weather conditions three aircraft bombed in the target area and one turned back. One aircraft could not drop its bombs because of a fault in the master switch and one did not take off because of brake trouble.

14/15 September

Each of four squadrons, Nos.103, 150, 300 and 301, sent three aircraft to attack barges and light craft in Boulogne harbour. Ten aircraft bombed in very bad weather conditions; two crews reported bursts seen in the dock area but the rest were unable to see the results of their efforts. One aircraft failed to find the target and returned and one aircraft returned early with engine trouble. Because of the bad weather several crews landed at bases away from their own.

15/16 September

Again twelve aircraft were detailed to attack barges and shipping at Boulogne, three from No.103 Squadron, three from No.150 Squadron and six from No.300 Squadron. Ten aircraft bombed and some bursts were seen in the target area. One aircraft bombed Le Touquet in error and one did not bomb because of pilot error.

17/18 September

Eighteen Battles were despatched to continue the attacks on Boulogne shipping. Nos.12, 103, 142 and 150 Squadrons each provided three aircraft and No.300 Squadron provided six. The target area was bombed by fifteen aircraft in low cloud conditions. One bombed an alternative target, Calais, and the bombs failed to release in two aircraft.

18 September

Two aircraft from No.300 Squadrom made a morning daylight attack on Boulogne; both bombed successfully.

18/19 September

Twelve aircraft, three from No.103 Squadron, three from No.150 Squadron and six from No.301 Squadron, attacked barges and shipping at Boulogne. Some bursts were seen in the target area.

20/21 September

Barges and shipping at Boulogne were once again the target for eighteen Battles. There were three each from Nos.12, 103, 142 and 150 Squadrons and six from No.301 Squadron. Ten aircraft bombed the target area and some bursts were observed. Two aircraft bombed a gun emplacement at Cap Gris Nez and one bombed Calais harbour. Three aircraft failed to find the target and did not bomb and two aircraft returned early with faults.

21/22 September

Barges at both Calais and Boulogne were the targets for six aircraft from the Polish squadrons and three aircraft each from Nos.103 and 150 Squadrons. The Polish squadrons cancelled the operation because of bad weather. Three aircraft from No.103 Squadron bombed Boulogne harbour and three from No.150 Squadron bombed Calais Harbour.

23/24 September

Shipping at Boulogne was the target for three aircraft from

No.103 Squadron, three aircraft from No.150 Squadron and six aircraft from No.300 Squadron. Ten aircraft bombed in the target area and fires were seen. One bombed the alternative target at Calais and one returned early with a W/T fault.

25 September

Three aircraft from No.103 Squadron, three from No.150 Squadron and six from No.301 Squadron took off for an early morning attack on barges and shipping at Boulogne. Ten aircraft bombed the target area and one bombed a gun emplacement at Cap Gris Nez. A No.301 Squadron Battle crashed at Brandon, Norfolk, on its outward flight.

27 September

The harbour and barges at Ostend were the target for seventeen Battles; three from No.103 Squadron, four from No.150 Squadron and ten from No.300 Squadron. The attack was made early in the morning and fifteen aircraft bombed the target area. Bomb bursts and some fires were seen. Two aircraft bombed Dunkirk harbour.

The September operations were regarded as successful. Though it is unlikely that the Battles caused major damage, the crews received valuable night flying and night bombing experience. Because of the difficulty of recognising targets on moonless nights, operations by the Battle squadrons were suspended until the new moon period.

9 October

Eight aircraft from No.301 Squadron made an evening attack on Calais harbour. All dropped their bombs in the target area.

10 October

Eight aircraft from No.300 Squadron made a further attack on Calais harbour and all bombed in the target area.

11 October

Operations for the Polish squadrons were cancelled because of bad weather. Six aircraft, three each from Nos.12 and 142 Squadrons, were detailed to make an evening attack on shipping and docks at Ostend. Four aircraft bombed successfully, one returned with a faulty compass and one misunderstood a signal and failed to take off.

12 October

Six aircraft from No.301 Squadron operated. Three bombed Calais and three bombed Ostend.

13 October

Three aircraft from No.12 Squadron, three from No.142 Squadron and six from No.300 Squadron took off to attack shipping and docks at Calais and Boulogne. Three aircraft bombed the target areas at Calais and three at Boulogne. The remaining aircraft failed to reach their targets and returned in the very bad weather. Three of the Battles crashed.

15/16 October

For the last No.1 Group operation by Battles, the targets were docks and shipping at Calais and Boulogne. Three aircraft from No.12 Squadron and two from No.142 Squadron were

briefed for Calais. Three aircraft bombed the target area, one was recalled because it had the wrong signal cartridge and one failed to take off because of a misunderstood signal. Six aircraft from No.301 Squadron all bombed the target area at Boulogne.

The six Battle squadrons made 289 sorties, many of which were abortive, between July and October 1940. Six Battles, four from No.142 Squadron, were missing from these operations.

Squadron Aircraft

No.12 Squadron

The squadron moved from Finningley to Binbrook on 3 July 1940 with 16 Battles. Eight of these were aircraft which had been flown from France after serving with the squadron in the AASF. They were: L5415, L5420, L5451, L5458, L5568, P2331, P5237 and P6597. The remaining eight had been received at Finningley from No.27 MU. They were: L5359, L5391, L5398-L5400, L5404, L5491 and L5495. A further 15 Battles and two Battle T.T. target tugs were on the squadron strength at some time during its period in 1 Group. They were: L5011, L5076, L5100, L5127, L5220, L5240, L5493, L5521, L5532, N2166, P2262, P2308, P2311, P5236 and P6571. The Battle T.T. target tugs were L5629 and L5630. On 1 August 1940, L5568, piloted by F/O B.E. Moss, was shot down by a British night fighter near Skegness, Lincs. It crashed into the sea and the three crew were killed. Several aircraft were lost during the detachment to Eastchurch, which was the target of repeated enemy raids. While visiting Martlesham on 15 August, L5493 was burned out after being hit by enemy bombs and the pilot, W/C V.Q. Blackden, was injured in the foot. During an attack on Boulogne on 17 August, P2331, piloted by P/O G.M. Hayton was damaged by AA fire and crashed on landing; two days later it was further damaged by enemy bombing and was subsequently removed to Austin for repair. In a bombing attack on Boulogne on 19/20 August, P6597 was missing. P/O P.W. Cook and his two crew were taken prisoner. Two aircraft, L5491 and P2311 were seriously damaged by bombing on 20 August. L5127 hit a bomb hole while taxying at Eastchurch on 25 August and was damaged beyond repair. The squadron started to re-equip with Wellingtons in November 1940 and the Battles had all left the unit by early January 1941.

No.142 Squadron

Twelve Battles were flown from France to Waddington on 15 June 1940. They were: L5113, L5453, L5456, L5464, L5533, L5582, L5584, L5586, P2177, P2321, P2325 and P6600. Five more Battles were collected from No.20 MU at Aston Down on 26 June. They were: L5501-L5504 and L5507. The squadron moved to Binbrook with its 17 Battles on 3 July 1940. A further 33 Battles and one Battle (T) trainer served with the squadron in No.1 Group, some for very brief periods. The Battles were: K7647, K7652, K9406, K9444, L5042, L5052, L5068, L5077, L5080, L5259, L5367, L5368, L5391, L5428, L5560, L5566, L5569, L5589, L5592, N2025, N2083, N2103, N2189, N2248, P2302, P2310, P2327, P2329, P5240, P6568, P6572, P6602 and P6603. The Battle (T) trainer was P6761. The squadron's first loss occurred on 28 July 1940 when two Aircraft, L5502 and L5584, failed to return from a raid on Evère aerodrome,

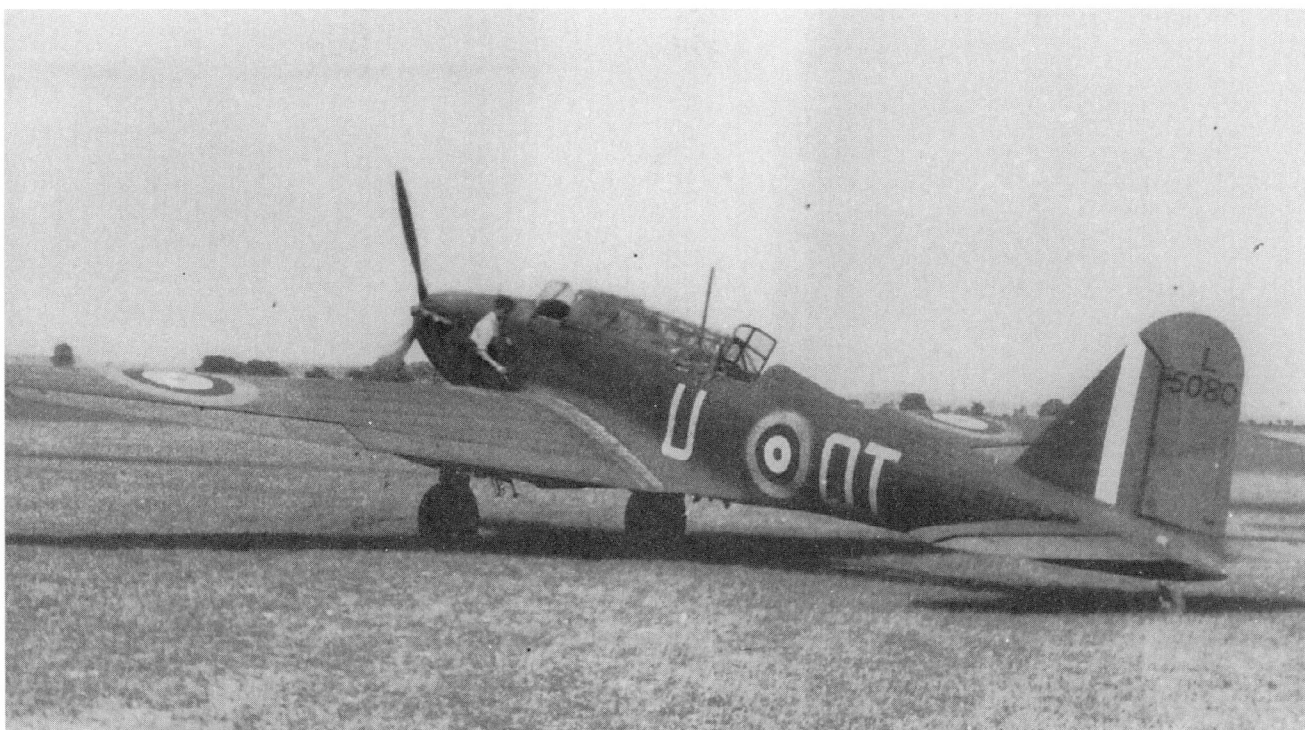

L3080 of No.142 Squadron at Binbrook in the late summer of 1940. (A Thomas collection)

Brussels. P/O R.H. Edwards and his crew in L5502 were taken prisoner and P/O M.J.A. Kirdy and his crew in L5584 were killed. On 4 August, L5113 dived into the ground at Middleton Stoney, Oxon., while on a night exercise. The three occupants, Sgt P.P. Duffy, Sgt F.K. Tremeger and Sgt H.E. Masters, were killed. During its detachment to Coastal Command at Eastchurch from 7 August to 6 September, the squadron was active operationally and it suffered several losses on the ground from enemy bombing. Two aircraft, L5503 and L5582, were missing from an attack on E-boats at Boulogne on 23 August. Midshipman Taylor and one of his crew in L5503 were taken prisoner and one was killed. One of L5582's crew was taken prisoner and the pilot, Sgt E.A. Pearce and the other member of the crew were killed. While landing at Eastchurch after an attempted raid on E boats at Calais on 27 August, P/O H.L. Oakley, piloting L5507, burst a tyre, ground-looped and the Battle was damaged beyond repair. The aircraft still had its bomb load on board! Several Battles were seriously damaged or destroyed in enemy air raids, the worst incident occurring on 2 September when the bomb dump at Eastchurch, after being hit by incendiary bombs, blew up during a raid and five of the squadron's aircraft were destroyed or damaged beyond repair. A few of the damaged aircraft were struck off charge on the unit and others were removed to Fairey, where some were repaired and others were written off. Some of the aircraft lost to the squadron as not repairable on the unit were: K7652, L5501, L5533, L5566, L5586, N2025, P2310, P6600 and P6603. The squadron returned to Binbrook from the much-bombed Eastchurch on 7 September 1940. In bad weather on 13 October, while returning from a raid on Calais, L5428, piloted by P/O Stevenson, ran out of fuel and was abandoned near Torksey, Lincs. The crew landed safely and the aircraft

was burned out after it crashed. Two aircraft crashed on 22 October: P/O P.E.A. Carr in L5391 belly-landed near Binbrook with no injuries to the crew and P/O McGregor Macdonald flew P2327 into the ground near Binbrook in bad visibility, slightly injuring two of the crew. The squadron started to re-equip with Wellingtons in November 1940 and the Battles were dispersed to various units, the last one leaving on 14 March 1941.

No.103 Squadron

After returning from France to Abingdon on 15 June 1940, the squadron re-formed at Honington on 18 June with twelve Battles, all of which had served with the AASF. They were: L5244, L5336, L5358, L5363, L5381, L5395, L5444, L5479, L5525, N2255, P2305 and P2311. Six Battles were received from No.8 MU on 26 June. They were: L5469, N2157, P2304 and P2306-P2308. The squadron moved to Newton with its eighteen Battles on 3 July 1940. On 7 July, three aircraft, L5444, L5479 and N2255 were sent to Rollasons for repair and three replacement aircraft, L5431-L5433, were collected from No.20 MU. Eleven other Battles, one Battle (T) trainer and two Battle T.T. target tugs served with the squadron in No.1 Group. The Battles were: K7671, K9247, K9460, K9471, L5010, L5011, L5038, L5125, L5237, L5532 and N2163. The Battle (T) trainer was P6759 and the Battle T.T. target tugs were L5629 and L5792. During night flying on 3 August, the pilot of L5433, Sgt S.C. Brams, mistook Cottesmore for Newton and climbed, stalled and hit trees on his approach. Sgt Brams and his observer were killed and the aircraft was burned out. L5010, piloted by Sgt F. Drinkwater, was missing from a raid on Calais on 9 September. It was reported to have been shot down by AA

K9264 was 'PM-L' of No.103 Squadron. (D Thompson collection)

fire and the three crew were killed. On 26 September, L5336 overshot the Newton flare path and hit the boundary on its return from Ostend. It was badly damaged and was sent to Fairey for repair. Flying on Battle aircraft ceased on 10 October 1940 as the squadron prepared to re-equip with Wellingtons. Most of the Battles had left the unit by the end of October 1940, the majority going to MUs.

No.150 Squadron

The squadron flew twelve Battles from France to Abingdon on 15 June 1940 and re-formed at Stradishall on 18 June. The twelve Battles, which had served with the squadron in the AASF, were: K9323, L5106, L5237, L5510, L5543, L5545, L5563, L5593, P2179, P2327, P5236 and P6602. Four more Battles received on 26 June were: L5042, L5057, L5058 and P2312. The squadron moved to Newton with its sixteen Battles on 3 July 1940. Ten other Battles and one Battle T.T. target tug served with the squadron at Newton. The Battles were: K7647, K9444, L5103, L5421, L5434, L5447, L5528, L5548, N2169 and P6568. The Battle T.T. target tug was L5630. There was a fatal accident at Newton on 27 July 1940 when a flare dropped to the ground from L5528 and ignited. The aircraft caught fire and its bomb load exploded, killing seven RAF personnel and injuring four others. Sadly, F/Lt W.M. Blom, DFC, and Sgt W.H. Franklin, EGM, veterans of No.150 Squadron's campaign in France, were killed in this incident. Sgt Franklin, a fitter/armourer, had made safe bombs on burning aircraft in two separate incidents in France. He was awarded the EGM on the second occasion. The squadron converted to Wellingtons in October/November 1940 and all its Battles had been transferred to other units by 17 October. None of No.150 Squadron's Battles were lost on operations between July and October 1940.

No.300 Squadron

No.300 Squadron, the first Polish squadron in the RAF, was

formed at Bramcote on 1 July 1940. Its aircraft establishment was sixteen Battles. The first fifteen were received on 1 July and they were: L5353, L5356, L5425-L5427, L5429, L5490, L5499, L5529, L5532, L5537, N2127, N2147, N2241 and P2309. The sixteenth aircraft, L5530, was received two days later. A Battle (T) trainer, R7402, was received on 31 July. The squadron moved to Swinderby on 22 August 1940 and training was continued there. Five other Battles served with the squadron at Swinderby, L5317, L5318, L5365, L5492 and L5567. During its return flight from operations over Boulogne on 13 October 1940, L5499 stalled and dived into the ground at Oxton, Notts. F/O Gebicki and his two crew were killed. On the same day, L5427 crashed at Sherwood, Nottingham, with no injuries. On 29 October, L5356 crashed at Sutton-on-Trent after a wing broke off while it was recovering from a dive; F/O Bielanski and his crew were killed. The squadron converted to Wellingtons in October/November 1940 and the Battles were dispersed to other units.

No.301 Squadron

The second Polish bomber squadron was formed at Bramcote on 22 July 1940. By 4 August, the squadron had received sixteen Battles and one Battle (T) trainer. The Battles were: L5075, L5316, L5351, L5392, L5445, L5448, L5449, L5535, L5536, L5549, L5551, L5555, L5556, L5597, P6567 and P6569 and the Battle (T) trainer was R7401. Battle L5575 was received on 7 August. The squadron moved to Swinderby on 28 August 1940. Battles received by the squadron at Swinderby were: K9247, L5048, L5193, L5237, L5557 and N2189. A fatal accident occurred on 8 August when L5597 flew into the ground at night near Bramcote. On 25 September, L5351, piloted by P/O J. Killinski, crashed at Brandon, Norfolk, on its outward flight to Boulogne. Training on Wellingtons started on 20 October and most of the Battles had left the squadron by the end of November 1940.

CHAPTER 11 - NORTHERN IRELAND

From France to Ulster

Two squadrons of the AASF in France, Nos.88 and 226, returned briefly to England in June 1940 before moving to Sydenham, Belfast, to carry out anti-invasion patrols along the coastline of Northern Ireland. No.88 Squadron Battles flew from Houssay to Driffield, via Abingdon, on 14 June 1940. The squadron's ground crews were evacuated from Brest in the S.S. *Vienna* and arrived at Locking, via Plymouth, on 17 June 1940. They joined the air party at Driffield on 18 June. The aircraft flew to Sydenham on 23 June and were joined by the squadron's main party four days later. No.226 Squadron flew their Battles from Artins to Thirsk on 15 June 1940, the main party following by sea from Brest to Plymouth, arriving at Weston-super-Mare on 17 June. They were re-united with the air party at Thirsk on the following day. The squadron moved to Sydenham on 27 June 1940.

Coastal Patrols

The purpose of the patrols was to search for anything unusual in the designated patrol areas. With invasion by the enemy a distinct probability, the RAF was on the lookout for any signs of hostile landings on the Ulster coast. The patrol duties were shared by Nos.88 and 226 Squadrons. There were two north patrols each day, at dawn and dusk, and two south patrols, also at dawn and dusk. The original route of the north patrols ran along the east coast of Ireland from Belfast to Cushendun; this was later extended to the Mull of Kintyre on the Scottish coast, then westwards as far as Lough Swilly. The south patrol route ran from Belfast to Bangor, then along the coast to Newry. The patrols, usually by single aircraft, were operated from July 1940 until the prospects of invasion had receded in May 1941, and in this period the two squadrons made over 1,100 individual sorties, the vast majority of which were completely uneventful. No.88 Squadron made 568 sorties and No.226 Squadron made 534, with little else to report than the movements of convoys. The squadrons were initially part of No.61 Group, which later became RAF Northern Ireland.

Other Activities

During their stay in Northern Ireland, both squadrons carried out training exercises, including practice bombing. Some exercises were conducted in collaboration with the Army and there were also fighter affiliation flights. The squadrons were on invasion standby during most of September 1940. On 2 September, at the height of the Battle of Britain, five of No.88 Squadron's pilots were posted to Fighter Command to help to alleviate the serious shortage of fighter pilots. Casualties among crews and aircraft in Ireland were light.

Engine failure caused P2159 of No.88 Squadron, piloted by Sgt. Pether, to crash near Ardglass on 20 March 1941; the crew were uninjured. The squadron also lost L5330 when it crashed at Upper Galwally, Belfast, with engine trouble, on 11 April 1941. L5544 crash-landed at Lisburn landing ground after an undercarriage failure on 22 June 1941 and there were also two less-serious landing accidents involving L5565 and L5015. During an air raid on Belfast on 5 May 1941, Sydenham aerodrome was bombed and three of No.88 Squadron's Battles were so badly damaged that they were written off (L5361, L5561 and L5572). Two more of the squadron's aircraft were damaged (K9437 and L5574). No.226 Squadron lost P6601 when it crashed into hills near Cushendall in County Antrim on 22 October 1940. The pilot was killed, one of the crew died later and the other member of the crew was slightly injured. The squadron had one aircraft badly damaged in the air raid on 5 May 1941 (L5452). Although the coastal patrols with Battles continued until May 1941, the crews of both squadrons started training on twin-engined Blenheims and Bostons early in the year. No.226 Squadron moved to Wattisham to re-equip with Blenheim IVs on 25 May 1941. No.88 Squadron moved to Swanton Morley in July 1941, then to Attlebridge on 1 August, where re-equipment with Bostons was completed.

No.88 Squadron Aircraft

The squadron flew six Battles to Sydenham when the air party moved there on 23 June 1940; these were L5330, L5361, L5393, L5561, P2159 and P2354. All of these except L5561 had recently returned from France. A further ten Battles from No.22 MU were added to the strength in July 1940, L5544, L5558, L5559, L5565, L5571, L5572, L5574, L5590, L5594 and L5596. The squadron acquired L5216 from No.22 MU in October 1940 and P5283 from No.12 MU in November. In April 1941, K9437 and P2268 were received from No.23 MU and in the following month four more Battles were received from the same source; these were K9450, L5015, L5051 and N2033. Finally, four Battles were taken over from No.226 Squadron in July 1941, L5122, L5419, L5576 and P6482. As already recorded, P2159 and L5330 were lost in crashes in March and April 1941 respectively. Three aircraft were damaged beyond repair in the air raid on Belfast on 5 May 1941, L5361, L5561 and L5572. During the squadron's stay in Northern Ireland, several Battles were disposed of by being sent to Short and Harland; these were L5559, L5216, L5574, L5544, L5594, P5283, P2268, L5558, L5596 and L5571. All the remaining Battles went to maintenance units when they were no longer required by the squadron; K9450, L5015, L5051, L5122, L5393, L5419, L5565, L5576, L5590, P2354 and P6482 to No.23 MU in September 1941, N2033 to No.23 MU in November 1941 and K9437 to No.27 MU in January 1942. Movements of Battles in and out of No.88 Squadron during its tour of duty in Northern Ireland are summarised in the following table.

No.88 Squadron Fairey Battles which served in Northern Ireland

Serial Number	Received Date	From	Disposal of Aircraft Date	To
L5330*	23.5.40	AASF	11.4.41	Crashed, Galwally
P2159*	23.5.40	AASF	20.3.41	Crashed, Ardglass
L5561*	6.6.40	Andover	5.5.41	Bombed, DBR
L5393*	9.6.40	AASF	5.9.41	23 MU
L5361*	15.6.40	AASF	5.5.41	Bombed, DBR
P2354*	15.6.40	AASF	5.9.41	23 MU
L5558	17.7.40	22 MU	30.10.41	S & H
L5565	17.7.40	22 MU	5.9.41	23 MU
L5574	17.7.40	22 MU	22.5.41	S & H
L5590	17.7.40	22 MU	5.9.41	23 MU
L5596	17.7.40	22 MU	?.41	S & H
L5559	21.7.40	22 MU	31.12.40	S & H
L5571	21.7.40	22 MU	?.41	S & H
L5572	21.7.40	22 MU	5.5.41	Bombed, DBR
L5544	21.7.40	22 MU	27.6.41	S & H
L5594	21.7.40	22 MU	6.9.41	S & H
L5216	6.10.40	22 MU	2.1.41	S & H
P5283	14.11.40	12 MU	8.9.41	S & H
K9437	21.4.41	23 MU	1.1.42	27 MU
P2268	21.4.41	23 MU	9.9.41	S & H
K9450	9.5.41	23 MU	5.9.41	23 MU
L5015	9.5.41	23 MU	5.9.41	23 MU
L5051	9.5.41	23 MU	5.9.41	23 MU
N2033	10.5.41	23 MU	16.11.41	23 MU
L5122	10.7.41	226 Sqn	5.9.41	23 MU
L5419	10.7.41	226 Sqn	5.9.41	23 MU
L5576	10.7.41	226 Sqn	5.9.41	23 MU
P6482	10.7.41	226 Sqn	5.9.41	23 MU

* Aircraft which moved with the squadron to Northern Ireland

No.226 Squadron Aircraft

On 27 June 1940 the squadron flew 14 Battles to Sydenham, all of which were recently returned from France. They were K9351, L5035, L5037, L5326, L5337, L5401, L5419, L5428, L5452, L5460, L5498, P5233, P5234 and P6601. Three Battles were received in July 1940, K9210 and K9211 from No.98 Squadron and L5468 returned from the AASF. P6482 was received from No.12 MU in November 1940, L5025 from No.23 MU in April 1941, L5463 from No.23 MU in May 1941 and L5122 from No.6 MU in May 1941. Three other Battles were received from No.22 MU on an unknown date; they were L5564, L5576 and L5595. Only one aircraft was lost in an accident in Northern Ireland, P6601, which crashed at Cushendall on 22 October 1940. Seven aircraft were disposed of to S & H; L5498 in January 1941, L5564 in April 1941, L5037 and L5452 in May 1941, L5460 in July 1941, L5035 and L5595 in August 1941. Ten aircraft were sent to Maintenance Units; K9351 to No.18 MU in July 1940, K9210 and K9211 to No.18 MU in August 1940, L5428 to No.20 MU in August 1940, L5025, L5326 and L5463 to 23 MU in August 1941, and L5337, L5401, P5233 and P5234 to No.47 MU in August 1941. In July 1941 L5122, L5419, L5576 and P6482 were transferred to No.88 Squadron. The remaining Battle, L5468 went to Dumfries for shipment to Canada. Movements of Battles in and out of No.226 Squadron during its stay in Northern Ireland are summarised in the following table.

No. 226 Squadron Fairey Battles which served in Northern Ireland

Serial Number	Received Date	From	Disposal of Aircraft Date	To
L5428*	17.5.40	AASF	3.8.40	20 MU
P5234*	17.5.40	AASF	6.8.41	47 MU
P6601*	17.5.40	AASF	22.10.40	Crashed
L5419*	20.5.40	AASF	10.7.41	88 Sqn
L5460*	20.5.40	AASF	31.7.41	S & H
K9351*	23.5.40	21 AD	26.7.40	18 MU
L5035*	23.5.40	AASF	14.8.41	S & H
L5498*	23.5.40	AASF	14.1.41	S & H
P5233*	26.5.40	AASF	6.8.41	47 MU
L5037*	26.5.40	AASF	14.5.41	S & H
L5452*	1.6.40	AASF	12.5.41	S & H
L5326*	9.6.40	AASF	19.8.41	23 MU
L5337*	9.6.40	AASF	6.8.41	47 MU
L5401*	9.6.40	AASF	6.8.41	47 MU
K9210	17.7.40	98 Sqn	2.8.40	18 MU
K9211	17.7.40	98 Sqn	13.8.40	18 MU
L5468	17.7.40	AASF	28.1.42	Dumfries
P6482	14.11.40	12 MU	10.7.41	88 Sqn
L5025	18.4.41	23 MU	11.8.41	23 MU
L5463	7.5.41	23 MU	1.8.41	23 MU
L5122	9.5.41	6 MU	10.7.41	88 Sqn
L5564	?	22 MU	10.4.41	S & H
L5576	?	22 MU	10.7.41	88 Sqn
L5595	?	22 MU	14.8.41	S & H

* Aircraft which moved with the squadron to Northern Ireland

Battles of No.11 Squadron in East Africa. (Ken Smy)

CHAPTER 12. EAST AFRICA

South African Air Force

Battles of the South African Air Force were used by the SAAF in the campaign which swept the Italians out of East Africa. They operated mainly over Kenya, Italian Somaliland and Ethiopia, with RAF squadrons from Aden and the Sudan covering Western Ethiopia, Eritrea and British Somaliland. Though their numbers were small - 27 aircraft in all - the Battles, operating with a mixed bag of veteran aircraft of other types, made a significant contribution to the success of the operations in East Africa.

In March 1940, South Africa offered to send troops and air squadrons to Kenya, and the first units of the SAAF started to arrive at the end of May 1940. South Africa declared war on Italy on 11 June 1940, and at that time Nos. 11 and 12 Bomber Squadrons in Kenya were equipped with Hartbees biplanes and Junkers Ju 86s respectively. Shortly after this, No.40 Squadron took over the Hartbees for army co-operation work and No.11 Squadron re-equipped with Battles. By September 1940, Nos.2 and 3 Fighter Squadrons, flying Fury, Gauntlet and Hurricane aircraft, had joined the South African Air Force in Kenya. This motley collection of mainly obsolete aircraft had as its objectives:

(i) The neutralisation of the *Regia Aeronautica* in Southern Ethiopia and Italian Somaliland

(ii) The defence of Mombasa, Nairobi and other centres

(iii) Co-operation with ground forces

No.11 Squadron, SAAF

The first Battle to see service with the SAAF, serial no. 901, was allocated to No.11 Squadron prior to the squadron being fully re-equipped with Battles. This aircraft left Eastleigh airfield on 19 June 1940 for a reconnaissance flight to Jumbo, Jelib and Afmadu in Italian Somaliland. The squadron's commanding officer, Major R.H. Preller, was the pilot and his main objective was to photograph landing grounds. After refuelling at Garissa, Preller continued to the Kismayu area and attacked Italian aircraft on Afmadu airfield. While doing so he suffered the misfortune of having the radiator of his aircraft hit by a single bullet. The engine seized and Preller crash-landed 12 miles from the target, sustaining a gash on his forehead in the process. The major and his two crew set the aircraft on fire then started out to reach the Kenya border. Suffering badly from heat and thirst, the three men arrived at a water hole, where Preller left his two crewmen and continued alone to the border. The crew were rescued on 4 July. As a postscript to his epic journey, Major Preller found the remains of his aircraft, with the interior burnt out, in a shed at Mogadishu airfield when it was occupied eight months later. Aircraft recognition was not a forte of the Italians; the aircraft was labelled "Wickers Wellesley".

The squadron's establishment of Battles was delivered

from South Africa to its base at Eastleigh, Nairobi, in early August 1940. The squadron moved north to Archer's Post, nearer to the Ethiopian border, on 10 August. In the meantime the Italians had occupied the fort of Moyale on the Kenya/Ethiopia border and a small part of northern Kenya. The Italians had great numerical superiority of land forces in East Africa and this led to the evacuation of British Somaliland, which was completed on 18 August. The Battles at Archer's Post went into action on 19 August when the whole squadron of thirteen aircraft mounted successful bombing raids on various targets in southern Ethiopia, including Yavello, Neghelli and Mega. Two days later, nine Battles set out to bomb the aerodrome at Mogadishu in Italian Somaliland. Three turned back because of bad weather, but the remaining aircraft attacked, destroying three Caproni aircraft, damaging six others and causing damage to airfield installations. All six of the attacking Battles were hit by AA fire from the ground. Two further attacks were made on Mogadishu during August, one on a fuel dump, where near misses were observed, and one on a motor transport concentration. This last attack, on 28 August, was hailed as an extremely successful raid with 750 vehicles claimed as destroyed. The Chief of the Air Staff in London congratulated the squadron on its achievement. Unfortunately, when Mogadishu was occupied some time later it was found that the mass of transport was a dump containing old vehicles abandoned after the Italian war on Abyssinia some years earlier. When flying from Archer's Post on the Mogadishu raids the Battles, because of their limited range, refuelled en route at a semi-desert landing strip at Habaswein near the border with Italian Somaliland. On a lighter note, on 30 August five Battles carrying 30 officers and men flew to Nairobi for weekend leave. This must have been a somewhat overcrowded journey! Operations continued during September with bombing attacks on targets in Italian Somaliland and southern Ethiopia, airfields receiving particular attention. Mogadishu was raided, also Shashamanna, in Ethiopia. At least three Battles were missing from these raids. Reconnaissance flights, mainly by single aircraft, and bombing attacks continued during October, with aerodromes and transport being the main targets. November was a relatively quiet month, with only 20 sorties by No.11 Squadron, from which three Battles were reported missing. One crew was reported by the Italians to be prisoners-of-war and another crew burned their crashed aircraft and escaped to safety over the frontier.

The strength of the Allied ground forces had been steadily increasing since the start of the war in East Africa and in December a "trial attack" was made on El Wak and El Uach, fortified villages on the Kenya/Italian Somaliland frontier. True to form, the Italian defenders fled and their commander was dismissed. El Wak was captured on 16 December 1940, after which the British force withdrew. Operations by the Battles of No.11 Squadron in December were limited; the aircraft were suffering from engine troubles, which was hardly surprising considering the adverse conditions in which they were used. Towards the end of the month several aircraft were flown to Eastleigh for inspection and engine changes. The Battles were grounded for some days while the inspections were made. The most notable operation of the month was a raid by six aircraft on Yavello aerodrome on 11 December against the Caproni 133 aircraft based there. Three enemy aircraft were believed to have been destroyed and three damaged. Several leaflet dropping sorties were made. When aircraft went missing on operations in East

Africa, a search was normally made to locate them, and particularly the crews. This work was not without its hazards and on 13 December, while searching for a missing Ju 86 with two other Battles, Battle 918 crashed and was burnt out. Lt. Macdonald and his two crew were killed.

The new year saw further attacks on Yavello and Shashamanna aerodromes and towards the end of January 1941 the squadron made reconnaissance flights and a raid on infantry and artillery positions at Moyale. Land forces were now advancing into southern Ethiopia and towards the port of Kismayu in Italian Somaliland. Mega, in Ethiopia, was captured on 18 February and Moyale was entered unopposed on 22 February. Early in February, No.11 Squadron moved to Husseini, where the airfield was a triangle cut out of the bush. In February 1941 several reconnaissance flights were made over Italian Somaliland to provide information for the advancing army, together with bombing attacks on Afmadu, Bardera, Jelib and the aerodrome at Isha Baidoa. Yavello and Neghelli in Ethiopia also received attention. The port of Kismayu, and Gobwen, were captured on 14 February and Jelib on 22 February. Three days later, on 25 February, British troops entered Mogadishu, the capital of Italian Somaliland, unopposed; the Italian defenders had fled from the city to the north. On 25 February, No.11 Squadron moved to Gobwen, near Kismayu, from where several reconnaissance sorties were made. On 2 March 1941, a "display of strength" flight over Mogadishu was made by nine Battles, accompanied by three Furies, five Hurricanes and nine Ju 86s. This aerial armada must have presented a unique spectacle, particularly as the Battles were flying with flaps and undercarriages down in order to slow them to the speed of the formation. On the same day, No.11 Squadron moved to Vittorio d'Afrika. The war in Italian Somaliland was now virtually over and the land forces moved quickly north into Ethiopia, capturing Jijiga on 17 March, then Harar on 29 March. The Italians retreated to Gondar. Six Battles bombed Harar on 8 March, refuelling at Belet Wen en route. The total distance flown on this mission was 1,200 miles and two of the aircraft had a flying time of over nine hours; all returned safely. In mid- March, one flight of No.11 Squadron was detached to Mogadishu for coastal defence duties. The remainder of the squadron moved to Belet Wen, which was little more than an airstrip, on 17 March, to be followed by the detached flight five days later. A shortage of aircraft was now restricting operations and reinforcements of more Battles were sent to the squadron from Nairobi. On 23 March, the squadron moved to Dagar Bur in Ethiopia, from where operations were carried out against road and railway targets in the Diredawa area. The squadron was again on the move on 29 March, this time to Gunbar Dug. Diredawa was captured on 30 March and attention was then turned westwards towards the Ethiopian capital, Addis Ababa. The main aerodrome at Addis Ababa was bombed on 4 April and the city fell on 6 April. During the rest of April, No.11 Squadron carried out reconnaissance flights and raided Dessye and Shashamanna. After two bombing raids on Shashamanna in early May 1941, the squadron moved to Maggio on 11 May. The loss of aircraft in action and the unserviceability caused by rough conditions left the squadron with only three serviceable Battles and these moved to Alagato on 14 May, from where raids were mounted on communications targets. The remainder of the squadron moved to Alagato on 27 May. The squadron's final operation was a bombing attack by three aircraft on motor transport on Squadron was absorbed into No.15 Squadron.

During its operational career the squadron used its ageing Battles to the full, carrying 20-lb bombs on some attacks and 250-lb bombs on others, and using dive bombing techniques in many raids to give greater accuracy. Some operations were carried out jointly with No.12 Squadron and fighter escorts were occasionally provided. The support given to the land forces by constant attacks on enemy aerodromes and transport and by the many reconnaissance missions undertaken was of great help in their rapid advances. No.11 Squadron's magnificent record is summed up in the dignified requiem note in its Operations Record Book: "11 Squadron today dies a natural death after 1 year and 12 days in the field. A general feeling of sadness prevailed today - and everyone feels that it is wrong that a squadron (the first South African squadron ever to proceed on active service) which has tried to build up a tradition should just disappear and completely lose its identity. During this year the squadron has undertaken 132 raids and over 400 sorties against the enemy. In raids against enemy aircraft it has officially destroyed 27 aircraft, damaged 21 and believed to have destroyed another four. Our casualties have been 14 killed, 13 prisoners of war (all since recaptured) and 3 wounded or injured."

No.15 Squadron, SAAF

On 1 June 1941, No.15 Squadron at Alagato absorbed what remained of No.11 Squadron. The strength of serviceable aircraft was three Battles. In the eight days from 1 June to 8 June, 22 sorties were made to bomb Italian troop concentrations on the River Omo and troops retreating from the River Omo towards Jimma. On each of the next three days, transport and troops at Cossa, north of Jimma, were attacked by three aircraft. The veteran Battle, no. 902, went missing on 11 June and crashed 40 miles north-west of Cossa, killing both crew members. Problems with the engines of the Battles were becoming serious and on investigation were diagnosed as faulty mixture controls. Wear and tear must also have been a contributory factor. The squadron moved to Addis Ababa on 13 June and one Battle crashed on landing with a collapsed undercarriage. The squadron returned to Alagato on 19 June. Hutments and AA installations at Dembi were bombed by two aircraft on 21 June. There were no operations in July and the squadron, with its two serviceable Battles, nos. 904 and 905, moved to Alomata on 5 August. On that day and on the three succeeding days the two Battles bombed buildings and the motor transport park at Gondar. Battle 905 force-landed on its return to Alomata with a defective undercarriage, leaving only one serviceable Battle, no. 904. This aircraft was out of action for a few days while it was sent to Addis Ababa for "minor adjustments". Eight sorties were made by the sole surviving usable Battle in the six days between 14 and 19 August; these consisted of bombing attacks on and near Gondar. After two raids on 14 August, the squadron Operations Record Book recorded: "With these two raids Captain Snyman brought his total to 25, a record for this type of aircraft in the South African Air Force and also a squadron record".

In its last operation on 19 August, the rudder of Battle 904 was badly damaged by AA fire. It was repaired in the next few days and after moving to Addis Ababa on 25 August it was flown to Eastleigh, Nairobi, on 30 August. The squadron returned to Eastleigh some days later and subsequently served in Egypt after converting to Marylands. During its operations in Ethiopia, the squadron used the very few remaining Battles to good effect and rendered material assistance to the ground forces.

Battles operational in East Africa

The table lists the Battles which were in action in East Africa, showing the SAAF serial number followed by the former RAF serial number.

901: ex-K9402 delivered to Capetown April 1939 for evaluation; 11 Sqn 6.40. Hit by ground fire, Afmadu airfield, and crashlanded 12m W of Kismayu, 19.6.40; crew walked home

902 ex-L5165; 11 Sqn 13.9.40; 15 Sqn 1.6.41. Flew into mountainside 40m NW of Cossa during search for missing Ju 86, 11.6.41; Lt E.J. Steyn and Sgt F.W. Kelly killed

903 ex-L5024; 11 Sqn 8.40. Hit by ground fire during attack on MT near Neghelli and engine cut; crashlanded 30m W of Marsabit, 17.10.40; Capt P. Robbertse and crew safe

904 ex-L5487; 11 Sqn 8.40; 15 Sqn 1.6.41; to SA 8.10.41; Air Armament School, Youngsfield; renamed 65 AS

905 ex-L5168; 11 Sqn 8.40; 15 Sqn 1.6.41; undercarriage jammed; bellylanded, Alomata, 8.8.41; sent to Eastleigh for repair

906 ex-L5172; 11 Sqn 8.40

907 ex-L5178; 11 Sqn 8.40

908 ex-L5088; 11 Sqn 8.40. Hit by ground fire, Neghelli, and crashlanded; aircraft blew up, 4.11.40; Lt B.L. Hutchinson and crew captured

909 ex-L5093; 11 Sqn 8.40. Crashed in bad weather near Dedai on return from raid on Shashamanna airfield, 10.4.41; Lt M.G.T. Ferreira and Sgt R. Grant killed

910 ex-L5097; 11 Sqn 8.40

911 ex-L5090; 11 Sqn 8.40. Shot down by CR.32s, Shashamanna, Somaliland, 12.9.40; Lt E.G. Armstrong and Sgt E. Adams killed

912 ex-L5375; 11 Sqn 8.40. Shot down by flak attacking Shashamanna airfield, 9.9.40; Capt R.A. Blackwell and Sgt F.A. van Zyl captured

913 ex-L5098; 11 Sqn 8.40. Shot down by CR.32s, Shashamanna, Somaliland, 12.9.40; Lt. J. Lindsey, Sgt N.P. McVicar and Sgt L. Feinberg captured

914 ex-L5174; 11 Sqn 8.40; 15 Sqn 1.6.41. Forcelanded 15m N of Sciola after raid on Dembi, 21.6.41; crew escaped

915 ex-L5074; 11 Sqn 8.40. Engine cut; crashlanded 30m NW of Archers Post on return from Yavello, 11.12.40; Lt. Matthias and crew safe

916 ex-L5078; 11 Sqn 8.40. Damaged by flak on reconnaissance in Todonyaug area and crashlanded, 16.11.40; Lt C.A. van Vliet and crew escaped; destroyed by crew

917 ex-R7359; 11 Sqn 2.3.41; dual control

918 ex-L5176; 11 Sqn 10.40. Crashed while searching for missing Ju 86, 13.12.40 and burnt out; Lt M. MacDonald, F/Sgt P.C. Marais and F/Sgt A. Schrooder killed

919 ex-N2161; 11 Sqn 3.41

920 ex-N2165; 11 Sqn 15.12.40; 15 Sqn 12.7.41; to SA 8.10.41; later Training HQ Communications Flight

922 ex-L5506; 11 Sqn 12.40; retd to SA; later 43 AS coded BA;

923 ex-P5246; 11 Sqn 2.41

924 ex-L5374; 11 Sqn 11.40; Hit by ground fire and crashlanded, Combolcia, 19.4.41; Capt J.F. Britz and Lt C.B. Hangar captured

925 ex-P6596; 11 Sqn 11.40; 15 Sqn 1.6.41; hit anthill on landing and undercarriage leg collapsed, Addis Ababa, 13.6.41; repaired and sent to South Africa; 44 Air School Grahamstown 7.43

926 ex-R3938; 11 Sqn 12.40

927 ex-R3945; 11 Sqn 11.40. Shot down by CR.42 on reconnaissance near Kismayu, 22.11.40; Capt D.W.J. Allam and crew captured but Allam later escaped

929 ex-L5525; 11 Sqn 1941

CHAPTER 13. ICELAND

No.98 Squadron

On their return from France, the squadron assembled at Gatwick in mid-June 1940, after the disastrous loss of many of its ground staff in the sinking of *Lancastria*. The original intention was that the squadron should be disbanded, but this decision was reversed early in July 1940 and the unit was reformed for anti-invasion operations in Iceland with No.15 Group, Coastal Command. The squadron received eighteen Battles from Maintenance Units in mid-July and these, together with L5628, made up the squadron's strength to nineteen aircraft. L5628, a Battle T.T. target tug, was a survivor of the squadron's stay in France. A move to Newton was made on 26 July 1940 and on the following day the ground party left for Kaldadarnes in Iceland, where they arrived on 31 July. Kaldadarnes is 30 miles east south-east of Reykjavik, near the south coast of Iceland, and is close to the river Olfusa. The prescribed duty of the squadron at Kaldadarnes was "to co-operate with British forces in Iceland in the frustration of enemy invasion of the island". This was amplified by an Air Council letter stating that the squadron should be trained in shallow dive bombing attacks against moving targets at sea in case enemy forces approached by sea. The squadron's ground staff was in Iceland for almost a month before any aircraft arrived and much of this time was spent in helping to level the airfield at Kaldadarnes.

On 27 August 1940, nine Battles, escorted by two Sunderland flying boats, flew via Wick to Kaldadarnes. They landed at 1730 after a flight of 5 hours 20 minutes. The squadron aircraft were L5063, L5066, L5073, L5099, L5331, L5332, L5343, L5505 and L5554. Four days later, on 31 August 1940, eight Battles flew in formation over Reykjavik to show the flag. The squadron Operations Record Book states that the flight "made a fine impression on the inhabitants". The local press reported that half of the population were enthusiastic but the other half were terrified because they thought the enemy had arrived! A large force of enemy ships was reported to be due east of the Humber on 31 August and the squadron was brought to immediate readiness. As with so many other reports of enemy activity, this one proved to be a false alarm. The next day, P/O A.K. Round made the squadron's first operational flight from Kaldadarnes, a 495-mile reconnaissance to the Djupivogur area, on the east coast of Iceland. Three aircraft were detached to Melgardi, near Akureyri, in the north of the island, on 12 September for a week. Early on the morning of Friday, 13 September 1940, L5343 set out to fly an army colonel to Akureyri. The weather was bad and on reaching Akureyri the pilot, F/O W. Wilcox, decided that it would be unsafe to attempt a landing because of heavy cloud cover over the area and he turned to fly back to Kaldadarnes. Engine trouble forced the pilot to land at Hsnfarver, 84 miles from Kaldadarnes. The landing was made near a lake on ground spread with boulders and the undercarriage collapsed and the starboard wing was damaged. F/O Wilcox and his passenger started to walk in the direction of Kaldadarnes. The journey would have been extremely difficult because of the rough terrain, the bitterly cold weather and an injury to the pilot's foot sustained during the landing. A rescue party which was making for the crash site found them after two days and they were returned safely to Kaldadarnes. Salvage of the aircraft was not feasible and an RAF party visited the crash site some time

later and recovered equipment from the wreck. To ensure that the Battle would be useless to the Germans if they invaded Iceland, a Very cartridge was fired into the fuselage centre section, burning it out. The remains of this aircraft were brought back to England in 1973 (see Chapter 20).

The squadron's remaining nine aircraft flew from Wick to Kaldadarnes on 14 September 1940, escorted by only one Sunderland on this occasion. The aircraft were Battles L5412, L5442, L5547, L5552, L5553, N2167, P2330 and P6570, and Battle T.T. L5628. P6570 made an undignified arrival by force-landing on the edge of the airfield and tipping over on its nose. It was struck off charge two months later. The Air Ministry issued an instruction on 21 September that six aircraft were to be maintained in flying condition with the remainder stored. Six crews and the necessary maintenance personnel were to remain in Iceland and the rest of the squadron personnel were to return to the U.K. in October for posting in Bomber Command. The ground party embarked for the U.K. on 26 October 1940.

In order that heavier aircraft could be accommodated in the spring, further levelling of Kaldadarnes aerodrome was carried out in late 1940 and early 1941, with the work impeded by a strike of local labour. Helping the British was not popular with some of the community; after many years of struggle for freedom from Danish domination, the Icelanders now found their island occupied by British forces and some were, not surprisingly, resentful of this. The station was declared operational in mid-January 1941 and the squadron commenced a series of coastal reconnaissance patrols. Living conditions for the squadron left much to be desired and further misery was caused by the weather. At the end of January it was reported that the new cookhouse was nearly completed. This had been partially constructed of sand-filled petrol tins which were alleged to be fireproof and sanitary; the old cookhouse had earth sides which harboured rats which were proving to be a nuisance. The winter of 1940/41 was a very severe one with frost, snow and gales. Flying was much curtailed in February because of the weather. On one day the weather was reported as cloudy with local dust storms in the morning, becoming overcast with frozen drizzle and soft hail. Goggles were needed to protect the eyes during the dust storms.

A patrol of two aircraft was sent out on 26 January 1941 to search for two large German warships possibly passing through the Denmark Straits. No ships were sighted. Patrols in the Denmark Straits continued for another two days without result. On 9 February a Battle took off to attempt to intercept an unidentified aircraft which was reported to have attacked army units then to have flown towards Kaldadarnes. The enemy aircraft was sighted but the Battle was too slow to catch it. The enemy aircraft then returned to Kaldadarnes and fired on the D/F hut without causing any damage. On 16 March, L5066 crashed while landing on the new runway at Kaldadarnes; it was struck off charge in May. On 31 March, a four-engined enemy aircraft was reported to be approaching Reykjavik but the five Battles which took off to intercept failed to make contact.

On 1 April 1941, RAF Kaldadarnes was officially formed. No.98 Squadron was reduced in strength in anticipation of the arrival of larger aircraft and its role was defined as:

(a) Coastal reconnaissance re approach of invading forces,
(b) Bombing invading forces,
(c) Reconnaissance for local forces.

Patrols continued in April and May and one Battle was fitted with target-towing equipment for AA co-operation work. Hudsons started to arrive in April. On 26 May, a Battle, P2330, flew into the side of a mountain and exploded, killing all the occupants. Early in June 1941 the station commander declared the Battles non-operational, but some patrols were carried out during the month together with photographic, AA co-operation and communication flights. A U-boat was attacked by L5547 on 26 June but no oil slicks were observed. On 15 July 1941, No.98 Squadron moved to Reykjavik, where it was disbanded because more suitable aircraft than the Battles were now in use for coastal patrol work. Two aircraft, L5099 and L5628, were transferred to No.1423 Flight, the latter for use as a target tug. Eleven of the remaining Battles were flown to Reykjavik between 19 and 26 July, dismantled and crated for transfer to Canada. No.98 Squadron's personnel returned to the U.K. for service in Bomber Command. The surviving No.98 Squadron Battle, L5547, was transferred to No.1423 Flight in November 1941. During its stay in Iceland, No.98 Squadron carried out a useful function with its regular anti-invasion patrols, the vast majority of which were uneventful. It would seem that the main hazards were the hard Icelandic weather and the spartan living conditions. The Battles which served with No.98 Squadron in Iceland are listed in the following table.

No.98 Squadron Fairey Battles in Iceland

Serial Number	Date to Iceland	Disposal of Aircraft Date	To
L5063	27.8.40	20.8.41	Canada
L5066	27.8.40	16.3.41	Crashed, Kaldadarnes
L5073	27.8.40	20.8.41	Canada
L5099	27.8.40	23.6.41	No.1423 Flight
L5331	27.8.40	20.8.41	Canada
L5332	27.8.40	20.8.41	Canada
L5343	27.8.40	13.9.40	Crashed, Hsnfarver, and abandoned
L5505	27.8.40	20.8.41	Canada
L5554	27.8.40	20.8.41	Canada
L5412	14.9.40	20.8.41	Canada
L5442	14.9.40	20.8.41	Canada
L5547	14.9.40	30.11.41	No.1423 Flight
L5552	14.9.40	20.8.41	Canada
L5553	14.9.40	20.8.41	Canada
L5628 (TT)	14.9.40	23.6.41	No.1423 Flight
N2167	14.9.40	20.8.41	Canada
P2330	14.9.40	26.5.41	Crashed into a mountain
P6570	14.9.40	14.9.40	Crashed, Kaldadarnes

No.1423 Fighter Flight

A new unit, No.1423 Fighter Flight, was formed at Kaldadarnes on 10 June 1941 with six Hurricanes for the defence of the Reykjavik area. Its operations were under the control of No.98 Squadron and three Battle pilots were transferred to the flight and trained on Hurricanes. The flight moved to Reykjavik with No.98 Squadron on 15 July 1941, where it became self-operating. Two Battles, L5099 and L5628, were taken over from No.98 Squadron, the latter being a target tug. The sole remaining No.98 Squadron Battle, L5547, was transferred to No.1423 Flight in November 1941. L5547 and L5628 were then used by No.269 Squadron. All three ended their days at Reykjavik; L5099 was SOC on 21 September 1943, L5547 was SOC on 21 October 1942 and L5628 was SOC on 30 April 1944. The unit ceased to be operational on 3 December 1941 and its personnel embarked for transfer to the UK on 31 December 1941. The Battles continued in use for some time, mainly for AA co-operation target-towing duties.

Other Battles in Iceland

Five other Battles were sent to Reykjavik, one of which, K7646, was lost at sea en route. The other four were:

N2058	Reykjavik 27.8.42;	SOC 7.12.43.
K7617	Reykjavik 7.11.42;	SOC 31.8.43.
L5746	Reykjavik 4.7.43;	SOC 30.4.44 (TT)
L5681	Reykjavik 4.7.43;	SOC 22.12.44 (TT)

Their main use was for towing drogues for AA co-opera

L5664 of No.2 Anti-Aircraft Co-operation Unit. Note blister in pilots canopy for better rearward view and target stowage under rear fuselage. (P Jarrett collection)

CHAPTER 14. UK TRAINING

Elementary and Reserve Flying Training Schools

Before World War II, elementary flying training was provided by Elementary and Reserve Flying Training Schools, which were run by civilian organisations. At the start of the war, these units were redesignated as Elementary Flying Training Schools. Several of the E&RFTS units had one or more Battles on their strength for use by their advanced flights. On the outbreak of war, or shortly after, the Battles were removed from these schools and nearly all of them were transferred to Flying Training Schools. The E&RFTS schools and aircraft concerned are listed below.

No.1 E&RFTS, Hatfield: K7575, K7616, K7672
No.3 E&RFTS, Hamble: K7559, K7610, K7640, K7641, K7643, K7687
No.4 E&RFTS, Brough: K7599
No.5 E&RFTS, Hanworth: K7602
No.8 E&RFTS, Woodley: K7565, K7604, K7645
No.9 E&RFTS, Ansty: N2046
No.11 E&RFTS, Perth: K7606
No.12 E&RFTS, Prestwick: K7607, K7608, K7614, K7626, K7627, K7646, K7648
No.13 E&RFTS, White Waltham: N2043, N2044, N2045
No.15 E&RFTS, Redhill: K7600, K7609, K7633, K7649
No.16 E&RFTS, Shoreham: K7612, K7613, K7617, K7688
No.18 E&RFTS, Fairoaks: K7683
No.19 E&RFTS, Gatwick: K7632
No.22 E&RFTS, Cambridge: K7618, K7622, K7625, L4992,

L4993, L5026, N2047, N2048, N2049
No.29 E&RFTS, Luton: K7638, K7639

During the short time that they were with the E&RFTS units the Battles had few accidents. At No.1 E&RFTS, K7616 bellylanded at Hatfield on 3 September 1939 after engine failure and was relegated to instructional airframe status shortly afterwards. No. 22 E&RFTS, Cambridge, lost K7618 when it bellylanded on the beach at Great Yarmouth, Norfolk, on 1 June 1939 after its engine cut.

Elementary Flying Training Schools

The only EFTS which used Battles was No. 15, at Redhill, where Polish pilots were trained. The aircraft were used by the Polish Flight of the unit between February and December 1940, though two were retained until March 1941. Most of the unit's Battles were disposed of to the Polish Flying Training School. The sixteen Battles and five Battle (T) trainers which were taken on the unit strength are listed below. The Battles, some of which were dual control machines, were: K7683, K9187, K9224, L4945, L5087, L5092, L5102, L5104, L5117, L5417, L5421, L5423, L5424, N2031, N2104 and P6572. The Battle (T) trainers were: P6616, P6637, P6639, R7383 and R7400. The first course for testing and grading Polish pilots started on 1 April 1940. The School moved to Carlisle on 3 June 1940, when its main training aircraft were Magisters, with the Battles being

P6728 of No.1 SFTS was built as a trainer with separate, but similar, cockpits. (R Sturtivant collection)

used for more advanced work in the Polish Flight. Instructions to stop flying the Battles were received on 7 November 1940 and the Poles were posted away shortly afterwards.

Flying Training Schools

Many Battles were used as training aircraft at the UK Flying Training Schools in the early part of the war, though the numbers involved were not nearly as great as those sent to Canada, Australia and South Africa for the Empire Air Training Schemes. At the start of World War II, the Flying Training Schools were designated Service Flying Training Schools but they will continue to be referred to here as Flying Training Schools. In all, ten of the FTSs used Battles and/or Battle (T) trainers and/or Battle T.T. target tugs, the number passing through each unit varying from one at No.3 FTS to well over 100 at No.1 FTS.

No.1 FTS, Netheravon

The unit was a prolific user of Battles and Battle (T) trainers between September 1939 and mid-1942. The first Battles arrived at the school on 10 September 1939 and 36 were on the strength by the end of the year. Many of these were in poor condition and it was difficult to obtain ground equipment and tool kits to maintain them. During the whole period when it used Battles, the unit complained about maintenance problems. The suggestion was made that Battles were unsuitable for flying training because they were unable to take the strains imposed by continuous short flights. The recurring take-offs and landings caused faults in hydraulic and brake systems and engine defects, particularly coolant leaks. By

April 1940, several of the original veteran Battles had left Netheravon and in that month it was decided to replace a Harvard flight by a flight of Battle (T) trainers, to be used for training Fleet Air Arm fighter pilots. By early July 1940, twenty-four of these had been received, most of them direct from Faireys. During the rest of 1940 and through 1941, many Battles and Battle (T)s arrived at 1 FTS and many left. In July 1941, the unit started to re-arm with Master III aircraft. Netheravon was taken over by Army Co-operation Command on 7 March 1942, by which time most of the Battles and Battle (T)s had been transferred to other units. There were a number of accidents during training and several instructors and pupils lost their lives. One of the worst of these was on 11 November 1941, when two Battles, L5294 and P6614, collided while L5294 was landing and P6614 was taking off at night at Shrewton. Two pupil pilots were killed. In July 1940, the unit decided that if the aerodrome was attacked by parachute and airborne troops, three Battles would be sent to bomb transport aircraft as they landed and to machine gun enemy aircraft and parachutists in the air. On 12 May 1941, P6671, a Battle (T) trainer, was taxying at Shrewton during night flying when it was hit by bombs dropped by a He 111 and was burnt out. A total of 62 Battles and 65 Battle (T) trainers served with 1 FTS. These were:
K7559, K7565, K7575, K7599, K7600, K7604, K7606-K7608, K7610, K7612-K7614, K7626, K7627, K7632, K7636, K7638-K7641, K7643, K7645, K7646, K7651, K7672, K7676, K7680, K7683, K7687, K7705, K9244, K9286, K9298, K9337, K9388, L4958, L4995, L4996, L5054, L5135, L5139, L5294, L5312, N2047-N2049, N2064, N2098, N2100, N2101, N2105, N2107, N2108, N2174, N2228, N2235, N2238, P2199, P2277, P2363 and P6614

The Battle (T) trainers were: P6617-P6619, P6621, P6622, P6625, P6627, P6632- P6635, P6645, P6664, P6665, P6667- P6669, P6671, P6673, P6677-P6684, P6687- P6691, P6720, P6722, P6723, P6725-P6729, P6733, P6735-P6737, P6750, P6752, P6754, P6757-P6759, P6764, P6765, P6767, P6768, R7356, R7365-R7368, R7375- R7377, R7385, R7402 and R7472

No.3 FTS, South Cerney

One Battle, L4993, was held by this unit for a short time in February 1940.

No.5 FTS, Sealand

The school received four Battles between December 1939 and April 1940. These were L5054, L5287, L5309 and P2277 and they had all left by early 1941. Two Battle T.T. target tugs were received, one in September 1940, (V1236), and one in October 1940, (V1237). These left on 1 November 1940.

No.7 FTS, Peterborough

Between 2 and 8 September 1939, the unit received 24 Battles from E&RFTSs. With three exceptions, they were all old Battles from the original K7000 series, and these veteran aircraft were very quickly transferred to other training units. The three more modern machines were retained until mid-1940. The 24 Battles were:
K7559, K7565, K7575, K7600, K7602, K7604, K7609, K7610, K7612, K7613, K7617, K7632, K7633, K7638, K7639, K7640, K7641, K7643, K7645, K7672, K7688 and N2043-N2045.
Fourteen Battle (T) trainers were received in February and March 1940, followed by 17 Battles and seven Battle (T) trainers between May and October 1940. The Battle (T) trainers were:
P6617-P6619, P6624, P6632-P6634, P6640-P6645, P6663, P6664, P6754, R7364, R7365, R7367, R7368 and R7385.
The Battles were:
K7634, K7638, K7676, K9298, L4994, L5069, L5132, L5303, L5308, L5310, N2047, N2048, N2107, N2174, N2175, N2177 and N2185.

The aircraft suffered a high level of unserviceability due to minor faults, e.g., leaking water radiators, magneto failures, plug trouble and bursting tyres. The situation was further worsened by peat moss, which had been used to fertilise the airfield, being sucked into the air intakes of the aircraft and restricting the inlet passage. The shortage of available Battles interfered with the unit's training programmes. In August 1940, a series of experiments in "synthetic" night flying in a Battle fitted with a special filter hood and screens were carried out. The results were described as very promising. It had been decided that the school was to be moved to Canada, to become No.31 SFTS at Kingston, and the first echelon left Peterborough in August 1940 and the final echelon left in January 1941. The Battles were despatched to various destinations, mainly other training units and MUs. During its stay at Peterborough the school had relatively few serious accidents involving Battles. Perhaps the most spectacular incident was on 14 November 1940, when the engine of L5303 caught fire during a height test over Pinchbeck, Lincs. Fortunately there was only one occupant and he parachuted to safety.

No.8 FTS, Montrose

Three Battle T.T. target tugs were received in September 1940 for target towing duties with the school's Advanced Training Squadron. They were V1238-V1240. All had been transferred to other training units by early December 1940.

No.9 FTS, Thornaby

Two Battles, K9385 and K9394, served with the unit from 24 November to 12 December 1938.

No.11 FTS, Shawbury

Twenty-one Battle (T) trainers and three Battles were received between February and May 1940, but these soon left the unit and all but one had been transferred elsewhere by the end of July 1940. The Battles were: L5007, L5008 and L5016. The Battle (T) trainers were: P6620-P6622, P6665-P6673, P6724, P6730, P6731, P6733-P6737 and R7360.

No.12 FTS, Grantham

The unit started to receive Battle (T) trainers to replace its Harts in February 1940. By the middle of June 1940, 41 Battle (T) trainers and 16 Battles had been sent to the school. Two more Battle (T) trainers and twelve more Battles were received, the last in April 1941. A number of the aircraft were involved in flying accidents and two Battle (T) trainers were shot down by enemy aircraft operating over England. P6674 was shot down near Harlaxton on 21 April 1941 and R7363 was shot down near Grantham on 18 May 1941. In mid-1941 the Battles started to be replaced by Oxfords and all the Battles had departed by the end of August. The Battle (T) trainers which served with the school were:
P6623-P6631, P6635, P6636, P6638, P6674-P6677, P6680, P6682-P6688, P6733, P6751, P6765-P6769, R7356, R7357 and R7361-R7370.
Battles which served with the school were:
K7602, K7606, K7619, K7622, K7670, K7676, K7690, K7710, K9296, K9392, L4954, L5018, L5054, L5060, L5067, L5132, L5138, L5183, L5287, L5300, L5307, N2047, N2107, N2109, N2177, N2238, N2242 and P2362.

No.15 FTS, Lossiemouth

At the start of World War II, sixteen Battles were received by No.15 FTS, mostly from E&RFTS units. This was a very temporary arrangement, as all the Battles but one had been transferred to other units by the middle of November 1939. The Battles were:
K7599, K7606-K7608, K7625, K7627, K7634, K7648, L4993, L4995, L4998, L5026 and N2046-N2049.

No.16(P)FTS, Newton

No. 1 (Polish) Flying Training School was formed at Hucknall in January 1941, equipped with Battles, Battle (T) trainers and Tiger Moths, to be joined later by Oxfords. In July 1941, the unit was redesignated No.16(P)FTS and moved to Newton. The Polish bomber squadrons converted to Wellingtons in late 1940, but No.16(P)FTS continued to use Battles and Battle (T)s until early in 1942, when they left the unit, most of them going to MUs. On 24 June 1941, P6630, a

L5598 served as the trials aircraft for the target-towing Battle, fitted with a wind-driven winch on the port side.
(D Thompson collection)

Battle (T), crashed at Hockenton, Newark, while attempting a practice forced landing. The engine of Battle K9221 cut and it crashed at Dore near Sheffield on 24 August 1941. A very serious accident occurred on 25 November 1941 when Battle N2177 was in mid-air collision with Battle (T) R7407. Both aircraft were wrecked and a flying instructor and two pupil pilots were killed. In all, 31 Battles and 35 Battle (T) trainers served with the unit. The Battles were:
K7599, K7604, K7670, K7676, K7683, K9221, K9224, L4945, L5013, L5018, L5060, L5067, L5137, L5138, L5140, L5183, L5252, L5287, L5311, L5417, L5423, L5424, N2031, N2045, N2104, N2107, N2109, N2177, N2243, P2362 and P6572.
The Battle (T) trainers were:
P6616, P6623, P6625-P6631, P6637-P6641, P6668, P6678, P6679, P6681, P6691, P6719, P6721, P6723, P6735, P6751, P6755, P6763, R7361, R7362, R7364, R7369, R7383, R7400, R7406, R7407 and R7477.

Operational Training Units

Battles were used by many OTUs for training and/or target towing duties. These are listed below.

No.1 OTU

No.1 OTU was formed as a Coastal Command crew training unit at Silloth in April 1940. Ten Battle T.T. target tugs served with the unit at various times between May 1940 and December 1942. They were:
L5632, L5633, L5667, L5680, L5681, L5682, L5691, L5717, L5771 and V1202.
Two of the Battle T.T.s were lost while with the unit; L5717 ditched in the Solway Firth after its engine cut on 11 July 1942 and L5667 was damaged beyond repair when it overshot a crash-landing after its engine cut near Carlisle on 20 October 1942. One Battle, L5209, was with the unit for a few days in December 1940.

No.2 OTU

No.2 OTU was formed as a Coastal Command twin-engine fighter and strike crew training unit at Catfoss in October 1940. Three Battle T.T. target tugs served with the unit at various times between December 1940 and May 1942. They were L5667, L5680 and V1270.

No.3 OTU

No.3 OTU was formed as a Coastal Command general reconnaissance training unit at Chivenor in November 1940. Two Battle T.T. target tugs served with the unit from December 1940. They were L5691 and L5771.

No.5/55 OTU

No.5 OTU was formed as a fighter training unit at Aston Down in March 1940 and was redesignated No.55 OTU on 1 November 1940. Two Battles, L5014 and L5133, were with the unit for a few months from May 1940. Nine Battle T.T. target tugs served with the unit at various times between June 1940 and December 1942. They were:

L5631, L5674, L5691, L5699, L5713, L5767, L5771, L5773 and V1202.

The unit moved to Usworth in March 1941 and to Annan in April 1942.

No.6/56 OTU

No.6 OTU was formed as a fighter training unit at Sutton Bridge in March 1940 and was redesignated No.56 OTU on 1 November 1940. Five Battle (T) trainers were received in June 1940 and were used for some months for pilot training. They were R7377-R7381. Ten Battle T.T. target tugs served with the unit at various times between July 1940 and May 1942. They were:
L5631, L5707, L5710, L5711, L5714, L5769, L5770, L5781, L5793 and V1204.
The unit moved to Tealing in March 1942.

No.7/57 OTU

No.7 OTU was formed as a fighter training unit at Hawarden in June 1940 and was redesignated No.57 OTU on 1 November 1940. Five Battle (T) trainers, R7372-R7376, were received in June 1940 and were used for some months for pilot training. Nine Battle T.T. target tugs served with the unit at various times between August 1940 and July 1943. They were:
L5625, L5631, L5705, L5706, L5709, L5714, L5716, L5770 and L5773.
The unit moved to Eshott in November 1942.

No.12 OTU

No.12 OTU was formed as a light bomber crew training unit at Benson in April 1940 from Nos.52, 63 and 207 Squadrons. In all, 66 Battles were transferred from these three squadrons, 13 from No.207 Squadron on 8 April, 26 from No.52 Squadron on 18 April and 27 from No.63 Squadron on 18 April. These are listed below.
Ex-207 Squadron: K9451, K9453-K9455, K9462-K9464, L4965, L4966, L5276, L5282, L5283 and L5482.
Ex-52 Squadron: K9308, K9393, K9399-K9401, K9403, K9405, K9407, K9410, K9413, K9419, K9436, K9442, K9444, K9460, K9468, K9481, L4968, L5203, L5264, L5272, N2022 and P2268-P2271.
Ex-63 Squadron: K9214, K9297, K9416, K9418, K9420, K9438, K9446, K9449, L4935, L4959, L4969-L4971, L4973, L5202, L5263, L5269, L5270, L5275, N2023, N2026, P2188, P2257, P2259, P2272, P2273 and P2275.
A further 32 Battles used by the unit during 1940 were:
K9395, L4943, L4976, L4977, L5030, L5040, L5045, L5055, L5061, L5062, L5071, L5079, L5091, L5101, L5124, L5182, L5184, L5314, L5421, L5432, L5441, L5447, L5500, L5562, L5570, L5573, N2106, N2148, N2164, N2168, N2249 and P2358.
In addition, 13 Battle (T) trainers were used by the unit. These were:
P6755, P6759, P6761-P6763, P6725, R7378-R7381, R7406, R7407 and R7373.
Of 111 Battles and Battle (T) trainers which served with the unit between April and December 1940, 25 crashed and were write-offs and one, P2269, was shot down by friendly AA fire. By the end of 1940, Battles had been almost entirely withdrawn from operational flying and the OTU changed to

night bomber training in December 1940, when the Battles were superseded by Wellingtons.

No.13 OTU

No.13 OTU was formed as a day bomber crew training unit at Bicester in April 1940 using Blenheims and Ansons. Three Battles were received in May 1940 and were on the strength of the unit for a short time. They were K9232, L4951 and N2023. On 10 June 1940, L4951 crashed into telephone wires while attempting a landing in bad visibility. The aircraft was burned out and the pilot and two passengers were killed.

No.17 OTU

No.17 OTU was formed as a light bomber crew training unit at Upwood in April 1940 using Blenheims and Ansons. In the same month eight Battles were received from No.35 Squadron, but they did not remain long with the unit. They were:
K7695, K9466, K9480, L4975, L4976, L5197, L5265 and L5266.
A further two Battles, K9290 and N2023, were received in October 1940 and left in 1941.

No.18 OTU

The Polish OTU was formed at Hucknall on 14 March 1940 to train Polish bomber crews. The first intake of 16 Polish pilots arrived at Hucknall for operational training on 22 March 1940. The unit was designated No.18 OTU in June 1940 and moved to Bramcote. Four Polish bomber squadrons, Nos. 300, 301, 304 and 305, were formed at Bramcote during 1940 and were equipped with Battles. Thirty-two Battles and four Battle (T) trainers served with this OTU between March and December 1940. The Battles were:
K9181, K9272, K9474, K9476, K9478, L4974, L5075, L5081, L5271, L5273, L5292, L5314, L5335, L5339, L5349, L5413, L5434, L5494, L5527, L5534, N2126, N2171, N2172, N2182, N2183, N2186-N2190, P2312 and P5230.
The Battle (T) trainers were:
P6692, P6718, P6719 and P6721.
Towards the end of 1940, the Polish bomber squadrons converted to Wellingtons and at No.18 OTU the Battles were superseded by Wellingtons.

No.24 OTU

No.24 OTU was formed as a night bomber crew training unit at Honeybourne in March 1942. Two Battles, K9384 and L5416, were in use from June to October 1942 for target towing duties.

No.30 OTU

No.30 OTU was formed as a night bomber crew training unit at Hixon in June 1942. One Battle, L5186, was used for target towing from August 1942 to January 1943.

No.52 OTU

No.52 OTU was formed as a single-seat fighter training unit at Debden in February 1941. It moved to Aston Down in

Battle Trainer P6728 of No.1 SFTS. (B Robertson collection)

August 1941. Nine Battle T.T. target tugs served in the unit at various times between March 1941 and September 1943. They were:
L5624, L5699, L5712, L5766, L5767, L5796, V1204, V1205 and V1249.
The unit also had a Battle (T) trainer, R7399, from March to October 1942.

No.53 OTU

No.53 OTU was formed as a single-seat fighter training unit at Heston in February 1941. Three Battle T.T. target tugs served in the unit at various times between March and October 1941. They were L5713, L5749 and L5781.

No.54 OTU

No.54 OTU was formed as a night fighter training unit at Church Fenton in November 1940. Two Battle T.T. target tugs served in the unit between March and December 1941. They were L5624 and L5625.

No.58 OTU

No.58 OTU was formed as a single-seat fighter training unit at Grangemouth in December 1940. Three Battle T.T. target tugs served with the unit at various times between March 1941 and June 1942. They were L5626, L5793 and V1210.

No.59 OTU

No.59 OTU was formed as a single-seat fighter training unit

at Crosby in February 1941. Eight Battle T.T. target tugs served with the unit at various times between March 1941 and July 1943. They were:
L5707, L5713, L5749, L5761, L5762, L5769, L5793 and V1204.
A Battle (T) trainer, P6685, was received by the unit in July 1942. The OTU moved to Milfield in August 1942

No.60 OTU

No.60 OTU was formed as a night fighter training unit at Leconfield in April 1941. Seven Battle T.T. target tugs served with the unit at various times between May 1941 and October 1942. They were:
L5624-L5626, L5707, L5793, L5796 and V1249.
The unit moved to East Fortune in June 1941.

No.61 OTU

No.61 OTU was formed as a single-seat fighter training unit at Heston in June 1941. Three Battle T.T. target tugs served with the unit at various times between July 1941 and July 1942. They were L5707, L5749 and V1204. The unit moved to Rednal in April 1942.

No.104 OTU

No.104 OTU was formed as a heavy bomber crew training unit at Nutts Corner in March 1943 and was disbanded in February 1944. One Battle, P2362, served with the unit.

Central Flying School

Battles N2085 and N2254 were received by the CFS in March and September 1939 respectively and both left the school in August 1940. A further Battle, P2277, was at the school from May 1940 to February 1941. Seven Battle (T) trainers were received between May and October 1940 and the last one left in April 1941. They were:
P6617, P6750, P6752-P6754, R7371 and R7382.
The CFS was based at Upavon.

Air Observer/Bombing and Gunnery Schools

Battles were used in the Air Observer and Bombing and Gunnery Schools for bombing and gunnery training and for the more mundane task of target towing. The Air Observer Schools became Bombing and Gunnery Schools on 1 November 1939 and reverted to the title Air Observer Schools on 19 July 1941.

No.1 AOS

Based at North Coates, the school received 12 Battles between the end of July and the beginning of September 1939. On the outbreak of war the school was moved from its vulnerable position in Lincolnshire to Penrhos in North Wales, where it became No.9 AOS. The Battles were:
L5251-L5253, L5255-L5262 and P2301.

No.2 B&GS/2 AOS

No. 2 B&GS at Millom was redesignated No.2 AOS in July 1941. Between January and July 1941, the school received two Battles, fourteen Battle T.T. target tugs and nine Battle (T) trainers. A further two Battle T.T. target tugs were received in October 1941. The Battles were N2105 and P2277. The Battle T.T. target tugs were:
L5633, L5745, L5750, L5754, L5755, L5777, L5780, L5783-L5785, L5787-L5789, L5795, L5797 and V1250. The Battle (T) trainers were:
P6617, P6667, P6752, R7367, R7371, R7378, R7381, R7382 and R7401.
The school had disposed of these aircraft by early 1942. There were two accidents in 1941 which resulted in aircraft being written off, both on 16 February. L5750 force-landed near Withington, Salop., after engine failure and hit a hedge; L5755 flew into a mountain near Llanrhaeadr-y-Mochnant, Denbighshire, while on a ferry flight.

No.3 AOS/3 B&GS

No. 3 AOS, based at Aldergrove, was redesignated No.3 B&GS on 1 November 1939. Between September 1939 and June 1940, 29 Battles were received by the school. They were:
K7646, L4995, L4998, L4999, L5009, L5011, L5014, L5017, L5020, L5023, L5027, L5046, L5054, L5128-L5130, L5136-L5138, L5141, L5142, L5380, L5386, N2225, N2226, N2228, N2240, P2322 and P2323.
The school was disbanded on 11 July 1940, by which time the Battles had been dispersed to other units.

No.4 AOS/4 B&GS/4 AOS

The former Armament Training Camp at West Freugh became No.4 AOS in April 1939. Many Battle aircraft arrived at West Freugh between September 1939 and April 1941 and many departed in the same period. The use of Battles at the school finished in early 1942. Most of the Battles were the bomber version, but several target tugs passed through the unit and a solitary Battle (T) trainer was with the school from August 1941 to February 1942. The Battles were:
K7575, K7600, K7606, K7612, K7625, K7633, K7641, K7644, K7645, K7708, K7709, K9177, K9184, K9226-K9228, K9233, K9243, K9248, K9285, K9288, K9303, K9307, K9347, K9359, K9362, K9415, K9423, K9443, K9447, K9457, K9470, L4982, L4984, L4993, L5084, L5086, L5130, L5141, L5290, L5291, L5295, L5298, L5299, L5304, L5309, N2024, N2052, N2054, N2056, N2057, N2060, N2062, N2089, N2094-N2096, N2181, N2229, N2254, P2266, P2276, P2278 and P2317, 64 in all.
The Battle T.T. target tugs were:
L5641, L5662, L5726, L5728, L5729, V1215-V1224 and V1246-V1249, 19 in all. The Battle (T) trainer was R7378.
In April 1940 the school was amalgamated into the Armament Training Wing and the Battles were being used for both bombing and gunnery training. The Battle T.T. target tugs arrived later in 1940. After April 1941, the school started to re-equip with Bothas and the remaining Battles and Battle T.T.s were used mainly for target towing. There were several serious accidents involving Battles at West Freugh. On 13 October 1940, the engine of K9347 cut and it bellylanded on sand dunes near West Freugh; the aircraft was struck off charge shortly afterwards. On 23 April 1941, K9359 crashlanded at East Freugh after its engine cut and it undershot the approach to West Freugh. On 15 May 1941, two target tugs, L5662 and V1223, collided in mid-air, resulting in four deaths. The engine of L5084 cut and it crash landed on its approach to Jurby on 20 May 1941. Three fatalities resulted when the engine of N2024 caught fire and the aircraft crashed in Luce Bay, Wigtown, on 13 July 1941. There were three deaths when N2060 flew into the ground while descending in low cloud near Portpatrick, Wigtown, on 14 July 1941. A target tug, V1222, was impounded by the Eire authorities when it landed at Waterford after the pilot, F/Lt Baranowski, got lost on a flight over the Irish Sea and landed at Waterford on 2 April 1941. The pilot was interned. No.4 AOS changed its designation to No.4 B&GS in November 1939 and changed it back to No.4 AOS in July 1941.

No.5 AOS/5 B&GS/5 AOS

No.5 AOS was opened at Jurby on the Isle of Man on 18 September 1939. It became No.5 B&GS in November 1939 and reverted to No.5 AOS in July 1941. The first Battles arrived at the station in November 1939 and they continued to arrive and depart up to mid 1941. The Battles were:
K7576, K7620, K7628, K7662, K7667, K7670, K7671, K7688, K9182, K9346, L5131, L5134, L5135, L5139, N2229, N2235, N2238, N2242, N2243, N2245, P2362 and P2363, 22 in all.
Ten Battle T.T. target tugs served at the school in 1940/41; L5642, L5669, L5670-L5672 and L5731-L5735.
Two Battle (T) trainers were at the school briefly in June

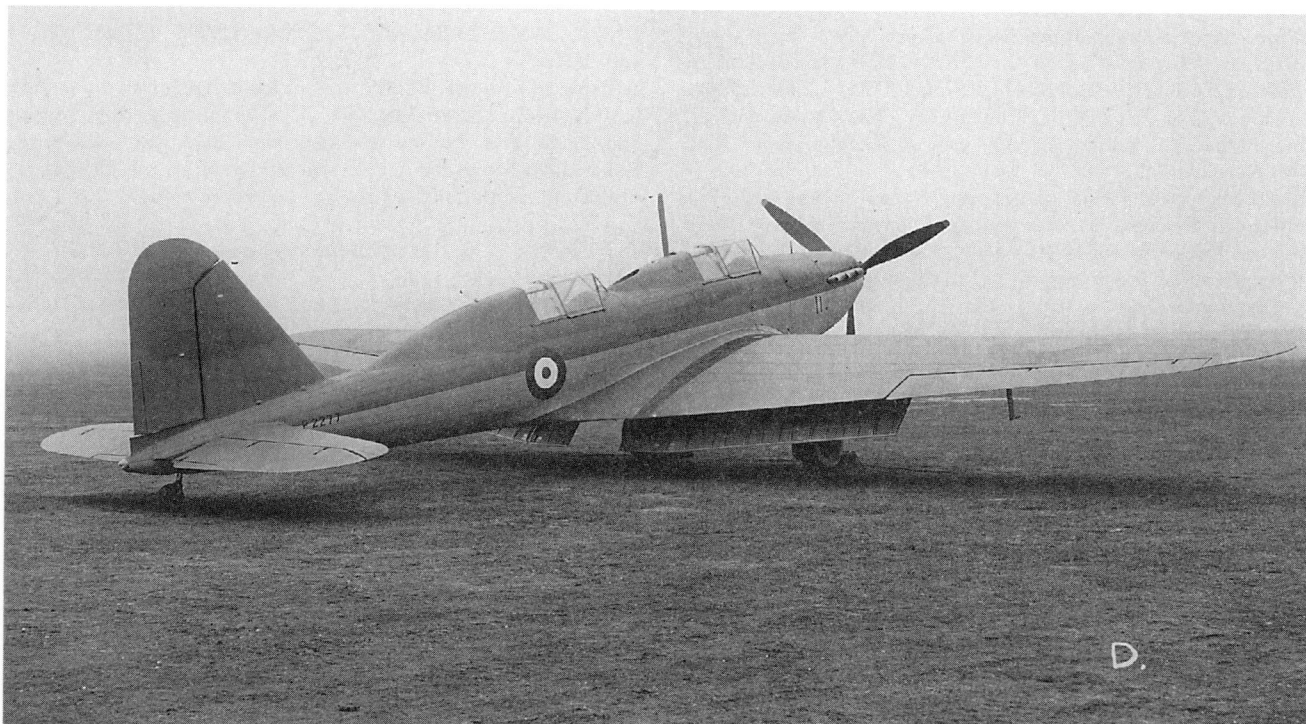

P2277 at the Aeroplane & Armament Experimental Establishment during trials of the Battle Trainer. (R Sturtivant collection)

1940; they were P6753 and R7371. After only three days at Jurby, K7620 was badly damaged when it undershot on landing and crashed into Henley L3391 on 9 November 1939. On 28 November 1939, K7628 bellylanded at Jurby and was extensively damaged. A Battle (T), P6753, crashed on a night approach to Jurby on 14 June 1940 and was damaged beyond repair. A target-towing aircraft, L5671, stalled while dropping its drogue on 1 October 1940 and dived into the ground at Hall Caine, Isle of Man. After the departure of all the original Battles, five Battle T.T. target tugs were assigned to the school in July 1942 and remained there until October/November 1942. They were:
L5636, L5748, V1273, V1266 and V1268.

No.6 B&GS

Although twenty Battles, nine Battle T.T. target tugs and one Battle (T) trainer were at No.6 B&GS, Pembrey, in 1940, most of them were only there for a few weeks. The Battles were:
K7690, L4999, L5007, L5008, L5016-L5018, L5060, L5067, L5069, L5084, L5086, L5300, L5305, L5307, L5310, L5311, N2109, N2176 and N2181.
The Battle T.T.s were L5634-L5642.
The Battle (T) was P6764. All of these aircraft were despatched from Pembrey to other training units by early June 1940, except for L5086, which remained at Pembrey until April 1941.

No.7 AOS/7 BGS

No.7 AOS, which became No.7 B&GS in November 1939, was based at Stormy Down in Wales. The first Battles arrived at the school in September 1939 and by June 1940, 23 had been received. Many of these were in use well into 1941. The Battles were:
K7599, K7604, K7608, K7639, K7672, K9291, K9371, L5001, L5002, L5019, L5021, L5025, L5053, L5065, L5069, L5072, L5293, L5305, L5311, L5313, N2051, N2125 and N2176.
In May 1940 the first of 26 Battle T.T. target tugs arrived at the school and these had been replaced by early 1942. The Battle T.T.s were:
L5635, L5637, L5638, L5640, L5663, L5673, L5687, L5688, L5736-L5741, L5782, L5786, V1211-V1214 and V1275- V1280.
A Battle (T) trainer, P6764, was at the school from May to September 1940.
The first accident to a Battle was on 18 January 1940, when L5065 bellylanded into trees near Cardiff after its engine cut. L5293 ditched in the sea off Porthcawl on 27 July 1940 when its engine cut. A Battle T.T., L5635, was seriously damaged when it bellylanded at Stormy Down on 25 November after its undercarriage jammed. L5019 was lost when it dived into the sea off Porthcawl on 4 March 1941. On 20 April 1941, L5072 dived into the ground near Kenfig Hill, Glamorgan. While approaching the drogue-dropping area at Kenfig on 2 May 1941, V1211, a Battle T.T., crashed and was completely wrecked.

No.8 AOS/8 B&GS/8 AOS

Battles started to arrive at the school at Evanton in Scotland in September 1939 and continued to arrive in small numbers until July 1940. They had all left by the end of 1941. The 21 Battles which served at the school were:
K7565, K7634, K7638, K7683, L4995, L4998, L5026, L5046, L5082, L5083, L5085, L5128, L5223, L5294, L5296, L5301, L5302, L5312, N2064, P2316 and P2318.
A total of 32 Battle T.T. target tugs served at the school at

various times between June 1940 and early 1942. They were: L5639, L5642, L5668-L5670, L5675-L5678, L5684-L5686, L5690, L5718, L5719, L5727, L5730-L5735, L5742-L5744, V1225, V1226, V1232, V1237, V1239, V1240 and V1275. One Battle (T) trainer, R7368, was at Evanton from June 1941 to May 1942.

On 20 May 1940 P2316 undershot a forced landing and hit a wall near Evanton; it was damaged beyond repair. There were no further serious accidents to the Battles until 25 April 1941, when the target tug V1240 crashed in a forced landing at Shandwick Bay in Ross. On 15 August 1941, L5301 overshot a forced landing after its engine cut at Aboyne, Aberdeenshire. It hit some trees and was wrecked. A target tug, V1275, was in a mid-air collision with Botha L6438 on 16 September 1941 and crashed into the sea.

No.9 AOS/9 B&GS

The school was based at Penrhos in North Wales. At the beginning of the war, No.1 AOS was moved there from North Coates and became No.9 AOS. The school was redesignated No.9 B&GS in November 1939 and reverted to its former title of No.9 AOS in July 1941. The twelve Battles received with the former No.1 AOS were:
L5251-L5253, L5255-L5262 and P2301.
Four more Battles were received in 1939; they were:
K7688, L5004, L5013 and L5029.
Between May and July 1940, a further 14 Battles were received. They were:
K7607, K7670, K9385, K9394, K9424-K9427, L5136, L5137 and N2043-N2046.
The first Battle T.T. target tugs were allotted to the school in June 1940 and by the beginning of November, 21 had arrived. They were:
L5718-L5721, L5745-L5747, V1227-V1233, V1236, V1237 and V1241-V1245.
A solitary Battle (T) trainer, P6676, arrived at the station in July 1941 and was retained until June 1942.
The Battles were used in all aspects of the school's work, i.e., bombing, gunnery and target towing. A serious accident occurred on 24 November 1939 when L5255 and L5256 collided in in the circuit of Penrhos and crashed; both were destroyed by fire and the crews were all killed. On 26 February 1940, K7688 crashed during a night forced landing in fog near Cardigan. V1228 stalled while dropping a drogue and crashed at Penrhos on 25 October 1940 and on 31 May 1941, L5004 flew into the sea off Pwllheli. The Battles and Battle (T)s were phased out by early 1942 and were replaced by Ansons and Blenheims.

No.10 AOS/10 B&GS/10 AOS

No.10 AOS was formed at Warmwell on 2 September 1939. It became No.10 B&GS in November 1939 and was moved to Dumfries in mid July 1940, where it became No.10 AOS on 13 September 1941. Six Battles arrived at the school in September 1939 followed by 14 others by July 1940 and six more in the first half of 1941. They left the school on various dates, the last leaving in October 1942. The 26 Battles were:
K7602, K7617, K7708, K9177, K9428-K9435, K9447, L4997, L5000, L5131, L5134, L5138, L5142, L5309, L5380, N2097, N2128, N2160, N2170 and N2223.
Battle T.T. target tugs served at the school at various dates between June 1940 and July 1942. The 18 Battle T.T.s were:

L5634, L5636, L5709, L5748, L5749, L5775, L5785, V1250 and V1265-V1274.
A Battle (T) trainer, P6666, was at the school from June 1941 to July 1942. On 18 July 1941, L5775, a target tug, looped and dived into the sea at Blackshaw Bank, Solway Firth. Battle L4997 crashed on 29 September 1941 at Closeburn, near Dumfries, after the pilot lost control in cloud.

Air Gunners Schools

Battles, Battle T.T. target tugs and Battle (T) trainers were all used in relatively small numbers by the Air Gunners Schools.

No.1 AGS

No.1 AGS at Pembrey received ten Battle T.T. target tugs between June and September 1941. All except one had left the school by the end of the year. They were:
L5674, L5728, L5745, L5783, L5784, V1219, V1230, V1243, V1250 and V1272.

No.2 AGS

No.2 AGS was formed at Dalcross in July 1941 and received five Battle (T) trainers between February and October 1942. They were: P6757, P6758, R7378, R7381 and R7410.
On 20 October 1942 R7410 crashed during a forced landing at Dalcross and it was struck off charge on 29 October 1942. None of the Battle (T)s stayed long at the school and the last one, P6758, left in April 1943.

No.3 AGS

The school was formed at Castle Kennedy in April 1942 and moved to Mona on Anglesey in December 1942. Between July and October 1942 the school received 27 Battle (T) trainers, four Battle T.T. target tugs and two Battles. The Battle (T)s were:
P6617-P6619, P6624, P6626, P6627, P6632, P6635, P6641, P6644, P6669, P6718, P6719, P6722, P6736, P6759, P6767, R7361, R7362, R7364, R7366, R7367, R7375, R7376, R7379, R7401 and R7406. The Battle T.T.s were: L5748, V1266, V1268 and V1273.
The Battles were K7565 and L5253.
All had left by early 1943. On 26 August 1942, P6644 collided with Botha L6173 on approach to Castle Kennedy. It was not repairable on the station and was sent to Rosenfields. P6632 force-landed in a lake at Cults Loch, Castle Kennedy on 9 November 1942.

No.4 AGS

Formed at Morpeth in Northumberland on 17 April 1942, No.4 AGS received one Battle (T) trainer, P6666, in July 1942 and retained it until November 1942.

No.7 AGS

The school was based at Stormy Down and received one Battle, L5001, and one Battle T.T. target tug, L5637, from No.7 BGS, which was also at Stormy Down. L5001 crashed after hitting a tree while low flying at Margam Castle, Glamorgan, on 22 June 1941 and L5637 dived into the sea off Porthcawl on 31 August 1941.

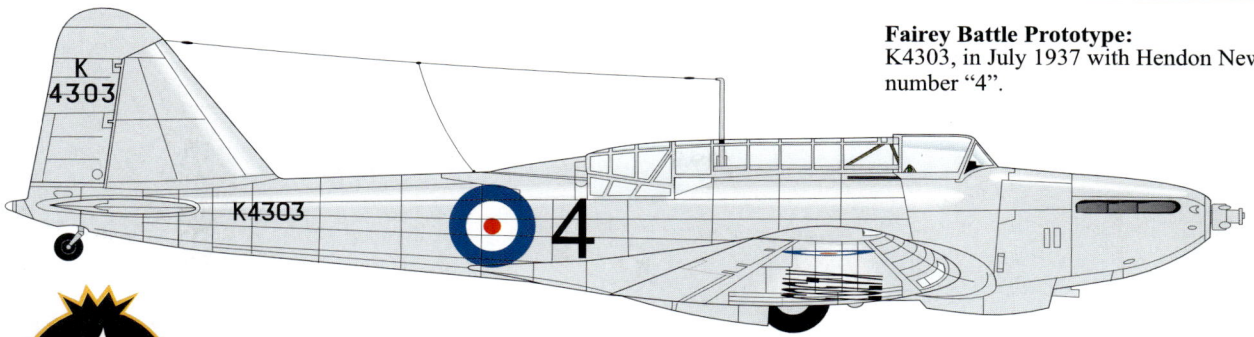

Fairey Battle Prototype:
K4303, in July 1937 with Hendon New Type number "4".

K
4303

K4303

4

Fairey Battle I:
K7578, 105-F of 105 Sqn., Harwell, circa 1937/38

105 Sqn., badge on fin of K7578.

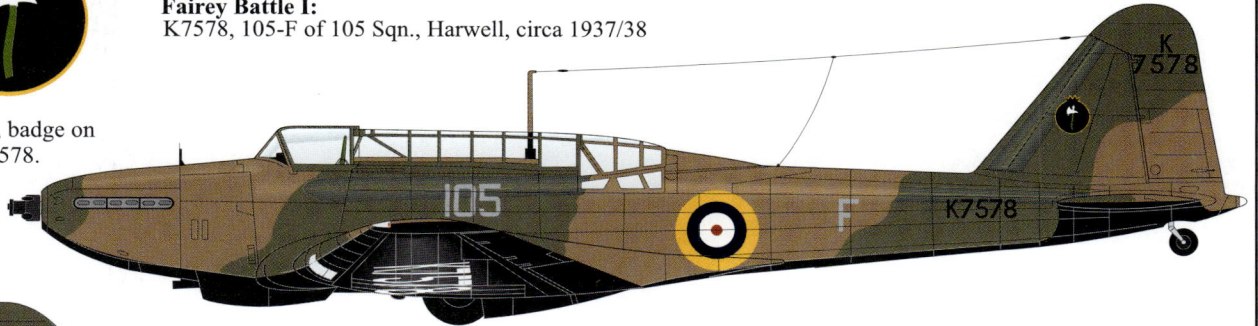

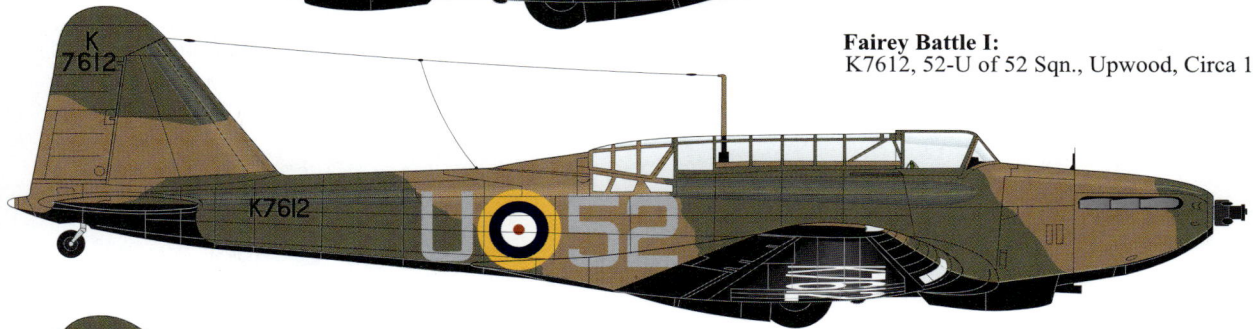

K
7578

105

F

K7578

Fairey Battle I:
K7612, 52-U of 52 Sqn., Upwood, Circa 1937/38.

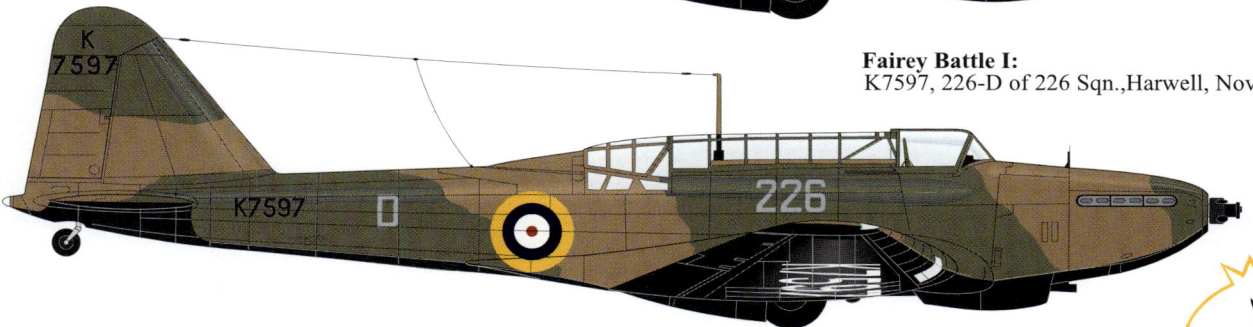

K
7612

K7612

U

52

Fairey Battle I:
K7597, 226-D of 226 Sqn.,Harwell, Nov 1937.

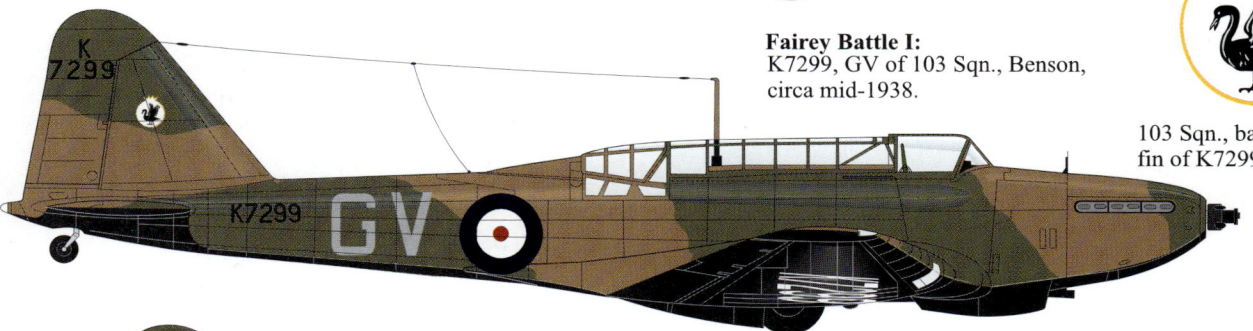

K
7597

K7597

D

226

Fairey Battle I:
K7299, GV of 103 Sqn., Benson, circa mid-1938.

103 Sqn., badge on fin of K7299

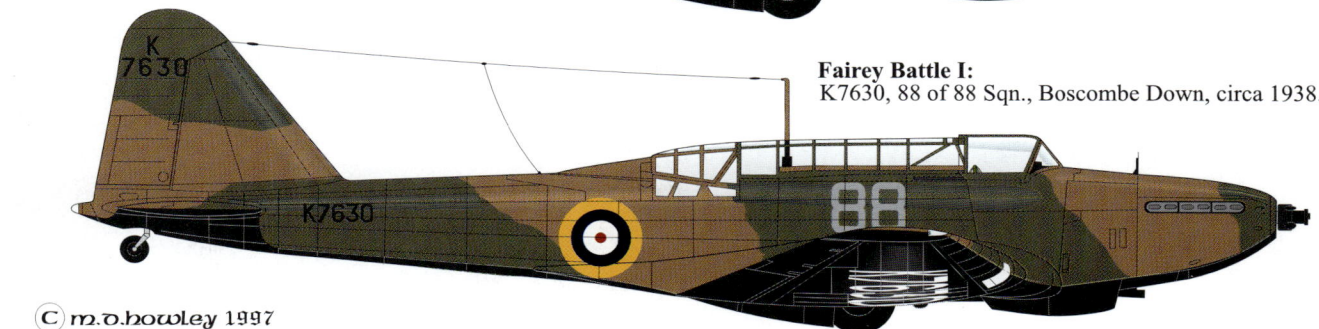

K
7299

K7299

GV

Fairey Battle I:
K7630, 88 of 88 Sqn., Boscombe Down, circa 1938.

K
7630

K7630

88

© m.o.howley 1997

Fairey Battle I:
K7650, 63-M of 63 Sqn., circa early 1938.

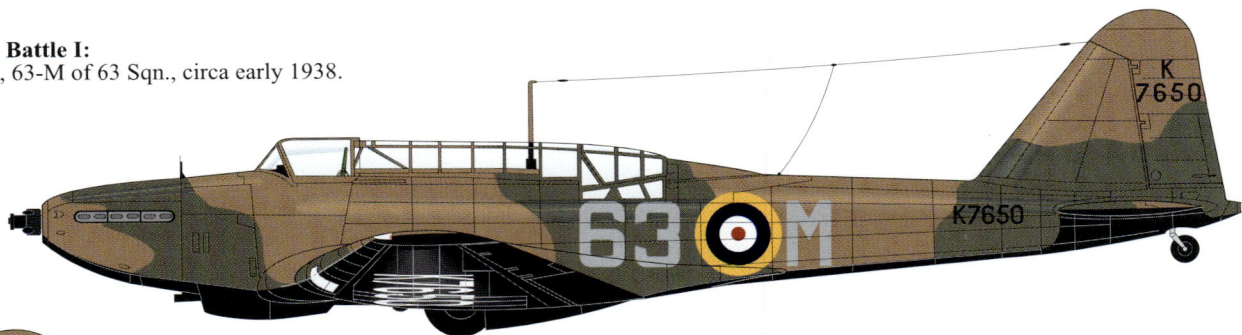

Fairey Battle I:
K7660, 218-L of 218 Sqn.,Boscombe Down 1938.

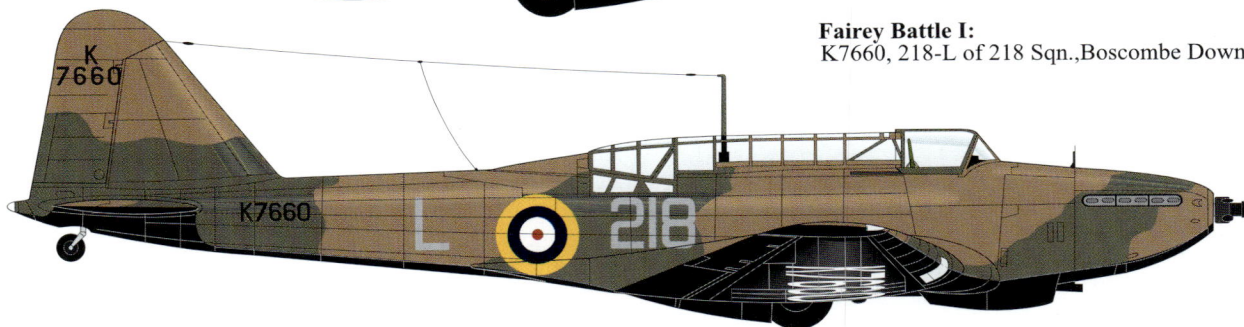

Fairey Battle I:
K9200, Z of 207 Sqn.,Cottesmore 1938.

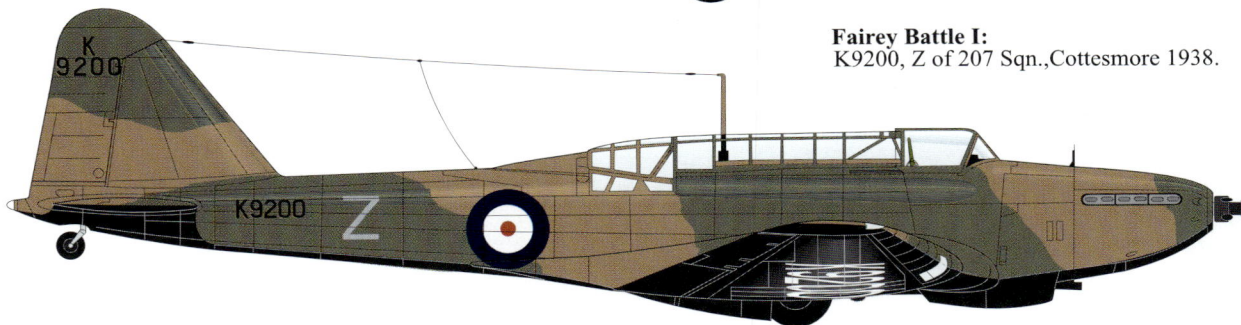

Fairey Battle I:
L4958, ON-R of 63 Sqn., circa 1938/39.

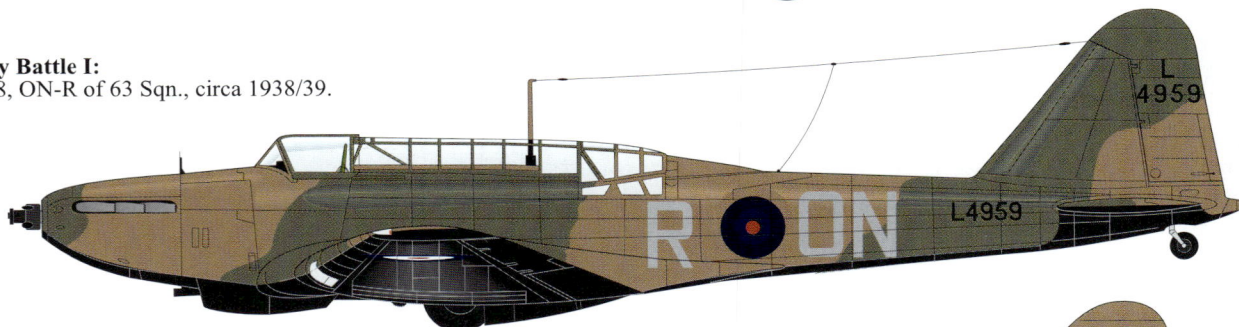

Fairey Battle II:
K9301, EF-L of 15 Sqn., Abingdon, circa early 1939.

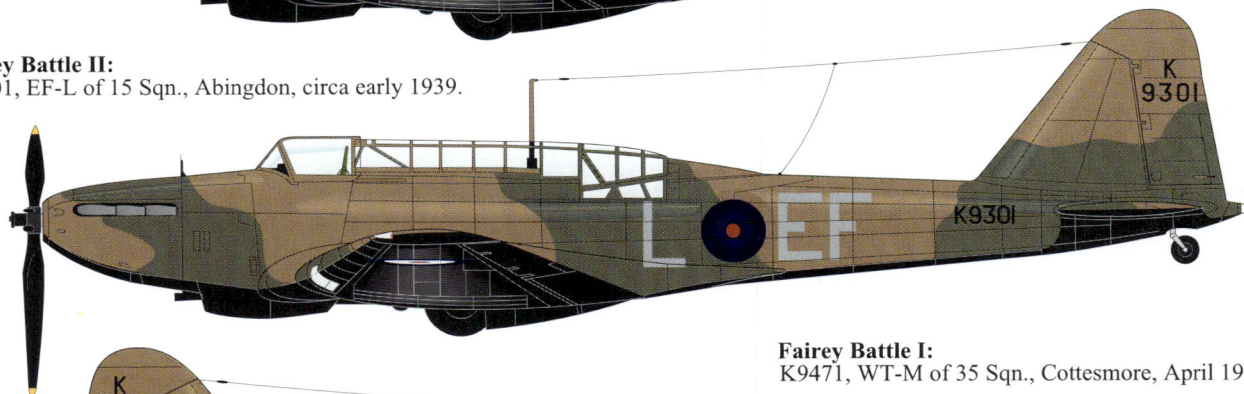

Fairey Battle I:
K9471, WT-M of 35 Sqn., Cottesmore, April 1939.

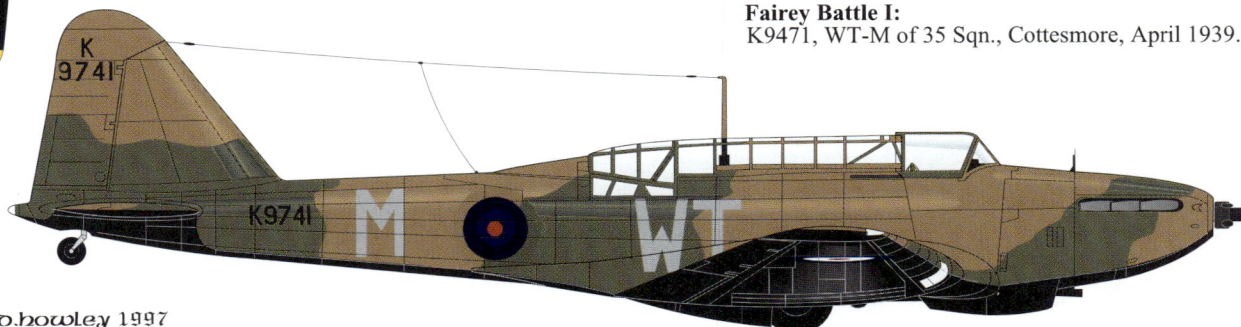

© m.o.howley 1997

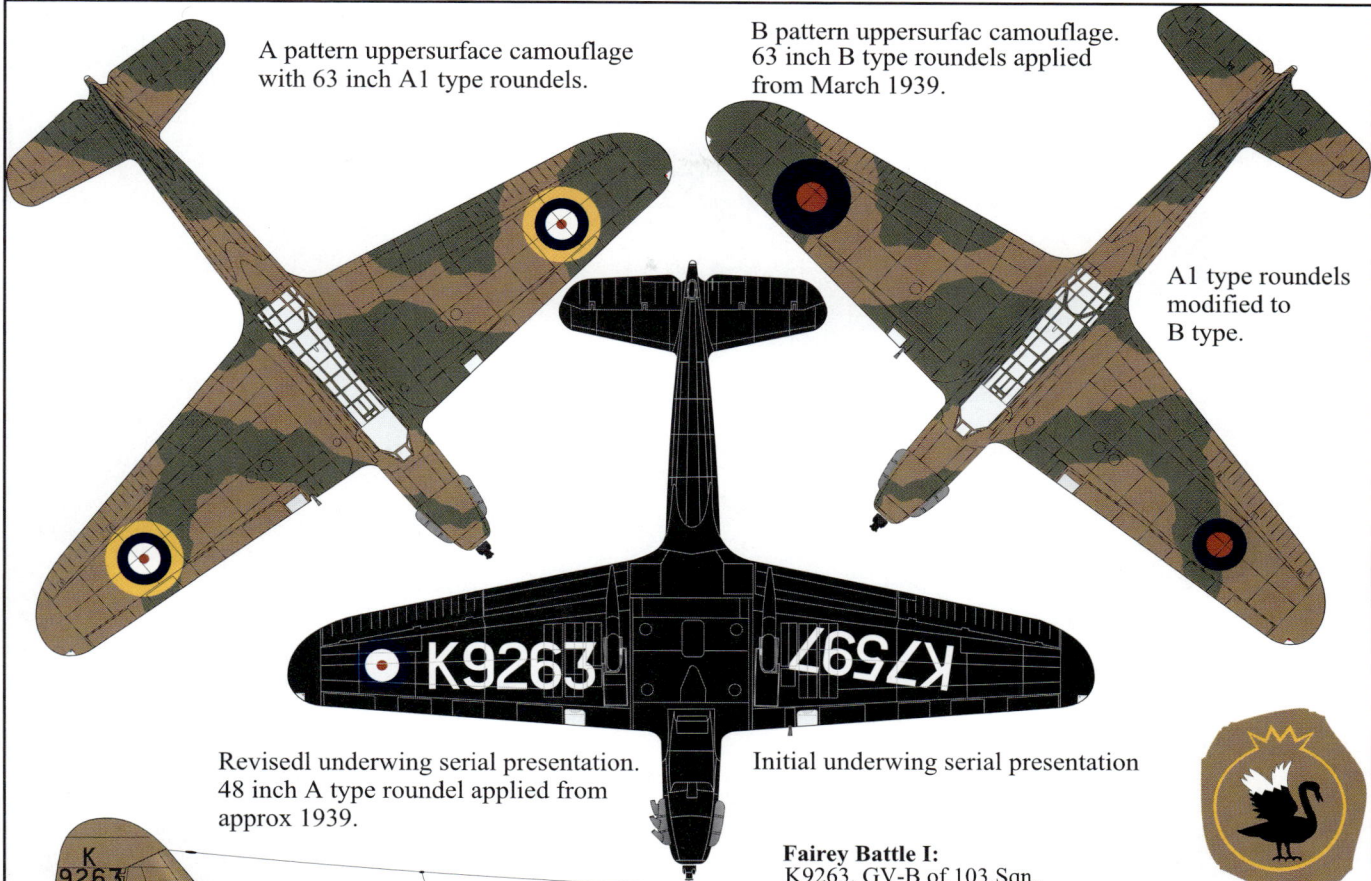

A pattern uppersurface camouflage with 63 inch A1 type roundels.

B pattern uppersurfac camouflage. 63 inch B type roundels applied from March 1939.

A1 type roundels modified to B type.

Revisedl underwing serial presentation. 48 inch A type roundel applied from approx 1939.

Initial underwing serial presentation

Fairey Battle I:
K9263, GV-B of 103 Sqn., Benson, 6 August 1939.

Variation of 103 Sqn., badge on fin of K9263.

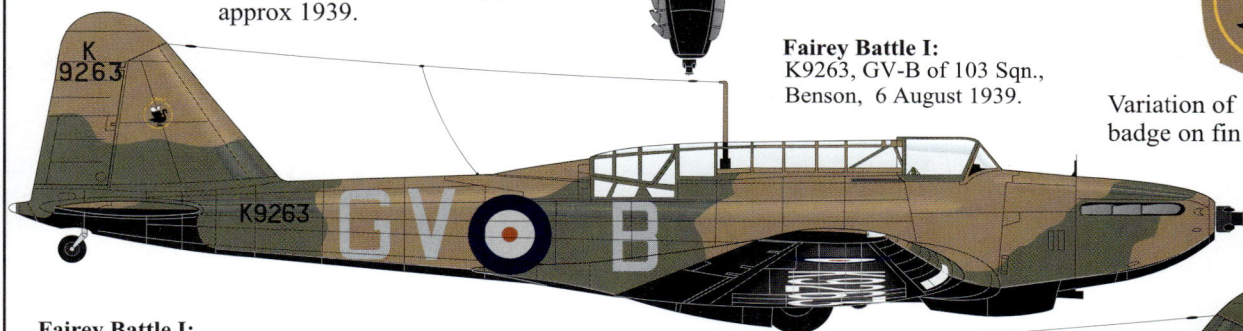

Fairey Battle I:
N2241, BH-G of 300 (Masovian)(Polish) Sqn., Bramcote, Aug.1939.

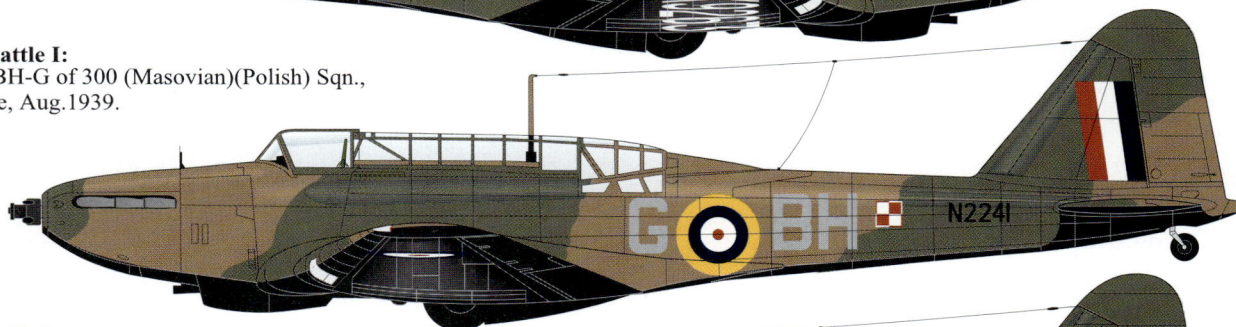

Fairey Battle I:
P2177, LS-Y , "Sylveste" of 15 Sqn., Conde-Vraux, France September 1939.

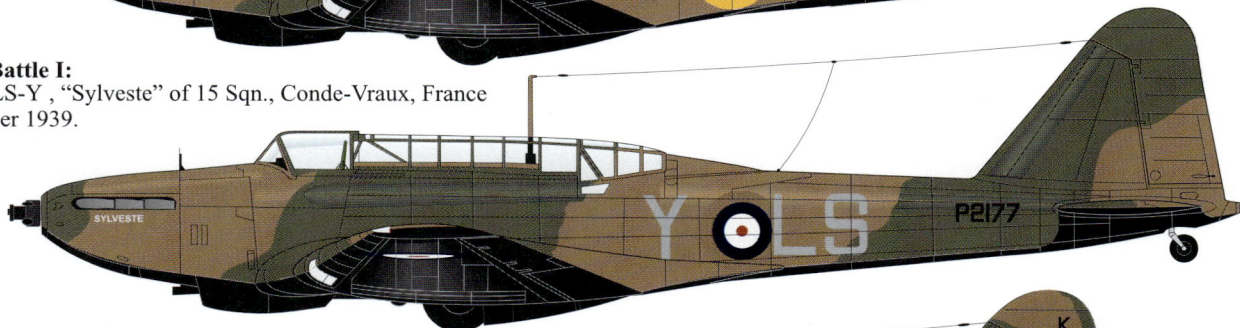

Fairey Battle I:
P9182, MQ-J of 226 Sqn., AASF, Reims, France Circa winter 1939/40.

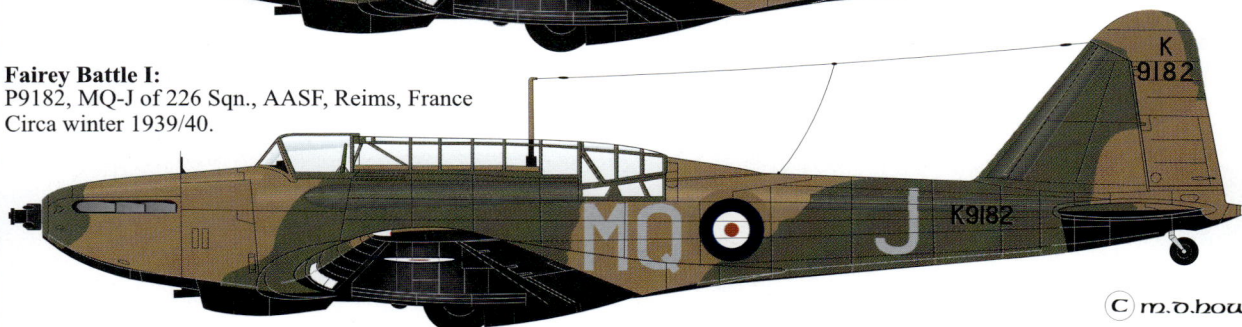

© m.o.howley 1997

Fairey Battle I:
K9282, RH-P of 88 Sqn., France winter 1939.

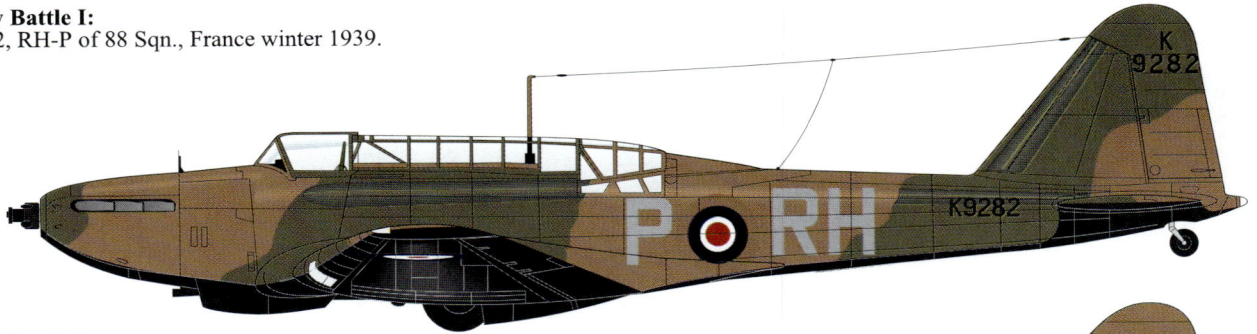

Fairey Battle I:
K9353, HA-J of 218 Sqn, AASF, France
circa late 1939/early 1940.

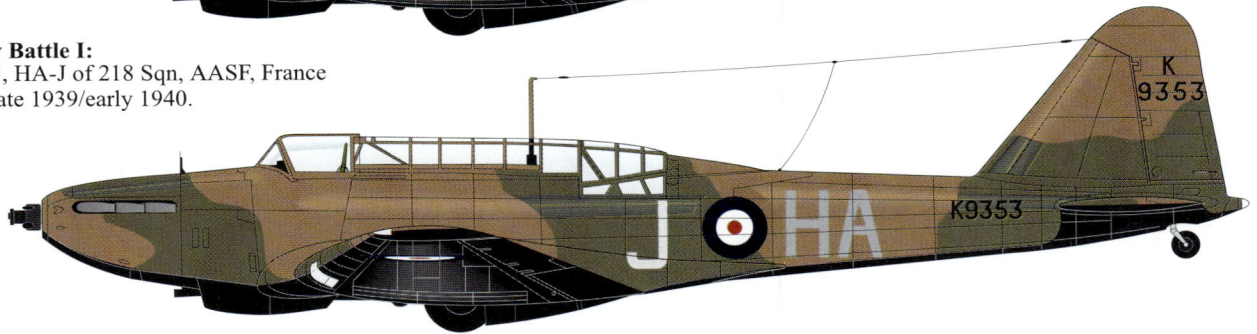

Fairey Battle I:
L5420, P of 12 Sqn., Berry au Bac, France,
early 1940.

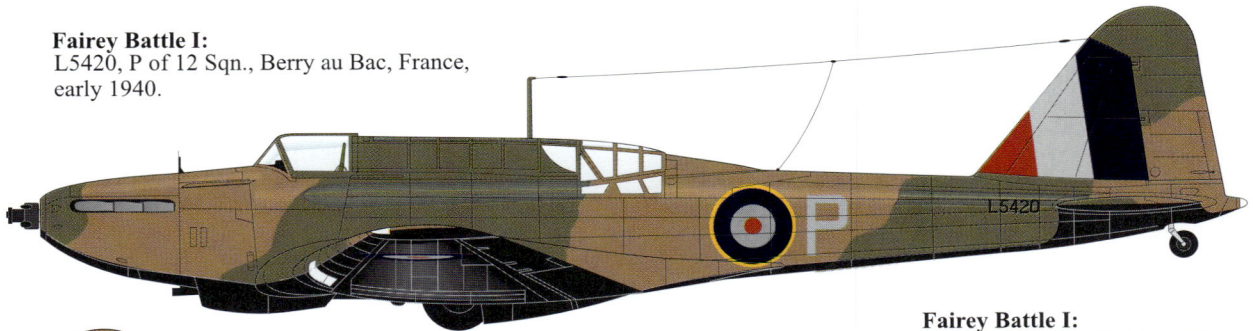

Fairey Battle I:
K7705, MQ-K of 226 Sqn., Reims, France
Circa early 1940.

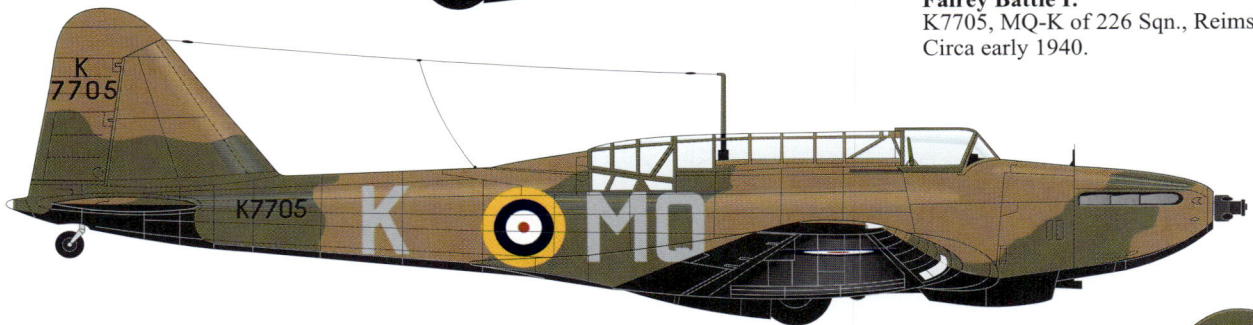

Fairey Battle I:
L5080, QT-U of 142 Sqn., Binbrook, 1940.

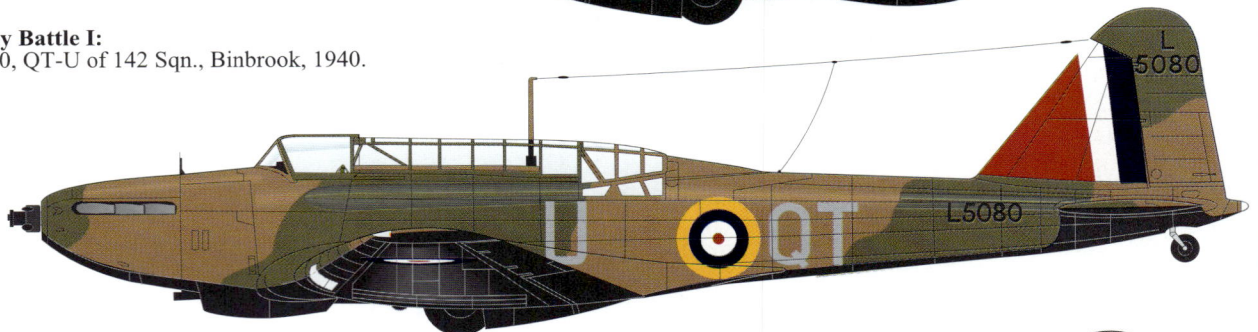

Fairey Battle I:
N2053 JQ-S of C Flt., No.2 AACU,
Roborough, 1940.

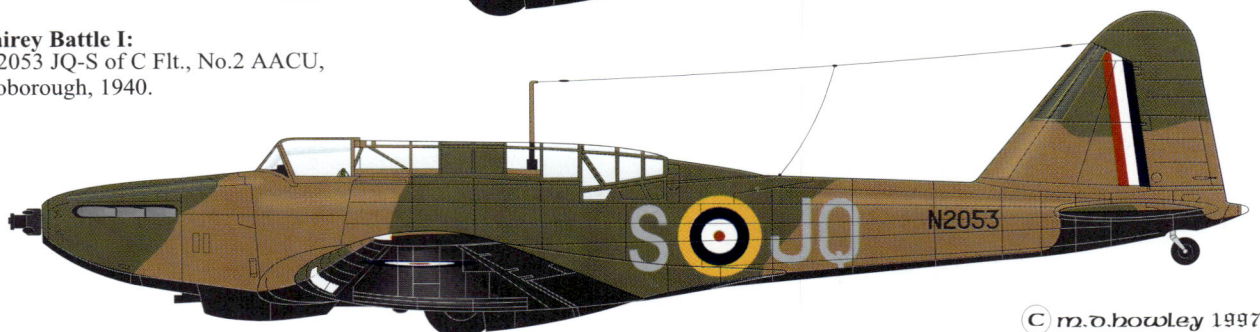

© m.o.howley 1997

Fairey Battle I:
L5360, RH-C abandoned by 88 Sqn., at Poitiers, France. Repaired by 212 (PR) Sqn., detachment and flown to Heston on 20 June 1940 by Flt.Lt."Tug" Wilson, with Sgt Walton, Sgt Ward, LAC Cook and LAC Jim Muncie as passengers.

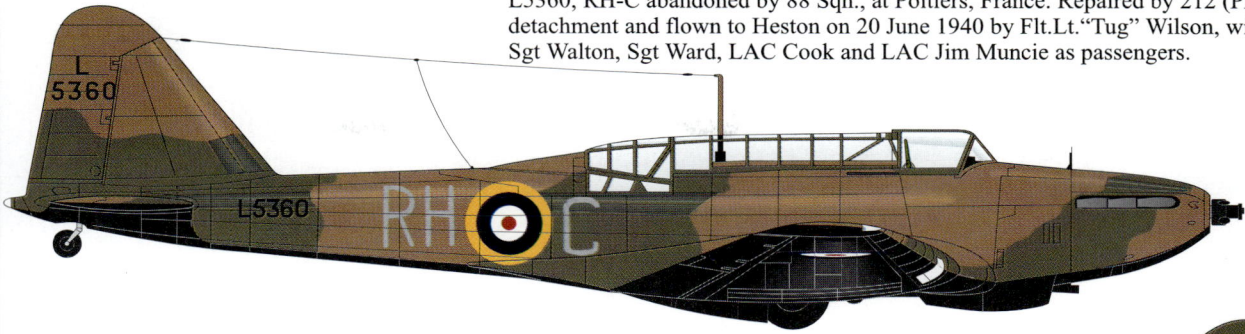

Fairey Battle I:
L5511, PM-L of 103 Sqn., France May 1940.

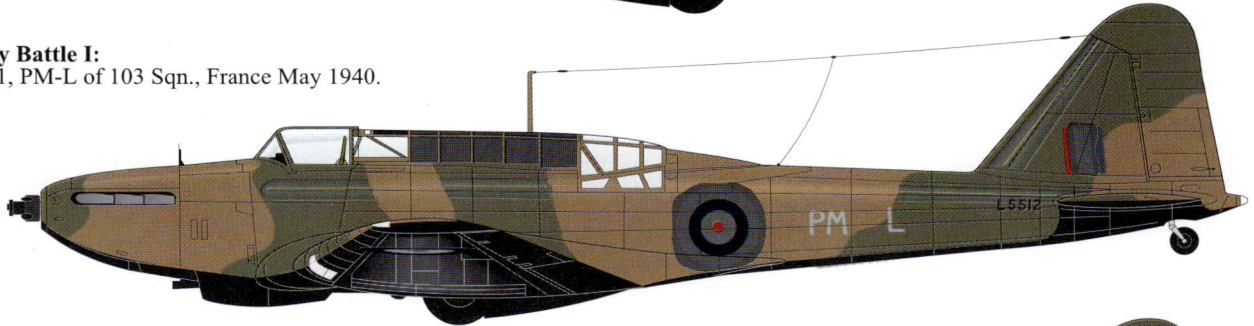

Fairey Battle I:
P2332, PH-F, A Flight 12 Sqn., France, 12 May 1940.
Flown by F/O Norman Thomas on the Maastricht Bridge raid.

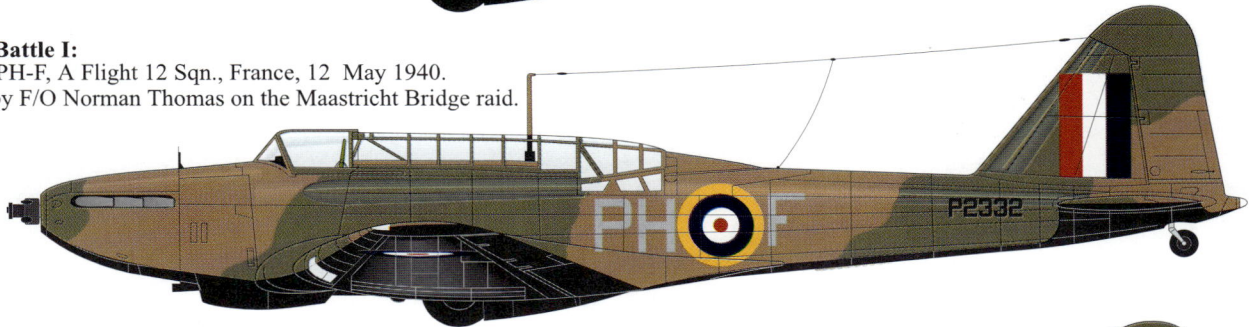

Fairey Battle I:
P6597, V of 12 Sqn., Berry au Bac, France early 1940.

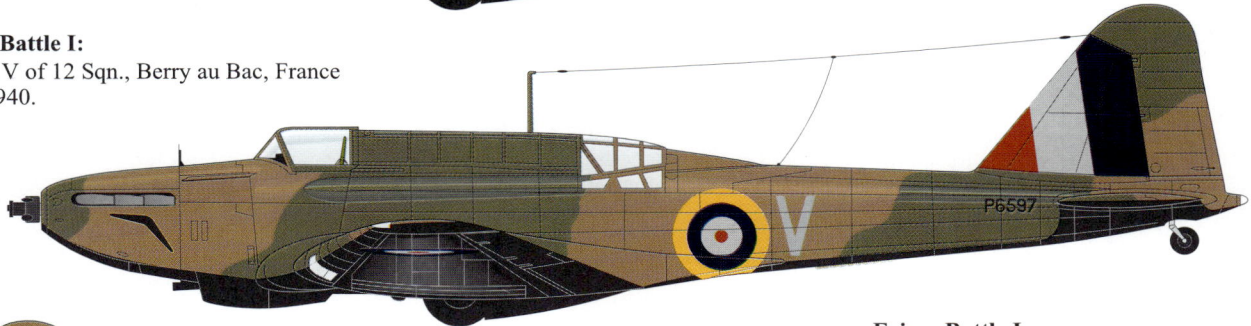

Fairey Battle I:
(Probably) 915, L of 11 Sqn., SAAF, British Somaliland circa August 1940.

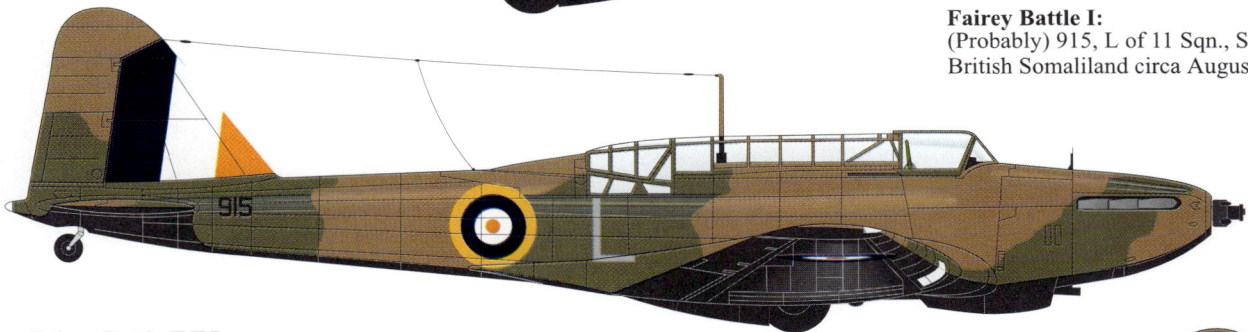

Fairey Battle T.T.I:
P6723, NZ-Y of 304(Silesian) (Polish) Sqn., Bramcote, circa late 1940.

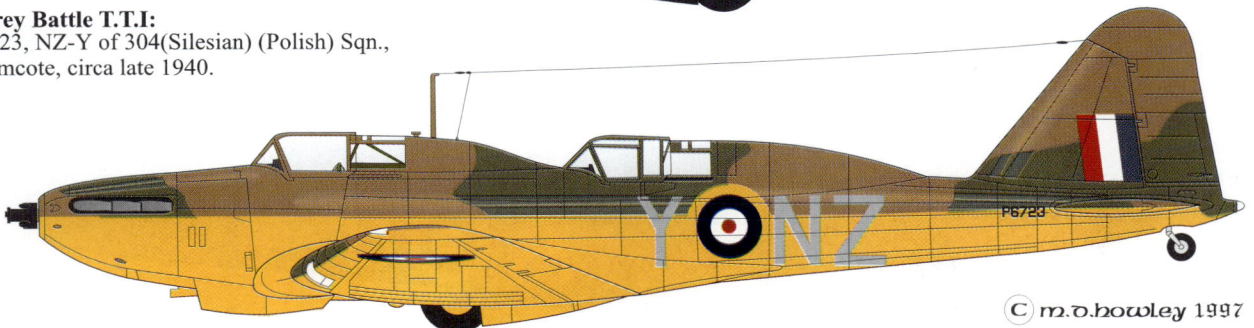

© m.d.howley 1997

Fairey Battle I:
2056, 28 of 8 Bombing & Gunnery School,
RCAF MacDonald, Manitoba, Canada, circa 1941.

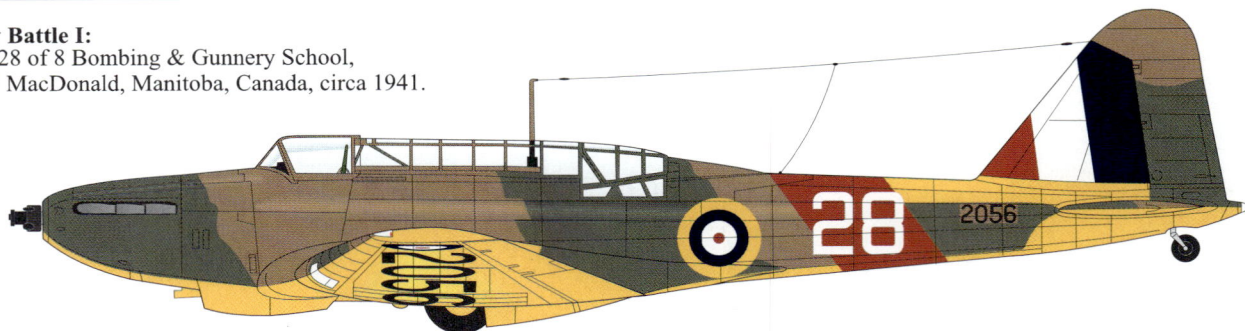

Fairey Battle I:
2095 (Ex-L5441), 72 of 8 Bombing & Gunnery School
RCAF Stataion MacDonald, Manitoba, Canada, 1941.

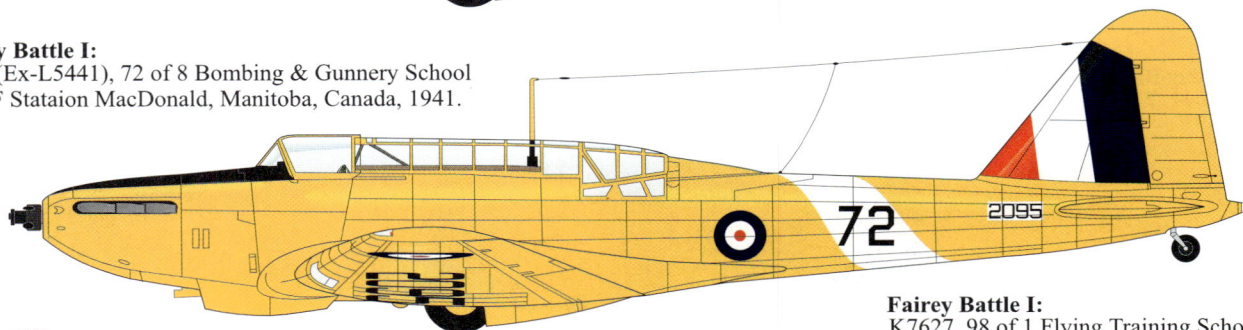

Fairey Battle I:
K7627, 98 of 1 Flying Training School,
Netheravon, circa ?????

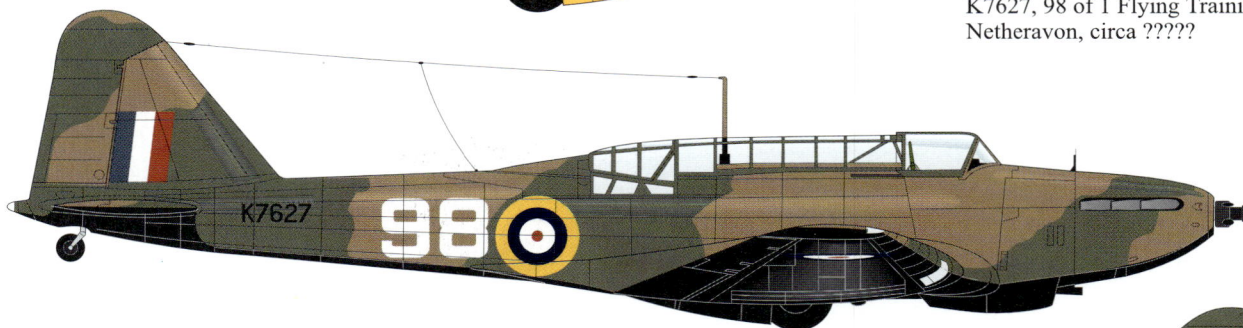

Fairey Battle I Engine test bed:
L5286, Napier Sabre engine.

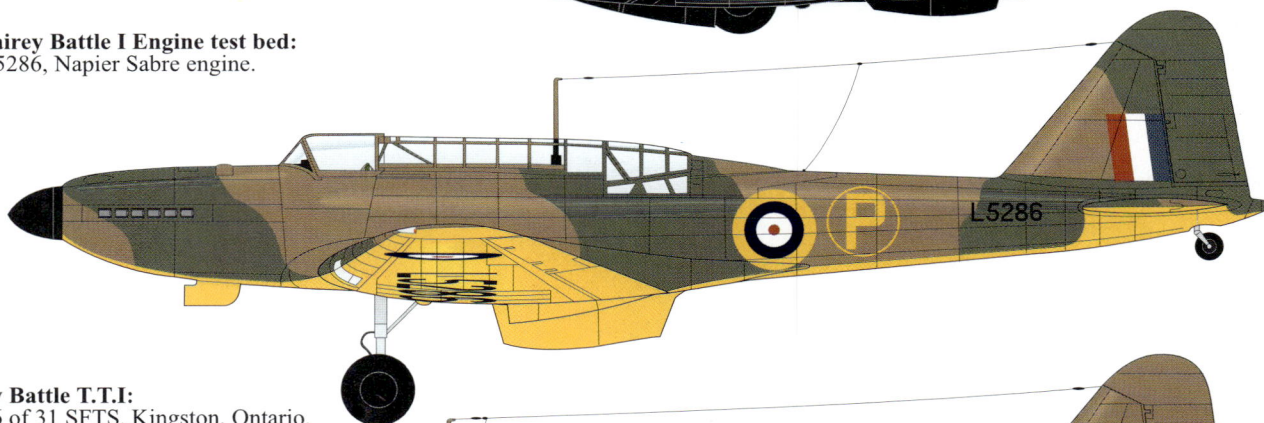

Fairey Battle T.T.I:
R7416 of 31 SFTS, Kingston, Ontario,
Canada, July 1941.

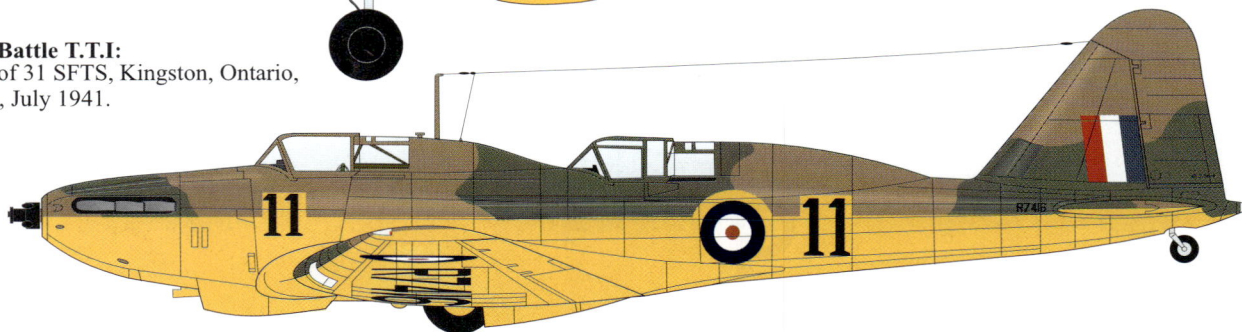

Fairey Battle I:
981, A-8 of 41 Air School, East London
South African Air Force, circa 1941/2.

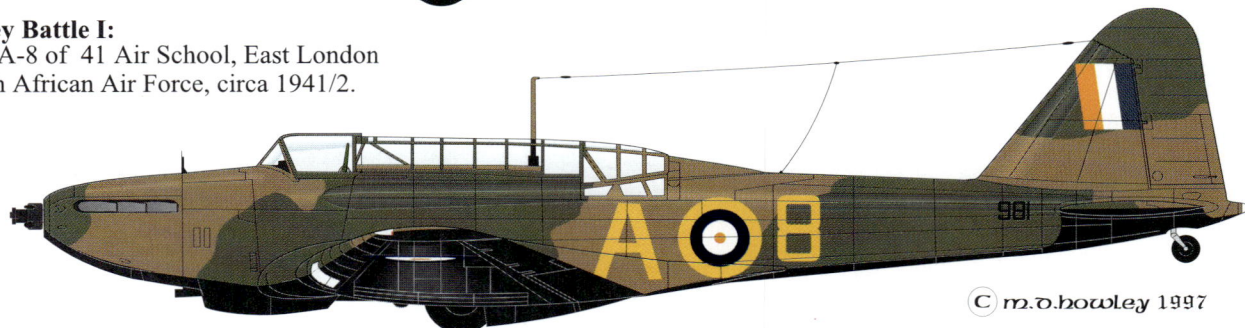

© m.o.howley 1997

Fairey Battle I (Engine test bed)
K9370, Fairey Prince engine, contra-rotating
propellers, shipped to the USA, 5 Dec. 1941.

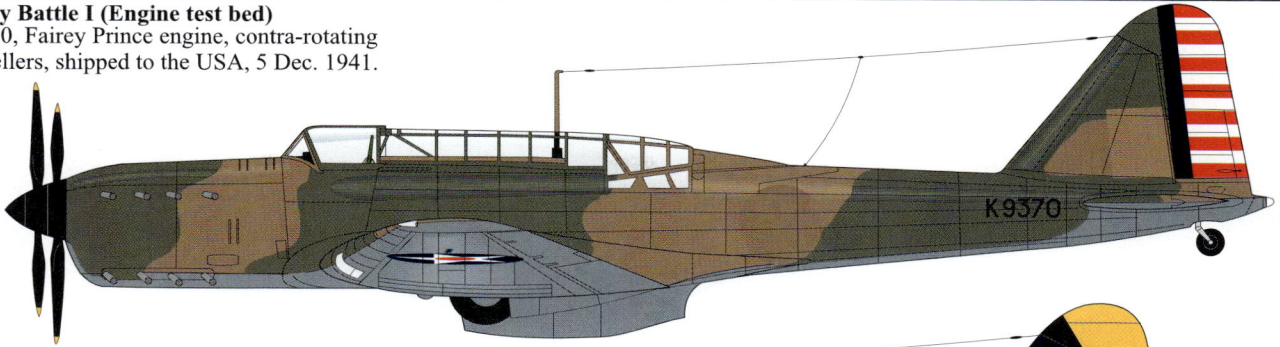

Fairey Battle I:
1639, 11 of No. 8 S.F.T.S., Moncton,
Canada circa 1943/44.

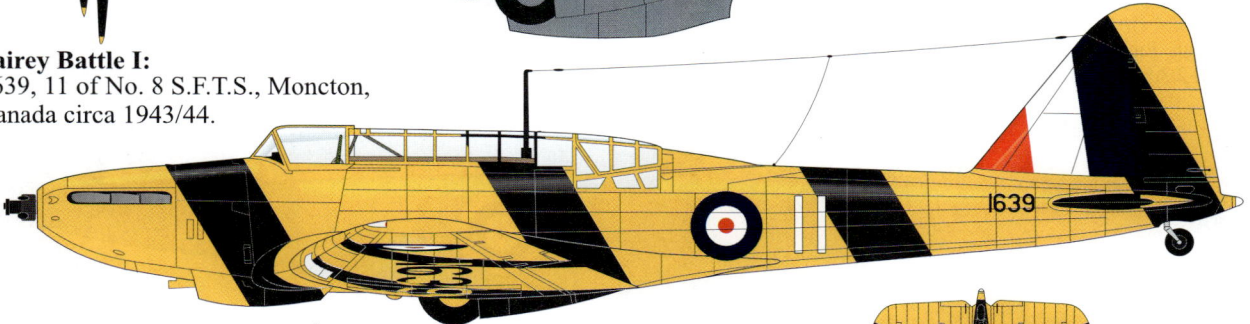

Upper and lower wing pattern on
Target Towing Battles.
Note:Starboard fuselage pattern
identical to Port.

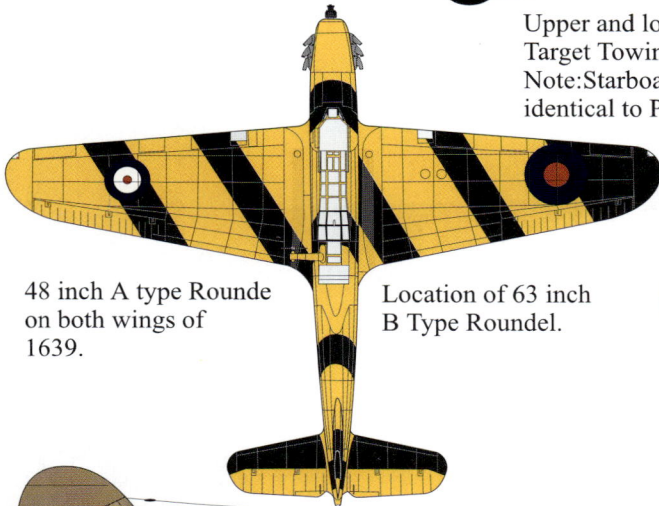

48 inch A type Rounde
on both wings of
1639.

Location of 63 inch
B Type Roundel.

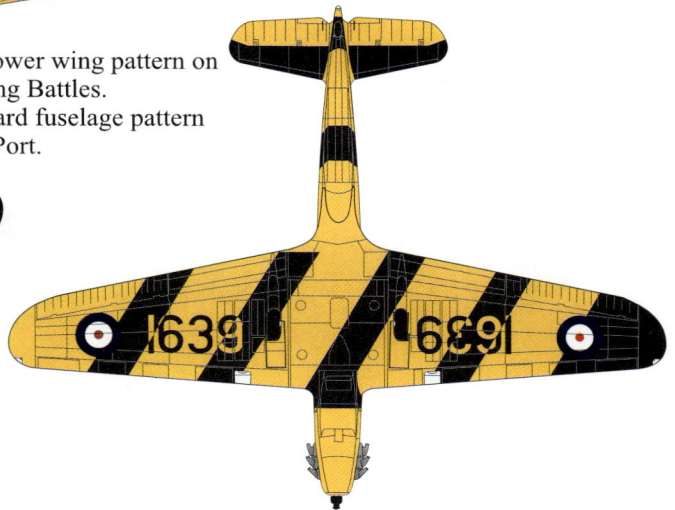

Fairey Battle T.I:
P6761, 5 of the Air Transport Auxiliary,
June 1942.

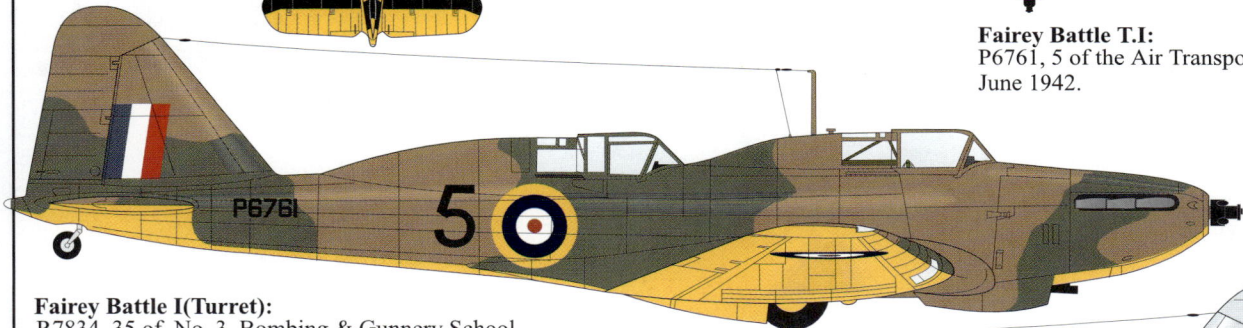

Fairey Battle I(Turret):
R7834, 35 of No. 3 Bombing & Gunnery School,
RCAF Macdonald, Manitoba, Canada, circa 1943/44.
(Note R of serial not applied).

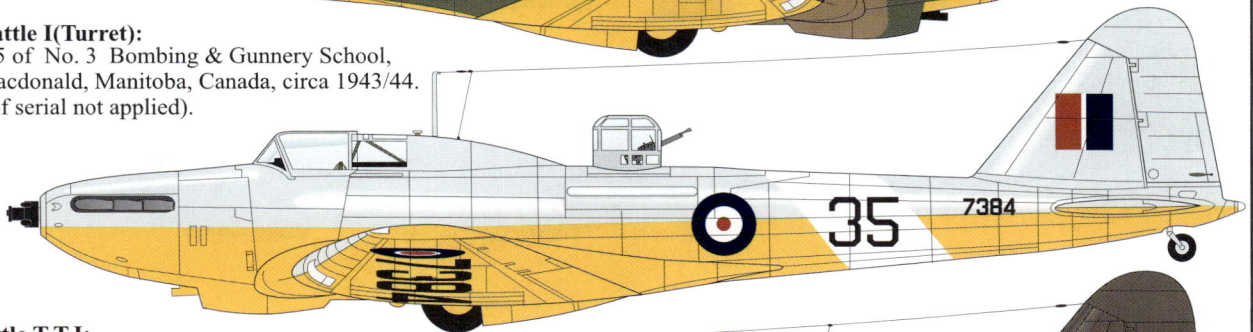

Fairey Battle T.T.I:
V1201, 01 of the Air Gunnery School, West Sale,
New South Wales, Australia, April.1944.

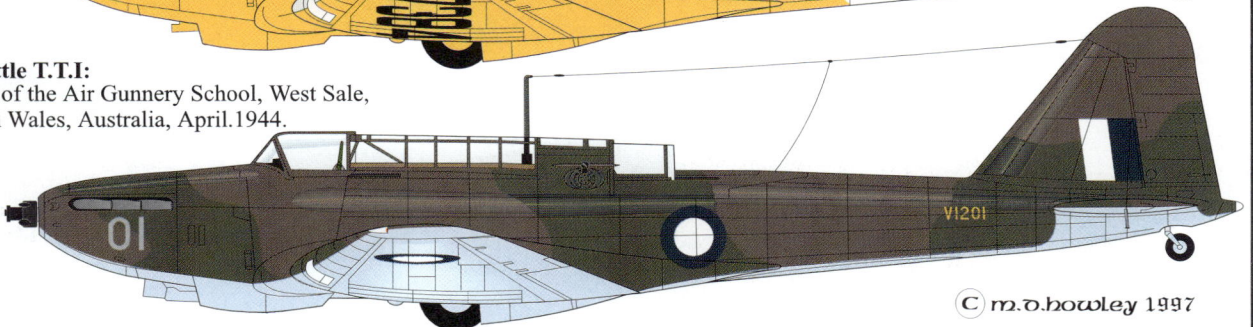

© m.o.howley 1997

Fairey Battle T.T.I:
V1238, 238 of the Air Gunnery School, West Sale,
New South Wales, Australia, 23 Dec.1944.

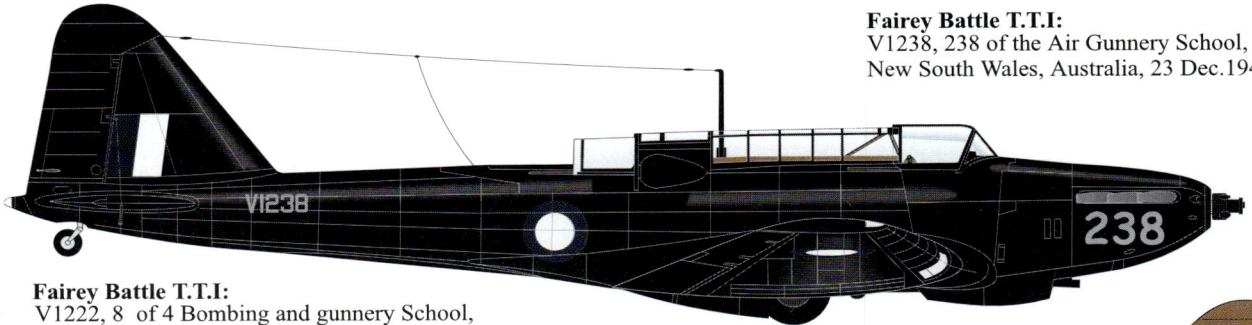

Fairey Battle T.T.I:
V1222, 8 of 4 Bombing and gunnery School,
West Freugh, force landed at Tramore, Waterford,
Ireland on 2 April 1941.

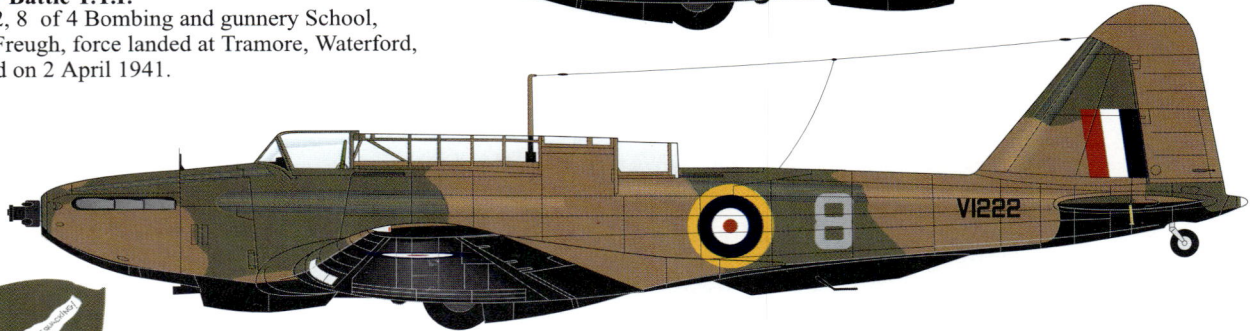

Donald Duck nose-art on 92.
Bullet holes in the banner read
"GET QUACKING".

Fairey Battle I:
92 (Ex-V1222) of the Irish Air Corps, 1941 to 1946.

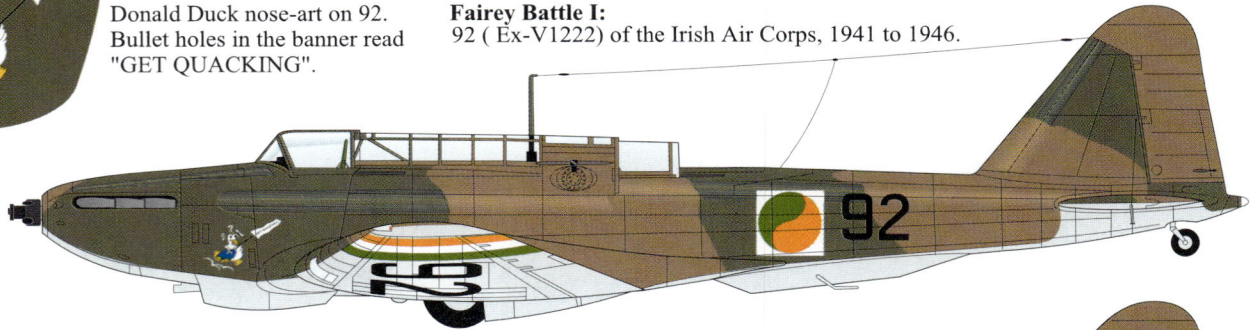

Fairey Battle I:
T66 of 3rd Air Regiment, Evere, Belgium.1939.

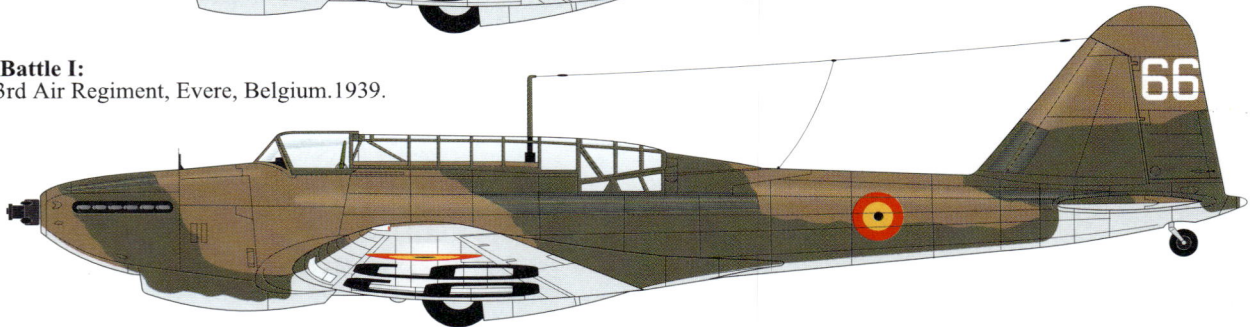

Fairey Battle I:
B282, 33 Mira, Royal Hellenic Air Force
circa 1939/40.

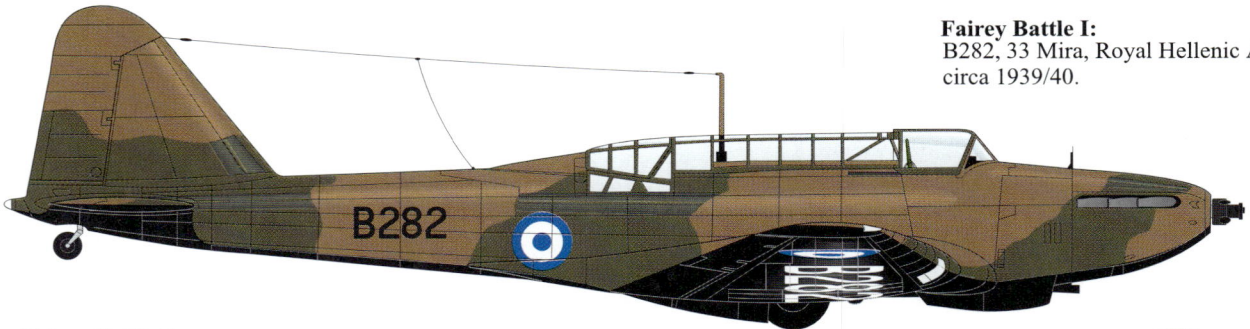

Fairey Battle I:
2829 (Ex-RAF ?????) of the Turkish Air Force
circa 1939/40.

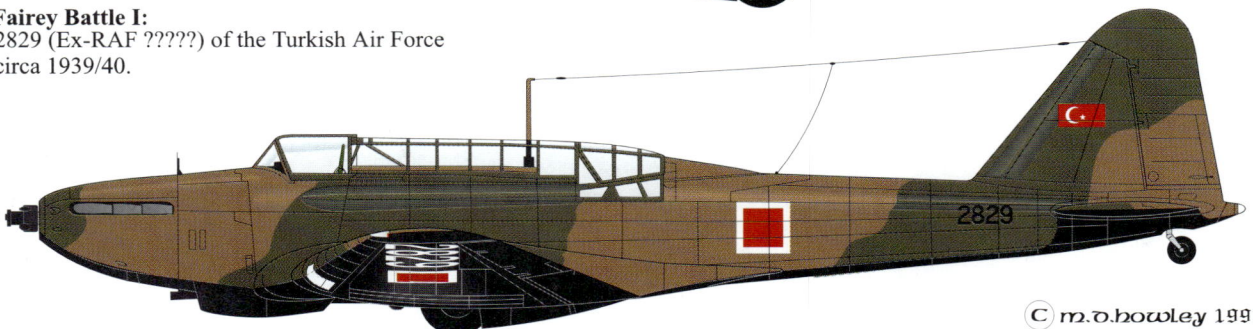

© m.o.howley 1997

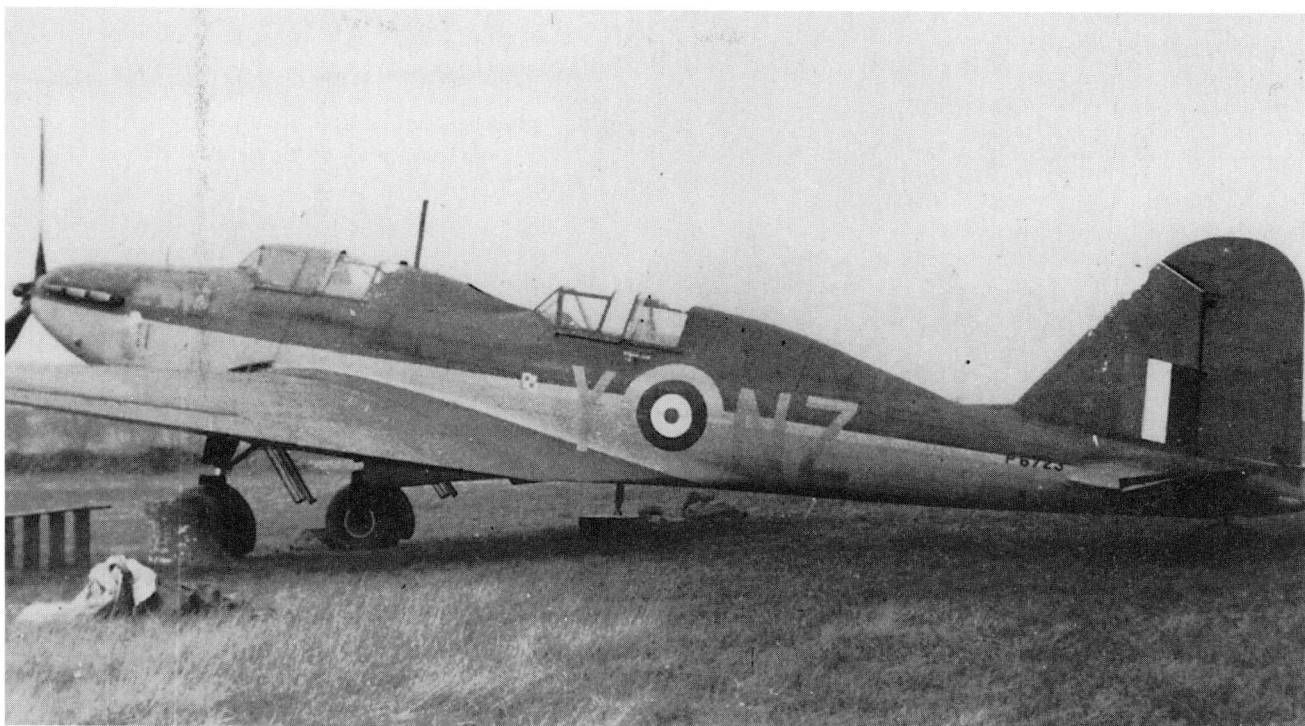

Battle Trainer P6723 served with No.304 Squadron of the Polish Air Force. (D Thompson collection)

No.8 AGS

Five Battle T.T. target tugs and one Battle were received from No.8 B&GS in 1941 when they were no longer needed by the B&GS. Both units were based at Evanton. The Battle T.T.s were:
L5670, L5678, L5732, V1226 and V1239.
The Battle was N2064.
The target tug V1239 crashed in a forced landing near Loth, Sutherland, on 20 August 1941 and was struck off charge shortly afterwards. The remaining aircraft were transferred to MUs late in 1941 to be prepared for sending overseas.

Air Armament School

No.1 AAS was transferred from Eastchurch to Manby in August 1938 and was the RAF's main armament training centre. Several types of aircraft, including Battles, were used there. The Battles started to arrive at Manby in December 1938 and continued to arrive until July 1939. Many of these had left the unit by January 1940, when more Battles started to arrive and continued to do so until July 1940. Most of these had been transferred to other units by the end of September 1941. One more Battle and three Battle T.T.s were received in mid 1941 but these were only with the school for a very short time. Three Battles were damaged beyond repair in accidents in October 1939. K7592 crashed at Manby when it stalled while landing and its wing hit the ground. K7598 bellylanded in a field after its engine failed on 10 October. K7593 crashed into the ground when its engine stalled during an air firing exercise at Theddlethorpe ranges on 13 October; all three occupants were killed. On 19 December 1939, K7658 was badly damaged when it belly-landed at South Cockerington Grange, Lincs., after engine failure. While on gunnery practice on 28 October 1940, L5027 stalled and

crashed into the sea near Donna Nook, Lincs. All three occupants were killed. The 58 Battles which served at the school were:
K7566, K7573, K7576, K7578, K7583, K7588, K7592, K7593, K7595, K7597, K7598, K7620, K7621, K7624, K7628, K7646, K7650, K7653, K7655, K7658, K7660, K7662, K7663, K7665, K7666-K7669, K7673-K7675, K7679, K7684-K7686, K9221, K9231, L4999, L5003, L5017, L5023, L5027, L5046, L5129, L5140, N2063, N2065, N2083, N2084, N2086, N2090-N2092, N2225, N2228, N2240, P2322 and P2323.
The three Battle T.T.s were L5666, L5709 and L5785.

Central Gunnery School

The CGS was formed at Warmwell in November 1939. Five Battles, K9267, K9291, K9296, K9298 and K9388, were received by the unit in November 1939 and L4996 was received in March 1940. All left the school in 1940. Battle P5248 was at the school from February 1941 to April 1942. Nine Battle T.T. target tugs served with the school at various times between June 1940 and March 1942. They were:
L5710, L5720, L5722-L5725, V1234, V1238 and V1243. L5724 was destroyed in an air raid on Warmwell on 1 April 1941.

Day Fighter Squadrons

From early 1939 into 1940, when the day fighter squadrons were re-equipping with modern aircraft, Battles and Battle (T) trainers were widely used to familiarise pilots with modern high-powered single-engined monoplanes. Most of the fighter squadrons had one or two Battles or Battle (T)s, some had three or four and three squadrons, Nos. 235, 253 and 266, were completely equipped with Battles pending the arrival of their Spitfires or Hurricanes. Many of these Battles were dual control versions.

No.235 Squadron

The squadron was reformed in October 1939 and received 17 Battles in December 1939 for training. Its brief use of the Battles ended in February 1940 when the crews converted to Blenheim Is. The Battles were:
L5005, L5007, L5008, L5014, L5016-L5018, L5032, L5132, L5133, L5312, L5379, L5381, L5383, L5406, L5412 and L5413.

No.253 Squadron

Also reformed in October 1939, the squadron received 16 Battles in December 1939 and these were used for training until they were replaced by Hurricanes early in 1940. The Battles were:
L5089, L5094-L5096, L5099, L5100, L5105, L5108-L5110, L5126, N2251, N2252 and N2256-N2258.
On 16 January 1940 the engine of N2258 cut in a snowstorm and the aircraft bellylanded near Manston. It was struck off charge shortly afterwards. The squadron retained a small number of Battles after its conversion to Hurricanes and on 3 August 1940, L5110 caught fire in the air and was abandoned near Newcastle.

No.266 Squadron

The squadron was reformed in October 1939 and received 20 Battles in December 1939 and January 1940. From January 1940 the Battles were replaced by Spitfires and the last Battle left the squadron in June 1940. The Battles were:
L5031, L5034, L5342, L5343, L5348, L5350, L5365, L5368, L5369, L5374, L5375, L5442, N2102, N2103, P5240, P5244, P5246, P5248, P5250 and P5251.
On 9 December 1939 L5350 landed with its undercarriage unlocked at Sutton Bridge. It was sent to Rollasons in January 1940 but did not re-enter RAF service. The engine of L5348 cut in a snowstorm on 16 January 1940 and it hit a hedge as it force landed at East Kirby, Notts. It was damaged beyond repair. On the following day P5244 crashed on take-off at Sutton Bridge and was badly damaged.

Battles were first allocated to fighter squadrons in February 1939. The squadrons receiving them, the aircraft received and the dates received are listed below. The list omits Nos.235, 253 and 266 Squadrons, which are dealt with above.

No.1 Squadron: K7580, 13.3.39.
No.3 Squadron: K7581, 9.5.39.
No.17 Squadron: K7582, 11.5.39; P6732, 25.6.40.
No.19 Squadron: K7656, 17.2.39.
No.32 Squadron: K7659, 21.2.39.
No.41 Squadron: K7651, 18.2.39.
No.43 Squadron: K7693, 15.2.39.
No.46 Squadron: K7652, 17.2.39.
No.54 Squadron: K7571, 13.2.39; K7629, 3.4.39.
No.56 Squadron: K7647, 10.2.39.
No.65 Squadron: K7680, 16.2.39.
No.66 Squadron: K7677, 16.2.39.
No.72 Squadron: K7676, 15.2.39.
No.73 Squadron: K7619, 15.2.39.
No.74 Squadron: K7629, 15.2.39; K7571, 3.4.39.
No.79 Squadron: K7590, 15.3.39.
No.87 Squadron: K7596, 15.2.39; K7654, 17.2.39;

K7636, 25.5.39.
No.111 Squadron: K7584, 18.2.39.
No.141 Squadron: L5133, L5406, 27.3.40;
L5014, 11.4.40.
No.151 Squadron: K7678, 16.2.39.
No.213 Squadron: K7586, 2.3.39.
No.234 Squadron: L5365, L5369, P5250, 14.2.40;
N2102, 24.2.40.
No.242 Squadron: L5014, L5133, L5406, 29.12.39.
No.245 Squadron: L5031, 9.2.40; P5240, 14.2.40.
P5251, 10.2.40.
No.264 Squadron: N2129, N2159, 16.12.39;
L5034, 16.3.40; L5105, 5.1.40.
No.302 Squadron: P6687, 19.7.40, Battle (T).
No.303 Squadron: R7399, 25.7.40, Battle (T)
No.306 Squadron: R7410, 10.9.40, Battle (T)
No.308 Squadron: P6687, 17.9.40; R7399, 25.9.40.
Battle (T)s.
No.310 Squadron: P6725, 20.7.40, Battle (T)
No.312 Squadron: R7409, 21.10.40, Battle (T)
No.316 Squadron: R7410, 23.7.41, Battle (T)
No.317 Squadron: R7399, 15.4.41, Battle (T)
No.501 Squadron: N2089, N2090, 17.3.39; N2094,
N2095, 20.3.39.
No.504 Squadron; N2091, 17.3.39. N2092, N2096,
N2097, 20.3.39.
No.602 Squadron: N2102, N2103, 23.3.39.
No.605 Squadron: N2108, N2109, 29.6.39.
No.609 Squadron: N2098, N2099, 10.5.39.
No.610 Squadron: N2106, N2107, 22.5.39.
N2064, N2066, 25.5.39.
No.611 Squadron: N2100, N2101, 10.5.39.
No.616 Squadron: N2027, N2031, N2104, N2105
16.5.39.

There were few serious accidents to the above aircraft while they were in the hands of the fighter squadrons. On 6 May 1939 K7654, No.87 Squadron, crashed on approach to a forced landing at Balsham, Cambs., after its engine cut. N2102 of No.234 Squadron was damaged beyond repair when its engine cut and it bellylanded and hit a hedge near York on 27 February 1940. On 16 December 1939 N2159 was abandoned over Hintlesham, Suffolk, when its engine cut. This aircraft was with No.264 Squadron, as was N2129 when it crashed near Braintree, Essex, during a forced landing in bad weather on 11 March 1940.

Night Fighter Squadrons

A small number of Battles, Battle (T) trainers and Battle T.T. target tugs were allocated to night fighter squadrons. The squadrons receiving them, the aircraft received and the dates received are shown below.

No.29 Squadron: L5781, L5796, 16.10.40.
L5778, L5779, 24.10.40. All
Battle T.T. target tugs
No.96 Squadron: R7409, 14.2.41. Battle (T)
No.255 Squadron: N2174, 27.7.42.
No.256 Squadron: P6685, 14.4.41, Battle (T)
No.307 Squadron: R7411, 7.9.40. P6685,
24.11.40, Battle (T)s
No.600 Squadron: L5032, 27.2.40.
The four Battle T.T.s with No.29 Squadron were used for flare towing trials, as described in Chapter 19. On 30 October 1940 R7411, No.307 Squadron, was abandoned near Goole, Yorks.

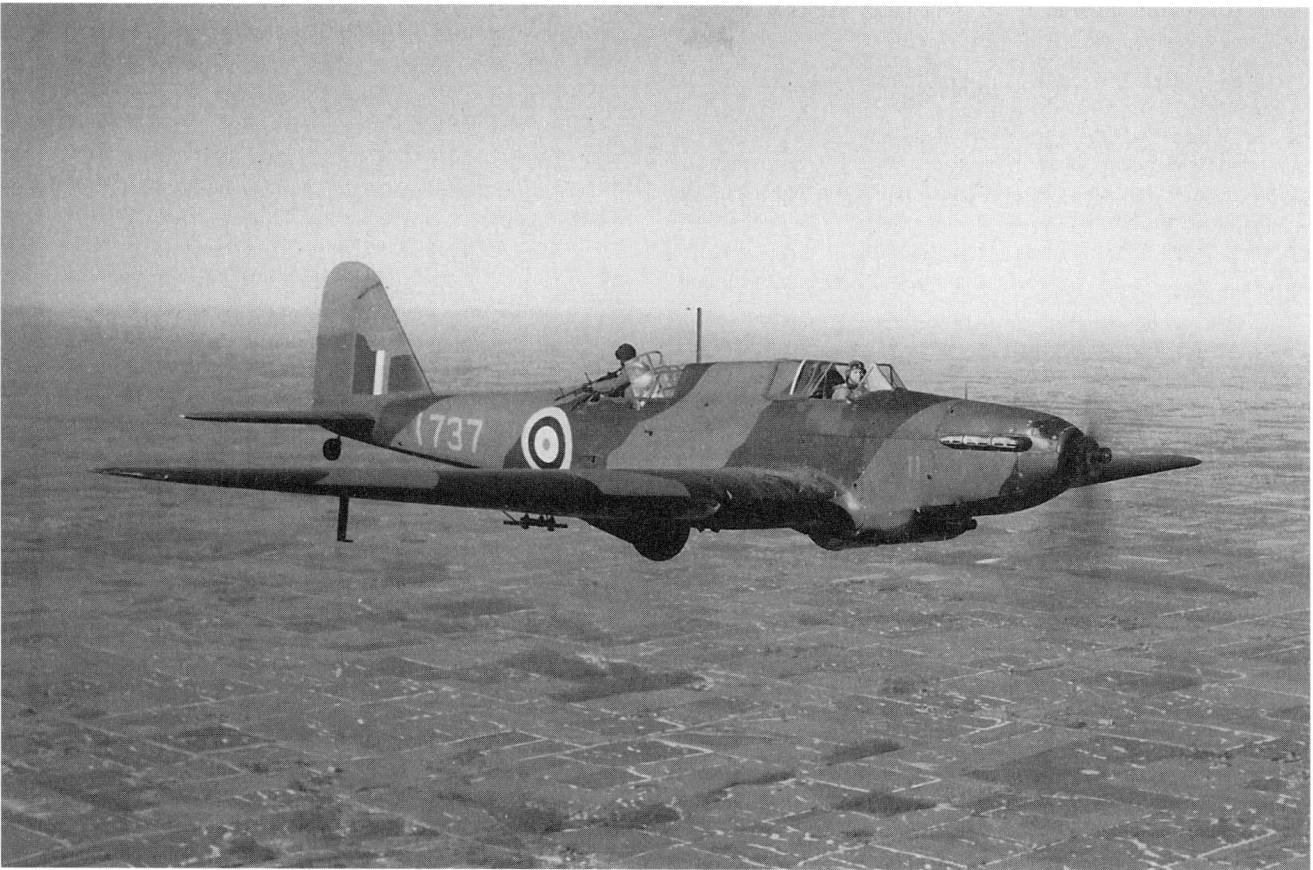

Battle 1737 of No.4 Bombing & Gunnery School, Fingal. (P Jarrett collection)

CHAPTER 15. CANADA

Canada was the largest provider of aircrew training facilities in the British Commonwealth Air Training Plan and large numbers of training aircraft were needed there. Early in the war there were large stocks of surplus Battles in the UK which could be used for aircrew training and many of these were sent to Canada. Over one-third of all the Battles built ended their lives in Canada.

The total number of Battles shipped to Canada was 754, nearly all of which were used in the Air Training Plan. Of these, 743 were sent from the UK and 11 were sent from Reykjavik in Iceland, where they had been serving with No.98 Squadron on anti-invasion patrols. Ten Battles which left the UK on 24 May 1941 failed to reach Canada and were presumably lost at sea. Four aircraft went to Canada and then on to Australia and they were not taken on charge by the RCAF. This left 740 Battles which were taken on the strength of the RCAF. The RCAF serial numbers 1301-1320 and 1601-2140 were allocated to 560 aircraft, RAF serial numbers were retained by 173 and RCAF 'A' series numbers were allotted to seven which were sent as ground instructional airframes. The RCAF received twenty Battles in 1939, 332 in 1940, 377 in 1941 and eleven in 1942.

In Canada most of the Battles were used by Bombing and Gunnery Schools in separate bombing, gunnery and target towing flights. The Service Flying Training Schools also used

a number of Battles. The first twenty Battles to go to Canada, Nos. 1301-1320, were sent in August 1939 and initially they were allotted to operational RCAF units, but most were later absorbed into the training organisation. The 740 RCAF Battles consisted of 632 bombers, 85 Battle (T) trainers and 23 Battle T.T. target tugs. Some of these aircraft were dual control. The RCAF converted 104 of the bomber Battles to target tugs. The open gunner's cockpit in the Battle was not considered suitable for gunnery training in Canada and 212 aircraft were fitted with Bristol single-gun manually-operated turrets. In 1943, it was feared that the supply of Merlin engines might run short and R7439 was fitted with a Wright Cyclone radial engine to see whether this engine could be substituted satisfactorily for the Merlin. The fear proved groundless and no further Cyclone engines were installed in Battles. Inevitably, many of the Battles were written off in training accidents and some were cannibalised when spare parts were in short supply. More modern types of aircraft were being supplied to the training schools in 1942 but Battles were in use in Canada throughout the war, though most of them had been put into storage then struck off charge by the end of the war. By 31 December 1943, 211 Battles had been struck off charge, followed by 224 in 1944, 197 in 1945 and 107 in 1946. One Battle, R7384, was preserved in Canada for the National Aviation Museum.

Training

A large organisation was set up to deal with the massive Canadian training plan. There were four Training Commands spread across Canada from Montreal in the east to Calgary in the west. Included in the structure were 11 Bombing and Gunnery Schools, all of which used Battles at some time. The Bombing and Gunnery Schools are listed below under their respective Training Commands.

No.1 Training Command, Toronto
No.1 B&GS, Jarvis
No.4 B&GS, Fingal
No.6 B&GS, Mountain View
No.31 B&GS, Picton

No.2 Training Command, Winnipeg
No.3 B&GS, Macdonald
No.5 B&GS, Dafoe
No.7 B&GS, Paulson

No.3 Training Command, Montreal
No.9 B&GS, Mont Joli
No.10 B&GS, Mount Pleasant.

No.4 Training Command, Calgary
No.2 B&GS, Mossbank
No.8 B&GS, Lethbridge.

The Schools numbered 1-10 were set up by the RCAF and No. 31 came under the control of the RCAF after it was transferred to Canada from the UK. The rugged construction of the Battle made it particularly suitable for training use and the Battles acquitted themselves well in Canada. There were, inevitably, maintenance problems in the tough northern winters, compounded in some instances by a shortage of trained personnel. Spare parts were sometimes difficult to obtain and much ingenuity was shown in manufacturing parts where this was possible.

No.1 B&GS, Jarvis, Ontario

Six Battles arrived at Jarvis on 9 August 1940, to be followed by others on succeeding days, and the first Air Observers course started on 19 August. There were four flights on the station, Maintenance, Gunnery, Bombing and Towing. By 31 March 1941, there were 58 Battles on charge and 31 other types, mainly Fleet Finches. The station's first fatal accident occurred on 6 July 1941, when Battle 1803 crashed and burst into flames. The pilot baled out, but two pupils, LACs C. Taggart and R. McNabb, were killed and the aircraft was a complete write-off. Two Battles collided in mid-air on 9 December 1941; 1814 crashed near Fisherville and its three occupants, FO E.J. Bounds, LAC J.S.W. Gray and LAC F.G. Barker, were killed. The other aircraft was 1604 which sustained damage to the port wing but landed at the aerodrome. Bolingbrokes started to arrive for training in the latter part of 1941 and by mid-1942 the station had a mixed bag of Battles, Bolingbrokes, Ansons and Lysanders on strength. Battle 1604 had another mid-air collision on 18 August 1942, this time with an Anson. The Battle crashed into Lake Erie, killing all three occupants, Sgt J.W. Whitehead, LAC A.C. Reed and LAC W.M. Kirby. The Battles were steadily replaced and by the end of 1942 there

were only nine on the station strength. The use of Battles at Jarvis ceased altogether in February 1943.

No.2 B&GS, Mossbank, Saskatchewan

The first three Battles flew into Mossbank from Trenton on 24 October 1940 and the School opened four days later. Flying exercises started on 7 November in very cold conditions and the School was handicapped by a lack of equipment. A steady stream of aircraft arrived at the station and the first air gunners course started operations on 27 November. While in transit from Winnipeg to Mossbank on 8 December, Battle 1730 suffered engine failure near Virden, Manitoba. The pilot was not able to attempt a forced landing because his vision was obscured by flames and smoke and he baled out and was injured on landing. The aircraft was a total loss. A subsequent Court of Enquiry decided that the trouble was caused by a glycol leak into the engine. Another transit accident occurred on 25 January 1941, when the pilot of Battle 1753 got lost in a snowstorm en route from Edmonton to Mossbank and made a wheels-up forced landing at Hanley. The aircraft was badly damaged and was later dismantled for freighting to Calgary.

The aircraft strength at 31 March 1941 was 55 Battles. Training continued and night flying started on 12 June 1941. On 11 April 1942 Battle 1900 caught fire in the air and the pilot force-landed on the bombing range. He was seriously injured and two pupils were slightly injured; the aircraft was burnt out. In mid-1942, replacement aircraft started to arrive at Mossbank and Lysanders were being used by the Towing Flight and Ansons by the Bombing Flight. Bolingbrokes were also brought into use. The pilot of Battle 1649 had a narrow escape on 18 May 1942 when he touched the bottom of Lake Johnstone with his wing tip while practising forced landings. At the time there were only a few inches of water in the lake. The wingtip of the aircraft was damaged, otherwise no harm was done. By the end of November 1942, there were only six Battles on the station strength and their use ceased completely in March 1943.

No.3 B&GS, Macdonald, Manitoba

The School opened on 10 March 1941 after the arrival of nine Battles during the preceding four days. Training commenced and by 30 April there were 64 Battles on the station. Following several minor mishaps, the first serious accident occurred on 23 June 1941, when Battle 1811 caught fire at 3,000 feet. The pilot, Sgt H.A. Switzer, made a good forced landing at St. Laurent and the crew escaped, but the aircraft was burnt out. Only four days later Battle 1806 crashed near the aerodrome, exploded and burned. The pilot and a trainee, Sgt W.G. Walker and LAC L. Fenner, were killed. A pilot was placed under open arrest when he failed to lower the undercarriage of Battle 1837 and belly-landed on the aerodrome on 11 August. It was recorded that there were no accidents at the school in October 1941 and that there had been 21 accidents since the School opened, including two fatalities. Training in bombing and gunnery continued until the end of June 1942, when notice was received that Macdonald was to become a straight gunnery school. On 11 July, Battle 1755 crashed near Longburn, 10 miles north-west of the station. All three occupants, Sgt N. Moss, LAC C. Off and AC2 J.P. Buzik, were killed and the aircraft was completely wrecked. The serviceability of the Battles was

An early arrival was 1628, seen at Camp Borden in the summer of 1940. (P Jarrett collection)

becoming a problem and it was recorded on 6 September 1942 that there had been "practically no flying today due to a shortage of serviceable aircraft". On 30 September, out of 71 Battles on the station, 43 were unserviceable. There was a serious incident on 14 October 1942 when Battle 1601 was alleged to have hit hydro-electric power cables, causing the death of two women by electrocution. At the subsequent trial, the pilot was found guilty of low flying and was reduced to the ranks and sentenced to six months hard labour. Battles fitted with gun turrets started to arrive on the station in November 1942 and there were 86 Battles on the strength at the end of the year, 69 of which were serviceable, showing a marked improvement on previous figures. Battles continued to be sent to Macdonald and on 31 January 1943 there was a total of 122 on strength. Technical troubles were being experienced with the operation of the gun turrets and spares were difficult to come by. Of 143 Battles on strength in mid-March, only 39 were serviceable, mainly because of operating and maintenance problems with the turret-equipped machines. The shortage of accommodation for the aircraft on the station was acute and in April all the free gun aircraft were picketed out in the open. The number of Battles on the station now started to decline and by 31 May 1943 it was down to 88, consisting of 64 turret Battles, 22 drogue towers and two dual-control versions. There was a mid-air collision between Battle 1736, a gunnery aircraft, and Battle 1886, a drogue aircraft, on 11 May 1943. Both aircraft were badly damaged but landed safely. On 17 August a fire started in the gunner's cockpit of Battle 2014 in mid-air. The pilot landed the aircraft on the aerodrome and the fire was extinguished, but the airframe was damaged and the Battle was sent to No. 8 Repair Depot and was written off. Another Battle, 1968,

caught fire in the air shortly after take-off on 6 November. The pilot landed the aircraft, the fire was put out but the Battle was a write-off. Another Battle, R4042, caught fire immediately after take-off on 4 December 1943. The pilot, WO A.T. Stevenson, landed blind with his wheels up and was badly burned but his crew were uninjured. The aircraft was a write-off.

There were 99 Battles on strength on 31 December 1943 and a further 31 Command Reserve Battles were stored at the station. Battle L5184 was wrecked on 22 January 1944 when it hit rocks after force-landing 8 miles north-west of the aerodrome. In early 1944, the Battles were being replaced by Bolingbrokes and Lysanders. By 31 March there were 66 Bolingbrokes and 32 Lysanders on strength and of the 106 Battles on the station, all but 23 were stored reserve aircraft. Use of Battles for training was discontinued and they remained in reserve until the school ceased operations in early 1945.

No.4 B&GS, Fingal, Ontario

The School opened on 25 November 1940 with a complement of Battles. On 8 December, Battle 1650 failed to return from a flight and two days later the wreckage of the aircraft was found on the beach at Fort Bruce. The aircraft had crashed into the lake and there were no survivors from the crew of FO L.A. Hood, AC2 E.W. Bourne and AC2 J.H. McNally.

The established training routine continued and there were the usual minor accidents to which all the schools were subject. Of 58 Battles on charge on 1 July 1941, 23 were in the Bombing Flight, 13 were in the Gunnery Flight and 22 were in the Drogue Flight. Night flying commenced in

1317 had a short flying life with the RCAF and is seen here at Camp Borden. (J McNulty via J Gradidge)

October 1941. Early in 1942 Bolingbrokes and Ansons started to arrive at the station and by the end of July the strength of Battles had fallen to 30. The Battles were steadily replaced by Bolingbrokes and Ansons for training and by Lysanders for target towing, and their use was discontinued by the end of 1942.

No.5 B&GS, Dafoe, Saskatchewan

Battles started to arrive at Dafoe on 8 May 1941 and training commenced at the School on 26 May. There were 37 Battles on charge on 31 May. On 16 September the airframe of Battle 1889 was seriously damaged when its drogue cable caught in the elevators. The aircraft was safely landed without casualties. The pilot, Sgt J.L.G. Cote, and two trainees, LAC C.A. Coles and LAC R.K. Crothers, were killed when Battle 2068 crashed into the ice on a lake on 1 December. Night bombing exercises started on 14 December. At the end of 1941, there were 56 Battles on the strength of the School. There was a mid-air collision between Battles 1892 and 2069 on 23 March 1942 which resulted in five fatalities. In aircraft 1892, LAC G.G.T. Hower, LAC E.P. Harris and LAC C.G. Harris were killed. In 2069, Sgt E. Naoum and LAC D.F. Hood were killed and Sgt W.M. Haggart baled out. Another fatal accident occurred on 23 July 1942 when Battles 1925 and 2066 collided in the air while landing. Both aircraft burst into flames on striking the ground. In 1925, LAC J.P.A. Bail was killed and LAC R.A. Ward and Sgt J.E. Parker seriously injured. In 2066, Sgt E.H. Dunn, LAC O.V. Nickerson were killed and LAC R.C. Parker injured. Ansons, Bolingbrokes and Lysanders started to replace the Battles in mid-1942 and by the end of April 1943 all Battles had left the station.

No.6 B&GS, Mountain View, Ontario

The School opened on 23 June 1941, when there were four Battles on charge. These were soon followed by others to bring the training complement up to strength. On 28 August there was an unusual assignment when 12 Battles were sent to Trenton for use in filming the propaganda film *Captains of the Clouds*. A film crew from Warner Bros. was at Mountain View in September for further work on the film. On 31 January 1942, there were 55 Battles on the station.

No.7 B&GS, Paulson, Manitoba

Paulson's first Battle arrived on 15 June 1941 and the School opened on 23 June 1941. There were 52 Battles on charge by 31 August. A bizarre incident occurred on 1 May 1942 when Battle 2039 was out on a routine bombing exercise. The pilot told his two pupils to look out but they thought he had told them to jump out and they took to their parachutes. Unfortunately one was injured. Ansons, Bolingbrokes and Lysanders started to arrive on the station to replace the Battles in mid-1942. There was a fatal accident on 2 September 1942 when Battle 1962 collided with Lysander 2389 and fell into Lake Dauphin. Sgt C.P.A. Lowe, LAC D.W. Duncan and LAC K.A. Lambert were killed. On 18 September, Battle 1877 crashed two miles from the station after engine failure. All three occupants, Sgt H.J.M. McNeill, LAC F.W.A. Musto and LAC W. Gilmour, were killed. By the end of January 1943, the School had stopped using Battles for training and the remaining 17 were in stored reserve. These had all been removed by 30 April 1943.

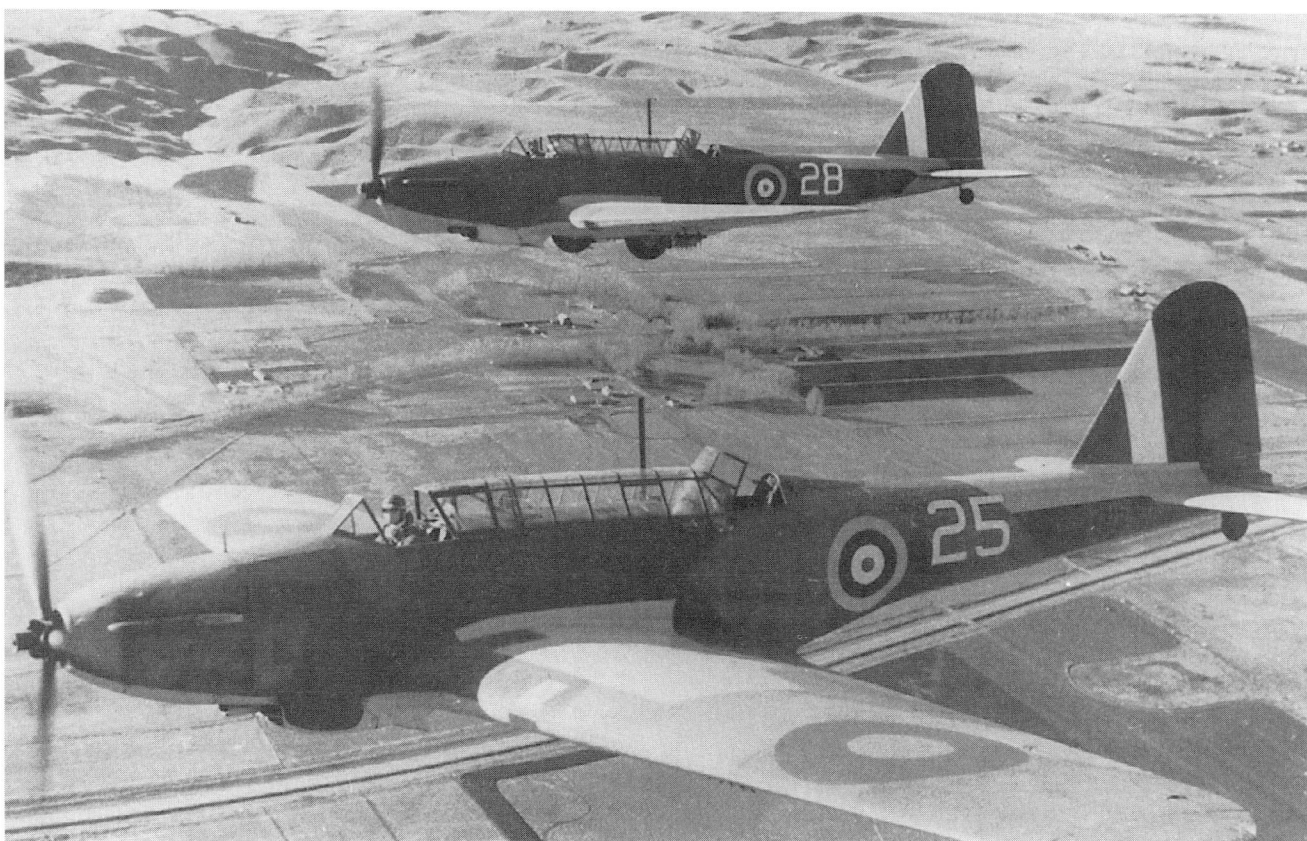

Battles of No.8 Bombing & Gunnery School, Lethbridge. (Bud Saunders via David Howley)

No.8 B&GS, Lethbridge, Alberta

The Lethbridge School opened on 13 October 1941 and there were 56 Battles on charge by 30 November. On 13 January 1942, Battle 2067 caught fire while on a camera gun exercise. The aircraft was totally destroyed but there were no injuries. Replacement of the Battles with Ansons, Bolingbrokes and Lysanders began in July 1942. Battle R4000 crashed after engine trouble on 19 August 1942 and the three occupants, Sgt L.P. Low, LAC G.G. Morin and LAC R.B. Sandman, were killed. On 4 December 1942, Battle 2070 was on routine camera gun exercises when it caught fire and crashed nine miles from the station. Sgt E.L. Williams and LAC E.T. Aikens were killed and LAC E.W. Armstrong seriously injured. The last of the Battles had been replaced in May 1943 and all had departed from Paulson by the end of that month.

No.9 B&GS, Mont Joli, Quebec

Opening day at Mont Joli was 15 December 1941 and there were 47 Battles on charge by the end of March 1942. The winter snow caused a number of minor accidents, mainly nosing over and damaging the propeller. While on a routine gunnery exercise on 19 May 1942, Battle 2022 crashed and burned, possibly because of a severe glycol leak. The pilot, PO A.F. Halamka, an instructor, Cpl C.J. Rooke and two trainees, LAC I.J. Shaw and LAC K.G. Weal, were killed. In response to a reported U-Boat attack on a convoy in the St. Lawrence River on 6 July 1942, two Battles and four Kittyhawks went to the scene but failed to find the U-Boat.

Each Battle was armed with two 250-lb depth charges. Battles continued to arrive at the station and on 31 January 1943 the aircraft strength was 121 Battles and 27 other types. There were 41 bomber Battles, 64 turret Battles, 15 drogue Battles and one dual control Battle. There was a fatality on 31 May 1943 when Battle 1960 crashed at Escourt, killing the pilot, Sgt G.W.M. Brochu. On 27 July, Battle 1648 crashed six miles from the station, killing F/Sgt D.J. McLean RNZAF and AC2 H. Revzen RCAF. In a collision between Battles 1949 and L5556 on 7 October 1943 both aircraft were destroyed and four were killed. In aircraft 1949, LAC S.G. Trueman was killed and LAC R.E. Peavoy seriously injured; in L5556, F/Sgt R. Dean, LAC E.W. Astell and LAC K. McKinstry were alll killed. Not all was sweetness and light between the RCAF and the local community; in January 1944 a farmer was fined 500 dollars for having 14 drogues in his possession. There was a tragic accident on 29 January 1944 when Cpl F.W. Jones became jammed in the turret of a Battle returning from a gunnery exercise and was strangled by the Bowden cable from the master hydraulic valve. The School continued to use Battles until training ceased; on 30 April 1945 there were still 75 Battles at Mont Joli.

No.10 B&GS, Mount Pleasant, Prince Edward Island

The Mount Pleasant School opened in November 1943, much later than the other Bombing and Gunnery Schools. Bolingbrokes were used for training, the Battles being confined to target towing duties. There were 22 drogue Battles on the station at the end of 1943. On 31 December 1943, Battle 2057 crashed near the station and its three

Turret-Battle R7384 of No. 3 Bombing & Gunnery School has lost its prefix letter, probably during conversion by CCF.
(P Jarrett collection)

occupants, Sgt W.J. Pearson, AC2 D.M. Scanlon and AC2 H.W. Huntula, were killed. Bolingbroke target tugs started to replace the Battles and all the Battles had left the School by 30 September 1944.

No.31 B&GS, Picton, Ontario

This was a RAF School transferred from the UK, arriving at Picton on 3 April 1941. Training started very shortly after arrival and night flying commenced on 1 August 1941. On 13 August, Battle 1907 collided with a Yale in the air; both of the pilots had "miraculous escapes". By the end of 1941 there were 55 Battles on charge. On 11 March 1942, K9194 force-landed on Wampoos Island after suffering engine failure and was completely wrecked.

The poor serviceability of the Battles caused problems in carrying out the training programme; night bombing training was cancelled in April until serviceability improved or until Bolingbrokes or Ansons were made available. By 30 June 1942, the 52 Battles on charge had been supplemented by 26 Ansons and 9 Lysanders. In July 1942 it was noted that the Battles were unable to fly more than two hours before becoming unserviceable, mainly because of glycol leaks and a lack of staff to repair them. This poor availability was still interfering with the training programme. On 14 August 1942 L5427 crashed into Lake Ontario and the pilot, Sgt B. Kempton-Werchie, RNZAF, and two trainees, LAC H.C. Pigerham and LAC D.N. JOnes, were killed. Towards the end of August 1942 Bolingbrokes started to arrive and with more Ansons and Lysanders available, the use of the Battles was much reduced. Of 45 Battles on charge, 22 were permanently unserviceable and were picketed out in the open. The run down of the number of Battles continued and all had left the station by 30 April 1943.

Aircraft Tables

The aircraft tables list the 740 Battles which were taken on charge by the RCAF. Seven of these were ex-RAF instructional airframes and were given RCAF numbers in the 'A' series. A further 46 Battles were reclassified as instructional airframes during their service with the RCAF.

Ten Battles left the UK for Canada on 24 May 1941 but did not arrive; they are presumed to have been lost at sea. They were: K9225, K9462, L5182, L5300, L5310, L5593, N2171, P6528, P6532, and P6551. Four Battles were sent to Canada on 11 May 1941 but they were not taken on charge by the RCAF and were subsequently sent on to Australia. They were: K7710, L5278, P5281 and P6493.

R7416 tips up in the snow at 31 B&GS, Kingston.
(M Lansman)

Two RAAF Battle target tugs at Pearce, WA, in 1942. (D Vincent collection)

CHAPTER 16. AUSTRALIA

Australia played a major part in the Commonwealth Air Training Plan and large numbers of aircraft were needed in the training schools. Many of these were sent from the UK and the rest were manufactured in Australia. The total number of Battles despatched to Australia was 367, of which 365 reached the RAAF. The remaining two, target tugs L5696 and L5698, were presumably lost en route to Australia. The numbers of Battles sent in each year are shown below.

1940 105 (incl. 45 Battle T.T. target tugs)
1941 125 (incl. 14 Battle T.T. target tugs and 7 Battle (T) trainers)
1942 126 (incl. 40 Battle T.T. target tugs and 4 Battle (T) trainers)
1943 11 (incl. 8 Battle T.T. target tugs)

Battles were used in the training schools mainly for bombing and gunnery training and target towing. Small numbers of Battles were used in pilot training, a few were in Communications Units and some Battle T.T.s were used by operational RAAF squadrons for target towing duties. While serving with the RAAF the aircraft retained their RAF serial numbers.

The first four Battles to be sent to the RAAF were despatched from the UK in March 1940 and they arrived at No.1 AP at Geelong, near Melbourne, at the end of April 1940. After assembly, flight testing commenced on 29 June 1940. Following this initial four, a steady stream of Battles

reached Australia in 1940, 1941 and 1942, with the numbers falling towards the end of 1942. The last Battle to be sent to Australia, target tug V1202, was despatched in October 1943. The use of Battles continued until after the end of the war, though many were withdrawn from service in 1944 and put into storage or written off. As is inevitable in any training organisation, several aircraft were lost in accidents. Some of the Battles suffered from severe corrosion and had to be written off. The write-off procedures for many of the aircraft were not completed until February 1949, but the RAAF had stopped using them well before that date.

Training

Battles served mainly at Nos.1, 2 and 3 Bombing and Gunnery Schools. In December 1943, there was a reorganisation of the Training Plan schools in Australia and No.1 Bombing and Gunnery School was merged with No.1 Air Observers School, No. 2 Bombing and Gunnery School was merged with No. 3 Air Observers School and No.3 Bombing and Gunnery School became the Air Gunnery School. Battles also served in smaller numbers at Central Flying School, Central Gunnery School, No. 4 Service Flying Training School, No. 6 Service Flying Training School, several Communications Units and in several RAAF squadrons.

Battles and Demons at No.1 Bombing & Gunnery School, Evan's Head, NSW, in November 1940. (P Jarrett collection)

No.1 BGS/1 AOS, Evans Head, New South Wales

This school was formed in August 1940 and it received its first 16 Battles in the following month. By the end of 1940, 44 Battles and 22 Battle T.T. target tugs had been delivered to the unit. Small numbers of aircraft, mainly replacements, continued to arrive at the school until November 1943. The school was merged with No.1 AOS when that unit moved to Evans Head in December 1943.

The school had its first major accident on 16 January 1941 when two target tugs, L5683 and L5700, collided in mid-air while being ferried from No.1 AD to Evans Head. Both aircraft crashed into the sea. In L5683 the pilot, P/O Norris, was killed. In L5700 the pilot, P/O Wright was killed and his passenger parachuted to safety. Two days later, on 18 January, Battle R3936 dived into the ground. The crew, P/O D.E. Allan and two trainees, were killed. While in flight from No.1 AD to Evans Head on 11 February 1941, Battle R4006 crashed at Moss Vale, New South Wales, killing the pilot, F/Lt Ross. After dropping its drogue on 30 March 1941, target tug L5609 was badly damaged in a forced landing. The pilot, F/O E. Bradbury and his one crew member were injured. The year 1942 seems to have been free of major accidents. On 10 February 1943, target tug V1232 dived into the ground one mile north-east of the airfield while towing a drogue. The crew of two, P/O M.A. Tait and one crewman were killed. There was a mid-air collision on 8 June 1943 when target tug L5650 hit Battle L4941. L5650 crashed into a swamp at Evans Head and the crew, Sgt G.W. Finch and one other were killed. L4941 managed to force-land and later continued in service. Battle L5082 was destroyed by fire when it force-landed at Evans Head after its engine failed

during a night take-off on 18 June 1943. While low flying on 14 January 1944, L5094 collided with a range hut, climbed to 400 feet, then crashed. The pilot, Sgt W.W. Hopper and two trainees were killed. Battle P2276 crashed on the beach at Disaster Bay while being ferried from Evans Head to No.1 CRD at Werribee, Victoria. The aircraft was salvaged and converted to components.

The Battles left the school in the first half of 1944, most of them destined for scrapping. In all, 87 Battles, 38 Battle T.T. target tugs and 4 Battle (T) trainers served in the unit.

No.2 BGS/3AOS, Port Pirie, South Australia

No.2 Bombing and Gunnery School was formed on 15 June 1941, and fifteen Battles had been received at Port Pirie immediately before that date. A further twelve Battles and ten Battle T.T. target tugs arrived at the unit in July 1940. By the end of October 1941, the school had 65 Battles, 17 Battle T.T. target tugs and one Battle (T) trainer. No more aircraft were received for a year, then small numbers of Battles and Battle T.T. target tugs were delivered to the unit, the last one being in November 1943. In December 1943, the school was redesignated No.3 AOS and only two Battles and one Battle T.T. target tug were received by the unit after that date. The school stopped using the Battles in early 1944, when most of them were sent for scrapping or were put into store.

The school was remarkably free from serious accidents in its first year of operation. On 13 August 1942, Sgt R.M. Plummer and his crewman were missing when target tug L5759 spun into the sea. On 22 November 1942, target tug L5760 stall turned and dived into the ground from 500 feet; the pilot, Sgt S.R. Scholz, and his crewman were killed.

L5387 in transit at Cootamundra, NSW, and apparently prepared for a gale. (Reg Lunnis via D Vincent)

After landing on 19 January 1943, a 20-lb bomb dropped off Battle K9426 and exploded. The aircraft's petrol tanks exploded and it was destroyed by fire, the crew and two ground crew being injured. Another Battle was destroyed by fire when L5070 force-landed because of a glycol leak and caught fire on 1 April 1943. After turning on its back, target tug L5640 spun and crashed on 20 May 1943. The pilot, Sgt L.J. Hampstead, and two others were killed. On 9 September 1943 there was a mid-air collision between Battle K9380 and target tug L5654. The pilots, Sgt R.A. Johns and Sgt G.N. Ninness, and the other four occupants of the two aircraft were all killed. On the same day, target tug L5653 took off with the starboard aileron locked. After climbing to 400 feet it dived into the ground and Sgt Scott and his crewman were killed. Engine failure forced L5710 to land on 8 October 1943 and it caught fire and was almost totally burned out.

Altogether, 114 Battles, 37 Battle T.T. target tugs and two Battle (T) trainers served in the unit.

No.3 BGS/AGS, East Sale, Victoria

No. 3 Bombing and Gunnery School was formed at East Sale on 12 January 1942. By mid-February 1942, 21 Battles, one Battle T.T. target tug and two Battle (T) trainers had been delivered to the school. Further aircraft, including 24 Battle T.T. target tugs, were received up to December 1943, when the school merged with the Air Gunnery School. After the formation of the AGS, the establishment of Battle T.T.s was increased and an additional 47 had been received by mid-March 1944. The school was disbanded at the end of 1945 but nearly all the Battles had been stored or sent for write-off by the middle of 1945.

After its engine caught fire on 16 September 1942, Battle K9375 force-landed and was burned out. The unit had its first serious accident on 22 October 1942 when Battle K9219 crashed two miles from West Sale after its engine failed. The crew, Sgt R. Rosevear and two trainees, sustained slight injuries after baling out. The aircraft was destroyed by fire. On 7 June 1943, flames were seen coming from the engine of Battle K9362 and it crashed at the Walla Wullock firing range. Sgt R.P. Stevens and two trainees were killed and the aircraft was destroyed by fire. During a forced landing on 17 November 1943, Battle P2263 hit some high tension wires and crashed. The pilot, F/Sgt J.S. Alexander was killed and two trainees were injured. The aircraft was burned out. After its engine started to smoke, target tug V1219 dived into the ground near Seaspring Safety Range on 18 August 1944. Sgt M.J. Fahey was killed and W/O G.F. Maley was uninjured.

Altogether 57 Battles, 80 Battle T.T. target tugs and six Battle (T) trainers served with the unit.

No.1 OTU

No. 1 Operational Training Unit moved from West Sale, Victoria, to Bairnsdale, Victoria on 12 June 1942, then to East Sale on 22 April 1943. Two Battle T.T. target tugs were received by the unit in December 1941, followed by a further seven in April 1942 and four in August 1942. A few more were received in 1942 and 1943, the last being delivered in August 1943. One Battle, N2228, was at the unit for a short time in March 1943 and a Battle (T) trainer, P6677, was there briefly in late 1943. One of the target tugs, L5765, was

Battles at West Sale, Victoria, home of No.1 Operational Training Unit. (Bill Penglase via D Vincent)

written off after it overran the runway at Mallacoota and hit a stump on 25 October 1942.

Altogether 23 Battle T.T. target tugs served with the unit. The Battle T.T.s had left the unit by January 1944, most of them going to the AGS.

CFS, Camden, New South Wales

The Central Flying School made very little use of Battles. Nine Battles were sent to the school in September 1940 but eight of them had left for No.1 BGS before the end of the month. The other Battle went to No.1 BGS in December 1940. A Battle T.T. target tug , L5751, was at the school for a few weeks in December 1940/January 1941 and a Battle (T) trainer, P6762, was there from November 1942 to January 1943 . A Battle was received by the unit in June 1944 but was designated an Instructional Airframe in September 1944.

Central Gunnery School

Seven Battle T.T. target tugs served with the Central Gunnery School. Three, L5617, L5657 and L5660, were received in August/September 1942. L5617 had sustained major damage in a forced landing shortly before it was sent to CGS and it was struck off charge within a few days of arrival. The other two stayed with the school until January 1945, when they were sent to the AGS. L5723 was received in May 1943 and L5655, L5697 and L5734 were received in June 1944. L5697 was sent to the AGS in January 1945 and the other two were sent to No.1 CRD in July 1945.

Communications Flights/Units

No.1 CF/CU, then based at Laverton, received five Battles and one Battle T.T. target tug in June/July 1941, but all had been sent to other units by the end of August 1941. The Battles were: K9322, K9468, L5529, L5551 and P6481. The Battle T.T. was L5791.

No.3 CF at Mascot had V1233, a target tug, on its strength for a few days in April 1943.

No.6 CU at Bachelor, Northern Territory, received three Battles in January 1944 and retained them until late April 1944. They were: L5390, P2317 and P6481.

No.7 CU at Pearce, Western Australia, received three target tugs in November 1943 and kept them until September/ October 1944, when they were sent to the AGS. The Battle T.T.s were L5774, L5778 and L5779.

Other Units

No.4 Service Flying Training School at Geraldton had two Battle T.T. target tugs; L5778 from May 1941 to February 1943, and L5779 from May 1941 to August 1942.

No.6 Service Flying Training School at Mallala received five Battles and a Battle T.T. target tug for brief periods in 1943 and 1944, apparently prior to them being written off. The Battles were: K9291, K9444, L4958, L5070 and N2045. The Battle T.T. was L5640.

L5156 of No.1 Bombing & Gunnery School over the coast near Evan's Head, NSW. (P Jarrett collection)

Several RAAF squadrons had one or two Battle T.T.s on their strengths at different times. L5791 was at No.12 Squadron at Darwin from July 1941 to March 1943. No.22 Squadron had L5764 from February 1942 to July 1942 and L5790 from July 1941 to July 1942. L5794 and V1232 were with No.24 Squadron from July 1941 to August 1942 and No. 35 Squadron held L5779 from September 1942 to November 1943.

There was a brief attempt to use a Battle T.T., V1235, for glider towing in late 1943. The project to tow gliders at No.2 AOS was abandoned after seven days, the aircraft being adjudged to be unsuitable for the work.

The gliders involved were probably de Havilland DHA.G1 troop-carriers but their production was halted after eight had been built.

Instructional Airframes

Thirteen Battles were taken out of service to be used as Instructional Airframes. Numbered 1 to 13, these were: L5142, K7705, K9297, L5529, ?, ?, ?, L5257, L5038, N2091, L5152, K9411 and K9324 respectively.

Disposal

After being put into storage in 1944 and 1945, most of the Battles were disposed of by being broken down into components, many of which were pushed into swamps, a sad end for an aircraft which had served its purpose in the Training Plan. A few Battles were sold for knockdown prices, e.g., £5, and some were used for testing the effects of incendiary bombs.

Surplus Battles in the boneyard at Port Pirie, SA. (Bill Penglase via D Vincent)

Battles of No.41 Air School in formation. (via Dave Becker)

CHAPTER 17. SOUTH AFRICA AND SOUTHERN RHODESIA

Training Schemes

Southern Rhodesia was the first country to operate the Empire Air Training Plan, later known as the British Commonwealth Air Training Plan, when the EFTS at Belvedere was opened on 25 May 1940. South Africa did not enter the main scheme, mainly for political reasons, but signed a separate agreement for the training of aircrew on 1 June 1940; this agreement established the Joint Air Training Scheme. Both countries used Fairey Battles as target tugs and the SAAF also used them for aircrew training. In addition, the SAAF used a number of Battles operationally in the East African campaign in 1940 and 1941, as described in Chapter 12. The training in South Africa was administered by the SAAF and that in Southern Rhodesia by the Rhodesian Air Training Group.

Southern Rhodesia

No. 24 Combined Air Observer School was formed at Moffat in August 1941 and was redesignated **No. 24 Bombing Gunnery and Navigation School** in May 1943. The school used Battle T.T. target tugs and 25 served there. The RATG records that eleven arrived in August/October 1941, followed by the rest in small numbers in 1942, 1943 and 1944. The Battle T.T.s were: L5641, L5642, L5668, L5686, L5688, L5690, L5716, L5720, L5722, L5732, L5733, L5737, L5742, L5783, V1212, V1226, V1229, V1247, V1265, V1268, V1276, V1279 and three others.

There were several accidents involving Battle T.T.s, none of which resulted in fatalities. On 1 September 1941 Sgt D.S. McGregor was piloting V1279 on drogue towing operations; while flying over Moffat aerodrome at 50 feet the aircraft stalled on to the ground with its undercarriage retracted. Engine problems caused several forced landings. The engine of L5686 overheated on 5 October 1943 causing the coolant to boil with subsequent loss of power; the pilot force landed in a small field but overshot, causing considerable damage to the aircraft. The other accidents at the school were fairly minor ones. In its Annual Training Report for 1944 the RATG commented on its Battle T.T.s as follows: "Other than the extreme age of these machines, calling for constant repairs and replacements, very little trouble has been experienced on the type". Three of the aircraft were struck off charge in 1943, eight in 1944, two early in 1945 and the remaining twelve in August 1945. The last courses of navigators and air gunners passed out of the school on 14 April 1945 and Moffat closed on 31 May 1945.

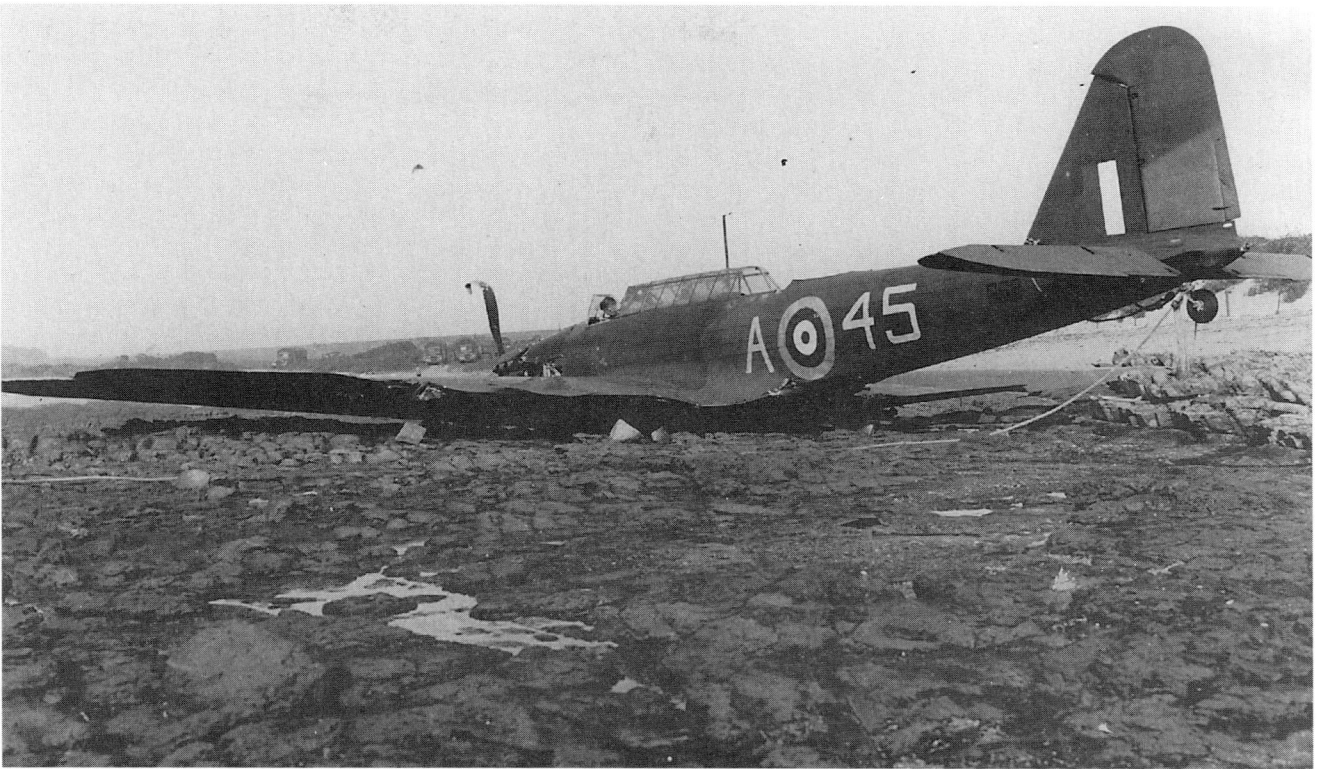

Battle 962 on the rocks near East London after ditching and being later washed ashore. (via Ken Smy)

South Africa

The SAAF made a major contribution to wartime aircrew training through its operation of the Joint Air Training Scheme, in which many different types of aircraft were used. Battles were used at the SAAF training schools for bombing, gunnery and navigation training and for target towing. The number of Battle aircraft shipped to the SAAF was 190, excluding four which were sent on to Australia, four sent on to India and eleven sent on to Southern Rhodesia. Eleven of the Battles were lost at sea en route to South Africa, leaving 179 for the SAAF. These bore the SAAF serial numbers 901-1082, excluding 1076-1078. The 179 aircraft consisted of 123 Battles, 51 Battle T.T. target tugs and five Battle (T) trainers. Some of the Battles were converted for target towing duties after arrival in South Africa. The main users of these aircraft were Nos. 1, 2 and 3 Combined Air Observer, Navigation, Bombing and Gunnery Schools, later redesignated as Air Schools.

The eleven aircraft lost at sea in transit to South Africa were Battles L5056, L5057, L5431, L5563, N2157 and N2169, on board SS *Huntingdon* lost February 1941; Battles K9389 and P5286, on board SS *City of Winchester* lost April 1941; Battle N2104 and Battle T.Ts L5748 and V1266, lost January 1943. It is likely that the three excluded SAAF serial numbers, 1076-1078, had been allotted to the last three of the aircraft lost at sea.

In 1940/41, 27 Battles were used operationally in the East African campaign. These were SAAF 901-920, 922-927 and 929. Most of the Battles in South Africa had been withdrawn from service by August 1944.

No.41 Air School

No. 1 Combined Air Observer, Navigator, Bombing and Gunnery School, based at Collondale, East London, was redesignated **41 Air School** on 30 April 1941. Battle aircraft started to arrive at the school in April 1941 and others followed. There was a shortage of aircraft for operational use if the war had spread to South Africa and Battles at Collondale were formed into a "shadow" squadron, No.141 Reserve Squadron, to operate as medium bombers if needed. Fortunately the necessity did not arise. Originally intended to be used as bombing and gunnery trainers, the Battles were used mainly for target towing and at the end of July 1943 there were 11 Battle T.T. target tugs and 1 Battle (T) trainer at the school. The increasing age of the aircraft, the shortage of spare parts and the rundown of the JATS led to the withdrawal of the aircraft in late 1944.

No.42 Air School

No. 2 CAONBGS, based at South End, Port Elizabeth, was redesignated **42 AS** on 30 April 1941. On that date there were 16 Battle aircraft at the school. By the end of 1941 there were 31 Battles on the strength of the unit.

No.43 Air School

No. 43 Air School was a Gunnery School and was formed at The Kowie, Port Alfred on on 12 January 1942. Battle aircraft started to arrive at the school in July 1942 and by July 1943 had 23 Battle target tugs and three Battle bombers there.

Battle 991, probably of No.41 Air School but it later served with 44 AS and 43 AS. (via Ken Smy)

No.44 Air School

The Navigation and Bombing School at Grahamstown was formed on 12 January 1942 and used Battles primarily for target towing. the school was using eleven Battles as target tugs at the end of July 1943. The use of Battles had been discontinued by the end of 1944.

No.45 Air School

This school was originally No. 5 Air Observer and Navigator School at Weston-super-Mare in England and was transferred to Oudtshoorn, where it opened on 1 December 1940. It was redesignated 45 AS on 30 April 1941. Battles were used as target tugs and the first five arrived in March 1943. By the end of July 1943 there were 14 Battle target tugs and one Battle (T) trainer on the strength. Use of the Battles was discontinued in the following year and the last of them left the unit in October 1944.

Nos.65 Air School and 66 Air Schools

No. 3 CAONBGS was formed at Youngsfield on 19 August 1940 and part of it became 65 AS, the Air Armament School, on 30 April 1941. Nos.65 and 66 Air Schools shared a pool of aircraft. Battles were in use there as target tugs.

Other Units

Small numbers of Battles were used by other units of the SAAF, as listed below.

62 AS, the former CFS, at Tempe, Bloemfontein.
68 AS, Technical Training School, at Voortrekkerhoogte.
69 AS, Technical Training School, at Germiston.
11 OTU, Fighter OTU, at Zwartkop then at Waterkloof.
THQ, Training Headquarters, Communications Flight.
71 Flight, Pilot Conversion Unit.

Kenya

Twelve Battles were transferred to No.133 MU at Eastleigh, Nairobi, Kenya, in February 1943. They were; K9269, K9286 (1064), L4945, L5014 (932), L5268 (975), L5543, L5549 (940), N2126 (938), P2179 (928), P6533, R4003 (933) and one other. Some more Battles were also transferred to Eastleigh and 17 serviceable Battles and two unserviceable Battles were held at the MU on 31 August 1943. No information is available about the use of these aircraft in Kenya, though one was held at 133 MU for locust spraying.

A formation of Belgian Battles over Evère. (via David Howley)

CHAPTER 18. EXPORTS

Battles for Export

Several countries showed an interest in the Battle before the Second World War and orders for a number of aircraft were received by the Fairey company, some of which were not fulfilled because of wartime conditions, or because war was threatened. All exported Battles were given RAF serial numbers before being sent abroad, with the exception of those sold to Belgium. There was an embargo on exports for some time during 1940 but this did not materially affect the release of Battles. Over half of all the Battles made were sent to countries operating the British Commonwealth Air Training Plan or, in South Africa's case, the Joint Air Training Scheme. Some of these were new aircraft, but many had seen service with the RAF.

Belgium

The Belgian Air Force bought 16 Battles (c/ns F3258 - F3273) which were delivered in 1938. Fairey owned a factory at Gosselies in Belgium but it was not equipped for building Battles and the 16 aircraft were made at the Stockport factory. These aircraft were fitted with an extended radiator intake and they had a smooth camouflage paint finish. They were powered by Merlin III engines and are reported to have been

marginally faster than the standard RAF Battles because of the smoother external finish. The Battles were used by 5eme Escadrille of IIIeme Groupe of the Belgian Air Force, based at Evère near Brussels. For identification, they carried the last two digits of the constructor's number on the fin.

Belgian pilots appreciated the increase in performance over their previous light bombers, the Fairey Fox biplanes built at Gosselies. Two Battles were lost in accidents before the German invasion, No.69 crashing near Eeklo on 8 December 1938 with the loss of the CO of the 5e Escadrille, Capt Jacques de Caters. He was succeeded by Capt Charly de Hepcée and, apart from the second-in-command and the adjutant, the pilots were NCOs. Most of the observers were from the Reserve.

When the Germans invaded on 10 May 1940, the escadrille had fourteen Battles on strength but Nos.65 and 67 were involved in a collision on the ground while No.63 was having engine maintenance. The eleven serviceable aircraft were dispersed to a landing ground at Belsele, midway between Ghent and Antwerp, to avoid damage from enemy air raids, in common with other units. This had little effect as small formations of German bombers attacked the field throughout the day, destroying No.66. The remainder moved quickly to Aalter where personnel from the 9eme Escadrille joined the 5eme. Orders came through to attack three bridges

Belgian Battle No.62 at Evère. (via David Howley)

over the Albert Canal next day.

However, in a gallant but hopeless attempt to bomb the bridges over the Albert Canal at Maastricht on 11 May 1940, six Battles out of nine dispatched were lost. Shortly after dawn, Nos. 58, 60 and 73, manned by crews for 9eme Escadrille and commanded by Capt Pierre, took off. Near Ghent, they encountered a formation of Do 17s and one Battle chased after them but was left behind as the Dorniers sped off, return fire wounding the pilot and gunner. No.60 was force-landed near Lebbeke.

The remaining two Battles continued towards Maastricht. No.58 was intercepted by three Bf 109s and shot down near Hasselt. No.73 reached the Veldwezelt bridge but the bombs hung up on the first run. Despite heavy flak, a second run was made and the bombs dropped a short distance from the bridge; the Battle escaped.

The second flight, consisting of Nos.61, 64 and 67, was only five minutes behind the first and its target was the bridge at Vroenhoven. Between Tongres and Maastricht, a column of enemy vehicles was met and machine-gunned. On arriving at the bridge, the Battles attacked in line astern. Two of the Battles had their bombs hang up while the third succeeded in dropping its bombs beside the bridge.

T70 went round for a second attempt and as the bombs were released by the pilot's control, it was hit by flak, caught fire and crashed. A similar fate met No.61 as it also tried for a second time.

Shortly afterwards, the third flight arrived, consisting of Nos.62, 68 and 71, aiming for the bridge at Briedgen. No.71 was hit by ground fire from Belgian troops and the observer badly injured; the pilot abandoned the mission and returned to base. No.62 was also hit and the crew baled out.

No.68 reached the bridge, being badly damaged by flak on the approach. After ordering the observer to jump, the pilot belly-landed the Battle and escaped.

Of the 18 crew members on this operation, five were killed and four injured. Only Nos. 64, 71 and 73 remained operational at Aalter while Nos.63, 65 and 67 were still at Evère.

An involuntary export took place on 13 May 1940 when a Battle from No.226 Squadron, P2353, force landed near Brussels after being hit by AA fire while on its way to attack enemy columns. The aircraft was taken over by the Belgian Air Force but could not be flown as it required 100-octane fuel while the Belgian Battles used 90-octane.

For a few more days, the surviving Battles undertook reconnaissance missions, which included some strafing attacks on German columns. No.73 landed at Aalter after a reconnaissance in the early hours of the 18th and soon afterwards German aircraft bombed and strafed the field, putting an end to the Battle's service in the Belgian Air Force.

Turkey

The delivery of four Battles, painted with Turkish colours, was stopped by the British Government in 1939, but later in the year the Government relented and 29 Battles were exported to Turkey between August and November of that year. These bore the serial numbers N2111-N2117, N2120-N2123, N2130, N2131, N2149, N2153-N2155, N2211-N2218, N2220-N2222 and N2224 and were new aircraft. A Battle T.T. target tug, L5623, went to the Turkish Air Force in May 1940. The 30 Battles were given Turkish Air Force

Greek Battle B282 of 33 Mira.
(Gen Kartalamakes via A Stamatopoulos)

The crew of a Greek Battle, Sophocles Baltatzes with his
gunner, Nikitides. (Gen Kartalamakes via A Stamatopoulos)

serial numbers 1-11 and 27-45. Early in 1940, four target towing Battles were allocated for export to Turkey, but these were not delivered. The fate of the Turkish Battles is not known but, given the flair of the Turkish pilots for exciting flying, it is a fair assumption that few survived to an honourable retirement.

Poland

Despite requests for assistance by Poland in 1939, no British aircraft reached there. There was a suggestion within the Air Ministry in June 1939 that a large number of Battles should be offered to Poland; 100-150 in June 1939, 50-100 in September/December 1939, 50 in April/May 1940 and up to 500 more in June/December 1940. This very magnanimous proposal was reduced in July 1939 to an offer to supply 100 Battles. With increasing German pressure on Poland, followed by the invasion, the need for aircraft became extremely urgent and the SS *Lassall* sailed for Constanza, in Romania, with aircraft and munitions for onward despatch to Poland. The cargo included nine Battles. Ships with a further 29 Battles were expected to leave the UK by 14 September 1939. In view of the desperate plight of the Poles as the Germans advanced into their country, the Chief of the Air Staff offered to release 20 Battles to be flown to France for collection by Polish pilots. The offer was made on 14 September 1939, but it was not taken up. As the defeat of Poland became imminent the Poles were informed on 20 September 1939, that the situation had developed so that it was impracticable to transport war material to the Polish forces. Ships carrying aircraft and stores destined for Poland would be diverted. Thus, of the sizeable force of Battles originally intended to be sent to Poland, none were delivered.

Greece

Shortly after the start of World War II in September 1939, a Greek order for nine Battles for the Royal Hellenic Air Force Combat Command was cancelled by the British Government and the aircraft were allocated to the RAF. In December 1939 the Government reversed its decision and agreed to release 12 Battles to Greece. In the event, 11 Battles, serial numbers P6604 - P6613 and P6615 were exported to Greece in March 1940; P6614 was originally destined for Greece but was re-

allocated to the RAF. These machines were used to form 33 Mira, one of the three squadrons comprising Combat Command. The other two squadrons were 31 Mira, equipped with Potez 633s, and 32 Mira with Blenheim IVs. The Battles were in standard RAF camouflage with Greek markings and they were given Greek serial numbers in the Beta series, B272 - B282. The Italian invasion of Greece from Albania started on 28 October 1940, when the Battles were based at Kouklaina. The initial successes of the Italians were soon reversed when the Greek counter offensive started in mid-November 1940. The Greek bomber squadrons were used in support of the land action and the Battles were in action against targets in Albania. On 15 November four Battles bombed Koritza North, in Albania, destroying a Caproni Ca 133 and damaging four fighters. On the same day, two Battles accompanied by two Blenheims attacked Koritza South. The Italian airfields were protected by Fiat CR 42 fighters and B272 piloted by Sgt Arnides, and B276 piloted by 2 Lt Kondides were shot down. Both aircraft crashed on Ivan mountain and the two pilots and an observer were killed. B274 was badly damaged but the pilot, Capt Pitsikas, flew it back to base. His observer, 2 Lt Papas, was badly wounded and died later in hospital. On 22 November three Battles successfully bombed and strafed a retreating Italian infantry column between Koritza and Pogradets. On 11 March 1941 a Battle piloted by Lt Col Stathakos, the CO of 33 Mira, was shot down by Italian fighters over Nivitsa-Slatinia. Both crew members were killed. Early in April 1941 the remnants of all three bomber squadrons were based at Menidi. The war situation changed dramatically on 6 April when the Germans invaded and moved rapidly through Greece. The end for the gallant Battles came on 20 April 1941, a day of very heavy air activity, when the remaining machines were destroyed on the ground at Tanagra in southern Greece by German air strikes. Little further information about the activities of the Battles in Greece is available because the Germans burned all Greek military records and photographs after they entered Athens in April 1941.

Finland

Air Ministry approval was given for the release of 20 Battles for delivery to Finland between January and March 1940, but none were sent.

Typical of the difficulties faced by the RCAF in winter, these Battles of No.9 Bombing & Gunnery School at Mont Joli require digging out before flying can begin. (R Sturtivant collection)

Eire

In response to a request from Eire for ten Harvards, 13 Hurricanes and three Battle target tugs, the Vice Chief of the Air Staff suggested, in January 1941, that an offer of ten Hector biplanes be made. The offer was approved by the Air Ministry and accepted by Eire. An involuntary export to Eire was V1222, a Battle T.T. target tug. The aircraft was on a training flight from West Freugh Air Observers School in Scotland on 2 April 1941 when it became lost and landed at Waterford in Eire. The Irish Government impounded the aircraft and it was used by the Irish Air Corps for several years.

Canada

By the outbreak of war in September 1939, ten Battles had been sent to the RCAF. Most of these were later transferred to training duties in the British Commonwealth Air Training Plan. After the start of the war over 700 more Battles were sent to Canada to be used as training aircraft. Further information about the Battles in Canada appears in Chapter 15.

Australia

Three hundred and sixty five Battles were sent to Australia, where they were used in the British Commonwealth Air Training Plan. Further information about the Battles in Australia appears in Chapter 16.

South Africa

A single Battle, K9402, was sent to South Africa for evaluation in April 1939. The report must have been favourable because more Battles were ordered for the South African Air Force and these saw action in East Africa. The original SAAF Battle, K9402, was shot down on a photographic reconnaissance mission in June 1940. Twenty-seven Battles were used operationally by the SAAF and another 152 were sent to South Africa for use in the Joint Air Training Scheme. Further information about the Battles in South Africa appears in Chapter 17.

Southern Rhodesia

Twenty five Battle T.T. target tugs were sent to the Southern Rhodesian Air Force for use by the Rhodesian Air Training Group in the training schools there. Further information about the Battles in Southern Rhodesia appears in Chapter 17.

India

One Battle and three Battle T.T. target tugs were sent to India in 1942 and were used for target towing duties at the Anti-Aircraft School at Karachi. The Battle was K7627 and the Battle T.T.s were L5661, L5663 and L5726.

New Zealand

Two Battles, both instructional airframes, were sent to the RNZAF. P6673 was sent to the RCAF in January 1941 and then to New Zealand, where it arrived in July 1941 and was given the serial Inst 42. K9177 was sent to the RNZAF in November 1942. It arrived in New Zealand in February 1943 and was numbered Inst 59.

U.S.A

The Battle used as a test bed for the 24-cylinder Fairey Prince engine, K9370, was sent to the USA in 1941 for evaluation of the engine. It was returned to the UK in 1943.

K9370 at Wright Field with a Fairey P.24 Prince engine driving contra-rotating propellers. (P Jarrett collection)

CHAPTER 19. TESTING AND SPECIALISED UNITS

ENGINE TESTING

The Battle was a tough undemanding aeroplane with no vicious characteristics in flight and its design allowed for different types of engine to be fitted fairly easily. It was therefore well suited for use as an aero engine test bed. Engines from several different manufacturers were installed and tested in Battles and at least 16 aircraft are known to have been used for this work. The engines and the aircraft in which they were tested are listed below

Rolls-Royce Merlin
K7572, K9257, K9406, K9477, N2058, N2110, N2234, P6752. There were a great many versions of the Merlin developed during its lifetime and various marks of this most successful engine were test flown in Battles.

Rolls-Royce Exe
K9222. The Exe was a 24 cylinder 1,200 hp air cooled sleeve valve engine, which, despite its promise, was cancelled in 1938. It had been intended to use the Exe in the naval Barracuda, but in the event the Merlin was fitted to this aircraft. After it was decided not to put the Exe into production, Rolls-Royce used their Exe-engined Battle as a communications aircraft for some years.

Napier Dagger
K9240. The 955 hp Mark VIII version of the air cooled H type 24 cylinder Dagger was tested during 1938 and 1939.

Whilst the Dagger was not a successful engine, the information derived from the tests was useful when the Sabre engine was being developed.

Napier Sabre
K9278, L5286. The Sabre was a large liquid cooled H type 24 cylinder engine developing over 2,000 hp. Both of the Battles in which it was tested were fitted with fixed undercarriages and both had large ventral radiators and an increased fin area. Testing commenced in May 1939 and the two Sabre Battles flew about 700 hours.

Bristol Taurus
K9331. The 14 cylinder air cooled Taurus radial engine began its flight tests in mid 1938, developing over 1,000 hp. In early 1939 a Mark III Taurus was installed in the aircraft for testing.

Bristol Hercules
N2042, N2184. The Hercules was a larger 1,375 hp 14 cylinder sleeve valve radial engine. Testing of the Mark II version commenced in February 1939. A Mark XI Hercules was later fitted to N2042. Both of these aircraft had fixed undercarriages.

Fairey P.24 Prince
K9370. The Prince was a 24 cylinder 2,000 hp liquid cooled

K9240 fitted with a Napier Dagger VIII engine. ((P Jarrett collection)

N2042 as a test-bed for the Bristol Hercules XI. (P Jarrett collection)

K9331 fitted with a Bristol Taurus TE-1M radial engine. (P Jarrett collection)

engine. It consisted of two combined 12 cylinder engines, each engine having a configuration of two banks of six vertically opposed cylinders. Both engines operated through the same crankcase with separate crankshafts driving two contra rotating propellers. Each half of the engine could be used independently of the other. A large ventral radiator was installed on this aircraft. Flight testing began in mid 1939 in this country and in 1941 the aircraft was sent to the USA for evaluation of the engine. This interesting power plant was not put into production in either the UK or the USA and K9370 was returned to this country in 1943. Altogether it flew for a total of over 300 hours.

OTHER TEST WORK

In addition to use as an engine test bed, several Battles were used for test work of various kinds. K9289 was used by Fairey in 1939 for testing a constant speed propeller and Rotol used three Battles for testing electrically controlled propellers. The Royal Aircraft Establishment at Farnborough used Battles K9258, K9371, K7698 and Battle T.T. target tugs L5598 and L5771 for test trials. Because of a shortage of suitable aircraft for towing gliders, a Battle was tested for this role in December 1941 at No.2 Glider Training School at Weston-on-the-Green. Not unexpectedly, it was found unsuitable.

AIRBORNE RADAR

Three Battles were used for testing early Air Interception radar. These were based at Martlesham Heath and formed one of the Performance Testing Units operating from there. Two Battles, K9207 and K9208, were received by the Flight on 3 June 1938 and a further aircraft, K9230, was received

on 30 June 1938. The aerial antennae were fixed on either side of the fuselage and the radar display units were installed in the rear cockpit of K9208. A scientist from the Airborne Radar Group, based at Bawdsey, flew with an RAF pilot during testing and one of the other Battles usually flew as the target aircraft. Development of the equipment progressed and by 1 June 1939 a complete working AI system was installed in K9208. The equipment had a maximum range of two miles and a minimum range of 1,000 yards. The success of this first rudimentary AI installation led to an instruction being given for 30 Battles to be fitted with the equipment by 1 September 1939. The Battles, however were superseded by Blenheims in July 1939 and the AI sets were installed in them. Battle K9208 was used to demonstrate the radar equipment in action and when a flying demonstration was given a plank of wood was put across the rear cockpit seat and the scientist and his visitor sat side by side in cramped discomfort to view the cathode ray tube screens. Among the many distinguished visitors who had airborne demonstrations of the equipment were the C-in-C Fighter Command, Sir Hugh Dowding, and Professor Lindemann. Mr. Winston Churchill attended for a ground demonstration. All three Battles were returned to MUs in November 1939.

FLARE TOWING TRIALS

Four Battle T.T. target tugs, L5778, L5779, L5781 and L5796 were received by No.29 Night Fighter Squadron at Wellingore in October 1940 to take part in towed flare trials. The object of the exercise was to illuminate target aircraft so that they could be seen and attacked by night fighters. The flares were attached to a 1,000 foot length of cable which was wound out from the winch in a Battle T.T. When the Battle T.T.reached the vicinity of the target aircraft a flare was lit and the night fighter following the Battle T.T. would see an illuminated target. Each cable carried a maximum of three flares and each flare burned for one minute. Several tests were made and their main effects were to dazzle the night fighter pilot, to light up the ground below and to show the position of the towing aircraft, making it vulnerable to attack. Despite the unpromising results of the tests, Fighter Command continued with them and trials were made using 500 feet of cable instead of 1,000 feet. The flares illuminated a comparatively small space and it was very difficult to get the aircraft into the right positions. The trials continued into 1941 but were finally abandoned as a failure. Two Battle T.T.s, L5778 and L5779 left the squadron in November 1940 and L5781 and L5796 left in March and April 1941 respectively.

AERIAL MINES

Long Aerial Mines, (LAM), codenamed *Pandora*, were modified bombs and it was intended that they should be suspended in a curtain from aircraft or parachutes on a 2,000 foot cable to destroy enemy aircraft. In September 1940, No.420 Flight was formed at Middle Wallop to carry out Pandora trials and in December 1940 the Flight became No.93 Squadron. Harrows were the original carriers, followed briefly by Wellingtons, then finally by Havocs. Two Battles and one Battle (T) trainer were allotted to the unit to be used for towing targets to test the "curtain"; P5248 arrived in September 1940 and L5049 and R7472 in November 1940. Trials were made without explosive charges in the mines then the device was used operationally with the mines charged. It was an extremely hazardous process and the results of its use were one Harrow aircraft damaged when a mine exploded near it, one air raid warden killed, several houses damaged and one enemy aircraft alleged to have been destroyed. The squadron persisted in the testing of Pandora until late 1941, when it was finally acknowledged to be a failure. Battle (T) R7472 left Middle Wallop on 23 November 1940, P5248 left on 8 February 1941 and L5049 left on 20 June 1941. The squadron was disbanded in December 1940.

AIR SUPPORT TRAINING

On 1 June 1942 Army Co-operation Command agreed to form No.1472 Flight to give air co-operation to the GHQ Home Forces Battle School at Barnard Castle in County Durham. The initial equipment was to be three Battles and three Tomahawks. Three Battles, L4978, L5140 and L5287, were received by the Flight at Dishforth in early June, followed shortly after by N2057. Three further Battles augmented the Flight, P2278 in October 1942 and P5288 and L5051 in February 1943. The Battles were used for simulated dive bombing and low level attacks during Battle School exercises and for some AA co-operation flights. Early in the life of the unit representations were made to No.33 Wing that the Battle was "hopeless" as a dive bomber and a wish was expressed that proper dive bombers should be provided. This was not to be and the unit continued to operate with the Battles. The Flight moved to Catterick on 17 January 1943. On 21 January 1943, L5140 suffered engine failure and crashed near Barnard Castle. The aircraft was a complete write-off but the pilot was unhurt. It was decided in March 1943 that the Battles and Tomahawks on the unit were to be replaced by Hurricane IIB bombers and the Battles departed in May 1943.

ANTI-AIRCRAFT CO-OPERATION

Anti-Aircraft Co-operation Units were set up to tow targets for coastal AA batteries to practice firing. They used a variety of aircraft types and four of them flew, inter alia, Battles.

No.1 AACU

The headquarters of this unit was at Farnborough, but its many flights were scattered far and wide in the UK. Three Battles were received in April 1939, but in September 1939 these were detached to No.2 AACU at Gosport until October 1940, when they returned to No.1 AACU's H Flight at Christchurch. They were N2118, N2119 and N2124. Other Battles which served with the unit were K9208, K9246, K9290, L4961, L4962, N2050 and P2245. Few of these stayed with the unit for long and all had departed by the end of 1941, most much earlier. The unit was split into independent flights on 1 October 1942 and four of the flights started to receive a small number of Battle (T) trainers after this. In November and December 1942, No.1600 Flight received P6637, P6682, P6733 and R7477. In 1943, P6637 and P6733 were transferred to No.1603 Flight, where they worked until they were struck off charge in September 1943. No.1609 Flight received P6727 and R7378 in November 1942 and transferred them to No.1606 Flight in June 1943, from where they were reclassified as ground instructional airframes in July 1943. Two other Battle (T) trainers, P6638 and P6643, served with No.1609 Flight for a short time in 1943.

No.2 AACU

Eleven Battles, seven Battle T.T. target tugs and one Battle (T) trainer served with the unit at various times between September 1939 and July 1943. The Battles were K7571, K7629, K9246, L4995, L5208, N2053, N2055, N2118, N2119, N2124 and P5277. The Battle T.T.s were L5663-L5666, L5679, L5689 and L5752. The Battle (T) was R7366. One aircraft, L5208, was destroyed in an air raid on Gosport on 16 August 1940 and N2055 crashed at Plympton, Devon, on 25 June 1941 after engine failure.

No.6 AACU

Eleven Battles were received by the unit between April and June 1940. They were K7659, K9246, L5034, L5205, L5206, L5208, L5209, L5211, L5215, L5217 and N2066. They left between December 1940 and April 1941. In December 1940 the unit received L5011 and it crashed at Low Meathop, Lancs., on 26 February 1941 after the engine cut on an approach to a forced landing in bad visibility.

No.7 AACU

Four Battles, L5205, L5211, L5215 and L5217 were received in May 1940. In September 1940 the unit received L5047 and on 30 September it crashed when it overshot on landing at Pembridge Landing Ground and hit a tree. A further Battle, L5011, was received in October 1940. All had left the unit by the end of May 1941.

TARGET TOWING

Several RAF Groups set up Target Towing Flights for air to air gunnery training and practice. A variety of types of aircraft, including Battles, were used by the TTFs. In November 1941 the Group TTFs were redesignated as

L5598 was the trials aircraft for the target-towing Battle.

numbered flights in the 1480 series. A few Battle T.T.s were allocated to the Group TTFs but most of the Battle aircraft used by them were standard Battles adapted for target towing.

No.2 Group TTF

The unit was formed on 22 February 1940 at West Raynham with six Battles from No.101 Squadron, the former Group Operational Training Unit. The Battles were: K9225, K9253, K9275, K9312, K9317 and K9358. Another Battle, L5268, was transferred to the flight on 15 March 1940 as a replacement for K9312, which was moved to No.47 MU. The Battles served in the unit until early in 1941, when they were sent to MUs after being replaced by Lysander target tugs.

No.3 Group TTF

Eight Battles and two Battle T.T.s served with the flight in 1940 and 1941. The Battles were K9178, K9262, K9277, K9320, K9375, L4978, L5214 and P2317. The Battle T.T.s were L5629 and L5788. Battle L5214 lost power and overshot a forced landing at East Winch, Norfolk, on 13 October 1940. It was struck off charge ten days later.

No.4 Group TTF

Battles were in use by No.4 Group as target tugs at Linton-on-Ouse in 1939. The TTF moved to Driffield on 1 October 1940 and was redesignated No.1484 Flight in November 1941. The Flight continued to use Battles until early in 1943. Eleven Battles and four Battle T.T.s served with the Flight. The Battles were K9178, K9200, K9384, L4981, L5039, L5228, L5416, N2151, N2152, P2157 and P2158. The Battle T.T.s were L5630, L5708, L5730 and L5792.

No.5 Group TTF

Battles were used by No.5 Group TTF from early in 1940 until mid-1942. The Flight was renamed No.1485 Flight in November 1941. Seven Battles and two Battle T.T.s served with the unit. The Battles were L4981, L5039, L5186, P2157, P2158, P2252 and P2253. The Battle T.T.s were L5629 and L5715.

ARMY CO-OPERATION

A shortage of suitable aircraft for army co-operation work led to trials of the Battle for this role. The trials were brief and conclusive; the Battle was not fitted for army co-operation duties. Single engine fighter aircraft, e.g. Tomahawks and Mustangs, came into use for army co-operation and several of the squadrons had Battles on their strength to give pilots experience in flying high-powered low-wing monoplanes. Army Co-operation squadrons which used Battles or Battle (T) trainers are listed below.

No.2 Squadron:	K7683, K9277, K9437 and P5288.
No.4 Squadron:	N2057, P2278, Battle (T) R7366.
No.13 Squadron:	L4996 and L5083.
No.16 Squadron:	K7574, K9208, L4996 and L5190.
No.26 Squadron:	L5051, L5460 and P5288.
No.53 Squadron:	N2090.
No.225 Squadron:	K7690 and L5035.
No.231 Squadron:	K7565, L5559, N2174, P2362, Battle (T)s P6681 and R7381.
No.239 Squadron:	L5025, P5283 and P6572.
No.241 Squadron:	K7614, K9199, N2089, P2158.
No.268 Squadron:	N2084 and N2086.
No.309 Squadron:	K9433, L5252, P2362, (T) P6733.

The Battle preserved at the Musée de l'Armée in Brussels still under restoration. (R W Simpson)

CHAPTER 20. PRESERVED BATTLES

Survivors

Of the 2,201 Battles built, only three are known to have survived and none of these are in flying condition. There are no surviving examples of several types of aircraft which were produced in quantity and used during World War II, therefore it may be considered to be fortunate that three Battles are still in existence. One is in England (L5343), one in Belgium (R3950) and one in Canada (R7384).

L5343

This Merlin III engined Battle was built by Austin Motors at the Longbridge shadow factory. It went into service in December 1939 with No.266 Squadron at Sutton Bridge in Lincolnshire, and was used for training pilots before they converted to Spitfires. It was transferred to No.20 MU in February 1940, then to No.98 Squadron at Newton in July 1940. On 27 August 1940, L5343 and eight other aircraft from the squadron flew via Wick to Kaldadarnes in Iceland for anti invasion coastal patrol duties. On 13 September 1940, while on a flight to Melgardi in northern Iceland, engine trouble forced L5343 to land near Hsnfarver, 84 miles from Kaldadarnes. The crew were rescued on 15 September. The aircraft suffered a collapsed undercarriage and a damaged

starboard wing. Because of the difficulty of salvaging the aircraft, it was decided to leave it where it was and to disable it to ensure that it did not fall into enemy hands in a repairable condition. The cockpit area was set alight with a Very pistol shot and severely damaged.

The aircraft remained there for thirty-three years until 1973 and during this period several parts were removed by souvenir collectors. In August 1973 a party from RAF Leeming set out to salvage the Battle. The Merlin engine and the propeller had been removed by a scrap merchant, who sold the engine to local aviation enthusiasts. The engine was bought back from its local owners. During August the remains of the Battle were transported to Keflavik. The Leeming party met many snags, which were overcome with considerable difficulty. There were no good roads in the crash area, there was no heavy lifting equipment available and the weather conditions were at times appalling. At the end of August the party and its vehicles flew in a Hercules aircraft to Leeming, leaving large parts of the Battle to be collected later when a larger transport aircraft would be available. The wings, rear fuselage and tailplane were transported to the UK by a Belfast aircraft in November 1973.

Restoration work was started at Leeming, the engine being the first item receiving attention. The work stopped when most of the project personnel were posted away from

L5343 in the Royal Air Force Museum at Hendon. (J Gradidge)

Leeming and the aircraft was transferred to the RAF Museum store at Henlow. The burnt out centre section of the fuselage needed replacing and a damaged fuselage from L5340 was acquired from the Strathallan Collection, who had received it from Canada. Nothing more was done until 1981, when L5343 and the spare fuselage were moved to St Athan and restoration work was restarted. The original propeller from L5343 was found in Iceland in 1989 and was flown to the UK. Restoration work was completed in March 1990 and the Battle was taken to the RAF Museum at Hendon, where it is on display in No.98 Squadron markings.

R3950

R3950, a standard Battle bomber, was built in 1939 by Austin Motors at Longbridge and was powered by a Merlin III engine. It did not enter squadron service with the RAF and was sent to Canada in March 1941, where it was taken on charge by the RCAF on 7 April 1941. Conversion to a target tug at No. 8 Repair Depot, Winnipeg, was completed by 1 July 1941. With the Canadian serial number 1899 the aircraft worked as a target tug for No. 2 Training Command of the RCAF in the Commonwealth Air Training Plan. It was struck off charge by the RCAF in February 1945 and found its way to the United States, where it was stored until it was purchased in 1972 by Sir William Roberts for the Strathallan Collection. The crated Battle was received at Strathallan estate in November 1972 and was stored until early 1977, when it was moved to Strathallan airfield. A considerable amount of work was done on the aircraft at Strathallan in restoring it. The aircraft was bought by the late Charles Church in 1987 and was entered for Christie's auction at Bournemouth in October 1987, where it failed to reach its price of £38,000. The Battle passed to the Historic Aircraft Collection of Jersey and in July 1990 the aircraft was acquired by the Belgian Ministry of Defence in exchange for a Spitfire XIV. It is appropriate that one of the remaining Battles should be in Belgium in view of Fairey's interest in that country with its former subsidiary company, Avions Fairey, at Gosselies. Battles were used operationally by the Belgian Air Force in 1940, in particular in the gallant attack on the Maastricht bridges on 11 May, when six out of the nine aircraft taking part were shot down. R3950 is now on display in the Brussels Military Museum.

R7384

This aircraft was a Battle Trainer with a Merlin III engine and it was built at Fairey's Heaton Chapel factory in 1940. It was sent to Canada in December 1940 and was taken on charge by the RCAF in January 1941. From January to December 1941 it was used at No.31 SFTS. It was then put into store until December 1942, when it was fitted with a gun turret and allotted to No.3 B&GS. In April 1943 the aircraft was again stored and it emerged in 1963, when it was restored at Calgary. It is now preserved in the markings of a gunnery trainer in yellow livery and is on display as part of the Canadian National Aeronautical Collection at Rockliffe, Ottawa.

N2188

In addition to the three aircraft mentioned above, Battle N2186 has been recovered from a swamp and is being slowly rebuilt at Port Adelaide, South Australia.

Newly-delivered Battles of No. 63 Squadron before receiving squadron identities. (P Jarrett collection)

K7650 of No.63 Squadron. (R Sturtivant collection)

AIRCRAFT TABLES

Royal Air Force

Fairey Battle prototype to specification P.23/35 delivered in May 1937. Contract 321541/35. Built at Hayes.

K4303   First flight 10.3.36; AAEE 21.10.36 for type tests; Fairey 1.12.36 for use as pattern aircraft at Stockport factory; RAE 4.6.37 for drag research; to 1475M at 5 SofTT 19.5.39. 182.10 hours.

155 Fairey Battle Is delivered by Fairey between May 1937 and May 1938. Contract 424738/35. K7558 built at Hayes, remaining 154 built at Stockport.

K7558   First flight 14.4.37; AAEE 6.7.37 for trials; RAE 25.4.38 for handling tests; Fairey 28.6.38 for flap development; 38 MU 21.6.40; RAE Exeter 4.8.40. Engine cut; bellylanded and burnt out near Tiverton, Devon, 27.8.40.; SOC 4.9.40.

K7559   63 Sqn 20.5.37; 106 Sqn 10.1.39; 3 ERFTS 10.6.39; 7 FTS 4.9.39; 1 FTS 30.11.39; 20 MU 10.2.41; 47 MU 3.3.41; to RCAF 23.6.41 as 2016. Dual Control.

K7560   63 Sqn 14.7.37; to 1033M at HAD 19.1.38; 4 SofTT; 429 Sqn ATC 29.3.43.

K7561   63 Sqn 1.7.37; to 1034M at HAD 21.1.38; 4 SofTT; SOC 7.12.43.

K7562   63 Sqn 16.6.37; Fairey 9.7.38; 88 Sqn 29.9.38; 106 Sqn 8.10.38. Engine cut; hit fence in forced landing and undercarriage collapsed near Thornaby 29.6.39. 575.40 hours.

K7563   63 Sqn 9.6.37; bellylanded in error, Upwood, 13.10.38; ROS; 106 Sqn 10.1.39. Bellylanded in error, Thornaby 18.4.39; DBR. 697.45 hours.

K7564   63 Sqn 6.7.37. Engine cut; overshot forced landing, Castle Bromwich 9.5.38; to 1110M at 2 SofTT 12.8.38; SOC 26.2.42. 96.40 hours.

K7565   63 Sqn 10.7.37; 8 ERFTS 12.1.39; 7 FTS 3.9.39; 1 FTS 10.9.39; 8 BGS 11.4.40; 27 MU 26.10.41; 3 AGS 6.8.42; 27 MU 26.8.42; 231 Sqn 12.9.42; 27 MU 22.1.43; SOC 30.6.43.

K7566   63 Sqn 22.6.37; 185 Sqn 10.1.39; 1 AAS 24.2.39; to 1939M 1.7.40; 1890 Sqn ATC 27.8.40; SOC 7.10.43.

K7567   63 Sqn 27.7.37; RAE 30.7.37; 63 Sqn 17.8.37. Flew into trees in bad weather and crashed, East Tisted, Hants., 25.11.38; PO J. Ellis killed, two injured. 219.10 hours.

K7568   63 Sqn 6.8.37; to 1035M at 1 SofTT 17.1.38; SOC 30.11.43.

K7569   63 Sqn 6.8.37; to 1036M at 1 SofTT 19.1.38; SOC 30.11.43.

K7570   63 Sqn 6.8.37; to 1037M at 3 SofTT 24.1.38; 6 SofTT 13.6.39; SOC 27.4.40.

K7571   105 Sqn 18.8.37; undercarriage leg collapsed on landing, Harwell, 24.3.38; ROS; 207 Sqn 4.11.38; 54 Sqn 13.2.39; 74 Sqn 3.4.39; 2 AACU 12.5.40; damaged in heavy landing, Roborough, 7.11.42; Rosenfield 19.11.42; 27 MU 9.1.43; SOC 30.11.43. Dual control.

K7572   AAEE 24.8.37 for oil cooling tests; R.Royce 23.8.37 for further tests; SOC 7.39. 555.00 hours.

K7573   105 Sqn 27.8.37; 207 Sqn 5.10.38; 1 AAS 2.2.39; 1 EWS 15.1.40; SOC 19.5.43.

K7574   4 Gp Exp Flt, Porton Down, 2.9.37; 3 Army personnel killed when container fell off aircraft, 18.1.40; AAEE 1.2.40; Western A/W 13.11.40; 38 MU 2.1.41; 16 Sqn 12.6.42; 27 MU 2.1.43; SOC 30.6.43.

K7575   105 Sqn 7.9.37; 6 MU 25.3.39; 1 ERFTS 19.6.39; 7 FTS 3.9.39; 1 FTS 12.9.39; 4 BGS 6.5.40; 47 MU 6.11.41; to RAAF 28.2.42.

K7576   105 Sqn 11.9.37; 207 Sqn 5.10.38; 1 AAS 2.2.39; 5 AOS 6.11.39; 30 MU 2.1.40; to 1955M at 3 SofTT

K7577   15.3.40; 1064 Sqn ATC 28.1.43; SOC 3.7.45.

K7577   AAEE 19.9.37 for bombing and armament tests; RAE 13.10.37; AAEE 11.7.38; RAE 4.8.39 for air defence trials; 5 MU 22.10.39; to 1792M 8.2.40; 1 EWS 19.4.40; SOC 19.5.43.

K7578   105 Sqn 21.9.37; 207 Sqn 5.10.38; 1 AAS 2.2.39; SF Eastchurch 14.12.39; to 1785M at 3 S of TT 2.2.40; SOC 17.3.44.

K7579   105 Sqn 22.9.37; to 1021M 17.11.37; 1 SofTT 11.1.38; 10 SofTT at 31.12.42; SOC 16.10.43.

K7580   105 Sqn 29.9.37; 207 Sqn 5.10.38; 1 Sqn 13.3.39; to 1640M; SOC 4.41. Dual control.

K7581   105 Sqn 26.9.37; 207 Sqn 5.10.38; 3 Sqn 9.5.39; 10 MU 21.11.39; to 1794M 8.2.40; 3 SofTT 20.3.40; SOC 17.3.44. Dual control.

K7582   105 Sqn 2.10.37; 207 Sqn 5.10.38; 17 Sqn 11.5.39; 20 MU 21.12.39; 9 MU 24.2.40; to 1924M at 2 SofTT 29.2.40. Dual control.

K7583   105 Sqn 2.10.37; 207 Sqn 5.10.38; 1 AAS 11.5.39; SF Eastchurch 18.12.39; to 1786M at 3 SofTT 2.2.40.

K7584   105 Sqn 2.10.37; 207 Sqn 9.12.38; 111 Sqn 18.2.39; to 1784M at 9 SofTT 24.4.40; later 1935M. Dual control.

K7585   105 Sqn 4.10.37; 207 Sqn 5.10.38. Undershot and hit tree on night approach, Cottesmore, 13.12.38; PO P.C. Rolls killed; to 1787M 6.2.39. 188.25 hours.

K7586   226 Sqn 14.10.37; 12 Gp HQ Flt 15.1.38; 213 Sqn 2.3.39; 20 MU 30.10.39; to 1797M 27.2.40; SOC 1.1.43. Dual control.

K7587   Austin (pattern aircraft) 8.10.37; Fairey for fitting TT gear 21.7.38; RAE for TT tests 26.7.39; Fairey 23.10.39; 49 MU 2.3.40; Fairey 6.6.40; 47 MU 24.9.40; to RCAF 27.10.40 as 1776.

K7588   226 Sqn 24.10.37; 35 Sqn 14.10.38; 1 AAS 17.2.39; 5 AAS 6.11.39; 30 MU 2.1.40; SOC 1.40; 3 SofTT as components 15.3.40.

K7589   226 Sqn 24.10.37. Flew into high ground in cloud on navex, Plynlimon, 8m W of Llanidloes, Wales, 6.10.38. 121.50 hours.

K7590   226 Sqn 24.10.37; 35 Sqn 24.10.38; 79 Sqn 15.3.39; 10 MU 7.9.39; to 1795M 8.2.40; 3 SofTT 20.3.40; SOC 17.3.44. Dual control

K7591   RAE 21.10.37; Fairey 27.1.38; RAE for balloon barrage experiments 12.2.38. Damaged in balloon cable experiments, Exeter, 11.11.39; SOC 28.1.40.

K7592   226 Sqn 26.10.37; 35 Sqn 15.10.38; 1 AAS 17.3.39. Stalled on landing and wing hit ground, Manby, 10.39; to 1774M at 1 EWS 22.2.40. SOC 19.5.43.

K7593   226 Sqn 26.10.37; 35 Sqn 15.10.38; 1 AAS 3.4.39. Engine cut during air firing exercise, stalled and hit ground, Theddlethorpe ranges, 13.10.39; Sgt W.E. Levitt and two others killed; SOC 29.10.39.

K7594   226 Sqn 26.10.37. Spun into lake off turn during air-to-ground rear gun training, Chesil Bank, Dorset, 11.12.37; Sgt A.W. Butler and gunner killed; to 1803M. 15.45 hours.

K7595   226 Sqn 28.10.37; 35 Sqn 14.10.38; 1 AAS 16.2.39; to 1872M 11.4.40; SOC 14.7.40.

K7596   226 Sqn 9.11.37; 35 Sqn 14.10.38; 87 Sqn 15.2.39; 20 MU 20.10.39; 36 MU 29.4.40; SOC 9.5.40; to RCAF 5.40 as instr. airframe A86. Dual control.

K7597   226 Sqn 9.11.37; 35 Sqn 14.10.38; 1 AAS 17.3.39; 5 SofTT 29.2.40; to 1875M 11.4.40; SOC 31.3.43.

K7598   226 Sqn 9.11.37; 35 Sqn 15.10.38; 1 AAS 16.2.39. Engine cut, bellylanded in field, 10.10.39; SOC 10.39. 166.10 hours.

K7599   52 Sqn 9.11.37; 4 ERFTS 5.1.39; 15 FTS 4.9.39; 1 FTS 27.9.39; 7 BGS 1.3.40; hit bowser taxying at Stormy Down, 19.3.41; 16(P)FTS 14.8.41; 18 MU 27.1.42; to SAAF 28.2.42.

K7600   226 Sqn 9.11.37; undercarriage collapsed on landing, Harwell, 10.5.38; 35 Sqn 15.10.38; 106 Sqn 9.3.39; 15 ERFTS 14.6.39; 7 FTS 2.9.39; 1 FTS 12.9.39; 4 BGS 1.3.40; Dumfries 8.8.41; to RAAF 15.10.41.

K7601   105 Sqn 9.11.37; 207 Sqn 5.10.38; to 1793M 8.2.40; 1 EWS 9.4.40; SOC 19.5.43.

K7602   52 Sqn 11.11.37; 5 ERFTS 4.2.39; 7 FTS 3.9.39; 10 AOS 19.9.39; 12 FTS 28.9.40; 47 MU 22.8.41; to RCAF 31.8.41 as 2074.

K7603   52 Sqn 12.11.37. Engine caught fire in air; crashlanded on railway, Ramsey, Hunts., 25.11.38; 233.15 hours.

K7604   52 Sqn 17.11.37; 8 ERFTS 2.1.39; 7 FTS 3.9.39; 1 FTS 10.9.39; 7 BGS 1.3.40; 16(P)FTS 14.8.41; 18 MU 17.3.42; Rosenfield 13.4.42; 38 MU 8.6.42; 19 Gp 27.6.42; 4 APC 26.7.42; SOC 11.8.43.

K7605   52 Sqn 13.11.37; AAEE for comparative trials 23.3.39; RAE for de-icing trials 13.6 39; 10 MU 10.12.39; to 1796M 8.2.40; 3 SofTT 20.2.40; SOC 17.3.44.

K7606   52 Sqn 17.11.37; 11 ERFTS 20.12.38; 15 FTS 2.9.39; 1 FTS 19.9.39; 4 BGS 22.7.40; 12 FTS 5.10.40; engine cut; forcelanded and hit obstructions, Saltby airfield, 28.2.41; Fairey 21.3.41; 47 MU 11.8.41; to RCAF 29.8.41 as 2072.

K7607   52 Sqn 17.11.37; 12 ERFTS 19.12.38; 15 FTS 2.9.39; 1 FTS 23.9.39; 9 BGS 3.5.40; undercarriage jammed; bellylanded, Penrhos, 22.2.41; ROS; engine cut; belly-landed 2½ miles N of Penrhos, 4.7.41; Fairey 9.7.41; Rosenfield 10.11.41; 47 MU 21.12.41; to RAAF 25.3.42.

K7608   52 Sqn 25.11.37; ran into trench on landing and undercarriage collapsed, Upwood, 29.4.38; ROS; 12 ERFTS 19.12.38; 15 FTS 4.9.39; 1 FTS 19.9.39; 7 BGS 1.3.40; 18 MU 3.9.41; 47 MU at 31.12.41; to RCAF 7.2.42.

K7609   52 Sqn 25.11.37; 15 ERFTS 15.1.39; 7 FTS 8.9.39. Hit ground in turn while low flying, Collingbourne Kingston, Wilts., 9.1.40; L/A H.E. Cook and passenger killed; SOC 23.4.40.

K7610   52 Sqn 8.12.37; 106 Sqn 30.3.39; 3 ERFTS 2.7.39; 7 FTS 3.9.39; 1 FTS 10.9.39. Engine cut; bellylanded 4m W of Boscombe Down, 13.12.40; SOC 1.1.41.

K7611   52 Sqn 27.11.37. Undershot landing and hit tender, Wittering, 19.11.38. 197.50 hours.

K7612   52 Sqn 13.12.37; 16 ERFTS 2.1.39; 7 FTS 2.9.39; 1 FTS 10.9.39; 4 BGS 13.2.40; to 1938M at 3 SofTT 26.2.40; SOC 17.3.44.

K7613   63 Sqn 29.11.37; 16 ERFTS 9.1.39; 7 FTS 2.9.39; 1 FTS 16.9.39; to RAAF 17.3.40.

K7614   63 Sqn 29.11.37; 12 ERFTS 5.1.39; 1 FTS 27.10.39; hit pillbox on landing, Stormy Down, 22.4.41; Rosenfield 7.5.42; 27 MU 28.5.42; 241 Sqn 22.6.42; damaged 3.11.42; Rosenfield 3.11.42; 18 MU 9.2.43; SOC 20.12.43.

K7615   105 Sqn 22.11.37. Undercarriage leg jammed; other leg collapsed on landing, Harwell, 4.4.38; SOC 10.6.38. 64.30 hours.

K7616   105 Sqn 8.12.37; 6 MU 6.4.39; 1 ERFTS 19.6.39. Engine cut; bellylanded in error, Hatfield, 3.9.39; SOC 17.11.39; to 2585M at S of AE Henlow 22.11.39; 14 SofTT 1.6.41.

K7617   52 Sqn 3.12.37; undercarriage collapsed after landing, Wyton, 17.5.38; ROS; 16 ERFTS 5.1.39; 7 FTS 2.9.39; 10 AOS 19.9.39; Rosenfield 3.9.42; 27 MU 7.10.42; 215 MU 24.10.42; 3 PATP 30.10.42; to Reykjavik 7.11.42; SOC 31.8.43.

K7618   52 Sqn 3.12.37; 22 ERFTS 20.12.38. Engine cut; bellylanded on beach, Great Yarmouth, Norfolk, 1.6.39; SOC 13.12.39. 400.10 hours.

K7619   226 Sqn 10.12.37; 35 Sqn 24.10.38; 73 Sqn 15.2.39; No. 1 FP Hucknall 19.10.39; 20 MU 28.3.40; 12 FTS 26.5.40; engine cut; forcelanded E of Grantham, Lincs., 7.4.41; 38 MU 25.8.41; 47 MU 15.11.41; to RAAF 5.1.42; Dual control.

K7620   226 Sqn 8.12.37; 35 Sqn 15.10.38; 1 AAS 16.2.39; 5 AOS 6.11.39; undershot landing and hit Henley L3391, Jurby, 9.11.39; Rollason 20.2.40; SOC 15.8.40.

K7621   63 Sqn 11.12.37; 185 Sqn 10.1.39; 1 AAS 4.3.39; to 1873M; broken up for scrap 14.7.40.

K7622   105 Sqn 13.12.37; 6 MU 5.4.39; 22 ERFTS 3.7.39; 8 MU 17.4.40; 12 FTS 7.6.40; 47 MU 27.7.41; to RAAF 27.8.41.

K7613 of No.63 Squadron at armament training camp, West Freugh, in 1938. (via A Thomas)

K7623   226 Sqn 8.12.37. Engine lost power; overshot into ditch 2m N of West Freugh, 22.3.38; SOC at 1 SofTT 12.4.38.

K7624   226 Sqn 16.12.37; 35 Sqn 15.10.38; 1 AAS 16.2.39; to 1871M 7.39; broken up 14.7.40.

K7625   52 Sqn 13.12.37; 22 ERFTS 19.12.38; 15 FTS 4.9.39; 4 BGS 15.11.39; to 1936M at 3 SofTT 26.2.40; SOC 17.3.44.

K7626   52 Sqn 12.12.37; 12 ERFTS 20.12.38; 1 FTS 27.10.39; bellylanded in error, Stormy Down, 3.10.40; ROS. Hit tree during forced landing while lost at night near Corsley Heath, Wilts., 10.3.41; SOC 20.3.41.

K7627   63 Sqn 12.12.37; 12 ERFTS 5.1.39; 15 FTS 4.9.39; 1 FTS 26.10.39; undercarriage collapsed after landing, Netheravon, 16.4.41; ROS; Rosenfield 30.3.42; 9 MU 1.7.42; 18 MU 22.7.42; 215 MU 7.8.42; EO Glasgow 11.8.42; to SAAF 11.8.42; to India 30.1.43.

K7628   105 Sqn 22.12.37; 207 Sqn 5.10.38; 1 AAS 2.2.39; 5 AOS 14.11.39; 5 BGS 1.12.39. Bellylanded in error, Jurby, 28.11.39; to 1894M at 9 SofTT 8.2.40; SOC 30.4.41.

K7629   88 Sqn 17.12.37; bellylanded in error, Boscombe Down, 3.6.38; ROS; 35 Sqn 21.11.38; 74 Sqn 15.2.39; 54 Sqn 3.4.39; 2 AACU 3.5.40; to 1925M 21.5.40. Dual control.

K7630   88 Sqn 17.12.37. Engine cut in bad weather; hit tree and crashed, Norton Heath, Essex, 7.8.38. 150.20 hours.

K7631   88 Sqn 21.12.37; 106 Sqn 8.10.38. Flew into sea in bad visibility 1m off Souter Point, Co. Durham, 13.1.39; Sgt E.J. Beer and AC2 W. Ingram killed. 251.05 hours.

K7632   88 Sqn 21.12.37; 106 Sqn 8.10.38; 19 ERFTS 10.6.39; 7 FTS 3.9.39; 1 FTS 10.9.39; overshot forced landing while lost and hit hedge, Roade, Northants., 25.1.40; Cranfield 1.3.40; Fairey 20.5.40; 8 MU 28.6.40; 305 Sqn 15.9.40; 9 MU 14.11.40; Austin 12.12.40; Parks 4.1.41; to RCAF 17.3.41.

K7633   88 Sqn 23.12.37; 106 Sqn 6.10.38; 15 ERFTS 14.6.39; 7 FTS 2.9.39; 4 AOS 28.11.39; overshot landing into pile of gravel, West Freugh, 6.3.41; ROS; 47 MU 6.11.41; to RCAF 24.12.41 as 2132.

K7634   88 Sqn 23.12.37; 106 Sqn 6.10.38; 15 FTS 4.9.39; 8 AOS 20.9.39; 7 FTS 2.10.40; 27 MU 20.2.41; damaged 27.6.41; Fairey 9.7.41; 47 MU 4.11.41; to RCAF 7.2.42 as 2128.

K7635   88 Sqn 23.12.37; 106 Sqn 8.10.38; 20 MU 29.10.39; to 1798M 27.2.40. SOC 18.1.43.

K7636   88 Sqn 6.1.38; 106 Sqn 6.10.38; 87 Sqn 25.5.39; 20 MU 20.10.39; 1 FTS 6.11.39; 36 MU 26.4.40; SOC 8.5.40; to RCAF as instr. airframe A87, 5.40. Dual control.

K7637   88 Sqn 6.1.38. Stalled on landing at night and hit ground, Boscombe Down, 18.6.38; to 1114M at EWS 15.8.38.

K7638   88 Sqn 6.1.38; 106 Sqn 6.10.38; 29 ERFTS 10.6.39; 7 FTS 3.9.39; 1 FTS 10.9.39; 8 BGS 11.4.40; 7 FTS 5.10.40; 20 MU 15.1.41; 47 MU 1.3.41; to RAAF 20.3.41.

K7639   88 Sqn 6.1.38; 106 Sqn 8.10.38; 29 ERFTS 10.6.39; 7 FTS 3.9.39; 1 FTS 10.9.39; 7 BGS 21.1.40; 18 MU 3.9.41; Western A/W 22.11.41; 38 MU 28.1.42; 4 APC 22.8.42; undercarriage collapsed in heavy landing, Carew Cheriton, 6.11.42; Austin 25.11.42; 38 MU 12.12.42; 4 APC 5.1.43; SOC 1.5.43.

K7640   88 Sqn 6.1.38; 106 Sqn 8.10.38; 3 ERFTS 10.6.39; 7 FTS 4.9.39; 1 FTS 28.11.39; engine cut; overshot forced landing and hit hedge, Margam ranges, Glam., 6.8.40; Fairey 14.8.40; 47 MU 14.11.40; to RCAF 16.12.40 as 1809.

K7641   88 Sqn 8.1.38; 106 Sqn 8.10.38; 3 ERFTS 2.7.39; 7 FTS 3.9.39; 1 FTS 10.9.39; hit bowser while taxying, Netheravon, 14.10.39; ROS; 4 BGS 13.2.40; to 1937M at 3 SofTT 26.2.40; SOC 17.3.44.

K7642   88 Sqn 7.1.38. Overshot forced landing while lost and fell into road, 7.1.38; 3 MU; SOC 9.5.38. 2.30 hours.

K7643   88 Sqn 7.1.38; 106 Sqn 6.10.38; 3 ERFTS 10.6.39; 7 FTS 3.9.39; 1 FTS 10.9.39; engine cut; bellylanded, Pepperbox Hill ranges, Wilts., 20.7.41; Rosenfield 27.7.41; 47 MU 22.11.41; to RAAF 5.1.42.

K7644 88 Sqn 13.1.38; 106 Sqn 6.10.38; 4 BGS 22.12.39; overshot landing and hit obstruction, West Freugh, 16.10.40; ROS; 9 MU 18.11.41; 18 Gp APC; undercarriage jammed; bellylanded, Leuchars, 9.8.42; ROS; 19 Gp APC 15.9.42; 540 Sqn 22.11.42; 3 APC; blown into tractor while taxying, Wick, 14.2.43; 18 MU 13.4.43; to 2476M at Blackpool TT Flt 27.11.43; 18 MU at 31.12.43. SOC 9.2.44.

K7645 63 Sqn 13.1.38; 8 ERFTS 11.1.39; 7 FTS 3.9.39; 1 FTS 16.9.39; 4 BGS 6.5.40; engine cut and undercarriage collapsed in forced landing, Sandmead, near West Freugh, 11.9.40; ROS; 4 AOS 14.6.41; 27 MU 13.1.42; 16 Gp APC 14.7.42; 18 Gp APC 10.10.42; 18 MU 3.3.43; to 2484M at 3 SofTT 10.12.43; SOC 14.7.44.

K7646 63 Sqn 14.1.38; 12 ERFTS 5.1.39; engine cut; bellylanded, Sydenham, 29.7.39; 3 BGS; 1 AAS 3.7.40; brakes failed, hit hangar, Manby, 7.11.40; ROS; Western A/W 22.8.41; 1 FTS at 31.12.41; 18 MU 18.3.42; 215 MU 5.6.42; 3 PATP 1.7.42; lost at sea en route to Iceland 8.10.42.

K7647 218 Sqn 17.1.38; 185 Sqn 10.10.38; 56 Sqn 10.2.39; 47 MU 24.4.40; Fairey 6.6.40; 8 MU 28.6.40; 142 Sqn 5.8.40; 150 Sqn 3.10.40; 27 MU 7.10.40; Austin 11.11.40; Parks 4.1.41; to RCAF 31.3.41. Dual control.

K7648 63 Sqn 16.1.38; 12 ERFTS 5.1.39; stalled on landing and wing hit ground, Prestwick, 27.8.39; 15 FTS 3.9.39; Scottish Avn 13.11.39; 30 MU 1.3.40; to 1831M at 3 SofTT 13.3.40; SOC 17.5.44.

K7649 63 Sqn 17.1.38; 15 ERFTS 9.1.39; hit by Audax K5593 while parked, Redhill, 7.5.39; ROS; Morris 27.11.39; 20 MU 30.3.41; 47 MU 28.4.41; to RAAF 4.6.41.

K7650 63 Sqn 17.1.38; 185 Sqn 10.1.39; 1 AAS 12.4.39; to 1877M at S of AE Henlow 14.4.40.

K7651 218 Sqn 20.1.38; 185 Sqn 10.10.38; 41 Sqn 18.2.39; 1 FTS 10.11.39. Failed to recover from dive during dive-bombing practice, Pepperbox Hill ranges, Wilts., 17.5.41; Lt H.G. Hunt RN killed; SOC 26.5.41. Dual control. 467.00 hours.

K7652 218 Sqn 20.1.38; engine cut; bellylanded, Upper Heyford, 29.3.38; ROS; 46 Sqn 17.2.39; 47 MU 24.2.40; Fairey 2.6.40; 6 MU 4.7.40; 142 Sqn 30.8.40; Fairey 26.9.40; 22 MU 9.1.41; 47 MU 14.2.41; to 2278M; to RCAF 11.3.41 as 1917. Dual control.

K7653 218 Sqn 21.1.38; 185 Sqn 10.10.38; 1 AAS 20.2.39; to 1881M at 1 SofTT 24.2.40; SOC 30.11.43.

K7654 218 Sqn 24.1.38; 185 Sqn 12.10.38; 87 Sqn 17.2.39. Engine cut; crashed on approach to forced landing, Balsham, Cambs., 6.5.39. Dual control. 180.35 hours.

K7655 218 Sqn 26.1.38; 185 Sqn 10.10.38; 1 AAS 4.3.39; to 1870M at 4 SofTT 7.3.40; SOC 14.7.40.

K7656 218 Sqn 26.1.38; 185 Sqn 12.10.38; 19 Sqn 17.2.39; 20 MU 20.10.39; to 1799M 27.2.40; SOC 5.6.42. Dual control.

K7657 218 Sqn 27.1.38. Undercarriage failed to lock and collapsed on landing, Boscombe Down, 27.8.38; to 1139M at EWS 1.10.38; at Hereford 31.12.42; SOC 30.6.43. 76.10 hours.

K7658 218 Sqn 31.1.38; 185 Sqn 10.10.38; 1 AAS 9.2.39. Engine cut; bellylanded, South Cockerington Grange, Lincs., 19.12.39; Rollason 25.1.40; SOC 26.8.40.

K7659 218 Sqn 31.1.38; 185 Sqn 11.10.38; 32 Sqn 21.2.39; 6 AACU 6.6.40; 32 MU 1.5.41; 47 MU 6.11.41; to RAAF 21.3.42. Dual control.

K7660 218 Sqn 31.1.38; 185 Sqn 10.10.38; 1 AAS 4.3.39; overshot landing into ditch, Manby, 12.10.39; Scottish Avn 16.11.39; Fairey 24.6.40; 47 MU 24.10.40; to RCAF 15.11.40 as 1738.

K7661 218 Sqn 3.2.38. Undercarriage jammed; bellylanded Boscombe Down, 18.5.38. 80.00 hours.

K7662 12 Sqn 11.2.38; 150 Sqn 30.9.38; 185 Sqn 19.11.38; 1 AAS 21.4.39; 5 AOS 6.11.39; 30 MU 26.3.40; to 1933M at 3 SofTT 27.4.40.

K7663 218 Sqn 10.2.38; 185 Sqn 10.10.38; 1 AAS 14.4.39; to 1879M at 1 SofTT 29.2.40; SOC 30.11.43.

K7664 218 Sqn 10.2.38; 185 Sqn 11.10.38. Took off in coarse pitch and hit hut, Henlow, 11.11.38; 13 MU 29.12.38; SOC 1.2.39.

K7665 218 Sqn 10.2.38; 185 Sqn 10.10.38; 1 AAS 20.2.39; to 1775M at 1 EWS 26.2.40; SOC 19.5.43.

K7666 218 Sqn 11.2.38; 185 Sqn 11.10.38; 1 AAS 4.3.39; 1 EWS 2.1.40; SOC 19.5.43.

K7667 12 Sqn 15.2.38; 150 Sqn 30.9.38; 1 AAS 6.2.39; 5 AOS 6.11.39; 30 MU 26.3.40; to 1934M at 3 SofTT 27.4.40; 400 Sqn ATC 21.1.43; SOC 21.9.45.

K7668 12 Sqn 15.2.38; 150 Sqn 30.9.38; 185 Sqn 19.11.38; 1 AAS 14.7.39; to 1878M at 1 SofTT 29.2.40.

K7669 12 Sqn 17.2.38; 150 Sqn 30.9.38; 185 Sqn 19.11.38; 1 AAS 4.3.39; to 1874M at 5 SofTT 29.2.40; SOC 29.4.44.

K7670 12 Sqn 17.2.38; 106 Sqn 8.1.39; 5 BGS 19.11.39; undercarriage jammed; bellylanded on ferry flight to 9 BGS, Sealand, 3.5.40; 12 FTS 28.9.40; 16(P)FTS 7.6.41; 18 MU 18.2.42; to SAAF 30.6.42.

K7671 12 Sqn 23.2.38; 106 Sqn 6.12.38; 5 BGS 17.11.39; 47 MU 18.3.40; Fairey 6.8.40; 27 MU 10.8.40; 103 Sqn 2.9.40; 27 MU 2.10.40; Austin 10.11.40; to RCAF 17.3.41.

K7672 12 Sqn 23.2.38; 6 MU 2.5.39; 1 ERFTS 19.6.39; 7 FTS 3.9.39; 1 FTS 10.9.39; 7 BGS 1.3.40; engine cut; bellylanded, Jurby, 2.3.40; ROS; Western A/W 29.9.41; 9 MU 8.11.41; 215 MU 26.4.42; 3 PATP 26.5.42; to RAAF 5.8.42.

K7673 12 Sqn 23.2.38; 150 Sqn 30.9.38; 35 Sqn 25.11.38; 1 AAS 16.2.39; 1 EWS 2.1.40; SOC 19.5.43.

K7674 12 Sqn 23.2.38; 105 Sqn 1.10.38; 207 Sqn 11.10.38; 1 AAS 16.2.39; to 1880M at 1 SofTT 24.2.40.

K7675 12 Sqn 25.2.38; 150 Sqn 30.9.38; 35 Sqn 12.1.39; 1 AAS 17.2.39. Undercarriage collapsed on landing, Manby, 31.12.39; to 1876M at 5 SofTT 29.2.40; SOC 29.4.44.

K7676 12 Sqn 1.3.38; 150 Sqn 30.9.38; 185 Sqn 19.11.38; 72 Sqn 15.2.39; 1 FTS 30.11.39; 7 FTS 16.5.40; 12 FTS 12.6.40; blown over taxying at Tollerton, 2.3.41; ROS; 16(P)FTS 15.6.41; undercarriage collapsed on landing, Hucknall, 11.7.41; ROS; engine cut; bellylanded near Long Clawson, Notts., 31.10.41; Rosenfield 10.11.41; 18 MU 26.2.42; 215 MU 16.4.42; 3 PATP 27.4.42; to RAAF 11.6.42. Dual control.

K7677 12 Sqn 1.3.38; 150 Sqn 30.9.38; 35 Sqn 12.1.39; 66 Sqn 16.2.39; 20 MU 20.10.39; to 1800M 27.2.40. Dual control.

K7678 12 Sqn 9.3.38; 150 Sqn 30.9.38; 35 Sqn 24.11.38; 151 Sqn 16.2.39; 20 MU 27.10.39; to 1801M 27.2.40. Dual control.

K7679 142 Sqn 4.3.38; 106 Sqn 17.11.38; 185 Sqn 19.11.38; 1 AAS 19.7.39; SF Eastchurch 14.12.39; to 1788M at 3 SofTT 2.2.40; SOC 17.3.44.

K7680 12 Sqn 9.3.38; 150 Sqn 30.9.38; 35 Sqn 24.11.38; 65 Sqn 16.2.39; 1 FTS 3.11.39. Engine cut due to fuel mishandling; bellylanded near Lopcombe Corner, Wilts., 10.2.41; to GI airframe at 2 SofTT 12.2.42.

K7681 Fairey for trial installations of modifications and equipment 23.3.38; 27 MU 11.8.42; Rosenfield 25.9.42; 18 MU 31.10.42; at Fairey 31.12.42; 18 MU 6.1.44; SOC 14.7.44.

K7682 AAEE for armament trials 21.3.38. Engine cut; bellylanded near Orfordness bombing range, Suffolk, 8.6.38; to 1119M at EWS 22.9.38; 11 SofTT; 1996 Sqn ATC 26.2.43.

K7683 142 Sqn 14.3.38; 88 Sqn 20.9.38; 106 Sqn 6.10.38; 18 ERFTS 10.6.39; 1 FTS 10.9.39; 8 BGS 26.2.40; 15 EFTS 12.10.40; 16(P)FTS 5.12.40; engine cut on take-off from Hucknall; crashlanded, Watnall, Derby, 1.3.41; ROS; overshot forced landing while lost and hit trees, Bunny, Notts., 22.7.41; Western A/W 28.7.41; Rosenfield 4.3.42; 27 MU 6.5.42; 2 Sqn 27.5.42; 27 MU 21.1.43; SOC 16.10.43.

K9263 of No.103 Squadron after a mid-air collision with K9373, Tollerton, 6 August 1939. (Harry Moyle via A Thomas)

K7684   142 Sqn 14.3.38; 105 Sqn 21.5.38; 207 Sqn 5.10.38; 1 AAS 2.12.38. Engine cut in circuit; crashlanded, Manby, 30.11.39; Rollason 25.1.40; Fairey 20.8.40; SOC 24.8.40.

K7685   142 Sqn 16.3.38; undercarriage collapsed on landing, Andover, 22.3.38; ROS; 105 Sqn 28.9.38; 207 Sqn 5.10.38; 1 AAS 2.2.39; SF Eastchurch 17.12.39.

K7686   142 Sqn 18.3.38; 63 Sqn 29.6.38; 185 Sqn 10.1.39; 1 AAS 24.2.39; 1 EWS 2.1.40; SOC 19.5.43.

K7687   142 Sqn 18.3.38; 88 Sqn 16.9.38; 106 Sqn 8.10.38; 3 ERFTS 10.6.39; 1 FTS 20.10.39; engine cut; bellylanded, Shalbourne, Wilts., 11.7.40; Fairey 15.7.40; 27 MU 8.10.40; 47 MU 3.5.41; to RAAF 9.6.41.

K7688   142 Sqn 22.3.38; 63 Sqn 29.9.38; 16 ERFTS 9.1.39; hit by Tiger Moth K4257 on landing, Shoreham, 26.7.39; ROS; 7 FTS 2.9.39; 9 MU 19.9.39; 5 AOS 6.11.39; 9 BGS 6.12.39. Crashed in forced landing in fog on night navex near Carnbica, 8m S of Cardigan, 26.2.40; 2 SofTT; SOC 14.3.40.

K7689   142 Sqn 22.3.38; 105 Sqn 21.5.38. Control lost during turn in cloud searchlight co-operation, abandoned, Lasham, Hants., 21.7.38. 73.55 hours.

K7690   12 Sqn 24.3.38; 105 Sqn 1.10.38; 207 Sqn 22.11.38; 8 MU 9.5.39; 6 BGS 14.5.40; 12 FTS 29.5.40; overshot night landing and hit pole, Harlaxton, 3.10.40; ROS; undercarriage collapsed in heavy landing, Harlaxton, 27.11.40; 32 MU 11.7.41; 38 MU 18.1.42; 225 Sqn 31.5.42; Rosenfield 25.1.43; 18 MU 24.6.43; SOC 14.7.44.

K7691   12 Sqn 1.4.38. Stalled and DBR in heavy landing, Andover, 5.9.38; to 1165M; West Drayton 31.10.38; 11 SofTT; 1022 Sqn ATC 14.7.42. 73.30 hours.

K7692   88 Sqn 1.4.38; 106 Sqn 6.10.38; 20 MU 29.10.39; 12 Gp Pool 3.12.39. Undercarriage not locked down and collapsed on landing, Aston Down, 3.12.39; to 1782M.

K7693   226 Sqn 7.4.38; 35 Sqn 15.10.38; 43 Sqn 15.2.39; 20 MU 15.11.39; to 1802M 27.2.40; SOC 6.42. Dual control.

K7694   226 Sqn 7.4.38; 35 Sqn 15.10.38. Stalled on approach due to icing and crashlanded, Cottesmore, 4.1.39; to 1341M at Locking 16.3.39; SOC 2.6.40. 99.45 hours.

K7695   35 Sqn 1.4.38; engine cut on take-off, bellylanded 1m NE of Cottesmore, 4.5.38; ROS; 17 OTU 22.4.40; 13 MU 2.5.40; Rollason 23.5.40; 38 MU 11.7.40; 47 MU 9.9.40; to RCAF 26.9.40 as 1708.

K7696   142 Sqn 7.4.38; 1 Salvage Section 10.3.40; 142 Sqn 12.5.40. Shot down near Laon, 19.5.40; PO H.H. Taylor, Sgt S. Lang and AC1 H. Long captured

K7697   142 Sqn 7.4.38; 22 MU 20.10.39; 47 MU 28.2.41; 18 MU 15.4.41; to SAAF 1941 as 971.

K7698   RAE for balloon barrage and aerial mine trials, also fire extinguishing tests 13.4.38; damaged in air raid, Exeter, 12.5.41; ROS; SOC 8.11.48 on Colerne scrap dump.

K7699   142 Sqn 13.4.38; 1 Salvage Section 9.10.39; 21 AD 11.12.39; SOC 3.40.

K7700   142 Sqn 14.4.38. Abandoned on evacuation of Berry-au-Bac, 17.5.40.

K7701   142 Sqn 14.4.38; Scottish Avn 15.1.40; 12 MU 26.11.40; Austin 6.2.41; to RCAF 4.5.41.

K7702   142 Sqn 20.4.38. Landed tail down in gusty wind conditions and DBR, West Freugh, 14.10.38.

K7703   142 Sqn 20.4.38; 1 Salvage Section 3.3.40; 21 AD 21.3.40; Fairey 26.6.40; 20 MU 28.8.40; 47 MU 18.9.40; to RCAF 18.10.40 as 1763.

K7704   142 Sqn 23.4.38; to 1613M at 2 SofTT 1.8.39.

K7705   35 Sqn 22.4.38; 226 Sqn 14.10.38; 8 MU 25.4.40; Western A/W 18.6.40; 27 MU 23.8.40; 1 FTS 5.10.40. Pilot overcome by fumes; crashlanded 2m E of Devizes, Wilts., 11.12.40; to 2546M 22.2.41; to RAAF 1941.

K7706   35 Sqn 25.4.38; 226 Sqn 14.10.38. Undershot landing and hit shelter, Harwell, 17.8.39; DBR.

K7707   35 Sqn 24.4.38; 226 Sqn 14.10.38; 1 Salvage Section 29.1.40; 21 AD 15.3.40; abandoned in France 5.40.

K7708   35 Sqn 27.4.38; 226 Sqn 14.10.38; 22 MU 20.10.39; 4 BGS 24.6.40; bellylanded in error, West Freugh, 6.9.40; ROS; 10 BGS 12.6.41; 10 AOS 9.41; 27 MU 21.10.42; SOC 30.6.43.

K7709   35 Sqn 29.4.38; 226 Sqn 14.10.38; 5 MU 10.12.39; 4 BGS 16.4.40; 27 MU 8.11.41; to 3555M at 12 SofTT 8.6.42; 250 Sqn ATC 6.2.43.

K7710   35 Sqn 30.4.38; 226 Sqn 14.10.38; 22 MU 31.10.39; 12 FTS 3.6.40; undershot landing and hit tree, Harlaxton, 10.11.40; Fairey 15.11.40; 47 MU 10.3.41; to Canada 11.4.41 then to RAAF.

K7711   35 Sqn 30.4.38; 226 Sqn 14.10.38. Engine cut; bellylanded and skidded into trees, Weatheroak Hill, Birmingham, 5.8.39; SOC 12.1.40.

K7712   35 Sqn 2.5.38; 226 Sqn 14.10.38; 1 Salvage Section 18.1.40; 21 AD 27.1.40; SOC 3.40.

311 Fairey Battle Is delivered by Fairey, Stockport, between May 1938 and February 1939. Contract 522745/36.

K9176   35 Sqn 20.5.38; 226 Sqn 14.10.38. Shot down, Montcornet, 20.5.40; Sgt A. Livingston killed; Sgt R.S. Annan and AC2 R.J. Jones captured

K9177   35 Sqn 5.5.38; 226 Sqn 24.10.38; 22 MU 20.10.39; 4 BGS 2.5.40; 10 BGS 12.6.41; 10 AOS 9.41; Rosenfield 8.7.42; 27 MU 31.8.42; 215 MU 8.10.42; 3 PATP 31.10.42; to RNZAF 21.11.42 as ground instr. airframe Inst59.

K9178   35 Sqn 11.5.38; 105 Sqn 24.1.39; Linton-on-Ouse 27.9.39; 4 Gp TTF; 3 Gp TTF 28.5.40; damaged taxying at Langham, 9.7.41; 47 MU 31.10.41; to RCAF 12.12.41 as 2117.

K9179   35 Sqn 6.5.38. Engine cut; hit trees and crashlanded on take-off from forced landing, Oulton Park, Cheshire, 20.6.38; to 1126M at RAF College 10.9.38; 215 Sqn ATC 2.7.42.

K9180   35 Sqn 6.5.38; 226 Sqn 24.10.38. Burnt on evacuation of Reims, 16.5.40.

K9181   207 Sqn 9.5.38; 105 Sqn 2.11.38; 22 MU 28.10.39; 18 OTU 9.6.40; 20 MU 27.11.40; Austin 9.1.41; Parks 6.2.41; to SAAF as 962.

K9182   35 Sqn 11.5.38; 226 Sqn 14.10.38; 22 MU 12.4.40; 5 BGS 4.8.40; 27 MU 21.9.40; 47 MU 14.1.41; to RCAF 5.2.41 as 1842.

K9183   35 Sqn 11.5.38; 226 Sqn 14.10 38. Shot down by ground fire, Luxembourg, 10.5.40; FO D.A. Cameron died of wounds; Sgt C.S. Hart and AC1 J.G. Ward captured; SOC 11.5.40

K9184   142 Sqn 12.5.38; 10 MU 25.2.40; 4 BGS 13.6.40; 9 MU 21.11.41; 18 Gp APC 22.7.42; tail damaged while taxying, Leuchars, 14.11.42; 9 MU 16.1.43; Rosenfield 6.4.43; SOC 30.4.43.

K9185   207 Sqn 12.5.38; 105 Sqn 5.10.38. Crashed near Issoudun, 17.12.39; 21 AD 17.12.39; SOC 12.39.

K9186   207 Sqn 12.5.38; 105 Sqn 5.10.38; presumed abandoned in France 5.40.

K9187   207 Sqn 14.5.38; 105 Sqn 21.11.38; 12 MU 23.7.40; 15 EFTS 13.8.40; undershot landing and hit fence, Kirkbride, 15.9.40; Fairey 23.9.40; 18 MU 24.4.41; Dumfries 9.7.41; to RCAF 19.8.41 as 2081.

K9188   207 Sqn 14.5.38; 105 Sqn 5.10.38; damaged by ground fire, Luxembourg, 10.5.40; LAC R.W. McCarthy wounded; abandoned at Villeneuve-les-Vertus, 16.5.40

K9189   207 Sqn 14.5.38; 105 Sqn 5.10.38; AASF 10.1.40; returned to 105 Sqn. Shot down, Donchery, 3m WSW of Sedan, 14.5.40; PO F.H. Ridley, Sgt G. Atkinson and AC1 J.S. Thomson killed

K9190   207 Sqn 19.5.38; 105 Sqn 5.10.38; 5 MU 10.12.39; 47 MU 8.2.41; to RCAF 11.3.41 as 1874.

K9191   207 Sqn 19.5.38; 105 Sqn 5.10.38; SF Mildenhall 29.9.39; 207 Sqn 2.11.39; Mildenhall 30.11.39; Fairey 6.6.40; 9 MU 14.7.40; 47 MU 15.8.40; to RCAF 6.9.40 as 1703.

K9192   207 Sqn 19.5.38. Engine cut; bellylanded 4m W of Wyton, 22.11.39; SOC 2.1.40.

K9193   207 Sqn 19.5.38; 105 Sqn 5.10.38. Engine cut; crashlanded on beach near St.Laurent-de-la-Salanque, Pyrénées Orientales, 20.2.40; SOC 6.3.40.

K9194   207 Sqn 21.5.38; 105 Sqn 5.10.38; 21 AD 21.12.39; 1 Salvage section 9.1.40; Fairey; 9 MU 22.11.40; Austin 21.2.41; Parks 28.3.41; to RCAF 10.4.41.

K9195   207 Sqn 21.5.38; 105 Sqn 5.10.38; crashlanded, Beausse, Maine-et-Loire, 15.2.40; 21 AD 2.3.40; presumed abandoned in France 6.40.

K9196   207 Sqn 21.5.38; 105 Sqn 5.10.38. Crashed near Harwell, 8.11.38; to 1196M. 94.30 hours.

K9197   207 Sqn 24.5.38; 105 Sqn 5.10.38. Crashed near Poix on ferry flight, 2.9.39; SOC 23.11.39; 223.00 hours.

K9198   207 Sqn 24.5.38; 105 Sqn 5.10.38; 21 AD 1.4.40; presumed abandoned in France 6.40.

K9199   98 Sqn 27.5.38; 88 Sqn 21.6.40; 22 MU 21.7.40; 18 MU 26.7.40; 241 Sqn 8.6.42; Rosenfield 12.10.42; 18 MU 29.4.42; SOC 13.10.43.

K9200   207 Sqn 26.5.38; 105 Sqn 11.10.38; Linton-on-Ouse 27.9.39; 4 Gp TTF; undershot landing, Driffield, 9.5.40; ROS; tipped up on take-off, Driffield, 27.3.41; Sunbeam Talbot 15.4.41; 4 Gp TTF; 1484 Flt 14.11.41; tail damaged taxying at Driffield, 1.4.42; ROS; tail damaged taxying at Driffield, 7.9.42; ROS; 18 MU 8.11.42; SOC 14.7.44.

K9201   98 Sqn 27.5.38; 21 AD 31.5.40; presumed abandoned in France; 302.45 hours.

K9202   98 Sqn 1.6.38; 21 AD 10.5.40; presumed abandoned in France; 283.45 hours.

K9203   98 Sqn 1.6.38; Scottish Avn 4.10.39; 38 MU 7.11.40; Austin 7.4.41; to RCAF 1941 as 2042

K9204   98 Sqn 1.6.38; 15 Sqn 16.9.39; 150 Sqn 9.10.39; 142 Sqn 13.11.39; 10 MU 22.2.40; Austin 1.5.41; Parks 28.5.41; to RCAF 7.9.41 as 2100.

K9205   98 Sqn 1.6.38. Engine cut; bellylanded, Wilmington, Sussex, 2.1.40; SOC 15.1.40.

K9206   98 Sqn 1.6.38; engine cut; bellylanded, Beeston, Notts., 3.10.38; ROS; SF Scampton 17.4.40; 20 MU 29.10.40; 47 MU 24.2.41; to RAAF 24.3.41.

K9207   AAEE for Exp Cooperation Unit 3.6.38; 32 MU 6.11.39; RAE 6.6.41; SOC 25.8.43.

K9208   AAEE 3.6.38; RAE 28.9.38; AAEE 30.9.38; 37 MU 11.11.39; 1 AACU; TFU at 31.12.41; 38 MU 26.1.42; 16 Sqn 27.5.42; 27 MU 9.1.43; SOC 30.6.43.

K9209   98 Sqn 8.6.38. Crashed, Old Sarum, 13.3.40; to 2553M 19.3.40; SOC 29.3.40.

K9210   98 Sqn 8.6.38; 226 Sqn 17.7.40; 18 MU 2.8.40; 47 MU 18.3.41; to RCAF 2.4.41 as 1907.

K9211   98 Sqn 8.6.38; 226 Sqn 17.7.40; 18 MU 13.8.40; 47 MU 6.2.41; to RCAF 21.2.41 as 1872.

K9212   98 Sqn 8.6.38; engine cut on take-off; bellylanded, Hucknall, 20.8.38; ROS; 15 Sqn 16.9.39; 12 Sqn at 30.11.39; 6 MU 1.3.40; Rollason 1.8.40; Fairey 2.9.40; 47 MU 23.10.40; to RCAF 28.11.40 as 1824.

K9213   98 Sqn 8.6.38; tyre burst on landing and undercarriage leg collapsed, Hucknall, 26.6.39; ROS; 9 MU 13.7.40; Austin 11.5.41; to RCAF 5.41 as 2036.

K9214   15 Sqn 13.6.38; 63 Sqn 13.9.39; 12 OTU 18.4.40; engine cut on take-off from Benson, bellylanded, Ingford Bridge, Oxon., 28.7.40; Fairey 20.8.40; 9 MU 29.12.40; 47 MU 14.2.41; to RCAF 2.3.41 as 1878.

K9215   98 Sqn 13.6.38; 9 MU 14.7.40; 47 MU 15.11.41; to RCAF 23.12.41 as 2122.

K9216   98 Sqn 14.6.38. Engine cut on take-off; flew into wood, Hucknall, 10.2.39. 42.35 hours.

K9217   98 Sqn 14.6.38; undershot landing, Weston Zoyland, 16.10.39; Scottish Avn 20.11.39; 12 MU 9.3.41; 47 MU 21.3.41; to RCAF 27.4.41 as 1978.

K9218   98 Sqn 17.6.38; 21 AD 22.5.40; SOC 5.40. 228.05 hours.

K9219   142 Sqn 17.6.38; 98 Sqn 7.10.39; 9 MU 13.7.40; Rollason 1.8.40; 9 MU; 47 MU 9.9.41; Austin 27.9.41; to RAAF 27.9.41.

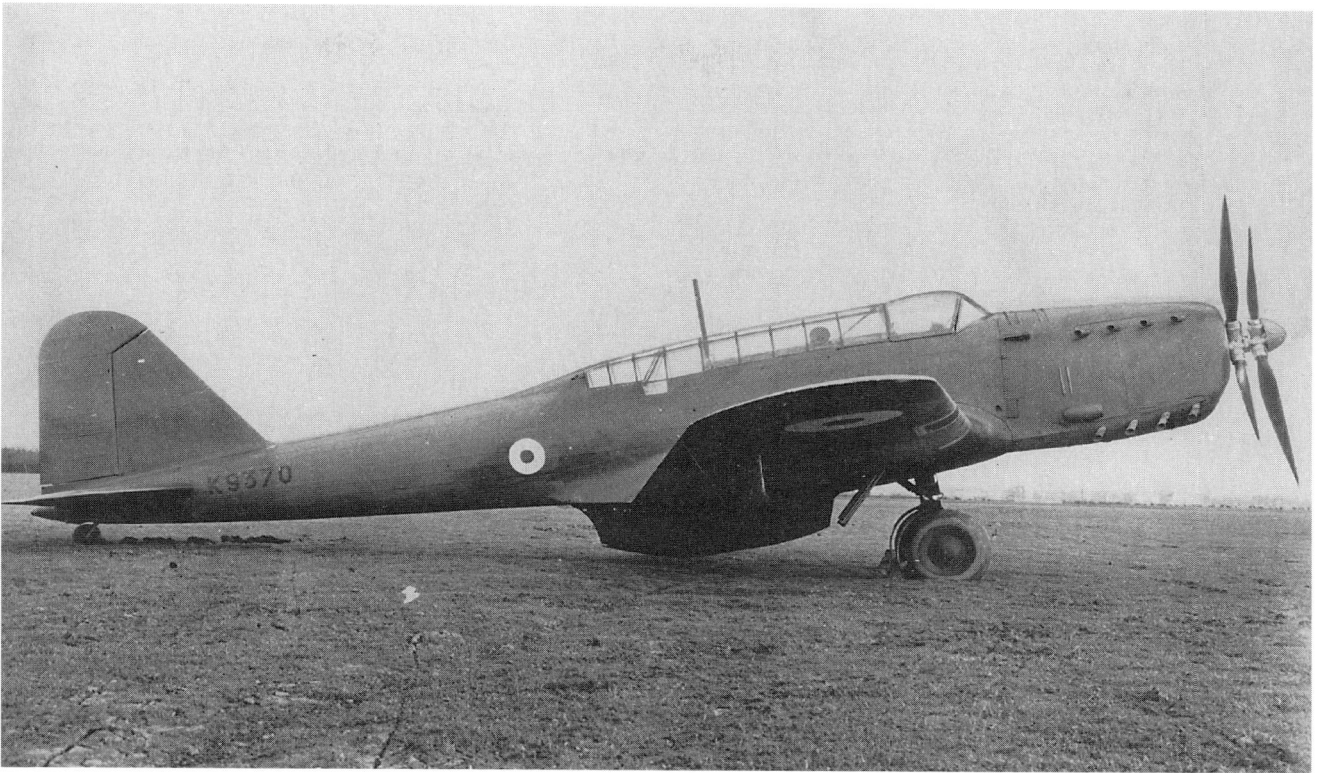

K9370 as the Prince test-bed in June 1939 prior to being shipped to the United States. (P Jarrett collection)

K9220   26 MU 17.6.38; damaged 21.11.38; 20 MU 22.6.39; to 1835M at 1 EWS 16.3.40; SOC 19.5.43.

K9221   AAEE for armament development work 20.6.38; 27 MU 30.5.40; 1 AAS 8.7.40; 16(P)FTS 19.8.41. Engine cut; crashlanded, Dore, near Sheffield, 24.8.41; Rosenfield 29.8.41; SOC 15.12.41.

K9222   Rolls-Royce for Exe test bed 21.6.38; SOC 29.1.46.

K9223   AAEE for armament development work 21.6.38; RAE for physiological tests and aerial mine tests 6.11.39. Became uncontrollable during aerial mine tests after tail chute accidentally released and crashed, Pawlett Hams, near Bridgwater, Somerset, 1.10.40; S/Ldr C.H.A. Colman killed; SOC 17.10.40.

K9224   15 Sqn 21.6.38; 22 MU 30.12.39; 15 EFTS 8.7.40; Polish FTS 11.12.40; 16(P)FTS 17.7.41; tailwheel broke on landing, Newton, 16.8.41; ROS; damaged in heavy landing, Newton, 18.3.42; Austin; 16(P)FTS 3.4.42; 18 MU 12.4.42; SOC 14.7.44.

K9225   15 Sqn 23.6.38; SF West Raynham 4.10.39; 101 Sqn at 30.11.39; 2 Gp TTF 22.2.40; 6 MU 9.1.41; 47 MU 24.2.41; to RCAF 24.5.41.

K9226   15 Sqn 23.6.38; 22 MU 30.12.39; 4 BGS 8.6.40; 32 MU 10.7.41; ATA; 38 MU 1.6.42; 18 MU 7.9.42; SOC 13.10.43.

K9227   15 Sqn 12.7.38; 22 MU 30.12.39; 4 BGS 24.8.40; 18 MU 15.8.41; 47 MU 8.12.41; to RAAF 29.1.42.

K9228   15 Sqn 23.6.38; 5 MU 10.12.39; 4 BGS 23.6.40; engine cut; overshot forced landing into ditch, Kidsdale LG, 15.5.41; 4 AOS 5.8.41; hit obstruction on landing, Ringway, 18.11.41; 9 MU 21.11.41; 215 MU 7.10.42; EO Liverpool 24.10.42; to RAAF 8.11.42.

K9229   15 Sqn 28.6.38; 98 Sqn 21.10.39; 9 MU 13.7.40; Austin 13.5.41; Parks 28.7.41; to RCAF 7.9.41.

K9230   AAEE for Exp Cooperation Unit 30.6.38; RAE 25.7.38; AAEE for Exp Cooperation Unit 28.9.38; 32 MU 10.11.39; SD Flt Christchurch. Engine cut; crashed in sea off Hengistbury Head, Hants., 28.4.41; PO A.C. James killed; SOC 31.5.41. 219.05 hours.

K9231   AAEE for armament development 30.6.38; 27 MU 10.6.40; 1 AAS 8.7.40; engine cut; bellylanded near Manby, 13.9.40; ROS; 47 MU 27.7.41; to RCAF 24.8.41 as 2083.

K9232   40 Sqn 30.6.38; Abingdon at 30.11.39; SF Abingdon 27.12.39; Bicester 6.3.40; 13 OTU; undercarriage jammed and collapsed on landing, Squires Gate, 3.5.40; 4 MU 11.5.40; Fairey 6.6.40; overshot forced landing on ferry flight from Ringway to Castle Bromwich, Whitley airfield, 5.4.41; Austin 5.4.41; 9 MU 16.7.41; 47 MU 2.9.41; to RAAF 27.9.41.

K9233   15 Sqn 1.7.38; 5 MU 10.12.39; 4 BGS 24.6.40; engine cut; overshot forced landing, West Freugh, 22.9.40; ROS; 4 AOS 14.6.41; 47 MU 8.1.42; Dumfries 26.1.42; to SAAF 2.3.42.

K9234   40 Sqn 1.7.38; to 1833M at 6 SofTT 13.3.40; SOC 29.3.44.

K9235   40 Sqn 5.7.38; to 1834M at 6 SofTT 13.3.40; SOC 4.12.43.

K9236   40 Sqn 4.7.38. Engine cut; bellylanded, Hallen, Glos., 10.2.39; to 1321M at 2 SofTT 7.3.39.

K9237   40 Sqn 5.7.38; to 1471M at 2 SofTT 14.4.39;

K9238   40 Sqn 7.7.38; 98 Sqn 9.10.39. Flew into ground in bad visibility near Stow-on-the-Wold, Glos., 7.11.39; FO D.K. Robertson, Sgt R.L. Harrison and AC2 F.J. Wilkes killed; complete write-off.

K9239   40 Sqn 7.7.38; to 1836M at 3 SofTT 13.3.40; 4 SofTT; SOC 30.6.43.

K9240   Fairey 28.6.38 for fitting Napier Dagger VIII engine; RAE for flight testing Dagger engine 3.12.38; to 2213M at 7 SofTT 12.9.40; SOC 21.11.44.

K9241   40 Sqn 7.7.38. Engine cut; bellylanded 6m SE of Cambridge, 7.12.38; to 1449M at 6 SofTT 24.4.39. 116.00 hours.

K9242   106 Sqn 11.7.38; 88 Sqn 8.10.38. Shot down by Bf 109s, Saarbrücken, 20.9.39; Sgt W.S. Everett and AC1 D.J. John killed; SOC 23.11.39. 217.55 hours.

K9243   106 Sqn 11.7.38; 88 Sqn 8.10.38; 5 MU 10.12.39; 4 BGS 19.6.40; 27 MU 8.11.41; SOC 30.6.43.

K9244   106 Sqn 11.7.38; 88 Sqn 6.10.38; 2 SF 23.4.40; 8 MU 29.4.40; Western A/W 13.7.40; 27 MU 23.8.40; 1 FTS 18.9.40; engine cut; bellylanded, Sandridge, near Melksham, Wilts., 26.11.40; Fairey 11.12.40; Austin 10.4.41; to RCAF 21.5.41.

K9245   106 Sqn 11.7.38; 88 Sqn 8.10.38. Shot down by Bf 109s, Saarbrücken, 20.9.39; F/Sgt D.A. Page, Sgt A.W. Eggington, AC1 E.A.W. Radford killed; SOC 23.11.39. 147.10 hours.

K9246   103 Sqn 18.7.38; 35 Sqn 28.9.39; 22 MU 21.10.39; 6 AACU 11.4.40; Gosport 22.6.40; 2 AACU 23.6.40; 1 AACU 30.10.40; 32 MU 21.4.41; 47 MU 27.8.41; to SAAF 10.9.41 as 998.

K9247   106 Sqn 15.7.38; 88 Sqn 8.10.38; 2 Salvage Section 21.2.40; 21 AD 12.3.40; Fairey 25.6.40; 27 MU 25.8.40; 301 Sqn 26.9.40; 103 Sqn 4.10.40; 27 MU 15.10.40; Austin 23.11.40; Parks 14.12.40; to RCAF 10.3.41.

K9248   106 Sqn 15.7.38; 88 Sqn 8.10.38; 5 MU 10.12.39; 4 BGS 16.4.40; engine cut on take-off, bellylanded, West Freugh, 22.5.40; Fairey 31.5.40; 18 MU 23.7.40; 47 MU 24.9.40; to RCAF 28.10.40 as 1767.

K9249   106 Sqn 15.7.38; 88 Sqn 8.10.38. Engine caught fire; abandoned, Netherhampton, Wilts., 20.6.39; Sgt H.G. Ing left in aircraft and killed; PO D.A.J. Foster and AC2 E.G. Williams unhurt; 111.40 hours.

K9250   106 Sqn 18.7.38; 88 Sqn 8.10.38; 8 MU 15.2.40; Western A/W 13.8.40; 47 MU 23.9.40; to RCAF 8.10.40 as 1735.

K9251   185 Sqn 21.7.38; 218 Sqn 10.10.38; presumed abandoned in France 6.40.

K9252   185 Sqn 21.7.38; 218 Sqn 11.10.38. Ran into bad weather on navex and crashed 40 N of Dijon, 1.3.40; 3 Salvage Section 8.3.40; presumed wreck abandoned in France, 6.40.

K9253   185 Sqn 22.7.38; 218 Sqn 11.10.38; bellylanded in error, Boscombe Down, 15.8.39; ROS; Abingdon 20.11.39; West Raynham 24.11.39; 101 Sqn 30.11.39; 2 Gp TTF 22.2.40; 38 MU 9.1.41; 47 MU 25.6.41; to RCAF 27.8.41 as 2103.

K9254   185 Sqn 22.7.38; 218 Sqn 11.10.38; 1 Salvage Section 17.1.40; 21 AD 10.3.40; presumed abandoned in France

K9255   185 Sqn 25.7.38; 218 Sqn 11.10.38; 6 MU 5.3.40; Rollason 1.8.40; Fairey 29.8.40; 47 MU 27.10.40; to RCAF 28.11.40 as 1815.

K9256   185 Sqn 25.7.38; 218 Sqn 11.10.38; 2 Salvage Section 7.3.40; 21 AD 25.3.40; presumed abandoned in France 6.40.

K9257   Rolls-Royce for Merlin X trials 25.7.38; to 1437M at 6 SofTT 18.4.39.

K9258   RAE for auto-control development 26.7.38; 22 MU 7.6.40; 47 MU 26.9.40; to RCAF 27.10.40 as 1769.

K9259   185 Sqn 26.7.38; 142 Sqn 21.9.38; damaged by bomb Berry-au-Bac, 12.5.40; allotted to 6 RSU 14.5.40; abandoned on evacuation, 16.5.40. SOC 20.5.40.

K9260   185 Sqn 28.7.38; 218 Sqn 11.10.38. Overshot landing at night, Boscombe Down, 11.4.39; to 1472M at Locking 2.5.39; 6 SofTT 8.6.39; SOC 12.4.40.

K9261   103 Sqn 30.7.38; Engine cut; hit trees and bellylanded E of Ditchling, Sussex, 19.10.38; SNC Ford 21.10.38; to 1189M at 4 SofTT 2.12.38.

K9262   106 Sqn 18.7.38; 88 Sqn 6.10.38; Abingdon at 30.11.39; 63 Sqn 12.12.39; Marham 8.4.40; 3 Gp TTF; bellylanded in error, Marham, 14.5.41; 215 MU 7.10.42; 3 PATP 6.11.42; to RAAF 3.1.43.

K9263   103 Sqn 30.7.38. Collided with K9373 over Nottingham, 6.8.39; Sgt. R.J.W. Williams killed; Sqn Ldr J. Coverdale and AC2 P.I. Bligh uninjured; 4 MU 20.11.39; SOC 5.3.40.

K9264   103 Sqn 1.8.38. Shot down by ground fire near Hotton, Luxembourg, 10.5.40; FO K.J. Drabble, Sgt T.D. Smith and LAC P.J. Lamble killed

K9265   103 Sqn 2.8.38; 2 SF 18.4.40; 8 MU 25.4.40; Western A/W 13.8.40; 47 MU 23.9.40; to RCAF 8.10.40 as 1737

K9266   103 Sqn 3.8.38; 6 ASP 21.1.40; 1 Salvage Section 24.1.40; 21 AD 28.2.40; presumed abandoned in France 6.40.

K9267   103 Sqn 3.8.38; 63 Sqn 20.10.39; CGS 20.11.39. Engine cut; bellylanded and hit bank, Drimpton, Dorset, 2.12.39; Rollason 25.1.40; DBR.

K9268   103 Sqn 3.8.38; 21 AD 3.6.40; 20 MU 19.6.40; 32 MU 28.7.40; 6 MU 21.11.40; 47 MU 28.2.41; to RCAF 7.4.41 as 1933.

K9269   103 Sqn 4.8.38; AASF 27.4.40; 10 MU 22.6.40; Gosport 14.7.40; damaged in air raid, Gosport, 16.8.40; Austin 6.9.40; 20 MU 18.3.41; Austin 16.4.41; to SAAF 15.6.41; to Middle East 30.1.43.

K9270   103 Sqn 4.8.38. Shot down by ground fire, Hotton, Luxembourg, 10.5.40; Sgt C.H. Lowne, Sgt C.J.S. Poole and LAC O.A. Hutchinson captured

K9271   103 Sqn 5.8.38. Damaged in action by Bf 109s and forcelanded near Rohrbach-les-Bitche, Moselle, 27.9.39; SOC 8.10.39.

K9272   150 Sqn 16.8.38; 52 Sqn 22.9.39; 22 MU 24.10.39; Polish OTU 8.4.40; 18 OTU; 38 MU 5.12.40; 47 MU 27.5.41; to RCAF 11.6.41 as 2009.

K9273   185 Sqn 16.8.38; 218 Sqn 11.10.38; presumed lost in France 5.40.

K9274   150 Sqn 16.8.38; 12 Sqn 30.9.38; 142 Sqn 30.11.39; 10 MU 22.2.40; Austin 2.4.40; 38 MU 30.7.40; 47 MU 18.9.40; to RCAF 18.10.40 as 1759.

K9275   150 Sqn 17.8.38; 12 Sqn 30.9.38; West Raynham 24.11.39; 101 Sqn 30.11.39; 2 Gp TTF 22.2.40; 38 MU 9.1.41; 47 MU 3.5.41; to RCAF 28.5.41 as 1972.

K9276   150 Sqn 17.8.38; bellylanded in error, Andover, 30.9.38; ROS; 12 Sqn 30.9.38; 2 Salvage Section 10.1.40; 21 AD 12.3.40; presumed abandoned in France 6.40.

K9277   150 Sqn 20.8.38; 12 Sqn 30.9.38; 3 Gp TTF; damaged taxying at Alconbury, 30.4.41; 9 MU 29.10.41; 2 Sqn 18.7.42; undercarriage collapsed at dispersal, Sawbridgeworth, 11.8.42; ROS; damaged in tail-down landing, Sawbridgeworth, 30.12.42; 27 MU 25.5.43; SOC 23.8.44.

K9278   Fairey for fitting Napier Sabre engine 15.8.38; First flight 31.5.39; Napier for flight development work 2.10.39; 18 MU 18.3.42; Napier at 31.12.42; 54 MU 22.5.44; SOC 31.5.44.

K9279   150 Sqn 20.8.38; 12 Sqn 30.9.38; 1 Salvage Section at 30.11.39; 1 SRU 3.12.39; 21 AD 9.12.39; SOC 3.40.

K9280   150 Sqn 20.8.38; 12 Sqn 30.9.38; 1 Salvage Section 22.11.39; 21 AD 3.12.39; presumed abandoned in France 6.40.

K9281   AAEE for development work 20.8.38; RAE for tests of Mk IV auto controls 11.1.39; 22MU 30.5.40; 47 MU 26.9.40; to RCAF 27.10.40 as 1771.

K9282   150 Sqn 24.8.38; 15 Sqn at 30.11.39; 88 Sqn 5.12.39; 8 MU 12.2.40; 47 MU 11.11.40; to RAAF 15.1.41.

K9283   150 Sqn 24.8.38. Crashlanded and burned, Ecury-sur-Coole, after damage in action with Bf 109s, 30.9.39; SOC 23.11.39. 214.55 hours.

K9284   150 Sqn 26.8.38; 12 Sqn 30.9.38; 6 RSU 25.4.40; 21 AD 6.5.40; Fairey 16.5.40; 18 MU 23.7.40; 47 MU 26.10.40; to RCAF 28.11.40.as 1791.

K9285   150 Sqn 29.8.38; 12 Sqn 30.9.38; 22 MU 20.10.39; 4 BGS 17.5.40; 9 MU 25.11.41; 18 MU 6.9.42; SOC 14.7.44.

K9286   150 Sqn 29.8.38; 12 Sqn 30.9.38; 8 MU 3.3.40; Western A/W 13.7.40; 27 MU 23.8.40; 1 FTS 9.9.40; overshot landing into trench, Netheravon, 4.3.41; ROS; Western A/W 6.11.41; 18 MU 8.3.42; 215 MU 14.5.42; 3 PATP 28.5.42; to SAAF 10.7.42 as 1064 ; to Middle East 30.1.43.

K9287   150 Sqn 29.8.38; 12 Sqn 30.9.38. Engine cut on take-off from forced landing; hit hedge, Grimley, 4m NNW of Worcester, 22.2.39; to 1326M at 2 SofTT 14.3.39; SOC 5.8.41.

K9288   150 Sqn 30.8.38; 12 Sqn 30.9.38; 22 MU 20.10.39; 4 BGS 17.5.40; engine caught fire; bellylanded,

K7612 of No.52 Squadron at Upwood in 1938. Harts and Blenheim in background with Heyford taking off.
(A Thomas collection)

Marshwood Beach, Wigtown, 15.10.40; ROS; stalled on landing in snowstorm, West Freugh, 16.1.41; Fairey 30.1.41; 9 MU 18.5.41; 47 MU 22.6.41; to RCAF 24.7.41 as 2054.

K9289 Fairey for target towing trials and variable pitch propeller tests 30.8.38; propeller went into reverse pitch in flight; bellylanded, 23.11.39; RAE for acceleration tests 18.1.40. Abandoned after glycol leak, Dursley, Hants., 29.6.44; SOC 29.6.44.

K9290 150 Sqn 30.8.38; 12 Sqn 30.9.38; 1 AACU 1.11.39; Abingdon 27.12.39; Bicester 6.3.40; undercarriage jammed and collapsed on landing, Bicester, 2.5.40; ROS; 17 OTU 20.10.40; 27 MU 23.2.41; 47 MU 6.11.41; to RAAF 28.2.42.

K9291 150 Sqn 1.9.38; 12 Sqn 30.9.38; CGS 15.11.39; 7 BGS; 47 MU 19.9.41; to RAAF 19.11.41.

K9292 142 Sqn 1.9.38; AASF 25.2.40; 10 MU 27.2.40; Western A/W 22.6.40; 47 MU 13.8.40; to RCAF 31.8.40 as 1715.

K9293 142 Sqn 1.9.38; 1 Salvage Section 17.1.40; 21 AD 16.2.40; presumed abandoned in France 6.40.

K9294 142 Sqn 5.8.38. Engine cut on take-off; hit fence, Andover, 2.3.39; DBR. 122.40 hours.

K9295 103 Sqn 5.9.38; 3 Salvage Section 2.2.40; 2 Salvage Section 13.2.40; 21 AD 20.3.40; presumed abandoned in France 6.40.

K9296 103 Sqn 8.9.38; Abingdon 21.10.39; CGS 20.11.39; 12 FTS 25.10.40; 13 MU 23.6.41; 18 MU 22.8.41; LEP 28.10.41; PATP 31.12.41; to SAAF 29.1.42 as 1006.

K9297 103 Sqn 8.9.38; Abingdon 3.11.39; 63 Sqn 13.1.40; 12 OTU 18.4.40; 20 MU 9.2.41; 47 MU 1.3.41; to RAAF 24.3.41.

K9298 103 Sqn 8.9.38; 52 Sqn 22.10.39; CGS 20.11.39; 7 FTS 7.8.40; 1 FTS 9.1.41; brakes failed, ran into hedge, Stormy Down, 4.4.41; ROS; overshot forced landing into ditch while lost, Shepstowe, Glos., 2.5.41; Fairey 8.5.41; 47 MU 25.10.41; to RCAF 24.12.41 as 2130.

K9299 103 Sqn 9.9.38; 8 MU 15.2.40; 47 MU 18.9.40; to RCAF 27.9.40 as 1722.

K9300 15 Sqn 9.9.38; 10 MU 22.11.39; 47 MU 2.6.41; to RCAF 11.6.41 as 2002.

K9301 15 Sqn 13.9.38; 2 Salvage Section 22.11.39; 142 Sqn 25.1.40; 20 MU 13.5.40; 32 MU 31.7.40; 6 MU 25.11.40; 5 FPP. Hit obstruction landing at Brize Norton, 25.11.40; DBR; to 2438M 22.12.40.

K9302 15 Sqn 13.9.38. Engine cut after take-off; stalled and crashlanded, Abingdon, 21.4.39; SOC 3.5.39. 55.35 hours.

K9303 15 Sqn 13.9.38; 22 MU 30.12.39; 4BGS 8.6.40; engine cut on approach to West Freugh, swung into sand dunes on landing, Luce Bay ranges, 21.11.40; ROS; 4 AOS 14.6.41; engine cut; undercarriage collapsed on landing, West Freugh, 8.7.41; 47 MU 28.11.41; to RCAF 21.12.41 as 2127.

K9304 15 Sqn 13.9.38; Abingdon at 30.11.39; 13 MU 7.5.40; Rollason 23.5.40; 38 MU 6.7.40; 47 MU 1.9.40; to RCAF 26.9.40 as 1707.

K9305 15 Sqn 13.9.38. Engine cut; crashlanded, Steppingley, Beds., 22.11.38; to 1353M at 4 SofTT 21.3.39; SOC 30.6.43. 17.00 hours.

K9306 40 Sqn 15.9.38. Engine cut; ditched in Naseby reservoir, Northants., 14.7.39.

K9307 40 Sqn 15.9.38; 5 MU 3.12.39; 4 BGS 16.4.40; 32 MU; 47 MU 1.7.41; to RCAF 27.8.41 as 2092.

K9308 40 Sqn 15.9.38; Abingdon at 30.11.39; 52 Sqn 5.1.40; 12 OTU 18.4.40; undershot night landing, Mount Farm, 22.11.40; Austin 27.11.40; Fairey 15.1.41; Austin 4.4.41; to SAAF 15.6.41.

K9309 40 Sqn 16.9.38; 5 MU 3.12.39; 47 MU 2.3.41; to RCAF 28.5.41 as 1989.

K9310 40 Sqn 16.9.38; 5 MU 3.12.39; 3 FPP 17.1.41; forcelanded while lost and tipped up, Poplar Hill, Stowmarket, Suffolk, 13.3.41; Fairey 4.7.41; HQ ATA 17.9.41; 38 MU 1.6.42; to 3631M 15.3.43; SOC 18.11.43.

K9311 15 Sqn 18.9.38; 22 MU 17.1.40; 47 MU 24.9.40; to RCAF 14.10.40 as 1753.

K9312 15 Sqn 18.9.38; West Raynham 4.10.39; 101 Sqn at

30.11.39; 2 Gp TTF 22.2.40; engine cut; bellylanded in marsh 2m NW of Dersingham, Norfolk, 7.3.40; 47 MU 15.3.40; Fairey 24.6.40; 27 MU 17.9.40; 47 MU 10.10.40; to RCAF 27.10.40 as 1743.

K9313 40 Sqn 19.9.38; to 1837M 13.3.40.

K9314 40 Sqn 20.9.38; to 1838M at 12 SofTT 13.3.40; RN Air Mech School at 31.12.42; SOC 25.4.44.

K9315 40 Sqn 20.9.38. Wing dropped on landing and undercarriage leg collapsed, West Freugh, 12.1.39; to 1293M at 2 SofTT 3.2.39; SOC 30.6.39. 40.50 hours.

K9316 106 Sqn 22.9.38; 88 Sqn 8.10.38; engine cut on navex, undershot forced landing NE of Waddington, 23.5.39; ROS; 8 MU 12.2.40; Western A/W 13.8.40; 47 MU 23.9.40; to RCAF 28.10.40 as 1768.

K9317 106 Sqn 22.9.38; 88 Sqn 6.10.38; West Raynham 24.11.39; 101 Sqn at 30.11.39; 2 Gp TTF 22.2.40; 9 MU 5.3.41; Austin 6.4.41; to RCAF 5.41 as 2048.

K9318 106 Sqn 22.9.38; 88 Sqn 6.10.38; 2 Salvage Section 13.1.40; 21 AD 8.3.40; presumed abandoned in France 6.40.

K9319 106 Sqn 27.9.38; 88 Sqn 6.10.38. Stalled on approach and hit ground; undercarriage collapsed, Evanton, 13.4.39. 114.00 hours.

K9320 106 Sqn 27.9.38; 88 Sqn 6.10.38; Mildenhall at 30.11.39; 3 Gp TTF; overshot landing and hit hedge, Langham, 27.5.41; Western A/W 26.11.41; LEP 10.1.42; to SAAF 29.1.42.

K9321 106 Sqn 27.9.38; 88 Sqn 6.10.38; 21 AD 8.6.40; Fairey 20.6.40; 18 MU 23.7.40; 47 MU 29.9.40; to RCAF 27.10.40 as 1773.

K9322 106 Sqn 27.9.38; 88 Sqn 6.10.38; 18 MU 18.9.40; 47 MU 22.12.40; to RAAF 15.1.41.

K9323 185 Sqn 27.9.38; 218 Sqn 10.10.38; 150 Sqn 31.5.40; Rollason 24.8.40; 9 MU 27.9.40; Austin 28.2.41; to RCAF 4.5.41.

K9324 185 Sqn 27.9.38; 218 10.10.38; 10 MU 7.3.40; Austin 2.4.40; 38 MU 17.7.40; 47 MU 1.9.40; to RAAF 19.9.40.

K9325 185 Sqn 27.9.38; 218 Sqn 10.10.38. Shot down, St. Vith, 11.5.40; FO A.J. Hudson, Sgt N.H. Thompson and AC1 A. Ellis captured

K9326 185 Sqn 27.9.38; 218 Sqn 10.10.38; AASF 12.3.40; 6 MU 12.4.40; Western A/W 22.6.40; 47 MU 13.8.40; to RCAF 31.8.40 as 1716.

K9327 185 Sqn 27.9.38; 218 Sqn 10.10.38; damaged in forced landing, Monchy, 10.1.40; ROS; K9329 collided with K9327 while landing at Auberive, 23.1.40; 2 Salvage Section 29.1.40; 21 AD 15.3.40; presumed abandoned in France 6.40.

K9328 185 Sqn 27.9.38; 218 Sqn 10.10.38. Hit pylon during low-level practice, Carlton, 10m NW of Bedford, 11.8.39; FO W. Kinane, Sgt P.A. Allan and AC1 I. Roberts killed

K9329 185 Sqn 29.9.38; 218 Sqn 10.10.38; collided with K9327 on landing due to flap failure, Auberive 23.1.40; 2 Salvage Section 29.1.40; 21 AD 15.3.40; 218 Sqn; Abandoned on evacuation, 5.40.

K9330 35 Sqn 29.9.38; 226 Sqn 14.10.38. Burnt on evacuation of Reims, 16.5.40.

K9331 Bristol 1.10.38 for Taurus II test bed; damaged and repaired at Bristols, 6.8.42; Rosenfield 14.6.43; SOC 16.6.43. 571.21 hours.

K9332 RAE 1.10.38; Fairey 2.6.40; 8 MU 4.7.40; 304 Sqn 26.8.40; 27 MU 23.12.40; 47 MU 17.1.41; to RCAF 7.3.41 as 1894.

K9333 142 Sqn 3.10.38; Damaged by flak, Sedan, 14.5.40, and forcelanded, Ecly, Ardennes; crew escaped

K9334 142 Sqn 3.10.38. Engine cut; bellylanded and hit hedge 2m NE of Honiton, Devon, 1.3.39; to 1354M at 5 SofTT 21.3.39.

K9335 142 Sqn 5.10.38. Engine cut; bellylanded and hit hedge, Tarrant Keynston, Dorset, 28.1.39; to 1292M at 4 SofTT 21.2.39.

K9336 142 Sqn 5.10.38; 207 Sqn; to 2434M at 2 SofTT 20.12.40; SOC 18.3.44.

K9337 142 Sqn 5.10.38; 2 Salvage Section 19.12.39; 226 Sqn 12.3.40; 10 MU 15.3.40; Western A/W 4.7.40; 27 MU 23.8.40; 1 FTS 5.10.40; Austin 1.2.42; 38 MU 5.7.42; 18 MU 7.9.42; SOC 14.7.44.

K9338 105 Sqn 8.10.38. Damaged in action, Luxembourg, 10.5.40 and abandoned on evacuation, 16.5.40.

K9339 105 Sqn 8.10.38; 21 AD 28.2.40; 105 Sqn. Damaged in action, Luxembourg, 10.5.40 and abandoned on evacuation, 16.5.40.

K9340 105 Sqn 8.10.38. Hydraulic pump burst and cockpit filled with fumes; bellylanded on beach, West Freugh, 31.1.39. 245 hours.

K9341 105 Sqn 14.10.38; 22 MU 28.4.40; 47 MU 9.11.40; to RCAF 16.12.40 as 1802.

K9342 105 Sqn 14.10.38. Shot down attacking bridge near Sedan, 14.5.40

K9343 226 Sqn 14.10.38. Hit by flak attacking bridge and crashed, Le Grandes Armoises, 11m SSW of Sedan, 14.5.40; Sgt V.H. Moseley, Sgt S.D. Hibberd and Cpl H.F. Little killed

K9344 226 Sqn 14.10.38; 98 Sqn 9.10.39; Finningley 1.4.40; 12 MU 3.9.40; 47 MU 13.1.41; to RCAF 5.2.41 as 1841.

K9345 226 Sqn 19.10.38; 98 Sqn 9.10.39. Burnt on evacuation, Chateau Bougon, Nantes, 15.6.40.

K9346 226 Sqn 14.10.38; 2 SF 24.4.40; 22 MU 2.5.40; 5 BGS 4.6.40; 27 MU 21.9.40; 47 MU 11.10.40; to RAAF 2.11.40.

K9347 226 Sqn 14.10.38; 22 MU 22.9.39; 4 BGS 17.5.40. Engine cut; bellylanded on sand dunes near West Freugh, 13.10.40; SOC 27.10.40.

K9348 88 Sqn 18.10.38; reported missing, Hirson, 19.5.40; presumed salvaged by 4 RSU 3.6.40; 21 AD 10.6.40; presumed abandoned in France, 6.40.

K9349 88 Sqn 18.10.38; presumed lost in France, 5.40.

K9350 88 Sqn 18.10.38; engine cut; bellylanded, Boscombe Down, 12.5.39; ROS; Abingdon at 30.11.39; 98 Sqn 12.4.40; 9 MU 13.7.40; 47 MU 20.7.41; to RCAF 29.8.41 as 2069.

K9351 88 Sqn 19.10.38; 21 AD 17.10.39; 226 Sqn 23.5.40; 18 MU 26.7.40; 47 MU 9.2.41; to RCAF 21.2.41 as 1870.

K9352 88 Sqn 20.10.38; presumed lost in France, 5.40.

K9353 218 Sqn 20.10.38. Hit by flak, Bouillon, and crashed, Sensenruth, 12.5.40; F/Sgt J.B. Horner, Sgt L.C. Flisher and LAC L.D. Davies killed

K9354 218 Sqn 24.10.38; 98 Sqn at 30 11.39; to 1869M, later 2554M.

K9355 218 Sqn 24.10.38; 8 MU 2.3.40; 47 MU 18.9.40; to RCAF 27.9.40 as 1723.

K9356 218 Sqn 26.10.38. Lost wing during dive bombing practice and dived into ground near Auberive, 13.11.39; PO R. Thynne, Sgt R.C.L. Pike and AC1 V.W.L. Richardson killed; wreck to 2 Salvage Section 13.11.39; SOC 27.1.40.

K9357 218 Sqn 26.10.38; crashed in forced landing 3m WNW of Soissons, Aisne, 12.1.40; 2 Salvage Section 20.1.40; 21 AD 10.3.40; presumed abandoned in France 6.40.

K9358 15 Sqn 27.10.38; West Raynham 4.10.39; 101 Sqn at 30.11.39; 2 Gp TTF 22.2.40; 38 MU 9.1.41; Austin 4.4.41; to RCAF 5.41 as 2039.

K9359 15 Sqn 27.10.38; PO P. Shennan fell out of aircraft and killed, 5.4.39; 22 MU 30.12.39; 4 BGS 17.5.40. Engine cut; undershot approach to West Freugh and crashlanded, East Freugh, Wigtown, 23.4.41; SOC 1.5.41.

K9360 40 Sqn 28.10.38; to 1839M 13.3.40.
K9361 40 Sqn 28.10.38; to 1840M 13.3.40.

K9362 40 Sqn 31.10.38; 5 MU 3.12.39; 4 BGS 12.6.40; 47 MU 9.12.41; to RAAF 28.2.42.

K9363 40 Sqn 31.10.38; to 1841M at 2 SofTT 13.3.40; SOC 18.3.44.

K9364 40 Sqn 31.10.38; to 1842M at 2 SofTT 13.3.40; SOC 26.10.43.

K9365 98 Sqn 1.11.38; 88 Sqn 21.6.40; 22 MU 21.7.40; 18 MU 27.7.40; 47 MU 9.2.41; to RCAF 21.2.41 as 1868.

K7635 of No. 88 Squadron. (P Jarrett collection)

K9366 98 Sqn 1.11.38; 15 Sqn 16.9.39; 142 Sqn at 30.11.39. Abandoned on evacuation of Berry-au-Bac 17.5.40.

K9367 98 Sqn 7.11.38; 15 Sqn 16.9.39; 142 Sqn at 30.11.39; 6 RSU 17.5.40; presumed abandoned in France 6.40.

K9368 98 Sqn 7.11.38; 15 Sqn 16.9.39; 12 Sqn at 30.11.39; 20 MU 7.5.40; 32 MU 6.9.40; 47 MU 1.3.41; to RAAF 3.4.41.

K9369 98 Sqn 7.11.38; 15 Sqn 20.9.39; 150 Sqn at 30.11.39; damaged by ground fire, Luxembourg, 10.5.40; presumed abandoned on evacuation, 5.40.

K9370 Fairey for P24 Prince test bed 7.11.38; RAE 12.7.41; USAAF Wright Field 15.1.42; retd to RAE 1943 and scrapped.

K9371 RAE for electrical development work 7.11.38; 22 MU 30.5.40; 7 BGS 4.6.40; 47 MU 25.10.41; to RAAF 19.11.41.

K9372 103 Sqn 7.11.38. Hit by ground fire and abandoned near Dippach, Luxembourg, 10.5.40; F/Lt M.C. Wells, Sgt H.F. Bullock and LAC T.H. Bowen captured

K9373 103 Sqn 7.11.38. Collided with K9273 and bellylanded, Hucknall, 6.8.39; to 1651M at 1 EWS 22.9.39.

K9374 103 Sqn 7.11.38; presumed lost in France 5.40.

K9375 12 Sqn 8.11.38; Mildenhall 30.10.39; 3 Gp TTF; 47 MU 30.10.41; to RAAF 5.1.42.

K9376 12 Sqn 7.11.38; 1 Salvage Section 22.11.39; 12 Sqn 18.1.40; 6 MU 1.3.40; Western A/W 22.6.40; 47 MU 13.8.40; to RCAF 31.8.40 as 1714.

K9377 12 Sqn 10.11.38; hit tree on approach, Andover 16.3.39; Mildenhall at 30.11.39; NFT.

K9378 150 Sqn 10.11.38; engine cut; bellylanded near Great Yarmouth, Norfolk, 14.7.39; Watton 21.7.39 and ROS; Scottish Avn 17.11.39; Fairey 24.6.40; 12 MU 17.8.40; 47 MU 15.10.40; to RCAF 28.11.40 as 1827.

K9379 150 Sqn 14.11.38; 20 MU 7.5.40; 32 MU 28.7.40; 6 MU 23.11.40; 47 MU 28.2.41; to RCAF 11.6.41 as 2010.

K9380 150 Sqn 14.11.38; 6 MU 29.4.40; Rollason 1.8.40; Fairey 2.9.40; 18 MU 10.2.41; 47 MU 28.2.41; to RAAF 3.4.41.

K9381 150 Sqn 17.11.38. Engine cut on approach; overshot and hit fence, Benson, 17.4.39; SOC 5.39. 72.00 hours.

K9382 226 Sqn 18.11.38; Scottish Avn 9.10.39; 47 MU 15.10.41; to RCAF 11.11.41 as 2109.

K9383 226 Sqn 18.11.38. Damaged in action, Sedan, 14.5.40 and burnt on evacuation of Reims/Champagne, 16.5.40.

K9384 218 Sqn 17.11.38; Linton-on-Ouse 27.9.39; 4 Gp TTF; 24 OTU 6.6.42; 27 MU 15.11.42; SOC 30.6.43.

K9385 9 FTS 24.11.38; 10 MU 12.12.38; 9 BGS 9.5.40; 18 MU 11.7.41; 47 MU 16.10.41; Dumfries 2.11.41; to SAAF 29.1.42 as 1005.

K9386 98 Sqn 19.11.38; 9 MU 13.7.40; Austin 22.5.41; to SAAF 11.7.41.

K9387 150 Sqn 19.11.38. Shot down by Bf 109s near Saarbrücken, 30.9.39; FO F.M.C. Corelli and AC1 K.V. Gay killed; SOC 23.11.39. 148.00 hours.

K9388 150 Sqn 17.11.38; Abingdon 24.10.39; CGS 20.11.39; 1 FTS 26.8.40; 32 MU 4.7.41; 1 FTS 22.8.41; engine cut; bellylanded 5m SE of Salisbury, Wilts., 6.11.41; ROS; 18 MU 23.3.42; undercarriage collapsed when engine started, Dumfries, 4.4.42; ROS; 215 MU 29.5.42; 3 PATP 29.6.42; to RAAF 5.8.42.

K9389 150 Sqn 19.11.38; 22 MU 2.5.40; Rollason 5.8.40; Fairey 2.9.40; 12 MU 10.12.40; Austin 30.1.41; Parks 24.3.41; to SAAF 12.4.41 but lost at sea en route in *City of Winchester.*

K9390 150 Sqn 19.11.38. Damaged by ground fire, Luxembourg, and crashed, Gosselies, near Charleroi, 10.5.40; crew escaped

K9391 150 Sqn 19.11.38. Flew into high ground descending in cloud on navex, Whitten Tor, near Two Bridges, Dartmoor, 4.7.39; SOC 7.39. 57.25 hours

K9392 150 Sqn 19.11.38; 103 Sqn 9.4.40; 2 SF 20.4.40; 8 MU 25.4.40; 12 FTS 16.5.40; engine cut; bellylanded, Casterton, Lincs., 25.8.40; Fairey 29.8.40; 18 MU 25.4.41; to SAAF 9.7.41 as 981.

K9393 52 Sqn 23.11.38; 12 OTU 18.4.40; stalled landing at night, Benson, 6.9.40; Austin 21.9.40; 12 MU 25.3.41; 47 MU 29.3.41; to RAAF 26.5.41.

K9394   9 FTS 24.11.38; 10 MU 12.12.38; 9 BGS 11.5.40; 18 MU 22.7.41; 215 MU 6.5.42; 3 PATP 28.5.42; to SAAF 16.7.42.

K9395   52 Sqn 23.11.38; RAE 20.2.39; 12 OTU 18.4.40; overshot forced landing in bad weather, Cowley, Oxford, 22.9.40; Fairey 28.9.40; Austin 14.4.41; to RCAF 30.4.41 as 2057.

K9396   52 Sqn 23.11.38. Engine cut; crashlanded near Andover, 11.3.40; SOC 17.3.40.

K9397   52 Sqn 26.11.38. Engine cut; overshot forced landing and hit shed near Trowbridge, Wilts., 29.10.39; SOC 7.11.39.

K9398   52 Sqn 24.11.38. Collided with K9399 in formation and crashed 1m NW of Dorchester, Oxon., 18.10.39; PO J.R. Anderson and AC1 R.A.W. Keogh killed; SOC 27.11.39.

K9399   52 Sqn 26.11.38; collided with K9398 but landed safely 18.10.39; ROS; hit tree on take-off and undercarriage collapsed on landing, Benson, 10.4.40; ROS; 12 OTU 18.4.40; Fairey 12.6.40; 12 MU 16.7.40; 305 Sqn 14.9.40; 9 MU 14.11.40; Austin 1.3.41; to RCAF 4.5.41.

K9400   52 Sqn 26.11.38; 12 OTU 18.4.40; 32 MU 23.1.41; Austin 25.4.41; to SAAF 15.6.41 as 968.

K9401   52 Sqn 26.11.38; 12 OTU 18.4.40; 18 MU 14.12.40; 47 MU 13.3.41; to RCAF 19.4.41 as 1948.

K9402   36 MU 28.11.38; to SAAF for evaluation 25.4.39 as 901.

K9403   52 Sqn 29.11.38; 12 OTU 18.4.40; undercarriage jammed; bellylanded, Shawbury, 2.2.41; 27 MU 12.2.41; 47 MU 17.7.41; to RCAF 27.8.41 as 2106.

K9404   52 Sqn 1.12.38; 103 Sqn 26.8.39. Abandoned on evacuation of Bétheniville, 16.5.40.

K9405   52 Sqn 1.12.38; 12 OTU 18.4.40; engine cut; bellylanded in trees, Budleigh Salterton, Devon, 21.5.40; Fairey 27.5.40; 20 MU 11.8.40; 47 MU 23.9.40; to RCAF 14.10.40 as 1762.

K9406   52 Sqn 2.12.38; engine iced up; undershot forced landing and hit hedge, Wootton Bassett, Wilts, 29.2.40; Rolls-Royce 5.4.40; Fairey 7.6.40; 20 MU 20.8.40; 142 Sqn 19.9.40; 27 MU 2.10.40; Austin 10.11.40; Parks 21.12.40; to RCAF 10.3.41.

K9407   52 Sqn 2.12.38; 12 OTU 18.4.40; engine cut; bellylanded 2m W of Abingdon, 5.3.40; Fairey 2.6.40; 9 MU 20.8.40; 47 MU 18.9.40; to RCAF 18.10.40 as 1754.

K9408   52 Sqn 2.12.38; 103 Sqn 26.8.39; 4 RSU 25.5.40; 21 AD 28.5.40; Fairey 24 .6.40; 20 MU 17.8.40; 47 MU 18.9.40; to RCAF 22.10.40 as 1727.

K9409   52 Sqn 2.12.38; 103 Sqn 26.8.39. Hit by ground fire, Vernon, but SOC on return as DBR, 10.6.40.

K9410   52 Sqn 6.12.38; 12 OTU 18.4.40; bellylanded in error, Benson, 3.5.40; ROS; undercarriage collapsed on landing, Benson, 17.6.40; ROS; 22 MU 12.1.41; 27 MU 5.2.41; 22 MU 16.2.41; 47 MU 16.10.41; Dumfries 2.11.41; to SAAF 29.1.42 as 1003.

K9411   52 Sqn 6.12.38; 103 Sqn 26.8.39; 8 MU 24.2.40; 13 MU 7.5.40; Rollason 23.5.40; 38 MU 30.6.40; 47 MU 1.9.40; to RAAF 19.9.40.

K9412   63 Sqn 10.12.38. Flew into ground on night navex, Great Massingham, Norfolk, 25.7.39; Sgt A.J. Shepherd, Sgt A.A. Sherriff and AC1 Roberts killed.

K9413   63 Sqn 10.12.38; 52 Sqn 28.1.40; 12 OTU 18.4.40; 20 MU 21.12.40; 47 MU 16.1.41; to RCAF 7.3.41 as 1895.

K9414   63 Sqn 10.12.38; engine cut after take-off for navex; hit fence in forced landing, Pyewike, Lincs., 7.3.39; ROS; 12 Sqn 26.8.39; 98 Sqn 9.10.39; 9 MU 13.7.40; 47 MU 8.7.41; to RCAF 27.8.41 as 2078.

K9415   63 Sqn 12.12.38; 12 Sqn 26.8.39; 22 MU 19.9.39; 4 BGS 2.5.40; 47 MU 21.12.41; Dumfries 26.1.42; to SAAF 15.4.43 as 1016.

K9416   63 Sqn 10.12.38; 12 OTU 18.4.40. Hit trees at night and crashed, Heath End, Oxon., 1.10.40; PO G. Sokolowski (PAF) killed; SOC 9.10.40.

K9417   63 Sqn 10.12.38; 12 Sqn 26.8.39; 150 Sqn 16.10.39; 6 ASP 27.4.40; 21 AD 6.5.40; 4 MU 16.5.40; Fairey 24.6.40; 12 MU 28.7.40; 305 Sqn 14.9.40; 9 MU 14.11.40; Austin 28.2.41; to RCAF 4.5.41.

K9418   63 Sqn 10.12.38; 12 OTU 18.4.40; to 2431M at 4 SofTT 20.12.40; SOC 30.6.43.

K9419   63 Sqn 10.12.38; 52 Sqn 28.1.40; 12 OTU 18.4.40; Engine cut; bellylanded, Shillingford, Oxon., 14.7.40. Engine cut; hit trees in forced landing, Milton, near Pewsey, Wilts., 28.8.40; SOC 11.9.40.

K9420   63 Sqn 12.12.38; 12 OTU 18.4.40. Engine cut on gunnery training; ditched off Seaton, Devon, 20.6.40.

K9421   63 Sqn 12.12.38; 12 Sqn 26.8.39; 98 Sqn 9.10.39; Finningley 1.4.40; 27 MU 12.12.40; 47 MU 16.7.41; to RCAF 8.8.41 as 2063.

K9422   63 Sqn 12.12.38; 15 Sqn 6.9.39; Abingdon 26.9.39; 98 Sqn 8.10.39; 18 MU 17.7.40; 47 MU 17.3.41; to RAAF 26.5.41.

K9423   63 Sqn 12.12.38; 12 Sqn 26.8.39; 22 MU 6.11.39; 4 BGS 2.5.40; Fairey 24.6.40; 27 MU 10.8.40; 12 MU 11.8.40; 47 MU 25.9.40; to RCAF 27.10.40 as 1749.

K9424   10 MU 19.12.38; 9 BGS 9.5.40; 47 MU 5.7.41; to RCAF 24.8.41 as 2094.

K9425   10 MU 19.12.38; 9 BGS 6.5.40; 47 MU 17.7.41; to RCAF 27.8.41 as 2089.

K9426   10 MU 19.12.38; 9 BGS 9.5.40; 10 MU 11.5.40; 9 BGS 20.5.40; 9 MU 22.2.41; 215 MU 26.4.42; 3 PATP 10.5.42; to RAAF 9.8.42.

K9427   10 MU 30.12.38; 9 BGS 9.5.40; 18 MU 23.7.41; Dumfries 31.7.41; to RCAF 19.8.41 as 2091.

K9428   10 MU 19.12.38; 10 BGS 11.5.40; 18 MU 19.11.41; 614 Sqn 8.6.42; 18 MU 16.9.42; SOC 14.7.44.

K9429   10 MU 19.12.38; 10 BGS 7.5.40; damaged in forced landing, Southwick, Kirkcudbright, 5.8.40; ROS; 10 AOS 9.41; 18 MU 3.8.42; 215 MU 18.8.42; 3 PATP 23.8.42; to RAAF 13.9.42.

K9430   10 MU 30.12.38; 10 BGS 15.4.40; 10 AOS 9.41; 18 MU 13.8.42; Rosenfield 1.10.42; 27 MU 9.12.42; SOC 30.6.43.

K9431   10 MU 31.12.38; 10 BGS 15.4.40; overshot landing and hit obstruction, Annan, 12.8.40; Fairey 20.8.40; 47 MU 5.2.41; to RCAF 13.3.41 as 1901.

K9432   10 MU 30.12.38; 10 BGS 16.4.40; 10 AOS 9.41; Rosenfield 8.7.42; 27 MU 17.9.42; 47 MU 6.10.42; to SAAF 6.4.43.

K9433   10 MU 30.12.38; 10 BGS 16.4.40; 10 AOS 9.41; 18 MU 18.11.41; 309 Sqn 2.6.42; Rosenfield 13.1.43; SOC 29.1.43.

K9434   10 MU 30.12 38; 10 BGS 22.4.40; 10 AOS 9.41; 18 MU 18.11.41; 614 Sqn 8.6.42; 18 MU 16.9.42; SOC 14.7.44.

K9435   10 MU 30.12.38; 10 BGS 15.4.40; overshot landing and tipped up, Dumfries, 13.11.40; ROS; 10 AOS 13.9.41; engine cut; crashlanded, North House Lane, St. Anns, Dumfries, 21.10.41; Rosenfield 10.11.41; 18 MU 19.2.42; 215 MU 20.4.42; 3 PATP 10.5.42; to RAAF 31.5.42.

K9436   185 Sqn 26.1.39; 63 Sqn 30.6.39; 52 Sqn 30.6.39; 12 OTU 18.4.40; 22 MU 12.1.41; Austin 14.4.41; to RCAF 5.41 as 2015.

K9437   9 MU 30.12.38; 185 Sqn 30.1.39; undercarriage collapsed when engine started, Thornaby, 23.3.39; ROS; 98 Sqn 10.9.39; overshot landing and hit shelter, Hucknall, 10.10.39; 13 MU 20.11.39; Scottish Avn at 31.12.39; Fairey 6.6.40; 20 MU 29.7.40; 23 MU 6.3.41; 88 Sqn 21.4.41; taxied into bomb crater, Sydenham, 7.5.41; ROS; 27 MU 1.1.42; 2 Sqn 16.9.42; 27 MU 11.2.43; SOC 30.11.43. 81.35 hours.

K9438   9 MU 30.12.38; 185 Sqn 30.1.39; 63 Sqn 3.7.39; 12 OTU 18.4.40; to 2432M at 2 SofTT 21.12.40; SOC 18.3.44. 594.00 hours.

K9439   9 MU 30.12.38; 185 Sqn 30.1.39; 63 Sqn 3.7.39; hit hedge in crashlanding while lost, Newnham Hill Farm, Oxon., 3.11.39; 18 MU 18.9.40; 47 MU 26.10.40; to RCAF 5.12.40 as 1789.

K9222 acting as a flying test-bed for the 1,200 hp Rolls-Royce Exe engine. (via D Birch)

K9440   9 MU 6.1.39; 185 Sqn 15.2.39; 63 Sqn 28.6.39; 52 Sqn 28.6.39. Hit trees on night take-off, Benson, 3.11.39; SOC 16.11.39.

K9441   9 MU 6.1.39; 185 Sqn 30.1.39; 88 Sqn 26.5.39; engine cut on bombing exercise, crashlanded, Morainvilliers, 29.2.40; 2 Salvage Section 1.3.40; 21 AD 17.3.40; presumed abandoned in France, 6.40.

K9442   9 MU 6.1.39; 185 Sqn 30.1.39; 63 Sqn 30.6.39; 52 Sqn 30.6.39; engine cut; bellylanded near Wallingford, Berks., 30.3.40; ROS; 12 OTU 18.4.40; 27 MU 9.12.40; 47 MU 19.9.41; to RAAF 14.10.41.

K9443   9 MU 6.1.39; 185 Sqn 30.1.39; 20 MU 29.10.39; 4 BGS 20.4.40; 18 MU 20.7.41; 215 MU 31.5.42; 3 PATP 1.7.42; to RAAF 4.8.42.

K9444   9 MU 6.1.39; 185 Sqn 15.2.39; 52 Sqn 17.7.39; 12 OTU 18.4.40; Fairey 1.6.40; 20 MU 23.7.40; 142 Sqn 19.9.40; 150 Sqn 3.10.40; 27 MU 7.10.40; 47 MU 5.2.41; to RAAF 18.2.41.

K9445   9 MU 9.1.39; 185 Sqn 15.2.39; 63 Sqn 3.7.39. Engine cut; overshot, skidded and hit hedge, Benson, 17.11.39; Morris Motors 15.1.40; SOC 26.8.40.

K9446   9 MU 9.1.39; 185 Sqn 31.1.39; 63 Sqn 3.7.39; 12 OTU 18.4.40; damaged 25.11.40; Fairey 11.12.40; 18 MU 12.5.41; Dumfries 19.6.41; to SAAF 24.7.41.

K9447   9 MU 9.1.39; 185 Sqn 30.1.39; 218 Sqn 27.8.39; 22 MU 14.9.39; 4 BGS 17.5.40; 10 AOS 9.41; 47 MU 21.12.41; to RAAF 7.4.42.

K9448   207 Sqn 13.1.39. Flew into hill in bad visibility, Winchcombe, Glos., 19.9.39; PO J.E. Hull and AC2 K. Malcolm killed; SOC 11.39.

K9449   9 MU 9.1.39; 185 Sqn 31.1.39; 52 Sqn 30.6.39; 63 Sqn 28.2.40; 12 OTU 18.4.40; engine cut on approach; stalled and undercarriage collapsed, Dorchester LG, Oxon., 24.6.40; Fairey 10.7.40; 9 MU 27.10.40; 47 MU 5.3.41; to RCAF 19.4.41 as 1947.

K9450   207 Sqn 10.1.39; 88 Sqn 26.8.39; 207 Sqn at 31.12.39; overshot landing, Penrhos, 24.5.40; Fairey 29.5.40; 20 MU 11.7.40; 23 MU 6.3.41; 88 Sqn 9.5.41; 23 MU 5.9.41; 613 Sqn 3.6.42; 27 MU 18.8.42; SOC 30.6.43. 487.05 hours.

K9451   207 Sqn 10.1.39; 12 OTU 8.4.40; engine cut; bellylanded, Great Haseley, Oxon., 10.9.40; Austin 21.9.40; 18 MU 11.2.41; 47 MU 27.2.41; to RCAF 13.3.41 as 1903.

K9452   207 Sqn 13.1.39; 88 Sqn 26.8.39; 98 Sqn 9.10.39. Crashed and presumed abandoned in France 5.40.

K9453   207 Sqn 13.1.39; 12 OTU 8.4.40; overshot night landing, swung and hit Chance light, Benson, 15.7.40; Fairey 20.7.40; 18 MU 15.9.40; 47 MU 30.9.40; to RCAF 27.10.40 as 1772.

K9454   207 Sqn 13.1.39; 12 OTU 8.4.40; engine cut; bellylanded, Turvey, Beds., 9.4.40; 4 MU 27.5.40; Fairey 6.6.40; 48 MU 8.9.40; 18 MU 18.9.40; 47 MU 26.10.40; to RCAF 5.12.40 as 1782.

K9455   207 Sqn 13.1.39; 12 OTU 8.4.40; engine cut; bellylanded on approach, Brize Norton, 8.7.40; Fairey 15.7.40; 47 MU 14.3.41; to RCAF 2.4.41 as 1908.

K9456   103 Sqn 23.1.39; 8 MU 16.2.40; 47 MU 21.9.40; to RCAF 8.10.40 as 1734.

K9457   35 Sqn 16.1.39; 15 Sqn 27.8.39; 22 MU 30.12.39; 4 BGS 2.5.40; engine cut; bellylanded and hit wall, Portpatrick, Kirkcudbright, 28.5.41; Fairey 4.6.41; 47 MU 16.8.41; to RCAF 29.8.41 as 2076.

K9458   207 Sqn 20.1.39; engine cut on approach; overshot into haystack, Cranfield, 3.10.39; Scottish Avn 10.39; 12 MU 21.4.41; Austin 13.5.41; to RCAF 7.9.41 as 2102.

K9459   207 Sqn 20.1.39; 18 MU 4.1.41; 47 MU 6.2.41; to RCAF 21.2.41 as 1873.

K9460   207 Sqn 20.1.39; 63 Sqn 10.12.39; 52 Sqn 17.12.39; 12 OTU 18.4.40; Fairey 5.6.40; 6 MU 15.7.40; 103 Sqn 5.8.40; 27 MU 2.10.40; Austin 10.11.40; to SAAF 15.6.41.

K9461   207 Sqn 20.1.39; 38 MU 30.12.40; 47 MU 11.6.41; to RCAF 23.6.41 as 2019.

K9462   207 Sqn 24.1.39; 12 OTU 8.4.40; 6 MU 19.12.40; 47 MU 28.2.41; to RCAF 24.5.41.

K9463   207 Sqn 24.1.39; 88 Sqn 26.8.39; 207 Sqn at 30.11.39; 12 OTU 18.4.40. Engine cut on take-off; spun and dived into ground SW of Benson, 11.6.40; PO B.P. Thomson (NZ), Sgt D.J. Craven and LAC P.A. Lewis killed.

K9464   207 Sqn 24.1.39; 12 OTU 8.4.40; engine cut; bellylanded near Harwell, 22.8.40; Fairey 2.9.40; 47 MU 13.11.40; to RAAF 15.1.41.

K9465   207 Sqn 24.1.39; forcelanded while lost and tipped up near Cottesmore, 30.12.39; 13 MU 9.1.40; Rollason 18.1.40; Fairey 18.8.40; 47 MU 2.11.40; to RCAF 28.11.40 as 1821.

K9466   35 Sqn 24.1.39; 17 OTU 22.4.40; 13 MU 2.5.40; Rollason 23.5.40; 38 MU 17.7.40; 47 MU 1.9.40; to RCAF 5.2.41 as 1848.

K9467   185 Sqn 24.1.39; 98 Sqn 10.9.39. Flew into ground in fog on navex 4m SW of Stow-on-the-Wold, Glos., 9.12.39; Sgt F. Hinson and AC1 L.R. Bull killed; pilot FO P.D.B. Stevens injured; SOC 27.1.40.

K9468   185 Sqn 24.1.39; 52 Sqn 30.6.39; 12 OTU 18.4.40; engine cut; crashlanded and fell into railway cutting, Marlborough, Wilts., 19.6.40; Fairey 21.8.40; 47 MU 22.11.40; to RAAF 15.1.41.

K9469   35 Sqn 24.1.39. Engine cut after take-off on night training flight; dived into ground, Cottesmore, 5.5.39; PO G.L. Cooper, Sgt J.F. Tompkins and AC2 J. Sweeney killed; SOC 5.5.39. 97.05 hours.

K9470   35 Sqn 24.1.39; engine cut; bellylanded, Cottesmore, 22.6.39; ROS; 63 Sqn 25.10.39; 22 MU 6.11.39; 4 BGS 2.5.40; Dumfries 8.8.41; presumed SOC 21.6.47.

K9471   35 Sqn 30.1.39; 47 MU 27.2.40; Fairey 6.6.40; 6 MU 8.7.40; 103 Sqn 6.8.40; 27 MU 2.10.40; Austin 10.11.40; Parks 21.12.40; to SAAF 5.2.41 as 937.

K9472   35 Sqn 30.1.39. Engine cut after take-off; lost height and flew into cliff, Carew Cheriton, 29.10.39; FO G.A.C. Rhind, AC1 E.W. Looker and AC2 B. Conner killed.

K9473   35 Sqn 30.1.39. Engine cut; tipped up in forced landing and undercarriage collapsed, Goldington, Beds., 5.11.39; SOC 28.11.39.

K9474   35 Sqn 30.1.39; Polish OTU 9.4.40; bellylanded in error, Hucknall, 6.5.40; ROS; 18 OTU 15.6.40; 22 MU 27.11.40; 47 MU 16.1.41; to RCAF 7.3.41 as 1879.

K9475   35 Sqn 30.1.39; engine cut; overshot forced landing, New Holland, Lincs., 29.8.39; Scottish Avn 22.11.39; Fairey 8.6.40; 9 MU 16.7.40; 47 MU 15.8.40; to RCAF 6.9.40 as 1705.

K9476   35 Sqn 30.1.39; engine cut; bellylanded, Cranfield, 24.11.39; ROS; Polish OTU 9.4.40; 18 OTU 15.6.40; 38 MU 5.12.40; Austin 23.2.41; Parks 29.3.41; to RCAF 10.4.41.

K9477   Rolls-Royce for Peregrine test bed 7.2.39; Southern Aircraft, Merlin XX engine, 5.5.42; 9 MU 16.6.42; SOC 4.10.43.

K9478   35 Sqn 30.1.39; Polish OTU 9.4.40; 18 OTU 15.6.40; 27 MU 10.2.41; 47 MU 24.2.41; to RAAF 3.4.41.

K9479   35 Sqn 6.2.39; 15 Sqn 27.8.39; Abingdon at 30.11.39; 6 MU 12.4.40; Western A/W 22.6.40; 47 MU 13.10.40; to RCAF 28.11.40 as 1816.

K9480   35 Sqn 6.2.39; 17 OTU 22.4.40. Lost height after take-off and flew into house, Ruffs Drive, Hucknall, 23.9.40; LAC E. Rozmiarek and five people in house killed.

K9481   35 Sqn 6.2.39; 52 Sqn 4.4.40; 12 OTU 18.4.40. Flew into hill in low cloud near Sidmouth, Devon, 24.5.40; PO W.D. Finlayson (NZ), A/Sgt E. Wigham and AC2 A.W.A. Coull killed; SOC 2.6.40.

K9482   150 Sqn 31.1.39. Crashed in forced landing near Aylesbury, Bucks., 7.2.39; to 1322M at 1 SofTT 6.3.39.

K9483   150 Sqn 31.1.39; bellylanded while lost in bad weather, Stone, Bucks., 7.2.39; ROS. Shot down attacking bridge, Sedan, 14.5.40; PO A.F. Posselt, Sgt D.J. Bowen and AC2 N.V. Vano killed.

K9484   150 Sqn 31.1.39. Shot down by Bf 109s, Saarbrücken, 30.9.39; FO J.R. Saunders and AC1 D.L. Thomas killed; SOC 23.11.39. 141.35 hours.

K9485   12 Sqn 5.2.39; 105 Sqn at 30.11.39. Hit by ground fire and flew into hill near Bouillon, 12.5.40; PO T. Hurst, Sgt W.J. Anning, LAC C.R. Wells killed.

K9486   12 Sqn 5.2.39; 105 Sqn at 30.11.39; 2 SF 24.3.40; 48 MU 21.7.40; 12 MU 25.7.40; 47 MU 13.6.41; to RAAF 15.7.41.

863 Fairey Battle Is delivered by Austin, Longbridge, between October 1938 and August 1940. Contract 540408/36. 200 (L5598-L5797) built as Battle T.T.s

L4935   A&AEE; 63 Sqn 31.1.39; 12 OTU 18.4.40; 9 MU 10.3.41; 32 MU 7.6.41; 9 MU 12.6.41; Dumfries 17.7.41; to RCAF 19.8.41 as 2096; manufactured with some non-standard parts and originally for use in the UK only.

L4936   142 Sqn 8.10.38; 1 Salvage Section 13.10.39; 21 AD 11.12.39; presumed lost in France 5.40; manufactured with some non-standard parts and originally for use in the UK only.

L4937   142 Sqn 3.10.38; 20 MU 8.5.40; 32 MU 31.7.40; 9 MU 16.1.41; 47 MU 1.3.41; to RCAF 25.4.41 as 1982; manufactured with some non-standard parts and originally for use in the UK only.

L4938   15 Sqn 26.10.38; 150 Sqn 27.9.39; 22 MU 24.10.39; 47 MU 10.11.40; to RCAF 28.11.40 as 1813.

L4939   15 Sqn 26.10.38. Engine cut on take-off; bellylanded, Abingdon, 20.2.39; DBR; 35.50 hours.

L4940   15 Sqn 26.10.38; 22 MU 30.12.39; 47 MU 13.10.40; to RCAF 1.11.40 as 1755.

L4941   103 Sqn 1.11.38; 63 Sqn 23.10.39; Abingdon at 30.11.39; Bicester 6.3.40; 27 MU 6.2.41; 47 MU 23.4.41; to RAAF 4.6.41.

L4942   103 Sqn 1.11.38; 150 Sqn 4.10.39; 22 MU 18.4.40; 47 MU 27.9.40; to RCAF 27.10.40 as 1747.

L4943   12 Sqn 14.11.38; 12 OTU. Flew into ground at night near Watlington, Oxon., 6.8.40; PO A.V. Fisher (NZ) killed; SOC 12.8.40.

L4944   12 Sqn 8.11.38. Destroyed on evacuation of Reims, 16.5.40.

L4945   150 Sqn 17.11.38; 22 MU 18.4.40; 15 EFTS 7.8.40; engine cut; bellylanded 1m N of Lockerbie, Dumfries, 2.11.40; 1 PFTS 28.3.41; 16(P)FTS 13.7.41; Prop went into fine pitch on take-off; overshot airfield, Newton, 24.7.41; Rosenfield 28.7.41; 47 MU 17.11.41; Dumfries 26.1.42; to SAAF 2.3.42; to Middle East 30.1.43.

L4946   150 Sqn 14.11.38. Shot down attacking bridge near Donchery, 3m WSW of Sedan, 14.5.40; FO J. Ing, Sgt J.D. Turner and AC1 W.J. Nolan killed.

L4947   150 Sqn 14.11.38; 22 MU 25.4.40; 47 MU 13.10.40; to RCAF 1.11.40 as 1757.

L4948   150 Sqn 14.11.38; engine cut on take-off; bellylanded, Boscombe Down, 24.1.39; ROS; hit by another aircraft while parked, Benson, 23.5.39; 21 AD 6.3.40; presumed lost in France, 5.40.

L4949   12 Sqn 17.11.38. Shot down by ground fire attacking troop columns, Luxembourg, 10.5.40; F/Lt W. Simpson and LAC R.T. Tomlinson injured.

L4950   12 Sqn 21.11.38. Shot down, Sedan, 14.5.40; FO E.R.D. Vaughan and Sgt C. Shelton-Jones killed; AC1 J.D. Wright captured.

L4951   12 Sqn 2.12.38; Abingdon at 30.11.39; 13 OTU 27.5.40. Sideslipped into ground in circuit and cart-wheeled, Squires Gate, 10.6.40; FO A. Chalmers, AC1 B.B.C. Smith and AC2 H.B. Bennett killed; SOC 14.6.40.

L4952   12 Sqn 21.11.38. Shot down attacking bridges and crashed, Pouru-St-Rémy, 5m ESE of Sedan, 14.5.40; Sgt K. Alderson and AC1 R.T. Ainsworth killed; F/Lt G.D. Clancy captured.

L4953   52 Sqn 22.11.38; 150 Sqn 26.8.39; Abingdon 3.11.39; undercarriage leg jammed; wing dug in on landing, Benson, 8.6.40; ROS; overshot landing and hit gun post, Benson, 24.9.40; 4 MU 30.9.40; 9 MU 20.11.40; 47 MU 14.2.41; to RCAF 8.3.41 as 1890.

L4954   52 Sqn 30.11.38; 88 Sqn 26.9.39; 8 MU 15.2.40; 12 FTS 13.6.40; undercarriage leg jammed; swung on landing, Grantham, 12.8.40; 4 MU 22.8.40; 47 MU 7.11.40; to RAAF 15.1.41.

L4955   52 and 63 Sqns 10.12.38; undercarriage collapsed in heavy landing, Benson, 25.11.39; ROS; undershot night

L5286 with a Napier Sabre. It had a ventral radiator, increased fin area and a fixed undercarriage. (P Jarrett collection)

	landing and hit hedge, bellylanded, Benson, 14.2.40; 50 MU 29.2.40; 4 MU 20.5.40; Fairey 12.6.40; 18 MU 23.7.40; 47 MU 24.9.40; to RCAF 28.10.40 as 1765.
L4956	52 Sqn 30.11.38; 88 Sqn 26.9.39. Damaged in air raid on Mourmelon 10.5.40 and abandoned
L4957	52 Sqn 5.12.38; 103 Sqn 26.8.39; 8 MU 17.2.40; 10 MU 1.6.40; FAA Gosport 14.7.40; 47 MU 8.7.41; to RCAF 24.7.41 as 2056.
L4958	52 Sqn 5.12.38; 63 Sqn 12.12.38; 12 Sqn 26.8.39; 10 MU 4.3.40; 4 MU 19.6.40; 27 MU 23.8.40; 1 FTS 9.9.40; overshot landing in rain and ran into pit, Netheravon, 3.4.41; 38 MU 17.6.42; 215 MU 5.10.42; EO Newcastle 18.10.42; to RAAF 22.10.42.
L4959	63 Sqn 14.12.38; 12 OTU 18.4.40. Engine cut; overshot forced landing and undercarriage collapsed 2m E of South Cerney, 20.7.40; SOC 29.7.40.
L4960	63 Sqn 10.12.38; damaged in heavy landing, Upwood, 24.4.39; ROS; 12 Sqn 26.8.39 22 MU 2.5.40; 47 MU 24.9.40; to RCAF 14.10.40 as 1761.
L4961	63 Sqn 10.12.38; 12 Sqn 26.8.39; 1 AACU 1.11.39; Abingdon 27.12.39; Bicester 6.3.40; 27 MU 5.2.41; Dumfries 14.7.41; to RCAF 19.8.41 as 2085.
L4962	207 Sqn 16.1.39; 88 Sqn 26.8.39; 1 AACU 1.11.39; Abingdon 27.12.39; Bicester 6.3.40; 27 MU 5.2.41; 47 MU 7.6.41; to RCAF 23.6.41 as 2017.
L4963	207 Sqn 16.1.39; Fairey 2.6.40; 8 MU 24.6.40; 305 Sqn 15.9.40; 9 MU 14.11.40; Austin 30.12.40; Parks 22.1.41; to RCAF 10.3.41.
L4964	207 Sqn 12.1.39; 27 MU 23.4.40; 47 MU 24.2.41; to RCAF 2.3.41 as 1881.
L4965	207 Sqn 12.1.39; 12 OTU. Bellylanded in error, Benson, 23.5.40; to 2433M 20.12.40; SOC 30.6.43.
L4966	207 Sqn 12.1.39; 12 OTU. Engine cut; hit trees on approach and crashed, Benson, 14.7.40; SOC 20.7.40.
L4967	207 Sqn 16.1.39; Marham 6.4.39. Stalled and crashed avoiding high ground while descending in cloud, Litcham, Norfolk, 23.3.39; PO G.C. Shepherd, Sgt F.C.T. Norman and AC1 J.T.S. Randle killed; SOC 5.39; 76.20 hours.
L4968	185 Sqn 20.1.39; 52 and 63 Sqns 28.6.39; 12 OTU 18.4.40; 38 MU 23.12.40; 47 MU 6.5.41; to RCAF 28.5.41 as 1987.
L4969	185 Sqn 24.1.39; 52 Sqn 30.6.39; 63 Sqn 30.11.39; hit fence in forced landing while lost, Great Missenden, Bucks., 13.1.40; ROS; 12 OTU 18.4.40; 32 MU 26.4.41; 47 MU 13.6.41; to RCAF 4.7.41 as 2028.
L4970	185 Sqn 20.1.39; 52 Sqn 28.6.39; 63 Sqn at 30.11.39; 12 OTU 18.4.40; hit Chance light on landing at night, Benson, 30.9.40; Fairey 4.10.40; 18 MU 30.1.41; 47 MU 28.2.41; to RAAF 3.4.41.
L4971	185 Sqn 6.2.39; 63 Sqn 4.8.39; 12 OTU 18.4.40. Crashed, Ewelme, Oxon., 2.8.40; PO R.O. Shuttleworth killed; SOC 9.8.40.
L4972	185 Sqn 24.1.39. Undercarriage collapsed in heavy landing in bad visibility, Thornaby, 13.3.39; 4 SofTT; to 1441M 20.4.39.
L4973	185 Sqn 20.1.39; 52 Sqn 17.7.39; 63 Sqn 26.8.39; engine cut; hit wires in forced landing, Stanton St. Bernard, Wilts., 16.4.40; ROS; 12 OTU 18.4.40; hit tree low flying, forcelanded, Yeovil, 31.7.40; ROS; 38 MU 16.12.40; Austin 12.4.41; to RCAF 21.5.41.
L4974	35 Sqn 4.2.39; Polish OTU 9.4.40; 18 OTU; Fairey 28.11.40; 43 Group 23.2.41; 9 MU 26.4.41; 47 MU 31.10.41; to RAAF 5.1.42.
L4975	35 Sqn 4.2.39; 17 OTU 22.4.40; Dumfries 1.9.41; 47 MU 30.9.41; to RAAF 4.12.41.
L4976	35 Sqn 4.2.39; 17 OTU 22.4.40; 12 OTU 27.6.40; 38 MU 16.12.40; RAE 14.4.41; 27 MU 14.8.42; SOC 30.6.43.
L4977	35 Sqn 4.2.39; 207 Sqn 2.3.40; 12 OTU. Flew into hill in low cloud on navex near Sidmouth, Devon, 24.5.40; PO P.N. Sigley (NZ), A/Sgt G.M. Stephens and AC1 R.R. Lamont killed; SOC 2.6.40.
L4978	35 Sqn 7.2.39; hit by K9274, Bicester, 26.6.39; ROS; 3 Group TTF 4.3.40; undercarriage jammed; bellylanded, Marham, 27.5.41; ROS; 9 MU 29.10.41; 1472 Flight 9.6.42; SOC 14.5.43.

L4979   6 MU 7.2.39; 40 Sqn 30.3.39. Ditched in English Channel en route to France, 2.9.39; SOC 23.11.39; 35.25 hours.

L4980   35 Sqn 7.2.39; 15 Sqn 27.8.39; 105 Sqn 6.12.39. Crashed on night training flight near Cheniers, 5m SW of Chalons-sur-Marne, 26.3.40; FO A.M. Edgar, Sgt H.E. Pettit and Cpl A.E. Jones killed; wreck to 2 Salvage Section 28.3.40 as DBR.

L4981   35 Sqn 7.2.39; 5 Group TTF 2.3.40; TTF Driffield 25.10.40; 5 Group TTF at 31.12.41; 18 MU 2.7.42; 215 MU 10.9.42; 3 PATP 16.9.42; to SAAF 28.9.42 as 1041.

L4982   6 MU 7.2.39; 40 Sqn 30.3.39; 4 BGS 20.4.40; 47 MU 9.12.41; to RAAF 26.2.42.

L4983   6 MU 10.2.39; 40 Sqn 30.3.39; to 1832M at 6 SofTT 13.4.40; SOC 31.7.43.

L4984   6 MU 10.2.39; 40 Sqn 30.3.39; 5 MU 7.12.39; 4 BGS 16.4.40; stalled on landing avoiding another aircraft, West Freugh, 1.1.41; Fairey 27.1.41; 18 MU 12.5.41; Dumfries 29.6.41; to RCAF 19.8.41 as 2090.

L4985   6 MU 13.2.39; 23 MU 3.3.41; 47 MU 21.9.41; to RAAF 19.11.41.

L4986   6 MU 16.2.39; 23 MU 28.2.41; 47 MU 10.9.41; to RCAF 14.11.41 as 2111.

L4987   6 MU 11.2.39; Austin 3.1.41; Parks 27.1.41; to RCAF 17.3.41.

L4988   6 MU 11.2.39; 23 MU 3.3.41; 47 MU 30.10.41; to RCAF 21.12.41 as 2125.

L4989   6 MU 16.2.39; RAE 15.2.41; to 3496M 9.1.42.

L4990   6 MU 13.2.39; 23 MU 3.3.41; 47 MU 1.7.41; to RCAF 27.8.41 as 2105.

L4991   6 MU 20.2.39; Austin 10.1.41; Parks 30.1.41; to SAAF 10.3.41 as 949.

L4992   6 MU 23.2.39; 22 ERFTS 29.7.39. Ditched in bad visibility off Porthtowan, Cornwall, 21.8.39; SOC 10.39; 101.35 hours.

L4993   6 MU 6.3.39; 22 ERFTS 29.7.39; 15 FTS 4.9.39; 4 AOS 20.9.39; 3 FTS 12.2.40; 4 BGS 29.2.40; brakes failed, hit hangar door, West Freugh, 3.3.40; Western A/W 10.12.41; 23 MU 6.4.42; 18 MU 8.11.42; SOC 14.7.44.

L4994   10 MU 11.5.39; 7 FTS 27.5.40; stalled on approach, Sibson, 1.10.40; Fairey 10.10.40; 22 MU 1.2.41; 18 MU 12.2.41; 47 MU 1.3.41; to RCAF 7.4.41 as 1944.

L4995   6 MU 20.2.39; 15 FTS 4.9.39; 3 AOS 25.9.39; 8 BGS 3.7.40; 1 FTS 31.5.41; 32 MU 17.6.41; 2 AACU 5.2.42; taxied into bowser, Roborough, 11.10.42; ROS; to 3969M at 2 SofTT 25.7.43.

L4996   20 MU 23.2.39; 9 MU 27.10.39; 2 SofTT; CGS 16.3.40; 1 FTS 17.9.40; 18 MU 20.4.42; 13 Sqn 9.6.42; 16 Sqn 5.9.42; 18 MU 30.11.42; SOC 14.7.44.

L4997   10 MU 20.2.39; 10 BGS 15.6.40; engine lost power, forcelanded and undercarriage collapsed, Glenluce, Wigtown, 12.7.40; ROS. Crashed after control lost in cloud, Lamb Hill, Closeburn, 6m N of Dumfries, 29.9.41; Capt J.R.C. Arnoux (Fr), PO J. Sokulski (PAF) and FO L. Rochowski (Pol) killed; SOC 6.10.41.

L4998   6 MU 20.2.39; 15 FTS 7.9.39; 3 AOS 25.9.39; engine cut; bellylanded, Aldergrove, 1.10.39; ROS; 8 BGS 3.7.40; engine cut; bellylanded, Easter Ross, 30.5.41; Fairey 14.6.41; 47 MU 19.10.41; to RAAF 4.12.41.

L4999   10 MU 20.2.39; 6 BGS 11.5.40; 3 BGS 2.6.40; 1 AAS 3.7.40; 18 MU 27.7.41; 47 MU at 31.12.41; to RAAF 31.5.42.

L5000   10 MU 20.2.39; 10 BGS 11.5.40; taxied into bowser, Warmwell, 13.6.40; ROS; tyre burst on take-off, swung and undercarriage collapsed, Annan, 25.9.40; 18 MU 3.8.42; SOC 14.7.44.

L5001   20 MU 20.2.39; 7 AOS 19.11.39; 7 AGS. Hit tree low flying, Margam Castle, Glamorgan, 22.6.41; F/Sgt G.T. Swann and PO Kitching killed; SOC 30.6.41; 490.15 hours.

L5002   20 MU 23.2.39; 7 AOS 19.11.39; undercarriage jammed; bellylanded, Porthcawl, 25.5.40; Fairey 29.5.40; 20 MU 22.7.40; 12 MU 25.7.40; 47 MU

L5003   12.10.40; to RCAF 1.11.40 as 1758.
   10 MU 6.3.39; 1 AAS 9.3.40; engine cut; ran into ditch in forced landing, Great Carlton, Lincs., 14.5.40; Fairey 7.6.40; 20 MU 28.7.40; RAE Exeter 14.10.40; 27 MU 14.2.43; SOC 30.11.43; 236.10 hours.

L5004   19 MU 24.2.39; 9 BGS 29.4.39. Flew into sea off Gimlet Rock, 2m S of Pwllheli, 31.5.41; presumed misjudged height; Sgt J.F. Cranston RCAF, LAC O. Cumins and LAC T. Froggatt missing; SOC 15.6.41.

L5005   19 MU 23.2.39; 235 Sqn 4.12.39; overshot forced landing in bad weather and hit hedge, Penshurst LG, 23.2.40; ROS; Fairey 6.6.40; 9 MU 14.7.40; 47 MU 15.8.40; to RAAF 6.9.40.

L5006   19 MU 27.2.39; to RAAF 11.5.40.

L5007   19 MU 1.3.39; 235 Sqn 21.12.39; 10 MU 22.2.40; 6 BGS 11.5.40; 11 FTS 24.5.40; 18 MU 13.7.40; 47 MU 29.9.40; to RCAF 27.10.40 as 1746.

L5008   19 MU 23.2.39; 235 Sqn 10.12.39; 10 MU 16.2.40; 6 BGS 11.5.40; 11 FTS 24.5.40; 18 MU 13.7.40; 47 MU 23.10.40; to RCAF 28.11.40 as 1833.

L5009   19 MU 24.2.39; 3 BGS 19.12.39; engine cut on take-off, bellylanded, Aldergrove, 16.4.40; 47 MU 26.4.40; 4 MU 27.5.40; Fairey 6.6.40; 27 MU 14.8.40; 305 Sqn 14.9.40; bellylanded in error, Bramcote, 24.9.40; 9 MU 14.11.40; Austin 28.2.41; Parks 26.3.41; to RCAF 10.4.41.

L5010   6 MU 21.3.39; 103 Sqn 17.7.40. Missing from raid on Calais, 9.9.40; Sgt F. Drinkwater, PO W.A. Cooper and S/Lt De Sanoual-Servier killed; SOC 11.9.40.

L5011   6 MU 1.3.39; 3 BGS 3.1.40; Fairey 17.6.40; 27 MU 16.8.40; 103 Sqn 27.9.40; 12 Sqn 4.10.40; 27 MU 10.10.40; 7 AACU 21.10.40; 6 AACU 19.12.40. Engine cut on approach to forced landing while lost in bad visibility; hit ground, Low Meathop, Grange-over-Sands, Lancs., 26.2.41; SOC 6.3.41.

L5012   19 MU 27.2.39; to RAAF 11.5.40.

L5013   19 MU 2.3.39; 9 BGS 29.12.39; 16 FTS 1.8.41; bellylanded in error, Newton, 19.9.41; ROS; 18 MU 23.2.42; 215 MU 14.8.42; 3 PATP 23.8.42; to RAAF 13.9.42.

L5014   19 MU 13.3.39; 235 Sqn 24.12.39; 242 Sqn 29.12.39; 3 BGS 11.1.40; hit ice hummock on landing and undercarriage collapsed, Church Fenton, 10.2.40; ROS; 141 Sqn 11.4.40; 5 OTU 17.5.40; 20 MU 11.9.40; Austin 6.11.40; Parks 13.11.40; to SAAF 5.2.41 as 932; to Middle East 30.1.43.

L5015   19 MU 1.3.39; 8 MU 28.6.40; 23 MU 17.3.41; 88 Sqn 9.5.41; overshot landing, Murlough LG, 31.5.41; ROS; 23 MU 5.9.41; 47 MU 8.12.41; to RAAF 21.2.42.

L5016   19 MU 17.3.39; 235 Sqn 4.12.39; 10 MU 22.2.40; 6 BGS 11.5.40; 11 FTS 24.5.40; 18 MU 13.7.40; 47 MU 28.9.40; to RCAF 27.10.40 as 1774.

L5017   19 MU 1.3.39; 235 Sqn 17.12.39; 10 MU 16.2.40; 6 BGS 11.5.40; 3 BGS 2.6.40; 1 AAS 3.7.40; 18 MU 14.8.41; Dumfries 11.11.41; at 3 PATP 31.12.41; to South Africa 17.1.42 then to RAAF.

L5018   19 MU 6.3.39; 235 Sqn 17.12.39; 10 MU 22.2.40; 6 BGS 11.5.40; 12 FTS 24.5.40; 16(P)FTS 15.6.41; Rosenfield 11.11.41; 18 MU 17.2.42; 215 MU 10.4.42; 3 PATP 27.4.42; to RAAF 23.5.42.

L5019   19 MU 6.3.39; 7 BGS 19.12.39. Dived into sea off Porthcawl, Glamorgan, 4.3.41; Sgt G. Tock, AC2 R. Sheperd and AC2 J. Staunch killed; SOC 1.4.41; 365.40 hours.

L5020   19 MU 2.3.39; 3 BGS 3.1.40; overshot landing in fog and wing dug in; undercarriage collapsed, Aldergrove, 3.3.40; 4 MU 18.5.40; 20 MU 6.8.40; 47 MU 18.9.40; to RCAF 27.9.40 as 1720.

L5021   19 MU 15.3.39; 7 BGS 19.12.39; undercarriage jammed; bellylanded, Porthcawl, 18.1.40; Rollason 25.1.40; Fairey 18.8.40; 9 MU 20.11.40; 47 MU 14.2.41; to RCAF 11.3.41 as 1935.

L5022   19 MU 15.3.39; to RAAF 11.5.40.

L5023   19 MU 15.3.39; 3 BGS 18.12.39; 1 AAS 3.7.40; undercarriage collapsed in heavy landing, Manby,

K7572 was used by Rolls-Royce for Merlin development at Hucknall. (Rolls-Royce via D Birch)

	27.3.41; ROS; 27 MU 30.9.41; 47 MU 30.11.41; to RAAF 5.1.42.	L5035	6 MU 21.3.39; AASF 20.5.40; 226 Sqn 23.5.40; Shorts 14.8.41; 38 MU 29.4.42; 225 Sqn 30.5.42; bellylanded, 25.7.42; Rosenfield 9.8.42; 18 MU 7.11.42; SOC 5.2.44.
L5024	6 MU 24.4.39; 47 MU 16.5.40; to SAAF 6.6.40 as 903.		
L5025	19 MU 2.3.39; 7 BGS 19.12.39; bellylanded in error, Porthcawl, 6.3.40; Fairey 29.5.40; 20 MU 14.8.40; 23 MU 6.3.41; 226 Sqn 18.4.41; 23 MU 11.8.41; 239 Sqn 6.6.42; Hurn at 31.12.42; 27 MU 25.1.43; SOC 30.6.43.	L5036	6 MU 25.3.39; Austin 18.4.41; Parks 14.5.41; to RCAF 5.41.
		L5037	6 MU 29.3.39; AASF 24.5.40; 226 Sqn 26.5.40; engine cut; bellylanded, Jordanstown, 25.4.41; Shorts 14.5.41; 18 MU 31.10.42; SOC 14.7.44.
L5026	6 MU 21.3.39; 22 ERFTS 4.8.39; 15 FTS 4.9.39; 8 AOS 20.9.39; 18 MU 7.8.41; to RCAF 11.9.41 as 2064.	L5038	6 MU 6.4.39; 103 Sqn 5.8.40; 38 MU 12.10.40; Austin 27.11.40; Parks 4.1.41; to RAAF 11.3.41.
L5027	19 MU 13.3.39; 22 MU 15.9.39; 3 BGS 15.12.39; 1 AAS 3.7.40. Stalled during gunnery practice and dived into sea 3m E of Donna Nook, Lincs., 28.10.40; FO D.M. Robertson, PO E.W. Blackwell, LAC F. Skryzpczak (PAF) killed; SOC 1.12.40; 345 hours.	L5039	6 MU 12.4.39; Finningley 11.1.40; 5 Group TTF 25.1.40; brakes failed, ran into hangar, Speke, 21.6.40; ROS; brakes failed, hit fire tender, Catfoss, 20.9.40; ROS; 4 Group TTF 25.10.40; Western A/W 7.11.41; 38 MU 14.5.42; 22 MU 11.10.42; 38 MU 31.12.42; 78 MU 30.11.44; SOC 4.12.44.
L5028	19 MU 15.3.39; 8 MU 26.7.40; 45 MU 12.3.41; Dumfries; to RAAF 15.10.41.	L5040	8 MU 6.4.39; 12 OTU 3.9.40; 32 MU 22.1.41; 47 MU 27.6.41; to RCAF 27.8.41 as 2079.
L5029	19 MU 15.3.39; 9 BGS 29.12.39; engine cut on approach, bellylanded, Hawarden, 3.9.41; 9 MU 3.9.41; Rosenfield 10.9.41; 47 MU 25.10.41; to RAAF 19.11.41.	L5041	8 MU 31.3.49; 305 Sqn 15.9.40; 9 MU 14.11.40; Austin 25.2.41; Parks 6.4.41; to RCAF 10.4.41.
		L5042	8 MU 15.4.39; 150 Sqn 26.6.40; 142 Sqn 3.10.40; Fairey 10.10.40; 20 MU 19.12.40; 47 MU 14.1.41; to RCAF 5.2.41 as 1847.
L5030	6 MU 25.3.39; 12 OTU 25.7.40; hit hut landing at night, Mount Farm, 17.11.40; 32 MU 5.2.41; Austin 25.5.41; to RCAF 5.41 as 2027.	L5043	8 MU 6.4.39; 304 Sqn 26.8.40; 47 MU 15.11.40; to RCAF 16.12.40 as 1830.
L5031	6 MU 29.3.39; 266 Sqn 18.1.40; 245 Sqn 9.2.40; 22 MU 2.5.40; engine cut; bellylanded in marshes, Skinburness, near Silloth, 5.3.41; ROS; undercarriage jammed, bellylanded Dumfries, 5.7.41; Dumfries 5.7.41; 47 MU 16.9.41; to RAAF 14.10.41.	L5044	8 MU 12.4.39; 304 Sqn 26.8.40; 47 MU 10.11.40; to RAAF 15.1.41.
		L5045	8 MU 6.4.39; 12 OTU 2.9.40; forcelanded short of fuel in low cloud, Holdenby, 6m NNW of Northampton, 15.11.40; Fairey 22.12.40; 47 MU 9.3.41; to RCAF 23.3.41 as 1913.
L5032	19 MU 18.3.39; 235 Sqn 17.12.39; 600 Sqn 27.2.40; 20 MU 9.8.40; 47 MU 18.9.40; to RCAF 23.10.40 as 1730.		
L5033	6 MU 25.3.39; 7 BGS; engine cut; forcelanded on soft sand and ran into river, Margam beach, Glam., 5.7.40; ROS; Austin 18.4.41; Parks 17.5.41; to RCAF 31.5.41 as 1996.	L5046	8 MU 6.4.39; 3 BGS; 1 AAS 3.7.40; 8 BGS; 47 MU 30.9.41; to RAAF 21.1.42.
		L5047	8 MU 31.3.39; 7 AACU 1.9.40. Overshot landing, swung to avoid obstruction and hit tree, Pembridge LG, 30.9.40; SOC 5.10.40.
L5034	6 MU 30.3.39; 266 Sqn 18.1.40; 264 Sqn 16.3.40; 6 AACU 27.4.40; Western A/W 28.2.41; 6 AACU 30.3.41; Austin 4.4.41; to SAAF 11.7.41 as 980.	L5048	8 MU 30.3.39; 304 Sqn 27.8.40; 301 Sqn 29.8.40; undercarriage collapsed in forced landing in bad weather

L5049   S of Annan LG, 21.9.40; Fairey 12.10.40; 9 MU 29.12.40; Austin 1.3.41; to RCAF 4.5.41.

L5049   8 MU 30.3.39; 420 Flight 29.11.40; 27 MU 20.6.41; 47 MU 6.11.41; to RAAF 21.2.42.

L5050   8 MU 31.3.39; 305 Sqn 15.9.40; 9 MU 14.11.40; Austin 11.12.40; Parks 4.1.41; to RAAF 11.3.41.

L5051   8 MU 6.4.39; 23 MU 24.3.41; 88 Sqn 9.5.41; 23 MU 5.9.41; 26 Sqn 28.5.42; 1472 Flight 15.2.43; 27 MU 13.5.43; SOC 23.8.44.

L5052   8 MU 30.3.39; 305 Sqn 15.9.40; 142 Sqn 1.11.40; 4 Group TTF; engine cut on approach, stalled and crashlanded, Manby, 2.1.41; Fairey 15.1.41; 47 MU 14.6.41; to RAAF 15.7.41.

L5053   8 MU 12.4.39; 7 AOS 5.9.39; tipped up taxying, Porthcawl, 6.9.39; ROS; 47 MU 19.9.41; to RCAF 14.11.41 as 2112.

L5054   8 MU 15.4.39; 10 FTS 22.11.39; 3 BGS; 5 FTS 18.12.39; 12 FTS 27.11.40; bellylanded in error, Hullavington, 5.5.41; ROS; 1 FTS 30.7.41; Rosenfield 29.8.41. Engine cut; bellylanded 1m W of Berwick St James, Wilts., 21.8.41; DBR

L5055   8 MU 12.4.39; 12 OTU 2.9.40; 32 MU 29.3.41; 47 MU 11.6.41; to RCAF 23.6.41 as 2004.

L5056   8 MU 6.4.39; 305 Sqn 15.9.40; 9 MU 14.11.40; Austin 21.12.40; Parks 7.1.41; to SAAF 24.2.41 but lost at sea en route in SS Huntingdon.

L5057   8 MU 6.4.39; 150 Sqn 26.6.40; 27 MU 10.10.40; Austin 8.12.40; Parks 7.1.41; to SAAF 24.2.41 but lost at sea en route in SS Huntingdon.

L5058   8 MU 18,4.39; 150 Sqn 26.6.40; 9 MU 11.10.40; Austin 22.11.40; Parks 28.12.40; to SAAF 28.2.41 as 947.

L5059   8 MU 6.4.39; 305 Sqn 15.9.40; 9 MU 14.11.40; Austin 1.1.41; to SAAF 5.2.41 as 935.

L5060   8 MU 6.4.39; 6 BGS 10.5.40; 12 FTS 29.5.40; bellylanded in error, Watchfield, 8.4.41; 16(P)FTS 22.8.41; 18 MU 18.2.42; to SAAF 30.6.42 as 1008.

L5061   8 MU 12.4.39; 12 OTU 3.9.40; 27 MU 24.12.40; 47 MU 30.4.41; to RAAF 4.6.41.

L5062   8 MU 12.4.39; 304 Sqn 26.8.40; 12 OTU 5.11.40; Fairey 11.12.40; 47 MU 18.5.41; to RCAF 11.6.41 as 2011.

L5063   20 MU 24.4.39; 98 Sqn 13.7.40; overshot landing and damaged undercarriage, Kaldadarnes, 31.3.41; to RCAF 20.8.41 (without tail assembly).

L5064   8 MU 19.4.39; 305 Sqn 15.9.40; 9 MU 14.11.40; Austin 12.12.40; Fairey 13.2.41; 47 MU 13.5.41; to RCAF 28.5.41 as 1990.

L5065   8 MU 18.4.39; 7 AOS 5.9.39. Engine cut; bellylanded into trees near Cardiff, 18.1.40; SOC 24.1.40.

L5066   20 MU 21.4.39; 98 Sqn 14.7.40; 20 MU 17.7.40; 98 Sqn 18.7.40. Landed with undercarriage unlocked, Kaldadarnes, 16.3.41; DBR; SOC 13.5.41.

L5067   8 MU 12.4.39; 6 BGS 14.5.40; 12 FTS 29.5.40; swung off flarepath and damaged, Harlaxton, 16.4.41; ROS; 16(P)FTS 15.6.41; undercarriage collapsed in forced landing, Ashbourne airfield, 24.11.41; Austin 1.12.41; 16(P)FTS 24.1.42; 27 MU 12.4.42; undercarriage jammed, bellylanded Shawbury, 26.10.42; ROS; SOC 30.6.43.

L5068   8 MU 18.4.39; 142 Sqn 4.9.40; 27 MU 17.12.40; 47 MU 16.1.41; to RCAF 26.2.41 as 1859.

L5069   8 MU 18.4.39; 6 BGS 10.5.40; 7 FTS 25.5.40; engine cut; tipped up in forced landing on boggy ground 4m W of Swansea, 26.5.40; ROS; 7 BGS 4.6.40; Western A/W 31.8.41; 47 MU 21.10.41; to RAAF 26.2.42.

L5070   8 MU 15.4.39; 304 Sqn 26.8.40; 47 MU 10.11.40; to RAAF 15.1.41.

L5071   8 MU 19.4.39; 12 OTU 3.9.40. Lost height after take-off and flew into ground 1m NW of Mount Farm, 26.11.40; PO W. Makarewicz, PO A. Ignaszal and Sgt F. Blyskal killed; SOC 18.12.40.

L5072   8 MU 19.4.39; 7 AOS 4.9.39. Dived into ground N of Kenfig Hill, Glamorgan, 20.4.41; Sgt K. Dindorf, AC1 Richardson and AC2 Elliott killed; SOC 29.4.41.

L5073   20 MU 26.4.39; 98 Sqn 14.7.40; to RCAF 20.8.41.

L5074   20 MU 21.4.39; 47 MU 19.5.40; to SAAF 19.6.40 as 915.

L5075   20 MU 26.4.39; 301 Sqn 20.7.40. Undercarriage collapsed on landing, Bramcote, 1.8.40; 5 SofTT; to 2204M; SOC 6.12.43.

L5076   20 MU 2.5.39; 12 Sqn 20.8.40; 38 MU 22.12.40; 47 MU 10.2.41; to RCAF 7.3.41 as 1897.

L5077   8 MU 19.4.39; 142 Sqn 4.9.40; 27 MU 2.12.40; Austin 1.1.41; Parks 16.1.41; to SAAF 16.2.41 as 939.

L5078   20 MU 26.4.39; 47 MU 20.5.40; to SAAF 19.6.40 as 916.

L5079   20 MU 21.4.39; 12 OTU 7.8.40. Engine lost power; hit trees on high ground, Streatley, Berks., 30.9.40; Sgt O. Odstreilek (Czech) killed; SOC 11.10.40.

L5080   20 MU 9.5.39; 142 Sqn 19.7.40; 32 MU 11.10.40; 47 MU 14.3.41; to RCAF 31.3.41 as 1905.

L5081   27 MU 21.4.39; Polish OTU 30.3.40; 18 OTU; damaged in forced landing in bad weather, Clifton Pastures bombing range, 3.10.40; Fairey 8.10.40; 9 MU 29.12.40; 47 MU 14.2.41; to RCAF 11.3.41 as 1902.

L5082   27 MU 24.4..39; 8 BGS 21.6.40; engine cut on take-off; swung and undercarriage collapsed, Evanton, 11.10.41; 27 MU 6.11.41; 18 MU 17.2.42; 215 MU 23.4.42; 3 PATP 10.5.42; to RAAF 14.6.42.

L5083   9 MU 27.4.39; 27 MU 29.9.39; 8 BGS 10.6.40; 18 MU 29.8.41; 13 Sqn 9.6.42; 400 Sqn 19.11.42; 27 MU 9.2.43; SOC 30.6.43.

L5084   9 MU 3.5.39; 27 MU 1.10.39; 6 BGS 13.4.40; 4 BGS 14.4.40; bellylanded in error, West Freugh, 1.8.40; ROS; engine cut; bellylanded on foreshore, Luce Bay, 16.4.41; ROS. Engine cut; crashlanded on approach, Jurby, 20.5.41; DBR; SOC 6.6.41; 245.45 hours.

L5085   9 MU 27.4.39; 27 MU 2.10.39; 8 BGS 21.6.40; 18 MU 15.8.41; Dumfries 11.11.41; 3 PATP at 31.12.41; to SAAF 29.1.42.

L5086   9 MU 27.4.39; 27 MU 2.10.39; 6 BGS 13.6.40; 4 BGS 14.4.41; 9 MU 19.11.41; to SAAF 2.3.42.

L5087   27 MU 24.4.39; 15 EFTS 11.8.40; overshot landing, Kingstown, 8.9.40; Austin 24.9.40; 47 MU 22.12.40; to RAAF 3.4.41.

L5088   6 MU 4.5.39; 47 MU 16.5.40; to SAAF 6.6.40 as 908.

L5089   6 MU 2.5.39; 253 Sqn 21.12.39; 36 MU 26.4.40; DBR 11.2.40; to RCAF 5.40 as Ground Instructional Airframe A88.

L5090   6 MU 26.4.39; 47 MU 16.5.40; to SAAF 6.6.40 as 911.

L5091   6 MU 3.5.39; 12 OTU 25.7.40. Dived into ground after night take-off from Benson, Wallingford, Oxon., 29.7.40; Sgt R. Hanna, Sgt R.C. Thomson and Sgt W. Robb killed; SOC 8.8.40.

L5092   6 MU 11.5.39; 15 EFTS 11.3.40; engine cut; hit trees and bellylanded, Pelutho, near Silloth, 17.8.40; Fairey 2.9.40; 22 MU 26.11.40; 47 MU 6.2.41; to RCAF 8.3.41 as 1884.

L5093   6 MU 4.5.39; 47 MU 16.5.40; to SAAF 6.6.40 as 909.

L5094   6 MU 2.5.39; 253 Sqn 13.12.39; 22 MU 24.2.40; 47 MU 12.8.40; to RAAF 6.9.40.

L5095   6 MU 2.5.39; 253 Sqn 17.12.39; 22 MU 23.2.40; 47 MU 20.9.41; to RCAF 14.11.41 as 2110.

L5096   6 MU 2.5.39; 253 Sqn 13.12.39; 22 MU 24.2.40; 47 MU 12.8.40; to RAAF 6.9.40.

L5097   6 MU 4.5.39; 47 MU 16.5.40; to SAAF 6.6.40 as 910.

L5098   6 MU 11.5.39; 47 MU 16.5.40; to SAAF 6.6.40 as 913.

L5099   6 MU 19.5.39; 253 Sqn 17.12.39; 22 MU 1.3.40; 20 MU 1.3.40; 98 Sqn 13.7.40; overshot landing, swung and undercarriage collapsed, Kaldadarnes, 16.1.41; ROS; 1423 Flight 23.6.41; undercarriage collapsed on landing, Kaldadarnes, 10.10.41; ROS; SF Kaldadarnes 8.12.41; SF Reykjavik 13.1.42; brakes failed, ran away, Keflavik, 25.10.42; ROS; Reykjavik for repair 24.7.43; SOC 21.9.43.

L5100   6 MU 12.5.39; 253 Sqn 17.12.39; engine cut after take-off; forcelanded 1m W of Manston, 27.12.39; 20 MU 15.6.40; 12 Sqn 22.8.40; 38 MU 22.12.40; Austin 7.4.41; Parks 5.5.41; to RCAF 24.7.41 as 2041.

K7682 fitted with a Bristol B1 Mk.III turret for trials at Boscombe Down in October 1941. (P Jarrett collection)

L5101 6 MU 8.5.39; 12 OTU 1.8.40; damaged in heavy landing, Penrhos, 5.12.40; 27 MU 8.3.41; 47 MU 13.5.41; to RCAF 28.5.41 as 1970.

L5102 6 MU 9.5.39; 15 EFTS 13.3.40; 22 MU 19.5.40; 47 MU 13.8.40; to RCAF 31.8.40 as 1713.

L5103 6 MU 4.5.39; 150 Sqn 29.7.40; 9 MU 11.10.40; Austin 20.11.40; Parks 14.12.40; to SAAF 5.2.41 as 930.

L5104 6 MU 7.5.39; 15 EFTS 11.3.40; engine lost power; undershot forced landing and hit bank, Kirkbride, 18.6.40; Fairey 24.6.40; 12 MU 16.8.40; 47 MU 14.10.40; to RCAF 27.11.40 as 1794.

L5105 6 MU 3.5.39; 253 Sqn 3.1.40; 264 Sqn 5.1.40; Fairey 12.6.40; 20 MU 28.7.40; 47 MU 7.11.40; to RAAF 15.1.41.

L5106 6 MU 9.5.39; AASF 18.5.40; 150 Sqn 19.5.40; 38 MU 12.10.40; 47 MU 10.11.40; to RCAF 16.12.40 as 1798.

L5107 6 MU 8.5.39; AASF 19.5.40; presumed lost in France.

L5108 6 MU 19.5.39; 253 Sqn 21.12.39; 22 MU 23.2.40; 47 MU 21.10.41; to RAAF 13.3.42.

L5109 6 MU 19.5.39; 253 Sqn 21.12.39; 22 MU 24.2.40; 47 MU 12.8.40; to RCAF 6.9.40 as 1706.

L5110 6 MU 17.5.39; 253 Sqn 21.12.39. Caught fire in the air and abandoned near Newcastle, 3.8.40; SOC 10.8.40.

L5111 6 MU 20.5.39; Austin 2.5.41; Parks 29.5.41; to RCAF 7.9.41 as 2099.

L5112 6 MU 8.5.39; AASF 18.5.40; 150 Sqn 19.5.40. Hit by ground fire, Hornoy, and crashed, Fallencourt, Seine-Maritime, 8.6.40; F/Lt R.A. Weeks, Sgt W.D.F. Pittar and LAC L.O. Grant killed

L5113 6 MU 12.5.39; AASF 20.5.40; 142 Sqn 21.5.40. Dived into ground on night navex, Middleton Stoney, near Bicester, 4.8.40; Sgt F.J. Tremeger, Sgt P.P. Duffy and Sgt H.E. Masters killed; SOC 16.8.40

L5114 6 MU 7.6.39; Austin 24.4.41; to SAAF 15.6.41.

L5115 6 MU 20.5.39; Austin 2.2.41; to RCAF 10.4.41.

L5116 6 MU 20.5.39; Austin 21.4.41; Parks 26.5.41; to RCAF 31.5.41 as 1993.

L5117 6 MU 4.5.39; 15 EFTS 13.3.40; 22 MU 7.5.40; 3 FPP 28.6.40; undercarriage damaged in heavy landing, White Waltham, 29.10.40; Fairey 6.11.40; 22 MU 22.1.41; 47 MU 15.5.41; to RAAF 9.6.41.

L5118 6 MU 9.5.39; 47 MU 24.2.41; to RCAF 17.5.41 as 1962.

L5119 6 MU 17.5.39; Austin 18.4.41; Parks 14.5.41; to RCAF 31.5.41 as 1992.

L5120 6 MU 19.5.39; 47 MU 8.11.40; to RCAF 27.11.40 as 1781.

L5121 6 MU 20.5.39; Austin 24.4.41; to RCAF 5.41 as 2046.

L5122 6 MU 20.5.39; 226 Sqn 9.5.41; 88 Sqn 10.7.41; 23 MU 5.9.41; 18 MU 23.2.42; 215 MU 20.4.42; 3 PATP 10.5.42; to RAAF 11.6.42.

L5123 6 MU 11.5.39; Austin 3.1.41; to SAAF 29.3.41 as 952.

L5124 6 MU 22.5.39; undercarriage leg jammed; skidded on landing, Brize Norton, 25.5.40; ROS; 12 OTU 1.8.40; damaged in forced landing while lost on navex, Watchfield, 5.11.40; ROS; 32 MU 26.4.41; at LEP 31.12.41; to South Africa 17.1.42 then to RAAF.

L5125 6 MU 22.5.39; 103 Sqn 17.7.40; 27 MU 8.10.40; Austin 25.11.40; engine cut; bellylanded W of Ratcliffe, 27.11.40; ROS; to SAAF 11.5.41 as 959.

L5126 6 MU 20.5.39; 253 Sqn 21.12.39; Rosenfield 23.5.41; 47 MU 14.7.41; to RCAF 8.8.41 as 2062.

L5127 6 MU 22.5.39; 12 Sqn 17.7.40. DBR taxying on rough ground, Eastchurch, 25.8.40; to 2210M; to RCAF 1941 as Instructional Airframe A133.

L5128 19 MU 23.5.39; 3 BGS 19.12.39; 8 BGS 3.7.40; 47 MU 29.9.41; to RAAF 5.1.42.

L5129 19 MU 19.5.39; 3 BGS 3.1.40; 1 AAS 3.7.40; 9 MU 4.9.41; 215 MU 26.4.42; 3 PATP 10.5.42; to RAAF 31.5.42.

L5130 19 MU 23.5.39; 3 BGS 3.1.40; 4 BGS 3.7.40; overshot landing, West Freugh, 15.7.41; Rosenfield 27.7.41; 47 MU 16.7.42; to RCAF 20.9.42 as 2140.

L5131 19 MU 23.5.39; 5 BGS 10.1.40; 10 BGS 8.1.41; 47 MU

L5132 23.11.41; LEP 26.1.42; to RCAF 21.3.42 as 2138.
19 MU 6.6.39; 235 Sqn 10.12.39; 10 MU 22.2.40; 7 FTS 3.6.40; 12 FTS 11.6.40; engine cut on take-off; bellylanded 1m W of Grantham, 27.8.40; Fairey 2.9.40; 22 MU 1.2.41; 18 MU 11.2.41; 47 MU 27.2.41; to RCAF 7.4.41 as 1943.

L5133 19 MU 26.5.39; 235 Sqn 17.12.39; 242 Sqn 29.12.39; 141 Sqn 27.3.40; 5 OTU 17.5.40. Hit ditch on landing in rain, Aston Down, 13.7.40; SOC 8.8.40; to GI airframe 2173M.

L5134 19 MU 23.5.39; 5 BGS 10.1.40; 10 BGS 8.1.41; Rosenfield 8.7.42; 27 MU 2.9.42; 215 MU 7.10.42; 3 PATP 4.11.42; to RAAF 21.11.42.

L5135 19 MU 26.5.39; 5 BGS 10.1.40; 1 FTS 26.1.41; engine cut; bellylanded 1m E of Shrewton, 17.4.41; Fairey 25.4.41; 47 MU 14.6.41; to RCAF 4.7.41 as 2024.

L5136 19 MU 24.5.39; 3 BGS 18.12.39; 9 BGS 3.7.40; Western A/W 7.9.41; Dumfries 25.10.41; 3 PATP at 31.12.41; to SAAF 29.1.42.

L5137 19 MU 19.11.39; 3 BGS 19.12.39; 9 BGS 3.7.40; 16(P)FTS 1.8.41; bellylanded in error, Newton, 10.10.41; 9 MU 13.2.42; 18 MU 6.9.42. Undercarriage leg broke through drain while being towed at 27 SLG, 9.3.43; DBR; SOC 14.7.44.

L5138 19 MU 2.6.39; 3 BGS 19.12.39; 10 BGS 3.7.40; 12 FTS 21.9.40; 16(P)FTS 12.6.41; 18 MU 27.1.42; to SAAF 2.3.42.

L5139 19 MU 26.5.39; 5 BGS 3.3.40; 1 FTS 26.1.41; overshot forced landing while lost, Preston, Wilts., 18.9.41; Rosenfield 29.9.41; 47 MU 11.1.42; to RCAF 13.4.42 as 2136.

L5140 19 MU 6.6.39; 1 AAS 20.7.40; 16(P)FTS 21.8.41; Rosenfield 13.2.42; 9 MU 2.5.42; 1472 Flight 9.6.42; taxied into starter and undercarriage leg collapsed, Dishforth, 3.12.42; ROS. Engine cut; hit tank on approach to forced landing and crashlanded near Durham, 21.1.43.

L5141 19 MU 6.6.39; 3 BGS 18.12.39; 4 BGS 3.7.40; 27 MU 7.11.42; to 3560M.

L5142 19 MU 6.6.39; 3 BGS 11.1.40; 10 BGS 2.7.40; overshot landing into ditch, Annan LG, 13.8.40; Fairey 20.8.40; 47 MU 22.11.40; to RAAF 15.1.41.

L5143 24 MU 16.6.39; 36 MU 9.5.40; to RAAF 22.5.40.

L5144 24 MU 2.6.39; 36 MU 5.5.40; to RCAF 16.5.40 as 1683.

L5145 24 MU 6.6.39; 36 MU 5.3.40; to RCAF 21.3.40 as 1622.

L5146 24 MU 7.6.39; 36 MU 2.3.40; to RCAF 21.3.40 as 1625.

L5147 24 MU 7.6.39; 36 MU 5.3.40; to RCAF 7.5.40 as 1670.

L5148 24 MU 6.6.39; 36 MU 2.3.40; to RCAF 29.3.40 as 1628.

L5149 24 MU 6.6.39; 36 MU 20.3.40; to RCAF 20.4.40 as 1661.

L5150 24 MU 6.6.39; to RCAF 2.2.40 as 1635.

L5151 24 MU 6.6.39; to RAAF 20.4.40.

L5152 24 MU 6.6.39; 36 MU 30.3.40; to RAAF 6.9.40.

L5153 24 MU 7.6.39; 36 MU 5.3.40; to RCAF 29.3.40 as 1630.

L5154 24 MU 6.6.39; to RCAF 2.2.40 as 1634.

L5155 24 MU 9.6.39; 36 MU 5.3.40; to RCAF 29.3.40 as 1629.

L5156 24 MU 15.6.39; 36 MU 30.3.40; to RAAF 1.5.40.

L5157 24 MU 15.6.39; 36 MU 2.3.40; to RCAF 21.3.40 as 1626.

L5158 24 MU 9.6.39; 36 MU 9.5.40; to RAAF 22.5.40.

L5159 24 MU 9.6.39; 36 MU 5.3.40; to RCAF 29.3.40 as 1627.

L5160 24 MU 21.6.39; 8 MU 10.7.40; 305 Sqn 15.9.40; 9 MU 14.11.40; Austin 14.2.41; to SAAF 29.3.41 as 954.

L5161 24 MU 15.6.39; to RCAF 2.2.40 as 1663.

L5162 24 MU 15.6.39; 36 MU 2.3.40; to RCAF 21.3.40 as 1623.

L5163 24 MU 21.6.39; 36 MU 30.3.40; to RAAF 17.5.40.

L5164 24 MU 21.6.39; to RCAF 2.2.40 as 1637.

L5165 24 MU 21.6.39; 47 MU 12.5.40; to SAAF 1.6.40 as 902.

L5166 24 MU 26.6.39; 36 MU 5.3.40; to RCAF 6.4.40 as 1636.

L5167 24 MU 15.6.39; to RCAF 2.2.40 as 1660.

L5168 24 MU 21.6.39; 36 MU 9.5.40; to SAAF 1.6.40 as 905.

L5169 24 MU 26.6.39; 36 MU 5.5.40; to RCAF 16.5.40 as 1680.

L5170 24 MU 26.6.39; 36 MU 30.3.40; to RAAF 10.5.40.

L5171 24 MU 21.6.39; 36 MU 5.5.40; to RCAF 16.5.40 as 1687.

L5172 24 MU 26.6.39; 47 MU 12.5.40; to SAAF 1.6.40 as 906.

L5173 24 MU 28.6.39; 8 MU 15.6.40; 304 Sqn 26.8.40; 47 MU 10.11.40; to RAAF 15.1.41.

L5174 24 MU 28.6.39; 47 MU 21.5.40; to SAAF 19.6.40 as 914.

L5175 24 MU 26.6.39; 36 MU 2.4.40; to RCAF 7.5.40 as 1669.

L5176 24 MU 26.6.39; 47 MU 21.5.40; to SAAF 19.6.40 as 918.

L5177 24 MU 26.6.39; 36 MU 27.3.40; to RCAF 20.4.40 as 1656.

L5178 24 MU 26.6.39; 36 MU 9.5.40; to SAAF 1.6.40 as 907.

L5179 24 MU 26.6.39; 36 MU 5.5.40; to RCAF 16.5.40 as 1691.

L5180 24 MU 28.6.39; to RCAF 2.2.40 as 1631.

L5181 24 MU 28.6.39; 36 MU 5.5.40; to RCAF 16.5.40 as 1684.

L5182 88 Sqn 27.6.39; 22 MU 17.9.39; 12 OTU 4.8.40; 20 MU 19.12.40; 47 MU 24.2.41; to RCAF 24.5.41; not received in Canada.

L5183 88 Sqn 27.6.39; 35 Sqn 24.10.39; bellylanded in bad visibility near Martlesham Heath, 10.12.39; Rollason 25.1.40; Fairey 1.9.40; 27 MU 8.10.40; 12 FTS 26.10.40; bellylanded in error, Harlaxton, 24.12.40; ROS; 16(P)FTS 12.6.41; engine cut; bellylanded, Newton, 14.8.41; 18 MU 27.1.42; to SAAF 28.2.42.

L5184 88 Sqn 5.7.39; 22 MU 18.9.39; 12 OTU 4.8.40; undercarriage collapsed on landing, Mount Farm, 22.11.40; 27 MU 26.12.40; Austin 2.4.41; to RCAF 19.5.41.

L5185 88 Sqn 27.6.39; Mildenhall 29.9.39; 207 Sqn 2.11.39; Mildenhall 30.11.39. Crashed in forced landing in bad visibility, 23.10.39; SOC 8.11.39.

L5186 88 Sqn 27.6.39; Catfoss 30.9.39; 106 Sqn 30.11.39; 5 Group TTF 25.1.40; 4 Group TTF 2.12.40; 5 Group TTF at 31.12.41; 1485 Flight; 30 OTU 1.8.42; 27 MU 28.1.43; SOC 30.11.43; 363.10 hours.

L5187 88 Sqn 24.7.39; 22 MU 19.9.39; 47 MU 10.11.40; to RCAF 28.11.40 as 1837.

L5188 88 Sqn 29.6.39; 12 Sqn 30.11.39. Shot down attacking bridge, Sedan, 14.5.40; Sgt H.R.W. Winkler, Sgt M.D. Smalley and AC1 L.R. Clarke captured

L5189 88 Sqn 29.6.39; 22 MU 17.9.39; 47 MU 16.6.41; to RCAF 4.7.41 as 2030.

L5190 88 Sqn 3.7.39; SAC 27.10.39; 88 Sqn 26.10.39; 16 Sqn 2.11.39; Abingdon at 30.11.39; AASF 1.3.40; 12 Sqn. Shot down by ground fire, Luxembourg, 10.5.40; PO A.W. Matthews, Sgt A.A. Maderson and LAC J.C. Senior captured

L5191 88 Sqn 5.7.39; 22 MU 17.9.39; Austin 14.3.41; to SAAF 11.5.41 as 958.

L5192 88 Sqn 12.7.39; Abingdon at 30.11.39; AASF 11.3.40; 218 Sqn 12.3.40; presumed lost in France 5.40.

L5193 218 Sqn 5.7.39; 22 MU 14.9.39; 301 Sqn 30.8.40; 47 MU 11.11.40; to RCAF 16.12.40 as 1799.

L5194 218 Sqn 3.7.39; 22 MU 18.9.39; 47 MU 9.11.40; to RCAF 24.12.40 as 1811.

L5195 218 Sqn 5.7.39; 22 MU 14.9.39; 18 MU 28.5.41; to RCAF 19.8.41 as 2084.

L5196 218 Sqn 5.7.39; 22 MU 19.9.39; Austin 12.1.41; to RCAF 4.5.41.

L5197 218 Sqn 3.7.39; 35 Sqn 24.10.39; 17 OTU 22.4.40; 12 MU 4.5.40; 305 Sqn 2.9.40; ran into hedge taxying,

K9348 of No.88 Squadron. (via D Thompson)

Bramcote, 18.9.40; 9 MU 14.11.40; Austin 1.1.41; Parks 28.1.41; to RCAF 17.3.41.

L5198   218 Sqn 12.7.39; 22 MU 14.9.39; 47 MU 24.8.41; to RCAF 31.8.41 as 2073.

L5199   218 Sqn 3.7.39; 22 MU 14.9.39; Austin 14.4.41; to SAAF 11.7.41 as 983.

L5200   218 Sqn 14.7.39; Abingdon at 30.11.39; 226 Sqn 21.12.39; 105 Sqn 23.12.39; 142 Sqn. Shot down, Les Andelys, Eure, 11.6.40; PO B.W. Peryman, Sgt J.N. Fraser and LAC J.H.Ledson captured

L5201   218 Sqn 10.7.39; 22 MU 17.9.39; 47 MU 11.6.41; to RCAF 23.6.41 as 2021.

L5202   218 Sqn 3.7.39; 35 Sqn 24.10.39; 63 Sqn 13.12.39; 12 OTU 18.4.40; undercarriage jammed; bellylanded Benson, 19.5.40; 4 MU 26.5.40; Fairey 2.6.40; 9 MU 14.7.40; 47 MU 29.8.40; to RAAF 19.9.40.

L5203   218 Sqn 12.7.39; 35 Sqn 24.10.39; 52 Sqn 4.4.40; 12 OTU 18.4.40; 32 MU 13.2.41; 47 MU 13.5.41; to RCAF 28.5.41 as 1986.

L5204   103 Sqn 9.7.39; 22 MU 16.9.39; 47 MU 16.6.41; to RCAF 4.7.41 as 2029.

L5205   103 Sqn 9.7.39; 22 MU 15.9.39; 110 Wing 11.4.40; 6 AACU 11.4.40; 7 AACU 3.5.40; undercarriage retracted in error while running up, Castle Bromwich, 9.6.40; ROS; Austin 25.2.41; Parks 4.4.41; to RCAF 10.4.41.

L5206   103 Sqn 12.7.39; 22 MU 15.9.39; 6 AACU 6.4.40; 27 MU 2.3.41; 47 MU 24.6.41; to RCAF 24.7.41 as 2055.

L5207   103 Sqn 9.7.39; 22 MU 15.9.39; 47 MU 12.6.41; to RCAF 23.6.41 as 2022.

L5208   103 Sqn 12.7.39; 22 MU 25.9.39; 110 Wing 9.4.40; 6 AACU 9.4.40; Gosport 22.6.40; 2 AACU 23.6.40; undercarriage collapsed on landing, Gosport, 2.7.40; ROS. Destroyed in air raid, Gosport, 16.8.40; SOC 23.9.40.

L5209   103 Sqn 9.7.39; 22 MU 16.9.39; 6 AACU 6.4.40; 1 OTU 18.12.40; 6 AACU 20.12.40; 27 MU 1.3.41; Austin 27.5.41; to RCAF 6.41 as 2008.

L5210   103 Sqn 12.7.39; 22 MU 19.9.39; Dumfries 22.4.41; to SAAF 30.9.41 as 970.

L5211   103 Sqn 12.7.39; 22 MU 25.9.39; 110 Wing 9.4.40; 6 AACU 9.4.40; 7 AACU 3.5.40; engine cut; overshot forced landing, East Keswick, near Leeds, 21.11.40; ROS; 32 MU 8.5.41; 47 MU 22.6.41; to RCAF 24.7.41 as 2032.

L5212   103 Sqn 12.7.39; 22 MU 19.9.39; overshot landing, Sealand, 9.11.40; 47 MU; to RAAF 4.6.41.

L5213   103 Sqn 12.7.39; 22 MU 19.9.39; 36 MU 29.2.40; 22 MU; 47 MU 16.6.41; to SAAF 15.7.41.

L5214   103 Sqn 12.7.39; 3 Group TTF. Lost power and overshot forced landing, East Winch, Norfolk, 13.10.40; SOC 23.10.40.

L5215   150 Sqn 12.7.39; 22 MU 15.9.39; 110 Wing 8.4.40; 6 AACU 8.4.40; 7 AACU 3.5.40; 9 MU 31.5.41; Dumfries 6.8.41; to RAAF 15.10.41.

L5216   150 Sqn 12.7.39; 22 MU 14.9.39; 88 Sqn 6.10.40; undershot landing and undercarriage leg collapsed, Sydenham, 8.11.40; Shorts 2.1.41; 47 MU 26.6.41; to RCAF 27.8.41 as 2098.

L5217   150 Sqn 15.7.39; 22 MU 14.9.39; 110 Wing 8.4.40; 6 AACU 8.4.40; 7 AACU 3.5.40; stalled on landing and tipped up, Castle Bromwich, 30.5.40; 9 MU 1.5.41; Dumfries 6.8.41; to RAAF 15.10.41.

L5218   150 Sqn 31.7.39; 22 MU 14.9.39; brakes failed; hit hangar door, Silloth, 27.1.41; 47 MU 1.3.41; to RCAF 25.4.41 as 1983.

L5219   150 Sqn 12.7.39; 22 MU 14.9.39; Austin 24.4.41; to RCAF 5.41 as 2026.

L5220   150 Sqn 22.7.39; 22 MU 19.9.39; 27 MU 19.9.39; engine cut; forcelanded in field, Hinton, Salop., 20.9.39; Scottish Avn 14.11.39; Fairey 8.6.40; 20 MU 28.7.40; 12 Sqn 27.8.40; 38 MU 16.12.40; 47 MU 22.2.41; to RCAF 2.3.41 as 1892.

L5221   150 Sqn 12.7.39; 22 MU 15.9.39; Austin 28.3.41; forcelanded in bad weather and tipped up, Twycross, Leics., 29.3.41; 47 MU 6.11.41; to RAAF 28.2.42.

L5222   150 Sqn 12.7.39; 22 MU 16.9.39; 47 MU 9.11.40; to RCAF 28.11.40 as 1825.

L5223   150 Sqn 15.7.39; 22 MU 23.9.39; 8 BGS 9.5.40; landed with undercarriage unlocked, Evanton, 24.7.40; ROS;

undercarriage jammed and collapsed on landing, Evanton, 19.11.40; ROS; 18 MU 7.9.41; 215 MU 31.8.42; 3 PATP 8.9.42; to RAAF 17.9.42.

L5224 150 Sqn 14.7.39; 22 MU 23.9.39; 47 MU 19.6.41; to SAAF 15.7.41 as 986.

L5225 150 Sqn 14.7.39. Engine cut; dived into ground on approach, Ecury-sur-Coole, 19.9.39; PO J.L. Calvert, Sgt T.B. Woodmason and AC1 J.L. Marsh killed; SOC 23.11.39; 6.45 hours.

L5226 15 Sqn 15.7.39; Abingdon at 30.11.39; AASF 16.2.40; 142 Sqn 17.2.40. Shot down, Dagny-Lambercy, during raid on Laon, 19.5.40; LAC W.D. Boyle killed; Sgt A.J. Godsell and Sgt B.A. Hopgood captured

L5227 142 Sqn 15.7.39; Abingdon at 30.11.39; AASF 8.3.40; 12 Sqn. Hit by ground fire attacking bridge over Albert Canal and crashed, Veldwezelt, Limburg, 12.5.40; Sgt F. Marland, Sgt K.D. Footner and LAC J.L. Ferrin killed

L5228 207 Sqn 26.7.39; 4 Group TTF 12.12.39; 18 MU 18.2.43; SOC 14.7.44.

L5229 15 Sqn 24.7.39; Abingdon at 30.11.39. Crashed in English Channel, 13.2.40.

L5230 15 Sqn 14.7.39; Abingdon at 30.11.39; AASF 21.2.40; 105 Sqn. Missing from attack on bridge, Sedan, 14.5.40; F/Lt H.C. Sammels. Sgt F.B. Abbott and LAC R.D. missing

L5231 15 Sqn 18.7.39; Abingdon at 30.11.39; AASF 16.2.40; 142 Sqn 17.2.40. Shot down by ground fire, Luxembourg, 10.5.40; FO M.H. Roth, Sgt W.F. Algie and Sgt H. Morris captured

L5232 15 Sqn 26.7.39; Abingdon at 30.11.39; AASF 4.3.40; 218 Sqn 5.3.40. Shot down, Sauville, during attack on bridge, Sedan, 14.5.40; Sgt N.B. Herriot, AC1 W. Robinson killed; PO W.A.R. Harris wounded but escaped

L5233 15 Sqn 24.7.39; Abingdon at 30.11.39; 88 Sqn 12.2.40. Damaged in action, Sedan, 14.5.40 and abandoned on evacuation, 16.5.40.

L5234 15 Sqn 24.7.39; Abingdon at 30.11.39; AASF 16.2.40; 103 Sqn 17.2.40. Abandoned on evacuation of Bétheniville, 16.5.40.

L5235 15 Sqn 24.7.39; Abingdon at 30.11.39; AASF 1.3.40; 142 Sqn; 218 Sqn. Shot down during attack on bridge, Thelonne, 5m S of Sedan, 14.5.40; LAC A.J. Taylor killed; PO A.M. Imrie captured

L5236 15 Sqn 26.7.39; Abingdon at 30.11.39; 103 Sqn 19.1.40; AASF 12.2.40; 103 Sqn. Hit tree during crashlanding on night navex, Chandon, near Amboise, Indre-et-Loire, 1.3.40; 21 AD 7.3.40; 2 Salvage Section 8.3.40; 21 AD 13.3.40. SOC 30.4.40.

L5237 15 Sqn 26.7.39; Abingdon at 30.11.39; 218 Sqn 18.2.40; 150 Sqn 21.5.40; overshot flarepath and hit fence, Newton, 11.9.40; ROS; 103 Sqn 30.9.40; 301 Sqn 4.10.40; Western A/W 23.11.40; 38 MU 2.1.41; 47 MU; to RCAF 7.3.41 as 1896.

L5238 15 Sqn 24.7.39; Abingdon at 30 11.39; AASF 21.2.40; 105 Sqn. Shot down attacking bridge, Sedan, 14.5.40; F/Lt R.N. Wall, Sgt A.C. Morgan and LAC H. Hatton killed

L5239 15 Sqn 24.7.39; Abingdon at 30.11.39; AASF 1.3.40; 4 RSU 14.5.40; presumed lost in France 5.40.

L5240 40 Sqn 24.7.39; Abingdon at 30.11.39; AASF 21.2.40; 142 Sqn 25.2.40; 1 Salvage Section 10.4.40; 21 AD 30.4.40; Fairey 25.6.40; 20 MU 26.7.40; 12 Sqn 19.9.40; 27 MU 7.10.40; Austin 29.11.40; Parks 28.12.40; to SAAF 28.2.41 as 946.

L5241 40 Sqn 24.7.39; Abingdon at 30.11.39; AASF 28.2.40; 12 Sqn. Damaged by flak attacking bridge, Vroenhoven, and crashlanded, St. Germaincourt, 12.5.40; AC1 G.N. Patterson captured

L5242 40 Sqn 24.7.39; Abingdon at 30.11.39; AASF 21.2.40; 142 Sqn 25.2.40. Damaged by ground fire, Luxembourg, 10.5.40; AC1 Cave injured; abandoned, Berry-au-Bac, 16.5.40.

L5243 40 Sqn 27.7.39; Abingdon at 30.11.39; 88 Sqn 25.2.40; 21 AD 10.5.40; abandoned in France 17.5.40.

L5244 40 Sqn 1.8.39; Abingdon at 30.11.39; AASF 4.3.40; 103 Sqn 5.3.40; Fairey 18.8.40; 9 MU 11.12.40; 47 MU 23.2.41; to RAAF 24.7.41.

L5245 40 Sqn 27.7.39; Abingdon at 30.11.39; 218 Sqn 18.2.40; 1 Salvage Section 19.4.40; 6 RSU 21.4.40; 21 AD 3.5.40; Fairey 25.6.40; 47 MU 1.11.40; to RCAF 28.11.40 as 1826.

L5246 40 Sqn 27.7.39; Abingdon at 30.11.39; AASF 21.2.40; 103 Sqn 24.2.40. Engine failed on night operation; crew abandoned aircraft, 9.6.40

L5247 40 Sqn 24.7.39; Abingdon at 30.11.39; AASF 12.2.40; 2SF 14.2.40; 226 Sqn 16.2.40. Shot down by ground fire, Luxembourg, 10.5.40; F/Lt B.R. Kerridge died of wounds; SOC 11.5.40.

L5248 40 Sqn 27.7.39; 15 Sqn 18.11.39; 88 Sqn 5.12.39; presumed lost in France 5.40.

L5249 40 Sqn 1.8.39; Abingdon at 30 11.39; AASF 28.2.40; 12 Sqn. Damaged by ground fire, Luxembourg, 10.5.40 but returned safely; Sgt A Young wounded; abandoned on evacuation

L5250 40 Sqn 27.7.39; Abingdon at 30.11.39; AASF 28.2.40; 105 Sqn. Damaged in action, Sedan: forcelanded and abandoned at Suippes, 14.5.40

L5251 1 AOS 9.8.39; 9 BGS; 32 MU 4.7.41; 18 MU 28.8.41; 215 MU 17.8.42; 3 PATP 5.9.42; to RAAF 17.9.42.

L5252 1 AOS 31.7.39; 9 BGS; 16(P)FTS 1.8.41; 9 MU 16.3.42; 309 Sqn 23.7.42; 27 MU 15.1.43; SOC 30.6.43.

L5253 1 AOS 1.8.39; 9 BGS; Western A/W 7.9.41; 9 MU 27.11.41; 3 AGS 28.7.42; 27 MU 3.12.42; SOC 30.6.43.

L5254 Crashed on landing, Longbridge, before delivery, 25.7.39.

L5255 1 AOS 9.8.39; 9 BGS; 9 AOS. Collided with L5256 and crashed 4m NNW of Penrhos, 24.11.39; PO K.P. Hamilton and 2 crew killed; SOC 6.12.39.

L5256 1 AOS 1.8.39; 9 BGS; 9 AOS. Collided with L5255 and crashed 4m NNW of Penrhos, 24.11.39; PO A.A. Dean and 2 crew killed; SOC 6.12.39.

L5257 1 AOS 9.8.39; 9 BGS; bounced on landing, swung and undercarriage collapsed, Penrhos, 4.6.40; ROS; 9 AOS; 18 MU 30.7.41; 47 MU 3.12.41; to RAAF 21.1.42.

L5258 1 AOS 31.7.39; 9 BGS; 9 AOS; 9 MU 1.9.41; 47 MU 15.11.41; to RAAF 5.1.42.

L5259 1 AOS 9.8.39; 9 BGS; engine cut on take-off, collided with Harvard N7121, Penrhos, 6.12.39; 4 MU 17.5.40; Fairey 13.6.40; 20 MU 25.7.40; 142 Sqn 31.8.40; Austin 26.5.41; to RCAF 6.41 as 2005.

L5260 1 AOS 9.8.39; 9 BGS; overshot landing and hit building, Penrhos, 21.11.39; ROS. Engine cut after take-off; undershot landing and hit hedge, Penrhos, 22.4.40; SOC 2.5.40.

L5261 1 AOS 5.9.39; 9 BGS; Western A/W 19.9.41; 47 MU 27.11.41; to RCAF 7.2.42.

L5262 1 AOS 9.8.39; 9 BGS; 18 MU 11.7.41; 215 MU 22.4.42; 3 PATP 27.5.42; to RAAF 14.6.42.

L5263 35 Sqn 1.8.39; 63 Sqn 12.12.39; tyre burst on landing, swung and undercarriage collapsed, Benson, 11.4.40; ROS; 12 OTU 18.4.40; engine cut on take-off; bellylanded, Brightwell Grove, Oxon., 12.7.40; Fairey 21.7.40; 22 MU 21.3.41; 47 MU 11.6.41; to RCAF 23.6.41 as 2020.

L5264 35 Sqn 8.8.39; 52 Sqn 5.3.40; 12 OTU 18.4.40; engine cut; overshot forced landing into ditch, Weston Zoyland, 17.5.40; ROS; engine cut; bellylanded, Kingston Blount, Oxon., 31.10.40; Fairey 6.11.40; 47 MU 26.3.41; to RCAF 17.5.41 as 1955.

L5265 35 Sqn 8.8.39; 17 OTU 22.4.40; Rollason 12.8.40; Fairey 2.9.40; 9 MU 20.11.40; Austin 28.2.41; to RCAF 4.5.41.

L5266 35 Sqn 10.8.39; 17 OTU 22.4.40; 32 MU 9.1.41; Austin 11.3.41; to RCAF 13.5.41.

L5267 35 Sqn 30.9.39; Fairey 15.8.40; 47 MU 7.11.40; to RAAF 15.1.41

N2034 was used by Rotols to test hollow-steel propellers. (R Sturtivant collection)

L5268 35 Sqn 16.8.39; 2 Group TTF 15.3.40; 38 MU 9.1.41; Dumfries 1.7.41; to SAAF 24.7.42 as 975; to Middle East 30.1.43.

L5269 35 Sqn 10.8.39; 63 Sqn 11.1.40; 12 OTU 18.4.40; engine cut; bellylanded, Bicester, 13.10.40; Fairey 25.10.40; 47 MU 14.3.41; to RCAF 31.3.41 as 1904.

L5270 35 Sqn 11.8.39; 63 Sqn 13.12.39; 12 OTU 18.4.40; engine cut; undercarriage collapsed in forced landing, Harwell, 11.6.40; ROS; undercarriage jammed, bellylanded, Benson, 29.9.40; 38 MU 30.12.40; Austin 26.3.41; to RCAF 13.5.41.

L5271 35 Sqn 1.9.39; Polish OTU 9.4.40; 18 OTU; 20 MU 27.11.40; 47 MU 1.3.41; to RCAF 25.4.41 as 1954.

L5272 35 Sqn 11.8.39; 52 Sqn 5.3.40; 12 OTU 18.4.40; swung in forced landing in bad weather 1m SE of Stratford-on-Avon, 30.10.40; 22 MU 4.1.41; 47 MU 3.3.41; to RCAF 25.4.41 as 1997.

L5273 35 Sqn 11.8.39; Polish OTU 9.4.40; 18 OTU; engine cut on take-off and undercarriage collapsed, Hucknall, 5.9.40; Austin 18.9.40; 18 MU 1.3.41; 47 MU 13.3.41; to RCAF 29.3.41 as 1910.

L5274 207 Sqn 8.8.39; Fairey 25.11.40; 18 MU 28.4.41; 9 MU 1.8.41; 47 MU 10.9.41; to RAAF 27.9.41.

L5275 207 Sqn 17.8.39; 63 Sqn 10.12.39; 12 OTU 18.4.40. Engine cut; bellylanded, Little Milton, Oxon., 6.8.40; to 2201M; SOC 27.8.40.

L5276 207 Sqn 10.8.39; 12 OTU; Austin 18.9.40; 20 MU 30.4.41; 47 MU 19.6.41; to SAAF 15.7.41.

L5277 207 Sqn 8.8.39; Rollason 27.1.41; Fairey 28.8.40. Undershot landing and undercarriage collapsed, Weston Zoyland, 2.1.40; DBR; SOC 26.9.40.

L5278 207 Sqn 16.8.39; 18 MU 19.12.40; 47 MU 12.3.41; to Canada 11.4.41 then to RAAF.

L5279 207 Sqn 11.8.39. Engine cut after take-off; stalled and crashlanded, Bassingbourn, 28.11.39; PO T.R. Williams killed; SOC 6.12.39.

L5280 207 Sqn 16.8.39; overshot landing in fog and hit hedge, Cranfield, 7.11.39; Scottish Avn at 30.11.39; Fairey 24.6.40; 12 MU 7.8.40; damaged 6.1.41; Rosenfield 23.2.41; SOC 23.2.41.

L5281 207 Sqn 11.8.39; engine cut; forcelanded Ashwell, Herts., 16.1.40; Rollason 23.1.40; Fairey 26.8.40; 9 MU 29.11.40; 47 MU 14.2.41; to RCAF 11.3.41 as 1921.

L5282 207 Sqn 17.8.39; 12 OTU. Lost height on night take-off and hit ground 1m E of Benson, 10.6.40; SOC 14.6.40.

L5283 207 Sqn 17.8.39; ran into Magister L8216 on landing, Cranfield, 3.10.39; ROS; 12 OTU. Engine cut on approach; crashlanded and hit wall, Aston Down, 29.8.40; Fairey 12.9.40; SOC 11.9.40.

L5284 207 Sqn 1.9.39; 22 MU 4.1.41; 47 MU 31.1.41; to RCAF 13.3.41 as 1919.

L5285 142 Sqn 12.8.39; Abingdon at 30.11.39; AASF 26.2.40; 88 Sqn 2.3.40; bellylanded in error, Sydenham, 11.7.40; ROS; 38 MU 16.11.40; Austin 11.5.41; to SAAF 9.7.41.

L5286 Northolt 18.8.39; RAE 8.9.39; Napier for installation and tests of Sabre engine; SOC 7.12.43.

L5287 9 MU 22.8.39; 27 MU 29.9.39; 5 FTS 2.4.40; 12 FTS 10.2.41; 16(P)FTS 7.6.41; hit pile of bricks in forced landing in bad weather, Church Broughton, 16.11.41; 9 MU 26.1.42; 1472 Flight 9.6.42; 18 MU 20.5.43; SOC 13.10.43.

L5288 9 MU 22.8.39; 19 MU 3.10.39; 27 MU 4.10.39; 10 MU 10.2.40; AASF 18.5.40; 150 Sqn 19.5.40. Shot down in attack on column near Vergies, 10 m SSE of Abbeville,

7.6.40; FO J.E. Vernon, Sgt G.A. Wilson and Sgt P.E.F. Adams killed

L5289 9 MU 15.8.39; AASF 19.1.40; 4 FPP. Stalled in circuit and dived into ground, Perpignan, 12.5.40; FO K.H. Dingle killed

L5290 9 MU 15.8.39; 27 MU 29.9.39; 4 BGS 11.4.40; engine cut; bellylanded on beach, Luce Bay, 26.9.40; ROS; Western A/W 11.12.41; LEP 12.2.42; to RCAF 13.4.42 as 2135.

L5291 9 MU 22.8.39; 27 MU 2.10.39; 4 BGS 11.4.40; undercarriage jammed; bellylanded, West Freugh, 19.11.40; ROS; 47 MU 30.11.41; to RAAF 5.1.42.

L5292 9 MU 10.9.39; 27 MU 29.9.39; Polish OTU 8.4.40; 18 OTU; 27 MU 15.12.40; Austin 17.1.41; to RCAF 10.3.41.

L5293 9 MU 23.8.39; 27 MU 3.10.39; 7 BGS 10.4.40. Engine cut; ditched off Porthcawl, Glamorgan, 27.7.40; FO H.T. Wheeler, AC2 M.A. Barringer and AC2 R.E. Barker killed; SOC 1.9.40; 128.50 hours.

L5294 9 MU 18.8.39; 8 AOS 5.9.39; 1 FTS 28.4.41. Control lost during night landing; crashed, Shrewton, 11.11.41; ALA S.H. Tyson (RN) killed, ALA R.G. Hallas seriously injured; SOC 15.11.41.

L5295 9 MU 23.8.39; West Freugh 4.9.39; Rollason 25.1.40; SOC 12.8.40.

L5296 9 MU 15.8.39; 8 AOS 5.9.39; engine cut; bellylanded, Arboll, 5m W of Tain, 13.1.41; Fairey 25.2.41; 47 MU 28.6.41; to RCAF 27.8.41 as 2104.

L5297 9 MU 22.8.39; SOC 8.11.39; to 2581M.

L5298 9 MU 30.8.39; West Freugh 4.9.39; 4 BGS; undercarriage jammed; bellylanded, West Freugh, 24.4.40; Fairey; 12 MU 21.7.40; 47 MU 26.10.40; to RCAF 15.11.40 as 1741.

L5299 9 MU 30.8.39; West Freugh 4.9.39; 4 BGS; 27 MU 8.11.41; to 3556M at 593 Sqn, ATC, 6.2.42; 12 SofTT 8.6.42; 27 MU 18.12.43.

L5300 9 MU 23.8.39; 27 MU 29.9.39; 10 MU 12.2.40; 6 BGS 11.5.40; 12 FTS 29.5.40; undershot night landing and hit hedge, Harlaxton, 3.10.40; Austin 6.10.40; 22 MU 22.1.41; 47 MU 16.4.41; to RCAF 24.5.41; not received in Canada.

L5301 27 MU 1.9.39; 8 BGS 16.5.40. Engine cut; overshot forced landing and hit trees, Aboyne, Aberdeenshire, 15.8.41; SOC 29.8.41.

L5302 27 MU 28.8.39; 8 BGS 16.5.40; 18 MU 21.8.41; 47 MU 11.11.41; to RAAF 5.1.42.

L5303 27 MU 28.8.39; 7 FTS 29.5.40. Engine caught fire; abandoned, Pinchbeck, Lincs., 14.11.40; SOC 1.12.40; 218.45 hours.

L5304 27 MU 28.8.39; 4 BGS 11.4.40; Fairey 27.6.40; 9 MU 29.12.40; 47 MU 14.2.41; to RCAF 11.3.41 as 1906.

L5305 27 MU 30.8.39; 6 BGS 4.5.40; 7 BGS 2.6.40; engine cut on take-off; crashlanded, Stormy Down, 26.5.41; Fairey 1.6.41; 47 MU 15.9.41; to RAAF 27.9.41.

L5306 27 MU 6.9.39; 23 MU 4.3.41; Dumfries 26.1.42; to RCAF 21.3.42 as 2139.

L5307 27 MU 30.8.39; 10 MU 14.2.40; 6 BGS 6.5.40; 12 FTS 29.5.40; engine cut; bellylanded, Ashfordby Station, near Melton Mowbray, Leics., 13.10.40; Fairey 18.10.40; 18 MU 18.4.41; Dumfries 2.5.41; to SAAF 1941 as 972.

L5308 27 MU 30.8.39; 7 FTS 20.5.40; Austin 10.4.41; to RCAF 21.5.41.

L5309 27 MU 10.9.39; 5 FTS 2.4.40; 4 BGS 7.11.40; 10 BGS 12.6.41; 10 AOS; Rosenfield 3.9.42; 27 MU 7.10.42; 215 MU 30.11.42; LEP 20.12.42; 3 PATP 21.1.43; to SAAF 6.4.43.

L5310 27 MU 1.9.39; 10 MU 14.2.40; 6 BGS 6.5.40; 7 FTS 26.5.40; undercarriage collapsed on landing, Newton Down, 4.9.40; ROS; 27 MU 20.2.41; 47 MU 18.4.41; to RCAF 24.5.41; not received in Canada.

L5311 27 MU 6.9.39; 6 BGS 4.5.40; 7 BGS 3.6.40; 16(P)FTS 14.8.41; engine cut; hit car on approach, Newton, 11.9.41; 18 MU 27.1.42; to RAAF 5.8.42.

L5312 27 MU 1.9.39; 235 Sqn 10.12.39; 8 BGS 10.6.40; 1 FTS 28.4.41; bellylanded in error, Stormy Down, 12.7.41; ROS; tyre burst on take-off; swung and undercarriage collapsed, Netheravon, 2.9.41; ROS; Western A/W 10.1.42; 23 MU 27.3.42; 15 APC 3.8.42; 27 MU 14.1.43; SOC 30.6.43.

L5313 27 MU 8.9.39; 7 BGS 10.4.40; 18 MU 3.9.41; Dumfries 11.11.41; 3 PATP at 31.12.41; to RAAF 18.1.42.

L5314 27 MU 30.8.39; 10 MU 15.2.40; 18 OTU 23.7.40; 12 OTU 16.11.40; 38 MU 4.1.41; 47 MU 8.2.41; to RCAF 8.3.41 as 1886.

L5315 27 MU 1.9.39; 305 Sqn 14.9.40; 9 MU 14.11.40; Austin 3.1.41; Parks 30.1.41; to RCAF 17.3.41.

L5316 27 MU 8.9.39; 301 Sqn 4.8.40; 47 MU 11.11.40; to RCAF 16.12.40 as 1803.

L5317 27 MU 5.9.39; 300 Sqn 26.8.40; 47 MU 10.11.40; to RCAF 18.12.40 as 1829.

L5318 27 MU 5.9.39; 300 Sqn 26.8.40; 47 MU 13.11.40; to RCAF 16.12.40 as 1808.

L5319 10 MU 10.9.39; 36 MU 6.5.40; to RCAF 18.5.40 as 1681.

L5320 10 MU 5.9.39; 36 MU 6.5.40; to RAAF 22.5.40.

L5321 10 MU 8.9.39; 36 MU 6.5.40; to RCAF 18.5.40 as 1685.

L5322 10 MU 8.9.39; 36 MU 6.5.40; to RAAF 22.5.40.

L5323 10 MU 15.9.39; tipped up while running up, Hullavington, 20.11.39; ROS; AASF 19.5.40; presumed lost in France, 5.40.

L5324 10 MU 6.9.39; 12 Sqn 19.5.40. Hit by ground fire attacking tanks in Forêt de Gault; crashed near St.Barthólemy, Seine-et-Marne, 13.6.40; Sgt N.C. Cotterell killed; PO J.S. Shorthouse wounded

L5325 10 MU 10.9.39; AASF 20.5.40. Swung on landing and undercarriage damaged, Beauvais, 19.5.40; presumed abandoned on evacuation.

L5326 10 MU 12.9.39; AASF 7.6.40; 226 Sqn 9.6.40; 23 MU 19.8.41; 18 MU 20.2.42; 215 MU 16.4.42; 3 PATP 27.4.42; to RAAF 11.6.42.

L5327 10 MU 8.9.39; AASF 21.5.40; 142 Sqn 21.5.40; presumed lost in France, 5.40.

L5328 10 MU 20.9.39; AASF 20.5.40; 12 Sqn 23.5.40; presumed lost in France, 6.40.

L5329 10 MU 12.9.39; 36 MU 6.5.40; to RCAF 18.5.40 as 1689.

L5330 10 MU 10.9.39; AASF 20.5.40; 88 Sqn 23.5.40. Engine cut; bellylanded, Upper Galwally, Belfast, 11.4.41; DBR; SOC 22.4.41; 172.00 hours.

L5331 10 MU 12.9.39; 98 Sqn 14.7.40; to RCAF 20.8.41.

L5332 10 MU 10.9.39; 98 Sqn 14.7.40; to RCAF 20.8.41.

L5333 10 MU 12.9.39; AASF 25.5.40; 88 Sqn 26.5.40; 6 RSU 3.6.40; presumed abandoned in France, 6.40.

L5334 10 MU 13.9.39; AASF 21.5.40; 88 Sqn 1.6.40. Hit by ground fire, St Valéry, and crashed, Beaurepaire, Oise, 12.6.40; F/Lt A.L. Pitfield and Sgt J. Ballantyne killed

L5335 10 MU 13.9.39; 18 OTU 23.7.40; 38 MU 5.12.40; Austin 15.1.41; to RCAF 4.5.41.

L5336 10 MU 13.9.39; AASF 12.6.40; 103 Sqn 16.6.40; overshot flarepath and hit hedge, Newton, 26.9.40; Fairey 4.10.40; 22 MU 14.12.40; 47 MU 30.1.41; to RCAF 13.3.41 as 1932.

L5337 10 MU 15.9.39; AASF 7.6.40; 226 Sqn 9.6.40; 47 MU 6.8.41; to RCAF 31.8.41 as 2068.

L5338 10 MU 13.9.39; AASF 7.6.40; presumed abandoned in France, 6.40.

L5339 10 MU 15.9.39; 18 OTU 23.7.40; taxied into pile of stones at night, Hucknall, 21.9.40; 18 MU 26.11.40; Austin 24.12.40; to SAAF 29.3.41 as 953.

L5340 24 MU 13.9.39; 36 MU 10.1.40; to RCAF 24.2.40 as 1614.

L5341 24 MU 15.9.39; 36 MU 8.1.40; to RCAF 1.40 as 1608.

L5342 24 MU 13.9.39; 266 Sqn 10.12.39; 36 MU 10.1.40; to RCAF 24.2.40 as 1618.

L5343 24 MU 13.9.39; 266 Sqn 9.12.39; 20 MU 24.2.40; 98

N2031 served as a conversion trainer with No.616 Squadron and is seen here at Manston. (R Sturtivant collection)

Sqn 13.7.40; crashed in Iceland, 13.9.40; SOC 20.1.41; salvaged and returned to England; now in RAF Museum, Hendon

L5344 24 MU 13.9.39; 36 MU 10.1.40; to RCAF 24.2.40 as 1615.

L5345 24 MU 17.9.39; 36 MU 10.1.40; to RCAF 20.2.40 as 1609.

L5346 24 MU 17.9.39; 36 MU 8.1.40; to RCAF 20.2.40 as 1610.

L5347 24 MU 17.9.39; 36 MU 3.1.40; to RCAF 24.2.40 as 1617.

L5348 24 MU 17.9.39; 266 Sqn 4.12.39. Engine cut in snowstorm; hit hedge on forced landing, East Kirkby, Notts., 16.1.40. SOC 29.1.40.

L5349 24 MU 19.9.39; Polish OTU 11.3.40; 18 OTU; Fairey 28.11.40; 9 MU 26.4.41; Dumfries 1.7.41; to RCAF 19.8.41 as 2097.

L5350 24 MU 20.9.39; 266 Sqn 4.12.39; landed with undercarriage locked, Sutton Bridge, 9.12.39; 47 MU 13.1.40; Rollason 25.1.40; Fairey 18.8.40; NFT

L5351 27 MU 29.9.39; 301 Sqn 3.8.40. Crashed near Brandon, Norfolk, en route to Boulogne, 25.9.40; PO J. Killinski killed; SOC 5.10.40.

L5352 27 MU 2.10.39; 305 Sqn 3.9.40; 9 MU 14.11.40; Austin 30.12.40; Parks 17.1.41; to RCAF 17.3.41.

L5353 27 MU 24.9.39; Bramcote 29.6.40; 300 Sqn 1.7.40; 47 MU 10.11.40; to RCAF 26.2.41 as 1860.

L5354 27 MU 24.9.39; 47 MU 27.2.41; to RAAF 3.4.41.

L5355 27 MU 21.9.39; 47 MU 10.10.40; to RCAF 27.10.40 as 1752.

L5356 27 MU 21.9.39; Bramcote 29.6.40; 300 Sqn 1.7.40. Wing broke off recovering from dive, Sutton-on-Trent, Notts., 29.10.40; FO Bileanski, Sgt Goebel and Sgt Szmajdowicz (all PAF) killed; SOC 10.11.40.

L5357 27 MU 21.9.39; 48 MU 22.8.40; 98 Sqn 21.8.40; 22 MU 30.11.40; 47 MU 15.9.41; to RAAF 27.9.41.

L5358 27 MU 21.9.39; 10 MU 13.2.40; AASF 19.5.40; 103

Sqn 23.5.40; hit by L5469, Newton, 3.8.40; 20 MU 21.10.40; 47 MU 7.11.40; to RAAF 15.1.41.

L5359 27 MU 29.9.39; 12 Sqn 27.6.40; 20 MU 28.11.40; 47 MU 28.2.41; to RCAF 1.4.41 as 1973.

L5360 27 MU 24.9.39; 10 MU 11.2.40; AASF 25.5.40; 88 Sqn 26.5.40; Fairey 24.6.40; 20 MU 23.7.40; 38 MU 1.1.41. Engine cut on air test; crashlanded near Llandow, 8.3.41; SOC 10.3.41.

L5361 27 MU 24.9.39; 10 MU 12.2.40; AASF 12.6.40; 88 Sqn 15.6.40. DBR in air raid, Sydenham, 5.5.41; SOC 18.5.51; 128.30 hours.

L5362 27 MU 24.9.39; 10 MU 12.2.40; AASF 7.6.40; lost in France 6.40.

L5363 27 MU 28.9.39; 10 MU 12.2.40; AASF 12.6.40; 103 Sqn 16.6.40; 27 MU 15.10.40; Austin 7.12.40; Parks 4.1.41; to SAAF 1941 as 963.

L5364 24 MU 6.10.39; 36 MU 11.1.40; to RCAF 15.3.40 as 1620.

L5365 24 MU 24.9.39; 266 Sqn 9.12.39; 234 Sqn 14.2.40; 22 MU 10.5.40; 300 Sqn 5.9.40; 47 MU 10.11.40; to RCAF 18.12.40 as 1795.

L5366 24 MU 24.9.39; 36 MU 10.1.40; to RCAF 9.3.40 as 1619.

L5367 24 MU 28.9.39; overshot landing in bad visibility and hit bank, Sealand, 8.1.40; 36 MU 8.1.40; 43 Group 28.2.40; Fairey 20.5.40; 8 MU 24.6.40; 142 Sqn 25.8.40; Fairey 29.9.40; 9 MU 8.12.40; Austin 6.3.41; to SAAF 11.5.41 as 956.

L5368 24 MU 24.9.39; 266 Sqn 10.12.39; 38 MU 7.5.40; 8 MU 15.6.40; 304 Sqn 26.8.40; 142 Sqn 1.11.40; 38 MU 16.12.40; overshot landing and undercarriage collapsed on ferry flight, Llandow, 16.12.40; passenger Sgt P. Malcolm killed; Rosenfield 23.2.41; SOC 1.7.41 as BER

L5369 24 MU 30.9.39; 266 Sqn 17.12.39; 234 Sqn 14.2.40; 22 MU 10.5.40; 47 MU 3.9.40; to RCAF 26.9.40 as 1725.

L5370 24 MU 20.10.39; 36 MU 10.1.40; to RCAF 24.2.40 as 1611.

L5371	24 MU 24.9.39; 36 MU 10.1.40; to RCAF 1.2.40 as 1601.
L5372	24 MU 28.9.39; 36 MU 10.1.40; to RCAF 24.2.40 as 1616.
L5373	24 MU 28.9.39; 36 MU 10.1.40; to RCAF 6.3.40 as 1612.
L5374	24 MU 30.9.39; 266 Sqn 4.12.39; 20 MU 24.2.40; 47 MU 23.5.40; to SAAF 2.7.40 as 924.
L5375	24 MU 23.10.39; 266 Sqn 10.12.39; 20 MU 24.2.40; 47 MU 19.5.40; to SAAF 6.6.40 as 912.
L5376	24 MU 19.10.39; 36 MU 2.3.40; to RCAF 29.3.40 as 1633.
L5377	24 MU 30.9.39; 36 MU 10.1.40; to RCAF 6.3.40 as 1613.
L5378	24 MU 23.10.39; 47 MU 4.9.40; to RCAF 26.9.40 as 1724.
L5379	19 MU 30.9.39; 235 Sqn 10.12.39; undercarriage collapsed in forced landing in bad weather, Ashford, Kent, 1.1.40; Rollason 9.1.40; Fairey 18.8.40; 47 MU 19.3.41; to RCAF 2.4.41 as 1930.
L5380	19 MU 30.9.39; 3 BGS 18.12.39; 10 BGS 15.7.40; engine cut; bellylanded near Kirkgunzeon, Dumfries, 10.12.40; Fairey 16.1.41; 47 MU 17.3.41; to RCAF 17.5.41 as 1956.
L5381	19 MU 6.10.39; 235 Sqn 10.12.39; 10 MU 22.2.40; AASF 19.5.40; 103 Sqn 23.5.40; to SAAF 1943.
L5382	19 MU 6.10.39; to RAAF 18.5.40.
L5383	19 MU 30.9.39; 235 Sqn 5.12.39; 10 MU 22.2.40; 12 Sqn 19.5.40. Shot down by fighters, Pacy-sur-Eure, 10m ESE of Evreux, 14.6.40; Sgt R.J. Wilcox, Sgt G.H. Emery and LAC J. Hislop killed
L5384	19 MU 9.39; to RCAF 2.2.40 as 1655.
L5385	19 MU 19.10.39; to RAAF 22.5.40.
L5386	19 MU 8.10.39; 3 BGS 18.12.39; overshot flarepath and damaged, Aldergrove, 15.6.40; Fairey 22.6.40; 47 MU 5.10.40; to RCAF 27.10.40 as 1766.
L5387	19 MU 20.10.39; to RAAF 2.5.40.
L5388	19 MU 8.10.39; to RCAF 2.2.40 as 1642.
L5389	19 MU 20.10.39; AASF 24.5.40; 88 Sqn 25.5.40; 18 MU 17.7.40; 47 MU 27.2.41; to RCAF 7.4.41 as 1939.
L5390	19 MU 20.10.39; to RAAF 11.5.40.
L5391	27 MU 8.10.39; 12 Sqn 26.6.40; Binbrook 21.8.40; 142 Sqn 10.9.40; damaged in forced landing 6m S of Binbrook, 22.10.40; Austin 27.10.40; 20 MU 7.4.41; Dumfries 10.8.41. Bellylanded in bad weather 6m N of Binbrook, 22.10.40; presumed SOC
L5392	27 MU 23.10.39; 301 Sqn 3.8.40; Rosenfield 1.1.41; Fairey 13.1.41; 47 MU 3.6.41; to RCAF 11.6.41 as 2012.
L5393	27 MU 23.10.39; AASF 7.6.40; 88 Sqn 9.6.40; 23 MU 5.9.41; Shorts 2.10.42; SOC 14.10.42.
L5394	27 MU 8.10.39; AASF 2.6.40; 98 Sqn 2.6.40; 9 MU 13.7.40; Austin 13.5.41; to RCAF 5.41 as 2047.
L5395	27 MU 23.10.39; AASF 7.6.40; 103 Sqn 16.6.40; 20 MU 10.10.40; Austin 28.11.40; Parks 28.12.40; to SAAF 28.2.41.
L5396	10 MU 12.2.40; 12 Sqn 19.5.40. Shot down by fighters, Colonges, Eure, during raid on Evreux, 14.6.40; PO P.H. Blowfield and LAC D.L. Grant killed; Sgt Batty escaped
L5397	27 MU 23.10.39; AASF 24.5.40; 142 Sqn. Damaged by enemy aircraft in battle area, 14.6.40, and abandoned at Faux-Villecerf.
L5398	27 MU 19.11.39; 12 Sqn 26.6.40; 38 MU 22.12.40; 47 MU 13.2.41; to RCAF 2.3.41 as 1877.
L5399	27 MU 20.10.39; 12 Sqn 26.6.40; Binbrook 21.8.40; 38 MU 22.12.40; 47 MU 11.6.41; to RCAF 23.6.41 as 2006.
L5400	27 MU 24.1.40; 12 Sqn 26.6.40; Binbrook 21.8.40; Fairey 25.9.40; Austin 13.4.41; to RCAF 5.41 as 2049.
L5401	AASF 7.6.40; 226 Sqn 9.6.40; 47 MU 6.8.41; to RCAF 31.8.41 as 2070.
L5402	27 MU 19.11.39; 218 Sqn 5.40. Damaged by ground fire near Luxembourg, 10.5.40 and abandoned on evacuation.
L5403	19 MU 20.10.39; to RAAF 11.5.40.
L5404	12 Sqn 27.6.40; overshot landing, Bramcote, 22.7.40; ROS; 20 MU 28.11.40; 47 MU 14.1.41; to RCAF 27.8.41 as 2077.
L5405	19 MU 20.10.39; to RCAF 2.2.40 as 1668.
L5406	235 Sqn 19.12.39; 242 Sqn 29.12.39; 141 Sqn 27.3.40; 6 MU 3.7.40; 23 MU 3.3.41; 47 MU 1.7.41; to RCAF 8.8.41 as 2061.
L5407	19 MU 20.10.39; to RAAF 20.4.40.
L5408	19 MU 20.10.39; to RCAF 2.2.40 as 1664.
L5409	19 MU 20.10.39; to RAAF 2.5.40.
L5410	19 MU 20.10.39; to RCAF 2.2.40 as 1658.
L5411	19 MU 20.10.39; to RCAF 2.2.40 as 1644.
L5412	19 MU 24.10.39; 235 Sqn 10.12.39; 10 MU 16.2.40; 98 Sqn 14.7.40; to RCAF 20.8.41.
L5413	19 MU 20.10.39; 235 Sqn 17.12.39; 10 MU 22.2.40; 18 OTU 23.7.40; 18 MU 26.11.40; Austin 9.1.41; Parks 30.1.41; to RCAF 17.3.41.
L5414	19 MU 24.10.39; to RCAF 2.2.40 as 1643.
L5415	6 MU 24.10.39; AASF 18.5.40; 12 Sqn 19.5.40; 20 MU 28.11.40; Austin 12.2.41; Parks 21.3.41; to SAAF 12.2.41.
L5416	6 MU 19.11.39; Linton-on-Ouse 12.1.40; undercarriage collapsed taxying, Linton-on-Ouse, 1.3.40; ROS; 1484 Flight at 31.12.41; undercarriage leg jammed; bellylanded, Driffield, 2.5.42; 24 OTU 21.6.42; 27 MU 12.10.42; SOC 30.6.43.
L5417	6 MU 24.2.40; 15 EFTS 29.2.40; Polish FTS 10.12.40; 16(P)FTS 13.7.41; Rosenfield 23.8.41; Fairey 26.8.41; 47 MU 6.12.41; to RAAF 5.1.42.
L5418	6 MU 6.3.40; AASF 22.4.40; 226 Sqn 23.4.40. Destroyed on evacuation of Reims, 16.5.40.
L5419	6 MU 6.3.40; AASF 19.5.40; 226 Sqn 20.5.40; 88 Sqn 10.7.41; 23 MU 5.9.41; 414 Sqn 28.5.42; Rosenfield 22.1.43; 18 MU 3.6.43; 14 MU 6.4.44; SOC 14.7.44.
L5420	6 MU 14.3.40; AASF 23.5.40; 12 Sqn 23.5.40; 20 MU 28.11.40; 47 MU 28.2.41; to RCAF 7.4.41 as 1942.
L5421	6 MU 16.2.40; 15 EFTS 8.3.40; engine cut on take-off, Redhill; bellylanded, Lonesome Lane, Reigate, 30.3.40; 47 MU 9.4.40; Fairey 6.6.40; 6 MU 4.7.40; 150 Sqn 12.8.40; 12 OTU 5.11.40; 22 MU 12.1.41; 47 MU 1.3.41; to RCAF 17.5.41 as 1966.
L5422	6 MU 14.3.40; 88 Sqn 8.5.40; 218 Sqn. Shot down attacking bridge, Noyers-Pont-Maugis, 4m S of Sedan, 14.5.40; FO J.F.R. Crane killed; AC1 T.W. Holloway captured
L5423	6 MU 16.2.40; 15 EFTS 6.3.40; undercarriage jammed, bellylanded, Kirkbride, 17.7.40; Polish FTS 10.12.40; 16(P)FTS 13.7.41; 27 MU 31.1.42; to 3558M at 12 SofTT 8.6.42.
L5424	6 MU 16.2.40; 15 EFTS 6.3.40; bellylanded in error, Redhill, 6.5.40; ROS; undercarriage collapsed on landing, Kirkbride, 21.6.40; Polish FTS 10.12.40; overshot forced landing in bad visibility and hit wall, Penistone, Yorks., 25.3.41; Fairey 19.4.41; 47 MU 14.7.41; to RCAF 27.8.41 as 2107.
L5425	20 MU 14.3.40; Bramcote 28.6.40; 300 Sqn 1.7.40; 47 MU 13.11.40; to RAAF 15.1.41.
L5426	20 MU 22.2.40; undershot landing and hit wall, Aston Down, 22.2.40; Bramcote 28.6.40; 300 Sqn 1.7.40; 47 MU 10.11.40; to RCAF 5.2.41 as 1850.
L5427	20 MU 11.3.40; Bramcote 28.6.40; 300 Sqn 1.7.40; forcelanded on return from raid near Hucknall, 13.10.40; Fairey 22.10.40; Austin 4.4.41; to RCAF 13.5.41.
L5428	20 MU 16.2.40; AASF 16.5.40; 226 Sqn 17.5.40; 20 MU 3.8.40; 142 Sqn 31.8.40. Ran out of fuel in bad weather, abandoned 2m NW of Torksey, Lincs., returning raid on Calais 13.10.40. SOC 23.10.40.
L5429	20 MU 21.2.40; Bramcote 23.6.40; 300 Sqn 1.7.40; taxied into hole and undercarriage collapsed, Bramcote, 2.8.40; 304 Sqn 12.9.40; 47 MU 10.11.40; to RCAF 5.2.41 as 1849.
L5430	20 MU 21.2.40; AASF 18.5.40; SOC 22.5.40.
L5431	20 MU 24.2.40; 103 Sqn 6.7.40; 38 MU 11.10.40;

Battle Trainer P6683 served with No.12 Service Flying Training School. (R Sturtivant collection)

L5432 Austin 10.11.40; Parks 28.12.40; to SAAF 24.2.41 but lost at sea en route, SS *Huntingdon*.
20 MU 24.2.40; 103 Sqn 6.7.40; 9 MU 12.10.40; 12 OTU 28.10.40. Hit tree on low flying exercise and bellylanded, Cuxham, Oxon., 2.12.40; SOC 20.12.40.

L5433 20 MU 20.3.40; 103 Sqn 6.7.40. Climbed, stalled and hit trees on approach after mistaking Cottesmore for Newton, 3.8.40; Sgt G.C. Brams and Sgt J.W. Mallard killed; SOC 9.8.40.

L5434 20 MU 23.2.40; 150 Sqn 19.7.40; 18 OTU 14.10.40; Western A/W 28.11.40; 38 MU 2.1.41; 47 MU 10.2.41; to RAAF 2.3.41.

L5435 24 MU 27.2.40; 8 MU 23.6.40; 304 Sqn 26.8.40; 47 MU 10.11.40; to RAAF 15.1.41.

L5436 8 MU 16.3.40; AASF 21.5.40; 142 Sqn 21.5.40; 21 AD 11.6.40; presumed abandoned in France 6.40.

L5437 8 MU 16.3.40; AASF 15.4.40; 150 Sqn 16.4.40. Shot down by Bf 109s during raid on roads, Vernon - Poix, and crashed near Merey, Eure, 13.6.40; PO R.C. Beale, Sgt. H.J.F. Tutt and Cpl D.B. Carter killed

L5438 8 MU 19.3.40; AASF 15.4.40; 226 Sqn. Hit by flak attacking bridge, Sedan, and crashed, 14.5.40; F/Sgt W.A. Dunn, Sgt A.F. Sedgwick and AC2 M.B. Millar killed

L5439 8 MU 15.3.40; AASF 16.4.40; 12 Sqn 25.4.40. Hit by ground fire, Veldwezelt, and crashed, Neerharen, Limburg, 12.5.40; PO I.A. McIntosh, Sgt N.T.W. Harper and LAC R.P. MacNaughton captured

L5440 8 MU 15.3.40; AASF 15.4.40; 142 Sqn 18.4.40. Abandoned on evacuation of Berry-au-Bac, 17.5.40.

L5441 24 MU 4.3.40; 8 MU 15.6.40; 304 Sqn 26.8.40; 12 OTU 5.11.40; 38 MU 15.12.40; Dumfries 2.7.41; to RCAF 19.8.41 as 2095.

L5442 24 MU 8.11.39; 266 Sqn 10.12.39; 20 MU 24.2.40; 98 Sqn 13.7.40; to RCAF 20.8.41.

L5443 27 MU 19.11.39; AASF 18.5.40; 142 Sqn; 6 RSU 22.5.40. Burnt on evacuation of Faux-Villecerf, 20.5.40.

L5444 27 MU 19.11.39; AASF 7.6.40; 103 Sqn 16.6.40; Rollason 2.7.40; 9 MU 9.8.40; 47 MU 29.8.40; to RAAF 19.9.40.

L5445 27 MU 19.11.39; 301 Sqn 3.8.40; 27 MU 20.11.40; 47 MU 3.5.41; to RCAF 28.5.41 as 1988.

L5446 27 MU 19.11.39; presumed struck off charge.

L5447 27 MU 8.11.39; 150 Sqn 11.7.40; 9 MU 11.10.40; 12 OTU 28.10.40; overshot night landing, swung and undercarriage collapsed, Mount Farm, 23.11.40; 32 MU 16.12.40; Fairey 15.1.41; Austin 4.4.41; to RCAF 13.5.41.

L5448 27 MU 22.11.39; 301 Sqn 3.8.40; Fairey 16.11.40; 47 MU 4.5.41; to RCAF 28.5.41 as 1968.

L5449 27 MU 22.11.39; 301 Sqn 3.8.40; 47 MU 11.11.40; to RCAF 18.12.40 as 1817.

L5450 20 MU 1.12.39; AASF 19.5.40; 226 Sqn 20.5.40; presumed lost in France, 6.40.

L5451 20 MU 14.11.39; AASF 19.5.40; 12 Sqn 21.5.40; engine cut on take-off; bellylanded 2m SE of Binbrook, 10.10.40; 20 MU 16.12.40; 47 MU 14.1.41; to RCAF 5.2.41 as 1843.

L5452 20 MU 1.12.39; AASF 19.5.40; 226 Sqn 1.6.40; Shorts 12.5.41; 23 MU 28.9.41; 215 MU 12.4.42; 3 PATP 27.4.42; to RAAF 23.5.42.

L5453 20 MU 24.11.39; AASF 19.5.40; 142 Sqn 15.6.40; hit bomb crater on take-off, Eastchurch, 17.8.40; 4 MU 16.9.40; 22 MU 22.1.41; 47 MU 14.2.41; to RCAF 11.3.41 as 1922.

L5454 20 MU 24.11.39; AASF; 142 Sqn; presumed lost in France, 6.40.

L5455 20 MU 24.11.39; AASF; presumed lost in France, 5.40.

L5456 20 MU 24.11.39; AASF 22.5.40; 142 Sqn 15.6.40; engine cut on approach; bellylanded, Eastchurch, 23.8.40; Fairey 18.9.40; 22 MU 10.12.40; Dumfries 2.8.41; to RCAF 11.9.41 as 2065.

L5457 20 MU 29.11.39; AASF 21.5.40; 142 Sqn 21.5.40; presumed lost in France, 5.40.

L5458 20 MU 29.11.39; AASF 24.5.40; 12 Sqn 16.6.40; 18 MU 17.12.40; 47 MU 18.3.41; to RCAF 17.5.41 as 1967.

L5459 20 MU 27.11.39; AASF 21.5.40; 150 Sqn 21.5.40. Damaged by Bf 110; forcelanded near Avioth, Meuse, 26.5.40; burnt by crew; FO J.G. Vernon escaped but Sgt G., Busby and LAC A.W. Rutland captured

L5460 8 MU 24.11.39; AASF 19.5.40; 226 Sqn 20.5.40; overshot landing and hit hedge, Aldergrove, 31.8.40; ROS; Shorts 31.7.41; 23 MU 14.11.41; 26 Sqn 28.5.42; undercarriage leg collapsed in heavy landing, Gatwick, 27.9.42; Rosenfield; SOC 3.5.43.

L5461   8 MU 24.11.39; AASF 19.5.40; 226 Sqn 20.5.40; 6 RSU 6.6.40; presumed abandoned in France, 6.40.

L5462   8 MU 29.11.39; AASF 19.5.40; 88 Sqn 20.5.40; 4 RSU 26.5.40; 21 AD 29.5.40; presumed abandoned in France, 6.40.

L5463   8 MU 29.11.39; AASF 19.5.40; 88 Sqn 20.5.40; 4 RSU 26.5.40; 21 AD 29.5.40; Fairey 26.6.40; 27 MU 13.9.40; 23 MU 4.3.41; 226 Sqn 7.5.41; 23 MU 1.8.41; Dumfries 26.1.42; to RCAF 21.3.42 as 2134.

L5464   8 MU 29.11.39; AASF 21.5.40; 142 Sqn 21.5.40; 38 MU 16.12.40; 47 MU 23.2.41; to SAAF 9.3.41 as 948.

L5465   8 MU 2.1.40; AASF 20.5.40; 103 Sqn 23.5.40; presumed lost in France 6.40.

L5466   8 MU 1.12.39; AASF 23.5.40; 88 Sqn 25.5.40; presumed lost in France 6.40.

L5467   8 MU 1.12.39; AASF 23.5.40; 88 Sqn 25.5.40. Shot down near Haraucort, 5m SSE of Sedan, 26.5.40; PO C.C.R. Anderson, Sgt R.W. Butler and Sgt E. Wilks killed

L5468   8 MU 24.1.40; 5 MU 25.1.40, 6 MU 6.3.40; AASF 14.5.40; 226 Sqn 17.7.40; undercarriage collapsed on landing, Sydenham, 23.11.40; ROS; Dumfries 28.1.42; to RCAF 21.3.42 as 2137.

L5469   8 MU 1.3.40; 150 Sqn 26.6.40; 103 Sqn 26.6.40; taxied into L5458, Newton, 3.8.40; 18 MU 29.11.40; Dumfries 16.4.41; to RCAF 22.5.41 as 1961.

L5470   19 MU 1.12.39; to RCAF 2.2.40 as 1667.

L5471   19 MU 24.1.40; to RAAF 11.5.40.

L5472   19 MU 24.1.40; to RCAF 2.2.40 as 1645.

L5473   19 MU 1.12.39; to RCAF 2.2.40 as 1666.

L5474   19 MU 1.3.40; AASF 24.5.40; 150 Sqn 25.5.40; presumed lost in France, 6.40.

L5475   19 MU 24.1.40; to RCAF 2.2.40 as 1657.

L5476   Loaned to Rotol Airscrew for tests 16.1.40; 38 MU 1.6.40; 8 MU 15.6.40; 305 Sqn 15.9.40; 9 MU 14.11.40; Austin 28.2.41; to RCAF 4.5.41.

L5477   19 MU 1.12.39; to RCAF 2.2.40 as 1679.

L5478   19 MU 16.2.40; 6 MU 5.4.40; AASF 7.6.40; 88 Sqn 8.6.40; 18 MU 17.7.40; 47 MU 3.2.41; to RAAF 24.2.41.

L5479   19 MU 21.2.40; 6 MU 5.4.40; AASF 7.6.40; 103 Sqn 16.6.40; Rollason 2.7.40; 9 MU 5.8.40; 47 MU 15.8.40; to RCAF 6.9.40 as 1702.

L5480   24 MU 25.1.40; to RCAF 2.2.40 as 1639.

L5481   24 MU 25.1.40; to RCAF 2.2.40 as 1638.

L5482   24 MU 4.3.40; 207 Sqn 15.6.40; 12 OTU. Hit HT cables after night take-off and dived into ground, North Stoke, Oxon., 24.7.40; Mid O.G. Mortimer RN, Sgt M.V. Everitt and Sgt E.P. Wood killed. SOC 31.7.40.

L5483   24 MU 27.2.40; 36 MU 5.5.40; to RCAF 18.5.40 as 1692.

L5484   24 MU 27.2.40; 36 MU 5.5.40; to RCAF 18.5.40 as 1688.

L5485   24 MU 25.1.40; to RCAF 2.2.40 as 1640.

L5486   24 MU 25.1.40; to RCAF 2.2.40 as 1641.

L5487   24 MU 26.1.40; 47 MU 12.5.40; to SAAF 6.6.40 as 904.

L5488   24 MU 27.2.40; 8 MU 15.6.40; 304 Sqn 26.8.40; undercarriage collapsed on landing, Bramcote, 15.9.40; 47 MU 10.11.40; to RAAF 15.1.41.

L5489   24 MU 29.2.40; 36 MU 28.3.40; to RCAF 20.4.40 as 1659.

L5490   27 MU 26.1.40; Bramcote 29.6.40; 300 Sqn 1.7.40; 47 MU 10.11.40; to RCAF 28.11.40 as 1790.

L5491   27 MU 24.1.40; 12 Sqn 27.6.40; damaged on ground 20.8.40; Fairey 26.9.40; SOC 26.9.40.

L5492   27 MU 6.3.40; 300 Sqn 1.9.40; 47 MU 13.11.40; to RCAF 18.12.40 as 1818.

L5493   27 MU 26.1.40; 12 Sqn 2.8.40; SOC 31.8.40.

L5494   27 MU 26.1.40; 10 MU 13.2.40; 18 OTU 23.7.40; 38 MU 29.11.40; Austin 24.3.41; to SAAF 11.5.41 as 961.

L5495   27 MU 26.1.40; 12 Sqn 26.6.40; 20 MU 1.1.41; 47 MU 23.2.41; to RCAF 25.4.41 as 1985.

L5496   RAE for tests of remote control 11.4.40; 22 MU 2.6.40; Austin 10.1.41; to RCAF 1.41 as 2044.

L5497   8 MU 19.3.40; AASF 15.5.40; presumed lost in France, 5.40.

L5498   8 MU 16.3.40; AASF 20.5.40; 226 Sqn 23.5.40; Shorts 14.1.41; undercarriage not locked and collapsed on landing, Sydenham, 11.2.41; ROS; 18 MU 1.3.42; 12 MU 7.1.43; SOC 29.12.44.

L5499   27 MU 29.2.40; Bramcote 29.6.40; 300 Sqn 1.7.40. Stalled and dived into ground Oxton, Notts., returning from raid on Boulogne, 13.10.40; FO Gebicki, Sgt Morawa and Sgt Egierski (all PAF) killed; SOC 30.10.40.

L5500   RAE for air defence trials (replacement for N2232); 20 MU 29.5.40; 12 OTU 7.8.40. Engine lost power; bellylanded 2m W of Llanbedrog, Caernarvon, 22.11.40; Fairey 18.12.40; SOC 13.1.41.

L5501   20 MU 25.1.40; 142 Sqn 26.6.40; Fairey 19.9.40; 22 MU 14.12.40; 47 MU 21.7,41; to RCAF 31.8.41 as 2075.

L5502   20 MU 25.1.40; 142 Sqn 26.6.40. Missing from raid on Brussels airfields, 28.7.40; F/Lt R.H. Edwards, Sgt R.W. Cornwell and Sgt R.E. Hotchkiss captured; F/Lt Edwards killed in escape attempt 26.9.42

L5503   20 MU 5.3.40; 142 Sqn 26.6.40. Missing from raid on E-boats at Boulogne, 22/23.8.40; Sgt L.M. Lowry killed; Midshipman Taylor RN and PO A.G. Middleton captured; SOC 10.9.40.

L5504   20 MU 25.1.40; 142 Sqn 26.6.40; 27 MU 19.12.40; 47 MU 6.2.41; to RCAF 21.2.41 as 1866.

L5505   20 MU 8.3.40; 98 Sqn 14.7.40; to RCAF without tail assembly 20.8.41.

L5506   20 MU 20.3.40; 47 MU 23.5.40; to SAAF 2.7.40 as 922.

L5507   20 MU 25.1.40; 142 Sqn 26.6.40. Tyre burst on landing at night; ground-looped, Eastchurch, 26.8.40; SOC 27.9.40.

L5508   8 MU 1.2.40; AASF 15.5.40; 103 Sqn 28.5.40; presumed lost in France, 6.40.

L5509   8 MU 2.3.40; AASF 15.5.40; 103 Sqn 18.5.40; presumed lost in France, 6.40.

L5510   8 MU 2.3.40; AASF 15.5.40; 150 Sqn 21.5.40; 38 MU 11.10.40; Austin 11.12.40; Parks 11.1.41; to RCAF 17.3.41.

L5511   8 MU 2.3.40; AASF 15.5.40; 103 Sqn 18.5.40; presumed lost in France, 6.40.

L5512   8 MU 2.3.40; AASF 15.4.40; 103 Sqn 18.4.40. Hit by flak, Bouillon, and crashed, Haraucort, Ardennes, 12.5.40; FO G.B. Morgan-Dean and AC1 H.B. Sewell killed

L5513   8 MU 2.3.40; AASF 15.5.40; 103 Sqn 18.5.40; presumed lost in France 6.40.

L5514   8 MU 5.3.40; AASF 15.5.40; 218 Sqn 18.5.40; 103 Sqn 21.5.40. Missing from raid on chateau, Roumont; crashed 3m NNW of Bouillon, 26.5.40; Sgt E.G. Hayward, AC1 W.F. Hubbard killed, F/Lt J.N. Leyden captured

L5515   8 MU 2.3.40; AASF 15.5.40; 103 Sqn 18.5.40. Damaged by ground fire in Abbeville area; forcelanded at Chalons and abandoned, 28.5.40.

L5516   19 MU 24.2.40; 6 MU 11.3.40; AASF 22.4.40; 103 Sqn 27.4.40. Shot down during attack on bridge, Remilly-Aillicourty, 3½m SE of Sedan, 14.5.40; crew escaped

L5517   19 MU 16.2.40; 6 MU 24.2.40; AASF 22.4.40; 142 Sqn 26.4.40. Hit by flak attacking bridge, Sedan, and crashed, Chéry, 14.5.40; F/Lt K.R. Rogers, Sgt H.F. Trescothic and Cpl H. Todd killed

L5518   19 MU 1.3.40; 8 MU 15.6.40; 304 Sqn 26.8.40; 47 MU 10.11.40; to RCAF 16.12.40 as 1796.

L5519   19 MU 23.2.40; 6 MU 9.3.40; AASF 25.5.40; 88 Sqn 26.5.40. Hit by flak during raid on Vernon and crashed, Perdreauville, Seine-et-Oise, 11.6.40; PO J.D.W. Gillam and Sgt R.C. Calder killed

L5520   19 MU 21.2.40; 6 MU 9.3.40; AASF 16.5.40; 12 Sqn 18.5.40. Crashlanded, Faux-Villecerf, and abandoned, 4.6.40.

Five Battles taxy out at Heath Row, in this case Belgian aircraft on the first delivery flight. (via D Howley)

L5521   19 MU 16.2.40; 6 MU 5.4.40; 12 Sqn 17.7.40; Fairey 25.9.40; to 2236M; to RCAF 22.3.41 as 1914.

L5522   Fairey "for 3 weeks to attempt to increase speed"; 38 MU 5.6.40; 8 MU 15.6.40; 304 Sqn 26.8.40; 47 MU 10.11.40; to RAAF 15.1.41.

L5523   20 MU 27.2.40; 6 MU 16.3.40; AASF 22.4.40; 105 Sqn 23.4.40. Shot down attacking bridge, Sedan, 14.5.40; PO H.E. White, Sgt G.A. Cartwright and AC1 J. Potter killed

L5524   8 MU 15.3.40; AASF 15.4.40; 150 Sqn 16.4.40. Shot down by Bf 109s attacking roads, Vernon - Poix, Aigleville, Eure, 13.6.40; PO A.R. Gulley killed; Sgt Berry and LAC D.L. Phillips captured

L5525   24 MU 27.2.40; 6 MU 16.3.40; AASF 24.5.40; 103 Sqn 16.6.40; 38 MU 12.10.40; Austin 10.11.40; Parks 4.1.41; to SAAF 5.2.41 as 929.

L5526   24 MU 29.2.40; 6 MU 16.3.40; AASF 22.4.40; 88 Sqn 23.4.40; 4 RSU 10.5.40; presumed abandoned in France, 6.40.

L5527   24 MU 29.2.40; 18 OTU 12.4.40; 18 MU 26.11.40; 32 MU 23.3.41; 47 MU 11.6.41; to RAAF 26.6.41.

L5528   27 MU 22.3.40; 150 Sqn 11.7.40. Flare ignited in aircraft on ground and bombs exploded, Newton, 27.7.40; FO W.M. Blom, Sgt W.H.J. Franklin, Sgt Gould, Cpl Sharpe, LAC Cann, LAC Hall, AC1 F. Stewart all killed; 8.20 hours.

L5529   27 MU 28.3.40; Bramcote 29.6.40; 300 Sqn 1.7.40; 47 MU 13.11.40; to RAAF 15.1.41.

L5530   27 MU 29.2.40; 300 Sqn 3.7.40; taxied into hole and undercarriage collapsed, Bramcote, 2.8.40; ROS; Western A/W 10.11.40; 18 MU 29.11.40; Austin 21.12.40; to RCAF 13.5.41.

L5531   27 MU 22.3.40; AASF 20.5.40; 12 Sqn 21.5.40. Shot down attacking tanks in Forêt de Gault, 13.6.40; PO J.F. McPhie, Sgt C.S.G. Beavers and LAC J.G. Thomson captured

L5532   27 MU 6.3.40; Bramcote 29.6.40; 300 Sqn 1.7.40; 103 Sqn 10.9.40; 12 Sqn 6.10.40; 20 MU 5.1.41; 47 MU 16.1.41; to RCAF 26.2.41 as 1863.

L5533   27 MU 22.3.40; AASF 19.5.40; 142 Sqn 15.6.40; Fairey 26.9.40; to RAAF 3.4.41.

L5534   27 MU 21.3.40; Polish OTU 1.4.40; 18 OTU; 20 MU 16.12.40; engine cut; overshot forced landing into trees 5m S of Bridgnorth, Salop., 14.1.41; Rosenfield 2.3.41; Austin 21.4.41; Parks 19.5.41; to RCAF 31.5.41 as 1991.

L5535   27 MU 22.3.40; 301 Sqn 3.8.40; Farnborough 20.11.40; RAE 14.2.41; 6 MU 5.4.41; Austin 9.5.41; to RCAF 5.41 as 2034.

L5536   27 MU 29.2.40; 301 Sqn 3.8.40; forcelanded in bad weather, West Felton, Salop., 14.11.40; 47 MU 15.11.40; to RCAF 16.12.40 as 1800.

L5537   27 MU 21.3.40; Bramcote 29.6.40; 300 Sqn 1.7.40; undershot approach and hit fence, Kingstown, 19.7.40; ROS; 20 MU 7.11.40; 47 MU 16.1.41; to RCAF 26.2.41 as 1858.

L5538   10 MU 1.3.40; AASF 25.4.40; 12 Sqn 6.5.40. Shot down by Bf 109s, St Fergau, 19.5.40; PO J.J. McElligott died of wounds and LAC T.O. Burgess wounded

L5539   10 MU 22.2.40; AASF 25.4.40; 150 Sqn 30.4.40. Shot down by ground fire, Luxembourg, 10.5.40; F/Lt E.R. Parker killed; Sgt J. Whalley and Cpl R.K. Rye unhurt but captured

L5540   10 MU 22.2.40; AASF 25.4.40; 6 RSU 1.5.40; 150 Sqn 3.5.40. Shot down by ground fire, Luxembourg, 10.5.40; FO A.C. Roberts, Sgt E.H. Ward and AC1 D. Meyrick captured

L5541   10 MU 21.2.40; AASF 25.4.40; 150 Sqn 26.4.40; 2 SF 27.4.40. Damaged by Bf 109s in battle area and crash-landed, La Ferté Vidame, Eure-et-Loir, 15.6.40; LAC Hillyard wounded

L5542   22 MU 28.3.40; 47 MU 10.6.41; to RCAF 23.6.41 as 2018.

L5543   10 MU 22.2.40; 142 Sqn 18.5.40; 150 Sqn 19.5.40; Rollason 19.7.40; 20 MU 13.8.40; 23 MU 6.3.41; 47 MU 10.1.42; to SAAF 16.3.42; to Middle East 30.1.43.

L5544   22 MU 28.3.40; 88 Sqn. Undercarriage leg jammed, crashlanded, Lisburn LG, 22.6.41; Shorts 27.6.41; SOC 24.8.41.

L5545   10 MU 24.2.40; AASF 25.4.40; 150 Sqn 28.4.40; 20 MU 10.10.40; Austin 4.12.40; Parks 28.12.40; to SAAF 28.2.41 as 944.

L5546   10 MU 1.3.40; 142 Sqn 18.5.40; 12 Sqn 21.5.40. Shot down by ground fire near Abbeville, 8.6.40; Sgt J.P. Boddington and LAC C.S. Burt killed; FO T.F.S. Brereton captured

L5547   20 MU 11.3.40; 98 Sqn 14.7.40; 1423 Flight 30.11.41; 269 Sqn 31.12.41; SOC 21.10.42.

L5548   20 MU 8.3.40; 150 Sqn 19.7.40; 38 MU 11.10.40; Austin 10.11.40; to SAAF 11.5.41 as 957.

L5549   20 MU 29.2.40; 301 Sqn 23.7.40; 27 MU 20.11.40; Austin 1.1.41; Parks 15.1.41; to SAAF 16.2.41 as 940; to Middle East 30.1.43.

L5550   20 MU 23.2.40; 98 Sqn 14.7.40; 4 MU 26.8.40; 47 MU 28.10.40; to RCAF 28.11.40 as 1831.

L5551   20 MU 24.2.40; 301 Sqn 24.7.40; 27 MU 20.11.40; 47 MU 5.2.41; to RAAF 18.2.41.

L5552   20 MU 21.2.40; 98 Sqn 14.7.40; to RCAF 20.8.41.

L5553   20 MU 5.3.40; 98 Sqn 14.7.40; to RCAF 20.8.41.

L5554   20 MU 29.2.40; AASF 22.5.40; 98 Sqn 14.7.40; to RCAF 20.8.41.

L5555   20 MU 5.3.40; AASF 22.5.40; 301 Sqn 23.7.40; 47 MU 11.11.40; to RCAF 16.12.40 as 1807.

L5556   20 MU 11.3.40; 301 Sqn 23.7.40; 27 MU 20.11.40; Austin 4.1.41; Parks 25.1.41; to RCAF 17.3.41.

L5557   22 MU 28.3.40; 301 Sqn 30.8.40; 47 MU 11.11.40; to RCAF 16.12.40 as 1804.

L5558   22 MU 28.3.40; 88 Sqn 17.7.40; Shorts 30.10.41; 9 MU 6.6.42; 18 MU 11.9.42; SOC 14.7.44.

L5559   22 MU 28.3.40; 88 Sqn 21.7.40; Shorts at 31.12.40; took off in coarse pitch; abandoned take-off and hit hedge, Lisburn LG, 2.9.41; 27 MU 8.10.42; 231 Sqn 9.1.43; to 3974M 7.7.43.

L5560   22 MU 28.3.40; 142 Sqn 8.8.40; 27 MU 3.11.40; Austin 15.1.41; to RCAF 3.41.

L5561   24 MU 10.4.40; 22 MU 16.5.40; Andover 26.5.40; 88 Sqn 6.6.40. Destroyed in air raid, Sydenham, 5.5.41; SOC 22.5.41.

L5562   24 MU 8.4.40; 22 MU 4.6.40; 12 OTU 4.6.40; 38 MU 26.3.41; 47 MU 6.6.41; to RCAF 11.6.41 as 2014.

L5563   24 MU 9.4.40; 22 MU 16.5.40; Andover 24.5.40; 150 Sqn 26.5.40; Rollason 19.7.40; 27 MU 31.7.40; 305 Sqn 14.9.40; 9 MU 14.11.40; Austin 16.12.40; Parks 4.1.41; to SAAF 24.2.41 but lost at sea en route, SS *Huntingdon*.

L5564   24 MU 8.4.40; 22 MU 24.5.40; 226 Sqn; engine cut on take-off; bellylanded Sydenham, 25.3.41; Shorts 10.4.41; SOC 28.5.42.

L5565   24 MU 6.4.40; 22 MU 19.5.40; 88 Sqn 17.7.40; overshot landing and skidded into hedge, Lisburn LG, 25.5.41; 23 MU 5.9.41; 613 Sqn 8.6.42; 27 MU 9.9.42; RAE 22.11.42; SOC 29.9.43.

L5566   24 MU 8.4.40; 22 MU 24.5.40; 142 Sqn 30.7.40; Fairey 22.9.40; SOC 9.2.41.

L5567   24 MU 9.4.40; 22 MU 19.5.40; 300 Sqn 30.8.40; 47 MU 13.11.40; to RCAF 5.2.41 as 1852.

L5568   24 MU 8.4.40; 22 MU 16.5.40; Andover 26.5.40; 12 Sqn 16.6.40. Shot down by British night fighter off Skegness, Lincs., 1.8.40; FO B.E. Moss. Sgt B.A. Long and Sgt T.J. Radley killed; SOC 9.8.40.

L5569   24 MU 8.4.40; 22 MU 27.5.40; swung on landing and undercarriage collapsed, Silloth, 27.5.40; 142 Sqn 8.8.40; Fairey 12.9.40; 47 MU 2.4.41; to RCAF 21.5.41.

L5570   24 MU 8.6.40; 22 MU 27.5.40; 12 OTU 4.8.40; 32 MU 12.1.41; 47 MU 18.3.41; to RCAF 2.4.41 as 1931.

L5571   24 MU 7.4.40; 22 MU 24.5.40; 88 Sqn 21.7.40; Shorts at 31.12.41; 38 MU 26.1.42; SOC 21.10.47.

L5572   24 MU 10.4.40; 22 MU 24.5.40; 88 Sqn 21.7.40. Destroyed in air raid, Sydenham, 5.5.41; SOC 22.5.41.

L5573   24 MU 6.4.40; 22 MU 23.5.40; 12 OTU 4.8.40; 38 MU 11.12.40; Austin 15.1.41; to RCAF 3.41.

L5574   24 MU 7.4.40; 22 MU 24.5.40; 88 Sqn 17.7.40; Shorts 22.5.41; 23 MU 11.4.42; 1 APC 3.8.42; SOC 13.4.43.

L5575   24 MU 9.4.40; 22 MU 24.5.40; 301 Sqn 7.8.40; 27 MU 22.11.40; 47 MU 16.1.41; to RCAF 26.2.41 as 1862.

L5576   24 MU 7.4.40; 22 MU 24.5.40; 226 Sqn; 88 Sqn 10.7.41; 23 MU 5.9.41; Dumfries 26.1.42; to SAAF 28.2.42.

L5577   6 MU 29.3.40; 105 Sqn 6.5.40; presumed lost in France

L5578   6 MU 14.3.40; 150 Sqn 3.5.40; 142 Sqn 8.5.40. Shot down by ground fire near Pétance, Luxembourg, 10.5.40; PO F.S. Laws, Sgt R.F. Miller and AC1 L.M. Langton killed

L5579   6 MU 15.3.40; AASF 13.5.40; 218 Sqn 14.5.40; 150 Sqn; 27 MU 13.10.40; Austin 8.12.40; to SAAF 11.5.41 as 960.

L5580   6 MU 15.3.40; 12 Sqn 19.5.40. Shot down attacking tanks in Forêt de Gault, 13.6.40; PO R.C.L. Parkhouse, Sgt A.R. Morris and AC1 D.A. MacDonald captured

L5581   6 MU 15.3.40; 88 Sqn 10.5.40. Shot down attacking bridge, St. Menges, 3m NNW of Sedan, 14.5.40; Sgt W.G. Ross, Sgt F.E. Beames and LAC J.H.K. Gegg killed

L5582   6 MU 20.3.40; 88 Sqn 10.5.40; 142 Sqn 29.5.40; 4 RSU 29.5.40; 142 Sqn 15.6.40. Missing from night raid on Boulogne, 23.8.40; Sgt E.A. Pearce, Sgt T.S. Duncan killed; Sgt G. Thompson captured; SOC 10.9.40.

L5583   24 MU 14.3.40; AASF 13.5.40; 150 Sqn 19.5.40. Damaged over battle area; forcelanded on Sommesousse airfield and abandoned, 19.5.40.

L5584   6 MU 27.3.40; AASF 22.5.40; 142 Sqn 15.6.40; Missing from raid on Brussels, 28.7.40; PO M.J.A. Kirdy, Sgt N. Longcluse, Sgt R.M. Hettle killed

L5585   6 MU 14.3.40; 105 Sqn 4.5.40; 6 RSU 5.5.40; 105 Sqn 14.5.40. Shot down attacking bridge, Sedan, 14.5.40; Sgt A.W.H. Hadley and AC1 W. Draper captured; FO C.F. Gibson evaded and wounded but later captured on French surrender.

L5586   6 MU 20.3.40; AASF 14.5.40; 142 Sqn 21.5.40; Fairey 25.9.40; 18 MU 10.2.41; 22 MU 10.2.41; 18 MU 11.2.41; 47 MU 28.2.41; to RCAF 3.4.41 as 1941.

L5587   24 MU 7.4.40; 22 MU 16.5.40; Andover 26.5.40; no further trace, presumed off charge.

L5588   24 MU 9.4.40; 2 MU 9.8.40; Dumfries 8.7.41; to RCAF 19.8.41 as 2086.

L5589   24 MU 9.4.40; 22 MU 27.5.40; 142 Sqn 30.7.40; 27 MU 1.1.41; 47 MU 17.1.41; to RCAF 7.3.41 as 1875.

L5590   24 MU 6.4.40; 22 MU 19.5.40; 88 Sqn 17.7.40; 23 MU 5.9.41; 15 APC 16.9.42; 1 APC 31.12.42; SOC 13.4.43.

L5591   24 MU 7.4.40; 22 MU 16.5.40; AASF 28.5.40; 150 Sqn. Damaged by Bf 109s over Forêt de Gault; crash-landed, Rebais, Seine-et-Marne, 13.6.40; LAC Rickard wounded

L5592   24 MU 9.4.40; 22 MU 27.5.40; 142 Sqn 7.8.40; 27 MU 19.12.40; 47 MU 6.2.41; to RCAF 21.2.41 as 1865.

L5593   24 MU 9.4.40; 22 MU 16.5.40; AASF 28.5.40; 150 Sqn 15.6.40; undercarriage leg jammed; bellylanded, Newton, 6.9.40; ROS; engine cut; bellylanded near Newton, 11.10.40; Fairey 17.10.40; 47 MU 23.3.41; to RCAF 24.5.41; not received in Canada.

K7627 of No.1 Service Flying Training School at Netheravon. (R Sturtivant collection)

L5594   24 MU 9.4.40; 22 MU 19.5.40; 88 Sqn; Shorts 6.9.41; 23 MU 13.12.41; 18 MU 25.2.42; 215 MU 12.4.42; 3 PATP 27.4.42; to RAAF 23.5.42.

L5595   24 MU 7.4.40; 22 MU 24.5.40; 226 Sqn; Shorts 14.8.41; 38 MU 21.12.41; 215 MU 17.9.42; 3 PATP 22.9.42; to RAAF 13.10.42.

L5596   24 MU 6.4.40; 22 MU 19.5.40; 88 Sqn 17.7.40; Shorts at 31.12.41; 18 MU 28.3.42; 215 MU 9.10.42; EO Liverpool 25.10.42; to RAAF 10.12.42.

L5597   20 MU 27.3.40; 301 Sqn 23.7.40. Flew into ground at night NW of Bramcote, 8.8.40; PO D. Fengler killed; SOC 15.8.40; 15.10 hours.

L5598   RAE 17.4.40; AAEE 13.5.40; engine cut; bellylanded Farnham, Surrey, 21.8.41; ROS; RAE at 31.12.41; SOC 26.4.43.

L5599   36 MU 13.4.40; to RAAF 1.5.40.

L5600   36 MU 12.4.40; to RAAF 1.5.40.

L5601   36 MU 18.4.40; to RCAF 26.4.40 as 1649.

L5602   36 MU 17.4.40; to RAAF 17.5.40.

L5603   36 MU 11.4.40; to RAAF 17.5.40.

L5604   36 MU 11.4.40; to RAAF 1.5.40.

L5605   36 MU 25.4.40; to RCAF 5.40 as 1686.

L5606   36 MU 17.4.40; to RCAF 17.5.40 as 1673.

L5607   36 MU 12.4.40; to RCAF 17.5.40 as 1674.

L5608   36 MU 12.4.40; to RCAF 26.4.40 as 1650.

L5609   36 MU 12.4.40; to RAAF 1.5.40.

L5610   36 MU 13.4.40; to RAAF 1.5.40.

L5611   36 MU 12.4.40; to RCAF 26.4.40 as 1651.

L5612   36 MU 22.4.40; to RCAF 17.5.40 as 1675.

L5613   36 MU 13.4.40; to RCAF 26.4.40 as 1648.

L5614   36 MU 17.4.40; to RCAF 17.5.40 as 1676.

L5615   36 MU 17.4.40; to RCAF 17.5.40 as 1677.

L5616   36 MU 22.4.40; to RCAF 17.5.40 as 1678.

L5617   36 MU 22.4.40; to RAAF 11.5.40;

L5618   36 MU 22.4.40; to RCAF 11.5.40 as 1671.

L5619   36 MU 24.4.40; to RCAF 11.5.40 as 1693.

L5620   36 MU 24.4.40; to RCAF 11.5.40 as 1682.

L5621   36 MU 24.4.40; to RCAF 11.5.40 as 1672.

L5622   36 MU 25.4.40; to RCAF 5.40 as 1690.

L5623   4 MU 29.4.40; to Turkish Air Force 7.5.40.

L5624   8 MU 26.6.40; Watchfield 13.9.40; 8 MU 22.10.40; 54 OTU 14.3.41; 60 OTU at 31.12.41; 52 OTU 24.10.42; Rosenfield 9.9.43; SOC 9.9.43; originally for Turkey but cancelled.

L5625   8 MU 26.6.40; Watchfield 13.9.40; 8 MU 22.10.40; 54 OTU 4.3.41; engine cut on take-off; bellylanded, Catfoss, 27.4.41; 57 OTU 11.9.41; 60 OTU 29.10.41; 57 OTU at 31.12.41; Rosenfield 18.5.43; SOC 23.6.43; originally for Turkey but cancelled.

L5626   8 MU 27.6.40; Watchfield 13.9.40; 8 MU 22.10.40; 58 OTU 21.3.41; 60 OTU 12.5.42; 58 OTU 17.5.42; Rosenfield 6.6.42; 215 MU 31.7.42; 3 PATP 29.8.42; to RAAF 13.9.42; originally for Turkey but cancelled.

L5627   36 MU 25.4.40; to RCAF 17.5.40 as 1694.

L5628   36 MU 26.4.40; 6 MU 4.5.40; AASF 10.5.40; 98 Sqn 17.5.40; 1423 Flight 23.6.41; 269 Sqn at 31.12.41; undercarriage collapsed on landing, Reykjavik, 30.1.42; ROS; SF Reykjavik 31.12.42. Undercarriage damaged on take-off; bellylanded, Kaldadarnes, 26.5.43; reduced to spares in Iceland; SOC 31.4.44; 315.20 hours.

L5629   36 MU 26.4.40; 6 MU 4.5.40; AASF 10.5.40; 98 Sqn 18.5.40; 12 Sqn 17.7.40; 103 Sqn 27.7.40; engine cut; bellylanded 2m N of Bridlington - Scarborough road, 7.10.40; ROS; 3 Group TTF 4.1.41; 5 Group TTF 23.8.41; Western A/W 12.12.41; 9 MU 25.2.42; LEP 20.4.42; to RAAF 31.5.42.

L5630   36 MU 26.4.40; 6 MU 4.5.40; AASF 10.5.40; 98 Sqn 17.5.40; 150 Sqn 16.7.40; 12 Sqn 24.8.40; 4 Group TTF 7.11.40; 9 MU 23.11.41; 215 MU 21.8.42; 3 PATP 11.9.42; to SAAF 31.12.42.

L5631   6 MU 7.5.40; 5 OTU 19.6.40; 56 OTU 6.4.41; 57 OTU 19.2.42; to 3962M at 2 SofTT 16.7.43.

L5632   22 MU 6.5.40; 1 OTU 6.5.40; undercarriage jammed; bellylanded Silloth, 15.3.41; ROS; bellylanded in error, Silloth, 5.4.42; ROS; 19 Group APC 9.12.42; 4 APC 20.12.42; Rosenfield 24.5.43; SOC 23.6.43.

L5633   22 MU 6.5.40; 1 OTU 6.5.40; forcelanded in bad visibility and hit hedge, Caersws, Mont., 10.1.41; ROS;

taxied into bowser, Millom, 24.1.41; Rosenfield 10.2.41; 27 MU 14.4.41; 2 BGS 10.5.41; 2 AOS; undercarriage leg jammed; damaged on landing, Millom, 13.10.41; 47 MU 5.1.42; to RAAF 26.2.42.

L5634   6 BGS 4.5.40; 10 BGS 2.6.40; overshot forced landing while lost and hit hedge, Fleetwood, Lancs., 14.7.40; ROS; engine cut; bellylanded 6m SE of Dalbeattie, Kirkcudbright, 8.7.41; ROS; 10 AOS 11.11.41; 9 MU 9.7.42; 27 MU 22.8.42; 215 MU 16.10.42; 3 PATP 4.11.42; to SAAF 28.11.42.

L5635   6 BGS 4.5.40; 7 BGS 24.5.40. Undercarriage jammed; bellylanded, Stormy Down, 25.11.40; SOC 22.12.40.

L5636   6 BGS 4.5.40; 10 BGS 2.6.40; 10 AOS; 5 AOS 4.7.42; 18 MU 23.11.42; 47 MU 29.3.43; to RAAF 10.5.43.

L5637   6 BGS 7.5.40; 7 BGS 24.5.40; 7 AGS. Dived into sea 5m off Porthcawl, Glamorgan, 31.8.41; Sgt C.L. Naylor, LAC Bond and AC2 Sullivan killed; SOC 30.9.41; 354.00 hours.

L5638   6 BGS 7.5.40; 7 BGS 2.6.40; 38 MU 24.4.42; 215 MU 1.9.42; 3 PATP 11.9.42; to SAAF 31.12.42.

L5639   6 BGS 7.5.40; 8 BGS 4.6.40; 9 MU 6.11.41; LEP 10.3.42; to RAAF 29.4.42.

L5640   6 BGS 7.5.40; 7 BGS 2.6.40; 38 MU 23.11.41; 36 MU 8.3.42; to RAAF 3.4.42.

L5641   6 BGS 7.5.40; 4 BGS 2.6.40; taxied into bowser, West Freugh, 12.3.41; ROS; engine cut; bellylanded, Glenluce, Wigtown, 9.7.41; ROS; 4 AOS 27.11.41; LEP 13.3.42; to SAAF 10.4.42; to SRAF 31.8.42.

L5642   6 BGS 7.5.40; 5 BGS 2.6.40; 8 BGS 28.11.40; 18 MU 6.4.41; 9 MU 8.11.41; LEP 10.3.42; to SAAF 31.3.42; to SRAF 9.7.42.

L5643   47 MU 7.5.40; to RCAF 19.7.40 as 1695.

L5644   47 MU 11.5.40; to RAAF 21.8.40.

L5645   47 MU 7.5.40; to RCAF 19.7.40 as 1696.

L5646   47 MU 7.5.40; to RCAF 19.7.40 as 1697.

L5647   47 MU 7.5.40; to RCAF 19.7.40 as 1698.

L5648   47 MU 7.5.40; to RCAF 19.7.40 as 1699.

L5649   47 MU 7.5.40; to RCAF 19.7.40 as 1700.

L5650   47 MU 11.5.40; to RAAF 7.8.40.

L5651   47 MU 11.5.40; to RAAF 7.8.40.

L5652   47 MU 19.5.40; to RAAF 21.8.40.

L5653   47 MU 11.5.40; to RAAF 7.8.40.

L5654   47 MU 11.5.40; to RAAF 26.7.40.

L5655   47 MU 11.5.40; to RAAF 7.8.40.

L5656   47 MU 11.5.40; to RAAF 21.8.40.

L5657   47 MU 19.5.40; to RAAF 26.7.40.

L5658   47 MU 11.5.40; to RAAF 21.8.40.

L5659   47 MU 14.5.40; to RAAF 21.8.40.

L5660   47 MU 14.5.40; to RAAF 26.7.40.

L5661   4 BGS 13.5.40; Rosenfield 10.11.41; 18 MU 23.3.42; 215 MU 31.5.42; EO Glasgow 10.8.42; to SAAF 18.8.42 as 1062; to India 30.1.43; 22 AACU. Undercarriage collapsed on landing, Drigh Road, 3.3.44.

L5662   4 BGS 20.5.40. Collided with Battle V1223, 15.5.41; SOC 27.5.41; 362.35 hours.

L5663   2 AACU 18.5.40; undercarriage collapsed on landing, Cleave, 11.12.40; ROS; overshot landing, swung and hit obstacle, St. Eval, 13.1.41; Fairey 3.3.41; 7 BGS 8.6.41; 38 MU at 31.12.41; 2 AACU 27.3.42; LEP 28.3.42; 1 PATP 23.5.42; to SAAF 30.6.42; to India 1.12.42.

L5664   2 AACU 18.5.40; stalled on landing, bounced and undercarriage collapsed, Gosport, 6.11.40; ROS; undercarriage collapsed on landing, Gosport, 16.6.41; ROS; 27 MU 12.12.41; 215 MU 23.5.42; 3 PATP 13.6.42; to SAAF 30.6.42 as 1048.

L5665   2 AACU 14.5.40; wheel came off on landing, Cleave, 24.2.41; Rosenfield 26.4.42; 215 MU 5.7.42; 3 PATP 2.9.42; to RAAF 17.8.42.

L5666   2 AACU 19.5.40; engine cut on take-off; bellylanded Gosport, 12.6.41; ROS; 1 AAS 30.9.41; Dumfries 11.11.41; 3 PATP at 31.12.41; to SAAF 30.9.41 as 1002.

L5667   22 MU 27.5.40; 1 OTU 19.6.40; overshot landing and hit hedge, Silloth, 16.9.40; ROS; 2 OTU 2.12.40;

engine cut; crashlanded on approach, Catfoss, 27.5.41; ROS; 1 OTU 27.11.41; skidded into car in forced landing in bad weather, Kidsdale, 7.4.42; ROS. Engine cut; overshot forced landing 4m S of Carlisle, 20.10.42; DBR; SOC 30.10.42; 395.55 hours.

L5668   12 MU 27.5.40; 8 BGS 19.6.40; 9 MU 14.2.42; 215 MU 25.11.42; LEP 21.12.42; 3 PATP 22.1.43; to SRAF 13.4.43.

L5669   5 BGS 21.5.40; 8 BGS 21.9.40; 9 MU 15.12.41; 8 BGS at 31.12.41; 9 MU; 215 MU 26.5.42; 3 PATP 27.6.42; to SAAF 19.7.42.

L5670   5 BGS 21.5.40; 8 BGS 24.10.40; 8 AGS; bellylanded in error, Evanton, 22.8.41; 9 MU 28.10.41; 215 MU 10.6.42; 3 PATP 19.6.42; to RAAF 9.7.42.

L5671   5 BGS 21.5.40. Stalled while dropping drogue and dived into ground W of Hall Caine, Isle of Man, 1.10.40; Sgt. S. Osmala and AC2 A. Sharp killed; SOC 17.10.40.

L5672   5 BGS 21.5.40. Engine cut; bellylanded on hillside near East Baldwin, Isle of Man, 27.9.40; Fairey 11.10.40; SOC 12.10.40.

L5673   7 BGS 21.5.40; 38 MU 13.12.41; 215 MU 5.6.42; 3 PATP 15.6.42; to SAAF 30.6.42 as 1046.

L5674   6 MU 19.5.40; 5 OTU 19.6.40; Western A/W 10.8.41; 1 AGS 1.9.41; 38 MU 15.11.41; 215 MU 25.5.42; 3 PATP 15.6.42; to SAAF 30.6.42 as 1042.

L5675   12 MU 27.5.40; 8 BGS 19.6.40; 9 MU 6.11.41; 215 MU 26.5.42; 3 PATP 16.6.42; to RAAF 9.7.42.

L5676   12 MU 27.5.40; 23 MU 21.6.40; 8 BGS 3.7.40; engine cut; forelanded on rough ground, Skelbo, Sutherland, 13.6.41; Fairey 18.7.41; 47 MU 21.10.41; 9 MU 26.10.41; LEP 10.3.42; to RAAF 4.4.42.

L5677   12 MU 27.5.40; 8 BGS 19.6.40; 9 MU 10.10.41; LEP 26.1.43; to RAAF 26.6.43.

L5678   12 MU 27.5.40; 8 BGS 19.6.40; brakes failed; hit hangar, Evanton, 19.3.41; ROS; landed with undercarriage unlocked, Evanton, 2.7.41; ROS; 8 AGS 11.10.41; 18 MU 17.12.41; LEP 10.3.42; to RAAF 4.4.42.

L5679   2 AACU 1.6.40; hit hedge in forced landing in bad weather, St. Cletter, near Launceston, Cornwall, 23.10.40; Fairey 31.10.40; 9 MU 29.12.40; 47 MU 27.2.41; to RAAF 26.5.41.

L5680   22 MU 27.5.40; 1 OTU 19.6.40; 2 OTU 2.12.40; undercarriage collapsed on landing, Catfoss, 4.7.41; ROS; 1 OTU 27.11.41; engine cut; bellylanded Silloth, 30.4.42; ROS; 18 MU 19.12.42; SOC 14.7.44.

L5681   22 MU 27.5.40; 1 OTU 19.6.40; Rosenfield 20.12.42; 18 MU 9.2.43; 16 Group APC 31.12.43; 47 MU 9.5.43; Reykjavik 4.7.43; SOC 22.12.44.

L5682   22 MU 27.5.40; 1 OTU 19.6.40; 16 Group APC 28.11.42; North Coates 2.12.42; bellylanded in error, North Coates, 1.3.43; ROS; Thorney Island; 18 MU 22.7.43; SOC 12.8.43.

L5683   22 MU 27.5.40; 47 MU 9.8.40; to RAAF 6.9.40.

L5684   22 MU 27.5.40; 8 BGS 26.6.40; 9 MU 2.12.41; 215 MU 4.8.42; 3 PATP 17.8.42; 1 PATP 29.8.42; to RAAF 14.9.42.

L5685   12 MU 27.5.40; 23 MU 21.6.40; 8 BGS 3.7.40; 27 MU 12.10.41; LEP 5.4.42; to SAAF 29.5.42.

L5686   12 MU 27.5.40; 23 MU 21.6.40; 8 BGS 3.7.40; 18 MU 31.3.41; Dumfries 23.4.41; to SAAF 21.5.41; to SRAF.

L5687   22 MU 27.5.40; 7 BGS 26.6.40; 38 MU 2.1.42; 215 MU 20.8.42; 3 PATP 23.8.42; 1 PATP 29.8.42; to RAAF 14.9.42.

L5688   12 MU 27.5.40; tipped up taxying, Kirkbride, 27.5.40; ROS; 7 BGS 24.9.40; bellylanded at Porthcawl, 21.10.40; ROS; 18 MU 31.3.41; Dumfries 2.5.41; to SRAF.

L5689   2 AACU 1.6.40; Rosenfield 30.1.43; 18 MU 13.4.43; 47 MU 4.6.43; to RAAF 15.7.43.

L5690   8 BGS 3.6.40; 27 MU 18.11.41; to SAAF 31.3.42; to SRAF 31.7.42.

L5691   1 OTU 3.6.40; 3 OTU 13.12.40; 5 OTU; landed with undercarriage unlocked, Chivenor, 7.12.41; ROS; 1447 Flight 26.4.42; undercarriage leg jammed; bellylanded

K7602 of No.52 Squadron being manhandled at Upwood. (P Jarrett collection)

Hooton Park, 29.4.42; ROS; 1 OTU; engine cut; bellylanded, Silloth, 25.9.42; ROS; 19 MU 16.3.43; Rosenfield 10.4.43; SOC 30.4.43.

L5692   22 MU 27.5.40; 47 MU 9.8.40; to RAAF 6.9.40.

L5693   6 MU 31.5.40; 47 MU 12.9.40; to RAAF 18.10.40.

L5694   6 MU 31.5.40; 47 MU 12.9.40; to RAAF 18.10.40.

L5695   6 MU 31.5.40; 47 MU 12.9.40; to RAAF 18.10.40.

L5696   6 MU 31.5.40; 47 MU 12.9.40; to RAAF 18.10.40. Lost at sea en route?

L5697   6 MU 12.6.40; 47 MU 2.8.40; to RAAF 19.8.40.

L5698   6 MU 31.5.40; 47 MU 12.9.40; to RAAF 18.10.40. Lost at sea en route?

L5699   6 MU 7.6.40; 5 OTU 19.6.40; 55 OTU; engine cut; bellylanded Tunstall, Staffs., 20.7.41; ROS; 52 OTU 21.4.42; hit by Spitfire P8147 while parked, Aston Down, 22.6.42; ROS. Crashed on beach while target towing, Bedwin Sands, Monmouth, 20.7.42; SOC 22.8.42.

L5700   6 MU 8.6.40; 47 MU 5.8.40; to RAAF 6.9.40.

L5701   6 MU 31.5.40; 47 MU 5.8.40; to RAAF 19.8.40.

L5702   6 MU 31.5.40; 47 MU 5.8.40; to RAAF 19.8.40.

L5703   6 MU 7.6.40; Watchfield 13.9.40; 47 MU 21.2.41; to RAAF 26.5.41.

L5704   6 MU 31.5.40; 47 MU 5.8.40; to RAAF 19.8.40.

L5705   9 MU 12.6.40; 47 MU 20.7.40; 9 MU 22.7.40; 7 OTU 5.8.40; 57 OTU at 31.12.41. Engine lost power; bellylanded near Boulmer, 21.1.43; to 3961M at 2 SofTT 16.7.43.

L5706   9 MU 7.6.40; 57 OTU 7.8.40; landed with undercarriage unlocked, Hawarden, 14.12.41; ROS; SOC 27.7.43.

L5707   9 MU 8.6.40; 47 MU 20.7.40; 9 MU 22.7.40; 6 OTU 26.7.40; 61 OTU 6.7.41; 56 OTU 29.7.41; 60 OTU 10.8.41; 59 OTU 27.2.42. Engine cut; bellylanded 2m N of Berwick, 31.12.42; to 3906M at 2 SofTT 7.7.43.

L5708   9 MU 8.6.40; TTF Waddington 26.9.40; 4 Group TTF 25.10.40; overturned in forced landing 7m NNE of Boston, Lincs., 22.8.41; Rosenfield 25.8.41; Fairey 29.8.41; 18 MU 25.11.41; LEP 17.1.42; to SAAF 28.2.42.

L5709   9 MU 12.6.40; 47 MU 20.7.40; 9 MU 22.7.40; 7 OTU 5.8.40; hit obstruction on take-off and elevator jammed, stalled and crashed, Hawarden, 2.3.41; Fairey 3.4.41; 1 AAS 23.6.41; 10 AOS 24.8.41; 1 AAS 29.8.41; 18 MU 1.12.41; LEP 8.3.42; to RAAF 3.4.42.

L5710   9 MU 14.6.40; 47 MU 20.7.40; 9 MU 22.7.40; 6 OTU 26.7.40; hit obstacle on landing, Holbeach LG, 5.2.41; Rosenfield 2.3.41; CGS 3.6.41; 18 MU 9.3.42; 215 MU 31.5.42; 3 PATP 4.9.42; to RAAF 17.8.42.

L5711   9 MU 7.6.40; 47 MU 20.7.40; 9 MU 22.7.40; 6 OTU 26.7.40. Engine cut on take-off; bellylanded 2m S of Sutton Bridge, 4.9.40; SOC 20.9.40.

L5712   9 MU 9.6.40; 2 School of Army Co-operation 13.6.40; 52 OTU 4.5.41; SOC 9.9.43.

L5713   9 MU 9.6.40; 2 School of Army Co-operation 13.6.40; 53 OTU 6.6.41; 55 OTU 17.9.41; 59 OTU 22.3.42; SOC 30.6.43.

L5714   9 MU 9.6.40; 47 MU 20.7.40; 9 MU 22.7.40; 6 OTU 26.7.40; bellylanded in error, Sutton Bridge, 20.8.40; ROS; undercarriage leg collapsed on landing, Holbeach LG, 1.3.41; ROS; 57 OTU 26.6.41; Rosenfield 12.5.43; SOC 23.6.43.

L5715 9 MU 9.6.40; 5 Group TTF 7.9.40. Engine cut; ditched 1m N of Hornsea, Yorks., 17.9.40; to 2260M at 6 SofTT.

L5716 9 MU 12.6.40; 47 MU 20.7.40; 9 MU 22.7.40; 7 OTU 27.8.40; engine cut; crashlanded and hit shed near Hawarden, 26.11.40; 34 MU 3.12.40; 32 MU 10.12.40; Fairey 15.1.41; 18 MU 24.4.41; Dumfries 2.5.41; to SRAF.

L5717 1 OTU 14.6.40. Engine cut; ditched in Solway Firth 3m E of Southerness Point, Dumfries, 11.7.42; Sgt J. Krzysztoszek (PAF) killed

L5718 9 BGS 14.6.40; 8 BGS 21.6.41; 27 MU 17.12.41; 215 MU 23.5.42; 3 PATP 25.6.42; to SAAF 19.7.42.

L5719 9 BGS 18.6.40; 8 BGS 21.6.41; 27 MU 10.10.41; 18 MU 16.2.42; 215 MU 14.10.42; 3 PATP 7.11.42; to SAAF 28.11.42 as 1072.

L5720 9 BGS 14.6.40; bellylanded in error, Penrhos, 15.7.40; ROS; CGS 3.11.41; LEP 14.3.42; to SAAF 10.4.42; to SRAF 31.8.42.

L5721 9 BGS 14.6.40; Fairey 26.2.41; 9 BGS 13.5.41; LEP 26.1.42; 18 MU 13.10.42; 47 MU 27.4.43; to RAAF 26.6.43.

L5722 CGS 17.6.40; 9 MU 19.3.42; 18 MU 31.8.43; 47 MU 12.9.43; to SAAF 23.11.43; to SRAF 31.3.44.

L5723 CGS 17.6.40; 18 MU 15.3.42; 215 MU 29.6.42; 3 PATP 18.8.42; 1 PATP 29.8.42; to RAAF 12.9.42.

L5724 CGS 17.6.40; undercarriage collapsed on landing, Warmwell, 18.2.41; ROS. Destroyed in air raid, Warmwell, 1.4.41. SOC 11.4.41; 119.00 hours.

L5725 CGS 25.6.40; engine cut; bellylanded, Chickerell, Dorset, 4.9.40; Austin 14.9.40; 9 MU 29.12.40; 47 MU 26.2.41; to RAAF 31.3.41.

L5726 4 BGS 21.6.40; 4 AOS at 31.12.41; Rosenfield 17.1.42; 27 MU 1.5.42; 215 MU 23.5.42; Rosenfield 4.6.42; 3 PATP 23.6.42; to SAAF 19.7.42 as 1058; to India 2.11.42; 22 AACU. Fumes entered cockpit; bellylanded near Drigh Road, 19.2.43.

L5727 8 BGS 18.6.40; 9 MU 28.10.41; landed with undercarriage locked, Ternhill, 13.3.42; LEP 13.3.42; to RAAF 5.8.42.

L5728 4 BGS 21.6.40; 1 AGS 26.6.41; engine cut; bellylanded, Burry Holme Sands, Rhosili Bay, Carmarthen, 8.8.41; Dumfries 15.11.41; taxied into obstruction, Llandow, 19.11.41; 38 MU at 31.12.41; Rosenfield 14.5.42; 215 MU 16.8.42; 3 PATP 19.8.42; 1 PATP 29.8.42; to RAAF 14.9.42.

L5729 4 BGS 21.6.40; engine cut; bellylanded and hit wall, Port Logan, Wigtown, 24.6.41; Fairey 30.6.41; LEP 11.12.41; to SAAF 16.1.43 as 1001.

L5730 8 BGS 18.6.40; 4 Group TTF 7.11.40; 8 BGS; 27 MU 15.12.41; 9 MU 24.12.41; 27 MU 2.1.42; LEP 3.3.42; to SAAF 29.7.42.

L5731 5 BGS 14.6.40; 8 BGS 8.4.41; undercarriage leg jammed; landed on one wheel, Evanton, 25.4.41; 27 MU 12.10.41; LEP 8.4.42; to SAAF 29.5.42.

L5732 5 BGS 21.6.40; 8 BGS 28.11.40; 8 AGS; 47 MU 16.12.41; to SRAF 9.1.42.

L5733 5 BGS 21.6.40; 8 BGS 21.9.40; 18 MU 31.3.41; to SAAF 21.5.41; to SRAF.

L5734 5 BGS 21.6.40; 8 BGS 11.9.40; 27 MU 2.12.41; LEP 3.5.42; 215 MU 20.5.42; 3 PATP 28.5.42; to RAAF 9.7.42.

L5735 5 BGS 21.6.40; 8 BGS 11.9.40; 27 MU 10.10.41; LEP 10.3.42; to RAAF 4.4.42.

L5736 7 BGS 22.6.40; bellylanded, Stormy Down, 4.2.41; 18 MU 31.3.41; Dumfries 5.6.41; to RAAF 11.7.41.

L5737 7 BGS 22.6.40; 38 MU 2.1.42; 215 MU 6.9.42; 3 PATP 13.9.42; to SAAF 8.10.42; to SRAF 6.4.43.

L5738 7 BGS 22.6.40; 38 MU 25.11.41; 215 MU 20.8.42; 3 PATP 30.8.42; to RAAF 17.8.42.

L5739 7 BGS 22.6.40; 18 MU 31.3.41; Dumfries 18.4.41; to SAAF 21.5.41.

L5740 7 BGS 22.6.40; 38 MU 23.11.41; 215 MU 10.7.42; EO Glasgow 10.8.42; to SAAF 18.8.42.

L5741 7 BGS 22.6.40; RAE 24.7.40; 7 BGS 9.9.40; bellylanded in error, Porthcawl, 29.10.40; ROS; 38 MU 13.12.41; 215 MU 17.7.42; 3 PATP 30.8.42; to RAAF 13.9.42.

L5742 8 BGS 21.6.40; 18 MU 31.3.41; Dumfries 15.4.41; to SRAF.

L5743 8 BGS 21.6.40; Western A/W 24.10.41; engine cut; overshot landing and undercarriage raised to stop, Whitchurch, 27.11.41; 9 MU 27.11.41; 18 MU 17.4.42; 215 MU 31.5.42; EO Glasgow 10.8.42; to SAAF 18.8.42 as 1065.

L5744 8 BGS 21.6.40; 27 MU 10.12.41; 215 MU 23.5.42; 3 PATP 9.6.42; to SAAF 30.6.42 as 1044.

L5745 9 BGS 24.6.40; 1 AGS 26.6.41; 2 AOS 31.10.41; 47 MU 9.1.42; to SAAF 20.3.42.

L5746 9 BGS 24.6.40; Rosenfield 16.1.42; 9 MU 10.5.42; 18 MU 24.9.42; 215 MU 16.11.42; LEP 31.12.42; 18 MU 17.3.43; 47 MU 4.5.43; to Iceland 14.6.43; Reykjavik 4.7.43; SOC 30.4.44; reduced to spares in Iceland; 274.55 hours.

L5747 9 BGS 24.6.40; landed with undercarriage unlocked, Penrhos, 28.3.41; ROS; 38 MU 5.1.42; 215 MU 30.5.42; 3 PATP 17.6.42; to SAAF 19.7.42.

L5748 10 BGS 25.6.40; 10 AOS at 31.12.41; 5 AOS 4.7.42; 3 AGS 29.10.42; 215 MU 1.12.42; EO Swansea 5.12.42; to SAAF 12.12.42; lost at sea en route.

L5749 10 BGS 25.6.40; engine cut; bellylanded near Bankend, Dumfries, 17.1.41; Fairey 12.2.41; 18 MU 28.4.41; Dumfries 16.6.41; 18 MU 19.6.41; 53 OTU 2.7.41; 61 OTU 5.7.41; Rosenfield 10.9.41; 59 OTU 29.9.41; engine cut; bellylanded, Allenby Ranges, near Silloth, 26.10.41; Dumfries 9.2.42; LEP 19.4.42; to SAAF 29.5.42.

L5750 6 MU 24.6.40; Watchfield 13.9.40; 6 MU 18.10.40; 2 BGS 16.2.41. Engine cut; hit hedge in forced landing 1m NW of Withington, Salop., 16.2.41; SOC 24.3.41.

L5751 6 MU 24.6.40; 47 MU 2.8.40; to RAAF 19.8.40.

L5752 6 MU 24.6.40; Watchfield 13.9.40; 6 MU 18.10.40; 2 AACU 8.11.40; LEP 27.4.42; to SAAF 29.7.42 as 1060.

L5753 6 MU 24.6.40; Watchfield 13.9.40; 6 MU 13.1.41; 47 MU 21.2.41; 18 MU 15.4.41; to SAAF 21.5.41.

L5754 6 MU 24.6.40; Watchfield 13.9.40; 6 MU 7.11.40; 2 BGS 16.2.41; 2 AOS; 47 MU 5.1.42; to RAAF 21.2.42.

L5755 6 MU 24.6.40; Watchfield 13.9.40; 6 MU 7.11.40; 2 BGS 16.2.41. Flew into mountain on ferry flight 6m NW of Llanrhaeadr-ym-Mochnant, Denbighshire, 16.2.41; PO D.S. Brooke killed

L5756 20 MU 24.6.40; 47 MU 5.9.40; to RAAF 1.10.40.

L5757 6 MU 2.7.40; 47 MU 2.8.40; to RAAF 19.8.40.

L5758 20 MU 5.7.40; 47 MU 28.2.41; to RAAF 26.5.41.

L5759 20 MU 5.7.40; 47 MU 22.2.41; to RAAF 31.3.41.

L5760 20 MU 5.7.40; 47 MU 28.2.41; to RAAF 26.5.41.

L5761 20 MU 5.7.40; 59 OTU 27.3.41; engine cut; overshot forced landing and undercarriage collapsed, Kingstown, 9.9.41; ROS. Missing on training flight, 15.11.42; F/Sgt J.B. MacDermott and passenger killed; SOC 15.11.42.

L5762 20 MU 5.7.40; 59 OTU 15.3.41; engine cut on take-off, bellylanded 2m W of Turnhouse, 19.7.42; Rosenfield 28.7.42; 215 MU 21.11.42; LEP 20.12.42; 3 PATP 21.1.43; to SAAF 13.4.43.

L5763 22 MU 16.7.40; 47 MU 31.7.41; to RAAF 27.8.41.

L5764 22 MU 16.7.40; 47 MU 26.8.41; to RAAF 22.9.41.

L5765 22 MU 16.7.40; 47 MU 5.8.41; to RAAF 27.8.41.

L5766 27 MU 16.7.40; 52 OTU 15.6.41; overshot landing into ditch, Holbeach LG, 27.6.41; ROS; elevator jammed; crashlanded, Roggiett, Mon., 16.5.42; Rosenfield 30.5.42; 215 MU 9.9.42; 3 PATP 16.9.42; to SAAF 31.12.42.

L5767 27 MU 16.7.40; 52 OTU 13.9.40; 55 OTU 13.4.41; 52 OTU 24.3.42; engine cut; hit wall in forced landing near Wooton-under-Edge, Glos., 27.8.42; ROS; Rosenfield 9.9.43; SOC 9.9.43.

L5768 27 MU 15.7.40; engine cut; overshot forced landing and hit ridge, Bewdley, Worcs., 15.7.40; Fairey 1.8.40; SOC 22.2.41.

N2234 was used by Rolls-Royce for Merlin development, shown here with a nose intake similar to that adopted for the Barracuda. (R Sturtivant collection)

L5769   27 MU 16.7.40; 6 OTU 14.9.40; undercarriage leg jammed; bellylanded, Sutton Bridge, 29.4.41; ROS; 59 OTU 29.7.41; engine cut; bellylanded, Brownrigg Hall, Cumberland, 24.3.42; ROS; undercarriage jammed, bellylanded, Crosby, 2.7.42; to 3907M at 2 SofTT 7.7.43.

L5770   27 MU 16.7.40; 7 OTU 13.9.40; Fairey 21.11.40; 27 MU 17.3.41; 56 OTU 9.7.41; bellylanded in error, Holbeach LG, 8.12.41; Rosenfield 17.12.41; LEP 1.4.42; to RAAF 14.6.42.

L5771   27 MU 16.7.40; 1 OTU 7.10.40; 3 OTU 13.12.40; 5 OTU; Rosenfield 9.12.42; 18 MU 31.3.43; RAE 4.5.43; SOC 5.11.43.

L5772   38 MU 17.7.40; 47 MU 26.2.41; to RAAF 31.3.41.

L5773   38 MU 17.7.40; 55 OTU 5.9.40; fumes entered cockpit; bellylanded, Acklington, 25.11.41; ROS; 57 OTU 11.2.42; trim tab jammed by drogue cable, bellylanded, Holy Island, 1.3.43; SOC 23.7.43.

L5774   38 MU 17.7.40; 47 MU 26.2.41; to RAAF 31.3.41.

L5775   18 MU 17.7.40; 10 BGS 9.6.41. Looped and dived into sea, Blackshaw Bank, Solway Firth, 18.7.41; Sgt H. Skowron (PAF) and LAC W. Wetherburn killed; SOC 27.7.41; 57.35 hours.

L5776   18 MU 17.7.40; Gunnery Research Unit 10.9.41; RAE 21.10.42; Gunnery Research Unit 31.12.42. Crashed 4.12.44; SOC 12.12.44.

L5777   12 MU 19.7.40; 18 MU 30.7.40; 2 AOS 1.7.41; 9 MU 15.1.42; 215 MU 4.6.42; 3 PATP 21.6.42; to SAAF 16.7.42 as 1051.

L5778   18 MU 17.7.40; 47 MU 24.10.40; 29 Sqn 24.10.40; 47 MU 2.11.40; to RAAF 10.11.40.

L5779   22 MU 19.7.40; 18 MU 26.7.40; 47 MU 24.10.40; 29 Sqn 24.10.40; 47 MU 2.11.40; to RAAF 10.11.40.

L5780   18 MU 28.7.40; 2 BGS 27.1.41; 2 AOS; 9 MU 15.1.42; to SAAF 28.2.42.

L5781   22 MU 19.7.40; 18 MU 26.7.40; Digby 11.10.40; 29 Sqn 16.10.40; 53 OTU 5.3.41; engine cut; bellylanded near Wick, Glam., 21.8.41; ROS; 56 OTU 20.10.41; overshot landing into dyke, Holbeach LG, 4.12.41; Rosenfield 9.12.41; LEP 1.4.42; to RAAF 14.6.42.

L5782   12 MU 22.7.40; 18 MU 23.7.40; 7 BGS 1.11.40; 38 MU 6.2.42; 18 MU 11.9.42; 215 MU 26.10.42; 3 PATP 3.11.42; to SAAF 28.11.42 as 1070.

L5783   12 MU 22.7.40; 18 MU 23.7.40; 2 BGS 27.1.41; 1 AGS 12.9.41; Dumfries 15.11.41; 3 PATP at 31.12.41;

to SRAF 5.1.42.

L5784   12 MU 22.7.40; 18 MU 23.7.40; 2 BGS 27.1.41; 1 AGS 12.9.41; Dumfries 7.11.41; 3 PATP at 31.12.41; 1 PATP 11.2.42; to SAAF 28.2.42.

L5785   18 MU 25.7.40; 12 MU 25.7.40; 18 MU 29.7.40; 2 BGS 11.2.41; Rosenfield 1.5.41; 1 AAS 23.6.41; 10 AOS 24.8.41; 1 AAS 29.8.41; 18 MU 28.10.41; LEP 8.3.42; to RAAF 4.4.42.

L5786   18 MU 25.7.40; 12 MU 25.7.40; 18 MU 29.7.40; 7 BGS 1.11.40; 38 MU 6.2.42; 27 MU 13.9.42; 215 MU 21.11.42; to SAAF 2.12.42.

L5787   18 MU 28.7.40; 2 BGS 27.1.41; 2 AOS; 9 MU 15.1.42; to SAAF 28.2.42.

L5788   18 MU 27.7.40; Marham 7.11.40; 3 Group TTF 8.11.40; Fairey 16.11.40; 27 MU 23.2.41; 2 AOS 18.7.41; 9 MU 15.1.42; to SAAF 28.2.42.

L5789   18 MU 25.7.40; 12 MU 25.7.40; 18 MU 29.7.40; 2 BGS 1.2.41; undercarriage jammed; bellylanded, Millom, 6.6.41; 2 AOS; 47 MU 5.1.42; to RAAF 21.2.42.

L5790   18 MU 27.7.40; 47 MU 31.10.40; to RAAF 11.12.40.

L5791   18 MU 1.8.40; 47 MU 21.10.40; to RAAF 11.12.40.

L5792   18 MU 27.7.40; Newton 23.10.40; 103 Sqn 26.10.40; 4 Group TTF 7.11.40; 1484 Flight at 31.12.41; 27 MU 29.1.43; 47 MU 8.6.43; to RAAF 15.7.43.

L5793   18 MU 28.7.40; Marham 1.11.40; hit sheep in forced landing while lost in bad weather SE of Weeton, Lancs., 1.11.40; Fairey 19.11.40; 9 MU 12.2.41; 56 OTU 12.5.41; taxied into bowser, Balado Bridge, 4.4.42; ROS; 58 OTU 1.5.42; 60 OTU 12.5.42; 59 OTU 19.5.42; SOC 30.6.43.

L5794   18 MU 31.7.40; 47 MU 21.10.40; to RAAF 11.12.40.

L5795   18 MU 28.7.40; 2 BGS 1.2.41; 18 MU 8.12.41; LEP 9.2.42; to SAAF 15.2.42 as 1010.

L5796   18 MU 31.7.40; Digby 11.10.40; 29 Sqn 16.10.40; 52 OTU 5.4.41; 60 OTU 12.5.41; SOC 9.9.43.

L5797   18 MU 1.8.40; engine cut after take-off; bellylanded Dumfries, 25.10.40; 2 BGS 17.5.41; 2 AOS; 47 MU 10.1.42; to RAAF 21.3.42.

189 Fairey Battle Is delivered by Fairey between February and June 1939. Contract 768880/38. Built at Stockport.

N2020   6 MU 6.2.39; 12 Sqn 31.3.39; 8 MU 25.4.40; 47 MU 18.9.40; to RCAF 22.10.40 as 1729.

N2021   63 Sqn 6.2.39. DBR in accident and collected by Martlesham Heath, 6.9.39; SOC 6.9.39.

N2022   63 Sqn 6.2.39; 52 Sqn 25.2.40; 12 OTU 18.4.40. Engine cut after take-off; crashlanded and hit hedge, Benson 21.11.40; Rosenfield 2.12.40; SOC 5.12.40.

N2023   63 Sqn 6.2.39; 12 OTU 18.4.40; 13 OTU 10.5.40; undercarriage leg jammed; bellylanded, Squires Gate, 30.9.40; ROS; 17 OTU 20.10.40; tipped up taxying, Upwood, 24.10.40; ROS; Austin 9.5.41; to RCAF 5.41 as 2050.

N2024   6 MU 6.2.39; 15 Sqn 31.3.39; 22 MU 20.12.39; 4 BGS 2.5.40; bellylanded in error, West Freugh, 28.3.41; ROS; became 4 AOS. Engine caught fire; crashed in Luce Bay, Wigtown, 13.7.41; Sgt Wells, LAC Dundera (Cz) and LAC Drcka (Cz) killed; SOC 8.8.41; 472.25 Hours.

N2025   6 MU 6.2.39; 15 Sqn 31.3.39; stalled on landing and undercarriage leg collapsed, Abingdon, 27.4.39; ROS; RAE 19.10.39; engine emitted smoke; hit obstruction in forced landing, Yeovilton, 11.5.40; Fairey 8.6.40; 8 MU 24.6.40; 142 Sqn 25.8.40. DBR when bomb dump blew up in air raid, Eastchurch, 2.9.40; SOC 12.9.40.

N2026   6 MU 6.2.39; 105 Sqn 21.4.39; 63 Sqn 7.7.39; 12 OTU 18.4.40. Engine cut; bellylanded in field 1m NW of Penrhos, 24.5.40; SOC 29.5.40.

N2027   6 MU 7.2.39; 616 Sqn 16.5.39; Rollason 7.6.40; 38 MU 9.7.40; 47 MU 1.9.40; to RAAF 19.9.40. Dual Control.

N2028   6 MU 7.2.39; 150 Sqn 7.4.39. Damaged by Bf 109s, Saarbrücken, and abandoned on return, 30.9.39; SOC 23.11.39.

N2029   6 MU 13.2.39; 47 MU 8.11.40; to RCAF 24.12.40 as 1812.

N2030   6 MU 16.2.39; Austin 1.1.41; Parks 15.1.41; to SAAF 16.2.41 as 942.

N2031   6 MU 16.2.39; 616 Sqn 16.5.39; 12 MU 25.7.40; 15 EFTS 28.8.40; engine cut; hit ditch in forced landing SSW of Kirkbride, 10.10.40; ROS; 1 PFTS 28.3.41; overshot landing in bad visibility and hit hedge, Hucknall, 19.5.41; ROS; undercarriage jammed, bellylanded Hucknall, 2.7.41; ROS; 16(P)FTS 13.7.41; 18 MU 14.2.42; to 2481M at 2 SofTT 9.11.43; 18 MU 29.11.43; SOC 14.7.44. Dual Control.

N2032   6 MU 16.2.39; 23 MU 28.4.41; 414 Sqn 28.5.42; undercarriage collapsed on landing, Croydon, 21.6.42; ROS; swung while taxying and hit barrels, Dunsfold, 29.12.42; Rosenfield 29.12.42; 18 MU 18.3.43; 14 MU 6.4.44; SOC 14.7.44.

N2033   6 MU 16.2.39; 23 MU 3.3.41; 88 Sqn 10.5.41; 23 MU 16.11.41; SOC 30.9.43.

N2034   6 MU 16.2.39; Rotol 17.9.40; RAE at 31.12.41; elevator damaged; tipped up on landing, Towyn, 21.11.42; ROS; SOC 19.4.44.

N2035   6 MU 15.2.39; Austin 7.5.41; to RCAF 5.41 as 2051.

N2036   6 MU 15.2.39; Austin 18.4.41; Parks 19.5.41; to RCAF 31.5.41 as 1995.

N2037   6 MU 15.2.39; RAE 7.2.41; 27 MU 27.2.43; SOC 20.11.43.

N2038   6 MU 16.2.39; RAE 17.9.40; Rosenfield 10.4.41; 18 MU 9.2.42; 215 MU 14.8.42; 3 PATP 21.8.42; 1 PATP 5.9.42; to RAAF 13.9.42.

N2039   6 MU 24.2.39; Austin 9.1.41; Parks 28.1.41; to RAAF 1.2.41.

N2040   6 MU 16.2.39; 47 MU 8.4.40; to RCAF 16.12.40 as 1797.

N2041   6 MU 16.2.39; Austin 18.4.41; Parks 16.5.41; to RCAF 31.5.41 as 1994.

N2042   RAE and Bristol 16.2.39; Hercules test bed with fixed undercarriage; SOC 16.4.45.

N2043   10 MU 20.2.39; 13 ERFTS 20.7.39; 7 FTS 4.9.39; 9 BGS 6.5.40; Fairey 26.2.41; 18 MU 3.5.41; Dumfries 19.6.41; to SAAF 11.7.41 as 993.

N2044   10 MU 20.2.39; 13 ERFTS 20.7.39; 7 FTS 4.9.39; 9 BGS 6.5.40; 18 MU 11.7.41; SOC 14.7.44.

N2045   10 MU 20.2.39; 13 ERFTS 27.7.39; 7 FTS 4.9.39; 9 BGS 5.7.40; engine cut; bellylanded, Morfa Nefyn,

N2046   Caernarvon, 11.6.41; ROS; 16(P)FTS 11.8.41; Rosenfield 28.9.41; 18 MU 1.4.42; 215 MU 14.8.42; 3 PATP 20.8.42; 1 PATP 29.8.42; to RAAF 14.9.42.

N2046   10 MU 20.2.39; 9 ERFTS 20.7.39; 15 FTS 4.9.39; 9 BGS 9.5.40; 47 MU 5.7.41; to RCAF 24.8.41 as 2088.

N2047   20 MU 24.2.39; 22 ERFTS 15.8.39; 15 FTS 4.9.39; 1 FTS 25.10.39; 7 FTS 21.5.40; 12 FTS 12.6.40; engine cut; hit HT cables 5m NW of Bourne, Lincs., 28.8.40; 47 MU 27.7.41; to RCAF 27.8.41 as 2087.

N2048   20 MU 24.2.39; 22 ERFTS 15.8.39; 15 FTS 4.9.39; 1 FTS 28.10.39; 7 FTS 21.5.40; 16 Group APC 9.7.42; 18 Group APC 10.10.42; flew into ground on landing, Leuchars, 21.12.42; 18 MU 3.3.43; SOC 14.7.44.

N2049   20 MU 24.2.39; 22 ERFTS 15.8.39; 15 FTS 4.9.39; 1 FTS 25.10.39; undercarriage jammed; bellylanded, Netheravon, 29.11.39; ROS; 22 MU 10.2.41; 47 MU 28.2.41; to RCAF 3.4.41 as 1927.

N2050   20 MU 27.2.39; 1 Ferry Pool 5.11.39; 1 AACU 10.4.40; Fairey 7.8.40; 18 MU 3.5.41; Dumfries 19.6.41; to SAAF 11.7.41 as 990.

N2051   20 MU 27.2.39; 7 AOS 19.11.39; Fairey 13.6.40; 12 MU 27.11.40; Austin 6.2.41; Parks 28.2.41; to SAAF 29.6.41 as 989.

N2052   20 MU 27.2.39; 4 BGS 20.4.40; 47 MU 9.12.41; to RCAF 24.12.41 as 2131.

N2053   20 MU 1.3.39; 2 AACU 5.1.40; 18 MU 20.4.42; 215 MU 22.5.42; 3 PATP 7.6.42; to RAAF 9.7.42.

N2054   20 MU 1.3.39; 4 BGS 20.4.40; 18 MU 26.11.41; 215 MU 14.8.42; 3 PATP 21.8.42; 1 PATP 29.8.42; to RAAF 13.9.42.

N2055   20 MU 1.3.39; 2 AACU 5.1.40. Engine cut; crashlanded near Plympton, Devon, 25.6.41; SOC 2.7.41.

N2056   20 MU 1.3.39; 4 BGS 20.4.40; engine cut; undershot forced landing into sand dunes, Luce Bay, Wigtown, 8.5.41; Fairey 12.5.41; 47 MU 8.8.41; to RCAF 29.8.41 as 2066.

N2057   20 MU 3.3.39; 4 BGS 20.4.40; hit truck taxying, West Freugh, 6.3.41; ROS; Western A/W 11.12.41; 18 MU 12.2.42; 4 Sqn 31.5.42; 1472 Flight 13.6.42; SOC 8.5.43.

N2058   Rolls-Royce for flight testing Merlin X 6.3.39; Rosenfield 17.12.41; 18 MU 4.4.42; 215 MU 31.5.42; 3 PATP 1.7.42; SF Reykjavik 27.8.42; SOC 7.12.43.

N2059   11 Group Pool 9.3.39; 22 Group Pool 15.5.39; bellylanded at Netheravon, 29.11.39; 19 MU 12.1.40; to 1791M 8.4.40; 4 SofTT 28.10.40; SOC 30.6.43.

N2060   11 Group Pool 3.3.39; 22 Group Pool 15.5.39; 20 MU 4.8.39; 4 BGS 15.6.40; became 4 AOS. Flew into ground descending in low cloud 3m N of Portpatrick, Wigtown, 14.7.41; PO Bylinski (PAF), LAC Hytkag (Cz) and LAC Marsalek (Cz) killed; SOC 23.7.41.

N2061   11 Group Pool 3.3.39; 22 Group Pool 15.5.39. Engine cut after take-off; bellylanded and ran into trees, Andover, 5.6.39; DBR

N2062   11 Group Pool 9.3.39; 22 Group Pool 15.5.39; 20 MU 11.1.40; 4 BGS 18.4.40; 18 MU 20.7.41; 215 MU 17.5.42; 3 PATP 29.5.42; to SAAF 16.7.42.

N2063   19 MU 8.3.39; 1 AAS 18.1.40; undercarriage leg jammed; bellylanded, Manby, 10.10.40; 18 MU 11.11.41; 215 MU 23.4.42; 3 PATP 10.5.42; to RAAF 11.6.42.

N2064   19 MU 9.3.39; 610 Sqn 25.5.39; 1 FTS 2.1.40; 8 BGS 26.2.40; engine cut; bellylanded 2m NE of Fearn, 18.7.41; ROS; 8 AGS 14.12.41; 47 MU 19.12.41; to RAAF 26.2.42.

N2065   19 MU 9.3.39; 1 AAS 20.1.40; 27 MU 2.10.41; 47 MU 31.12.41; to RAAF 26.2.42.

N2066   19 MU 13.3.39; 610 Sqn 25.5.39; 6 AACU 19.5.40; 27 MU 10.4.41; 47 MU 7.9.41; to RAAF 27.9.41.

N2082   Fairey 13.3.39; 820 Sqn Gosport 25.4.39 with trial installation of equipment for flight investigations relating to Fulmar; 6 MU 2.5.39; Austin 2.5.41; to RCAF 5.41 as 2037.

Battle K7516 of No.105 Squadron. (P Jarrett collection)

N2083 19 MU 14.3.39; 1 AAS 18.1.40; engine cut; bellylanded E of Grimoldby Station, Lincs., 8.4.40; 54 MU 18.4.40; Fairey 6.6.40; 6 MU 4.7.40; 142 Sqn 30.8.40; damaged in forced landing while lost, Wainfleet, Lincs., 10.10.40; Fairey 18.10.40; 9 MU 3.12.40; 47 MU 26.2.41; to RCAF 11.3.41 as 1924.

N2084 19 MU 14.3.39; 1 AAS 20.1.40; 9 MU 4.9.41; 268 Sqn 23.5.42; 54 MU 26.3.43; Rosenfield 29.3.43; SOC 29.3.43.

N2085 CFS 17.3.39; overshot landing and tipped up, Upavon, 8.5.40; ROS; 20 MU 29.8.40; 47 MU 18.9.40; to RCAF 22.10.40 as 1731.

N2086 19 MU 23.3.39; 1 AAS 25.1.40; 9 MU 4.9.41; 268 Sqn 23.5.42; 54 MU 26.3.43; SOC 29.3.43.

N2087 142 Sqn 17.3.39; SD Flight Boscombe Down 1.2.40; 9 MU 23.7.40; 47 MU 18.9.40; to RCAF 8.10.40 as 1733.

N2088 142 Sqn 17.3.39. Crashed on navex 5m S of Neufchatel 8.4.40; FO P.A.L. Farrell, Sgt L.A. Raper and Cpl C.E. Wilburn killed; destroyed by fire; remains to 1 Salvage Section 11.4.40

N2089 501 Sqn 17.3.39; 6 MU 5.12.39; 20 MU 27.12.39; 4 BGS 18.4.40; 47 MU 28.2.41; 18 MU at 31.12.41; 241 Sqn 7.6.42; 18 MU 27.6.42; 215 MU 14.8.42; 3 PATP 19.8.42; 1 PATP 29.8.42; to RAAF 14.9.42

N2090 501 Sqn 17.3.39; 53 Sqn 26.5.39; 8 MU 23.9.39; 1 AAS 24.1.40; 27 MU 30.9.41; 47 MU 8.2.42; to RAAF 7.4.42.

N2091 504 Sqn 17.3.39; 5 MU 27.7.39; 1 AAS 29.2.40; Fairey 20.5.41; 47 MU 4.8.41; to RAAF 27.8.41.

N2092 504 Sqn 20.3.39; 5 MU 27.7.39; 1 AAS 6.4.40; 18 MU 14.8.41; Dumfries 11.11.41; 3 PATP at 31.12.41; to South Africa 17.1.42 then to RAAF.

N2093 150 Sqn 21.3.39. Shot down by Bf 109s near Saarbrücken and crashed, Metzig, Moselle, 30.9.39; Sgt W.F.L. Cole killed; SOC 23.11.39.

N2094 501 Sqn 20.3.39; 6 MU 15.11.39; 20 MU 13.12.39; 4 BGS 20.4.40; 32 MU 10.4.41; 47 MU 15.6.41; to RCAF 4.7.41 as 2025. Dual Control.

N2095 501 Sqn 20.3.39; 6 MU 15.11.39; 4 BGS 12.4.40; 4 AOS at 31.12.41; 27 MU 6.1.42; to 3309M at 6 SofTT 5.8.42. Dual Control.

N2096 504 Sqn 20.3.39; undercarriage raised in error after landing, Exeter, 13.8.39; ROS; Rollason 25.1.40; Fairey 2.9.40; 4 BGS 26.10.40; 47 MU 9.12.41; to RAAF 21.2.42. Dual Control.

N2097 504 Sqn 22.3.39; 10 MU 2.10.39; 10 BGS 1.5.40; engine cut; bellylanded, Kirkbean, Dumfries, 29.4.41; 10 AOS 2.9.41; Rosenfield 2.9.42; 27 MU 30.9.42; 215 MU 8.10.42; 3 PATP 25.11.42; to SAAF 2.12.42. Dual Control.

N2098 6 MU 22.3.39; 609 Sqn 10.5.39; 1 FTS 20.11.39; to 1882M 11.4.40; SOC 24.3.40. Dual Control.

N2099 6 MU 22.3.39; 609 Sqn 10.5.39; 152 Sqn 18.10.39; 38 MU 19.5.40; 47 MU 9.9.40; to RCAF 27.10.40 as 1748. Dual Control.

N2100 6 MU 24.3.39; 611 Sqn 10.5.39; 1 FTS 10.11.39; engine cut; bellylanded, Wardour, near Tisbury, Wilts., 2.3.40; ROS; engine cut; bellylanded, Margam bombing range, Glam., 20.4.41; Rosenfield 22.2.42; 9 MU 4.6.42; 18 Group APC 27.6.42; 3 APC 19.3.43; 18 MU 23.3.43; SOC 14.7.44. Dual Control.

N2101 6 MU 23.3.39; 611 Sqn 10.5.39; 1 FTS 10.11.39; overshot forced landing while lost in bad visibility and hit tree, Grayhurst, near Newport Pagnell, Bucks., 13.2.40; SOC 19.2.40; to 2555M; Dual Control.

N2102 602 Sqn 23.3.39; hit house on approach, Abbotsinch, 4.5.39; ROS; 266 Sqn 8.1.40; 234 Sqn 24.2.40. Engine cut; bellylanded and hit hedge 10m SE of York, 27.2.40; DBR; SOC 7.3.40. Dual Control.

N2103 602 Sqn 23.3.39; braked while taxying and tipped up, Abbotsinch, 12.4.39; ROS; 266 Sqn 8.1.40; engine cut; undercarriage collapsed in forced landing, Thornton Hill, near East Kilbride, 10.2.40; ROS; Fairey 12.6.40; 8 MU 4.7.40; 142 Sqn 4.9.40; 18 MU 1.1.41; 47 MU 9.1.41; to RCAF 5.2.41 as 1856. Dual Control.

N2104 6 MU 24.3.39; 616 Sqn 16.5.39; 12 MU 25.7.40; 15 EFTS 17.8.40; 1 PFTS 10.12.40; undershot approach and hit hedge, Hucknall, 10.6.41; ROS; 16(P)FTS 13.7.41; 18 MU 20.2.42; 215 MU 16.11.42; EO Swansea 3.12.42; to SAAF 12.12.42 but lost at sea en route 28.1.43. Dual Control.

N2105 6 MU 30.3.39; 616 Sqn 16.5.39; undercarriage would not lock down and collapsed on landing, Doncaster, 23.9.39; ROS; 27 MU 8.10.40; 2 BGS 2.5.41; 1 FTS 11.10.41; overshot landing and hit hedge, Stormy Down, 29.12.41; ROS; 18 MU 2.4.42; 400 Sqn 15.6.42; Rosenfield 22.1.43; 27 MU 2.4.43; SOC 30.6.43. Dual Control.

N2106 5 MU 29.3.39; 610 Sqn 22.5.39; ran into ditch on landing, Carlisle/Kingstown, 17.5.40; Fairey 1.6.40; 8 MU 19.6.40; 304 Sqn 26.8.40; 12 OTU 5.11.40; 20 MU 30.12.40; 47 MU 14.1.41; to RCAF 5.2.41 as 1844. Dual Control.

N2107 5 MU 29.3.39; 610 Sqn 22.5.39; 1 FTS 16.12.39; 7 FTS 21.5.40; 12 FTS 11.6.40; bellylanded in error, Harlaxton, 29.12.40; 16(P)FTS 20.7.41; 18 MU 27.1.42; to RAAF 9.7.42.

N2108 5 MU 29.3.39; 605 Sqn 29.6.39; 1 FTS 4.11.39. Flew into ground in fog SE of Upavon, 11.3.40; to 1868M 9.4.40. Dual Control.

N2109 5 MU 6.4.39; 605 Sqn 29.6.39; 20 MU 3.3.40; 6 BGS 1.5.40; 12 FTS 29.5.40; 16(P)FTS 15.6.41; 27 MU 30.1.42; to 3316M at 6 SofTT 8.8.42; 27 MU 31.12.42; 5 SofTT 26.1.43. Dual Control.

N2110 Rolls-Royce 24.3.39; 3 SofTT 11.11.41; Rolls-Royce 24.1.42; SOC 2.42.

N2111 5 MU 24.3.39; 36 MU 24.7.39; to Turkish Air Force 26.8.39; originally for Poland.

N2112 5 MU 29.3.39; 36 MU 27.7.39; to Turkish Air Force 26.8.39; originally for Poland.

N2113 5 MU 30.3.39; 36 MU 25.7.39; to Turkish Air Force 26.8.39; originally for Poland.

N2114 5 MU 30.3.39; 36 MU 25.7.39; to Turkish Air Force 26.8.39; originally for Poland.

N2115 5 MU 30.3.39; 36 MU 1.8.39; to Turkish Air Force 16.9.39; originally for Poland.

N2116 5 MU 30.3.39; 36 MU 31.7.39; to Turkish Air Force 16.9.39; originally for Poland.

N2117 5 MU 30.3.39; 36 MU 25.7.39; to Turkish Air Force 16.9.39; originally for Poland.

N2118 1 AACU 6.4.39; 2 AACU; 1 AACU 30.10.40; 1 SD Flight 26.11.41; TFU 29.10.41; 38 MU 23.11.41; 4 APC 26.7.42; Rosenfield 24.3.43; SOC 28.3.43.

N2119 1 AACU 6.4.39; 2 AACU; 1 AACU 30.10.40; TFU 29.10.41; 38 MU 23.11.41; Rosenfield 8.5.42; 9 MU 26.7.42; 18 Group APC 10.9.42; 18 MU 3.3.43; SOC 5.2.44.

N2120 5 MU 6.4.39; 36 MU 31.7.39; to Turkish Air Force 16.9.39; originally for Poland.

N2121 5 MU 6.4.39; 36 MU 24.7.39; to Turkish Air Force 16.9.39; originally for Poland.

N2122 5 MU 6.4.39; 36 MU 25.7.39; to Turkish Air Force 16.9.39; originally for Poland.

N2123 5 MU 6.4.39; 36 MU 31.7.39; to Turkish Air Force 16.9.39; originally for Poland.

N2124 1 AACU 6.4.39; 2 AACU; 1 AACU 30.10.40; TFU 29.9.40; 47 MU 6.12.41; to RAAF 12.3.42.

N2125 8 MU 6.4.39; 7 AOS 5.9.39; engine cut; hit hedge in forced landing, St Brides Major, Glam., 9.5.41; 47 MU 19.9.41; to RCAF 14.11.41 as 2113.

N2126 8 MU 6.4.39; Polish OTU 19.3.40; 18 OTU; 20 MU 26.11.40; Austin 1.1.41; to SAAF 5.2.41 as 938; to Middle East 30.1.43.

N2127 8 MU 6.4.39; Bramcote 29.6.40; 300 Sqn 1.7.40; 47 MU 10.11.40; to RCAF 16.12.40 as 1801.

N2128 8 MU 6.4.39; 10 AOS 4.9.39; tyre burst on take-off and undercarriage collapsed, Annan LG, 23.9.40; ROS; engine cut; bellylanded 1m S of New Abbey, Dumfries, 29.4.41; ROS; landed with undercarriage unlocked, Silloth, 7.10.41; 18 MU 7.9.42; SOC 14.7.44.

N2129 8 MU 14.4.39; 264 Sqn 16.12.39. Wing hit ground in forced landing while lost in bad weather near Braintree,

Essex, 11.3.40; SOC 29.3.40; to 1887M 11.4.40; Cosford 20.12.42.

N2130 8 MU 14.4.39; 36 MU 10.8.39; to Turkish Air Force 16.9.39; originally for Poland.

N2131 8 MU 14.4.39; 36 MU 10.8.39; to Turkish Air Force 16.9.39; originally for Poland.

N2147 8 MU 14.4.39; Bramcote 29.6.40; 300 Sqn 1.7.40; 47 MU 10.11.40; to RCAF 11.12.40 as 1820.

N2148 8 MU 15.4.39; 12 OTU 3.9.40. Flew into ground in bad visibility, Cadeleigh, 3m SSW of Tiverton, Devon, 12.9.40; Sgt R.A. Jooris, Sgt L.G. Mitchell and Sgt H.E.M. Long killed; SOC 2.10.40.

N2149 8 MU 15.4.39; 36 MU 10.8.39; to Turkish Air Force 15.11.39.

N2150 6 MU 15.4.39; AASF 23.5.40; 12 Sqn 23.5.40. Burnt on evacuation of Chateau Bougon airfield, Nantes, 16.6.40.

N2151 6 MU 15.4.39; Linton-on-Ouse 8.1.41; engine cut; bellylanded 1m S of Cottam airfield, 11.8.41; ROS; 1484 TTF at 31.12.41; 18 MU 8.11.42; SOC 14.7.44.

N2152 6 MU 15.4.39; Linton-on-Ouse 17.1.40; 1484 TTF at 31.12.41; 18 MU 8.11.42; SOC 5.2.44.

N2153 8 MU 15.4.39; 36 MU 10.8.39; to Turkish Air Force 15.11.39.

N2154 8 MU 15.4.39; 36 MU 11.8.39; to Turkish Air Force 15.11.39.

N2155 8 MU 15.4.39; 36 MU 11.8.39; to Turkish Air Force 15.11.39.

N2156 8 MU 18.4.39; 36 MU 11.8.39; to RCAF 20.1.40 as 1606.

N2157 8 MU 18.4.39; 103 Sqn 26.6.40; 38 MU 11.10.40; Austin 9.12.40; Parks 8.1.41; to SAAF 24.2.41 but lost at sea en route SS *Huntingdon*.

N2158 8 MU 18.4.39; 36 MU 11.8.39; to RCAF 20.1.40 as 1604.

N2159 20 MU 19.4.39; 8 MU at 30.11.39; 264 Sqn 16.12.39. Engine cut; abandoned over Hintlesham, Suffolk, 16.12.39; PO H.G. Tipple bailed out too late and killed; SOC 16.12.39.

N2160 20 MU 19.4.39; 10 AOS 4.9.39; engine cut on approach; overshot forced landing, Kirkbean, near Dumfries, 27.11.40; Fairey 14.1.41; 47 MU 18.6.41; to RCAF 4.7.41 as 2031.

N2161 20 MU 21.4.39; 47 MU 19.5.40; to SAAF 19.6.40 as 919.

N2162 20 MU 21.4.39; 47 MU 6.11.40; to RCAF 27.11.40 as 1780.

N2163 20 MU 21.4.39; 103 Sqn 26.7.40; 20 MU 10.10.40; 47 MU 28.11.40; to RAAF 15.1.41.

N2164 20 MU 21.4.39; 12 OTU 7.8.40. Hit pillbox in forced landing when lost, Fairoaks, 17.9.40; SOC 25.9.40.

N2165 20 MU 25.4.39; 47 MU 20.5.40; to SAAF 19.6.40 as 920.

N2166 20 MU 23.4.39; 12 Sqn 22.8.40; 18 MU 17.12.40; 215 MU 22.5.42; 3 PATP 7.6.42; to RAAF 9.7.42.

N2167 20 MU 25.4.39; 98 Sqn 14.7.40; to RCAF 20.8.41.

N2168 20 MU 25.4.39; 12 OTU 7.8.40; overshot flarepath and hit hedge, Benson, 13.8.40; ROS; engine cut; overshot landing and hit truck, Benson, 8.11.40; Fairey 14.11.40; Austin 10.4.41; to SAAF 11.7.41.

N2169 20 MU 8.5.39; 150 Sqn 26.7.40; 9 MU 11.10.40; Austin 23.11.40; Parks 28.12.40; to SAAF 24.2.41 but lost at sea en route SS *Huntingdon*.

N2170 9 MU 26.4.39; 10 AOS 4.9.39; engine cut; overshot forced landing into ditch 4m NE of Dundrennan, Kirkcudbright, 22.5.41; Rosenfield 8.7.42; 27 MU 31.8.42; 215 MU 7.10.42; EO Newcastle 18.10.42; to RAAF 18.10.42.

N2171 27 MU 25.4.39; Polish OTU 2.4.40; 18 OTU; 20 MU 15.12.40; Austin 7.2.41; 5 MU 20.2.41; 47 MU 11.5.41; to RCAF 24.5.41; not received in Canada.

N2172 27 MU 26.4.39; Polish OTU 2.4.40; 18 OTU; 20 MU 15.12.40; 47 MU 28.2.41; to RCAF 25.4.41 as 1951.

N2173 9 MU 27.4.39; AASF 19.1.40; 98 Sqn 12.5.40; Austin 2.4.41; to RCAF 13.5.41.

An unidentified Battle with a Hind and a Tutor, presumably at an armament training camp. (P Jarrett collection)

N2174   9 MU 27.4.39; 27 MU 2.10.39; 10 MU 12.2.40; 7 FTS 27.5.40; 1 FTS 21.4.41; Rosenfield 10.2.42; 27 MU 21.6.42; 255 Sqn 27.7.42; 27 MU 15.11.42; 231 Sqn 27.12.42; to 3946M at 2 SofTT 7.7.43.

N2175   9 MU 27.4.39; 27 MU 1.10.39; 10 MU 10.2.40; 7 FTS 27.5.40; DBR in accident, 8.11.40; SOC 1.12.40.

N2176   9 MU 1.5.39; 27 MU 29.9.39; 6 BGS 4.5.40; 7 BGS 2.6.40; 47 MU 25.10.41; to RAAF 4.12.41.

N2177   9 MU 1.5.39; 27 MU 29.9.39; 10 MU 11.2.40; 7 FTS 27.5.40; undershot night landing and undercarriage collapsed, Sibson, 7.8.40; ROS; 12 FTS 3.3.41; 16(P)FTS 7.6.41; DBR in accident, 25.11.41; SOC 29.11.41.

N2178   9 MU 1.5.39; 6 MU 13.5.40; 12 Sqn. Shot down by Bf 109s, Hannogne area, 19.5.40; Sgt E.J. Belcher killed; FO P.R. Barr and LAC V.C. Rawlings wounded

N2179   9 MU 1.5.39; 27 MU 29.9.39; 47 MU 30.4.41; to RAAF 9.6.41.

N2180   9 MU 4.5.39; AASF 9.5.40; abandoned in France, 6.40.

N2181   9 MU 4.5.39; 27 MU 1.10.39; 6 BGS 11.1.40; 4 BGS 14.4.40; ran out of fuel, hit bank in forced landing, East Freugh, 26.5.40; Fairey 31.5.40; 12 MU 25.8.40; 47 MU 17.10.40; to RCAF 11.12.40 as 1839.

N2182   27 MU 4.5.39; 18 OTU 13.5.40; Fairey 28.11.40; 43 Group 3.2.41; 12 MU 26.4.41; Fairey 19.9.41; 47 MU 1.12.41; to RAAF 5.1.42.

N2183   RAE 8.5.39; 22 MU 7.6.40; 18 OTU 13.9.40; 20 MU 27.11.40; 47 MU 7.2.41; to RCAF 21.2.41 as 1871.

N2184   Fairey and RAE 8.5.39; Bristol 18.10.39; SOC 16.4.45; Hercules test bed with fixed undercarriage.

N2185   27 MU 4.5.39; 7 FTS 20.5.40. Stalled on approach to Sibson and hit ground, Chesterton, Hunts., 29.7.40; SOC 5.8.40.

N2186   27 MU 8.5.39; Polish OTU 1.4.40; 18 OTU; Fairey 28.11.40. 43 Group 23.2.41; 12 MU 27.4.41; 47 MU 11.5.41; to RCAF 28.5.41 as 1971.

N2187   27 MU 8.5.39; Polish OTU 30.3.40; 18 OTU; hit obstruction on landing, Hucknall, 27.7.40; ROS; Fairey 28.11.40; 43 Group 23.2.41; 12 MU 27.4.41; Austin 10.5.41; to RCAF 5.41 as 2035.

N2188   27 MU 8.5.39; 18 OTU 13.5.40; 20 MU 28.11.40; Austin 17.1.41; to RAAF 25.3.41.

N2189   27 MU 8.5.39; Polish OTU 30.3.40; 18 OTU; overshot landing and hit hedge, Hucknall, 14.6.40; Fairey 17.6.40; 20 MU 16.8.40; 142 Sqn 19.9.40; 301 Sqn 25.9.40; 47 MU 11.11.40; to RCAF 16.12.40 as 1805.

N2190   27 MU 8.5.39; Polish OTU 30.3.40; 18 OTU; 38 MU 29.11.40; Austin 4.4.41; to RCAF 5.41 as 2052.

N2211   8 MU 11.5.39; 36 MU 1.8.39; to Turkish Air Force 16.9.39; originally for Poland.

N2212   8 MU 11.5.39; 36 MU 1.8.39; to Turkish Air Force 16.9.39; originally for Poland.

N2213   8 MU 11.5.39; 36 MU 1.8.39; to Turkish Air Force 16.9.39; originally for Poland.

N2214   8 MU 11.5.39; 36 MU 1.8.39; to Turkish Air Force 16.9.39; originally for Poland.

N2215   8 MU 11.5.39; 36 MU 1.8.39; to Turkish Air Force 16.9.39; originally for Poland.

N2216   8 MU 11.5.39; 36 MU 1.8.39; to Turkish Air Force 16.9.39; originally for Poland.

N2217   8 MU 11.5.39; 36 MU 3.8.39; to Turkish Air Force 16.9.39; originally for Poland.

N2218   8 MU 15.5.39; 36 MU 3.8.39; to Turkish Air Force 16.9.39; originally for Poland.

N2219   8 MU 15.5.39; to Polish Air Force 10.8.39.

N2220   8 MU 15.5.39; 36 MU 3.8.39; to Turkish Air Force 16.9.39; originally for Poland.

N2221   8 MU 16.5.39; 36 MU 10.8.39; to Turkish Air Force 16.9.39; originally for Poland.

N2222   8 MU 16.5.39; 36 MU 10.8.39; to Turkish Air Force 16.9.39; originally for Poland.

N2223   8 MU 16.5.39; 10 AOS 5.9.39; undershot landing and hit wall, Annan LG, 27.9.40; ROS; engine cut; hit wall in forced landing, Shambellie, Dumfries, 28.10.41; Rosenfield 6.11.41; 215 MU 15.4.42; 3 PATP 27.4.42; to RAAF 23.5.42.

N2224   8 MU 16.5.39; 36 MU 3.8.39; to Turkish Air Force 16.9.39; originally for Poland.

N2225   8 MU 22.5.39; 19 MU 22.8.39; 3 BGS 3.1.40; 1 AAS 7.7.40; 27 MU 30.9.41; 18 MU 15.2.42; 215 MU 23.4.42; 3 PATP 10.5.42; to RAAF 14.6.42.

N2226   19 MU 19.5.39; 3 BGS 1.1.40; overshot forced landing in bad weather, Wallby, Cambs., 12.1.40; ROS; Fairey 6.6.40; 20 MU 2.9.40; 47 MU 18.9.40; to RCAF 27.9.40 as 1718.

N2227   19 MU 19.5.39; 36 MU 12.8.39; to RCAF 20.1.40 as 1605.

N2228   19 MU 19.5.39; 3 BGS 11.1.40; 1 AAS 3.7.40; 1 FTS 5.8.41; undercarriage collapsed in forced landing in bad weather 3m W of Stormy Down, 10.2.42; Rosenfield 18.5.42; 27 MU 4.8.42; 215 MU 24.8.42; 3 PATP 2.9.42; to RAAF 17.8.42.

N2229   19 MU 22.5.39; 5 BGS 24.2.40; 4 BGS 4.2.41; undercarriage jammed; landed on one wheel, West Freugh, 2.3.41; ROS; bellylanded in bad weather, Ballantrae, Ayrshire, 13.7.41; ROS; 4 AOS 14.10.41; 47 MU 21.12.41; LEP 25.1.42; to RAAF 31.5.42.

N2230   19 MU 19.5.39; 36 MU 12.8.39; to RCAF 20.1.40 as 1607.

N2231   RAE for Air Defence trials 22.5.39; brakes failed to hold on wet grass, Aberporth, 19.11.41; ROS; Rosenfield 13.5.43; SOC 13.5.43.

N2232   RAE for Air Defence trials 22.5.39. Crashed 28.11.39; SOC 22.2.40.

N2233   19 MU 24.5.39; 36 MU 12.8.39; 8 MU 9.9.39; 304 Sqn 26.8.40; 47 MU 10.11.40; to RAAF 15.1.41

N2234   Rolls-Royce 24.5.39; Fairey 21.6.41; 47 MU 4.10.41; Dumfries 2.11.41; to SAAF 29.1.42.

N2235   19 MU 24.5.39; 5 BGS; 1 FTS 26.1.41; undershot flarepath and hit obstruction, Shrewton, 19.10.41; 27 MU 30.9.42; 18 MU 17.7.40; 47 MU; SOC 30.6.43.

N2236   19 MU 24.5.39; 36 MU 19.8.39; 8 MU 9.9.39; Andover 25.5.40; 88 Sqn 26.5.40; overshot landing and hit obstruction, Kingstown, 18.7.40; ROS; 47 MU 17.12.40; to RAAF 15.1.41.

N2237   19 MU 25.5.39; 36 MU 12.8.39; 8 MU 9.9.39; Andover 25.5.40; 88 Sqn 26.5.40; 22 MU 21.7.40; 18 MU 28.7.40; 47 MU 6.2.41; to RCAF 11.3.41 as 1891.

N2238   19 MU 25.5.39; 5 BGS 10.1.40; 12 FTS 26.2.41; 1 FTS 30.6.41; 27 MU 30.5.42; SOC 30.6.43.

N2239   19 MU 25.5.39; 36 MU 12.8.39; to RCAF 21.1.40 as 1602.

N2240   19 MU 26.5.39; 3 BGS 3.1.40; 1 AAS 3.7.40; undercarriage collapsed on landing, Manby, 7.10.40; ROS; 9 MU 1.9.41; 215 MU 26.4.42; 3 PATP 10.5.42; to RAAF 9.8.42.

N2241   19 MU 26.5.39; 36 MU 12.8.39; 8 MU 9.9.39; AASF 14.6.40; 8 MU 16.6.40; Bramcote 29.6.40; 300 Sqn 1.7.40; 47 MU 10.11.40; to RCAF 11.12.40 as 1810.

N2242   19 MU 26.5.39; 5 BGS 10.1.40; 12 FTS 20.3.41; 27 MU 3.8.41; to RCAF 21.12.41 as 2126.

N2243   19 MU 26.5.39; 5 BGS 16.1.40; 16(P)FTS 11.6.41; 27 MU 1.6.42; 16 Group 27.6.42; 18 Group APC 15.10.42; 18 MU 13.3.43; SOC 4.6.43.

N2244   19 MU 31.5.39; to RAAF 11.5.40.

N2245   19 MU 31.5.39; 5 BGS 16.1.40; engine cut; bellylanded Bride, Isle of Man, 26.8.40; Fairey 18.9.40; 12 MU 22.11.40; Austin 7.2.41; to RCAF 17.3.41.

N2246   19 MU 31.5.39; 36 MU 12.8.39; to RCAF 20.1.40 as 1603.

N2247   19 MU 31.5.39; to RAAF 2.5.40.

N2248   6 MU 1.6.39; 142 Sqn 17.7.40; 4 MU 2.9.40; 38 MU 2.1.41; 47 MU 10.1.41; to RCAF 7.3.41 as 1898.

N2249   6 MU 1.6.39; 12 OTU 17.8.40; 20 MU 27.5.41; 47 MU 14.7.41; to RCAF 24.8.41 as 2082.

N2250   6 MU 1.6.39; AASF 25.5.40; 9 MU 13.7.40; 47 MU 16.10.41; to RAAF 4.12.41.

N2251   6 MU 5.6.39; 253 Sqn 10.12.39; 22 MU 29.2.40; 47 MU 30.9.41; Dumfries 2.11.41; to RAAF.

N2252   6 MU 5.6.39; 253 Sqn 12.12.39; 20 MU 23.2.40. Engine cut; hit tree in forced landing SW of Carlisle, 23.2.40; SOC 18.3.40.

N2253   6 MU 7.6.39; AASF 24.5.40; 103 Sqn 26.5.40. Damaged while attacking Ju 87s and crashlanded S of Paris, 8.6.40; Sgt G. Beardsley, Sgt G. Avery and LAC G. F. Lewis captured

N2254   6 MU 7.6.39; CFS 8.9.39; 20 MU 1.8.40; 4 BGS 29.10.40; 18 MU 20.7.41; 400 Sqn 7.6.42; 27 MU 31.12.42; SOC 30.6.43.

N2255   6 MU 12.6.39; AASF 25.5.40; 103 Sqn 16.6.40; Rollason 2.7.40; 9 MU 23.7.40; 47 MU 15.8.40; to RAAF 6.9.40.

N2256   6 MU 12.6.39; 253 Sqn 10.12.39; skidded into hedge in forced landing in bad weather 1m N of Oswestry, Salop., 23.2.40; 22 MU 23.2.40; 47 MU 5.9.41; to RAAF 27.9.41.

N2257   6 MU 12.6.39; 253 Sqn 7.12.39; overshot landing and tipped up, Manston, 14.12.39; ROS; 22 MU 20.3.40; 47 MU 1.11.41; to RCAF 19.12.41 as 2124.

N2258   6 MU 13.6.39; 253 Sqn 10.12.39. Engine cut in snowstorm; belly landed 5m SW of Manston, 16.1.40; SOC 23.1.40.

150 Fairey Battle Is delivered by Fairey between June and October 1939. Contract 768880/38. Built at Stockport.

P2155   36 MU 16.6.39; to RCAF 8.39 as 1301.

P2156   6 MU 16.6.39; AASF 7.6.40; 88 Sqn 9.6.40; 18 MU 29.7.40; 47 MU 27.9.40; to RCAF 27.10.40 as 1750.

P2157   6 MU 16.6.39; Finningley 11.1.40; 5 Group TTF 25.1.40; Driffield TTF 27.10.40; undercarriage jammed; landed on one wheel, Coningsby, 28.6.41; Fairey 3.7.41; 47 MU 23.10.41; to RAAF 21.3.42.

P2158   6 MU 16.6.39; Finningley 11.1.40; 5 Group TTF 25.1.40; Driffield TTF 25.10.40; 5 Group TTF at 31.12.41; 9 MU 1.6.42; 241 Sqn 21.6.42; 18 MU 10.11.42; SOC 19.11.43.

P2159   6 MU 16.6.39; AASF 19.5.40; 88 Sqn 23.5.40. Engine cut; bellylanded and hit hedge 2m N of Ardglass, Northern Ireland, 20.3.41; SOC 13.4.41.

P2160   6 MU 16.6.39; AASF 7.6.40; 88 Sqn 8.6.40; presumed lost in France, 6.40.

P2161   6 MU 19.6.39; AASF 19.5.40; 226 Sqn 20.5.40. Shot down in battle area near La Chapelle-Moutils, Seine-et-Marne, 13.6.40; Sgt J.B. Callaghan and Sgt L. Turner killed

P2162   6 MU 19.6.39; AASF 21.5.40; 12 Sqn 23.5.40. Shot down by Bf 109s attacking tank column, Poix, 7.6.40; Sgt F. Field, Sgt H.C. Bevan and LAC McKrill killed

P2163   6 MU 20.6.39; AASF 23.5.40; 103 Sqn 26.5.40; presumed lost in France, 6.40.

P2164   24 MU 20.6.39; 36 MU 10.1.40; to RCAF 15.3.40 as 1621.

P2165   24 MU 20.6.39; 47 MU 25.2.41; to RCAF 11.3.41 as 1936.

P2166   24 MU 20.6.39; 36 MU 27.2.40; to RAAF 4.4.40.

P2167   24 MU 20.6.39; 36 MU 27.2.40; to RAAF 21.3.40.

P2168   24 MU 20.6.39; 36 MU 29.2.40; to RAAF 18.4.40.

P2169   24 MU 21.6.39; 36 MU 27.2.40; to RAAF 21.3.40.

P2170   24 MU 23.6.39; 36 MU 2.3.40; to RCAF 21.3.40 as 1624.

P2171   36 MU 23.6.39; to RCAF 8.39 as 1302.

P2172   36 MU 23.6.39; to RCAF 8.39 as 1303.

P2173   36 MU 23.6.39; to RCAF 8.39 as 1304.

P2174   12 Sqn 27.6.39; 22 MU 19.9.39; Dumfries 24.8.41; to SAAF 9.41.

P2175   12 Sqn 27.6.39; 22 MU 19.9.39; 18 MU 17.8.41; SOC 8.41.

P2176   12 Sqn 27.6.39; Abingdon at 30.11.39; 105 Sqn 1.4.40; badly damaged by ground fire, Bouillon, 12.5.40; 6 RSU 24.5.40; abandoned in France, 6.40.

P2177   12 Sqn 27.6.39; 15 Sqn at 30.11.39; 105 Sqn 7.12.39; 142 Sqn 15.6.40; 27 MU 27.10.40; Austin 13.2.41; to SAAF 29.3.41 as 950.

P2178   12 Sqn 27.6.39; 22 MU 19.9.39; 47 MU 26.8.41; to SAAF 10.9.41.

P2179   12 Sqn 27.6.39; 150 Sqn 5.10.39; 9 MU 11.10.40; Austin 20.11.40; Parks 14.12.40; to SAAF 5.2.41 as 928; to Middle East 30.1.43.

P2180   12 Sqn 30.6.39; 15 Sqn 29.9.39; 226 Sqn at 30.11.39. Destroyed on evacuation of Reims, 16.5.40.

P2181   12 Sqn 30.6.39; 22 MU 19.9.39; 43 Group; engine cut; hit hedge in forced landing, Mowbray, near Silloth, 20.9.41; Rosenfield 26.9.41; 47 MU 4.1.42; LEP 25.1.42; to SAAF 2.3.42.

P2182   12 Sqn 30.6.39; 150 Sqn 4.10.39. Shot down during attack on bridge near Douzy, 5m ESE of Sedan,

K7673 served first with No.1 Air Armament School, Manby and then at No.1 Electrical & Wireless School at Cranwell.
(R Sturtivant collection)

	14.5.40; PO J. Boon, Sgt T. Fortune and AC1 S. Martin killed
P2183	12 Sqn 30.6.39; 150 Sqn 5.10.39; 1 Salvage Section 16.10.39; 218 Sqn at 30.11.39. Damaged by ground fire, Bouillon, and crashed, Nouvion-sur-Meuse, 12.5.40; PO F.S. Bazalgette killed; Sgt W.H. Harris and LAC H.B. Jones escaped
P2184	12 Sqn 30.6.39; 150 Sqn 4.10.39; presumed lost in France, 6.40.
P2185	36 MU 3.7.39; to RCAF 8.39 as 1305.
P2186	36 MU 6.7.39; to RCAF 8.39 as 1306.
P2187	36 MU 6.7.39; to RCAF 8.39 as 1307.
P2188	142 Sqn 6.7.39; Abingdon at 30.11.39; 63 Sqn 18.1.40; 12 OTU 18.4.40; 18 MU 14.12.40; 47 MU 21.3.41; to RCAF 2.4.41 as 1909.
P2189	142 Sqn 6.7.39; Abingdon at 30.11.39; AASF 4.3.40; 218 Sqn 5.3.40; presumed lost in France, 6.40.
P2190	142 Sqn 6.7.39; Abingdon at 30.11.39; AASF 9.4.40; 105 Sqn 11.4.40; badly damaged by ground fire, Luxembourg, 10.5.40; 21 AD 1.6.40; abandoned in France, 6.40.
P2191	142 Sqn 6.7.39; Abingdon at 30.11.39; AASF 12.2.40; 103 Sqn 13.2.40. Shot down by Bf 109 near Sedan, 14.5.40; Sgt G. Beardsley and LAC G.F. Lewis escaped
P2192	142 Sqn 6.7.39; Abingdon at 30.11.39; AASF 11.3.40; 218 Sqn 12.3.40; presumed lost in France, 6.40.
P2193	142 Sqn 10.6.39; Abingdon at 30.11.39; AASF 12.2.40; 103 Sqn 12.2.40. Hit by flak, Bouillon, and crashed, Sensenruth, 12.5.40; PO E.E. Morton and AC1 A.S. Ross killed
P2194	142 Sqn 10.6.39; Abingdon at 30.11.39; 142 Sqn 13.12.39; 6 RSU 10.5.40; presumed abandoned in France, 6.40.
P2195	142 Sqn 10.6.39. Missing 14.5.40; SOC 15.6.40.
P2196	36 MU 11.7.39; to RCAF 8.39 as 1308.

P2197	36 MU 11.7.39; to RCAF 8.39 as 1309.
P2198	36 MU 11.7.39; to RCAF 8.39 as 1310.
P2199	142 Sqn 12.7.39; Abingdon at 30.11.39; AASF 22.2.40; 1 Salvage Section 11.3.40; 21 AD 21.3.40; Fairey 25.6.40; 9 MU 26.8.40; 1 FTS 17.9.40; 22 MU 3.3.41; Austin 3.4.41; to RCAF 13.6.41 as 2058.
P2200	142 Sqn 15.7.39; Abingdon at 30.11.39; 226 Sqn 21.12.39; 105 Sqn. Shot down by ground fire, Luxembourg, 10.5.40; PO D.G. O'Brien, Sgt D.F. Eastick and AC1 S.R. Wright captured; SOC 31.5.40.
P2201	142 Sqn 18.7.39; Abingdon at 30.11.39; AASF 5.3.40; 218 Sqn 6.3.40. Shot down on reconnaissance near Kreilsheim, 20.4.40; PO H.D. Wardle captured; Sgt E. Davidson and AC1 A Bailey killed
P2202	105 Sqn 27.7.39; 218 Sqn 10.10.39; 88 Sqn 11.10.39. Hit by ground fire, Bouillon, and crashed, St.Vith, 11.5.40; PO A.W. Mungovan, Sgt F. Robson and AC1 E.W. Maltby captured
P2203	105 Sqn 27.7.39; 63 Sqn 25.10.39; Abingdon at 30.11.39; 218 Sqn 17.1.40. Hit by ground fire, St. Vith, and crashed, Troisvierges, 11.5.40; Sgt C.J.E. Dockrill, Sgt F.F. Dormer and AC1 K.G. Gregory killed; SOC 31.5.40.
P2204	105 Sqn 27.7.39; 12 Sqn at 30.11.39. Shot down by ground fire attacking bridge, Veldwezelt, 12.5.40; FO D.E. Garland, Sgt T. Gray and LAC L.R. Reynolds killed
P2233	36 MU 26.7.39; to RCAF 8.39 as 1311.
P2234	36 MU 26.7.39; to RCAF 8.39 as 1317.
P2235	36 MU 26.7.39; to RCAF 8.39 as 1312.
P2236	36 MU 26.7.39; to RCAF 8.39 as 1313.
P2237	36 MU 26.7.39; to RCAF 8.39 as 1318.
P2238	36 MU 27.7.39; to RCAF 8.39 as 1314.
P2239	36 MU 26.7.39; to RCAF 8.39 as 1319.
P2240	36 MU 27.7.39; to RCAF 8.39 as 1315.

P2241 36 MU 27.7.39; to RCAF 8.39 as 1316.

P2242 36 MU 27.7.39; to RCAF 8.39 as 1320.

P2243 105 Sqn 1.8.39; AASF 28.11.39; 12 Sqn 1.12.39; damaged by ground fire, Luxembourg; forcelanded, Piennes, 10.5.40; salvaged and to 2483M 6.40; 18 MU 29.11.43

P2244 226 Sqn 31.7.39; Abingdon at 30.11.39; AASF 6.3.40; 150 Sqn. Flew into ground on night bombing practice near St. Hilaire-le-Grand, 31.3.40; FO D. Devoto, Sgt C. Wall, AC1 W.F. Taylor killed; wreck to 2 Salvage Section 2.4.40 and presumed abandoned in France, 6.40.

P2245 226 Sqn 1.8.39; 63 Sqn 25.10.39; 1 AACU 1.11.39; overshot landing and skidded on to road, Weston Zoyland, 18.11.39; Abingdon 27.12.39; Bicester 6.3.40; 27 MU 22.2.41; undercarriage jammed; landed on one wheel, Sealand, 18.4.41; 47 MU 18.4.41; to RAAF 4.6.41.

P2246 226 Sqn 1.8.39; Abingdon at 30.11.39; AASF 8.3.40; 142 Sqn. Damaged by Bf 109s, Sedan, and crashlanded, 14.5.40; 6 RSU 17.5.40; presumed abandoned in France, 6.40.

P2247 105 Sqn 1.8.39; Abingdon at 30.11.39; 88 Sqn 12.2.40. Crew abandoned aircraft with radio U/S when lost, Pont-sur-Yonne, 23.3.40; 1 Salvage Section 28.3.40; SOC 23.4.40.

P2248 105 Sqn 4.8.39; Abingdon at 30.11.39; AASF 21.2.40; presumed lost in France 6.40.

P2249 105 Sqn 4.8.39; Abingdon at 30.11.39; AASF 24.1.40; 218 Sqn 26.1.40. Shot down, St. Vith, 11.5.40. SOC 31.5.40; PO H.M. Murray, Sgt P. Stubbs and AC2 I.G. Adams captured

P2250 226 Sqn 4.8.39; Abingdon at 30.11.39; AASF 11.3.40; 1 Salvage Section 12.3.40; 105 Sqn 21.3.40. Spun into ground at night, Champigneul, Marne, 31.3.40; F/Lt C.R. Mace and Cpl F. Coughtrey killed; wreck to 1 Salvage Section 1.4.40; SOC 23.4.40.

P2251 226 Sqn 4.8.39; 63 Sqn 25.10.39; Abingdon at 30.11.39; AASF 11.3.40; 1 Salvage Section 12.3.40; 88 Sqn 26.3.40. Hit by ground fire near Bouillon and crashed near Bercheux, 11.5.40; Sgt E.J.M. Whittle killed; F/Lt A.J. Madge and Cpl A.C. Collyer captured

P2252 226 Sqn 7.8.39; Catfoss 30.9.39; 106 Sqn at 30.11.39; 5 Group TTF 25.1.40; swung on landing and hit hut, Catfoss, 18.6.40; Austin 14.8.40; engine cut; undershot forced landing, Swaton, Lincs., 31.8.40; 12 MU 19.12.40; Austin 6.2.41; to RCAF 17.3.41.

P2253 226 Sqn 7.8.39; Catfoss 30.9.39; 106 Sqn at 30.11.39; 5 Group TTF; undercarriage collapsed in forced landing in bad weather, Siggleshorne Grange, Catfoss, 16.1.40; Rollason 23.1.40; Fairey 26.8.40; SOC 26.9.40.

P2254 226 Sqn 7.8.39; 63 Sqn 25.10.39; Abingdon at 30.11.39; 226 Sqn 14.1.40; presumed abandoned in France, 6.40.

P2255 226 Sqn 7.8.39; 15 Sqn 22.11.39; Abingdon at 30.11.39; 226 Sqn 5.12.39; destroyed on evacuation of Reims, 16.5.40.

P2256 226 Sqn 9.8.39; Abingdon at 30.11.39; 103 Sqn 19.1.40. Hit tree on ranges, St. Hilaire-le-Grand, 27.3.40; PO I.P. Hinton, Sgt D.C. Findley and AC2 J.A. Sharpe killed; wreck to 1 Salvage Section 29.3.40; SOC 23.4.40.

P2257 226 Sqn 9.8.39; Abingdon at 30.11.39; 63 Sqn 18.1.40; 12 OTU 18.4.40; undercarriage jammed and collapsed on landing, Benson, 10.10.40; 38 MU 21.12.40; 20 MU 22.12.40; 47 MU 10.2.41; to RCAF 8.3.41 as 1888.

P2258 105 Sqn 9.8.39; Abingdon at 30.11.39; 88 Sqn 12.2.40; abandoned on evacuation, 21.5.40; SOC 3.6.40.

P2259 105 Sqn 9.8.39; Abingdon at 30.11.39; 63 Sqn 18.1.40; 12 OTU 18.4.40; bullet fired into coolant system while clearing stoppage; bellylanded, Penrhos, 20.5.40; 4 MU 28.5.40; 18 MU 23.7.40; 47 MU 24.9.40; to RCAF 27.10.40 as 1778.

P2260 105 Sqn 9.8.39; Mildenhall 29.9.39; 207 Sqn 2.11.39; Mildenhall TTF at 30.11.39. Control lost in cloud; dived into ground, Gosberton, Lincs., 26.2.40; Sgt T. Owens and AC2 W. Mahon killed; SOC 12.3.40.

P2261 105 Sqn 9.8.39; Abingdon at 30.11.39; 88 Sqn 12.2.40. Hit by ground fire near Bouillon and crashed near St.Vith, 11.5.40; PO B.M. Skidmore, Sgt R.A.P. Kirby and AC1 W.L. Parsons killed

P2262 40 Sqn 10.8.39; Abingdon at 30.11.39; AASF 26.2.40; 20 MU 15.5.40; Fairey 22.6.40; 20 MU 23.7.40; 12 Sqn 19.9.40; 38 MU 1.1.41; 47 MU 14.6.41; to RCAF 23.6.41 as 2023.

P2263 88 Sqn 10.8.39; Abingdon at 30.11.39; 88 Sqn 12.1.40; 4 RSU 25.5.40; 21 AD 28.5.40; Fairey 26.6.40; 20 MU 24.8.40; AMDP for Refuelling Flight 3.9.40; RAE 7.2.41; AMDP 23.5.41; Fairey 22.8.41; 47 MU 23.10.41; to RAAF 13.3.42.

P2264 218 Sqn 10.8.39; 22 MU 14.9.39; 47 MU 5.12.41; to RAAF 5.1.42.

P2265 105 Sqn 10.8.39; 226 Sqn 14.8.39. Crashed on night training flight 7.4.40; Sgt J.R. Branton and LAC P.K. Davies killed; wreck to 1 Salvage Section 10.4.40; SOC 25.4.40.

P2266 150 Sqn 10.8.39; 22 MU 16.9.39; 4 BGS 17.4.40; 32 MU 10.7.41; 18 MU 5.9.41; RAE 16.10.41; Flight Refuelling 17.4.42; SOC 8.8.43; 572.25 hours.

P2267 52 Sqn 11.8.39; 105 Sqn 26.8.39; 226 Sqn 7.11.39. Shot down by ground fire, Sedan, 14.5.40; Sgt F.J. Percival and Cpl R.S. Clark killed; S/Ldr C.E.S. Lockett captured; SOC 31.5.40.

P2268 52 Sqn 11.8.39; 12 OTU 18.4.40; engine cut; bellylanded in field, Trent, Somerset, 28.6.40; Fairey 5.7.40; 20 MU 10.8.40; 23 MU 6.2.41; 88 Sqn 21.4.41; Shorts 9.9.41; 23 MU 1.1.42; 18 MU 8.11.42; SOC 13.10.43.

P2269 52 Sqn 11.8.39; engine cut in circuit; bellylanded Benson, 22.2.40; ROS; 12 OTU 18.4.40. Hit by AA fire while lost on navex, Portsmouth; abandoned and crashed, Ryde, Isle of Wight, 3.6.40; PO A.G. McIntyre (NZ) injured; Sgt G.H. Hudson and AC1 D.L. Leonard drowned; SOC 10.6.40.

P2270 52 Sqn 11.8.39; 12 OTU 18.4.40. Undershot night landing, stalled and DBR, Benson, 19.7.40; to 2143M; to RCAF 9.40 as instructional airframe A164.

P2271 52 Sqn 11.8.39; engine cut; damaged in forced landing 1m W of Blandford, 15.2.40; ROS; 12 OTU 18.4.40; undercarriage jammed, bellylanded Benson, 23.5.40; ROS. Abandoned after control lost at night, South Moreton, 3m SW of Benson, 5.8.40; SOC 27.8.40.

P2272 63 Sqn 26.8.39; 12 OTU 18.4.40. Engine cut; bellylanded and hit tree, Boro Corner, near Tiverton, Devon, 21.7.40; to 2159M.

P2273 63 Sqn 26.8.39; 12 OTU 18.4.40. Control lost after night take-off from Benson; dived into ground, Ewelme, Oxon., 8.4.40; PO M.E.F. Barnett killed; SOC 24.4.40.

P2274 63 Sqn 26.8.39. Hit trees on high ground in bad visibility, Checkendon, Berks., 3.11.39; PO G.F.A. Barwell killed; SOC 30.11.39.

P2275 63 Sqn 26.8.39; 12 OTU 18.4.40; SOC 29.5.40.

P2276 150 Sqn 27.8.39; 22 MU 16.9.39; 4 BGS 7.4.40; overshot landing and undercarriage collapsed, West Freugh, 8.5.40; ROS; 47 MU 6.11.41; to RAAF 28.2.42.

P2277 AAEE 26.8.39; CFS 15.5.40; 2 BGS 11.2.41; 5 FTS 6.41; 1 FTS 11.8.41. Undershot landing, hit tree and overturned, Shrewton, 25.10.41; PO A.J.T. Boddam-Whetham and A/L/A Brooks killed; SOC 29.10.41.

P2278 103 Sqn 27.8.39; 22 MU 22.9.39; 4 BGS 17.4.40; undercarriage would not lock down and collapsed on landing, West Freugh, 11.8.40; ROS; 18 MU at 31.12.41; 4 Sqn 1.6.42; 1472 Flight 24.10.42; 27 MU 13.5.43; Airspares 20.2.44; SOC 10.3.44.

P2300 5 MU 30.8.39; 105 Sqn 23.12.39; 8 MU 12.6.40; 304 Sqn 26.8.40; 47 MU 10.11.40; to RAAF 15.1.41.

P2301 1 AOS 30.8.39; 9 BGS; 18 MU 11.7.41; to RCAF 12.12.41 as 2115.

P2302 5 MU 29.8.39; 8 MU 12.6.40; 142 Sqn 25.8.40; Fairey 26.9.40; 47 MU 5.2.41; to RCAF 13.3.41 as 1900.

K7564 soon after delivery to No.63 Squadron alongside Hind K5395 of No.12 Squadron. (P Jarrett collection)

P2303   103 Sqn 27.8.39; 22 MU 20.9.39; 47 MU 1.10.41; to RCAF 12.12.41 as 2114.

P2304   5 MU 29.8.39; 8 MU 2.10.39; 103 Sqn 26.6.40; engine cut; bellylanded, Smallwood, Cheshire, 31.8.40; Fairey 10.9.40; 9 MU 20.11.40; Austin 28.2.41; to RCAF 4.5.41.

P2305   5 MU 29.8.39; 8 MU 27.9.39; AASF 10.6.40; 103 Sqn 16.6.40; 20 MU 10.10.40; Austin 7.12.40; Parks 4.1.41; to RAAF 11.3.41.

P2306   5 MU 30.8.39; 8 MU 2.10.39; 103 Sqn 26.6.40; 20 MU 10.10.40; Austin 27.11.40; Parks 21.12.40; to RCAF 1940 as 1998.

P2307   5 MU 30.8.39; 8 MU 2.10.39; 103 Sqn 26.6.40; 9 MU 12.10.40; Austin 22.11.40; Parks 21.12.40; to SAAF 5.2.41 as 936.

P2308   5 MU 1.9.39; 8 MU 26.9.39; 103 Sqn 26.6.40; 27 MU 15.10.40; 12 Sqn 26.10.40; 27 MU 17.12.40; 47 MU 16.1.41; to RCAF 26.2.41 as 1861.

P2309   5 MU 3.9.39; 8 MU 27.9.39; Bramcote 29.6.40; 300 Sqn 1.7.40; landed with one wheel up, Swinderby, 30.8.40; ROS; 47 MU 10.11.40; to RCAF 5.2.41 as 1851.

P2310   5 MU 31.8.39; 8 MU 12.6.40; 142 Sqn 25.8.40; SOC 4.9.40.

P2311   5 MU 3.9.39; 8 MU 29.9.39; AASF 14.6.40; 103 Sqn 16.6.40; 12 Sqn 21.8.40; Austin 13.9.40; 12 MU 8.12.40; Austin 6.2.41; Parks 24.2.41; to RCAF 10.4.41.

P2312   5 MU 3.9.39; 8 MU 23.9.39; 103 Sqn 26.6.40; 150 Sqn 26.6.40; 18 OTU 14.10.40; Western A/W 28.11.40; 47 MU 12.2.41; to RCAF 11.3.41 as 1934.

P2313   5 MU 3.9.39; 8 MU 27.9.39; AASF 15.5.40; 88 Sqn 20.5.40. Blew up on take-off, Les Grandes Chappelles, 29.5.40; FO H.G. Evitt, Sgt E.W.J. Chapman and AC1 C.A. Edwards killed

P2314   5 MU 3.9.39; 8 MU 27.9.39; AASF 15.5.40; 103 Sqn 18.5.40; presumed lost in France, 5.40.

P2315   5 MU 6.9.39; 8 MU 26.9.39; AASF 15.5.40; 218 Sqn 18.5.40; 103 Sqn 21.5.40. Damaged attacking Ju 87s, Poix, and forcelanded south of Paris, 8.6.40; PO Webber wounded

P2316   9 MU 5.9.39; 8 AOS 5.9.39; 8 BGS; ran on to soft ground on landing and tipped up, Donibristle, 8.11.39; ROS. Engine cut; bellylanded and hit wall 10m NE of Evanton, 20.5.40; SOC 30.5.40.

P2317   9 MU 3.9.39; West Freugh 4.9.39; 4 BGS; 3 Group TTF 12.2.40; 4 BGS 29.2.40; 47 MU 6.11.41; to RAAF 5.1.42.

P2318   9 MU 5.9.39; 8 AOS 5.9.39; 8 BGS; 47 MU 23.3.41; to RCAF 19.4.41 as 1949.

P2319   9 MU 5.9.39; AASF 19.1.40; 9 MU 14.7.40; 47 MU 30.9.41; to RCAF 12.12.41 as 2116.

P2320   9 MU 5.9.39; AASF 19.1.40; 98 Sqn 17.5.40; 88 Sqn 21.6.40; 22 MU 21.7.40; 18 MU 27.7.40; 47 MU 11.2.41; to RCAF 21.2.41 as 1869.

P2321   9 MU 5.9.39; 27 MU 1.10.39; AASF 20.5.40; 142 Sqn 22.5.40; 27 MU 2.12.40; Dumfries 8.5.41; to SAAF 11.7.41.

P2322   9 MU 6.9.39; 3 AOS 6.9.39; 1 AAS 7.7.40; Western A/W 28.8.41; LEP 21.10.41; 3 PATP at 31.12.41; to South Africa 17.1.42 then to RAAF.

P2323   9 MU 6.9.39; 3 AOS 6.9.39; 1 AAS 7.7.40; ran into bowser taxying, Manby, 22.2.41; ROS; Western A/W 28.8.41; 27 MU 30.9.41; 47 MU 3.1.42; LEP 26.1.42; to SAAF 2.3.43.

P2324   9 MU 8.9.39; 27 MU 30.9.39; AASF 12.4.40; 6 RSU 20.4.40; 218 Sqn 22.4.40. Shot down attacking bridge, Sedan, 14.5.40; FO D.A.J. Foster and AC1 T.J. Bryan captured

P2325   9 MU 8.9.39; 27 MU 1.10.39; AASF 18.5.40; 142 Sqn 15.6.40; 4 MU 1.9.40; 47 MU 11.2.41; to RCAF 2.3.41 as 1876.

P2326   9 MU 8.9.39; 27 MU 2.10.39; AASF 12.4.40; 218 Sqn 19.4.40. Hit by ground fire and abandoned, St. Vith, 11.5.40; Sgt C.M. Jennings killed; FO C.A.R. Crews, Sgt T.S. Evans captured

P2327   9 MU 8.9.39; 27 MU 30.9.39; 10 MU 11.2.40; AASF 18.5.40; 150 Sqn 19.5.40; 142 Sqn 3.10.40. Stalled at night on air test; flew into ground in bad visibility, Binbrook, 22.10.40; Sgt Woodruff and Sgt Duckers injured; SOC 29.10.40.

P2328   9 MU 16.9.39; 27 MU 1.10.39; 10 MU 11.2.40; AASF 12.4.40; 103 Sqn 20.4.40. Hit by flak, Vernon, and crashed, Gasny, Eure, 10.6.40; FO C.V. Thomas and LAC P.I. Bligh killed

P2329   9 MU 16.9.39; 27 MU 1.10.39; 10 MU 11.2.40; 142 Sqn 29.8.40; 27 MU 1.1.41; 47 MU 27.2.41; to RCAF 7.4.41 as 1946.

P2330   9 MU 16.9.39; 27 MU 1.10.39; 10 MU 10.2.40; 98 Sqn 14.7.40; missing 26.5.41; SOC 11.6.41.

P2331   9 MU 16.9.39; 27 MU 2.10.39; AASF 18.5.40; 226 Sqn 20.5.40; 12 Sqn 16.6.40; crashlanded on return from Boulogne, 17.8.40; Austin 17.9.40; Fairey 22.9.40; 47 MU 13.3.41; to RCAF 27.4.41 as 1981.

P2332   20 MU 16.9.39; AASF 15.4.40; 12 Sqn 16.4.40. Shot down attacking bridge, Vroenhoven, 12.5.40; FO N.M. Thomas, Sgt B.T.P. Carey and Cpl T.S. Campion captured

P2333   20 MU 16.9.40; AASF 15.4.40; 142 Sqn 18.4.40. Shot down by Bf 109s, Sedan, 14.5.40; Sgt J. Brookes and LAC R.H. Nugent killed; Sgt A.N. Spear escaped.

P2334   20 MU 16.9.39; AASF 15.4.40; 150 Sqn 16.4.40. Destroyed in air raid, Ecury-sur-Coole, 11.5.40.

P2335   20 MU 16.9.39; AASF 15.4.40; 226 Sqn. Shot down in battle area, Breux-sur-Avre, Eure, 14.6.40; FO K.M. Rea killed.

P2336   20 MU 19.9.39; AASF 15.4.40; 150 Sqn 16.4.40. Shot down by flak, Neufchateau, Luxembourg, 12.5.40; PO I. Campbell-Irons, Sgt N.J. Ingram and LAC H.R. Figg killed

P2353   20 MU 19.9.39; AASF 15.4.40; 226 Sqn. Damaged by ground fire attacking roads in Boeimeer/Rijsbergen area and forcelanded near Brussels, 13.5.40; PO W.M. Waddington wounded; handed over to Belgian Air Force

P2354   20 MU 19.9.39; AASF 12.5.40; 88 Sqn 15.6.40; 23 MU 5.9.41; 18 MU 12.3.42; 215 MU 16.11.42; 3 PATP 28.11.42; 215 MU 22.12.42; to RAAF 3.1.43.

P2355   20 MU 21.9.39; AASF 18.5.40; 88 Sqn 19.5.40. Destroyed in air raid in France.

P2356   20 MU 21.9.39; AASF 16.5.40; 88 Sqn 20.5.40. Missing over battle area, 23.5.40; PO A.E. Wickham, Sgt E. Hibbert and AC1 M. Whelan killed

P2357   20 MU 21.9.39; AASF 18.5.40; 103 Sqn 18.5.40; presumed lost in France, 5.40.

P2358   20 MU 21.9.39; AAEE; engine cut; bellylanded Wilton, Wilts., 9.3.40; ROS; 12 OTU 17.8.40; undershot night landing into wire entanglement, Benson, 28.9.40; Fairey 7.10.40; 9 MU 8.12.40; Austin 25.2.41; Parks 4.4.41; to RCAF 10.4.41.

P2359   20 MU 25.9.39; engine cut on take-off; undercarriage collapsed on landing, Aston Down, 12.5.40; ROS; AASF 18.5.40; 142 Sqn; presumed lost in France, 5.40.

P2360   20 MU 25.9.39; AASF 12.5.40; 218 Sqn 13.5.40. Missing during attack on bridge, Sedan, 14.5.40; PO R.T.L. Buttery and AC2 W.C. Waterston missing, presumed killed

P2361   19 MU 25.9.39; to RCAF 2.2.40 as 1665.

P2362   19 MU 27.9.39; 5 BGS 24.2.40; 12 FTS 1.3.41; 16(P)FTS 7.6.41; 309 Sqn 13.6.42; 63 MU 27.6.42; Rosenfield 30.6.42; 27 MU 2.9.42; 231 Sqn 22.12.42; 104 OTU 11.1.43; SOC 28.4.44.

P2363   19 MU 27.9.39; 5 BGS 3.3.40; 1 FTS 20.8.41; 9 MU 22.6.42; 27 MU 2.9.42; 18 MU 6.9.42; 215 MU 7.10.42; EO Liverpool 24.10.42; to RAAF 8.11.42.

P2364   19 MU 27.9.39; to RAAF 2.5.40.

P2365   19 MU 25.9.39; to RAAF 11.5.40.

P2366   19 MU 27.9.39; to RCAF 2.2.40 as 1653.

P2367   19 MU 27.9.39; to RCAF 2.2.40 as 1646.

P2368   19 MU 27.9.39; to RCAF 2.2.40 as 1647.

P2369   19 MU 4.10.39; to RCAF 2.2.40 as 1654.

50 Fairey Battle Is delivered by Fairey in October and November 1939. Contract 768880/38. Built at Stockport.

P5228   19 MU 4.10.39; 36 MU 27.3.40; to RCAF 19.4.40 as 1652.

P5229   27 MU 30.9.39; 6 RSU 20.4.40; 12 Sqn 25.4.40. Shot down attacking bridge 5m ESE of Sedan, 14.5.40; Sgt A.G. Johnson, Sgt E.F. White killed; AC1 F.T. Spencer captured

P5230   27 MU 30.9.39; 10 MU 12.2.40; 18 OTU 23.7.40; undercarriage collapsed on landing on rough ground, Hucknall, 4.9.40; 18 MU 26.11.40; Dumfries 30.6.41; to SAAF 24.7.41.

P5231   27 MU 30.9.39; 12 Sqn 11.5.40; 21 AD 7.6.40; abandoned in France, 6.40.

P5232   27 MU 3.10.39; 150 Sqn 26.4.40. Shot down attacking bridge, Sedan, 14.5.40; F/Sgt G.T. Barker and Sgt J.D.F. Williams killed; LAC A.K. Summerson escaped to own lines

P5233   27 MU 3.10.39; AASF 24.5.40; 226 Sqn 26.5.40; 47 MU 6.8.41; to RCAF 29.8.41 as 2067.

P5234   27 MU 4.10.39; AASF 16.5.40; 226 Sqn 17.5.40; 47 MU 6.8.41; to RAAF 27.8.41.

P5235   27 MU 3.10.39; 150 Sqn 19.4.40. Shot down in battle area, 19.5.40; PO D.E.T. Osment, Sgt G.W. Clifford and AC1 W.G. Slade captured

P5236   27 MU 5.10.39; 10 MU 15.2.40; 150 Sqn 26.4.40; 12 Sqn 29.8.40; 20 MU 16.12.40; 47 MU 7.2.41; to RCAF 8.3.41 as 1885.

P5237   27 MU 4.10.39; 103 Sqn 14.5.40; 12 Sqn 16.6.40; 38 MU 22.12.40; 47 MU 7.7.41; to RCAF 27.8.41 as 2108.

P5238   27 MU 5.10.39; AASF 16.5.40; 142 Sqn 18.5.40; damaged by enemy aircraft, Laon, 19.5.40; Sgt T. Jones killed; 4 RSU 21.5.40; 21 AD 11.6.40. Abandoned at Chateau Bougon, Nantes, 16.6.40.

P5239   24 MU 5.10.39; 36 MU 27.2.40; to RAAF 21.3.40.

P5240   24 MU 10.10.39; 266 Sqn 19.12.39; 245 Sqn 14.2.40; 12 MU 7.5.40; 142 Sqn 6.8.40; 20 MU 9.1.41; 47 MU 10.2.41; to RAAF 2.3.41.

P5241   24 MU 10.10.39; 36 MU 29.2.40; to RCAF 29.3.40 as 1632.

P5242   24 MU 10.10.39; 36 MU 29.2.40; to RAAF 18.4.40.

P5243   24 MU 10.10.39; 36 MU 29.2.40; to RAAF 4.4.40.

P5244   24 MU 16.10.39; Sutton Bridge 9.12.39; 266 Sqn 9.12.39; engine cut after take-off; hit ditch in forced landing, Sutton Bridge, 17.1.40; Rollason 25.1.40; Fairey 18.8.40; SOC 26.9.40.

P5245   24 MU 10.10.39; 36 MU 20.3.40; to RCAF 20.4.40 as 1662.

P5246   24 MU 16.10.39; 266 Sqn 10.12.39; tailwheel collapsed in heavy landing, Sutton Bridge, 12.12.39; 20 MU 26.2.40; 47 MU 19.5.40; to SAAF 2.7.40 as 923.

P5247   24 MU 16.10.39; 36 MU 27.2.40; to RAAF 21.3.40.

P5248   24 MU 16.10.39; 266 Sqn 10.12.39; 32 MU 27.3.40; 266 Sqn 1.4.40; Experimental Flight Martlesham Heath 12.4.40; 420 Flight 24.9.40; undercarriage jammed; bellylanded, Middle Wallop, 22.10.40; CGS 8.2.41; Warmwell 8.2.41; Rosenfield 11.4.42; 9 MU 19.7.42; 18 MU 7.9.42; SOC 10.12.44.

P5249   24 MU 16.10.39; 36 MU 29.2.40; to RAAF 18.4.40.

P5250   24 MU 16.10.39; 266 Sqn 19.12.39; 234 Sqn 14.2.40; Rollason 6.6.40; 38 MU 17.7.40; 47 MU 18.9.40; to RCAF 18.10.40 as 1760.

P5251   24 MU 14.10.39; 266 Sqn 17.12.39; 245 Sqn 10.2.40; 22 MU 2.5.40; 47 MU 16.6.41; to SAAF 15.7.41.

P5252   12 MU 19.10.39; 47 MU 14.3.41; to RCAF 2.4.41 as 1937.

P5270   12 MU 19.10.39; Dumfries 20.4.41; to RCAF 22.5.41 as 1958.

P5271   12 MU 19.10.39; 47 MU 15.3.41; to RCAF 17.5.41 as 1963.

P5272   12 MU 19.10.39; 47 MU 5.3.41; to RCAF 25.4.41 as 1977.

P5273   12 MU 27.10.39; 47 MU 28.2.41; to RAAF 4.6.41.

P5274   12 MU 19.10.39; 47 MU 11.2.41; to RCAF 11.3.41 as 1918.

P5275   12 MU 22.10.39; 47 MU 11.2.41; to RAAF 3.4.41.

P5276   12 MU 22.10.39; 47 MU 21.5.41; to RCAF 10.6.41 as 2033.

L5424 of No.15 Elementary Flying Training School after bellylanded in error at Redhill on 6 May 1940. (C A Nepean Bishop)

P5277   12 MU 22.10.39; 2 AACU 13.3.41; FAA Gosport 6.5.42; 2 AACU 12.9.42; 27 MU 16.4.43; SOC 10.3.44.

P5278   12 MU 22.10.39; 47 MU 4.3.41; to RCAF 2.4.41 as 1864.

P5279   12 MU 22.10.39; 47 MU 2.3.41; to RCAF 25.4.41 as 1950.

P5280   12 MU 24.10.39; 47 MU 28.2.41; to RCAF 3.4.41 as 1940.

P5281   12 MU 24.10.39; 47 MU 1.3.41; to Canada 11.4.41 then to RAAF.

P5282   12 MU 26.10.39; 47 MU 14.3.41; to RCAF 2.4.41 as 1938.

P5283   12 MU 28.10.39; 88 Sqn 14.11.40; Shorts 8.9.41; 23 MU 9.1.42; 239 Sqn 29.5.42. Crashed in forced landing, Watchlaw, Northumberland, 25.7.42; SOC 31.7.42.

P5284   12 MU 28.10.39; 47 MU 1.3.41; to RCAF 1.4.41 as 1975.

P5285   12 MU 28.10.39; Dumfries 5.6.41; to RCAF 19.8.41 as 2080.

P5286   12 MU 28.10.39; Austin 30.1.41; Parks 6.3.41; to SAAF 12.4.41 but lost at sea en route, *City of Winchester*.

P5287   12 MU 27.10.39; 47 MU 12.3.41; to RCAF 29.3.41 as 1911.

P5288   12 MU 29.10.39; 2 Sqn 6.6.42; bellylanded after oil pressure dropped, Herts., 9.6.42; ROS; 27 MU 9.9.42; 26 Sqn 31.12.42; 1472 Flight 3.2.43; 18 MU 20.5.43; SOC 13.10.43.

P5289   12 MU 27.10.39; 47 MU 8.9.40; to RAAF 1.10.40.

P5290   12 MU 1.11.39; 47 MU 16.7.41; to RCAF 8.8.41 as 2059.

P5291   12 MU 29.10.39; Austin 9.4.41; to RCAF 4.41 as 2013.

P5292   12 MU 1.11.39; 47 MU 8.9.40; to RCAF 27.9.40 as 1721.

P5293   12 MU 1.11.39; 47 MU 19.9.40; to RCAF 28.10.40 as 1764.

P5294   12 MU 1.11.39; Austin 14.4.41; to RCAF 5.41 as 2045.

200 Fairey Battle Is delivered by Fairey between November 1939 and May 1940. Contract 768880/38. Built at Stockport. 100 (from P6616) built as Battle Trainers.

P6480   12 MU 6.11.39; 47 MU 3.5.41; to RCAF 28.5.41 as 1969.

P6481   12 MU 6.11.39; 47 MU 6.11.40; to RAAF 15.1.41.

P6482   12 MU 6.11.39; 226 Sqn 14.11.40; 88 Sqn 10.7.41; 23 MU 5.9.41; 18 MU 14.2.42; SOC 29.6.43.

P6483   12 MU 6.11.39; tipped up taxying in strong wind, 6.11.39; ROS; 47 MU 1.3.41; to RAAF 24.3.41.

P6484   12 MU 6.11.39; 47 MU 5.3.41; to RAAF 3.4.41.

P6485   12 MU 6.11.39; 47 MU 1.3.41; to RCAF 25.4.41 as 1953.

P6486   12 MU 6.11.39; 47 MU 22.7.41; to RCAF 29.8.41 as 2071.

P6487   12 MU 6.11.39; Austin 3.6.41; to SAAF 9.7.41.

P6488   12 MU 6.11.39; 47 MU 27.6.41; to RCAF 27.8.41 as 2093.

P6489   12 MU 6.11.39; 47 MU 6.11.40; to RAAF 15.1.41.

P6490   12 MU 8.11.39; Austin 13.5.41; to RCAF 5.41 as 2038.

P6491   12 MU 8.11.39; 3 School of General Reconnaissance 1.1.41; Parks 15.1.41; to SAAF 16.2.41 as 943.

P6492   12 MU 8.11.39; 47 MU 1.11.40; to RCAF 28.11.40 as 1814.

P6493   12 MU 8.11.39; 47 MU 6.3.41; to Canada 11.4.41 then to RAAF.

P6494   12 MU 10.11.39; 47 MU 1.11.40; to RCAF 28.11.40 as 1834.

P6495   12 MU 8.11.39; Austin 3.2.41; to RCAF 4.5.41.

P6496   12 MU 12.11.39; 47 MU 6.9.40; to RCAF 27.9.40 as 1719.

P6497   12 MU 13.11.39; 47 MU 5.9.40; to RCAF 26.9.40 as 1726.

P6498   12 MU 13.11.39; 47 MU 5.3.41; to RCAF 25.4.41 as 1984.

P6499   12 MU 12.11.39; Austin 10.2.41; to RAAF 25.3.41.

P6500   12 MU 13.11.39; 47 MU 10.2.41; to RCAF 11.3.41 as 1928.

P6501   12 MU 13.11.39; Austin 6.2.41; to SAAF 29.3.41 as 951.

P6502   Fairey; 12 MU; 47 MU 12.9.40; to RCAF 26.9.40 as 1712.

P6503   12 MU 13.11.39; 47 MU 6.3.41; to RAAF 3.4.41.

P6504   12 MU 18.11.39; 47 MU 13.3.41; to RCAF 29.3.41 as 1912.

P6505   12 MU 18.11.39; 47 MU 13.3.41; to RCAF 19.4.41 as 1945.

P6506   12 MU 18.11.39; 27 MU 9.5.41; Austin 21.5.41; to SAAF 11.7.41.

P6507   12 MU 20.11.39; 47 MU 1.3.41; to RCAF 23.3.41 as 1916.

P6508   12 MU; 47 MU 15.3.41; to RCAF 16.5.41 as 1964.

P6509   12 MU 18.11.39; 47 MU 25.2.41; to RAAF 3.4.41.

P6523   12 MU 18.11.39; 47 MU 14.2.41; to RCAF 11.3.41 as 1925.

P6524   12 MU 20.11.39; Dumfries 22.4.41; to RCAF 22.5.41 as 1957.

P6525   12 MU 20.11.39; Austin 8.5.41; to RCAF 5.41 as 2043.

P6526   12 MU 20.11.39; Dumfries 19.4.41; to RCAF 22.5.41 as 1959

P6527   12 MU 29.11.39; Austin 27.4.41; to RCAF 5.41 as 2040.

P6528   12 MU 28.11.39; 47 MU 20.4.41; to RCAF 24.5.41; not received in Canada.

P6529   12 MU 28.11.39; Austin 6.4.41; to SAAF 15.6.41.

P6530   12 MU 28.11.39; 47 MU 8.1.41; to RCAF 5.2.41 as 1853.

P6531   12 MU 28.11.39; 47 MU 28.2.41; to RAAF 3.4.41.

P6532   12 MU 28.11.39; 47 MU 26.2.41; To RCAF 24.5.41; not received in Canada.

P6533   12 MU 4.12.39; 22 MU 5.3.40; Dumfries 3.5.41; to SAAF 11.7.41; to Middle East 30.1.43.

P6534   12 MU 4.12.39; Austin 3.6.41; to RCAF 6.41 as 2007.

P6535   12 MU 4.12.39; 47 MU 10.2.41; to RCAF 2.3.41 as 1893.

P6536   12 MU 4.12.39; Austin 5.1.41; to RAAF 25.3.41.

P6537   12 MU 4.12.39; undercarriage collapsed taxying, Kirkbride, 10.2.41; 47 MU 21.3.41; to RCAF 17.5.41 as 1965.

P6538   12 MU 16.12.39; 47 MU 30.9.40; to RCAF 27.10.40 as 1779.

P6539   12 MU 4.12.39; 47 MU 21.9.40; to RCAF 8.10.40 as 1736.

P6540   12 MU 4.12.39; 22 MU 5.3.40; 12 MU 10.4.40; 47 MU 12.1.41; to RCAF 5.2.41 as 1857.

P6541   12 MU 4.12.39; Austin 9.1.41; Parks 6.2.41; to RCAF 10.4.41.

P6542   12 MU 4.12.39; 47 MU 8.2.41; to RCAF 8.3.41 as 1887.

P6543   12 MU 4.12.39; 47 MU 6.2.41; to RCAF 8.3.41 as 1883.

P6544   12 MU 4.12.39; 47 MU 8.9.40; to RCAF 26.9.40 as 1710.

P6545   12 MU 4.12.39; 47 MU 28.2.41; to RCAF 3.4.41 as 1926.

P6546   12 MU 4.12.39; 47 MU 8.9.40; to RCAF 9.40 as 1717.

P6547   12 MU 4.12.39; 47 MU 10.2.41; to RCAF 8.3.41 as 1889.

P6548   12 MU 18.12.39; 47 MU 20.3.41; to RCAF 27.4.41 as 1980.

P6549   12 MU 18.12.39; Austin 8.1.41; Parks 23.1.41; to SAAF 29.6.41 as 978.

P6550   12 MU 14.12.39; Dumfries 22.4.41; to RCAF 22.5.41 as 1960.

P6551   12 MU 14.12.39; 47 MU 14.3.41; to RCAF 24.5.41; not received in Canada.

P6552   12 MU 14.12.39; 47 MU 13.1.41; to RCAF 5.2.41 as 1840.

P6553   12 MU 14.12.39; 47 MU 9.1.41; to RCAF 5.2.41 as 1855.

P6554   12 MU 18.12.39; to RCAF 29.3.41 as 1915.

P6555   12 MU 18.12.39; Austin 3.2.41; to SAAF 29.3.41 as 955.

P6556   12 MU 16.12.39; 47 MU 24.9.40; to RCAF 14.10.40 as 1742.

P6557   12 MU 20.12.39; 47 MU 12.9.40; to RCAF 26.9.40 as 1709.

P6558   12 MU 16.12.39; 47 MU 13.3.41; to RCAF 25.4.41 as 1979.

P6559   12 MU 16.12.39; 47 MU 9.1.41; to RCAF 5.2.41 as 1854.

P6560   12 MU 16.12.39; 3 School of General Reconnaissance 1.1.41; Parks 15.1.41; to SAAF 5.2.41 as 934.

P6561   12 MU 16.12.39; Austin 27.12.40; Parks 14.1.41; to SAAF 16.2.41 as 941.

P6562   12 MU 19.12.39; Austin 30.1.41; to RCAF 13.5.41.

P6563   12 MU 20.12.39; 47 MU 15.3.41; to RCAF 27.4.41 as 1952.

P6564   12 MU 19.12.39; Austin 6.2.41; Parks 26.3.41; to RCAF 10.4.41.

P6565   12 MU 4.1.40; Austin 27.12.40; Fairey 10.2.41; 47 MU 26.5.41; to RCAF 11.6.41 as 2000.

P6566   12 MU 4.1.40; 47 MU 1.3.41; to RCAF 1.4.41 as 1976.

P6567   20 MU 2.1.40; 301 Sqn 24.7.40; 27 MU 20.11.40; 47 MU 6.2.41; to RCAF 21.2.41 as 1867.

P6568   20 MU 2.1.40; 150 Sqn 26.7.40; 142 Sqn 28.8.40; 18 MU 1.1.41; 47 MU 3.2.41; to RCAF 13.3.41 as 1920.

P6569   20 MU 2.1.40; 301 Sqn 24.7.40; 47 MU 11.11.40; to RCAF 16.12.40 as 1806.

P6570   20 MU 2.1.40; 98 Sqn 14.7.40. Engine cut in circuit; crashlanded in bog, Kaldadarnes, Iceland, 14.9.40; SOC 26.11.40.

P6571   20 MU 2.1.40; 12 Sqn 26.7.40; Binbrook. Engine cut; crashed in forced landing, Wainfleet Sands, Lincs., 11.7.41; SOC 25.7.41.

P6572   20 MU 29.2.40; 142 Sqn 26.7.40; overshot forced landing and undercarriage collapsed, Binbrook, 4.8.40; Fairey 14.8.40; 15 EFTS 11.10.40; Polish FTS 27.12.40; undershot approach and hit hedge, Hucknall, 23.3.41; ROS; 16(P)FTS 13.7.41; 18 MU 19.3.42; De Havilland 18.4.42; Rosenfield 19.5.42; 27 MU 15.7.42; 239 Sqn 5.8.42; 27 MU 31.12.42; SOC 11.3.44.

P6596   20 MU 10.3.40; 47 MU 23.5.40; to SAAF 2.7.40 as 925.

P6597   19 MU 14.2.40; 6 MU 11.3.40; AASF 13.5.40; 12 Sqn 16.6.40. Missing on night raid on Boulogne, 19.8.40; PO F.W. Cook, Sgt J. Stewart and Sgt S.I. Harrison captured

P6598   19 MU 14.2.40; 6 MU 11.3.40; AASF 19.5.40; 226 Sqn 20.5.40. Crashed during raid on Vernon, St.Pierre-d'Autils, Eure, 11.6.40; Sgt G.P. McLoughlin, Sgt E. Marrows and F.Sgt J.A., Russell killed

P6599   19 MU 14.2.40; 6 MU 15.3.40; AASF 18.5.40; 88 Sqn 23.5.40; 4 RSU 26.5.40; 21 AD 29.5.40; Fairey 26.6.40; 47 MU 27.10.40; to RCAF 28.11.40 as 1832.

P6600   19 MU 29.2.40; AASF 21.5.40; 142 Sqn 21.5.40; Fairey 22.9.40; SOC 26.9.40.

P6601   19 MU 14.2.40; 6 MU 15.3.40; AASF 16.5.40; 226 Sqn 17.5.40. Lost formation in bad weather and flew into high ground descending in cloud 4m SW of Cushendall, Co. Antrim, 22.10.40; Sgt P.F. Morris killed, Sgt J.C. Pearce and Sgt J. McMaster; one killed one injured; SOC 4.11.40.

P6602   19 MU 14.2.40; 6 MU 15.3.40; AASF 21.5.40; 150 Sqn 21.5.40; 142 Sqn 30.9.40; 27 MU 2.12.40; 47 MU 1.3.41; to RAAF 3.4.41.

P6603   613 Sqn for Army Co-operation trials 7.5.40; 8 MU 4.7.40; 142 Sqn 25.8.40; to GI airframe 16.9.40.

P6604   Fairey 13.2.40; to RHAF 3.40.

P6605   Fairey 23.2.40; to RHAF 3.40.

P6606   To RHAF 3.40.

Battle Trainer P6631, with damage to wing-tip while with No.12 Service Flying Training School. (via Wg Cdr C G Jefford)

P6607	To RHAF 3.40.
P6608	To RHAF 3.40.
P6609	To RHAF 3.40.
P6610	To RHAF 3.40.
P6611	To RHAF 3.40.
P6612	To RHAF 3.40.
P6613	To RHAF 3.40.
P6614	Fairey; originally for Greece but returned to RAF standard and re-allocated to RAF; 9 MU 9.9.40; 1 FTS 17.9.40. Control lost on night take-off; dived into ground, Shrewton, 11.11.41; SOC 18.11.41.
P6615	To RHAF 3.40.
P6616	15 EFTS 20.2.40; Hucknall 7.11.40; Polish FTS 4.12.40; 16(P)FTS 13.7.41; 27 MU 30.1.42; to 3312M at 6 SofTT 5.8.42.
P6617	7 FTS 27.2.40; CFS 26.10.40; 2 BGS 11.2.41; landed with undercarriage unlocked, Millom, 14.3.41; ROS; undercarriage jammed, bellylanded Millom, 3.6.41; ROS; 1 FTS 26.9.41; 9 MU 24.5.42; 3 AGS 11.8.42; 18 MU 24.1.43; SOC 14.7.44.
P6618	7 FTS 27.2.40; 1 FTS 22.1.41; bellylanded in error, Netheravon, 12.3.41; ROS; Western A/W 10.1.42; 23 MU 25.3.42; 3 AGS 30.7.42; taxied into crane, Castle Kennedy, 28.10.42; ROS; Mona 27.2.43; SOC 14.7.44.
P6619	7 FTS 27.2.40; ran out of fuel and bellylanded Marholm, near Peterborough, 5.8.40; Fairey 12.8.40; 9 MU 11.12.40; 1 FTS 7.4.41; undercarriage leg jammed, bellylanded, Netheravon, 31.8.41; ROS; engine cut; bellylanded NE of Boscombe Down, 9.11.41; Rosenfield 14.11.41; 23 MU 18.3.42; 3 AGS 30.7.42; taxied into roller and undercarriage leg collapsed, Castle Kennedy, 23.11.42; 27 MU 6.3.43; SOC 23.8.44.
P6620	11 FTS 27.2.40; 18 MU 13.7.40; Austin 16.10.40; to RCAF 5.1.41.
P6621	11 FTS 27.2.40; 1 FTS 24.6.40; undercarriage leg collapsed in heavy landing, Stormy Down, 15.3.41; Austin 18.12.41; 18 MU 27.1.43; SOC 19.11.43.
P6622	11 FTS 27.2.40; 1 FTS 21.6.40; bellylanded in error, Netheravon, 21.7.40; ROS; bellylanded in error, Netheravon, 19.3.41; ROS; bellylanded in error, Shrewton, 20.9.41; Rosenfield 24.9.41; 47 MU 25.1.42; to RAAF 7.4.42.
P6623	12 FTS 28.2.40; 16(P)FTS 15.6.41; 27 MU 8.2.42; to 3557M at 12 SofTT 8.6.42; 771 Sqn, ATC, 6.2.43.
P6624	12 FTS 28.2.40; 7 FTS 23.8.40; undercarriage collapsed on landing, Sibson, 8.12.40; ROS; HQ ATA, 26.3.41; bellylanded, White Waltham, 12.6.41; ROS; engine cut on take-off, bellylanded near White Waltham, 2.10.41; ROS; engine cut on take-off, bellylanded Snow Hill, Berks., 3.3.42; Rosenfield 4.3.42; 27 MU 29.4.42; 3 AGS 14.7.42; 27 MU 15.12.42; SOC 30.6.43.
P6625	12 FTS 29.2.40; undercarriage jammed; bellylanded, Grantham, 13.6.40; 1 FTS 2.7.40; 12 FTS 28.1.41; 16(P)FTS 7.6.41; undershot forced landing, Newton, 27.11.41; Austin 1.12.41; 16(P)FTS 9.12.41; 9 MU 16.3.43; SOC 9.9.44.
P6626	12 FTS 28.2.40; bellylanded in error, Barkston LG, 11.6.40; ROS; undercarriage collapsed in heavy landing at night, Harlaxton, 17.12.40; ROS; 16(P)FTS 15.6.41; bellylanded in error, Hucknall, 5.7.41; ROS; Rosenfield 13.2.42; 9 MU 4.8.42; 27 MU 17.8.42; 3 AGS 27.8.42; 18 MU 18.2.43; SOC 19.11.43.
P6627	12 FTS 5.3.40; wheel ran into hole taxying and torn off, Desford, 5.4.40; ROS; 16(P)FTS 12.6.41; engine cut; hit trees in forced landing, Wood Lane, Hucknall, 11.7.41; Fairey 18.7.41; 1 FTS 13.10.41; Rosenfield 11.2.42; 38 MU 23.2.42; 3 AGS 3.9.42; 27 MU 9.2.43; SOC 23.8.44.

P6628   12 FTS 5.3.40; 16(P)FTS 16.7.41; undercarriage leg jammed; bellylanded, Newton, 15.8.41; ROS; undercarriage collapsed after landing, Newton, 2.11.41; ROS; 27 MU 10.4.42; 29 MU 1.12.42; SOC 30.9.44.

P6629   12 FTS 5.3.40; bellylanded Harlaxton, 29.10.40; 16(P)FTS 7.6.41; 23 MU 29.3.42; 18 MU 16.10.42; SOC 14.7.44.

P6630   12 FTS 5.3.40; undercarriage leg jammed; bellylanded, Grantham, 21.5.40; ROS; undercarriage jammed; bellylanded Grantham, 31.7.40; ROS; undercarriage collapsed on landing, Harlaxton, 21.9.40; ROS; overshot flarepath into ditch, Grantham, 16.2.41; ROS; 16(P)FTS 15.6.41. Stalled in practice forced landing, Grange Farm, Hockenton, Newark, Notts., 24.6.41; SOC 30.6.41.

P6631   12 FTS 8.3.40; bellylanded in error, Harlaxton, 14.10.40; ROS; 16(P)FTS 12.6.41; bellylanded in error, Hucknall, 19.6.41; Fairey 24.6.41; 47 MU 16.10.41; to RAAF 5.12.41.

P6632   7 FTS 16.3.40; engine cut; bellylanded, Langtoft, near Market Deeping, Lincs., 17.10.40; Rosenfield 1.1.41; Fairey 10.1.41; 22 MU 23.3.41; 1 FTS 24.4.41; Fairey 24.5.41; 1 FTS 20.8.41; 23 MU 22.4.42; 18 MU 22.4.42; 3 AGS 16.8.42. Engine cut; forcelanded in lake, Colts Loch, Castle Kennedy, 9.11.42; SOC 7.12.42.

P6633   7 FTS 16.3.40; undercarriage collapsed on landing, Peterborough, 28.5.40; ROS; undercarriage jammed, bellylanded, Sibson, 31.10.40; Rosenfield 4.1.41; Fairey 10.1.41; 22 MU 6.4.41; 1 FTS 24.4.41; hit hedge in forced landing in bad weather, Llandrindod Wells, Radnor, 7.8.41; Rosenfield 22.8.41; 47 MU 21.11.41; to RCAF 19.12.41 as 2120.

P6634   7 FTS 16.3.40; overshot landing, Sibson, 22.8.40; Fairey 4.9.40; 22 MU 10.2.41; 1 FTS 14.5.41; Western A/W 11.12.41; LEP 30.1.42; 18 MU 4.2.42; SOC 14.7.44.

P6635   12 FTS 8.3.40; engine cut after take-off; bellylanded, St Gonerby, near Grantham, 29.8.40; Austin 8.9.40; 9 MU 13.2.41; 1 FTS 4.4.41; 23 MU 27.2.42; 3 AGS 27.7.42; 18 MU 29.1.43; SOC 16.10.43.

P6636   12 FTS 8.3.40. Engine lost power on approach to forced landing while lost; hit trees, Cossington, Leics., 21.12.40; SOC 2.1.41.

P6637   15 EFTS 10.3.40; Hucknall 7.12.40; Polish FTS 5.12.40; 16(P)FTS 13.7.41; 23 MU 26.2.42; 18 MU 11.9.42; 1600 Flight 18.11.42; 1603 Flight 12.2.43; SOC 11.9.43.

P6638   12 FTS 18.3.40; 16(P)FTS 7.6.41; 23 MU 29.3.42; hit drogue and forcelanded, Cark, 21.12.42; ROS; 1609 Flight 8.2.43; SOC 7.5.43.

P6639   15 EFTS 10.3.40; Polish FTS 19.12.40; 16(P)FTS 13.7.41; Rosenfield 27.8.41; Fairey 24.8.41; 47 MU 15.11.41; to RCAF 21.12.41 as 2118.

P6640   7 FTS 15.3.40; engine cut; forcelanded, Edgebolton, Salop., 2.12.40; 27 MU 2.12.40; 16(P)FTS 26.7.41; overshot forced landing and hit fence, Newton, 18.12.41; Austin 21.12.41; 16(P)FTS at 31.12.41; 27 MU 2.4.42; to 3317M at 5 SofTT 8.8.42.

P6641   7 FTS 15.3.40; undershot flarepath and undercarriage collapsed, Sibson, 1.10.40; ROS; 27 MU 10.2.41; 16(P)FTS 16.9.41; 23 MU 2.4.42; 3 AGS 5.8.42; 27 MU 6.3.43; SOC 23.8.44.

P6642   7 FTS 15.3.40; undershot landing and hit obstruction, Peterborough, 27.7.40; ROS; 22 MU 11.2.41; 47 MU 6.9.41; to RAAF 27.9.41.

P6643   7 FTS 15.3.40; 27 MU 2.12.40; HQ, ATA, 1.6.42; 1609 Flight ; 27 MU 8.2.43; SOC 30.6.43.

P6644   7 FTS 15.3.40; engine cut; hit tree in forced landing, Walton, 2m N of Peterborough, 7.10.40; Fairey 12.10.40; PRU 2.3.41; landed with undercarriage unlocked, Benson, 12.5.41; ROS; Western A/W 6.11.41; 9 MU 8.12.41; 3 AGS 28.7.42; collided with Botha L6173 on approach, Castle Kennedy, 26.8.42; Rosenfield 4.9.42; 18 MU 7.11.42; SOC 14.7.44.

P6645   7 FTS 16.3.40; hit tree on night approach, Peterborough, 13.5.40; ROS; 1 FTS 17.11.40; bellylanded at night near Shrewton, 27.11.40; ROS; Rosenfield 11.2.41; 9 MU 4.5.41; HQ, ATA, 21.8.41; Southern A/C 10.1.42; HQ, ATA, 9.3.42; 27 MU 1.6.42; Southern A/C 23.7.43; SOC 10.3.44.

P6663   7 FTS 16.3.40; undercarriage collapsed on landing, Dishforth, 2.12.40; ROS; 27 MU 24.3.41; 47 MU 5.7.41; to RCAF 24.7.41 as 2053.

P6664   7 FTS 21.3.40; 1 FTS 21.11.40; Western A/W 6.11.41; 47 MU 11.12.41; to RAAF 21.1.42; SOC 13.3.45.

P6665   11 FTS 15.3.40; 1 FTS 2.7.40; engine cut; hit wall in forced landing, Turkdean, Glos., 8.11.40; ROS; damaged in heavy landing, Netheravon, 12.7.41; Fairey 18.7.41; 47 MU 17.11.41; to RCAF 19.12.41 as 2121.

P6666   11 FTS 20.3.40; Fairey 25.6.40; 22 MU 20.12.40; 10 BGS 5.6.41; 10 AOS; 4 AGS 15.7.42; 27 MU 26.11.42; SOC 30.6.43.

P6667   11 FTS 20.3.40; undercarriage collapsed after landing, Shawbury, 17.4.40; Fairey 22.6.40; 18 MU 10.2.41; 22 MU 10.2.41; 18 MU 12.2.41; 2 BGS 25.5.41; 1 FTS 19.9.41; 23 MU 8.4.42; 18 MU 15.9.42; SOC 16.10.43.

P6668   11 FTS 20.3.40; 1 FTS 21.6.40; bellylanded in error, Shrewton, 5.2.41; Fairey 25.2.41; 6 MU 6.5.41; overshot landing and hit hedge, Hucknall, 30.6.41; ROS; 16(P)FTS 30.6.41; 23 MU 18.2.42; SOC 22.9.43.

P6669   11 FTS 20.3.40; 1 FTS 2.7.40; engine cut; bellylanded Shoddesdon, 3m SE of Ludgershall, Wilts., 29.11.40; Fairey 18.12.40; 9 MU 23.3.41; 1 FTS 7.4.41; engine cut; bellylanded, High Post, 23.10.41; ROS; hit by P6725 while parked, Netheravon, 25.1.42; Rosenfield 2.2.42; 38 MU 17.4.42; 3 AGS 14.7.42; 27 MU 15.12.42; SOC 21.1.44; 471.55 hours.

P6670   11 FTS 21.3.40; 18 MU 13.7.40; Austin 10.8.40; Parks 6.9.40; to RCAF 8.10.40.

P6671   11 FTS 21.3.40; 1 FTS 21.6.40; engine lost power; overshot flarepath and hit obstruction, Shrewton, 22.8.40; ROS; SOC 12.5.41.

P6672   11 FTS 21.3.40; 18 MU 13.7.40; Austin 10.8.40; Parks 30.8.40; to RCAF 3.10.40.

P6673   11 FTS 21.3.40; 1 FTS 21.6.40. Undershot night approach and hit tent, Shrewton, 1.1.41; to 2545M; to RCAF 1.41 as instructional airframe A125; to RNZAF 1941 as instructional airframe Inst42.

P6674   12 FTS 21.3.40; hit tractor in forced landing, Shrewton, 11.2.41; ROS. Shot down by enemy aircraft, Stroxton, 1½m SE of Harlaxton, 21.4.41; Sgt. R. Kilbuern and LAC A.J.E. Foster killed; SOC 26.4.41; 592.20 hours.

P6675   12 FTS 27.3.40. Control lost after take-off; dived into ground on night training flight near Harlaxton, 27.4.40; Sgt B.O. Whiteley killed; 58 MU 29.4.40; SOC 2.5.40; 22.55 hours.

P6676   12 FTS 27.3.40; engine cut on take-off; bellylanded 1m W of Barkston LG, 20.8.40; ROS; undercarriage collapsed in heavy landing, Harlaxton, 2.5.41; Fairey 10.5.41; 9 BGS 25.7.41; 27 MU 16.6.42; Rosenfield 19.10.42; 18 MU 6.12.42; SOC 19.11.43.

P6677   12 FTS 27.3.40; undercarriage leg collapsed taxying at night, Grantham, 6.5.40; ROS; 9 MU 23.3.41; 1 FTS 20.4.41; engine cut; bellylanded near Upavon, 20.7.41; Rosenfield 27.7.41; 47 MU 24.11.41; to RAAF 5.12.41.

P6678   1 FTS 29.3.40; bellylanded in error, Netheravon, 13.5.40; Fairey 18.5.40; 38 MU 7.7.40; 304 Sqn 26.8.40; 27 MU 7.12.40; 16(P)FTS 14.7.41; bellylanded in error, Newton, 14.9.41; ROS; 27 MU 8.2.42; to 3310M at 6 SofTT 5.8.42.

P6679   1 FTS 5.4.40; bellylanded in error, Shrewton, 27.10.40; ROS; Western A/W 16.4.41; 16(P)FTS 6.5.41; 23 MU 15.3.42; SOC 14.9.43.

P6680   12 FTS 2.4.40; 1 FTS 11.7.41. Bellylanded in error, Shrewton, 8.11.41; to 2934M at 4 SofTT 11.2.42; 2 SofTT 3.4.43.

P6681   1 FTS 29.3.40; undercarriage collapsed in heavy landing, Netheravon, 23.3.41; Western A/W 16.4.41; 1

Battle Trainer R7366 with No.1 Service Flying Training School which trained both RAF and Fleet Air Arm pilots.

FTS 1.5.41; 16(P)FTS 23.7.41; undercarriage raised in error while taxying, Netheravon, 21.10.41; ROS; 1 FTS 16.7.42; 27 MU 12.8.42; 231 Sqn 12.9.42; 27 MU 21.12.42; SOC 23.8.44.

P6682   12 FTS 2.4.40; engine cut on take-off; swung and undercarriage collapsed, Barkston LG, 30.5.40; Fairey 8.6.40; 9 MU 6.3.41; 1 FTS 7.4.41; engine cut; bellylanded, Shrewton, 22.8.41; ROS; 23 MU 27.2.42; 18 MU 16.10.42; 1600 Flight 21.11.42; 27 MU 14.3.43; SOC 23.8.44.

P6683   12 FTS 2.4.40; engine lost power on approach; hit hedge, Barkston LG, 30.5.40; ROS; landed with undercarriage unlocked, Barkston LG, 8.8.40; ROS; 1 FTS 11.7.41; 23 MU 27.2.42; SOC 14.9.43.

P6684   12 FTS 2.4.40; skidded in forced landing while lost and hit dyke, Gosberton Marsh, Lincs., 24.6.40; Fairey 1.7.40; 27 MU 12.4.41; 1 FTS 8.6.41; Western A/W 6.11.41; 47 MU 11.12.41; To RCAF 7.2.42 as 2129.

P6685   12 FTS 2.4.40; damaged in heavy landing, Grantham, 8.5.40; Burtonwood 22.5.40; Fairey 2.6.40; 12 MU 16.7.40; 305 Sqn 1.9.40; 307 Sqn 24.11.40; 256 Sqn 14.4.41; engine cut on take-off; overshot approach and crashed, Squires Gate, 1.5.42; ROS; 59 OTU 5.7.42; SOC 30.6.43.

P6686   12 FTS 4.4.40; tipped up taxying, Grantham, 21.4.40; ROS; bellylanded in error, Harlaxton, 26.3.41; ROS. Hit high ground while low flying 2m N of Melton Mowbray, 11.6.41; SOC 15.6.41; 428.15 hours.

P6687   12 FTS 4.4.40; engine cut; bellylanded near Whittlesey, Cambs., 3.5.40; 54 MU 5.40; Fairey 27.5.40; 38 MU 4.7.40; 302 Sqn 19.7.40; 308 Sqn 17.9.40; engine cut; overshot landing, Christchurch, 15.6.41; Rosenfield 20.6.41; Fairey 23.6.41; 1 FTS 26.8.41; to 2933M at 4 SofTT 11.2.42.

P6688   12 FTS 5.4.40; engine cut; bellylanded, Besford, near Pershore, 15.2.41; Fairey 21.3.41; 1 FTS 21.5.41;

bellylanded in error, High Post, 26.8.41; ROS; Rosenfield 19.1.42; 27 MU 1.5.42; Rosenfield 13.10.42; 27 MU 15.11.42; SOC 23.8.44.

P6689   1 FTS 5.4.40; engine cut; bellylanded 1m NW of Winterbourne, Wilts., 17.10.40; Fairey 24.10.40; 47 MU 6.3.41; to RCAF 1.4.41 as 1974.

P6690   1 FTS 10.4.40; bellylanded in error, Netheravon, 24.5.40; stalled on landing and damaged, Netheravon, 13.9.40; Austin 3.10.40; 9 MU 13.4.41; 1 FTS 25.5.41; bellylanded in error, Shrewton, 2.11.41; 23 MU 27.2.42; SOC 22.9.43.

P6691   1 FTS 5.4.40; Western A/W 24.6.41; 16(P)FTS 26.7.41; hit obstruction in forced landing while lost, Burnaston, Derby, 4.9.41; Rosenfield 19.9.41; 47 MU 11.11.41; to RCAF 24.12.41 as 2133.

P6692   Polish OTU 6.4.40; 18 OTU; 32 MU 18.5.41; 47 MU 16.7.41; to RCAF 8.8.41 as 2060.

P6718   Polish OTU 6.4.40; 18 OTU; 38 MU 29.11.40; 3 AGS 28.7.42; Mona; 18 MU 27.2.43; SOC 19.11.43.

P6719   Polish OTU 6.4.40; 18 OTU; 20 MU 27.11.40; 16(P)FTS 7.9.41; 9 MU 20.5.42; 3 AGS 28.7.42; 18 MU 15.12.42; SOC 14.7.44.

P6720   1 FTS 10.4.40; bounced on landing and wing hit ground, Shrewton, 10.1.41; ROS; tyre burst on landing; swung and undercarriage collapsed, Shrewton, 24.3.41; ROS; undercarriage jammed; bellylanded, Stormy Down, 20.6.41; Fairey 30.6.41; 47 MU 15.11.41; to RAAF 17.12.41.

P6721   18 OTU 10.4.40; Fairey 28.11.40; 16(P)FTS 23.4.41; undercarriage jammed; landed on one wheel, Hucknall, 13.6.41; ROS; undercarriage collapsed in heavy landing, Newton, 16.12.41; Austin 21.12.41; 16(P)FTS at 31.12.41; 23 MU 15.3.42; SOC 8.9.43.

P6722   1 FTS 10.4.40; 23 MU 27.2.42; 3 AGS 30.8.42; 27 MU 15.12.42; SOC 23.8.44.

P6723   1 FTS 10.4.40; engine cut; bellylanded High Post LG, 7.5.40; Fairey 6.6.40; 38 MU 8.7.40; 304 Sqn 26.8.40; 27 MU 7.12.40; 16(P)FTS 17.7.41; 23 MU 20.2.42; SOC 22.9.43.

P6724   11 FTS 21.4.40; 18 MU 13.7.40; Austin 7.8.40; Parks 26.8.40; to RCAF 1.10.40 (fuselage) and 21.10.40 (wings).

P6725   1 FTS 17.4.40; overshot landing and hit hedge, Netheravon, 30.5.40; Fairey 7.6.40; 38 MU 4.7.40; 310 Sqn 20.7.40; undercarriage leg jammed up; crashlanded Dumfries, 5.9.40; ROS; 12 OTU 13.9.40; undercarriage collapsed on landing, Benson, 27.11.40; 20 MU 22.12.40; 1 FTS 19.4.41; bellylanded in error, Shrewton, 18.11.41; ROS; ran into P6669 taxying, Netheravon, 25.1,42; 23 MU 10.3.42; SOC 8.9.43.

P6726   1 FTS 17.4.40. Bellylanded in error, Netheravon 18.7.40; to 2144M 7.40; to RCAF 9.40 as instructional airframe A99.

P6727   1 FTS 17.4.40; taxied into ditch, Netheravon, 9.9.40; Fairey 11.10.40; 9 MU 2.3.41; 1 FTS 6.4.41; lost wheel in heavy landing, Netheravon, 29.5.41; engine cut after take-off, bellylanded 2m SW of Netheravon, 11.8.41; ROS; Western A/W 10.1.42; 23 MU 29.3.42; 18 MU 28.10.42; 1609 Flight 13.11.42; 1606 Flight 22.6.43; to 3910M at 2 SofTT 15.7.43.

P6728   1 FTS 17.4.40; undercarriage jammed; bellylanded Aberfield Hall, 2m NE of Shinfield, Berks., 7.10.40; Fairey 13.10.40; 27 MU 23.2.41; 1 FTS 2.5.41; 38 MU 26.1.42; 27 MU 22.10.42; SOC 1.12.42.

P6729   1 FTS 17.4.40; taxied into ditch at night, Shrewton, 24.2.41; ROS; ran away while taxying, Netheravon, 16.7.41; Fairey 21.7.41; 47 MU 24.11.41; to RAAF 17.12.41.

P6730   11 FTS 17.4.40; 18 MU 13.7.40; Austin 10.8.40; Parks 6.9.40; to RCAF 12.10.40.

P6731   11 FTS 21.4.40; 18 MU 13.7.40; Austin 19.8.40; Parks 6.9.40; to RCAF 8.10.40.

P6732   12 MU 9.5.40; 98 Sqn 12.5.40; 17 Sqn 25.6.40; 5 MU 11.7.40; Andover 17.7.40; 18 MU 26.7.40; Austin 3.2.41; Parks 2.4.41; to RCAF 10.4.41.

P6733   11 FTS 21.4.40; Fairey 23.6.40; 12 FTS 13.4.41; undercarriage collapsed in heavy landing, Harlaxton, 22.4.41; ROS; 1 FTS 30.6.41; damaged in heavy landing, Netheravon, 1.10.41; Rosenfield 2.10.41; 18 MU 7.3.42; 309 Sqn 2.6.42; 1 AACU 17.11.42; 1600 Flight 31.12.42; 1603 Flight 22.6.43; SOC 11.9.43.

P6734   11 FTS 21.4.40; 18 MU 13.7.40; Austin 10.8.40; Parks 14.9.40; to RCAF 12.10.40.

P6735   11 FTS 2.5.40; 1 FTS 2.7.40; overshot landing and hit obstruction, Netheravon, 31.7.40; ROS; ran into ditch taxying at night, Shrewton, 7.12.40; ROS; bellylanded in error, Netheravon, 4.4.41; ROS; 16(P)FTS 5.8.41; 27 MU 13.2.42; to 3311M at 6 SofTT 5.8.42.

P6736   11 FTS 2.5.40; bellylanded in error, Shawbury, 2.6.40; ROS; 1 FTS 10.9.40; bellylanded in error at night, Shrewton, 23.3.41; ROS; Rosenfield 27.11.41; 23 MU 11.4.42; 3 AGS 25.7.40; Mona; 18 MU 27.2.43; SOC 19.11.43.

P6737   11 FTS 2.5.40; 1 FTS 2.7.40; bellylanded in error, Porthcawl, 8.8.40; ROS; Western A/W 16.4.41; 1 FTS 19.4.41; engine cut; bellylanded, Netheravon, 31.7.41; Fairey 5.8.41; 47 MU 15.11.41; to RCAF 19.12.41 as 2123.

P6750   CFS 3.5.40; engine cut; bellylanded and hit wall, Glen Truan, Isle of Man, 6.10.40; Fairey 17.10.40; 9 MU 2.3.41; 1 FTS 4.4.41; engine cut; overshot forced landing, Stormy Down, 25.6.41; Fairey 30.6.41; 47 MU 6.11.41; to RCAF 19.12.41 as 2119.

P6751   12 FTS 3.5.40; bellylanded in error, Harlaxton, 25.11.40; ROS; undercarriage collapsed in heavy landing, Harlaxton, 8.1.41; ROS; 16(P)FTS 7.6.41; ROS; undershot landing and undercarriage torn off, Newton, 10.1.42; Austin 19.1.42; 16(P)FTS 4.4.42; 23 MU 5.5.42; SOC 29.9.42.

P6752   CFS 3.5.40; bellylanded in error, Jurby, 10.6.40; Rolls-Royce 17.7.40; 2 BGS 11.2.41; 1 FTS 26.9.41; 38 MU 31.1.42; 14 MU 19.2.42; 38 MU; 5 MU 20.12.42; SOC 15.1.45.

P6753   CFS 3.5.40; 5 BGS. Engine cut on night approach; hit bank and undercarriage collapsed, Jurby, 14.6.40; SOC 25.6.40.

P6754   CFS 3.5.40; 7 FTS 30.5.40; 1 FTS 22.1.41; bellylanded on flarepath in error, Shrewton, 25.2.41; ROS; bellylanded in error, Netheravon, 30.7.41; ROS; landed with undercarriage unlocked, Shrewton, 8.9.41; ROS. Failed to recover from dive bombing attack on range and hit ground, Pepperbox Hill ranges, Wilts., 28.10.41; ALA D. Stewart RN killed; SOC 3.11.41.

P6755   12 MU 9.5.40; 98 Sqn 17.5.40; 12 OTU 25.6.40; swung on take-off and undercarriage collapsed, Benson, 12.8.40; Fairey 22.8.40; 6 MU 5.4.41; 16(P)FTS 30.6.41; 23 MU 17.3.42; SOC 12.9.43.

P6756   12 MU 9.5.40; 98 Sqn 17.5.40; 4 FPP, Engine cut; overshot forced landing into trees, East Lockinge, Wantage, Berks., 13.6.40; SOC 18.6.40.

P6757   12 MU 9.5.40; 98 Sqn 17.5.40; 6 MU 15.6.40; 1 FTS 30.8.40; bellylanded in error, Shrewton, 10.11.40; ROS; 23 MU 11.2.42; taxied into Spitfire EP980, Prestwick, 6.9.42; ROS; 2 AGS 6.9.42; 18 MU 21.10.42; SOC 14.7.44.

P6758   12 MU 9.5.40; 98 Sqn 17.5.40; 6 MU 17.6.40; 3 FPP 27.6.40; landed with one wheel up, Whitchurch, 19.7.40; 1 FTS 17.9.41; bellylanded in error, Shrewton, 14.10.41; ROS; 23 MU 24.3.42; 18 MU 30.9.42; 2 AGS 24.10.42; 18 MU 3.4.43; SOC 14.7.44.

P6759   12 MU 9.5.40; 98 Sqn 17.5.40; 12 OTU 25.6.40; 103 Sqn 16.7.40; 12 OTU 7.11.40; 20 MU 14.12.40; 1 FTS 17.4.41; bellylanded in error, Shrewton, 17.9.41; ROS; undercarriage collapsed after landing, Netheravon, 10.10.41; Austin 10.11.41; 1 SFTS 24.12.41; 23 MU 1.3.42; 3 AGS 20.8.42; 18 MU 2.2.43; SOC 14.7.44.

P6760   12 MU 9.5.40; 98 Sqn 17.5.40; 6 MU 15.6.40; 3 FPP 31.8.40; bellylanded in error, Whitchurch, 7.9.40; ROS; 32 MU 14.2.41; 47 MU 22.5.41; to RCAF 10.6.41 as 2001.

P6761   12 MU 9.5.40; 98 Sqn 17.5.40; 12 OTU 25.6.40; 142 Sqn 19.7.40; 2 Sqn RCAF 9.1.41; 38 MU 19.3.41; HQ ATA 24.8.41; Rosenfield 22.6.42; 27 MU 4.8.42; 215 MU 2.9.42; 3 PATP 13.9.42; to SAAF 31.12.42.

P6762   12 MU 10.5.40; 98 Sqn 17.5.40; 12 OTU 25.6.40; 22 MU 15.12.40; 47 MU 12.9.41; to RAAF 27.9.41.

P6763   12 MU 10.5.40; 98 Sqn 17.5.40; 12 OTU 25.6.40; 20 MU 19.12.40; 16(P)FTS 16.7.41; 27 MU 16.2.42; to 3559M at 359 Sqn ATC 6.2.43.

P6764   6 BGS 10.5.40; 7 BGS 25.5.40; 1 FTS 18.9.40; bellylanded in error, Netheravon, 24.10.40; ROS; force-landed while lost and ran into hedge, Swallowcliffe, Wilts., 26.12.40; ROS. Flew into Town Quarry, Weston-super-Mare, in bad visibility, 25.1.41; F/Lt T.P. de la Rue killed; SOC 4.2.41.

P6765   12 FTS 14.5.40; Fairey 2.10.40; 9 MU 10.4.41; 1 FTS 20.4.41; bellylanded in error, Shrewton, 19.8.41; ROS; Austin 15.3.42; 1 FTS 3.10.42; Netheravon 6.12.42; 27 MU 6.12.42; 1 FTS; undercarriage collapsed on landing, Shrewton, 6.1.43; ROS; SOC 23.8.44.

P6766   12 FTS 14.5.40. Overshot forced landing while lost and hit railway embankment near Hubberts Bridge, 3m W of Boston, Lincs., 29.12.40; SOC 8.1.41.

P6767   12 FTS 14.5.40; undercarriage collapsed in heavy landing, Harlaxton, 15.4.41; ROS; 1 FTS 30.6.41; 23 MU 1.3.42; 3 AGS 12.8.42; 18 MU 15.12.42; SOC 16.10.43.

P6768   12 FTS 20.5.40; engine cut on take-off, bellylanded 1m S of Barkston LG, 10.9.40; Austin 23.9.40; 9 MU 15.3.41; 1 FTS 20.4.41; bellylanded in error, Shrewton, 2.9.41; ROS; 23 MU 9.3.42; 18 MU 6.10.42; SOC 19.11.43.

P6769   12 FTS 20.5.40. Engine cut; overshot forced landing and hit gun post, Harlaxton 7.4.41; Rosenfield 15.4.41; SOC 1.5.41.

R7439 was selected as the first Battle to be re-engined with a Wright Cyclone in Canada. As the supply of Merlins remained adequate, plans for further conversions were abandoned. (via Don Hannah)

100 Fairey Battle Is delivered by Austin, Longbridge, between October 1939 and May 1940. Contract B2580/39.

R3922	36 MU 31.10.39; 9 MU 12.6.40; 47 MU 5.10.40; to RCAF 27.10.40 as 1744.
R3923	36 MU 28.10.39; 9 MU 12.6.40; 47 MU 30.9.40; to RCAF 27.10.40 as 1770.
R3924	36 MU 28.10.39; to RAAF 18.8.40.
R3925	36 MU 20.11.39; to RAAF 2.11.40.
R3926	36 MU 28.10.39; 9 MU 12.6.40; 47 MU 10.10.40; to RCAF 27.10.40 as 1777.
R3927	36 MU 31.10.39; 9 MU 29.6.40; 47 MU 30.8.40; to RAAF 18.9.40.
R3928	36 MU 8.11.39; 9 MU 12.6.40; 47 MU 29.8.40; to RAAF 27.10.40.
R3929	36 MU 30.10.39; 9 MU 29.5.40; 47 MU 11.10.40; to RAAF 2.11.40.
R3930	36 MU 8.11.39; 9 MU 29.5.40; 47 MU 27.9.40; to RCAF 27.10.40 as 1751.
R3931	36 MU 31.10.39; 9 MU 12.6.40; 47 MU 17.10.40; to RAAF 14.11.40.
R3932	36 MU 8.11.39; 9 MU 29.5.40; 47 MU 10.10.40; to RCAF 27.11.40 as 1823.
R3933	36 MU 8.11.39; 9 MU 29.5.40; 47 MU 27.9.40; to RCAF 27.10.40 as 1775.
R3934	36 MU 31.10.39; 9 MU 29.6.40; 47 MU 30.8.40; to RAAF 18.8.40.
R3935	36 MU 16.11.39; 47 MU; to RCAF 6.9.40 as 1701.
R3936	36 MU 14.11.39; to RAAF 19.9.40.
R3937	36 MU 8.11.39; 9 MU 29.5.40; 47 MU 27.9.40; to RCAF 27.10.40 as 1745.
R3938	36 MU 8.11.39; 47 MU; to SAAF 19.7.40 as 926.
R3939	36 MU 8.11.39; to RAAF 19.9.40.
R3940	36 MU 14.11.39; 47 MU; to RCAF 22.10.40 as 1732.
R3941	36 MU 14.11.39; to RCAF 28.11.40 as 1836.
R3942	36 MU 16.11.39; 9 MU 29.6.40; 47 MU 2.9.40; to RCAF 26.9.40 as 1711.
R3943	36 MU 16.11.39; to RCAF 28.11.40 as 1793.
R3944	36 MU 22.11.39; to RAAF 19.8.40.
R3945	36 MU 16.11.39; 47 MU; to SAAF 19.7.40 as 927.
R3946	36 MU 14.11.39; 47 MU; to RCAF 22.10.40 as 1728.
R3947	9 MU 9.12.39; Austin 26.9.40; 9 MU 5.12.40; 47 MU 14.2.41; to RCAF 11.3.41 as 1923.
R3948	9 MU 6.12.39; Austin 22.9.40; 47 MU 13.11.40; to RAAF 15.1.41.
R3949	9 MU 11.12.39; Austin 26.9.40; 9 MU 28.11.40; 47 MU 23.2.41; to RAAF 24.3.41.
R3950	9 MU 12.12.39; Austin 26.9.40; 9 MU 27.11.40; 47 MU 23.2.41; to RCAF 7.3.41 as 1899; restored and now in Brussels Military Museum as 70.
R3951	9 MU 11.12.39; Austin 26.9.40; 9 MU 8.11.40; 47 MU 23.2.41; to RAAF 24.3.41.
R3952	9 MU 16.12.39; Austin 22.9.40; 9 MU 8.11.40; 47 MU 15.1.41; to RCAF 7.2.41 as 1845.
R3953	9 MU 12.12.39; Austin 26.9.40; 9 MU 26.11.40; 47 MU 25.2.41; to RCAF 11.3.41 as 1929.
R3954	9 MU 12.12.39; Austin 22.9.40; 47 MU 5.11.40; 9 MU 23.11.40; 47 MU 26.2.41; to RAAF 4.6.41.
R3955	9 MU 20.12.39; Austin 26.9.40; 47 MU 5.11.40; to RCAF 28.11.40 as 1828.
R3956	9 MU 12.12.39; Austin 26.9.40; 47 MU 13.11.40; to RAAF 15.1.41.
R3957	9 MU 29.12.39; Austin 26.9.40; 47 MU 13.11.40; to RAAF 15.1.41.
R3958	9 MU 22.12.39; Austin 22.9.40; Parks 5.10.40; to RCAF 3.12.40.
R3959	9 MU 1.1.40; Austin 12.9.40; Parks 21.9.40; to RCAF 8.10.40.
R3960	9 MU 9.1.40; Austin 22.9.40; Parks 5.10.40; to RCAF 21.10.40.
R3961	9 MU 8.2.40; Austin 26.9.40; 9 MU 7.12.40; Austin 28.2.41; to RCAF 4.5.41.
R3962	9 MU 29.12.39; Austin 22.9.40; Parks 23.9.40; to RCAF 28.12.40.

R3963	9 MU 10.1.40; Austin 22.9.40; Parks 21.9.40; to RCAF 28.12.40.
R3964	9 MU 21.12.39; Austin 22.9.40; Parks 5.10.40; to RCAF 28.12.40.
R3965	9 MU 4.1.40; Austin 22.9.40; Parks 12.10.40; to RCAF 26.10.40.
R3966	9 MU 15.1.40; Austin 22.9.40; Parks 21.9.40; to RCAF 29.12.40.
R3967	9 MU; Austin 22.9.40; Parks 12.10.40; to RCAF 26.10.40.
R3968	9 MU 15.1.40; Austin 26.9.40; 9 MU 13.11.40; 47 MU 23.2.41; to RCAF 2.3.41 as 1882.
R3969	9 MU 15.1 40; Austin 22.9.40; Parks 21.10.40; to RCAF 28.12.40.
R3970	9 MU 10.1.40; Austin 26.9.40; 47 MU 16.11.40; to RCAF 11.12.40 as 1838.
R3971	9 MU 4.3.40; Austin 26.9.40; 47 MU 16.11.40; to RCAF 18.12.40 as 1819.
R3990	9 MU 12.1.40; Austin 22.9.40; Parks 21.10.40; to RCAF 28.12.40.
R3991	9 MU 16.1.40; Austin 13.9.40; Parks 24.9.40; to RCAF 28.12.40.
R3992	9 MU; Austin 26.9.40; Parks 30.11.40; to RCAF 28.12.40.
R3993	9 MU; Austin 26.9.40; Parks 30.11.40; to RCAF 20.3.41.
R3994	9 MU; Austin 13.9.40; Parks 14.9.40; to RCAF 23.10.40.
R3995	9 MU 6.2.40; Austin 26.9.40; Parks 14.12.40; to RCAF 31.3.41.
R3996	9 MU 15.1.40; Austin 26.9.40; Parks 7.12.40; to RCAF 31.3.41.
R3997	9 MU 24.1.40; Austin 26.9.40; Parks 30.11.40; to RCAF 31.3.41.
R3998	9 MU 25.1.40; Austin 26.9.40; Parks 7.12.40; to RCAF 15.3.41.
R3999	9 MU 25.2.40; 47 MU 17.10.40; to RCAF 5.12.40 as 1784.
R4000	9 MU 7.2.40; to RCAF 24.8.40.
R4001	9 MU 9.2.40; Austin 26.9.40; Parks 28.12.40; to RCAF 11.6.41 as 1999.
R4002	9 MU 10.2.40; Austin 26.9.40; Parks 28.12.40; to RAAF 11.3.41.
R4003	9 MU 25.1.40; Austin 26.9.40; Parks 14.12.40; to SAAF 5.2.41 as 933; to Middle East 30.1.43.
R4004	9 MU 7.2.40; Austin 26.9.40; Parks 14.12.40; to SAAF 5.2.41 as 931.
R4005	9 MU 25.2.40; 47 MU 17.10.40; to RCAF 1.11.40 as 1756.
R4006	9 MU 25.2.40; 47 MU 17.10.40; to RAAF 14.11.40.
R4007	9 MU 7.3.40; Austin 26.9.40; 9 MU 16.11.40; 47 MU 14.2.41; to RCAF 2.3.41 as 1880.
R4008	9 MU 22.2.40; 47 MU 17.10.40; to RAAF 14.11.40.
R4009	9 MU 22.2.40; 47 MU 17.10.40; to RAAF 14.11.40.
R4010	9 MU 3.3.40; Austin 22.9.40; 9 MU 16.11.40; 47 MU 15.1.41; to RCAF 7.2.41 as 1846.
R4011	9 MU 8.3.40; Austin 22.9.40; 47 MU 21.10.40; to RCAF 3.12.40 as 1786.
R4012	9 MU 23.2.40; 47 MU 17.10.40; to RAAF 14.11.40.
R4013	9 MU 29.2.40; Austin 13.9.40; Parks 24.9.40; to RCAF 8.10.40.
R4014	9 MU 10.4.40; Austin 13.9.40; Parks 24.8.40; to RCAF, fuselage 1.10.40, wings 21.10.40.
R4015	9 MU 5.3.40; Austin 13.9.40; Parks 31.8.40; to RCAF 12.10.40.
R4016	9 MU 1.3.40; Austin 22.9.40; Parks 12.10.40; to RCAF 26.10.40.
R4017	9 MU 6.3.40; Austin 19.9.40; Parks 21.9.40; to RCAF 21.10.40.
R4018	9 MU 6.3.40; Austin 13.9.40; Parks 26.9.40; to RCAF 3.10.40.
R4019	9 MU 19.3.40; Austin 22.9.40; 47 MU 21.10.40; to RAAF 15.1.41.
R4035	9 MU 15.3.40; Austin 22.9.40; 47 MU 21.10.40; to RCAF 5.12.40 as 1783.

R4036	9 MU 29.3.40; Austin 22.9.40; 47 MU 25.10.40; to RCAF 15.11.40 as 1739.
R4037	9 MU 8.4.40; Austin 13.9.40; Parks 16.9.40; to RCAF 8.10.40.
R4038	9 MU 11.3.40; Austin 22.9.40; 47 MU 17.10.40; to RCAF 5.12.40 as 1785.
R4039	9 MU 21.3.40; Austin 22.9.40; Parks 5.10.40; to RCAF 28.12.40.
R4040	9 MU 14.3.40; Austin 22.9.40; 47 MU 21.10.40; to RCAF 5.12.40 as 1788.
R4041	9 MU 16.4.40; to RCAF 24.8.40.
R4042	9 MU 8.4.40; Austin 13.9.40; Parks 21.9.40; to RCAF 3.11.40.
R4043	9 MU 15.3.40; Austin 22.9.40; Parks 5.10.40; to RCAF 12.10.40.
R4044	9 MU 15.3.40; Austin 22.9.40; 47 MU 25.10.40; to RCAF 15.11.40 as 1740.
R4045	9 MU 16.4.40; Austin 22.9.40; 47 MU 5.11.40; to RCAF 28.11.40 as 1822.
R4046	9 MU 31.3.40; Austin 13.9.40; Parks 14.9.40; to RCAF 21.10.40.
R4047	9 MU 16.4.40; Austin 22.9.40; 47 MU 5.11.40; to RCAF 28.11.40 as 1835.
R4048	9 MU 27.4.40; Austin 22.9.40; 47 MU 5.11.40; to RCAF 28.11.40 as 1792.
R4049	9 MU 23.4.40; Austin 22.9.40; 47 MU 12.10.40; to RAAF 2.11.40.
R4050	9 MU 28.3.40; Austin 22.9.40; Parks 28.9.40; to RCAF 28.12.40.
R4051	9 MU 8.4.40; Austin 13.9.40; Parks 31.5.41; to RCAF 3.10.41.
R4052	9 MU 13.4.40; to RCAF 24.8.40.
R4053	9 MU 4.4.40; Austin 13.9.40; Parks 27.9.40; to RCAF 21.10.40.
R4054	9 MU 16.5.40; Austin 22.9.40; 47 MU 21.10.40; to RCAF 3.12.40 as 1787.

100 Fairey Battle Trainers delivered by Fairey between May and November 1940. Built at Stockport. Contract 15447/39.

R7356	12 FTS 20.5.40; 1 FTS 11.7.41. Lost height in turn at night and hit ground 2m E of Shrewton, 15.12.41; SOC 17.12.41.
R7357	12 FTS 20.5.40; DBR 30.12.40; Rosenfield 11.2.41; NFT
R7358	47 MU 22.5.40; to SAAF 19.6.40 as 921.
R7359	47 MU 22.5.40; to SAAF 19.6.40 as 917.
R7360	11 FTS 25.5.40; 18 MU 25.7.40; Austin 24.10.40; to RCAF 21.12.40.
R7361	12 FTS 3.6.40; engine cut; undershot landing and hit bowser, Grantham, 1.8.40; ROS; bellylanded in error, Barkston LG, 20.8.40; ROS; 16(P)FTS 7.6.41; Southern A/C 13.2.42; 23 MU 20.4.42; 3 AGS 30.8.42; 27 MU 4.2.43; SOC 21.1.44. 747.55 hours.
R7362	12 FTS 3.6.40; 16(P)FTS 7.6.41; undercarriage leg jammed, landed on one wheel, Hucknall, 5.7.41; ROS; engine cut; bellylanded, 21.10.41; Rosenfield 10.11.41; 23 MU 16.2.42; 3 AGS 15.7.42; undercarriage jammed, landed on one wheel, Castle Kennedy, 8.9.42; ROS; 18 MU 20.12.42; SOC 14.7.44.
R7363	12 FTS 11.6.40. Shot down by enemy aircraft 3m S of Grantham, 18.5.41; FO B.K. Thomas killed; SOC 30.5.41; 449.40 hours.
R7364	12 FTS 9.6.40; 7 FTS 12.6.40; undercarriage collapsed on landing, Peterborough, 24.10.40; ROS; 12 FTS 3.3.41; 16(P)FTS 7.6.41; Rosenfield 27.2.42; 9 MU 28.5.42; 3 AGS 28.7.42; 18 MU 18.2.43; SOC 8.44.
R7365	12 FTS 9.6.40; 7 FTS 12.6.40; 1 FTS 22.1.41; Western A/W 19.4.41; 47 MU 27.5.41; to RCAF 11.6.41 as 2003.
R7366	12 FTS 11.6.40; 1 FTS 11.7.41; bellylanded in error, Netheravon, 26.11.41; Rosenfield 19.1.42; 27 MU 29.4.42; 18 MU; 4 Sqn 31.5.42; 2 AACU 6.8.42; 27 MU; 3 AGS 9.9.42; 27 MU 6.3.43; SOC 30.6.43.

Battle trainer R7412 with No.31 Service Flying Training School at Kingston, Ontario. (B Robertson collection)

R7367   12 FTS 9.6.40; 7 FTS 11.6.40; 27 MU 2.12.40; 2 BGS 4.6.41; hit car while taxying, Millom, 19.6.41; ROS; 2 AOS 29.8.41; 1 FTS 19.9.41; 27 MU 16.5.42; 3 AGS 19.8.42; 27 MU 9.2.43; SOC 30.6.43.

R7368   12 FTS 9.6.40; 7 FTS 11.6.40; undercarriage leg jammed, bellylanded Sibson, 26.10.40; Fairey 4.11.40; 1 FTS 6.4.41; Fairey 3.5.41; 8 BGS 30.6.41; 27 MU 7.5.42; SOC 7.12.44.

R7369   12 FTS 9.6.40; bellylanded, Grantham, 15.6.40; ROS; 16(P)FTS 16.7.41; 23 MU 19.2.42; SOC 22.9.43.

R7370   12 FTS 11.6.40; taxied into concrete post at night and undercarriage collapsed, Harlaxton, 9.7.40; Fairey 28.8.40; 38 MU 2.9.40; Austin 25.10.40; Parks 9.11.40; to RCAF 8.1.41.

R7371   5 BGS 14.6.40; CFS 14.6.40; 2 BGS 15.4.41; 2 AOS; 38 MU 15.3.42; SOC 28.12.44.

R7372   7 OTU 15.6.40; 27 MU 11.9.40; 3 FPP 9.10.40; 27 MU 1.6.42; HQ ATA 14.7.43; SOC 12.7.44.

R7373   7 OTU 15.6.40; 12 OTU 10.10.40; 20 MU 19.12.40; Austin 1.3.41; Parks 4.4.41; to RCAF 10.4.41.

R7374   7 OTU 15.6.40; 27 MU 5.11.40; Austin 9.1.41; to RCAF 1.4.41.

R7375   7 OTU 15.6.40; engine cut after take-off from Hawarden; bellylanded, Buckley, 28.6.40; Fairey 9.7.40; 27 MU 11.3.41; 1 FTS 17.5.41; bellylanded in error, Shrewton, 11.6.41; Rosenfield 10.2.42; 9 MU 15.5.42; 3 AGS 28.7.42; 18 MU 19.2.43; to 2485M at 3 SofTT 10.12.43; 18 MU 31.12.43; SOC 14.7.44.

R7376   7 OTU 15.6.40; undercarriage collapsed after landing, Shawbury, 1.2.41; ROS; engine cut on take-off, bellylanded, Northolt, 2.6.41; Fairey 7.6.41; 1 FTS 16.8.41; engine cut on take-off; bellylanded 1m N of Netheravon, 12.9.41; Rosenfield 23.9.41; 23 MU 18.3.42; 3 AGS 10.8.42; 27 MU 15.12.42; SOC 23.8.44.

R7377   6 OTU 15.6.40; 27 MU 23.3.41; 1 FTS 2.5.41; damaged in heavy landing, Shrewton, 6.8.41; Rosenfield 17.8.41; 47 MU 5.2.42; to RAAF 7.4.42.

R7378   6 OTU 15.6.40; 12 OTU 21.9.40; 18 MU 17.12.40; 2 BGS 7.5.41; 4 AOS 14.8.41; 2 AGS 22.2.42; Rosenfield 12.8.42; 18 MU 29.9.42; 1609 Flight 17.11.42; 1606 Flight 23.6.43; to 3909M at 2 SofTT 15.7.43.

R7379   6 OTU 15.6.40; 12 OTU 21.9.40; undercarriage retracted in error on landing, Benson, 30.9.40; ROS; undercarriage collapsed on landing, Benson, 25.11.40; 38 MU 30.12.40; HQ ATA 22.8.41; 38 MU 3.6.42; 3 AGS 7.9.42; 18 MU 15.12.42; SOC 14.7.44.

R7380   6 OTU 23.6.40; 12 OTU 21.9.40; PRU 16.12.40; overshot forced landing into ditch, Crosshall, 1m N of Eaton Socon, Beds., 17.2.41; Western A/W 24.4.41; 47 MU 17.5.41; to RAAF 9.6.41.

R7381   6 OTU 22.6.40; 12 OTU 21.9.40; landed with undercarriage unlocked, 26.10.40; 18 MU 17.12.40; 2 BGS 3.5.41; 2 AOS; 2 AGS 13.2.42; Rosenfield 10.5.42; 27 MU 26.9.42; 231 Sqn 30.9.42; 27 MU 21.12.42; HQ ATA 9.7.43; Rosenfield 8.7.44; SOC 8.7.44.

R7382   CFS 23.6.40; undercarriage jammed, bellylanded Dumfries, 3.2.41; ROS; 2 BGS 16.2.41; 2 AOS; 23 MU 5.4.42; 18 MU 8.11.42; SOC 14.7.44.

R7383   15 EFTS 22.6.40; 1 (P)FTS 7.12.40; bellylanded in error, Hucknall, 18.4.41; ROS; 16(P)FTS 13.7.41; bellylanded in error, Newton, 10.8.41; ROS; 9 MU 23.3.42; 9 MU 17.2.44; SOC 28.3.46.

R7384   6 MU 29.6.40; Austin 20.10.40; to RCAF 21.12.40; restored 1963 and now in Canadian National Aeronautical Collection, Rockliffe, Canada.

R7385 6 MU 27.6.40; 7 FTS 27.7.40; 22 MU 23.3.41; 1 FTS 10.5.41; engine cut; bellylanded, Beckfoot, near Silloth, 10.5.41; Fairey 15.5.41; engine cut; bellylanded,

Irington, near Leominster, Hereford, 29.8.41; 1 FTS 17.9.41; Rosenfield 16.10.41; 47 MU 2.1.42; to RAAF 7.4.42.

R7399   20 MU 22.6.40; 303 Sqn 25.7.40; 308 Sqn 25.9.40; 317 Sqn 15.4.41; 52 OTU 23.3.42; Rosenfield 12.10.42; 27 MU 29.11.42; SOC 30.6.43.

R7400   15 EFTS 6.7.40; bellylanded in error, Kirkbride, 8.8.40; ROS; 1(P)FTS 4.12.40; 16(P)FTS 13.7.41; 23 MU 29.3.42; SOC 14.9.43.

R7401   20 MU 7.7.40; 301 Sqn 31.7.40; 27 MU 20.11.40; 2 BGS 3.6.41; taxied into camouflage sprayer, Millom, 23.8.41; ROS; overshot landing and hit wall, Brougham, Cumberland, 3.12.41; ROS; 2 OAFU 4.4.42; 23 MU 6.4.42; 3 AGS 4.8.42; 27 MU 15.12.42; SOC 21.1.44.

R7402   20 MU 16.7.40; 300 Sqn 31.7.40; undercarriage leg jammed; bellylanded Swinderby, 16.9.40; 22 MU 16.12.40; 1 FTS 24.4.41; Rosenfield 23.9.41; 47 MU 17.1.42; to SAAF 20.3.42 as 1034.

R7403   20 MU 11.7.40; Austin 5.8.40; Parks 27.8.40; to RCAF 8.10.40.

R7404   20 MU 16.7.40; Austin 5.8.40; Parks 24.8.40; to RCAF 3.10.40.

R7405   18 MU 1.8.40; Austin 7.8.40; Parks 26.8.40; to RCAF , fuselage 1.10.40, wings 21.10.40.

R7406   48 MU 4.8.40; 18 MU 7.8.40; 12 OTU 28.9.40; 6 MU 17.12.40; 16(P)FTS 30.6.41; engine cut; bellylanded, Wiverton, near Bingham, Notts., 31.10.41; Rosenfield 8.11.41; 23 MU 7.3.42; 3 AGS 15.7.42; bellylanded in error, West Freugh, 26.7.42; ROS; 27 MU 27.1.43; HQ ATA 24.7.43; SOC 17.5.44.

R7407   18 MU 5.8.40; 12 OTU 28.9.40; 6 MU 21.12.40; 16(P)FTS 30.6.41; undercarriage jammed; bellylanded Newton, 21.7.41; ROS; DBR 25.11.41; SOC 29.11.41.

R7408   18 MU 31.7.40; Austin 7.8.40; Parks 6.9.40; to RCAF. fuselage 1.10.40, wings 21.10.40.

R7409   48 MU 4.8.40; 18 MU 5.8.40; 312 Sqn 21.10.40; 96 Sqn 14.2.41; Pocklington 15.7.42; presumed SOC 21.6.47.

R7410   27 MU 5.8.40; 306 Sqn 10.9.40; 316 Sqn 23.7.41; Western A/W 30.8.41; 316 Sqn 10.10.41; engine cut; bellylanded, Buckland Farm, Wellington, Somerset, 8.4.42; Rosenfield 18.4.42; 18 MU 27.6.42; 2 AGS 20.9.42. Crashed in forced landing, Dalcross, 20.10.42; SOC 29.10.42.

R7411   27 MU 4.8.40; 307 Sqn 7.9.40; abandoned 5m E of Goole, Yorks., 30.10.40; SOC 3.1.41.

R7412   27 MU 5.8.40; Austin 12.1.41; Parks 7.2.41; to RCAF 1.4.41.

R7413   Austin 8.8.40; Parks 30.8.40; to RCAF 3.10.40.

R7414   Austin 11.8.40; Parks 6.9.40; to RCAF 12.10.40.

R7415   Austin 14.8.40; Parks 30.8.40; to RCAF, fuselage 1.10.40, wings 21.10.40.

R7416   Austin 20.8.40; Parks 14.9.40; to RCAF 12.10.40.

R7417   Austin 20.8.40; Parks 21.9.40; to RCAF 8.10.40.

R7418   Austin 25.8.40; Parks 21.9.40; to RCAF 21.10.40.

R7419   Austin 25.8.40; Parks 21.9.40; to RCAF 28.12.40.

R7420   Austin 25.8.40; Parks 28.9.40; to RCAF 28.12.40.

R7421   Austin 26.8.40; Parks 21.9.40; to RCAF 21.10.40.

R7422   Austin 27.8.40; Parks 21.9.40; to RCAF 12.10.40.

R7423   Austin 28.8.40; Parks 28.9.40; to RCAF 3.11.40.

R7424   Austin 29.8.40; Parks 28.9.40; to RCAF 16.11.40.

R7425   Austin 30.8.40; Parks 28.9.40; to RCAF 28.12.40.

R7426   Austin 31.8.40; Parks 5.10.40; to RCAF 28.12.40.

R7427   Austin 2.9.40; Parks 5.10.40; to RCAF 28.12.40.

R7428   Austin 3.9.40; Parks 5.10.40; to RCAF 3.11.40.

R7429   Austin 3.9.40; Parks 5.10.40; to RCAF 3.12.40.

R7430   Austin 9.9.40; Parks 5.10.40; to RCAF 21.10.40.

R7431   Austin 5.9.40; Parks 12.10.40; to RCAF 16.11.40.

R7432   Austin 6.9.40; Parks 12.10.40; to RCAF 16.11.40.

R7433   Austin 7.9.40; Parks 12.10.40; to RCAF 16.11.40.

R7434   Austin 7.9.40; Parks 12.10.40; to RCAF 21.10.40.

R7435   Austin 10.9.40; Parks 12.10.40; to RCAF 21.10.40.

R7436   Austin 11.9.40; Parks 12.10.40; to RCAF 3.11.40.

R7437   Austin 13.9.40; Parks 12.10.40; to RCAF 16.11.40.

R7438   Austin 15.9.40; Parks 19.10.40; to RCAF 26.10.40.

R7439   Austin 15.9.40; Parks 19.10.40; to RCAF 26.10.40.

R7440   Austin 23.9.40; Parks 12.10.40; to RCAF 21.10.40.

R7441   Austin 18.9.40; Parks 17.10.40; to RCAF 23.10.40.

R7442   Austin 20.9.40; Parks 19.10.40; to RCAF 16.11.40.

R7443   Austin 22.9.40; Parks 19.10.40; to RCAF 16.11.40.

R7444   Austin 23.9.40; Parks 12.10.40; to RCAF 21.10.40.

R7445   Austin 24.9.40; Parks 26.10.40; to RCAF 16.11.40.

R7446   Austin 25.9.40; Parks 26.10.40; to RCAF 28.12.40.

R7447   Austin 27.9.40; Parks 26.10.40; to RCAF 16.11.40.

R7448   Austin 28.9.40; Parks 26.10.40; to RCAF 28.12.40.

R7461   Austin 29.9.40; Parks 26.10.40; to RCAF 16.11.40.

R7462   Austin 8.10.40; Parks 26.10.40; to RCAF 28.12.40.

R7463   Austin 28.9.40; Parks 2.11.40; to RCAF 28.12.40.

R7464   Austin 1.10.40; Parks 26.10.40; to RCAF 16.11.40.

R7465   9 MU 8.10.40; Austin 20.10.40; Parks 2.11.40; to RCAF 28.12.40.

R7466   9 MU 10.10.40; Austin 20.10.40; Parks 9.11.40; to RCAF 28.12.40.

R7467   9 MU 12.10.40; Austin 20.10.40; Parks 9.11.40; to RCAF 28.12.40.

R7468   9 MU 14.10.40; Austin 20.10.40; Parks 9.11.40; to RCAF 21.12.40.

R7469   38 MU 20.10.40; Austin 15.11.40; Parks 21.12.40; to RCAF 8.1.41.

R7470   38 MU 20.10.40; Austin 24.11.40; 38 MU 25.11.40; Austin 22.12.40; to RCAF 10.3.41.

R7471   38 MU 20.10.40; Austin 21.12.40; Parks 13.1.41; to RCAF 10.3.41.

R7472   9 MU 23.10.40; 420 Flight 8.11.40; 1 FTS 23.11.40; bellylanded in error, Netheravon, 7.2.41; ROS. Crashed after control lost in fog near Shrewsbury, Salop, 27.3.41; PO H.J. Craig and ALA G.J.B. Kendall killed

R7473   9 MU 23.10.40; Austin 12.11.40; Parks 7.12.40; to RCAF 21.12.40.

R7474   9 MU 25.10.40; Austin 12.11.40; Parks 30.11.40; to RCAF 5.1.41.

R7475   9 MU 27.10.40; Austin 13.11.40; Parks 7.12.40; to RCAF 5.1.41

R7476   9 MU 31.10.40; Austin 13.11.40; Parks 30.11.40; to RCAF 5.1.41.

R7477   20 MU 21.11.40; 16(P)FTS 3.7.41; damaged in heavy landing, Newton, 23.10.41; ROS; 23 MU 29.3.42; 18 MU 8.9.42; 1600 Flight 20.11.42; 18 MU 13.4.43; SOC 14.7.44.

R7478   20 MU 19.11.40; Austin 19.12.40; Parks 2.1.41; to SAAF 28.2.41 as 945.

R7479   20 MU 21.11.40; Austin 2.3.41; Parks 2.4.41; to RCAF 10.4.41.

R7480   20 MU 21.11.40; Pembridge 3.1.41; 20 MU 31.3.41; Austin 8.4.41; Parks 2.5.41; to RCAF 31.5.41.

66 Fairey Battle Target Tugs delivered by Austin, Longbridge, between August and October 1940. Contract B2580/39.

V1201   12 MU 1.8.40; 47 MU 3.2.41; to RAAF 18.2.41.

V1202   12 MU 1.8.40; 1 OTU 20.8.40; 5 OTU at 31.12.41; 18 Group APC 9.11.42; Rosenfield 5.4.43; 47 MU 18.7.43; to RAAF 11.10.43.

V1203   12 MU 6.8.40; 47 MU 3.2.41; to RAAF 18.2.41.

V1204   12 MU 8.8.40; 52 OTU 16.3.41; 56 OTU 2.4.41; landed with undercarriage unlocked, Sutton Bridge, 2.4.41; ROS; 59 OTU 5.12.41; 61 OTU 9.6.42; 59 OTU 8.7.42; to 3908M at 2 SofTT 7.7.43.

V1205   12 MU 6.8.40; 52 OTU 12.3.41; SOC 9.9.43.

V1206   20 MU 8.8.40; 47 MU 6.9.40; to RAAF 1.10.40.

V1207   20 MU 5.8.40; 47 MU 5.9.40; to RAAF 19.9.40.

V1208   20 MU 5.8.40; 47 MU 5.9.40; to RAAF 1.10.40.

V1209   20 MU 8.8.40; 47 MU 5.9.40; to RAAF 19.9.40.

V1210   20 MU 8.8.40; 58 OTU 13.3.41; engine cut; bellylanded Whitekirk, 2m ENE of East Fortune, 14.12.41; Rosenfield 25.12.41; LEP 4.4.42; to RAAF 31.5.42.

V1211   7 BGS 8.8.40. Crashed on approach to drogue dropping area, Kenfig, 2.5.41; PO J. Puklo (PAF) and AC2 E.J. Williams killed; SOC 12.5.41.

Members of the management pose in front of target tug V1249 as it emerges from the Austin production line at Longbridge.
(P Jarrett collection)

V1212   7 BGS 8.8.40; bellylanded in error, Stormy Down, 21.7.41; ROS; 38 MU 7.12.41; 215 MU 25.4.42; 3 PATP 26.5.42; to SRAF 14.6.42.

V1213   7 BGS 10.8.40; undercarriage leg jammed; bellylanded Stormy Down, 11.12.40; ROS; 38 MU 6.2.42; 215 MU 16.6.42; 3 PATP 24.6.42; to SAAF 19.7.42.

V1214   7 BGS 8.8.40; undershot approach and hit bank, Stormy Down, 5.12.40; ROS; 38 MU 6.2.42; LEP 22.2.42; 215 MU 10.6.42; 3 PATP 22.6.42; to SAAF 19.7.42.

V1215   4 BGS 8.8.40; 4 AOS at 31.12.41; Rosenfield 25.1.42; 9 MU 27.4.42; 215 MU 26.5.42; 3 PATP 13.6.42. to SAAF 30.6.42 as 1047.

V1216   48 MU 18.8.40; 4 BGS 19.8.40; 4 AOS at 31.12.41; LEP 15.2.42; to SAAF 2.3.42.

V1217   4 BGS 15.8.40; 4 AOS at 31.12.41; LEP 20.2.42; to SAAF 21.3.42.

V1218   48 MU 10.8.40; 4 BGS 12.8.40; 4 AOS at 31.12.41; LEP 2.3.42; to SAAF 21.3.42.

V1219   4 BGS 4.9.40; 32 MU 10.4.41; 1 AGS 21.6.41; LEP 17.3.42; to RAAF 29.4.42.

V1220   48 MU 18.8.40; 4 BGS 21.8.40; 4 AOS at 31.12.41; LEP 15.2.42; to SAAF 2.3.42.

V1221   4 BGS 15.9.40; 4 AOS at 31.12.41; 18 MU 2.3.42; Rosenfield 25.7.42; 215 MU 24.9.42; 52 MU 2.10.42; to RAAF 22.10.42.

V1222   48 MU 18.8.40; 4 BGS 19.8.40; 4 AOS. Landed near Waterford, Eire, while lost, 2.4.41; interned then sold to Irish Air Corps.

V1223   48 MU 18.8.40; 4 BGS 21.8.40. Collided with L5662 15.5.41; SOC 27.5.41; 258.25 hours.

V1224   48 MU 18.8.40; 4 BGS 23.8.40; 4 AOS at 31.12.41; to SAAF 21.3.42.

V1225   48 MU 30.8.40; 8 BGS 31.8.40; 18 MU 6.4.41; Dumfries 13.4.41; to SAAF 23.6.41.

V1226   8 BGS 22.8.40; overshot landing into ditch, Evanton, 28.2.41; 8 AGS; 47 MU 15.12.41; to SRAF 9.1.42.

V1227   9 BGS 22.8.40; Western A/W 8.1.42; 18 MU 24.2.42; 215 MU 9.9.42; to RAAF 17.9.42.

V1228   9 BGS 22.8.40. Stalled while dropping drogue, Penrhos 25.10.40; PO T. Dabrowski, Sgt W. Ustyanowski and AC1 E. Evans killed; SOC 13.11.40.

V1229   9 BGS 24.8.40; 38 MU 6.1.42; LEP 9.2.43; 3 PATP 2.3.43; to SRAF 13.4.43.

V1230   9 BGS 24.8.40; stalled on landing, Penrhos, 12.4.41; ROS; 1 AGS 22.6.41; LEP 28.12.41; to SAAF 28.2.42.

V1231   9 BGS 29.8.40; 18 MU 16.2.42; 215 MU 2.9.42; 3 PATP 15.9.42; to SAAF 31.12.43.

V1232   9 BGS 29.8.40; 8 BGS 13.6.41; 47 MU 8.12.41; to RAAF 2.3.42.

V1233   9 BGS 29.8.40; engine cut; bellylanded Abersoch, 5m W of Penrhos, 20.8.41; ROS; LEP 5.1.42; 18 MU 6.2.42; LEP 29.4.42; to RAAF 5.8.42.

V1234   CGS 4.9.40; engine cut; bellylanded E of Warmwell, 22.11.40; ROS; 9 MU 14.3.42; de Havilland 8.4.42; Rosenfield 19.6.42; de Havilland 4.8.42; SOC 9.2.45.

V1235   47 MU 9.9.40; to RAAF 18.10.40.

V1236	5 FTS 4.9.40; 9 BGS 1.11.40; SOC 10.12.40.
V1237	5 FTS 9.10.40; 9 BGS 1.11.40; 8 BGS 13.6.41; 27 MU 18.11.41; to RAAF 29.4.42.
V1238	8 FTS 7.9.40; CGS 5.12.40; 18 MU 12.3.42; 215 MU 29.6.42; 3 PATP 28.8.42; to RAAF 13.9.42.
V1239	48 MU 11.9.40; 8 FTS 14.9.40; 8 BGS 10.11.40; 8 AGS. Crashed in forced landing N of Loth, Sutherland, 20.8.41; SOC 8.9.41.
V1240	8 FTS 7.9.40; 8 BGS 10.11.40. Crashed in forced landing, Shandwick Bay, Ross, 25.4.41; SOC 10.5.41.
V1241	9 BGS 6.9.40; 47 MU 19.12.41; to RAAF 28.2.42.
V1242	9 BGS 6.9.40; bellylanded in error, Penrhos, 1.1.41; ROS; LEP 10.2.42; to RAAF 29.4.42.
V1243	9 BGS 11.9.40; 1 AGS 22.6.41; CGS 7.11.41; 18 MU 12.3.42; 215 MU 7.10.42; 3 PATP 10.10.42; to RAAF 8.11.42.
V1244	9 BGS 16.9.40; DBR 13.11.40; SOC 2.12.40.
V1245	9 BGS 7.10.40; LEP 26.1.41; to SAAF 7.10.41 as 1012.
V1246	4 BGS 15.9.40; 4 AOS at 31.12.41; 18 MU 15.2.42; 215 MU 11.10.42; 3 PATP 30.10.42; to SAAF 28.11.42 as 1073.
V1247	4 BGS 23.9.40; 4 AOS at 31.12.41; LEP 11.3.42; to SRAF 31.3.42.
V1248	4 BGS 25.9.40; 4 AOS at 31.12.41; LEP 2.3.42; to SAAF 21.3.42.
V1249	4 BGS; 27 MU 15.3.41; 60 OTU 24.6.41; tyre burst on landing; swung and undercarriage collapsed, East Fortune, 20.6.42; ROS; 52 OTU 9.9.42; Rosenfield 9.9.43; SOC 9.9.43.
V1250	10 BGS 24.9.40; Fairey 29.4.41; 1 AGS 21.7.41; 2 AOS 31.10.41; 47 MU 7.1.42; to RAAF 13.3.42.
V1265	10 BGS 5.10.40; 18 MU 1.4.41; Dumfries 6.4.41; to SRAF.
V1266	10 BGS 25.9.40; 10 AOS at 31.12.41; 5 AOS 10.7.42; 3 AGS 24.10.42; 215 MU 1.12.42; EO Swansea 5.12.42; to SAAF 12.12.42 but lost at sea en route.
V1267	10 BGS 26.9.40; 18 MU 1.4.41; LEP 4.4.41; presumed SOC 21.6.47.
V1268	10 BGS 24.9.40; 10 AOS at 31.12.41; 5 AOS 10.7.42; 3 AGS 29.10.42; Bristol 20.12.42; 18 MU 21.12.42; 47 MU 29.3.43; to SRAF 3.7.43.
V1269	10 BGS 27.9.40; 18 MU 1.4.41; LEP 4.4.41; to SAAF 21.5.41.
V1270	10 BGS 5.10.40; 10 AOS at 31.12.41; 2 OTU 31.1.42; 10 OAFU. Engine cut; bellylanded on approach, Southerness Point, Kirkcudbright, 5.5.42; SOC 15.5.42; 18 MU; LEP 20.12.42; 3 PATP 21.1.43; to RAAF 9.3.43.
V1271	10 BGS 27.9.40; 10 AOS at 31.12.41; Southern A/C 30.4.42; 18 MU 1.6.42; undercarriage jammed, bellylanded, Dumfries, 29.10.42; ROS; LEP 15.12.42; to RAAF 3.1.43.
V1272	10 BGS 5.10.40; engine cut; crashlanded Dumfries, 16.5.41; Fairey 23.5.41; 1 AGS 27.6.41; Dumfries 7.11.41; Austin 1.12.41; Dumfries 6.12.41; to SAAF 16.1.42.
V1273	10 BGS 5.10.40; engine cut; forcelanded Portobello, Kirkcudbright, 8.4.41; ROS; bellylanded in error, Dumfries, 20.8.41; ROS; 10 AOS at 31.12.41; 5 AOS 5.7.42; 3 AGS 24.10.42; 215 MU 1.12.42; LEP 22.12.42; 3 PATP 21.1.43; to SAAF 13.4.43.
V1274	10 BGS 5.10.40; 10 AOS at 31.12.41; Southern A/C 1.5.42; 9 MU 13.6.42; 215 MU 16.7.42; 3 PATP 13.8.42; to SAAF 31.12.42.
V1275	7 BGS 11.10.40; bellylanded in bad weather near Brendon, Somerset, 7.3.41; Rosenfield 7.4.41; 8 BGS 5.7.41. Collided with Botha L6438 and crashed in sea, 16.9.41; SOC 27.9.41.
V1276	7 BGS 12.10.40; 38 MU 7.12.41; 215 MU 20.4.42; 3 PATP 27.4.42; 1 PATP 23.5.42; to SRAF 8.10.42.
V1277	7 BGS 10.10.40; 38 MU 26.1.42; Rosenfield 2.5.42; 215 MU 27.7.42; 3 PATP 13.8.42; to RAAF 17.8.42.
V1278	7 BGS 12.10.40; Western A/W 12.11.41; LEP 17.12.41; to SAAF 18.1.42 as 1011.
V1279	7 BGS 14.10.40; 18 MU 6.4.41; Dumfries 18.4.41; to SRAF.
V1280	7 BGS 30.10.40; 38 MU 7.12.41; 18 MU 20.4.42; 215 MU 4.6.42; 3 PATP 17.6.42; to SAAF 29.7.42.

Eight (or nine) Fairey Battles taken over by RAF in the Middle East. Believed to be those ex-SAAF aircraft left at Eastleigh and only serials known to have been used were as follows. Remainder may have been used for spares and did not carry serials

HK931	Recorded on strength of No.25 AACU but no further trace after December 1943.
HK932	No record of service
HK933	Recorded on strength of No.25 AACU; forcelanded in September 1943 and thereafter no further trace
HK934 to	
HK938	Allotted but no trace of use
HK958	Allotted but no record of service

In addition to the above aircraft, 16 Battles were supplied direct by Fairey to the Belgian Air force. These aircraft were not allocated RAF serial numbers; their Belgian serial numbers were T58 to T73, corresponding to the last two digits of the contructor's numbers.

One Battle, AR625, was built from the fuselage of K9192 and two other aircraft. This aircraft went to 9 MU on 14.7.40, to 47 MU on 15.8.40 and to Canada as 1704 on 6.9.40.

One Battle was "impressed" in the Middle East and given the serial number HK931; this was possibly one of the aircraft originally supplied to the RHAF.

2095 with No.8 Bombing & Gunnery School at Lethbridge, Manitoba. (via D Howley)

Royal Canadian Air Force

The Battles shipped to Canada are listed below under their original serial number. A conversion table to RCAF serials can be found at the end of the tables.

From the time of shipment from the UK, it took up to three months for Battles to be taken on charge (TOC), depending on delays in sailing, time taken to cross the Atlantic, unloading, transfer by road or rail to the assembly point and unpacking. Included among the aircraft were some which were intended for RAF-manned units, No.31 Service Flying Training School and No.31 Bombing & Gunnery School. These retained their original serials but all surviving aircraft were eventually transferred to the Empire Air Training Scheme pool, usually referred to in contemporary RCAF records as JATS for Joint Air Training Scheme. New RCAF serials were not applied retrospectively to these and they spent the rest of their service still with RAF serials.

Initially, the Battles went to Camp Borden and Trenton but some were transported to civilian factories for assembly. These were Fleet Aircraft, Fort Erie, MacDonald Bros., Winnipeg, Aircraft Repair, Edmonton, Ottawa Car Ltd., De Havilland, Downsview, and Central Aircraft, Crumlin. Repairs were also carried out at these plants. Where no transfer after an accident is shown, it may be assumed that the aircraft was repaired by unit.

The dates are those of allocation, normally to Training Commands for issue to their respective units. Arrival of the aircraft could be delayed due to weather, unserviceability and transit time. Each Command held a stored reserve (indicated by SR in the tables) of aircraft surplus to establishment which could be drawn on to replace wastage or increase the number of aircraft on the unit. Training Commands involved were No.1 at Toronto, No.2 at Winnipeg, No.3 at Montreal and No.4 at Calgary. These became Air Commands in 1944 but by then most of the Battles had been replaced.

Repair Depots, originally Aircraft Repair Depots, repaired and modified aircraft and also held a reserve, termed workshop reserve. Those dealing with Battles were No.4 at Scoudouc, No.6 at Trenton, No.8 at Winnipeg, No.9 at St.

John, Quebec, and No.10 at Calgary.

Other units using Battles included the Air Armament School at Trenton and the Training & Development Flight at Rockliffe.

In particular, No.9 RD was responsible for aircraft being fitted with turrets by Canadian Car and Foundry's Turcot Works, Montreal. In these cases, the wings were removed and only the fuselage passed over to CCF, the aircraft being re-assembled on completion of the work. These were then designated Battle IT. CCF overhauled and modified 263 Battles during World War Two. Since Battles were fitted with Grumman target towing gear, it is probably CCF's connection with building Grumman FF-1s that brought this about.

Fairchild, Longueuil, near Montreal, received a contract to fit Battles with Wright R-1830-G3B radial engines but this was cancelled after only one, R7439, had been equipped. Although the Merlin IIIs and Vs had long been replaced by later marks, there were still enough in store, and available by cannibalisation, to keep the Battles flying in adequate numbers.

Fleet Aircraft were mainly engaged in the production of its own trainer designs at Fort Erie but also undertook overhaul and repair work on Battles. MacDonald Bros. Aircraft Ltd at Winnipeg Airport were mainly engaged in the construction of Anson wings and the overhaul of various types, including Battles. Central Aircraft at Crumlin, Ontario, also undertook repair and modification work.

For final disposal, surviving Battles were passed on to the War Assets Corporation (WAC) which tried, without much success, to sell Battles. A 1,000 hp three-seater had no economically-viable role in the post-war world. Many went for scrap and others rotted away in fields, the latter fortunately providing some of the basic material for the few Battle reconstructions that survive today.

The first item in the tables show original RAF serial/RCAF serial. A few were delivered with RAF ground instructional airframe (M) serials and received only RCAF A-numbers.

K7559/2016	TOC 22.7.41 at Fleet Acft; 1 TC 27.8.41 for 1 B&GS; cv to TT by 25.4.42; 6 RD 18.1.43; SOC 12.1.43 for spares
K7587/1776	TOC 16.11.40 at Aircraft Repair; 4 TC 14.1.41 for 2 B&GS; engine cut in circuit; bellylanded ½m S of Mossbank, 3.5.42; engine cut on take-off; bellylanded, Mossbank, 2.7.41; engine cut; bellylanded ½m S of Mossbank, 4.5.42; Central Acft 17.6.43; SOC 23.2.44
K7596/A086	TOC 30.5.40 at TTS St.Thomas as GI airframe A086; SOC 21.7.44 as scrap
K7602/2074	TOC 24.9.41 at 8 RD; 2 TC 18.2.42; Central Acft 15.4.43; 1 TC SR 29.9.43; SOC 15.5.46 for WAC [856 hrs]
K7606/2072	TOC 24.9.41 at 8 RD; 2 TC 11.11.41 for 3 B&GS; 9 RD 22.5.43; cv to GI airframe A330 19.10.43; SOC 30.3.46
K7608	TOC 10.3.42 at Fleet Acft; 3 TC 9.4.42 for 9 B&GS; hit by R7431 while parked, Mont Joli, 13.1.43; collided with N2167 on icy taxiway, Mont Joli, 27.2.43; 9 RD 31.5.43; SOC 7.3.45 for WAC [606 hrs]
K7632	TOC 17.4.41 at 6 RD; 1 TC 10.5.41 for 31 B&GS; 6 RD 14.12.42; SOC 23.3.44 for spares
K7633/2132	TOC 22.1.42 at 4 RD; SOC 8.6.43
K7634/2128	TOC 10.3.42 at Fleet Acft; 3 TC 18.4.42 for 9 B&GS. Engine cut on take-off; overshot runway down embankment, Mont Joli, 27.8.42; Central Acft 1.10.42; SOC 13.1.43 for spares
K7636	TOC 30.5.40 at 1 TTS St. Thomas as GI airframe AO87; SOC 14.2.45
K7640/1809	TOC 7.1.41 at Fleet Acft; 1 TC 7.2.41 for 1 B&GS; 9 RD 21.9.42; CCF for turret fitment 26.9.42; 3 TC 20.12.42 for 9 B&GS; SR 22.1.44; sold 17.6.46 for WAC [1557 hrs]
K7647	TOC 18.4.41 at Fleet Acft; 1 TC 5.5.41 for 31 SFTS; hit by R3995 while running up, Kingston, 21.5.41; 6 RD 9.8.41; 3 TC 8.12.41 for CTS Rockliffe; 6 RD 9.3.42; 9 RD 12.4.42; SOC 20.4.44
K7652/1917	TOC 7.4.41 at Acft Repair; 2 TC 7.5.41 for 5 B&GS; GI airframe number A261 allotted 9.1.43 but apparently not used; SOC 11.3.43 for spares
K7660/1738	TOC 6.12.40 at Fleet Acft; 1 TC 14.1.41; 3 TC for cv to TT 4.2.42; 9 RD 11.11.43; SOC 15.5.44
K7671	TOC 17.4.41 at 6 RD; 1 TC 6.5.41 for 31 B&GS; 6 RD 18.1.43; SOC 26.2.44 for spares
K7695/1708	TOC 15.10.40 at Trenton; 1 TC 12.11.40 for 4 B&GS; 3 TC 8.12.41; 6 RD 13.2.42; Fleet 20.5.42; 9 RD 18.7.42 for tf to CCF; turret fitted at CCF 9.11.42; 3 B&GS 22.2.43; SR 21.3.44; 2 TC 23.5.44; SOC for WAC 16.2.45 [488 hrs]
K7701	TOC 26.5.41 at 6 RD; 1 TC 10.6.41 for 31 B&GS; 9 RD 29.10.42 for turret fitment by CCF; 3 TC SR 10.3.43; SOC 4.11.44 for WAC [613 hrs]
K7703/1763	TOC 8.11.40 at Acft Repair; 4 TC 16.12.40 for 2 B&GS; engine cut; bellylanded, Mossbank, 16.3.41; undercarriage leg collapsed taxying, Mossbank, 10.4.42; ran off runway and undercarriage collapsed, Mossbank, 31.7.42; 8 RD 21.11.42; 9 RD 13.3.43 for turret fitment; SOC 6.11.44 for WAC
K9178/2117	TOC 31.12.41 at Fleet Acft; 3 TC 9.2.42 for 9 B&GS; 9 RD 14.6.43; SOC 7.3.45 for WAC [961 hrs]
K9182/1842	TOC 6.3.41 at Acft Repair; 2 TC 4.4.41 for 3 B&GS; Central Acft 15.4.43; 3 TC SR 2.8.43; cv to TT 27.11.43; 1 AC SR 15.1.45; SOC 12.6.46 for WAC [1274 hrs]
K9187/2081	TOC 16.9.41 at Acft Repair; 4 TC 11.10.41 for 8 B&GS; SR 18.11.42; Central Acft 1.4.43; cv to TT; 3 TC SR 29.7.43; issued to 10 B&GS 26.11.43; SR 17.4.44; issued to 9 B&GS 10.7.44;
	SR 9.4.45; sold 17.6.46 to WAC [918 hrs]
K9190/1874	TOC 5.4.41 at Acft Repair; cv to TT by Mackenzie Air Services 5.6.41; 4 TC 25.9.41 for 8 B&GS; Central Acft 8.6.43; 3 TC SR 7.2.44; 9 B&GS 7.8.44; bellylanded with engine failure 2m W of Baie des Sables, 6.2.45; SR 9.4.45; sold 17.6.46 to WAC [906 hrs]
K9191/1703	TOC 23.9.40 at Trenton; 4 TC for 2 B&GS 25.10.40; tipped up while running up, Mossbank, 4.11.41; SR 13.10.42; SOC 11.1.43 for spares
K9194	TOC 8.5.41 at 6 RD; 1 TC 27.5.41 for 31 B&GS. Engine lost power; hit tree in forced landing, Wampoos Island, in St.Lawrence near Prescott, Ont., 11.3.42; SOC 5.5.42
K9203/2042	TOC 22.7.41 at 8 RD; 2 TC 26.8.41 for 7 B&GS. Engine lost power; overshot forced landing and hit trees 1½m NE of Paulson, Man., 8.8.42; to 10 RD for spares recovery and SOC 2.11.42
K9204/2100	TOC 9.10.41 at Acft Repair; 4 TC 5.11.41 for 8 B&GS; SR 18.11.42; Central Acft 1.4.43; cv to TT; 3 TC SR 26.6.43; issued to 10 B&GS 1.11.43; overshot landing into ditch, Mount Pleasant, 7.2.44; SR 17.4.44; issued to 10 B&GS 13.6.44; SR 9.4.45; sold 17.6.46 to WAC [723 hrs]
K9210/1907	TOC 22.4.41 at Fleet Acft; 1 TC 8.5.41 for 6 B&GS; CTS/31 B&GS. Engine cut on take-off; crashlanded, Picton, 13.8.41; not repaired and SOC 4.12.41 [155 hrs]
K9211/1872	TOC 24.3.41 at Fleet Acft; 1 TC 28.4.41 for CTS Picton; 3 TC 8.12.41; 6 RD 13.2.42; Fleet Acft 20.5.42; 9 RD 18.7.42 for turret fitment by CCF; 2 TC 18.2.43 for 3 B&GS; SR 21.3.44; SOC 16.2.45 for WAC
K9212/1824	TOC 8.1.41 at Fleet Acft; 1 TC 29.1.41 for 1 B&GS; CCF for turret fitment 24.8.42; 3 TC for 9 B&GS 7.11.42; 3 TC SR 16.3.43; 9 B&GS 2.6.43; SR 23.9.44; 1 AC 15.1.45; sold 17.6.46 to WAC [1654 hrs]
K9213/2036	TOC 22.7.41 at 8 RD; 2 TC for 7 B&GS 20.8.41; 8 RD 15.12.42; 9 RD 13.3.43; SOC 4.11.44 for WAC [610 hrs]
K9214/1878	TOC 7.4.41 at 8 RD; 2 TC 16.5.41; to 5 B&GS 19.5.41; SR 26.1.43; 9 RD 26.3.43 for turret fitment by CCF; Central Acft 28.4.43; 3 TC SR 19.1.44; SOC 4.11.44 for WAC [961 hrs]
K9215/2122	TOC 9.1.42 at Fleet Acft; 3 TC 24.2.42 for 9 B&GS; cv to GI airframe A267 9.1.43; 9 RD 23.3.44; SOC 9.6.44 for spares
K9217/1978	TOC 27.5.41 at Acft Repair and cv to TT by MacKenzie Air Services 5.6.41; 2 TC 9.7.41 for 3 B&GS; hit by 1845 while parked, MacDonald, 27.9.41; engine cut; bellylanded 7m NE of MacDonald, 16.2.44; SR 21.3.44; SOC 16.2.45 for WAC [1692 hrs]
K9229/2101	TOC 9.10.41 at Acft Repair; 4 TC 5.11.41 for 8 B&GS; Central Acft 4.8.43; SOC 25.3.44 for spares
K9231/2083	TOC 22.9.41 at Acft Repair; 4 TC 16.10.41; SR 18.11.42; Central Acft 10.6.43; 1 TC SR 10.12.43; SOC 13.2.45 for WAC [444 hrs]
K9244	TOC 11.6.41 at Fleet Acft; 1 TC 3.7.41 for 31 SFTS; 6 RD 10.9.41; 9 RD 10.9.42 for turret fitment by CCF; 2 TC 27.1.43 for 3 B&GS; SR 21.3.44; SOC 16.2.45 for WAC [475 hrs]
K9247	TOC 29.3.41 at Fleet Acft and cv to TT; 1 TC 21.4.41 for 31 B&GS; 9 RD 15.10.42; 6 RD 13.11.42; SOC 24.3.44 for spares
K9248/1767	TOC 13.11.40 at Acft Repair; 4 TC 27.12.40 for 2 B&GS; engine cut on take-off; bellylanded 5½m E of Mossbank, 23.3.41; SR 13.10.42; SOC 11.1.43
K9250/1735	TOC 24.10.40 at Trenton; 1 TC 12.11.40 for 31 B&GS; CTS Picton. Hydraulics burst and pilot

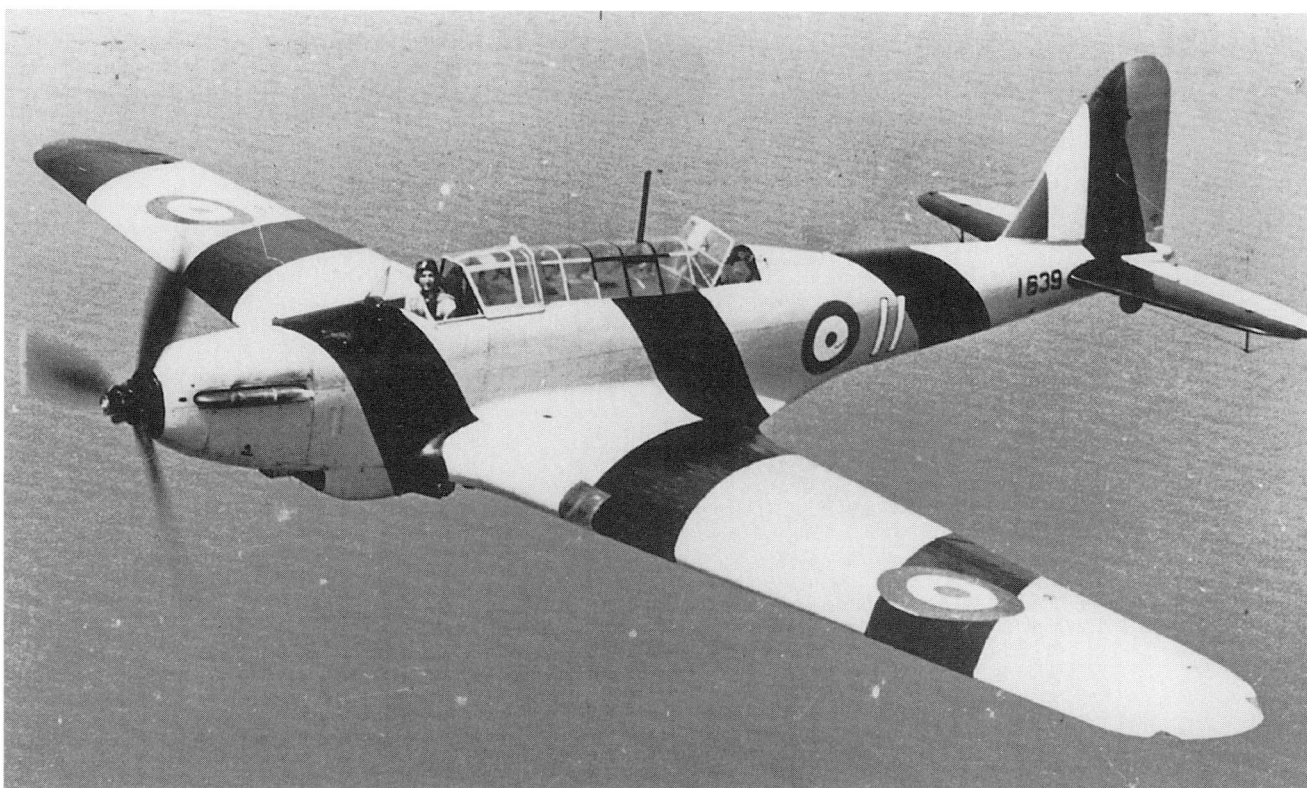

Battle target tug 1639 with the Test & Development Establishment at Trenton. (via Bruce Robertson)

temporarily blinded; abandoned, South Bat, 8m SE of Picton, Ont., 23.4.41; SOC 13.6.41; GI airframe A264 not used

K9253/2103 TOC 11.9.41 at Acft Repair; 4 TC 5.11.41 for 8 B&GS; Central Acft 3.6.43; 3 TC SR 1.2.44; SOC 7.3.45 for WAC [942 hrs]

K9255/1815 TOC 8.1.41 at Fleet Acft; 1 TC 22.1.41 for 4 B&GS; taxied into bowser, Fingal, 9.11.41; engine cut on take-off; bellylanded, Fingal, 11.5.42; Fleet Acft 21.5.42; 9 RD 19.10.42; CCF for turret fitment 19.10.42; 3 TC SR 28.4.43; SOC 4.11.44 for WAC

K9258/1769 TOC 16.11.40 at Aircraft Repair; 4 TC 14.1.41 for 2 B&GS; engine lost power due to glycol leak; bellylanded 3m NE of Ardill, Sask., 9.3.43; 8 RD 14.5.43; Central Acft 25.7.43; SOC 23.3.44 for spares

K9265/1737 TOC 24.10.40 at Trenton; 1 TC 12.11.40 for 4 B&GS; engine cut; crashlanded 3m S of Melbourne; 2.2.42; Central Acft 10.5.42; 9 RD 20.1.43; 3 TC 26.7.44; SOC 8.11.44 for WAC

K9268/1933 TOC 22.4.41 at Acft Repair; 2 TC 17.5.41 for 5 B&GS; brakes failed; taxied into hangar, Dafoe, 13.9.41; SR 26.1.43; SOC 16.2.45 for WAC [479 hrs]

K9272/2009 TOC 1.7.41; at 8 RD; 2 TC 5.8.41; to 5 B&GS 10.8.41; taxied into 1924, Dafoe, 18.2.42; SR 16.11.42; SOC 16.2.45 for WAC [662 hrs]

K9274/1759 TOC 8.11.40 at Aircraft Repair; 4 TC 11.12.40 for 2 B&GS; engine cut on take-off; bellylanded 1m E of Mossbank, 12.3.42; Acft Repair 23.3.42; Central Acft 28.1.43; Fairchild 26.4.43 for cv to Battle II but cancelled; 3 TC SR 24.8.43 and cv

TT; 3 TC 9.11.43; SR 12.9.44; 1 AC SR 15.1.45; sold 17.6.46 to WAC [1103 hrs]

K9275/1972 TOC 11.6.41 at Fleet Acft; 1 TC 3.7.41 for 6 B&GS; 9 RD 10.10.42; 3 TC SR 26.7.44; SOC 4.11.44 for WAC [535 hrs]

K9281/1771 TOC 16.11.40 at Acft Repair; cv TT by Acft Repair during erection; 2 TC 5.3.41 for 3 B&GS; bellylanded in error, MacDonald, 24.4.41; 2 TC SR 21.3.44; SOC 16.2.45 for WAC [1525 hrs]

K9284/1791 TOC 8.1.41 at Fleet Acft; 1 TC 16.1.41 for 4 B&GS; 6 RD 18.1.43; SOC 12.1.43

K9288/2054 TOC 12.8.41 at 8 RD; 4 TC 12.9.41 for 8 B&GS; SR 18.11.42; SOC 11.1.43 for spares

K9292/1715 TOC 14.10.40 at Trenton but arrived 6 ARD as damaged by sea water en route; SOC 19.4.41

K9298/2130 TOC 22.1.42 at 4 RD; 3 TC 13.4.42 for 9 B&GS; tyre burst on landing; ground-looped and tipped up, Mont Joli, 29.10.42; 9 RD 14.6.43; SOC 4.11.44 for WAC [982 hrs]

K9299/1722 TOC 17.10.40 at Trenton; 1 TC 12.11.40 for 4 B&GS; 6 RD 14.12.42; SOC 29.9.43 for spares

K9300/2002 TOC 3.7.41 at 8 RD; 2 TC 30.7.41; to 7 B&GS 4.8.41; 8 RD 7.1.43; 2 TC SR 16.4.43; issued to 3 B&GS 17.1.44; SR 21.3.44; SOC 16.2.45 for WAC [855 hrs]

K9303/2127 TOC 9.1.42;at Fleet Acft; 9 RD 4.5.42 for turret fitment by CCF; 3 TC 22.9.42 for 9 B&GS. Engine failed on approach; hit fence and crashlanded ¼m E of Mont Joli, 7.10.43; to 9 RD for spares recovery, 15.10.43; SOC 24.2.44

K9304/1707 TOC 15.10.40 at Trenton; 1 TC 12.11.40; cv TT 29.4.41; 3 TC 24.2.42 for 9 B&GS; ran into 7608 on runway, Mont Joli, 20.10.42; bellylanded in

K9307/2092 — error, Mont Joli, 30.11.42; cv crew trainer 1.6.43; cv back to TT 1.6.43; 1 AC 15.1.45; EAC 3.5.45; sold 17.6.46 to WAC [1754 hrs]

K9307/2092 TOC 11.9.41 at Acft Repair; 4 TC 16.10.41; Central Acft 22.5.43; 1 TC SR1.12.43; SOC 13.2.45 for WAC [504 hrs]

K9309/1989 TOC 11.6.41 at Fleet Acft; 1 TC 8.7.41 for 6 B&GS; 3 TC 6.2.42 for 9 B&GS; 9 RD 31.5.43; 3 TC SR 26.7.44; SOC 6.11.44 for WAC [810 hrs]

K9311/1753 TOC 5.11.40 at Acft Repair; 4 TC 10.12.40 for 2 B&GS. Became lost in bad weather on ferry flight; ran out of fuel and bellylanded 3m N of Hanley, Sask., 25.1.41; to Acft Repair for salvage, 17.4.41 and SOC 1.7.41

K9312/1743 TOC 16.11.40 at Fleet Acft; 1 TC 9.12.40 for 4 B&GS. Engine cut; undercarriage collapsed in forced landing near Fingal, 22.3.41; to Fleet for spares recovery 29.4.41; SOC 26.2.42 [370 hrs]

K9316/1768 TOC 13.11.40 at Aircraft Repair; 4 TC 16.1.41 for 2 B&GS; hit by 1777 while parked, Mossbank, 22.4.41. Tyre burst on take-off; swung off runway and wing hit ground, Mossbank, 11.10.42; SOC 11.1.43

K9317/2048 TOC 22.7.41 at 8 RD; 2 TC 3.9.41 for 5 B&GS; undercarriage jammed; bellylanded, Dafoe, 7.8.42; SR 16.11.42; Central Acft 27.4.43; 3 TC SR 17.8.43; cv to TT; issued to 10 B&GS 11.11.43; engine cut on attempted overshoot; forcelanded, Mount Pleasant, 22.2.44; 4 RD 28.3.44; SOC 15.9.44

K9321/1773 TOC 16.11.40 at Aircraft Repair; 2 TC 5.3.41 for 3 B&GS; cv TT 25.4.41; bellylanded with engine trouble 2½m NE of MacDonald, 7.2.43; 2 TC SR 21.3.44; SOC 16.2.45 for WAC [1424 hrs]

K9323 TOC 27.5.41 at Fleet Acft; 1 TC 12.6.41 for 31 B&GS; engine cut; damaged in forced landing near Picton, 28.10.41; engine cut; bellylanded, South Milford, Ont., 29.1.42; Fleet Acft 11.2.42; 9 RD 3.6.42 for turret fitment by CCF; 2 TC 10.10.42 for 3 B&GS; SR 11.5.44; SOC 16.2.45 for WAC [837 hrs]

K9326/1716 TOC 14.10.40 at Trenton; 1 TC 12.11.40 for 4 B&GS; hydraulics failed; bellylanded ½m SE of Fingal, 8.6.42; Central Acft 24.6.42; 9 RD 1.2.43 for turret fitment; 3 TC SR 7.9.43; SOC 4.11.44 for WAC [5 hrs]

K9332/1894 TOC 18.4.41 at MacDonald Acft; 4 TC 6.10.41 for 8 B&GS; Central Acft 10.6.43; 3 TC SR 23.2.44; SOC 6.11.44 for WAC [473 hrs]

K9341/1802 TOC 7.1.41 at Fleet Acft; 2 TC 17.2.41 for 3 B&GS; 8 RD 14.2.43; 2 TC SR 13.8.43; SOC 16.2.45 for WAC [967 hrs]

K9344/1841 TOC 6.3.41 at Aircraft Repair; 2 TC 3.4.41 for 3 B&GS. Hit by 1966 while parked, MacDonald, 14.1.43; 8 RD 12.2.43 and SOC 17.4.43 for spares

K9350/2069 TOC 24.9.41 at 8 RD; 2 TC 11.11.41 for 5 B&GS. Collided with 1892 during gunnery exercise and abandoned 6m SE of Dafoe, 23.3.42; Sgt E. Naoum and LAC D.F. Hood killed; Sgt W.M. Haggart bailed out safely; SOC 31.3.42

K9351/1870 TOC 24.3.41 at Fleet Acft; 2 TC 3.4.41 for 3 B&GS; undercarriage leg jammed up; damaged on landing, MacDonald, 8.5.41; bellylanded in error, MacDonald, 11.8.41; SR 17.4.43; SOC 16.2.45 for WAC [536 hrs]

K9355/1723 TOC 17.10.40 at Trenton; 1 TC for CTS Picton; brakes failed; ran into fence, Picton, 25.6.41; taxied into Oxford 1521, Picton, 31.7.41; 3 TC 8.12.41; 6 RD 9.3.42; Fleet Acft 20.5.42; 9 RD 18.7.42 for turret fitment by CCF; 2 TC 10.10.42; 3 B&GS 20.12.42; hit by R7420 on runway, MacDonald, 11.8.43; SR 21.3.44; SOC 16.2.45 for WAC [514 hrs]

K9358/2039 TOC 22.7.41 at 8 RD; 2 TC 20.8.41 for 7 B&GS; SOC 11.1.43 for spares

K9365/1868 TOC 24.3.41 at Fleet Acft; 1 TC 9.4.41 for 4 B&GS; 3 TC 11.12.41 for 9 B&GS; overshot landing into deep snow and tipped up, Mont Joli, 14.3.42; tyre burst on landing; ground-looped, Mont Joli, 30.9.42. Bellylanded in bad weather, Keegan, 4m NW of Van Buren, Maine, 2.4.43; 9 RD 10.7.43; SOC 9.12.43

K9376/1714 TOC 14.10.40 at Trenton; Fleet Acft 11.11.40 for winter cv; 4 TC 22.10.41 for 8 B&GS; SR 8.11.42; Central Acft 11.5.43; SR at 3 TC 5.8.43; cv TT 26.11.43; 10 B&GS; Cat. A accident, Mount Pleasant, 28.5.44 but no record found; to 4 RD for salvage, 9.6.44; SOC 29.7.44

K9378/1827 TOC 8.1.41 at Fleet Acft; 1 TC 7.2.41 for 4 BGS; 3 TC 17.6.42 for 9 B&GS; 9 RD 14.6.43; SOC 6.11.44 for WAC [991 hrs]

K9379/2010 TOC 13.7.41 at 8 RD; 2 TC 5.8.41; to 5 B&GS 10.8.41; SOC 11.1.43 for spares

K9382/2109 TOC 9.12.41 at CCF fitted with Blenheim turret; normal Bristol turret fitted by CCF; 3 TC 7.7.42 for 9 B&GS; collided with R7443 5m SSW of Mont Joli, 19.6.43; landed safely; SR 9.4.45; sold 17.6.46 for WAC [1179 hrs]

K9395/2057 TOC 14.7.41 at MacDonald Bros; 2 TC 13.9.41 for 3 B&GS; Central Acft 15.4.43; cv to TT; 3 TC 24.11.43 for 10 B&GS. Dived into ground after streaming drogues 3m S of Mount Pleasant, 31.12.43; Sgt W.J. Pearson, AC2 D.M. Scanlon and H.W. Huntula were killed; to 4 RD for salvage, 11.1.44; SOC 28.3.44 as scrap

K9399 TOC 26.5.41 at 6 RD; 1 TC 10.6.41 for 31 B&GS; 9 RD 1.10.42; SOC 7.3.45 for WAC [766 hrs]

K9401/1948 TOC 14.5.41 at Fleet Acft; 1 TC 4.6.41 for 6 B&GS; taxied into Bolingbroke 9109, Mountain View, 12.8.42; 6 RD 11.1.43; SOC 12.1.43 for spares

K9403/2106 TOC 16.9.41 at Acft Repair; 8 RD 12.11.41; 9 RD 5.8.42 for turret fitment by CCF; 2 TC 10.10.42 for 3 B&GS; SR 12.5.44; SOC 16.2.45 for WAC [1286 hrs]

K9405/1762 TOC 5.11.40 at Acft Repair; 4 TC 1.11.41 for 8 B&GS as TT; 10 RD 17.12.42; Central Acft 22.5.43; 1 TC SR 1.12.43; sold 20.10.44 to WAC [563 hrs]

K9406 TOC 29.3.41 at Fleet Acft; 1 TC 21.4.41 for 31 B&GS; Fleet Acft 14.5.42; 9 RD 29.9.42 for turret fitment by CCF; 3 TC 1.2.43 for 9 B&GS; SR 9.4.45; sold 17.6.46 to WAC [1080 hrs]

K9407/1754 TOC 8.11.40 at Acft Repair; 4 TC 10.12.40 for 2 B&GS; SR 13.10.42; Central Acft 3.5.43; 9 RD 17.1.44 and cv TT; 3 TC 18.7.44 for 9 B&GS; 3 TC SR 23.9.44; sold 17.6.46 to WAC [900 hrs]

K9408/1727 TOC 5.11.40 at MacDonald Bros; 4 TC 2.12.40 for 2 B&GS; brakes failed taxying and tipped up in snowbank, Mossbank 27.2.42; SR 13.10.42; Central Acft 10.6.43; 3 TC SR 13.3.44; 9 RD; SOC 7.3.45 for WAC [257 hrs]

K9413/1895 TOC 7.4.41 at 8 RD and cv to TT; 2 TC 5.7.41 for 3 B&GS; CCF 11.12.41; 10 RD 2.2.42; 4 FC 17.6.42; Central Acft 10.6.43; SR 6.3.44; SOC 7.3.45 for WAC [1006 hrs]

K9414/2078 TOC 11.9.41 at Acft Repair; 4 TC 11.10.41 for 8 B&GS; lost power in circuit and bellylanded 1½m SW of Lethbridge, 7.9.42; engine cut; bellylanded in Old Man River 10m N of Coaldale, Alta., 28.9.42; SOC 20.7.43

K9417 TOC 27.5.41 at Fleet Acft and cv to TT; 1 TC 12.6.41 for 31 B&GS; 6 RD 10.9.42; 1 TC 1.11.41; 6 RD 28.1.43; SOC 27.4.43 for spares

Turret trainer R7384 with No.3 Bombing & Gunnery School, Macdonald, Manitoba. (P Jarrett collection)

K9421/2063   TOC 21.8.41 at Acft Repair; 9 RD 24.8.42 for turret fitment by CCF; 2 TC 20.12.42 for 3 B&GS; SR 21.3.44; SOC 16.2.45 for WAC

K9423/1749   TOC 16.11.40 at Fleet Acft; 1 TC 9.12.40 for 4 B&GS; 9 RD 10.10.42; CCF 10.10.42 for turret fitment 18.2.43; 2 TC 18.2.43 for 3 B&GS; SR 21.3.44; SOC 16.2.45 for WAC [1360 hrs]

K9424/2094   TOC 11.9.41 at Acft Repair; 4 TC 16.10.41 for 8 B&GS; SR 18.11.42; Central Acft 10.6.43; 1 TC SR 14.12.43; SOC 13.2.45 for WAC [420 hrs]

K9425/2089   TOC 11.9.41 at Acft Repair; 4 TC 5.11.41 for 8 B&GS; SR 18.11.42; allotted GI airframe A273 9.1.43 but not taken up; SOC 26.1.43 for spares

K9427/2091   TOC 11.9.41 at Acft Repair; 4 TC 16.10.41; Central Acft 10.6.43; SOC 15.2.44

K9431/1901   TOC 5.4.41 at Acft Repair; 4 TC 30.4.41 for 2 B&GS; hit by 1316 while parked, Mossbank, 11.3.42; SR 13.10.42; 9 RD 20.4.43; SOC 6.11.44 for WAC [730 hrs]

K9436/2015   TOC 14.7.41 at MacDonald Bros; 2 TC 21.8.41 for 7 B&GS; 8 RD 15.12.42; 2 TC SR 16.4.43; issued to 3 B&GS 17.1.44; SR 21.3.44; SOC 16.2.45 for WAC [758 hrs]

K9439/1789   TOC 27.12.40 at De Havilland; 2 TC 19.2.41 for 3 B&GS; landed with undercarriage unlocked, MacDonald, 28.3.41; SR 17.4.43; SOC 16.2.45 for WAC [501 hrs]

K9449/1947   TOC 14.5.41 at Fleet Acft; 1 TC 6.6.41; to 6 B&GS 26.6.41; 9 RD 18.8.42 for turret fitment by CCF; 3 TC 5.12.42 for 9 B&GS; SR 16.3.43; hit by 2111 while parked, Mont Joli, 12.6.43; sold 17.6.46 for WAC [1767 hrs]

K9451/1903   TOC 5.4.41 at Acft Repair; 2 TC for 5 B&GS 19.5.41; engine lost power on take-off; overshot, Dafoe, 30.4.42. Engine lost power after take-off; crashlanded into trees 1m NE of Dafoe, 21.10.42; to 8 RD 3.11.42 and cv to GI airframe A258 9.1.43 for 3 WS; 8 RD 1.9.43 and SOC 11.12.43

K9453/1772   TOC 16.11.40 at Aircraft Repair; 2 TC 5.3.41 for 3 B&GS; cv TT 25.4.41 at 3 B&GS. Engine failed while target towing; bellylanded 7m N of MacDonald, 6.11.43; 8 RD 11.11.43; SOC 27.11.43 for spares

K9454/1782   TOC 27.12.40 at De Havilland; 2 TC 15.3.41 for 3 B&GS; Central Acft 15.4.43; 9 RD 7.1.44 for cv to TT; 3 TC SR 24.10.44; SOC 7.3.45 for WAC [922 hrs]

K9455/1908   TOC 22.4.41 at Fleet Acft; 1 TC for AAS, later 5 B&GS; damaged in forced landing 22m SW of Dafoe, Sask., 2.6.42. Brake failed; swung into hangar, Mountain View, 8.8.42; not repaired, sent to 6 RD and SOC 12.1.43 for spares

K9456/1734   TOC 24.10.40 at Trenton; 1 TC 12.11.40 for 31 B&GS. Collided with Yale 3359 on approach and lost elevator; crashlanded, Picton, 15.1.41; PO C.W. Hickerson severely injured; to spares and SOC 12.5.41 [392 hrs]

K9457/2076   TOC 24.9.41 at 8 RD; 2 TC 3.11.41 for 7 B&GS; SR 17.11.42; SOC 11.1.43 for spares

K9458/2102   TOC 9.10.41 at Acft Repair; 4 TC 5.11.41 for 8 B&GS; SR 18.11.42; Central Acft 11.5.43; 1 TC SR 23.9.43; SOC 13.2.45 for WAC [566 hrs]

K9459/1873   TOC 24.3.41 at Fleet Acft; 1 TC 28.4.41 for CTS Picton; 3 TC 8.12.41 for CTS Rockliffe; taxied into Oxford 1521, Rockliffe, 9.1.42; 6 RD 1.4.42; Fleet Acft 20.5.42; 9 RD 26.8.42 for turret fitment by CCF; 2 TC 10.10.42 for 3 B&GS. Hit by 1680 on runway, MacDonald, 17.2.43; 8 RD 23.3.43 and SOC 28.4.43 for spares

K9461/2019   TOC 22.7.41 at Fleet Acft; 1 TC 3.9.41 for 6 B&GS; 9 RD 24.8.42 for turret fitment by CCF; 3 TC 7.11.42 for 9 B&GS; jumped chocks running up and hit Nomad 3508, Mont Joli, 19.1.43; 9 RD 24.8.43; SOC 4.11.44 for WAC

K9465/1821   TOC 8.1.41 at Fleet Acft; 1 TC 23.1.41 for 4 B&GS; CCF 10.10.42 for turret fitment; 3 TC SR 10.3.43; SOC 4.11.44 for WAC [725 hrs]

K9466/1848   TOC 6.3.41 at MacDonald Bros; 2 TC 8.5.41 for 5 B&GS. Bellylanded while drogue towing 2m

K9474/1879   NW of Dafoe, Sask., 11.6.41; DBR and SOC 7.3.42

K9474/1879   TOC 7.4.41 at 8 RD and cv to TT; 2 TC 15.7.41; 4 TC 8.9.41 for 8 B&GS; SR 18.11.42; Central Acft 10.6.43; 9 RD 10.6.44; 3 TC 12.7.44 for 9 B&GS; SR 9.4.45; sold 17.6.46 to WAC [629 hrs]

K9475/1705   TOC 23.9.40 at Trenton; 4 TC 25.10.40 for 2 B&GS, 32 SFTS; SR 25.11.42; SOC 11.1.43

K9476   TOC 8.5.41 at 6 RD; 1 TC 27.5.41 for 31 B&GS; hit by P2304 while taxying, Picton, 8.3.42; cv to TT; 10.7.41; 6 RD 28.1.43; SOC 27.4.43 for spares

K9479/1816   TOC 8.1.41 at Fleet Acft; 1 TC 22.1.41 for 4 B&GS; landed with wheels up and prop hit runway; took overshoot action and landed OK, Fingal, 12.6.42; 3 TC 17.6.42 for 9 B&GS; SOC 11.1.43

L4935/2095   TOC 16.9.41 at Acft Repair; 4 TC 21.10.41 for 8 B&GS; collided with 2095 10m W of Lethbridge, 18.5.42; returned safely; Central Acft 7.8.43; SOC 17.2.44

L4937/1982   TOC 13.5.41 at Acft Repair; cv to TT by MacKenzie Air Services 5.6.41; 4 TC 9.7.41 for 2 B&GS; engine overheated; bellylanded on shore of lake 6m NW of Mossbank, 20.9.42; SR 13.10.42; SOC 11.1.43 for spares

L4938/1813   TOC 8.1.41 at Fleet Acft; 1 TC 22.1.41 for 1 B&GS; engine cut; forcelanded 3m W of Port Dover, 7.9.41; CCF 26.8.42 for turret fitment; 3 TC 12.11.42; 9 B&GS 6.12.42; SR 16.3.43; 9 B&GS 19.6.43; belly-landed with engine failure, Baie des Sables, Que., 27.11.44; 1 AC 15.1.45; sold 17.6.46 to WAC [1599 hrs]

L4940/1755   TOC 27.11.40 at MacDonald Bros; 2 TC 1.3.41 for 3 B&GS; cv to TT 25.4.42. Control lost at low altitude; dived into ground 10m N of MacDonald, 11.7.42; Sgt N. Moss, LAC C. Off and AC2 J.P. Buzik killed; to spares 30.7.42; SOC 12.8.42

L4942/1747   TOC 16.11.40 at Fleet Acft; 1 TC 9.12.40 for 4 B&GS; engine failed; crashlanded, Melbourne range, near Fingal, 15.4.42; not repaired; 6 RD 11.1.43; SOC 12.1.43

L4947/1757   TOC 27.11.40 at MacDonald Bros; 2 TC 1.3.41 for 3 B&GS; cv TT 25.4.41; SR 24.3.44; SOC 16.2.45 for WAC [472 hrs]

L4953/1890   TOC 7.4.41 at 8 RD and cv to TT; 2 TC 1.7.41 for 3 B&GS; 4 TC 6.10.41 for 7 B&GS; Central Acft 3.8.43; SOC 19.3.44 for spares

L4955/1765   TOC 13.11.40 at Aircraft Repair; 4 TC 27.12.40 for 2 B&GS; SR 3.10.42; Central Acft 12.4.43; 3 TC SR 8.6.43; cv TT; 10 B&GS 4.11.43; SR 24.8.44; sold 17.6.46 to WAC [963 hrs]

L4957/2056   TOC 25.8.41 at 8 RD; 4 TC 10.9.41 for 8 B&GS; taxied into Delta 689, Lethbridge, 19.11.41; overshot night landing into fence, Lethbridge, 4.12.41; SR 18.11.42; SOC 11.1.43 for spares

L4960/1761   TOC 5.11.40 at Acft Repair; 4 TC 11.12.40 for 2 B&GS; 7 B&GS 25.6.41; engine cut after take-off; crashlanded ½m E of Paulson, Man, 4.2.42; MacDonald Acft 2.3.42; CCF 12.9.42 for turret fitment; 3 TC SR 1.6.43; sold 17.6.46 to WAC [443 hrs]

L4961/2085   TOC 16.9.41 at Acft Repair; 4 TC 16.10.41 for 8 B&GS; SR 18.11.42; Central Acft 1.4.43; cv to TT; 3 TC SR 8.7.43; issued to 10 B&GS 11.11.43; later to 9 B&GS; SR 24.8.44; sold 17.6.46 to WAC [861 hrs]

L4962/2017   TOC 22.7.41 at Fleet Acft; 1 TC 25.8.41 for 1 B&GS; cv to GI airframe A160 18.7.42; SOC 21.1.44 for spares

L4963   TOC 29.3.41 at Fleet Acft and fitted as TT; 1 TC 28.4.41 for 31 B&GS; 6 RD 24.11.42; Central Acft 17.6.43; SOC 17.2.44

L4964/1881   TOC 7.4.41 at 8 RD; 2 TC 16.5.41; to 5 B&GS

L4968/1987   22.5.41; 8 RD 13.3.42; SOC 10.6.42 for spares

L4968/1987   TOC 11.6.41 at Fleet Acft; 1 TC 8.7.41 for 6 B&GS; 3 TC 6.2.42 for 9 B&GS; to GI airframe A256 25.1.43; SOC 15.9.44 for spares

L4969/2028   TOC 24.7.41 at Fleet Acft; 1 TC 11.8.41 for 6 B&GS; brakes failed; ran into 2330 and 1990, Mountain View, 11.10.41; 6 RD 13.11.41; 9 RD 21.7.42 for turret fitment by CCF; 2 TC 10.10.42 for 3 B&GS; SR 2.4.44; SOC 16.2.45 for WAC [658 hrs]

L4973   TOC 11.6.41 at Fleet Acft; 1 TC 8.7.41 for 31 SFTS; 6 RD 19.9.41; cv to GI airframe A187 25.9.42; SOC 26.4.44

L4984/2090   TOC 11.9.41 to Acft Repair; 4 TC 16.10.41 for 8 B&GS; SR 18.11.42; Central Acft 11.5.43; cv to TT; 3 TC SR 9.7.43; issued to 10 B&GS 4.11.43; SR 18.9.44; SOC 11.6.46 for WAC [603 hrs]

L4986/2111   TOC 13.12.41 at Fleet Acft; 3 TC 17.1.42 for 9 B&GS; swung into snowbank taxying and tipped up, Mont Joli, 6.4.42; taxied into 1947, Mont Joli, 12.6.43; 9 RD 8.7.43; 3 TC SR 1.3.44; issued to 9 B&GS 9.8.44; engine cut; bellylanded 2m E of Mont Joli, 8.12.44; SR 9.4.45; sold 17.6.46 to WAC [618 hrs]

L4987   TOC 17.4.41 at Ottawa Car Co; 1 TC 10.5.41 for 31 B&GS; landed without flaps and overshot landing; undercarriage leg collapsed, Picton, 14.7.41; tyre burst on landing; swung off runway and tipped up, Picton, 12.4.42; 9 RD 15.10.42 for turret fitment by CCF; 3 TC SR 1.6.43; SOC 4.11.44 for WAC [290 hrs]

L4988/2125   TOC 9.1.42 at Fleet Acft; 3 C&F Flt St.Hubert; ran into snowbank taxying, Mont Joli, 24.1.42; 3 TC 24.2.42 for 9 B&GS; undercarriage collapsed during take-off run, Mont Joli, 15.5.42; cv to GI airframe A265 9.1.43; 9 RD 28.8.44; SOC 15.9.44 for spares

L4990/2105   TOC 11.9.41 at Acft Repair; 4 TC 5.11.41 for 8 B&GS; Central Acft 3.6.43; 3 TC SR 23.2.44; SOC 4.11.44 for WAC [358 hrs]

L4994/1944   TOC 22.4.41 at Acft Repair; 2 TC 2.6.41; to 7 B&GS 22.6.41; SOC 11.1.43 for spares

L5002/1758   TOC 27.11.40 at MacDonald Bros; 4 TC 8.2.41 for 2 B&GS; cv TT 25.4.41; engine cut; bellylanded 8m NW of Mossbank, 24.7.41; 4 TC SR 13.10.42; cv to GI airframe A268 at 2 WS 9.1.43 SOC 1.12.43

L5007/1746   TOC 16.11.40 at Fleet Acft; 1 TC 9.12.40 for 4 B&GS; engine lost power; bellylanded, Fingal, 1.2.41; hydraulic fluid blinded pilot; bellylanded, Fingal, 14.4.42; Fleet Acft 11.5.42; CCF 28.9.42 for turret fitment; 3 TC SR 6.5.43; 9 B&GS 22.11.44; engine lost power; bellylanded, Mont Joli, 7.1.45; engine cut; bellylanded, Luceville, Que., 5.3.45; SOC 1.4.46 for WAC [95 hrs]

L5008/1833   TOC 8.1.41 at Fleet Acft; 2 TC 15.3.41 for 3 B&GS; ran into drilling machine on landing on icy runway, Fort Erie, 25.3.41; SR 17.4.43; SOC 16.2.45 for WAC [664 hrs]

L5009   TOC 8.5.41 at Fleet Acft; 1 TC 6.6.41 for 31 B&GS; 6 RD 4.1.43; SOC 1.3.44 for spares

L5016/1774   TOC 16.11.40 at Acft Repair; 2 TC 5.3.41 for 3 B&GS; cv TT 25.4.41; 3 B&GS 30.9.43. Engine lost power while towing drogue; belly-landed 3½m NE of MacDonald, 25.9.43; SOC 6.10.43 for spares

L5020/1720   TOC 17.10.40 at Trenton; 1 TC 12.11.40; 2 TC 19.3.41 for 3 B&GS; brakes failed; hit 1820 and bowser, MacDonald, 4.3.42; cv TT 22.4.43; SR 21.3.44; SOC 16.2.45 for WAC [910 hrs]

L5021/1935   TOC 7.4.41 at Acft Repair; 2 TC 17.5.41; to 5 B&GS 22.5.41; SR 26.1.43; SOC 16.2.45 for WAC [723 hrs]

L5026/2064   TOC 25.9.41 at 8 RD; 4 TC 23.11.41 for 8

1855 was a target tug attached to No.5 Bombing & Gunnery School, Fingal, Ontario. (Bud Saunders via D Howley)

	B&GS; SR 18.11.42; SOC 11.1.43 for spares
L5030/2027	TOC 22.7.41 at Fleet Acft; 1 TC 25.9.41 for 8 B&GS; SR 18.11.42; allotted GI airframe number A272 9.1.43 but SOC 26.1.43 for spares
L5032/1730	TOC 5.11.40 at MacDonald Bros. Engine cut in transit from MacDonald Acft to 2 B&GS; pilot bailed out due to fumes 14m from Virden, Man., 8.12.40; SOC 12.3.41
L5033/1996	TOC 1.7.41 at 6 RD; 1 TC 15.7.41 for 6 B&GS; 9 RD 10.10.42 for turret fitment by CCF; 2 TC 1.2.43 for 3 B&GS; SR 21.3.44; SOC 16.2.45 for WAC
L5036	TOC 1.7.41 at 6 RD; 1 TC 21.8.41 for 31 B&GS; cockpit filled with glycol fumes; crashlanded on No.3 Range, Picton, 17.3.42; 6 RD 17.4.42; Central Acft 23.6.42; 9 RD 28.12.42 for turret fitment by CCF; 3 TC SR 7.9.43; SOC 7.3.45 for WAC [166 hrs]
L5040/2079	TOC 11.9.41 at Acft Repair; 4 TC 11.10.41 for 8 B&GS; SR 18.11.42; SOC 16.2.45 for WAC [324 hrs]
L5041	TOC 8.5.41 at 6 RD and cv to TT; 1 TC 27.5.41 for 31 B&GS; 9 RD 23.9.42 and cv to standard; 3 TC SR 5.10.43; SOC 4.11.44 for WAC
L5042/1847	TOC 6.3.41 at Acft Repair; 2 TC 8.4.41 for 3 B&GS; undercarriage jammed; bellylanded, MacDonald, 24.7.41; 124 Ferry Sqn; tipped up in deep snow taxying, Armstrong, Ont., 22.3.43; Central Acft 3.6.43; 1 TC SR 2.11.43; SOC 13.2.45 for WAC [711 hrs]
L5043/1830	TOC 7.1.41 at Fleet Acft; 1 TC 11.2.41 for 4 B&GS; engine cut; bellylanded, Fingal 17.5.41; 9 RD 7.10.42; engine cut on ferry flight; bellylanded

	among trees near Richmond, Ont., 28.9.42; Central Acft 24.10.42; 9 RD 29.3.43; SOC 6.11.44 for WAC [261 hrs]
L5045/1913	TOC 16.4.41 at 8 RD and cv to TT; 2 TC 3.7.41 for 3 B&GS; SR 16.11.42; 2 TC 16.2.43 for 3 B&GS; SR 21.3.44; SOC 16.2.45 for WAC [1256 hrs]
L5048	TOC 26.5.41 at 6 RD; 1 TC 10.6.41 for 31 SFTS; 6 RD 9.8.41; 4 TC 6.10.41; SR 18.11.42; Central Acft 11.5.43; 1 TC SR 13.10.43; SOC 13.2.45 for WAC [370 hrs]
L5053/2112	TOC 13.12.41 at Fleet Acft; 3 TC 17.1.42 for 9 B&GS; 9 RD 14.6.43; SOC 7.3.45 for WAC [971 hrs]
L5055/2004	TOC 22.7.41 at Fleet Acft; 1 TC 8.9.41 for 6 B&GS; 6 RD 11.1.43; SOC 12.1.43 for spares
L5062/2011	TOC 1.7.41 at 8 RD; 2 TC 8.8.41; SOC 11.1.43 for spares
L5063	TOC 16.9.41 at Fleet Acft; received without various parts at 6 RD 3.11.41 and cv to GI airframe A186 25.9.42; SOC 4.8.44
L5064/1990	TOC 11.6.41 at Fleet Acft; 1 TC 8.7.41 for 6 B&GS; hit by 2028 on taxiway, Mountain View, 11.10.41; 3 TC 11.12.41 for 9 B&GS; hit by 2116 while parked, Mont Joli, 16.8.42; 9 RD 14.6.43; SOC 6.11.44 for WAC [824 hrs]
L5068/1859	TOC 20.3.41 at 8 RD; 2 TC 14.5.41; to 5 B&GS 19.5.41; SR 4.4.44; SOC 16.2.45 for WAC [491 hrs]
L5073	TOC 16.9.41 at Fleet Acft; 1 TC 3.12.41 for 31 B&GS; 6 RD 24.11.42; 1 TC 21.6.43 for tests at 6 RD; SOC 15.5.46 for WAC [297 hrs]
L5076/1897	TOC 7.4.41 at 8 RD; 2 TC for 7 B&GS 27.6.41;

	SOC 11.1.43 for spares
L5080/1905	TOC 21.4.41 at Fleet Acft; 1 TC 2.5.41 for 4 B&GS; bellylanded, Fingal, 15.1.42; 3 TC 4.2.42 for 9 B&GS; engine lost power on overshoot; landed in deep snow and tipped up 1m SE of Mont Joli, 3.3.42; cv to GI airframe A266 25.1.43; 9 RD 28.8.44; SOC 15.9.44
L5081/1902	TOC 7.4.41 at Acft Repair 4 TC 30.4.41 for 2 B&GS; engine failed; bellylanded 10m NW of Mossbank, 29.7.42; SOC 20.7.43 for spares [793 hrs]
L5089	TOC 30.5.40 at TTS St.Thomas as GI airframe A088; SOC 14.2.45
L5092/1884	TOC 7.4.41 at 8 RD; 2 TC 12.6.41 for 3 B&GS; SR 16.11.42; 9 RD 24.3.43; SOC 6.11.44 for WAC [865 hrs]
L5095/2110	TOC 13.1.41 at Fleet Acft; 1 TC 10.1.42 for 1 B&GS; 9 RD 10.10.42 for turret fitment by CCF; 3 TC SR 7.9.43; SOC 7.3.45 for WAC [375 hrs]
L5100/2041	TOC 12.8.41 at Fleet Acft; 1 TC 27.8.41 for 1 B&GS; 9 RD 26.9.42 but turret fitment by CCF cancelled; 3 TC SR 22.2.44; sold 17.6.46 to WAC [529 hrs]
L5101/1970	TOC 11.6.41 at Fleet Acft; 1 TC 3.7.41 for 6 B&GS; 6 RD 11.2.43; SOC 24.3.44 for spares
L5102/1713	TOC 14.10.40 at Trenton; 1 TC 12.11.40 for 4 B&GS; 6 RD 18.1.43; SOC 12.1.43
L5104/1794	TOC 8.1.41 at Fleet Acft; 1 TC 18.1.41 for 4 B&GS; 3 TC 11.12.41 for 9 B&GS; swung on take-off into snow and tipped up, Mont Joli, 3.3.42; tyre burst on landing; swung and tipped up, Mont Joli, 5.5.42; hit fence on take-off and undercarriage collapsed on landing, Mont Joli, 4.7.42; Central Acft 1.8.42; not repaired and SOC 13.1.43 for spares
L5106/1798	TOC 7.1.41 at Fleet Acft; 1 TC 5.2.41 for 2 B&GS; 6 RD 12.12.42; SOC 1.5.44 for spares
L5109/1706	TOC 23.9.40 at Trenton; 4 TC 25.10.40 for 2 B&GS; 8 RD 21.11.42; 9 RD 27.2.43 for turret fitment; SOC 6.11.44 for WAC [724 hrs]
L5111/2099	TOC 9.10.41 at Acft Repair; 4 TC 27.10.41 for 8 B&GS; SR 18.11.42; Central Acft 10.6.43; 1 TC SR 11.11.43; SOC 13.2.45 for WAC [951 hrs]
L5115	TOC 8.5.41 at 6 RD; 1 TC 27.5.41 for 31 B&GS; cv to TT; undercarriage collapsed on landing, Picton, 12.2.42; 9 RD 27.10.42; 6 RD 18.12.42; SOC 23.3.44 for spares
L5116/1993	TOC 1.7.41 at 6 RD; 1 TC 15.7.41 for 6 B&GS; 3 TC 11.12.41 for 9 B&GS; bellylanded after engine failure ¼m S of Mont Joli, 3.3.42; undercarriage leg fell off on take-off; bellylanded, Mont Joli, 16.9.42; lost power on take-off; ran into ditch, Mont Joli, 1.12.42. Engine cut; bellylanded, Little Metis, PQ, 5m E of Mont Joli, 18.5.43; SOC 26.8.43
L5118/1962	TOC 3.6.41 at 6 RD; 2 TC 23.6.41; to 7 B&GS 1.7.41; pilot blinded by glycol leak; overshot landing across road, Paulson, 7.10.41; MacDonald Bros 20.10.42; retd to 7 B&GS 7.7.42. Collided with Lysander 2389 and lost tail; fell into Lake Dauphin 10m NW of Dauphin, Man., 2.9.42; Sgt C.P.A. Lowe, LAC D.W. Duncan and LAC K.A. Lambert killed; SOC 8.10.42
L5119/1992	TOC 1.7.41 at 6 RD; 1 TC 15.7.41 for 6 B&GS; 3 TC 17.6.42 for 9 B&GS; swung on landing and undercarriage leg collapsed, Mont Joli, 30.10.42; 9 RD 31.5.43 for cv to TT; 3 TC SR 13.7.44; retd to 9 B&GS 13.11.44; SOC 12.6.46 for WAC [693 hrs]
L5120/1781	TOC 21.12.40 at Fleet Acft; 1 TC 13.1.41 for 4 B&GS; engine cut in circuit; overshot forced landing, Fingal, 18.6.42; 6 RD 23.11.42; Central Acft 17.6.43; SOC 31.3.44 for spares
L5121/2046	TOC 22.7.41 at 8 RD; 2 TC 3.9.41 for 3 B&GS; Central Acft 15.4.43; 1 TC SR 12.10.43; SOC
L5126/2062	13.2.45 for WAC [539 hrs] TOC 21.8.41 at Acft Repair; 4 TC 15.3.42 for 2 B&GS; 6 RD 21.11.42; 3 TC SR 2.5.43; issued to 9 B&GS 15.7.43; to 10 B&GS by 3.44; blown off taxiway and undercarriage leg collapsed, Mount Pleasant, 10.3.44; SR 18.7.44; sold 17.6.46 to WAC [639 hrs]
L5127	TOC 19.5.41 at TTS St.Thomas after being reduced to spares at Fleet Acft; remains to GI purposes as A133; SOC 21.1.44
L5130/2140	TOC 14.10.42 at 9 RD; sent to CCF for turret fitment; 3 TC 5.12.42 for 9 B&GS; SR 16.3.43; issued to 9 B&GS 19.4.43; SR 22.1.44; sold 17.6.46 to WAC [654 hrs]
L5131/2138	TOC 10.4.42 at 4 RD; 3 TC 24.6.42 for 9 B&GS; SOC 11.1.43 for spares
L5132/1943	TOC 22.4.41 at Acft Repair; 2 TC 2.6.41; to 5 B&GS 3.6.41; SR 16.11.42; SOC 11.1.43 for spares
L5135/2024	TOC 24.7.41 at Fleet Acft; 1 TC 19.8.41 for 6 B&GS; 9 RD 14.9.42 for turret fitment by CCF; 2 TC 5.12.42 for 3 B&GS; engine cut; bellylanded 8m NE of MacDonald, 2.11.43; SR 16.5.44; SOC 16.2.45 for WAC [1120 hrs]
L5139/2136	TOC 7.5.42 at 9 RD and sent to CCF for turret fitment; Fairchild 10.8.42 for conversion to Battle II but cancelled; 9 RD 8.12.42; SOC 2.4.43 for spares
L5144/1683	TOC 7.6.40 at Trenton; 1 TC 23.9.40 for 4 B&GS; engine lost power; bellylanded, Mountain View, 9.4.42; Fleet Acft 25.4.42; 9 RD 25.8.42 for turret fitment by CCF; 2 TC 27.1.43 for 3 B&GS; SR 24.4.44; SOC 16.2.45 for WAC [481 hrs]
L5145/1622	TOC 11.4.40 at Trenton; 1 TC 13.5.40 for 4 B&GS; 4 TC 1.11.40 for 2 B&GS. Engine cut on air test; bellylanded 5m S of Mossbank, 7.8.42; SOC 11.1.43 for spares
L5146/1625	TOC 11.4.40 at Trenton; 1 TC 6.8.40 for 1 B&GS; 6 RD 16.10.40; 1 TC SR 12.11.40; tipped-up while running-up, Jarvis, 2.11.41; 3 TC 4.2.42 for 9 B&GS; cv GI airframe A263 25.1.43; 9 RD 23.3.44; SOC 9.6.44
L5147/1670	TOC 29.5.40 at Trenton; 1 TC 23.9.40 for 4 B&GS; 3 TC 4.2.42 for 9 B&GS; swung taxiing in snow and tipped up, Mont Joli, 3.3.42; tyre burst on landing; swung and tipped up, Mont Joli, 4.6.43; collided with 2031 on ground, Mont Joli, 17.4.43; to GI airframe A329 19.10.43 at 1 TC; SOC 14.2.45
L5148/1628	TOC 18.4.40 at Trenton; Camp Borden 2.6.40; undershot landing and wing dug in, Camp Borden, 26.8.40; 6 ARD SR 16.10.40; Fleet Acft 1.11.40; 1 TC 2.8.41; T&DE 9.8.41; 9 RD 29.8.42 for turret fitment by CCF; 2 TC 5.12.42 for 3 B&GS; SR 21.3.44; SOC 16.2.45 for WAC [678 hrs]
L5149/1661	TOC 13.5.40 at Trenton; 1 TC 12.8.40 for 1 B&GS; 9 RD 10.10.42; Central Acft 26.1.43; Fairchild 16.4.43 for cv to Battle II but cancelled; 3 TC SR 24.8.43; SOC 6.11.44 for WAC [1751 hrs]
L5150/1635	TOC 23.4.40 at Trenton; 1 TC 10.6.40 for 1 B&GS; 3 TC 24.2.42 for 9 B&GS. Undercarriage damaged on take-off; bellylanded, Mont Joli, 25.9.42; cv to GI aircraft A255 25.1.43; SOC 15.9.44
L5153/1630	TOC 18.4.40 at Trenton; 1 TC 5.6.40 for ATS Trenton; undercarriage leg jammed; ground-looped on landing, Trenton, 8.8.40; passed to CFS; collided with Anson 6165 on take-off, Trenton, 16.4.41; Fleet Acft 25.4.41; not repaired and SOC 21.2.42 for spares
L5154/1634	TOC 23.4.40 at Trenton; Rockliffe 19.6.40; 1 TC 29.7.40 for 1 B&GS; hit by 1803 while parked, Jarvis, 8.4.41. Flaps failed; overshot landing on to

2054, from No. 8 Bombing & Gunnery School, flies over the outskirts of Lethbridge. (Bud Saunders via D Howley)

rough ground and ground-looped, Jarvis, 23.7.41; Fleet Acft 7.8.41; not repaired and SOC 19.11.41 for spares [294 hrs]

L5155/1629 TOC 18.4.40 at Trenton; 1 TC 5.6.40 for 4 B&GS; 9 RD 10.10.42 for turret fitment by CCF; 2 TC for 3 B&GS 17.10.42; SR 3.4.43; 3 B&GS 16.4.43; SR 24.4.44; SOC 16.2.45 for WAC [1402 hrs]

L5157/1626 TOC 11.4.40 at Trenton; Camp Borden 2.6.40. Stalled off turn and dived into ground near Bear Point, Lake Simcoe, Ont., 2.9.40; PO M.L. Stephen killed; SOC 29.11.40 [145 hrs]

L5159/1627 TOC 28.4.40 at Trenton; Camp Borden 2.6.40; 6 B&GS 23.6.41; 6 RD 12.11.41; 9 RD 20.3.42 for turret fitment; 3 TC for 6 B&GS 7.7.42, later 9 B&GS; hit by L5332 while parked, Mont Joli, 7.11.42; hit by P6734 while parked, Mont Joli, 26.6.43. Engine failed; crashlanded near Rimouski, Que., 15.11.43; 9 RD 1.12.43; not repaired and SOC 6.3.44

L5161/1663 TOC 13.5.40 at Trenton; 1 TC 10.8.40 for 1 B&GS; 2 TC 24.3.41 for 3 B&GS; SR 4.4.44; SOC 16.2.45 for WAC [590 hrs]

L5162/1623 TOC 11.4.40 at Trenton; 1 TC 4.5.40 for 4 B&GS; 4 TC 28.10.40 for 2 B&GS; taxied into Hurricane 5423, Mossbank, 14.8.42; 9 RD 17.10.42 for turret fitment; 3 TC SR 10.3.43; SOC 4.11.44 for WAC [757 hrs]

L5164/1637 TOC 29.4.40 at Trenton; 1 TC 5.6.40 for 1 B&GS; 4 TC 1.11.40 for 2 B&GS; SR 13.10.42; SOC 11.1.43 for spares

L5166/1636 TOC 29.4.40 at Trenton; 1 TC 5.6.40; 6 ARD SR 16.10.40; 4 TC 2.11.40 for 2 B&GS; 4 TC 22.3.41 for 3 B&GS; SR 4.4.44; SOC 16.2.45 for WAC [327 hrs]

L5167/1660 TOC 13.5.40 at Trenton; 1 TC 12.8.40 for 1 B&GS; 9 RD 28.9.42; SOC 6.11.44 for WAC

L5169/1680 TOC 7.6.40 at Trenton; 4 TC 22.10.40 for 2 B&GS; 2 TC 22.3.41 for 3 B&GS; tyre burst on

landing; swung and tipped up, MacDonald, 18.6.41; bellylanded after engine trouble 2½m E of MacDonald, 4.1.43; taxied into K9459 on runway, MacDonald, 17.2.43; SR 17.4.43; SOC 16.2.45 for WAC [503 hrs]

L5171/1687 TOC 7.6.40 at Trenton; 1 TC 3.9.40 for 1 B&GS; 2 TC 1.3.41 for 3 B&GS; Central Acft 5.4.43; 1 TC SR 7.9.43; SOC 13.2.45 for WAC [805 hrs]

L5175/1669 TOC 29.5.40 at Trenton; 1 TC 21.9.40 for AAS; undercarriage collapsed on landing, 3.12.40; 9 RD 10.10.42 for turret fitment by CCF; 2 TC 17.10.42 for 3 B&GS; SR 24.4.44; SOC 16.2.45 for WAC [891 hrs]

L5177/1656 TOC 9.5.40 at Trenton; WAC 18.7.40 for Patricia Bay; damaged, Patricia Bay, 16.8.41; 4 TC 11.4.42; SR 18.11.42; SOC 11.1.43 for spares

L5179/1691 TOC 7.6.40 at Trenton; 1 TC 16.10.40 for 1 B&GS; hit by 1682 while being towed, Jarvis, 22.12.41; Central Acft 25.8.42; 9 RD 26.2.43 for turret fitment; 3 TC SR 7.9.43; 1 AC SR 15.1.45; SOC 7.3.45 for WAC [549 hrs]

L5180/1631 TOC 18.4.40 at Trenton; 1 TC 5.6.40 for 1 B&GS; ran into 1607 while taxying, Trenton, 19.8.40; crashlanded with glycol leak 2½m S of Victoria, Ont., 1.2.42; 6 RD for repair 25.2.42; CCF 23.11.42 for turret fitment; 3 TC SR 7.9.43; 9 RD 15.1.45; SOC 7.3.45 for WAC [585 hrs]

L5181/1684 TOC 7.6.40 at Trenton; 1 TC 26.10.40 for 1 B&GS; 9 RD 26.9.42; 9 RD 4.2.43 for turret fitment by CCF; 3 TC SR 7.9.43; SOC 7.3.45 for WAC [1003 hrs]

L5184 TOC 9.6.41 at 6 RD; 1 TC 2.7.41 for 31 SFTS; 6 RD 3.9.41; 9 RD 25.7.42 for turret fitment by CCF; 2 TC 6.10.42 for 3 B&GS; engine cut; bellylanded 5m NE of MacDonald, 21.2.43. Oil pressure lost; bellylanded 8m N of MacDonald, 22.1.44; 8 RD 26.1.44; SOC 7.2.44

L5187/1837 TOC 27.12.40 at Fleet Acft; 2 TC 1.3.41 for 3 B&GS; swung into 1836 taxying, MacDonald,

14.4.41; damaged, MacDonald, 11.8.41; taxied into 1785, MacDonald, 7.11.42; cv TT 22.4.43; SR 4.4.44; SOC 16.2.45 for WAC [738 hrs]

L5189/2030 TOC 24.7.41 at Fleet Acft; 1 TC 11.8.41 at 6 B&GS; hit by 2030 on taxiway, Mountain View, 1.10.41; hit by 2025 while parked, Mountain View, 15.3.42; 9 RD 18.8.42 for turret fitment by CCF; 3 TC 20.12.42 for 9 B&GS; SR 16.3.43; issued to 9 B&GS 19.4.43; SR 9.4.45; sold 17.6.46 to WAC [1119 hrs]

L5193/1799 TOC 7.1.41 at Fleet Acft; 1 TC 5.2.41 for 1 B&GS; engine cut; bellylanded 6m E of Selkirk, Ont., 10.2.42; 6 RD 18.1.43; SOC 12.1.43 for spares

L5194/1811 TOC 13.1.41 at Fleet Acft; 2 TC 17.2.41 for 3 B&GS. Caught fire in air; bellylanded on road 35m NE of MacDonald, Man., 23.6.41; DBF; SOC 9.9.41 [224 hrs]

L5195/2084 TOC 16.9.41 at Acft Repair; 4 TC 16.10.41 for 8 B&GS; SR 18.11.42; Central Acft 1.4.43; cv to TT; 3 TC SR 11.6.43; issued to 10 B&GS 11.11.43; tyre burst on landing; swung and tipped up, Mount Pleasant, 8.4.44; SR 18.8.44; sold 17.6.46 to WAC [557 hrs]

L5196 TOC 27.5.41 at Fleet Acft; 1 TC 12.6.41 for 31 B&GS; forcelanded in blizzard on No.3 Range, Picton, 12.1.42; 6 RD 29.1.42; Central Acft 23.6.42; 9 RD 28.11.42; SOC 4.11.44 for WAC

L5197 TOC 17.4.41 at 6 RD; 1 TC 10.5.41 for 31 B&GS; ran into fuel tanker taxying at Picton, 29.5.41; 6 RD 26.1.43; SOC 23.3.44 for spares

L5198/2073 TOC 24.9.41 at 8 RD; 4 TC 28.10.41 for 8 B&GS. Undercarriage leg collapsed on landing; ground-looped, Lethbridge, 8.10.42; SR 18.11.42 and SOC 11.1.43

L5201/2021 TOC 22.7.41 at Fleet Acft; 1 TC 25.8.41 for 1 B&GS; 9 RD 26.9.42 for turret fitment by CCF; 3 TC SR 1.6.43; sold 17.6.46 to WAC [509 hrs]

L5203/1986 TOC 11.6.41 at Fleet Acft; 9 RD 18.8.42 for turret fitment by CCF; 3 TC 5.12.42 for 9 B&GS; SR 16.3.43; retd to 9 B&GS 10.7.44; SR 9.4.45; sold 17.6.46 to WAC [1424 hrs]

L5204/2029 TOC 24.7.41 at Fleet Acft; 1 TC 11.8.41 for 6 B&GS; 6 RD 11.1.43; SOC 12.1.43 for spares

L5205 TOC 8.5.41 at 6 RD; 1 TC 27.5.41 for 31 B&GS; 9 RD 20.9.42 for turret fitment by CCF; 2 TC 5.12.42 for 3 B&GS; tipped up taxying, MacDonald, 3.5.43; engine cut; bellylanded 7m N of MacDonald, 2.1.44; SR 21.3.44; SOC 16.2.45 for WAC [725 hrs]

L5206/2055 TOC 12.8.41 at 8 RD; 4 TC 12.9.41 for 2 B&GS; engine cut; bellylanded 2m N of Mossbank, 22.7.42; SR 13.10.42; SOC 11.1.43 for spares

L5207/2022 TOC 22.7.41 at Fleet Acft; 1 TC 19.8.41 for 6 B&GS; 3 TC 6.2.42 for 9 B&GS. Flew into ground on gunnery exercise 5m SW of St.Luce, PQ, 19.5.42; DBF; PO A.F. Halamka, Cpl C.J. Rooke, LAC I.J. Shaw and LAC K.G. Weal killed; SOC 3.7.42

L5209/2008 TOC 22.7.41 at Fleet Acft; 1 TC 5.9.41 for 6 B&GS; taxied into Harvard 2759, Mountain View, 9.6.42; taxied into 1608 on runway, Mountain View, 1.7.42; allotted GI airframe number A254 9.1.43 but not taken up; 6 RD 15.3.43; SOC 11.3.43 for spares

L5211/2032 TOC 12.8.41 at 8 RD; 2 TC 3.9.41 for 3 B&GS; SR 17.4.43; SOC 16.2.45 for WAC [460 hrs]

L5216/2098 TOC 11.9.41 at Acft Repair; 4 TC 27.10.41 for 8 B&GS; SR 18.11.42; Central Acft 10.6.43; SOC 13.2.45 for WAC [110 hrs]

L5218/1983 TOC 13.5.41 at Acft Repair; cv to TT by MacKenzie Air Services 5.6.41; 4 TC 9.7.41 for 2 B&GS; 6 RD 21.11.42; 9 RD 19.2.43 for turret fitment by CCF; 3 TC SR 7.9.43; SOC 7.3.45 for WAC [602 hrs]

L5219/2026 TOC 22.7.41 at Fleet Acft; 1 TC 19.8.41 for 6 B&GS; 9 RD 18.8.42 for turret fitment by CCF; 2 TC 9.11.42 for 3 B&GS; SR 21.3.44; SOC 16.2.45 for WAC [783 hrs]

L5220/1892 TOC 7.4.41 at 8 RD; 2 TC 14.5.41 for 5 B&GS. Collided with 2069 during gunnery exercise and crashed 6m SE of Dafoe, 23.3.42; LACs G.G.J. Hower, E.P. Harris and C.G. Harris killed; SOC 31.3.42

L5222/1825 TOC 8.1.41 at Fleet Acft; 1 TC 30.1.41 for 1 B&GS; swung on landing and tipped up, Jarvis, 2.4.42; pilot blinded by glycol leak; bellylanded, Cheapside, 4m E of Jarvis, 1.6.42; Central Acft 9.6.42; allotted CCF 16.12.42 for turret fitment; apparently not carried out; 9 RD 16.3.43; 3 TC SR 26.7.44; SOC 6.11.44 for WAC [156 hrs]

L5237/1896 TOC 7.4.41 at 8 RD; 2 TC 17.6.41 for 5 B&GS; SR 26.1.43; 9 RD 24.3.43; SOC 6.11.44 for WAC [597 hrs]

L5245/1826 TOC 27.12.40 at Fleet Acft; 1 TC 27.1.41 for 4 B&GS; engine lost power; forcelanded 1m E of Fingal, 14.4.41; 6 RD 23.11.42; SOC 21.3.44 for spares

L5259/2005 TOC 22.7.41 at Fleet Acft; 4 TC 1.10.41 for 8 B&GS; SR 18.11.42; Central Acft 18.6.43; 1 TC SR 14.12.43; SOC 13.2.45 for WAC [280 hrs]

L5261 TOC 10.3.42 at Fleet Acft; 3 TC 8.4.42; Fleet Acft 27.5.42; 9 RD 30.10.42 for turret fitment by CCF; 2 TC 1.2.43 for 3 B&GS; SR 16.5.44; SOC 16.2.45 for WAC [681 hrs]

L5263/2020 TOC 22.7.41 at Fleet Acft; 1 TC 6.9.41 for 6 B&GS; 9 RD 18.8.42 for turret fitment by CCF; 2 TC 5.12.42 for 3 B&GS; engine cut on take-off; forcelanded in field ½m W of MacDonald, 3.4.44; SR 16.5.44; SOC 16.2.45 for WAC [1282 hrs]

L5264/1955 TOC 3.6.41 at 6 RD; 2 TC 17.6.41; to 7 B&GS 24.6.41. Engine cut; stalled in forced landing, Paulson, 11.10.42; 8 RD 20.10.42; SOC 28.12.42 for spares

L5265 TOC 27.5.41 at Fleet Acft; 1 TC 12.6.41 for 31 B&GS; 9 RD 23.9.42; SOC 4.11.44 for WAC [609 hrs]

L5266 TOC 9.6.41 at 6 RD; 1 TC 5.7.41 for 31 B&GS; 6 RD 16.9.41; Central Acft 23.6.42; 9 RD 27.1.43; 3 TC SR 26.7.44; SOC 4.11.44 for WAC [300 hrs]

L5269/1904 TOC 21.4.41 at Fleet Acft; 1 TC for 3 B&GS; 6 RD 1.12.42; 9 RD 8.3.43; SOC 4.11.44 for WAC [919 hrs]

L5270 TOC 9.6.41 at 6 RD; 1 TC 5.7.41 for 31 B&GS; 6 RD 28.12.42; SOC 27.4.43 as spares

L5271/1954 TOC 13.5.41 at Acft Repair; 2 TC 13.6.41 for 7 B&GS; engine cut; bellylanded 1½m E of Fairville, Man., 31.7.41; SOC 11.1.43 for spares

L5272/1997 TOC 13.5.41 at Acft Repair; Boeing 6.8.41; Trapp Tech Sch 16.2.43; SOC 12.3.46 for WAC

L5273/1910 TOC 16.4.41 at 8 RD and cv TT; 2 TC 9.7.41; to 5 B&GS 12.7.41; 4 TC 6.10.42 as SR; GI airframe as A271 for 2 WS apparently not taken up; SOC 26.1.43 for spares

L5281/1921 TOC 7.4.41 at Acft Repair; 2 TC 13.5.41; to 5 B&GS 15.5.41; SR 16.11.42; Central Acft 27.4.43; 1 TC SR 13.9.43; SOC 13.2.45 for WAC [767 hrs]

L5284/1919 TOC 5.4.41 at Acft Repair; 2 TC 10.5.41; to 5 B&GS 15.5.41; brakes failed taxying; hit hangar, Dafoe, 14.6.41; 7 B&GS 16.7.41; cv to GI airframe A259 9.1.43; 8 RD 1.9.43 and SOC 11.12.43 for spares

L5290/2135 TOC 7.5.42 at 9 RD; turret fitted by CCF; 2 TC 18.2.43 for 3 B&GS; Central Acft 19.4.43; 3 TC SR 28.2.44; SOC 4.11.44 for WAC [544 hrs]

L5292 TOC 29.3.41 at Fleet Acft and cv to TT; 1 TC 21.4.41 for 31 B&GS. Collided with P6541 while towing target near Picton, Ont., 16.11.41; 6

1319 at No.9 Bombing & Gunnery School in the snow at Mont Joli. (Bruce Robertson collection)

RD 8.12.41; cv to GI airframe A154 2.2.42; SOC 12.8.44 for spares

L5296/2104 TOC 4.9.41 at Acft Repair; 4 TC 5.11.41 for 8 B&GS; overshot landing on to road, Lethbridge, 12.6.42; SR 18.11.42; SOC 26.1.43 for spares

L5298/1741 TOC 6.12.40 at Fleet Acft; 1 TC 13.1.41 for 4 B&GS; 9 RD 5.11.42 for turret fitment by CCF; 3 TC SR 17.9.43; SOC 7.3.45 for WAC [541 hrs]

L5304/1906 TOC 7.4.41 at Acft Repair; 2 TC 2.5.41 for 3 B&GS; 5 B&GS; undercarriage jammed; crash-landed, Dafoe, 1.4.42; lost power and forcelanded 2m SW of Dafoe, 2.6.42; SOC 11.12.42 for spares

L5306/2139 TOC 10.4.42 at 4 RD; 9 RD 6.8.42 for turret fitment by CCF; 3 TC 20.12.42 for 9 B&GS; SR 16.3.43; issued to 9 B&GS 19.4.43. Baulked on landing and overshot in coarse pitch with flaps and undercarriage down; lost height and crashlanded ¼m SE of Mont Joli, 5.8.43; to 9 RD; SOC 9.12.43 for spares

L5308 TOC 11.6.41 at Fleet Acft; 1 TC 8.7.41 for 31 B&GS; overshot landing, Picton, 29.5.42; taxied into Lysander 2339 on runway, Picton, 1.10.42; 6 RD 26.1.43; SOC 26.2.44 for spares

L5314/1886 TOC 7.4.41 at 8 RD and cv to TT; 2 TC 9.7.41 for 3 B&GS; collided with 1736 10m NE of MacDonald, 11.5.43, but returned safely; SR 21.3.44; SOC 16.2.45 for WAC [1349 hrs]

L5315 TOC 17.4.41 at 6 RD; 1 TC 10.5.41 for 31 B&GS; 6 RD 4.1.43; SOC 24.3.44 for spares

L5316/1803 TOC 7.1.41 at Fleet Acft; 1 TC 7.2.41 for 1 B&GS; swung by wind into 1634 while taxying, Jarvis, 8.4.41. Pilot abandoned aircraft after smoke came from engine and crashed, St. Catharines, Ont., 6.7.41; LAC C. Taggart and LAC R. McNabb killed; SOC 22.8.41 [256 hrs]

L5317/1829 TOC 7.1.41 at Fleet Acft; 1 TC 17.2.41 for 4 B&GS; bellylanded while lost 1½m W of Eagle, Ont., 15.2.41; 9 RD 10.10.42; 6 RD 13.11.42; allotted CCF for turret fitment 30.3.43; 9 RD

3.4.43; 3 TC SR 26.7.44; SOC 6.11.44 for WAC [379 hrs]

L5318/1808 TOC 7.1.41 at Fleet Acft; 1 TC 7.2.41; cv to GI airframe A251 18.2.43 for TTS St.Thomas; SOC 7.2.45

L5319/1681 TOC 7.6.40 at Trenton; 1 TC 21.10.40 for 1 B&GS; engine cut; bellylanded, Cayuga LG, Ont., 6.12.40; 6 RD 12.12.42; SOC 1.5.44 for spares

L5321/1685 TOC 7.6.40 at Trenton; 1 TC 23.9.40 for 6 B&GS; ground-looped and hit Lockheed 212 7642, Trenton, 12.11.40; hit by 2031 while parked, Mountain View, 6.6.42; 9 RD 18.8.42 for turret fitment by CCF; 3 TC for 9 B&GS 7.11.42. Hydraulic line broke and pilot overcome by fumes; crashlanded 2m W of Mont Joli, 7.12.43; to 9 RD 16.12.43 and SOC 20.4.44

L5329/1689 TOC 7.6.40 at Trenton; 1 TC 16.10.40 for 1 B&GS; 9 RD 28.9.42 for turret fitment by CCF; 3 TC 1.2.43 for 9 B&GS; SR 16.3.43; 9 B&GS 19.6.43; SR 22.1.44; sold 17.6.46 to WAC [1358 hrs]

L5331 TOC 16.9.41 at Fleet Acft; 6 RD 3.11.41; Central Acft 23.6.42; 9 RD 5.1.43 for turret fitment by CCF; 124 Ferry Sqn; undercarriage leg collapsed on landing on ferry flight, Kingston, 18.2.43; 3 TC 10.4.43 for 9 B&GS. Engine cut; damaged in forced landing 1m SW of Luceville, 4.10.44; 9 RD 7.10.44; SOC 27.10.44

L5332 TOC 16.9.41 at Fleet Acft; 6 RD 3.11.41; 9 RD 5.4.42 for turret fitment by CCF; hit 1627 taxying, Mont Joli, 7.11.42; 3 TC 1.10.42 for 9 B&GS; engine failed; crashlanded 1m SW of Baie des Sables, Que., 23.1.44; 9 RD 1.2.44; SOC 23.5.44 for spares

L5335 TOC 27.5.41 at Fleet Acft; 1 TC 12.6.41 for 31 SFTS; both tyres burst on landing; tipped up, Kingston, 29.7.41; 6 RD 19.9.41; 9 RD 18.1.43; engine cut after take-off; bellylanded, St.John, Que., 8.7.43; SOC 23.5.44 for spares

L5336/1932 TOC 5.4.41 at Acft Repair; 2 TC 15.5.41; to 5

L5337/2068   B&GS 19.5.41; damaged 3.2.42 at Dafoe; SR 26.1.43; 124 Ferry Sqn; ran into snow taxying and tipped up, Kapuskasing, 6.3.43; 9 RD 24.3.43; SOC 4.11.44 for WAC [781 hrs]

L5337/2068   TOC 24.9.41 at 8 RD; 2 TC 3.11.41 for 5 B&GS 3.11.41. Lost height in turn during gunnery exercise and flew into ice in Quill Lake, 5m SE of Dafoe, Sask., and sank, 1.12.41; Sgt J.L.G. Cote (Aust), LAC C.A. Coles and LAC R.K. Crothers (Aust) killed; SOC 27.12.41

L5340/1614   TOC 2.4.40 at Trenton; 1 TC 28.3.40 at Trenton; 2 TC 19.3.41 for 3 B&GS; SR 17.4.43; SOC 16.2.45 for WAC [472 hrs]

L5341/1608   TOC 24.2.40 at Trenton; 6 B&GS; hit by 1008 on runway, Mountain View, 1.7.42; 6 RD 10.1.43; SOC 26.2.44 for spares

L5342/1618   TOC 16.3.40 at Trenton; 1 TC 5.4.40 4 B&GS; 2 TC 19.3.41 for 3 B&GS; SOC 11.1.43 for spares

L5344/1615   TOC 16.3.40 at Trenton; 1 TC 23.4.40 for 1 B&GS; 4 TC 1.11.40 for 2 B&GS; SR 13.10.42; Central Acft 19.6.43; SOC 24.4.44

L5345/1609   TOC 16.3.40 at Camp Borden; 6 ARD SR 16.10.40; 1 TC 12.11.40 for 4 B&GS; engine cut on take-off; bellylanded, Fingal, 19.10.42; 9 RD for CCF turret fitment 10.10.42; 3 TC SR 6.7.44; SOC 6.11.44 for WAC

L5346/1610   TOC 16.3.40 at Camp Borden; 6 ARD SR 16.10.40; 1 TC 12.11.40 for 1 B&GS; 3 TC 19.2.42 for 9 B&GS; engine cut; bellylanded 1½m SE of Mont Joli, 29.10.42. Engine failed due to glycol leak; hit rocks in bellylanding, St.Octave, Metis, Que., 8.7.43; 9 RD 13.7.43; SOC 18.11.43 for spares

L5347/1617   TOC 28.3.40 at Trenton; 1 TC 17.4.40 for 4 B&GS; 6 ARD SR 16.10.40; 1 TC 12.11.40 for 4 B&GS; engine cut on take-off; bellylanded 1m SE of Fingal, 2.4.42; 9 RD for turret fitment, 25.11.42 by CCF; 3 TC SR 18.6.43; 9 B&GS 5.7.43 for test of Mk.IV turret; 9 RD 9.9.43; 3 TC 16.9.43 for 9 B&GS; blown off taxiway into ditch, Mont Joli, 10.9.44; engine cut during gunnery exercise; bellylanded, Mont Joli, 8.2.45; SOC 21.4.45

L5349/2097   TOC 11.9.41 at Acft Repair; 4 TC 27.10.41 for 8 B&GS; SR 18.11.42; SOC 11.1.43 for spares

L5352   TOC 17.4.41 at Ottawa Car Ltd; 1 TC 13.5.41 for 31 B&GS; bellylanded after hydraulic failure, Picton, 23.9.41. Engine lost power; forcelanded on ferry flight 1m N of Brockville, Ont., 2.10.42; 9 RD 17.10.42; Central Acft 27.10.42; SOC 11.1.43 for spares

L5353/1860   TOC 20.3.41 at 8 RD; 2 TC 16.5.41; to 7 B&GS 18.6.41; swung off runway into ditch on ferry flight, Stevensons Field, Winnipeg, 20.5.41; swung on landing and undercarriage collapsed, Dauphin LG, Paulson, 1.8.41; SOC 11.1.43 for spares

L5355/1752   TOC 16.11.40 at Fleet Acft; 1 TC 9.12.40 for 4 B&GS; 3 TC 25.3.42 for 9 B&GS; 9 RD for cv to TT 31.5.43; 3 TC SR 23.12.43; SOC 4.11.44 for WAC [562 hrs]

L5359/1973   TOC 22.4.41 at 8 RD; 2 TC 15.7.41 for 5 B&GS; SOC 26.1.43 for spares

L5364/1620   TOC 8.4.40 at Trenton; 1 TC 1.5.40 for 4 B&GS; 4 TC 28.10.40 for 2 B&GS; SR 13.10.42; SOC 11.1.43 for spares

L5365/1795   TOC 7.1.41 at Fleet Acft; 2 TC 7.2.41 for 3 B&GS; SR 6.4.44; SOC 16.2.45 for WAC [672 hrs]

L5366/1619   TOC 28.3.40 at Trenton; 1 TC 17.4.40 for 4 B&GS; engine cut during low-level bombing run; bellylanded, Consecon, Ont., 27.5.40; 4 TC 1.11.40 for 2 B&GS; SR 13.10.42; SOC 11.1.43 for spares

L5369/1725   TOC 17.10.40 at Trenton; 1 TC 12.11.40 for 4

L5370/1611   B&GS; 6 RD 29.1.43; SOC 26.2.44

L5370/1611   TOC 6.4.40 at Trenton; 1 TC 30.4.40 for 4 B&GS; 4 TC 8.11.40 for 2 B&GS; SR 13.10.42; SOC 11.1.43

L5371/1601   TOC 16.2.40 at Trenton; 6 ARD SR 16.10.40; 1 TC 12.11.40; 2 TC 24.3.41 for 3 B&GS; flew into HT wires 15m W of Portage la Prairie, 14.10.42; two civilians hit by wires and electrocuted; cv to TT 22.4.43; SR 21.3.44; SOC 16.2.45 for WAC [915 hrs]

L5372/1616   TOC 16.3.40 at Trenton; 1 TC 5.4.40 for 4 B&GS; 4 TC 1.11.40 for 2 B&GS; nosed over while running up, Mossbank, 3.5.42; SR 13.10.42; SOC 26.1.43 for spares

L5373/1612   TOC 6.4.40 at Trenton; 1 TC 26.4.40 for 4 B&GS; 6 ARD 16.10.40; 1 TC 12.11.40 for 4 B&GS; CCF for turret fitment 10.10.42; 3 TC SR 1.6.43; hit by 1940 while parked, Mont Joli, 13.8.43; sold 17.6.46 to WAC [573 hrs]

L5376/1633   TOC 18.4.40 at Trenton; 1 TC 18.8.40 for 1 B&GS; undercarriage leg collapsed on landing, Jarvis, 26.2.41; 9 RD 24.9.42 for turret fitment by CCF; 3 TC 27.1.43; SR 16.3.43; 3 TC 1.6.43 for 9 B&GS; SR 22.1.44; sold 17.6.46 to WAC [1582 hrs]

L5377/1613   TOC 6.4.40 at Trenton; 1 TC 1.5.40 for 4 B&GS; 6 ARD SR 16.10.40; 1 TC for 4 B&GS 12.11.40; 6 RD 14.12.42; SOC 17.1.44 for spares

L5378/1724   TOC 17.10.40 at Trenton; 1 TC 12.11.40 for 4 B&GS; 9 RD 10.10.42 for turret fitment by CCF; 2 TC 8.3.43; SR 3.4.43; 3 B&GS 30.4.43; SOC 16.2.45 for WAC [609 hrs]

L5379/1930   TOC 22.4.41 at Fleet Acft; 1 TC 13.5.41 for 1 B&GS; 9 RD 9.11.42 for turret fitment by CCF; 3 TC SR 6.5.43; sold 17.6.46 to WAC [308 hrs]

L5380/1956   TOC 3.6.41 at 6 RD; 2 TC 19.6.41; to 7 B&GS 24.6.41; Central Acft 15.4.43; 1 TC SR 26.11.43; SOC 13.2.45 for WAC [1093 hrs]

L5384/1655   TOC 9.5.40 at Trenton; EAC 18.7.40; HWE 18.7.41; cv to TT; 31 SFTS 27.9.41; CCF 24.8.42 for turret fitment; 9 RD 13.11.42; 3 TC SR 26.7.44; SOC 6.11.44 for WAC

L5386/1766   TOC 16.11.40 at Acft Repair; 4 TC 27.12.40 for 2 B&GS; engine lost power on take-off; crashlanded 2½m SW of Mossbank, 18.10.41; undercarriage leg collapsed taxying, Mossbank, 11.4.42; 8 RD 21.11.42; 9 RD 18.2.43; 2 TC SR 26.7.44; SOC 6.11.44 for WAC [877 hrs]

L5388/1642   TOC 2.5.40 at Trenton; Fleet Acft 24.8.40; 1 TC 14.6.41; to 6 B&GS 23.6.41; taxied into Anson 8214, Mountain View, 15.5.42; 9 RD 18.8.42 for turret fitment by CCF; 2 TC 5.12.42 for 3 B&GS; bellylanded after glycol leak 10m NE of MacDonald, 14.2.43; SR 16.5.44; SOC 16.2.45 for WAC [1154 hrs]

L5389/1939   TOC 22.4.41 by Acft Repair; 2 TC 17.5.41; to 5 B&GS 20.5.41; SR 26.1.43; 9 RD 24.3.43; 3 TC SR 26.7.44; SOC 4.11.44 for WAC [602 hrs]

L5392/2012   TOC 3.7.41 at 8 RD; 2 TC 8.8.41; 8 RD 15.12.42; 9 RD 26.3.43; 3 TC SR 26.7.44; SOC 4.11.44 for WAC [418 hrs]

L5394/2047   TOC 22.7.41 at 8 RD; 2 TC 3.9.41 for 3 B&GS; SOC 11.1.43 for spares

L5398/1877   TOC 7.4.41 at 8 RD; 2 TC 12.6.41 for 7 B&GS; engine cut; bellylanded 6m W of Paulson, 26.8.42. Engine cut after take-off; spun into ground 2m SW of Dauphin LG, 18.9.42; Sgt H.J.M. McNeill, LAC F.W.A. Musto and LAC W. Gilmour killed; SOC 21.10.42

L5399/2006   TOC 22.7.41 at Fleet Acft; 1 TC 8.9.41 for 6 B&GS; engine cut on test flight; crashlanded in field 11m W of Mountain View, 10.12.41; 6 RD 30.12.41; 9 RD 7.7.42 for turret fitment by CCF; 2 TC 8.10.42 for 3 B&GS; SR 3.4.43; issued to 3 B&GS 16.4.43; SR 24.4.44; SOC 16.2.45 for

A Battle crew trainer keeps company with a Stinson 105 at Paulson. (via D Howley)

WAC [331 hrs]

L5400/2049 TOC 22.7.41 at 8 RD; 2 TC 8.9.41 for 5 B&GS; 8 RD 14.1.43; 124 Ferry Sqn; engine cut; bellylanded ½m W of Mattice, Ont., 12.3.43; 1 TC 3.5.43; Central Acft 14.5.43; 3 TC SR 2.8.43; cv to TT; issued to 10 B&GS 26.11.43; SR 18.8.44; sold 17.6.46 to WAC [903 hrs]

L5401/2070 TOC 24.9.41 at 8 RD; 4 TC 28.10.41 for 8 B&GS. Caught fire in air and crashed on approach to forced landing 9 m E of Lethbridge, 4.12.42; Sgt E.L. Williams and LAC E.T. Aitkens killed; SOC 12.3.43

L5404/2077 TOC 11.9.41 at Acft Repair; 4 TC 11.10.41 for 8 B&GS; SR 18.11.42; allotted A270 as GI airframe 9.1.43 but not taken up; SOC 26.1.43 for spares

L5405/1668 TOC 29.5.40 at Trenton; 1 TC 10.8.40 for 1 B&GS; hit by Lysander 2308 while parked, Jarvis, 1.4.42; Fleet Acft 6.5.42; 9 RD 25.7.42 for turret fitment by CCF; 3 TC 1.2.43 for 9 B&GS; 1 AC SR 15.1.45; sold 17.6.46 to WAC [876 hrs]

L5406/2061 TOC 21.8.41 at Acft Repair; 4 TC 1.10.41 for 8 B&GS; SR 18.11.42; SOC 11.1.43 for spares

L5408/1664 TOC 13.5.40 at Trenton; 1 TC 16.10.40; 4 TC 11.11.40 for 2 B&GS; SR 13.10.42; 8 RD 2.6.43; brakes failed; hit bowser, St.John, 27.8.43; 2 TC SR 7.9.43; SOC 16.2.45 for WAC [549 hrs]

L5410/1658 TOC 9.5.40 at Trenton; 1 TC 10.8.40 for 4 B&GS; 6 ARD 16.10.40; 4 TC 7.11.40 for 2 B&GS; tyre burst on take-off and damaged undercarriage; leg collapsed on landing, Mossbank, 10.9.42; 9 RD 17.10.42 for turret fitment by CCF; 2 TC SR 25.3.43; 3 B&GS 17.8.43; tyre burst on landing; swung and tipped up, MacDonald, 27.8.43; 2 TC SR 21.3.44; SOC 16.2.45 for WAC [319 hrs]

L5411/1644 TOC 2.5.40 at Trenton; 1 TC 10.8.40 for 1 B&GS; overshot landing into fence, Jarvis, 13.3.41; 3 TC 17.6.43 for 9 B&GS; SOC 11.1.43 for spares

L5412 TOC 16.9.41 at Fleet Acft; 1 TC 29.12.41 for 31

B&GS; 9 RD 23.9.42 for turret fitment by CCF; 3 FC 20.12.42 for 9 B&GS; SR 16.3.43; issued to 9 B&GS 28.5.43; bellylanded with glycol leak, Mont Joli, 15.8.44; undercarriage leg jammed; swung on landing into snowbank, Mont Joli, 11.1.45; SR 9.4.45; sold 17.6.46 for WAC [1137 hrs]

L5413 TOC 17.4.41 at Ottawa Car Ltd as TT; 1 TC 8.5.41 for 31 SFTS; 6 RD 12.9.41; 9 RD 23.9.42; cv to standard by 13.11.42; SOC 4.11.44 for WAC [405 hrs]

L5414/1643 TOC 2.5.40 at Trenton; 1 TC 9.8.40 for 1 B&GS. Engine cut; crashlanded 2m E of Jarvis, 23.2.41; Fleet Acft 24.4.41; SOC 18.11.41 for spares [357 hrs]

L5420/1942 TOC 22.4.41 at Acft Repair; 2 TC 20.5.41; to 5 B&GS 23.5.41; cv to GI airframe A260 9.1.43; SOC 11.12.43

L5421/1966 TOC 3.6.41 at 6 RD; 2 TC 15.6.41; to 7 B&GS 13.7.41, later 3 B&GS; ran off taxying into snowdrift and tipped up, 27.12.42; taxied into 1841, MacDonald, 14.1.43; 9 RD 13.3.43 for turret fitment by CCF; Central Acft 28.4.43; 3 TC SR 7.2.44; SOC 4.11.44 for WAC [974 hrs]

L5424/2107 TOC 11.9.41 at Acft Repair; 2 TC 8.11.41 for 3 B&GS; overshot landing and nosed over, MacDonald, 31.1.43; SR 17.4.43; SOC 16.2.45 for WAC [515 hrs]

L5426/1850 TOC 6.3.41 at MacDonald Bros; 2 TC 7.7.41; to 7 B&GS 30.7.41, later 3 B&GS; 9 RD 10.8.42 for cv to TT; SR after cv to standard 13.11.42; 3 TC SR 9.7.43; 7 B&GS; SOC 6.11.44 for WAC [635 hrs]

L5427 TOC 9.6.41 at 6 RD; 1 TC 5.7.41 for 31 B&GS; engine starved of fuel and undershot landing, Picton, 13.3.42. Spun into lake during air-to-ground firing exercise 10m S of Picton, 14.8.42; Sgt B. Kempton-Werchie (NZ), LAC H.C. Pigerham and LAC D.N. Jones killed; SOC 17.11.42

L5429/1849	TOC 6.3.41 at MacDonald Bros; 2 TC 10.6.41 for 3 B&GS; MacDonald Acft for cv to TT 10.6.41; retd 3 B&GS; bellylanded with engine failure 7m NE of MacDonald, 7.5.43; SR 21.3.44; SOC 16.2.45 for WAC [1512 hrs]
L5441/2095	TOC 16.9.41 at Acft Repair; 4 TC 21.10.41 for 8 B&GS; collided with 2096 10m W of Lethbridge, 18.5.42; returned safely; SR 18.11.42; SOC 11.1.43 for spares
L5442	TOC 16.9.41 at Fleet Acft; 6 RD 3.11.41; 9 RD 9.1.42 for turret fitment by CCF; 2 TC SR 25.3.43; issued to 3 B&GS 13.1.44; taxied into Anson FP744, MacDonald, 17.4.44; SR 16.5.44; SOC 16.2.45 for WAC [90 hrs]
L5445/1988	TOC 11.6.41 at Fleet Acft; 1 TC 8.7.41 for 6 B&GS; undercarriage leg jammed; ground-looped on landing, Mountain View,.2.12.41; 9 RD 18.8.42 for turret fitment by CCF; 2 TC 5.12.42 for 3 B&GS; SR 24.4.44; SOC 16.2.45 for WAC [877 hrs]
L5447	TOC 9.6.41 at 6 RD; 1 TC 5.7.41 for 31 B&GS; 9 RD 29.10.42; 6 RD 18.12.42; SOC 23.3.44 for spares
L5448/1968	TOC 11.6.41 at Fleet Acft; 1 TC 3.7.41 for 6 B&GS; 9 RD 18.8.42 for turret fitment by CCF; 2 TC 22.10.42 for 3 B&GS. Electrics caught fire after take-off; crashlanded, Mont Joli, 6.10.43; 8 RD 8.10.43 and SOC 15.10.43
L5449/1817	TOC 7.1.41 at Fleet Acft; 2 TC 1.3.41 for 3 B&GS. Ran into tractor on taxiway, MacDonald, 11.11.42; SOC 11.1.43 for spares
L5451/1843	TOC 6.3.41 at Acft Repair; 2 TC 8.4.41 for 3 B&GS; SR 4.4.44; SOC 16.2.45 for WAC [457 hrs]
L5453/1922	TOC 7.4.41 at Acft Repair; 2 TC 13.5.41; 5 B&GS 15.5.41; SR 26.1.42; 9 RD 24.3.43 for cv to TT; 3 TC 24.7.43 for 10 B&GS; collided with Anson 11855 taxying, Summerside, 17.2.44; SR 17.4.44; 3 TC 10.7.44 for 9 B&GS; SR 9.4.45; sold 17.6.46 to WAC [1148 hrs]
L5456/2065	TOC 25.9.41 at 8 RD; 4 TC 23.10.41; Central Acft; 3 TC SR 21.5.43; issued to 9 B&GS 15.7.43; later to 10 B&GS; SR 24.8.44; sold 17.6.46 to WAC [691 hrs]
L5458/1967	TOC 3.6.41 at 6 RD; 2 TC 2.7.41 for 7 B&GS; 6 RD 21.11.42; SOC 23.3.44 for spares
L5463/2134	TOC 10.4.42 at 4 RD; 9 RD 21.5.42 for turret fitment by CCF; 3 TC 7.11.42 for 9 B&GS; SR 13.3.43; issued to 9 B&GS 19.4.43. Engine cut after take-off; bellylanded, Mont Joli, 22.11.43; to 9 RD for spares and SOC 6.3.44
L5468/2137	TOC 10.4.42 at 4 RD; 7 B&GS 13.7.41; 9 RD 28.5.42; 3 TC SR 18.6.43; SOC 4 11.44 for WAC [196 hrs]
L5469/1961	TOC 9.6.41 at Fleet Acft; 1 TC 25.6.41 for 6 B&GS; SOC 28.11.42 for spares
L5470/1667	TOC 29.5.40 at Trenton; 1 TC 12.11.40 for 1 B&GS. Engine cut after take-off; crashlanded, Resort Bay, 2½m NW of Jarvis, Ont., 9.3.41; to Fleet Acft 29.4.41 for spares recovery and SOC 23.10.41 [50 hrs]
L5472/1645	TOC 2.5.40 at Trenton; 1 TC 20.9.40 for 4 B&GS; cv to TT by 25.4.42; 6 RD 11.1.43; SOC 12.1.43 for spares
L5473/1666	TOC 29.5.40 at Trenton; 1 TC 10.8.40 for 1 B&GS; 6 RD 23.11.42; 9 RD 3.4.43; SOC 6.11.44 for WAC [682 hrs]
L5475/1657	TOC 9.5.40 at Trenton; 1 TC 10.8.40 for 1 B&GS; 3 TC 11.12.41 for 9 B&GS; bellylanded with glycol leak, Mont Joli, 8.10.42; Central Acft 17.10.42; 9 RD 24.3.43 for turret fitment; 3 TC SR 9.7.43; SOC 4.11.44 for WAC [1050 hrs]
L5476	TOC 27.5.41 at Fleet Acft; 1 TC 12.6.41 for 31 B&GS; tyre burst on landing and wing damaged; overshot and landed, Picton, 24.3.42; Fleet Acft
	10.4.42; 9 RD 24.6.42 for turret fitment by CCF; 2 TC 17.10.42 for 3 B&GS; engine cut; bellylanded 12m NW of MacDonald, 23.12.43; SR 16.5.44; SOC 16.2.45 for WAC [677 hrs]
L5477/1679	TOC 7.6.40 at Trenton; 1 TC 21.10.40 for 4 B&GS; 3 TC 4.2.42 for 9 B&GS; landed with flat tyre; swung off runway, Mont Joli, 13.5.42; to GI airframe A264 25.1.43; 9 RD 23.3.44; SOC 9.6.44 for spares
L5479/1702	TOC 23.9.40 at Trenton; 4 TC 25.10.41 for 2 B&GS; crashed on ferry flight to 8 RD 27.8.41; 2 TC 6.9.41; SR 16.11.42; cv to TT by 7.12.42; 8 RD 15.2.43; 2 TC SR 14.8.43; 3 B&GS 10.1.44; SR 1.4.44; SOC 16.2.45 for WAC [800 hrs]
L5480/1639	TOC 29.4.40 at Trenton; T&D Flt 1.6.40; 1 TC 20.6.40; 9 RD 1.4.42; CCF for turret fitment; 3 TC 5.8.42 for 9 B&GS; SR 22.1.44; 9 B&GS 7.8.44; SR 9.4.45; sold 17.6.46 to WAC [1437 hrs]
L5481/1638	TOC 29.4.40 at Trenton; 1 TC 9.8.40 for 1 B&GS; to GI airframe A249 9.1.43; SOC 15.10.43 for spares
L5483/1692	TOC 7.6.40 at Trenton; 1 TC 23.9.40 for AAS; engine failed after take-off; bellylanded in field 4m W of Mountain View, 4.5.41; 6 RD 7.7.41; 1 TC 30.7.41 for 6 B&GS; skidded into bowser, Mountain View, 20.1.42; 6 RD 20.1.43; SOC 21.3.44
L5484/1688	TOC 7.6.40 at Trenton; 1 TC 16.10.40 for 1 B&GS; 9 RD 5.12.42 for turret fitment by CCF; 2 TC 27.1.43 for 3 B&GS; SR 21.3.44; SOC 16.2.45 for WAC [1433 hrs]
L5485/1640	TOC 29.4.40 at Trenton; 1 TC 6.9.40 for 1 B&GS; 3 TC 11.12.41 for 9 B&GS; swung taxying into snowbank and tipped up, Mont Joli, 20.3.42. Engine failed; bellylanded and hit rock, St.Flavie, 3m W of Mont Joli, 29.4.43; SOC 5.7.43 for spares
L5486/1641	TOC 29.4.40 at Trenton; 1 TC 9.8.40 for 1 B&GS; 3 TC C&F Flt; forcelanded in field with glycol leak, Cotau Landing, Que., 16.1.42; 9 RD 8.7.43; 3 TC SR 26.7.44; SOC 6.11.44 for WAC
L5489/1659	TOC 9.5.40 at Trenton; 1 TC 10.8.40 for 1 B&GS; engine cut on take-off; forcelanded, Jarvis 16.2.42; engine cut; bellylanded ¼m NE of Koklev Field, 7.3.42; brakes failed; taxied into Bolingbroke 9949, Jarvis, 9.9.42; 9 RD 28.9.42; SOC 8.6.43
L5490/1790	TOC 8.1.41 at Fleet Acft; 1 TC 16.1.41 for 4 B&GS; Fleet Acft 24.5.41; 4 TC 3.11.41 for 8 B&GS; Central Acft 25.5.43; 1 TC SR 1.12.43; SOC 13.2.45 for WAC [573 hrs]
L5492/1818	TOC 7.1.41 at Fleet Acft; 2 TC 17.2.41 for 3 B&GS. Engine lost power on take-off; crashlanded ½m N of MacDonald, 13.8.42; 8 RD 21.8.42; SOC 2.11.42 for spares
L5495/1985	TOC 13.5.41 at Acft Repair; cv to TT by MacKenzie Air Services 5.6.41; 4 TC 9.7.41 for 2 B&GS; undercarriage leg collapsed taxying, Mossbank, 30.7.42; Central Acft 21.5.43; 1 TC SR 22.11.43; SOC 13.2.45 for WAC [753 hrs]
L5496/2044	TOC 22.7.41 at 8 RD; 4 TC 27.8.41; 6 RD 21.11.42; Fairchild 17.4.43 for cv to Mk.II but cancelled; 3 TC SR 24.8.43 and cv to TT; issued to 10 B&GS 4.11.43; SR 9.8.44; issued to 9 B&GS 30.8.44. Oil pressure dropped and windscreen obscured by oil while target towing; bellylanded, Mont Joli, 19.1.45; SOC 10.4.45
L5501/2075	TOC 24.9.41 at 8 RD; 4 TC 23.10.41 for 8 B&GS; SR 18.11.42; Central Acft 10.6.43; 9 RD 21.12.43 and cv to TT; 3 TC 18.7.44 for 9 B&GS; SR 9.4.45; sold 17.6.46 to WAC [570 hrs]
L5504/1866	TOC 24.3.41 at Fleet Acft; 1 TC 15.4.41 for AAS; 6 B&GS; 6 RD 13.12.42; cv to GI airframe

Target tug 1694 awaits delivery to No.2 Bombing & Gunnery School. (R Sturtivant collection)

	A277 24.3.43; SOC 4.8.44
L5505	TOC 16.9.41 at Fleet Acft; received without various components at 6 RD 3.11.41; cv to GI airframe A185 25.9.42; SOC 2.12.44 for spares
L5510	TOC 17.4.41 at 6 RD; 1 TC 10.5.41 for 31 B&GS; engine cut; undershot landing, Picton, 8.3.42; 9 RD 23.9.42 for turret fitment by CCF; 3 TC SR 1.6.43; issued to 9 B&GS 27.4.44; SR 9.4.45; sold 17.6.46 to WAC [852 hrs]
L5518/1796	TOC 7.1.41 at Fleet Acft; 1 TC for 1 B&GS. Engine failed due to glycol leak; bellylanded 2½m SE of Selkirk, Ont., 28.9.42; Central Acft 2.10.42; SOC 13.1.43 for spares
L5521/1914	TOC 16.4.41 at 8 RD; 2 TC 26.8.41 for 3 B&GS; 9 RD 12.2.43; SOC 4.11.44 for WAC [616 hrs]
L5530	TOC 9.6.41 at 6 RD; 1 TC 2.7.41 for 31 SFTS; 6 RD 9.9.41; 9 RD 7.7.42 for turret fitment by CCF; 3 TC 8.10.42 for 9 B&GS; SR 9.4.45; sold 17.6.46 to WAC [1415 hrs]
L5532/1863	TOC 20.3.41 at 8 RD; 2 TC 16.5.41; to 5 B&GS 22.5.41; engine lost power; landed with undercarriage unlocked and crashlanded in field 1m S of Dafoe, 7.8.42; SR 4.4.44; SOC 16.2.45 for WAC [680 hrs]
L5534/1991	TOC 1.7.41 at 6 RD; 1 TC 15.7.41 for 6 B&GS; 9 RD 18.8.42; SOC 4.11.44 for WAC [769 hrs]
L5535/2034	TOC 22.7.41 at 8 RD; 2 TC 16.8.41; to 7 B&GS 20.8.41; SR 16.11.42; issued to 7 B&GS 7.12.42; Central Acft 15.4.43; 1 TC SR 23.9.43; SOC 13.2.45 for WAC [697 hrs]
L5536/1800	TOC 7.1.41 at Fleet Acft; 1 TC 1.2.41 for 1 B&GS; overshot landing and hit fence, Jarvis, 8.6.42; 6 RD 18.1.43; SOC 12.1.43 for spares
L5537/1858	TOC 20.3.41 at 8 RD; 2 TC 14.5.41; to 5 B&GS 19.5.41; undercarriage leg jammed; landed on one wheel, Dafoe, 11.9.41; engine cut on take-off; bellylanded 4½m NW of Dafoe, 28.7.42; SR 26.1.43; 9 RD 24.3.43; 3 TC SR 26.7.44; SOC 6.11.44 for WAC [568 hrs]
L5542/2018	TOC 22.7.41 at Fleet Acft; 1 TC 28.8.41 for 6 B&GS; 6 RD 20.1.43; SOC 24.3.44 for spares
L5550/1831	TOC 8.1.41 at Fleet Acft; 1 TC 9.4.41 for 1 B&GS; 3 TC 4.2.42 for 9 B&GS; landed with wheels partly down, Mont Joli, 15.11.42; 9 RD 8.7.43; 3 TC SR 26.8.44; SOC 6.11.44 for WAC [994 hrs]
L5552	TOC 16.9.41 at Fleet Acft; 1 TC 3.12.41 for 31 B&GS; engine caught fire; forcelanded, Picton, but badly damaged by fire after landing, 19.4.42; Fleet Acft 9.5.42; 9 RD 3.9.42 for turret fitment by CCF; 2 TC 1.2.43 for 3 B&GS; SR 21.3.44; SOC 16.2.45 for WAC [511 hrs]
L5553	TOC 16.9.41 at Fleet Acft but incomplete; 6 RD 3.11.41; Central Acft 23.6.42; 9 RD 23.1.43; 1 TC SR 25.9.43; SOC 13.2.45 for WAC [100 hrs]
L5554	TOC 16.9.41 at Fleet Acft; 1 TC 26.1.42 for 31 B&GS; hit by Crane 8189 while parked, Picton, 25.3.42; Fleet 6.5.42; 9 RD 26.8.42 for turret fitment by CCF; 2 TC 9.11.42 for 3 B&GS; SR 16.5.44; to display airframe 10.7.46; 10 RD 14.7.50; sold to Ajax Aircraft Parts, 22.10.53 [678 hrs]
L5555/1807	TOC 7.1.41 at Fleet Acft; 2 TC 17.2.41 for 3 B&GS; engine cut; bellylanded in ploughed field 1m S of MacDonald, 19.5.41; MacDonald Bros 6.6.41; 2 TC 13.4.42; SR 26.1.43; 9 RD 26.3.43; 3 TC SR 26.7.44; SOC 6.11.44 for WAC [363 hrs]
L5556	TOC 17.4.41 at 6 RD; 1 TC 10.5.41 for 31 B&GS; undercarriage leg collapsed on landing, Picton, 6.4.42; 9 RD 4.9.42 for turret fitment by CCF; 2 TC 7.11.42 for 9 B&GS. Collided with 1949 while drogue towing and lost tail, 3m E of Mont Joli, 7.10.43; F/Sgt R. Dean, LAC E.W. Astell RAF and LAC K. McKinstry killed; 9 RD 14.10.43; SOC 24.2.44
L5557/1804	TOC 7.1.41; 2 TC 17.2.41 for 3 B&GS; SR 4.4.44; SOC 16.2.45 for WAC [824 hrs]

L5560 — TOC 10.4.41 at 6 RD as TT; 1 TC 25.4.41 for 31 SFTS; overshot forced landing into wall after loss of power 10m ENE of Kingston, 26.5.41; 6 RD 7.7.41; 9 RD 4.9.42 for turret fitment by CCF; 2 TC 5.12.42 for 3 B&GS; SR 21.3.44; SOC 16.2.45 for WAC [645 hrs]

L5562/2014 — TOC 3.7.41 at 8 RD; 2 TC 16.8.41; to 5 B&GS26.8.41; bellylanded in error, Dafoe, 10.10.41; 9 RD 10.8.42 for turret fitment by CCF; 2 TC 9.11.42 for 3 B&GS; engine cut; bellylanded 35m S of MacDonald, 5.8.43. Caught fire in air; force-landed, MacDonald, 17.8.43; SOC 31.8.43 for spares

L5567/1852 — TOC 6.3.41 by MacDonald Acft; 2 TC 31.7.41; 4 TC 8.9.41 for 8 B&GS; Central Acft 28.6.43; SOC 17.4.44 for spares

L5569 — TOC 11.6.41 at Fleet Acft; 1 TC 8.7.41 for 31 SFTS; 6 RD 9.9.41; 9 RD 17.9.42 for turret fitment by CCF; 2 TC 27.1.43 for 3 B&GS; SR 7.8.43; SOC 4.11.44 for WAC [315 hrs]

L5570/1931 — TOC 22.4.41 at Fleet Acft; 1 TC 13.5.41 for 1 B&GS; engine lost power on approach; belly-landed, Jarvis, 28.5.42; Central Acft 3.6.42; 9 RD 5.1.43 for turret fitment by CCF; 3 TC SR 7.9.43; SOC 4.11.44 for WAC [5 hrs]

L5573 — TOC 10.4.41 at 6 RD; 1 TC 25.4.41 for 31 B&GS. Engine cut during bombing practice; forcelanded in field 1m S of Picton, 16.10.41; 6 RD 12.11.41; cv to GI airframe A163 18.7.42; SOC 14.2.45

L5575/1862 — TOC 20.3.41 at 8 RD; 2 TC 12.6.41; to 7 B&GS 18.6.41. flew into ground in circuit 1m NW of Paulson, 1.7.41; SOC 1.8.41

L5586/1941 — TOC 28.4.41 at Fleet Acft; 1 TC 23.5.41 for 4 B&GS; 6 RD 29.1.43; SOC 24.3.44 for spares

L5588/2086 — TOC 16.9.41 at Acft Repair; 4 TC 16.10.41 for 8 B&GS; taxied into Harvard 3818, Lethbridge, 10.7.42; SR 18.11.42; Central Acft 10.6.43; 1 TC SR 25.10.43; SOC 13.2.45 for WAC [377 hrs]

L5589/1875 — TOC 7.4.41 at 8 RD; 2 TC 16.5.41; to 5 B&GS 26.5.41; SR 26.1.43; 9 RD 24.3.43 for turret fitment by CCF; Central Acft 28.4.43; 3 TC SR 26.1.44; SOC 4.11.44 for WAC [725 hrs]

L5592/1865 — TOC 24.3.41 at Fleet Acft; 1 TC 9.4.41 for 4 B&GS; 9 RD 21.9.42 for turret fitment by CCF; 3 TC 20.12.42 for 9 B&GS; SR 16.3.43; 9 B&GS 1.6.43; SR 9.4.45; sold 17.6.46 to WAC [1606 hrs]

L5601/1649 — TOC 6.5.40 at Trenton; Rockliffe 27.6.40 as TT; 6 ARD 22.8.40; 4 TC 1.11.40 for 2 B&GS; SR 13.10.42; Central Acft 19.6.43; SOC 21.4.44 for spares

L5605/1686 — TOC 7.6.40 at Trenton as TT; 4 TC 1.11.40 for 2 B&GS; hit flagpole and undercarriage jammed; landed on one wheel, Mossbank, 1.11.41; SR 13.10.42; Central Acft 10.6.43; SOC 23.2.44

L5606/1673 — TOC 3.6.40 at Trenton; 1 TC 14.8.40 for 1 B&GS; 3 TC 21.3.42 for 9 B&GS; lost height on overshoot in coarse pitch; forcelanded and hit fence 2m W of Mont Joli, 11.10.43; 9 RD 15.10.43; SOC 24.2.44

L5607/1674 — TOC 3.6.40 at Trenton; 1 TC 14.8.40 for 1 B&GS; SR 1.8.42; 3 TC 2.9.42 for 9 B&GS; later 10 B&GS; SR 3.8.44; SOC 4.11.44 for WAC [1281 hrs]

L5608/1650 — TOC 6.5.40 at Trenton; 1 TC 6.6.40 for 4 B&GS as TT. Missing 8.12.40 and two days later found crashed on beach, Fort Bruce; FO L.A. Hood, AC2 E.W. Bourne and AC2 J.H. McNally had been killed in the crash; SOC 28.2.41 [203 hrs]

L5611/1651 — TOC 6.5.40 at Trenton; 1 TC 24.5.40 for 4 B&GS as TT; Fleet Acft 29.4.41; 2 TC 19.3.42; 124 Ferry Sqn; hit snowdrift on landing and damaged, Kapuskasing, 26.3.42; SOC 11.1.43

L5612/1675 — TOC 3.6.40 at Trenton; 1 TC for 1 B&GS as TT;

4 ARD 8.1.41; 1 TC 31.1.41 for 1 B&GS; 3 TC 11.12.41 for 9 B&GS; 1 AC SR 9.4.45; sold 17.6.46 to WAC [1536 hrs]

L5613/1648 — TOC 6.5.40 at Trenton; 1 TC 24.5.40 for 4 B&GS; 3 TC 23.3.42 for 9 B&GS. Control lost while towing drogue; dived into ground, Mont Joli, 27.7.43; F/Sgt D.J. McLean RNZAF and AC2 H. Revzen RCAF killed; to 9 RD 16.8.43 for spares recovery and SOC 15.12.43

L5614/1676 — TOC 3.6.40 at Trenton; 1 TC 10.8.40 for 1 B&GS, later 4 B&GS; taxied into roller, Fingal, 11.9.41; Fleet Acft 29.9.41; 2 TC 19.3.42 for 7 B&GS; SR 8.8.42; 2 TC 28.8.42 for 3 B&GS; SR 16.11.42; 3 B&GS 7.12.42; engine cut; bellylanded 11m NE of MacDonald, 17.8.43; SR 21.3.44; SOC 16.2.45 for WAC [836 hrs]

L5615/1677 — TOC 3.6.40 at Trenton; 1 TC 14.8.40 for 1 B&GS; 3 TC 9.12.41 for 9 B&GS; engine caught fire; bellylanded 8m W of Mont Joli, 5.9.42; Central Acft 29.9.42; 3 TC 12.3.43 for 10 B&GS; brakes failed; ran into ditch, Mont Joli, 22.5.43; SR 12.9.44; sold 17.6.46 to WAC [1295 hrs]

L5616/1678 — TOC 3.6.40 at Trenton; 1 TC 14.8.40 for 1 B&GS as TT; EAC Dartmouth 16.12.40; engine cut on take-off; crashlanded into trees, Dartmouth, 26.2.41; CCF for repair 24.3.41; CCF for turret installation experiments 17.7.41; 9 RD 6.6.42; SOC 28.9.42 for spares

L5618/1671 — TOC 29.5.40 at Trenton; 1 TC 14.8.40 for 1 B&GS as TT; 3 FC 1.9.42 for 9 B&GS, later 10 B&GS; SR 9.8.44; 124 Ferry Sqn 15.8.44; taxied into Anson 11680, Ancienne Lorette, 25.8.44; retained at 3 TC; 1 AC SR 9.4.45; sold 17.6.46 to WAC [607 hrs]

L5619/1693 — TOC 7.6.40 at Trenton; 4 TC 1.11.40 for 2 B&GS; brakes failed taxying; swung into ditch, Mossbank, 3.9.42; Central Acft 10.6.43; to GI airframe A374 4.2.44 at WETP School, Galt, Ont.; 1 TC SR 6.4.44; 6 RD 23.2.45 for write-off; SOC 7.3.45

L5620/1682 — TOC 7.6.40 at Trenton; 1 TC 14.8.40 for 1 B&GS as TT; taxied into 1691, Jarvis, 2.12.41; Fleet Acft 11.4.42; 1 TC 26.4.42; SR 1.8.42; 3 TC 2.9.42 for 9 B&GS; engine cut; bellylanded 4m E of Quebec City Bridge, 31.3.43; 9 RD 1.3.44; SOC 26.5.44

L5621/1672 — TOC 29.5.40 at Trenton; 1 TC 29.5.40 for 1 B&GS as TT; SR 1.8.42; 3 TC 2.9.42 for 9 B&GS, later 10 B&GS; SR 18.5.44; sold 17.6.46 to WAC [1283 hrs]

L5622/1690 — TOC 7.6.40 at Trenton; 4 TC 1.11.40 for 2 B&GS; engine cut while towing drogue; bellylanded 15m NW of Mossbank, 21.5.41; tyre burst on landing; swung and tipped up, Mossbank, 21.4.42; SR 13.10.42; Central Acft 3.5.43; 9 RS 11.1.44; 3 TC SR 10.7.44; sold 17.6.46 to WAC [994 hrs]

L5627/1694 — TOC 7.6.40 at Trenton; 4 TC 1.11.40 for 2 B&GS as TT; SR 25.11.42; Central Acft 18.5.43; 1 TC SR 8.11.43; SOC 22.6.45 for WAC [951 hrs]

L5643/1695 — TOC 5.8.40 at Trenton; 1 TC for 1 B&GS as TT; 3 TC 4.12.42; 3 TC SR 22.1.43; 9 B&GS 11.3.44; Pilot overcome by hydraulic fumes; bellylanded 2m E of Mont Joli, 20.7.44; 9 RD 31.7.44; not repaired and SOC 29.8.44

L5645/1696 — TOC 5.8.40 at Trenton; 1 TC 14.8.40 for 1 B&GS as TT; SR 1.8.42; 3 TC 2.9.42 for 9 B&GS; taxied into truck, Mont Joli, 13.7.43; SR 22.1.44; 3 TC 11.3.44 for 9 B&GS; 8 SFTS; 1 AC SR 9.4.45; sold 17.6.46 to WAC [1842 hrs]

L5646/1697 — TOC 5.8.40 at Trenton; 1 TC 14.8.40 for 1 B&GS as TT; 3 TC 9.4.42; SOC 11.1.43

L5647/1698 — TOC 5.8.40 at Trenton; 1 TC 14.8.40 for 1 B&GS as TT; forcelanded with electrical fault near Selkirk, 6.3.41; 3 TC 21.3.42 for 9 B&GS; engine

Battle Trainer R7418 with No.31 Service Flying Training School at Kingston, Ontario. (R Williams via R Sturtivant)

cut; bellylanded 1½m SW of Mont Joli, 7.6.44. Engine cut; bellylanded, St.Luce, Que., 21.8.44; not repaired and SOC 1.9.44

L5648/1699 TOC 5.8.40 at Trenton; 1 TC 14.8.40 for 1 B&GS as TT; undercarriage leg collapsed on landing, Jarvis, 16.8.41; 9 RD 5.1.42; 9 RD for turret fitment 5.11.42; apparently not fitted; 6 RD 18.12.42; SOC 17.1.44

L5649/1700 TOC 5.8.40 at Trenton; 1 TC 14.8.40 for 1 B&GS as TT; SR 1.8.42; 3 TC 2.9.42 for 9 B&GS. Hydraulics burst and temporarily blinded pilot; crashlanded, Mont Joli, 12.10.42; SOC 11.1.43 for spares

N2020/1729 TOC 5.11.40 at MacDonald Bros; 4 TC 26.11.40 for 2 B&GS; Acft Repair 19.2.41; 4 TC 16.2.42; 10 RD 22.7.43; SOC 22.12.43

N2023/2050 TOC 22.7.41 at 8 RD; 4 TC 11.11.41 for 8 B&GS; SR 18.11.42; Central Acft 10.6.43; 9 RD 10.1.44; SOC 7.3.45 for WAC [566 hrs]

N2029/1812 TOC 13.1.41 at Fleet Acft; 2 TC 21.2.41 for 3 B&GS; SR 4.4.44; SOC 16.2.45 for WAC [799 hrs]

N2035/2051 TOC 14.7.41 at MacDonald Bros; 2 TC 26.8.41 for 3 B&GS; SR 17.4.43; SOC 16.2.45 for WAC [642 hrs]

N2036/1995 TOC 1.7.41 at 6 RD; 1 TC 15.7.41 for 6 B&GS; 6 RD 12.2.43; SOC 1.5.44 for spares

N2040/1797 TOC 7.1.41 at Fleet Acft; 2 TC 17.2.41 for 3 B&GS; 9 RD 13.3.43; 3 TC SR 26.7.44; SOC 6.11.44 for WAC [703 hrs]

N2041/1994 TOC 1.7.41 at 6 RD; 1 TC for 6 B&GS. Engine cut; crashed in forced landing 2m E of Trenton, 24.7.42; to spares and SOC 20.10.42

N2046/2088 TOC 11.9.41 at Acft Repair; 4 TC 16.10.41 for 8 B&GS; SR 18.11.42; Central Acft 1.4.43; cv to TT; 3 TC SR 24.6.43; issued to 9 B&GS 18.11.43; SR 18.9.44; sold 17.6.46 to WAC [481 hrs]

N2047/2087 TOC 11.9.41 at Acft Repair; 2 TC 22.11.41 for 5 B&GS; SR 17.11.42; SOC 16.2.45 for WAC

[494 hrs]

N2049/1927 TOC 28.4.41 at Fleet Acft; 1 TC 17.5.41 for 4 B&GS; forcelanded after engine failure 12m SW of Fingal, 28.5.41; engine failed on test flight; bellylanded 8m NE of Fingal, 13.5.42; Fleet Acft 2.6.42; 9 RD 2.11.42 for turret fitment by CCF; 3 TC SR 7.9.43; SOC 7.3.45 for WAC

N2052/2131 TOC 22.1.42 at 4 RD; 3 TC 11.4.42 for 9 B&GS; brakes failed; taxied into 1937, Mont Joli, 12.8.42; brakes failed; taxied into R7429, Mont Joli, 12.4.43; 9 RD 31.5.43; SOC 4.11.44 for WAC [1203 hrs]

N2056/2066 TOC 24.9.41 at 8 RD; 2 TC 3.11.41 for 5 B&GS. Collided with 1925 on approach and crashed, Dafoe, Sask., 23.7.42; Sgt E.H. Dunn and LAC O.V. Nickerson killed, LAC R.C. Parker injured; SOC 23.10.42 as scrap

N2082/2037 TOC 22.7.41 at 8 RD; 2 TC 21.8.41 for 5 B&GS; lost glycol and bellylanded, Arborfield, Sask., 31.10.41; MacDonald Bros 6.11.41; 9 RD 28.11.42; SOC 4.11.44 for WAC [152 hrs]

N2083/1924 TOC 7.4.41 at Acft Repair; 2 TC 14.5.41 for 5 B&GS; taxied into 1977, Dafoe, 20.11.41; hit by 2009 while parked, Dafoe, 18.2.42; SR and cv to TT 12.4.43; 2 TC 10.1.44 for 3 B&GS; SR 1.4.44; SOC 16.2.45 for WAC [638 hrs]

N2085/1731 TOC 5.11.40 at MacDonald Bros; 4 TC 2.12.40 for 2 B&GS; 2 TC 22.3.41 for 3 B&GS; engine cut on take-off; bellylanded, MacDonald, 29.10.42; cv TT 22.4.43; SR 21.3.44; SOC 16.2.45 for WAC [566 hrs]

N2087/1733 TOC 24.10.40 at Trenton; 1 TC 12.7.41 for 6 B&GS; 6 RD 11.12.42; Fairchild 17.4.42 for cv to Battle II; 9 RD 24.8.43; SOC 7.3.45 for WAC [358 hrs]

N2094/2025 TOC 24.7.41 at Fleet Acft; 1 TC 11.8.41 for 6 B&GS; taxied into 2030, Mountain View, 25.3.42; 9 RD 10.10.42 for turret fitment; 2 TC 8.3.43 for 3 B&GS; SR 21.3.44; SOC 16.2.45 for WAC [999 hrs]

N2099/1748	TOC 16.11.40 at Fleet Acft; 1 TC 9.12.40 for 4 B&GS; 3 TC 8.12.41 for 9 B&GS; 6 RD 9.3.42; Fleet Acft 20.5.42; 9 RD 19.10.42 for turret fitment by CCF; 2 TC SR 25.3.43; 3 B&GS 13.1.43; 2 TC SR 4.4.44; SOC 16.2.45 for WAC [43 hrs]
N2103/1856	TOC 6.3.41 at MacDonald Acft and cv to TT; 2 TC 13.8.41 for 3 B&GS. Oil pressure dropped and engine vibrated; forcelanded 10m N of MacDonald, 27.10.42; SOC 11.1.43 for spares
N2106/1844	TOC 6.3.41 at Acft Repair; 2 TC 8.4.41 for 3 B&GS; 9 RD 13.3.43 for turret fitment; not carried out; SOC 6.11.44 for WAC [704 hrs]
N2125/2113	TOC 13.12.41 at Fleet Acft; 3 TC 17.1.42 for 9 B&GS; missed runway landing in bad visibility and tipped up in snow, Mont Joli, 20.2.42; swerved into ditch taxying, Mont Joli, 8.8.42; 9 RD 14.6.43; SOC 4.11.44 for WAC [1070 hrs]
N2127/1801	TOC 7.1.41 at Fleet Acft; 2 TC 17.2.41 for 3 B&GS; pilot overcome by fumes; bellylanded, MacDonald, 23.5.41; SR 4.4.44; SOC 16.2.45 for WAC [245 hrs]
N2147/1820	TOC 11.2.41 at MacDonald Bros; 2 TC 30.4.41 for 3 B&GS; hit by 1720 while parked, MacDonald, 4.3.42; engine cut on take-off; bellylanded in field 2m W of MacDonald, 13.4.42; SR 21.3.44; SOC 16.2.45 for WAC [1421 hrs]
N2156/1606	TOC 16.2.40 at Trenton; 6 RD 3.11.42; 9 RD 6.3.43 for turret fitment; 3 TC SR 6.7.44; SOC 6.11.44 for WAC
N2158/1604	TOC 24.2.40 at Trenton; 1 TC for AAS; later 1 B&GS; collided with 1814 3m W of Fisherville, Ont., 9.12.41; landed safely. Collided with Anson 8207 and spun into Lake Erie, Evans Point, 18.8.42; Sgt J.W. Whitehead, LACs A.C. Reed and W.M. Kirkby killed; SOC 27.10.42
N2160/2031	TOC 24.7.41 at Fleet Acft; 1 TC 11.8.41 for 6 B&GS; brakes failed; ran into 1685, Mountain View, 6.6.42; 9 RD 18.8.42 for repair and turret fitment by CCF; 3 TC 9.11.42 for 9 B&GS; collided with 1670 on ground, Mont Joli, 17.4.43; SR 9.4.45; sold 17.6.46 to WAC [1795 hrs]
N2162/1780	TOC 21.12.40 at Fleet Acft; 1 TC 13.1.41 for 4 B&GS; 3 TC 6.3.42 for 9 B&GS; skidded on ice taxying and undercarriage collapsed, Mont Joli, 4.4.42; Fleet Acft 5.5.42; 9 RD 29.7.42 for turret fitment by CCF; 2 FC for 3 B&GS 20.12.42. Engine cut on take-off; overshot runway into ditches, MacDonald, 11.8.43; 8 RD 23.8.43; SOC 27.8.43
N2167	TOC 16.9.41 at Fleet Acft; 1 TC 24.1.42 for 31 B&GS; 9 RD 20.8.42 for turret fitment by CCF; 3 TC 9.11.42 for 9 B&GS; collided with 7608 on icy taxiway, Mont Joli, 27.2.43; SOC 21.6.43
N2172/1951	TOC 13.5.41 at Acft Repair; 2 TC 11.6.41; to 7 B&GS 22.7.41; ran out of fuel, and bellylanded 13m from Paulson, 18.8.41; 8 RD 10.2.43; Central Acft 24.7.43; SOC 12.4.44 for spares
N2173	TOC 9.6.41 at 6 RD; 1 TC 5.7.41 for 31 B&GS; 6 RD 14.12.42; SOC 1.5.44 for spares
N2181/1839	TOC 11.2.41 at MacDonald Bros; 2 TC 25.4.41; to 5 B&GS 8.5.41 as TT; bellylanded in error, Dafoe, 21.11.41; forcelanded with engine failure, Dafoe, 7.5.42; brakes failed; taxied into Crane 7862, Dafoe, 22.5.42; brakes failed; hit Crane 7862, Saskatoon, 22.8.42; 5 B&GS; ran into 1853 taxying, Dafoe, 22.6.42; SOC 26.1.43 for spares
N2183/1871	TOC 24.3.41 at Fleet Acft and cv to TT; 1 TC 9.4.41 for 4 B&GS; 9 RD 10.10.42; 6 RD 13.11.42; 3 TC 4.11.43 for 10 B&GS; Cat A at Mt. Pleasant 24.5.44; no record traced; 4 RD 7.6.44 for salvage; SOC 17.4.44
N2186/1971	TOC 11.6.41 at Fleet Acft; 1 TC 3.7.41 for 6 B&GS; 9 RD 18.11.42; 3 TC SR 26.7.44; SOC 4.11.44 for WAC [551 hrs]
N2187/2035	TOC 22.7.41 at 8 RD; 2 TC 16.8.41; to 7 B&GS 25.8.41; SOC 11.1.43 for spares
N2189/1805	TOC 7.1.41 at Fleet Acft; 2 TC 25.2.41 for 3 B&GS. Undercarriage leg collapsed on landing and wing hit ground, MacDonald, Man., 1.8.42; not repaired and SOC 11.1.43
N2190/2052	TOC 14.7.41 at MacDonald Bros; 2 TC 23.8.41 for 5 B&GS; engine lost power; bellylanded, Dafoe, 9.4.42; SR 26.1.43; SOC 16.2.45 for WAC [795 hrs]
N2226/1718	TOC 17.10.40 at Trenton; 1 TC 12.11.40 for 4 B&GS; cv TT 29.4.41; 12 FS Rockliffe; bellylanded with engine trouble on ferry flight, Fingal, 7.3.42; Fleet Acft 31.3.42; 1 TC 24.6.42; 9 RD 9.11.42 for turret fitment; retd to standard 30.3.43; 2 TC as SR 25.3.43; 3 B&GS 13.1.44; SR at 2 TC 24.4.44; SOC 16.2.45 for WAC [198 hrs]
N2227/1605	TOC 16.2.40 at Trenton; 4 TC for 2 B&GS; 4 B&GS; bellylanded with engine failure, Fingal, 17.4.42; SOC 12.1.43
N2230/1607	TOC 24.2.40 at Trenton; 1 TC 4.40 for 4 B&GS; hit by 1631 while parked, Trenton, 8.8.40; later 1 B&GS; 9 RD 6.9.42 for turret fitment by CCF; 6 RD 13.11.42; SOC 1.5.44 for spares
N2237/1891	TOC 8.4.41 at 4 RD Dartmouth and cv to TT; EAC Halifax 24.7.41 for HWE; 1 TC 9.9.41; to 31 SFTS 27.9.41. Engine cut while drogue towing; bellylanded on Amherst Is., 4m SW of Kingston, Ont., 5.11.41; not repaired and SOC as spares, 12.6.42
N2239/1602	TOC 16.2.40 at Trenton; 1 TC for 4 B&GS; engine cut; bellylanded in field 2m S of Fingal, 23.6.42; 9 RD 5.11.42 for turret fitment by CCF; 3 TC SR 6.4.43; SOC 4.11.44 for WAC [720 hrs]
N2241/1810	TOC 11.2.41 at MacDonald Bros; 2 TC 16.5.41 for 5 B&GS; pilot blinded by glycol leak; bellylanded 2½m NE of Dafoe, 20.7.41; MacDonald Acft 29.7.41; 9 RD 13.8.42 for turret fitment by CCF; 3 TC SR 17.12.42; 3 TC 19.6.43 for 9 B&GS; sold 17.6.46 to WAC [1042 hrs]
N2242/2126	TOC 9.1.42 at Fleet Acft; 3 TC 24.2.42 for 9 B&GS; swerved on take-off and undercarriage torn off, Mont Joli, 26.3.42; 9 RD 14.6.43; SOC 4.11.44 for WAC [999 hrs]
N2245	TOC 17.4.41 at Ottawa Car Ltd; 1 TC 10.5.41 for 31 B&GS; 9 RD 20.8.42 for turret fitment by CCF; 3 TC 5.12.42 for 9 B&GS; SR 16.3.43; issued to 9 B&GS 28.5.43; SR 22.1.44; sold 17.6.46 to WAC [1014 hrs]
N2246/1603	TOC 16.2.40 at Trenton; AAS; taxied into Nomad 3492, Mountain View, 26.8.41; 6 B&GS; hydraulics blew on take-off; bellylanded, Mountain View, 18.2.42; ground-looped on landing at night, Mountain View, 20.3.42; swung on landing and wing hit ground, Mountain View, 17.5.42; 6 RD 1.12.42; SOC 1.5.44 for spares
N2248/1898	TOC 7.4.41 at 8 RD; 2 TC for 7 B&GS 27.6.41; 9 RD 10.8.42 for turret fitment by CCF; 3 TC 7.11.42 for 9 B&GS. Developed glycol leak after take-off; crashlanded 1½m E of Mont Joli, 3.4.44; 9 RD 27.4.44 for salvage; SOC 9.8.44
N2249/2082	TOC 22.9.41 at Acft Repair; 4 TC 16.10.41 for 8 B&GS; SR 18.11.42; SOC 26.1.43 for spares
N2257/2124	TOC 9.1.42 at Fleet Acft; 3 TC 24.2.42 for 9 B&GS; 9 RD 14.6.43; 3 TC 23.6.44 for 9 B&GS; SR 9.4.45; sold 17.6.46 to WAC [728 hrs]
P2155/1301	TOC 21.8.39 at Camp Borden; ATS Trenton 3.9.39; ATS 12.1.40; 115(F) Sqn 23.1.40; Trenton 9.5.40; 4 TC 1.11.40 for 2 B&GS; SR 13.10.42; SOC 11.1.43 for spares
P2156/1750	TOC 27.10.40 at Fleet Acft; 1 TC 9.12.40 for 4 B&GS; engine cut; forcelanded ½m NE of Fingal,

This target tug from No.3 Bombing & Gunnery School at Macdonald appears to have lost its serial number. (via D Howley)

	29.4.42; 6 RD 23.11.42; SOC 23.3.44 for spares
P2164/1621	TOC 8.4.40 at Trenton; 1 TC 9.5.40 for 1 B&GS; to GI airframe A250 9.1.43 but not taken up; 6 RD 4.2.43; SOC 3.3.43
P2165/1936	TOC 7.4.41 at Acft Repair; 4 TC 20.8.41 for 2 B&GS; Central Acft 1.7.43; SOC 19.3.44 for spares
P2170/1624	TOC 11.4.40 at Trenton; 1 TC 1.5.40 for 1 B&GS; 4 TC 28.10.40 for 2 B&GS; SR 13.10.42; SOC 11.1.43 for spares
P2171/1302	TOC 21.8.39 at Camp Borden; ATS Trenton 3.9.39; ATS Camp Borden 8.1.40; 1 TC 1.4.40 for ATS Trenton; undercarriage collapsed during engine run-up, Trenton, 8.8.40; passed to 4 B&GS; 6 RD 2.2.43; SOC 17.1.44 for spares
P2172/1303	TOC 21.8.39 at Camp Borden; ATS Trenton 3.9.39; ATS Camp Borden 12.1.40; 115(F) Sqn 13.1.40; FAD St.Hubert 19.3.40; Trenton 9.5.40; 4 TC 11.11.40 for 2 B&GS; hit snowdrift and tipped up, Mossbank, 20.11.41; Central Acft 20.9.43; 9 RD 6.1.44; 3 TC SR 6.7.44; SOC 6.11.44 for WAC
P2173/1304	TOC 21.8.39 at Camp Borden; ATS Trenton 7.9.39. Dived into ground in bad visibility 10m SW of Snow Road, Sharbot Lake, Ont., 14.10.39; PO G.J. Oldstead and PO H.K. Corbett killed; SOC 4.12.39 [48 hrs]
P2185/1305	TOC 21.8.39 at Camp Borden; ATS Trenton 4.9.39; Ottawa 6.9.39; Trenton 25.9.39; ATS Camp Borden 22.1.40; 1 TC 1.4.40 for 4 B&GS; 4 TC 28.10.40 for 2 B&GS; SR 13.10.42; SOC 11.1.43 for spares
P2186/1306	TOC 21.8.39 at Camp Borden; ATS Trenton 3.9.39; ATS Camp Borden 8.1.40; 1 TC 1.4.40 for CTE and 4 B&GS; forcelanded while lost at De France, Ohio, 29.5.42; 9 RD 26.9.42 for turret fitment by CCF; 3 TC 5.12.42 for 9 B&GS; SR

	6.3.43; sold 17.6.46 to WAC
P2187/1307	TOC 21.8.39 at Camp Borden; ATS Trenton 1.9.39; ATS Camp Borden 2.40; 1 TC 2.11.40 for 4 B&GS; 4 TC 2.11.40 for 2 B&GS; 2 TC 19.6.41 for 7 B&GS; SOC 11.1.43 for spares
P2188/1909	TOC 22.4.41 at Fleet Acft; 1 TC 8.5.41 for CTS Picton; 3 TC 8.12.41; 6 RD 23.3.42; Fleet Acft 10.5.42; 9 RD 18.7.42 for turret fitment by CCF; 2 TC 8.10.42 for 3 B&GS; engine cut; bellylanded 15m NW of MacDonald, 12.3.43; engine cut; bellylanded 3m N of MacDonald, 12.4.43; SR 16.5.44; SOC 16.2.45 for WAC [514 hrs]
P2196/1308	TOC 21.8.39 at Camp Borden; ATS Trenton 4.9.39; ATS Camp Borden 8.1.40; 1 TC 4.40; 3 TC 7.6.40 for AES; Fleet Acft 10.8.40; 4 TC 22.10.41 for 8 B&GS; SR 18.11.42; SOC 26.1.43 for spares
P2197/1309	TOC 29.8.39 at Camp Borden; ATS Trenton 9.9.39; ATS Camp Borden 8.1.40; 1 TC 1.4.40 for 1 B&GS; 4 TC 28.10.40 for 2 B&GS; 2 TC 22.3.41 for 3 B&GS; SOC 11.1.43 for spares
P2198/1310	TOC 29.8.39 at Camp Borden; ATS Trenton 7.9.39; ATS Camp Borden 8.1.40; forcelanded, Cooks Bay, Ont., 21.3.40; damaged, Camp Borden, 29.3.40; 1 TC 1.4.40 for 4 B&GS; 6 ARD 16.10.40; 1 TC 2.11.40 for 4 B&GS; engine cut on take-off; bellylanded ¼m S of Fingal, 23.4.42; Central Acft 5.6.42; 9 RD 23.1.43 for turret fitment by CCF; 3 TC SR 7.9.43; SOC 4.11.44 for WAC
P2199/2058	TOC 14.7.41 at MacDonald Acft; 4 TC 22.9.41 for 8 B&GS; SR 18.11.42; Central Acft 10.6.43; 1 TC SR 13.12.43; SOC 13.2.45 for WAC [240 hrs]
P2233/1311	TOC 20.9.39 at Camp Borden; ATS Trenton 3.11.39; 1 TC 1.4.40 for 1 B&GS; 3 TC 4.12.41 for 9 B&GS; engine lost power; hit fence in forced

P2234/1317 landing 12m E of St.Anaclet, Que. 29.1.42; Fleet Acft 3.5.42; 9 RD 8.10.42 for turret fitment by CCF; 2 TC 18.2.43 for 3 B&GS; SR 8.4.43; 2 TC 6.4.43 for 3 B&GS; SOC 16.2.45 for WAC [583 hrs]

P2234/1317 TOC 3.11.39 at FIS Camp Borden; ATS Camp Borden 2.2.40; damaged, Camp Borden, 2.3.40; to GI airframe A56 20.4.40 for 1 TTS St.Thomas; SOC 12.9.40 as components

P2235/1312 TOC 26.9.39 at Camp Borden; ATS Trenton 27.10.39; crashed, North Port, 30.12.39; to GI airframe A52 15.5.40 at 1 TTS St.Thomas; SOC 9.5.46

P2236/1313 TOC 20.9.39 at Camp Borden; FIS Camp Borden 5.1.40; ATS Camp Borden 6.2.40; 1 TC 1.4.40 for 1 B&GS; 6 ARD 6.10.40; 4 TC 7.11.40 for 2 B&GS; SR 3.10.42; to GI airframe A269 9.1.43 for 2 WS; SOC 1.12.43 for spares

P2237/1318 TOC 3.11.39 at Camp Borden; ATS Camp Borden 3.2.40; 1 TC 1.4.40 for ATS; bellylanded in error, Trenton, 27.9.40; later to 1 B&GS; 9 RD 18.8.42 for turret fitment by CCF; 2 TC SR 17.10.42; SOC 16.2.45 for WAC [1045 hrs]

P2238/1314 TOC 20.9.39 at Camp Borden; ATS Trenton 29.10.39; ATS Camp Borden 18.1.40; to GI airframe A51 18.5.40 at 1 TTS St.Thomas; SOC 24.8.40 as components

P2239/1319 TOC 3.11.39 at Camp Borden; 115(F) Sqn 23.1.40; T&D Flt Ottawa 10.4.40; 1 TC 4.5.40 for 1 B&GS; 3 TC 1.12.41 for 9 B&GS; swung into ditch on landing, Mont Joli, 3.9.42; taxied into 7431, Mont Joli, 9.4.43; SR 1.4.45; sold 17.6.46 to WAC [1581 hrs]

P2240/1315 TOC 20.9.39 at Camp Borden; ATS Trenton 1.11.39; ATS Camp Borden 18.1.40; T&DF Ottawa 7.3.40. Engine cut after take-off; crashlanded 2m NE of Rockliffe, 1.8.41; to 6 RD 5.7.41 for spares and SOC 8.12.41

P2241/1316 TOC 20.9.39 at Camp Borden; ATS Camp Borden; engine cut due to fuel starvation; bellylanded, Cook's Bay, Ont., 9.3.40; 1 TC 1.4.40 for 1 B&GS; 4 TC 12.10.40 for 2 B&GS; overshot forced landing in fog 8m NW of Mossbank, 5.7.41; taxied into 1901, Mossbank, 11.3.42; SR 13.10.42; Central Acft 9.6.43; SOC 12.4.44 for spares

P2242/1320 TOC 3.11.39 at Camp Borden; ATS Camp Borden 6.2.40; 6 ARD 16.10.40; 1 TC 12.11.40 for 4 B&GS; allotted A252 9.1.43 but not used; 6 RD 4.2.43; SOC 26.1.43 for spares

P2252 TOC 17.4.41 at Ottawa Car Ltd; 1 TC 17.11.41 for 31 B&GS; 9 RD 1.10.42 for turret fitment by CCF; 2 TC 27.3.43 for 3 B&GS; SR 21.3.44; SOC 16.2.45 for WAC [512 hrs]

P2257/1888 TOC 7.4.41 at 8 RD; 2 TC 17.6.41 for 3 B&GS; Central Acft 15.4.43; 9 RD 16.1.44 for cv to TT; 3 TC 18.7.44 for 7 B&GS, later 9 B&GS; undercarriage leg collapsed after landing, Mont Joli, 9.3.45; sold 17.6.46 to WAC [1371 hrs]

P2259/1778 TOC 16.11.40 at Acft Repair; 4 TC 14.1.41 for 2 B&GS; engine cut; bellylanded 5m S of Mossbank, 13.8.42; SR 13.10.42; SOC 17.6.44

P2262/2023 TOC 22.7.41 at Fleet Acft; 1 TC 19.8.41 for 6 B&GS; taxied into building, Mountain View, 10.9.41; later with 31 B&GS; 6 RD 12.2.43; SOC 23.3.44 for spares

P2270/2143M TOC 23.9.40 at Aero Engineering School as GI airframe A104; SOC 6.9.44

P2301/2115 TOC 31.12.41 at Fleet Acft; AHQ Ferry Sqn. Control lost on ferry flight to 9 B&GS; dived into ground, Clappisons Corners, near Hamilton, Ont., 10.2.42; FO E. Montgomery killed; SOC 9.5.42

P2302/1900 TOC 5.4.41 at Acft Repair; 4 TC 30.4.41 for 2 B&GS. Caught fire and crashlanded, Johnston Lake, 5m N of Mossbank, Sask., 11.4.42; SOC 29.5.42

P2303/2114 TOC 31.12.41 at Fleet Acft; 3 TC 20.1.42 for 9 B&GS; landed with wheels partly down, Mont Joli, 15.11.42; 9 RD 8.7.43; SOC 7.3.45 for WAC [335 hrs]

P2304 TOC 26.5.41 at 6 RD; 1 TC 10.6.41 for 31 B&GS; taxied into K9476, Picton, 8.3.42; undercarriage leg collapsed on landing, Picton, 28.5.42; 9 RD 10.9.42 for turret fitment by CCF; 2 TC 5.12.42 for 3 B&GS; SR 16.5.44; SOC 16.2.45 for WAC [847 hrs]

P2306/1998 TOC 26.7.41 at 6 RD; 1 TC 26.7.41 for 6 B&GS. Engine lost power; hit ridge in forced landing, Mountain View, 21.1.42; to spares and SOC 11.6.42

P2308/1861 TOC 20.3.41 at 8 RD; 2 TC 17.5.41; to 5 B&GS 22.5.41; SR 16.11.42; SOC 11.1.43 for spares

P2309/1851 TOC 6.3.41 by MacDonald Bros and cv to TT; 2 TC 19.7.41 for 3 B&GS; SR 21.3.44; SOC 16.2.45 for WAC [1322 hrs]

P2311 TOC 9.5.41 at Fleet Acft; 1 TC 2.6.41 for 31 B&GS; bellylanded in error, Picton, 29.8.41; 9 RD 10.9.42 for turret fitment by CCF; 2 TC 8.3.43 for 3 B&GS; SR 21.3.44; SOC 16.2.45 for WAC [604 hrs]

P2312/1934 TOC 7.4.41 at Acft Repair; 2 TC 17.5.41; to 5 B&GS 22.5.41; SR 26.1.43; SOC 16.2.45 for WAC [758 hrs]

P2318/1949 TOC 14.5.41 at Fleet Acft; 1 TC 6.6.41; to 6 B&GS 26.6.41; 9 RD 18.8.42 for turret fitment by CCF; 3 TC 7.11.42 for 9 B&GS. Collided with L5556 and pilot bailed out 3m E of Mont Joli, 7.10.43; LAC S.G. Trueman killed and LAC R.E. Peavoy seriously injured; wreck to 9 RD 13.10.43 and SOC 24.2.44

P2319/2116 TOC 31.12.41 at Fleet Acft; 3 TC 9.2.42 for 9 B&GS; rock jammed wheel; swung into 1990 taxying, Mont Joli, 16.8.42; 9 RD 31.6.43; SOC 1.3.45 for WAC [683 hrs]

P2320/1869 TOC 24.3.41 at Fleet Acft; 1 TC 28.4.41 for 1 B&GS; 9 RD 28.9.42; 6 RD 13.11.42; Fairchild Acft 27.4.43 for cv to Battle II not carried out; 124 Ferry Sqn; engine cut on take-off on ferry flight; crashlanded 2m NE of Longueuil, 3.9.43; 9 ED 21.9.45; SOC 18.1.44

P2325/1876 TOC 7.4.41 at 8 RD; 2 TC 16.5.41; to 5 B&GS 20.5.41; SOC 11.1.43 for spares

P2329/1946 TOC 22.4.41 at Acft Repair; 2 TC 2.6.41; to 7 B&GS 17.6.41; SOC 11.1.43

P2331/1981 TOC 27.5.41 at Acft Repair; cv to TT by MacKenzie Air Services 5.6.41; 2 TC 9.7.41 for 3 B&GS; SR 16.11.42; retd to 3 B&GS 7.12.42; engine cut; tipped up in forced landing 40m SE of MacDonald, 20.6.43; engine cut; bellylanded 1m S of MacDonald, 6.12.43; SR 21.3.44; SOC 16.2.45 for WAC [1486 hrs]

P2358 TOC 8.5.41 at 6 RD; 1 TC 27.5.41 for 31 B&GS; forcelanded in bad weather and undercarriage collapsed, Stouts Farm, Crosley, Ont., 13.6.41; 6 RD 7.7.41; 4 TC SR 18.11.42; SOC 11.1.43 for spares

P2361/1665 TOC 29.5.40 at Trenton; 1 TC 16.10.40; 4 TC 22.10.40 for 2 B&GS; hydraulics failed; bellylanded, Mossbank, 1.8.41; McKenzie Air Services 8.8.41; 4 TC SR 16.2.42; 10 RD 22.7.43; SOC 18.3.44 for spares [192 hrs]

P2366/1653 TOC 9.5.40 at Trenton; 1 TC 16.10.40; 4 TC 1.11.40 for 2 B&GS; 7 B&GS 25.6.41; Central Acft 15.4.43; 1 TC SR 12.11.43; SOC 13.2.45 for WAC [898 hrs]

P2367/1646 TOC 2.5.40 at Trenton; 1 TC 10.8.40 for 1 B&GS; 2 TC 24.3.41 for 3 B&GS; Central Acft 15.4.43; 1 TC SR 12.11.43; SOC 13.2.45 for WAC [669 hrs]

P2368/1647 TOC 2.5.40 at Trenton; 1 TC 16.10.40 for 1

B&GS as TT; tipped up taxying in high wind, Jarvis, 8.12.41; mod to standard by 25.4.42; engine cut; crashlanded, South Cayuga, Ont., 17.6.42; Central Acft 30.6.42; 9 RD 13.3.43; SOC 6.11.44 for WAC

P2369/1654 TOC 9.5.40 at Trenton; 1 TC 10.8.40 for 1 B&GS; undercarriage leg collapsed on landing, Jarvis, 16.9.40; 3 TC 17.6.42 for 9 B&GS; SOC 11.1.43 for spares

P5228/1652 TOC 9.5.40 at Trenton; 1 TC 16.10.40; 4 TC 22.10.40 for 2 B&GS; tyres burst on landing; swung off runway, Mossbank, 7.6.41; 7 B&GS 19.6.41; SOC 21.1.43 for spares

P5233/2067 TOC 24.9.41 at 8 RD; 4 TC 11.11.41 for 8 B&GS. Caught fire in air and forcelanded 8m NE of Pitcurebutte, Alta., 13.1.42; DBF; SOC 25.3.42

P5236/1885 TOC 7.4.41 at 8 RD and cv to TT; 2 TC 9.7.41; to 7 B&GS 12.7.41; SR 26.3.44; SOC 16.2.45 for WAC [1315 hrs]

P5237/2108 TOC 11.9.41 at Acft Repair; 4 TC 22.11.41 for 2 B&GS; SR 13.10.42; 9 RD 19.1.43 for turret fitment by CCF; 3 TC SR 15.1.44; issued to 9 B&GS 27.4.44; SR 9.4.45; sold 17.6.46 to WAC [411 hrs]

P5241/1632 TOC 18.4.40 at Trenton; 1 TC 5.6.40; 5 B&GS; allotted CCF 18.8.42 for turret fitment; apparently not carried out and remained at 9 RD; 3 TC SR 26.7.42; SOC 8.11.44 for WAC

P5245/1662 TOC 13.5.40 at Trenton; 1 TC 14.8.40 for 1 B&GS; 3 TC 21.3.42 for 9 B&GS. Engine failed due to glycol leak; bellylanded 6m E of Mont Joli, 15.8.44; 9 RD 28.8.44; SOC 15.9.44 for spares

P5250/1760 TOC 8.11.40 at Acft Repairs; 4 TC 11.12.40; 3 B&GS; 3 TC for turret fitment 17.10.42; 3 TC SR 7.9.43; SOC 7.3.45 for WAC [761 hrs]

P5252/1937 TOC 22.4.41 at Fleet Acft; 1 TC 15.5.41 for AAS; 3 TC 17.6.42 for 9 B&GS; hit by 2131 while parked, Mont Joli, 12.8.42; 9 RD 31.5.43; SOC 4.11.44 for WAC [833 hrs]

P5270/1958 TOC 9.6.41 at Fleet Acft; 1 TC 25.6.41; 6 RD 19.1.43; SOC 12.1.43 for spares

P5271/1963 TOC 3.6.41 at 6 RD; 2 TC 23.6.41; to 7 B&GS 1.7.41. Hit trees low flying and bellylanded 40m W of Clear Lake, Man., 29.6.42; SOC 4.8.42 for spares

P5272/1977 TOC 13.5.41 at Acft Repair; 2 TC 9.7.41; to 5 B&GS 15.7.41. Hit by 1924 while parked, Dafoe, 20.11.41; SOC 6.4.42 for spares

P5274/1918 TOC 7.4.41 at Acft Repair; 2 TC 9.5.41; to 5 B&GS 22.5.41; SR 12.4.43 and cv to TT; 2 TC 10.1.44; for 3 B&GS; SR 1.4.44; SOC 16.2.45 for WAC [877 hrs]

P5276/2033 TOC 8.7.41 at 8 RD; 2 TC 12.8.41; to 5 B&GS 15.8.41; bellylanded with engine failure, Poplar Point, Man., 29.12.42; 8 RD 14.1.43; 2 TC SR 16.4.43; issued to 3 B&GS 17.1.44; SR 21.3.44; SOC 16.2.45 for WAC [409 hrs]

P5278/1864 TOC 22.4.41 at Fleet Acft; 1 TC 8.5.41 for 6 B&GS; 9 RD 10.10.42; 3 TC SR 26.7.44; SOC 6.11.44 for WAC [555 hrs]

P5279/1950 TOC 13.5.41 at Acft Repair; 2 TC 11.6.41 for 5 B&GS; 9 RD 10.8.42 for turret fitment by CCF; 3 TC 5.12.42 for 9 B&GS; 1 AC SR 9.4.45; sold 17.6.46 to WAC [1657 hrs]

P5280/1940 TOC 28.4.41 at Fleet Acft; 1 TC 23.5.41 for 4 B&GS; 9 RD 10.10.42 for turret fitment by CCF; 3 TC SR 6.5.43; taxied into 1612, Mont Joli, 13.8.43; 1 AC SR 15.1.45; sold 17.6.46 to WAC

P5282/1938 TOC 22.4.41 at Fleet Acft; 1 TC 15.5.41 for AAS; 6 B&GS; swerved taxiing and hit Bolingbroke 9103, Mountain View, 23.9.42; 9 RD 10.10.42 for turret fitment by CCF; 3 TC SR 28.4.43; SOC 4.11.44 for WAC [471 hrs]

P5284/1975 TOC 22.4.41 at 8 RD and cv to TT; 2 TC 15.7.41 for 7 B&GS; 4 TC 6.10.41 for 8 B&GS; SR

18.11.42; 124 Ferry Sqn; hydraulics failed; landed on one wheel and ground-looped, Armstrong, Ont., 20.1.43; 9 RD 11.12.43; SOC 4.11.44 for WAC [550 hrs]

P5285/2080 TOC 16.9.41 at Acft Repair; 4 TC 11.10.41 for 8 B&GS; SR 18.11.42; Central Acft 11.5.43; 1 TC SR 8.1.44; SOC 22.6.45 for WAC [204 hrs]

P5287/1911 TOC 16.4.41 at 8 RD and cv TT; 9 RD 10.8.42 for turret fitment by CCF; 3 TC 10.11.42 for 9 B&GS; SR 5.5.43; 2 TC 13.1.44 for 3 B&GS; SR 24.4.44; SOC 16.2.45 for WAC [648 hrs]

P5290/2059 TOC 21.8.41 at Acft Repair; 4 TC 25.9.41 for 8 B&GS; SR 18.11.42; Central Acft 10.6.43; 1 TC SR 3.12.43; SOC 13.2.45 for WAC [154 hrs]

P5291/2013 TOC 14.7.41 at MacDonald Bros; 2 TC 16.8.41 for 7 B&GS; SR 16.11.42; 8 RD 2.3.43; 9 RD 26.3.43; 3 TC SR 26.7.44; SOC 4.11.44 for WAC [575 hrs]

P5292/1721 TOC 17.10.40 at Trenton; 1 TC 12.11.40 for 4 B&GS; taxied into 1750, Fingal, 13.2.41; 3 B&GS; 31 B&GS; damaged, 6.11.41; 4 B&GS; swung on landing in hole and tipped up, Fingal, 2.4.42; 9 RD 10.10.42 for turret fitment by CCF; 6 RD 13.11.42; Central Acft 17.6.43; 3 TC SR 6.3.44; SOC 6.11.44 for WAC [953 hrs]

P5293/1764 TOC 16.11.40 at Edmonton; 4 TC 16.12.40 for 2 B&GS; engine cut; undershot landing, Mossbank, 10.4.41; Acft Repair 18.4.41; 4 TC SR 16.2.42; 10 RS 22.7.43; SOC 22.12.43 for spares [181 hrs]

P5294/2045 TOC 22.7.41 at 8 RD; 4 TC 27.8.41 for 2 B&GS; landed with undercarriage partly down, Mossbank, 11.8.42; SR 13.10.42; 9 RD 19.1.43; SOC 4.11.44 for WAC [500 hrs]

P6480/1969 TOC 11.6.41 at Fleet Acft; 1 TC 3.7.41 for 6 B&GS; hit fence on overshoot, Mountain View, 16.7.41; 9 RD 10.10.42; 3 TC SR 9.7.43; SOC 4.11.44 for WAC [413 hrs]

P6485/1953 TOC 13.5.41 at Acft Repair; 2 TC 13.6.41 for 7 B&GS; 6 RD 21.11.42; Central Acft 17.6.43; 3 TC SR 28.2.44; SOC 7.3.45 for WAC [895 hrs]

P6486/2071 TOC 24.9.41 at 8 RD; 4 TC 28.10,.41 for 8 B&GS; SR 18.11.42; Central Acft 1.4.43; 3 TC SR 3.6.43; cv to TT; issued to 10 B&GS 1.12.43; 10 B&GS, later to 9 B&GS; SR 12.9.44; sold 17.6.46 to WAC [318 hrs]

P6488/2093 TOC 11.9.41 at Acft Repair; 4 TC 16.10.41; SR 18.11.42; Central Acft 11.5.43; cv to TT; 3 TC SR 5.8.43; issued to 10 B&GS 4.11.43. Developed glycol leak; overshot bellylanding in field 16m N of Mount Pleasant, 30.11.43; 4 RD 8.12.43 and SOC 27.3.44

P6490/2038 TOC 22.7.41 at 8 RD; 2 TC 21.8.41 for 7 B&GS; SR 16.11.41; 2 TC 7.12.42; 8 RD 15.2.43; Central Acft 31.3.43; 3 TC SR 4.6.43; issued to 10 B&GS 25.10.43; throttle disconnected; forcelanded in field 1m SW of Mount Pleasant, 8.4.44; SR 18.9.44; sold 17.6.46 to WAC [660 hrs]

P6492/1814 TOC 8.1.41 at Fleet Acft; 1 TC 22.1.41 for 1 B&GS. Collided with 1604 on gunnery exercise and crashed 3m W of Fisherville, Ont., 9.12.41; FO E.J. Bounds, LAC J.S.W. Gray and LAC F.G. Barber killed; SOC 18.4.42

P6494/1834 TOC 8.1.41 at Fleet Acft; 1 TC 9.4.41 for 1 B&GS; 6 RD 18.1.43; SOC 12.1.43 for spares

P6495 TOC 26.5.41 at 6 RD; 1 TC 10.6.41 for 31 B&GS; 6 RD 26.1.43; SOC 26.2.44 for spares

P6496/1719 TOC 17.10.40 at Trenton; 1 TC 12.11.40 for 4 B&GS; bellylanded with glycol leak, Fingal, 3.9.41. Engine cut on approach; stalled and hit ground, Fingal, 23.2.42; to GI airframe A162 18.7.42; SOC 21.1.44

P6497/1726 TOC 17.10.40 at Trenton; 1 TC 12.11.40 for 1 B&GS; 2 TC 19.3.41 for 3 B&GS; flew through trees on shore, L. Manitoba, 10.4.41; landed OK;

A Battle attacking a drogue is caught by the camera. Unfortunately, one can see that both have the same serial number!

SOC 11.1.43 for spares

P6498/1984 TOC 13.5.41 at Acft Repair; cv to TT by MacKenzie Air Services 5.6.41; 4 TC 9.7.41 for 2 B&GS; engine cut; bellylanded, Mossbank bombing range, 6.7.42; SR 13.10.42; SOC 11.1.43 for spares

P6500/1928 TOC 7.4.41 by Acft Repair; 2 TC 15.5.41 for 5 B&GS; cv to GI airframe A257 9.1.43; 8 RD 1.9.43; SOC 11.12.43 for spares

P6502/1712 TOC 15.10.40 at Trenton; 1 TC 12.11.40; cv TT 29.4.41; 3 TC 4.2.42 for 9 B&GS; engine cut; bellylanded 2½m SE of Mont Joli, 26.3.43. Engine developed glycol leak in circuit; bellylanded ½m S of Mont Joli, 25.7.43; to 9 RD for spares recovery 29.7.43 and SOC 4.10.43

P6504/1912 TOC 16.4.41 at 8 RD; 2 TC 5.7.41; to 7 B&GS 13.7.41; SOC 11.1.43 for spares

P6505/1945 TOC 14.5.41 at Fleet Acft; 1 TC 6.6.41; to 6 B&GS 23.6.41. Engine cut; forcelanded in ice, Nicholson Island, 12m SW of Mountain View, 20.2.42; salvaged and to A161 18.7.42; SOC 21.1.44

P6507/1916 TOC 16.4.41 at 8 RD and cv to TT; 2 TC 5.7.41 for 3 B&GS; SR 21.3.44; SOC 16.2.45 for WAC [1116 hrs]

P6508/1964 TOC 3.6.41 at 6 RD; 2 TC 25.6.41; to 7 B&GS 4.7.41. Engine cut due to glycol leak; crashlanded 3m E of Paulson, 1.11.41; DBF; SOC 10.1.42

P6523/1925 TOC 7.4.41 at Acft Repair; 2 TC 14.5.41; to 5 B&GS 15.5.41. Collided with 2066 on approach and crashed, Dafoe, Sask., 23.7.42; LAC J.P.A. Bail killed; Sgt J.E. Parker and LAC R.A. Ward seriously injured; SOC 23.10.42

P6524/1957 TOC 9.6.41 at Fleet Acft; 1 TC 19.6.41; to 6 B&GS 23.6.41; undercarriage leg jammed up; landed on one wheel, Mountain View, 4.5.42; Fleet Acft 18.5.42; 9 RD 8.10.42 for turret fitment by CCF; 3 TC 28.4.43 for 7 B&GS; SOC 4.11.44 for WAC [1 hr]

P6525/2043 TOC 22.7.41 at 8 RD; 2 TC 26.8.41; to 7 B&GS 28.8.41; 8 RD 6.1.43; Central Acft 8.5.43; 1 TC SR 24.8.43; SOC 13.2.45 for WAC

P6526/1959 TOC 9.6.41 at Fleet Acft; 1 TC 25.6.41 for 6 B&GS; 9 RD 10.10.42 for turret fitment by CCF; 2 TC SR 27.3.43; 3 B&GS 17.8.43; SR 21.3.44; SOC 16.2.45 for WAC [612 hrs]

P6527/2040 TOC 22.7.41 at 8 RD; 2 TC 21.8.41 for 7 B&GS; SR 17.4.43; SOC 16.2.45 for WAC [227 hrs]

P6530/1853 TOC 6.3.41 at MacDonald Acft; 2 TC for 5 B&GS 7.6.41; 9 RD 10.8.42 for turret fitment by CCF; 3 TC 7.11.42 for 9 B&GS; SR 16.3.43; 3 TC 28.5.43 for 9 B&GS; sold 17.6.46 to WAC [1389 hrs]

P6534/2007 TOC 22.7.41 at Fleet Acft; 1 TC 27.8.41 for 1 B&GS; tyre burst on take-off; swung and tipped up, Jarvis, 8.5.42; 9 RD 28.9.42; 6 RD 13.11.42; 9 RD 19.2.43; 3 TC SR 26.7.44; SOC 4.11.44 for WAC [598 hrs]

P6535/1893 TOC 7.4.41 at 8 RD; 2 TC 14.5.41; to 5 B&GS 19.5.41; 9 RD 25.3.43; 3 TC SR 26.7.44; SOC 6.11.44 for WAC [561 hrs]

P6537/1965 TOC 3.6.41 at 6 RD; 2 TC 25.6.41; to 7 B&GS 4.7.41; SR 16.11.42; 8 RD 15.2.43 for turret fitment by CCF; 9 RD 27.3.43; 3 TC SR 15.1.44; 3 TC 27.4.44; 9 RD 11.9.44; 3 TC 26.9.44; 3 Comm Flt; SR 15.1.45; sold 17.6.46 to WAC

R7416 hangared for the night at No.1 SFTS, Kingston. (M Langman via R Sturtivant)

[494 hrs]

P6538/1779 TOC 16.11.40 at Acft Repair; 4 TC 14.1.41 for 2 B&GS; engine cut; bellylanded 5m E of Mossbank, 4.5.42; SR 25.11.42; SOC 11.1.43 for spares

P6539/1736 TOC 24.10.40 at Trenton; 1 TC 12.11.40 for RFT Flt Picton; pilot temporarily blinded by hydraulic burst; flew into ground, Picton, 1.3.41; CTS Picton; nosed over taxying, Picton, 21.11.41; 3 TC 8.12.41; 6 RD 18.3.42; Fleet Acft 20.5.42; 9 RD 18.7.42 for turret fitment by CCF; 2 TC 9.11.42 for 3 B&GS; collided with 1886 10m NE of MacDonald, 11.5.43, but returned safely; SR 24.4.44; SOC 16.2.45 for WAC [699 hrs]

P6540/1857 TOC 6.3.41 at MacDonald Acft and cv to TT; 2 TC 24.6.41 for 3 B&GS; SR 21.3.44; SOC 16.2.45 for WAC [1202 hrs]

P6541 TOC 8.5.41 at 6 RD; 1 TC 27.5.41 for 31 B&GS; overshot landing, Picton, 10.1.42; 6 RD 28.1.43; SOC 1.5.44 for spares

P6542/1887 TOC 7.4.41 at 8 RD and cv to TT; 2 TC for 7 B&GS 27.6.41 ; SR 16.11.42; 7 B&GS 7.12.42; SR 21.3.44; SOC 16.2.45 for WAC [1309 hrs]

P6543/1883 TOC 7.4.41 at 8 RD; 2 TC 16.5.41; to 5 B&GS 19.5.41; SR 16.11.42; SOC 11.1.43 for spares

P6544/1710 TOC 15.10.40 at Trenton; 1 TC 12.11.40 for 4 B&GS; hit HT wires 10m NE of Fingal, 4.5.41; returned OK; engine cut; crashlanded 4m SE of Wallacetown, Ont., 8.7.42; Central Acft 14.7.42; 9 RD 15.2.43; cv TT at 3 TC; 4.11.43; SR 17.4.44; 3 TC 6.7.44 for 9 B&GS; 1 AC 15.1.45; EAC 3.5.45; sold 17.6.46 to WAC [1023 hrs]

P6545/1926 TOC 28.4.41 at Fleet Acft; 1 TC 17.5.41 for 4 B&GS; engine failed; bellylanded, Fingal, 17.4.42; 9 RD 5.11.42 for turret fitment by CCF; 3 TC SR 7.9.43; SOC 7.3.45 for WAC [513 hrs]

P6546/1717 TOC 9.10.40 at Trenton; 1 TC 2.11.40 for 4 B&GS; cv TT 29.4.41; 6 RD 6.11.41; to GI airframe A155 2.2.42; SOC 12.8.44

P6547/1889 TOC 7.4.41 at 8 RD as TT; 2 TC 3.7.41 for 5 B&GS; drogue cable caught on elevator; undercarriage leg collapsed in heavy landing, Dafoe, 16.9.41; 9 RD 10.8.42 for turret fitment by CCF; 3 TC 9.11.42; SR 12.7.43; SOC 4.11.44 for WAC [358 hrs]

P6548/1980 TOC 27.5.41 at Acft Repair; cv to TT by MacKenzie Air Service 5.6.41; 2 TC 9.7.41; to 5 B&GS 12.8.41 ; transferred to 3 B&GS; engine cut; bellylanded 20m NW of MacDonald, 13.12.41; engine cut; forcelanded in swamp 10m NW of Langruth, Man., 21.7.42; SR 21.3.44; SOC 16.2.45 for WAC [1240 hrs]

P6550/1960 TOC 9.6.41 at Fleet Acft; 1 TC 25.6.41 for 6 B&GS; 9 RD 18.8.42 for turret fitment by CCF; 3 TC 5.12.42 for 9 B&GS. Hit wires while circling pilot's home; hit house and crashed on wharf at East Court, Que., 31.5.43; Sgt G.W.M. Brochu killed; to spares and SOC 26.8.43

P6552/1840 TOC 6.3.41 at Acft Repair; 2 TC 2.4.41 for 3 B&GS; 9 RD 12.2.43 for turret fitment; Central Acft 28.4.43; 3 TC SR 23.2.44; SOC 4.11.44 for WAC [798 hrs]

P6553/1855 TOC 6.3.41 at MacDonald Acft and cv TT; 2 TC for 5 B&GS 1.6.41; cable damaged tailplane, 11.6.41; 4 TC 6.10.42; SR 18.11.42; Central Acft 11.5.43; 3 RC SR 21.8.43; 3 TC 4.11.43 for 10 B&GS; SR 9.8.44; sold 17.6.46 for WAC [355 hrs]

P6554/1915 TOC 16.4.41 at 8 RD and cv to TT; 2 TC 3.7.41 for 3 B&GS; 124 Ferry Sqn; engine failed after take-off for ferry flight, Winnipeg, 29.8.42; retd to 3 B&GS; engine cut; bellylanded 1½m NE of

	MacDonald, 6.11.43; SR 21.3.44; SOC 16.2.45 for WAC [1347 hrs]
P6556/1742	TOC 5.11.40 at Acft Repair; 4 TC 7.12.40 for 2 B&GS; 9 RD for cv to TT 22.5.43; 3 TC 24.11.43 for 10 B&GS; SR 17.4.44; 3 TC 13.6.44 for 10 B&GS; SR 9.4.45; sold 17.6.46 to WAC [1079 hrs]
P6557/1709	TOC 15.10.40 at Trenton; 1 TC 12.11.40 for 4 B&GS; cv TT 29.4.41; 6 RD 29.1.43; SOC 1.5.44
P6558/1979	TOC 13.5.41 at Acft Repair; cv to TT by MacKenzie Air Services 5.6.41; 2 TC 9.7.41; to 5 B&GS 13.8.41; SOC 11.1.43 for spares
P6559/1854	TOC 6.3.41 at MacDonald Acft; 2 TC 5.6.41 for 5 B&GS; undercarriage leg jammed; crashlanded, Jarvis, 8.5.42; SR 16.11.42; SOC 11.1.43 for spares
P6562	TOC 9.6.41 at 6 RD; 1 TC 5.7.41 for 31 SFTS; 9 RD 18.8.42; SOC 23.5.44 for spares
P6563/1952	TOC 27.5.41 at Acft Repair; 2 TC 17.6.41; 6 RD forcelanded with engine trouble 5m N of Dafoe, 13.2.42; FA 21.11.42; SOC 23.3.44 for spares
P6564	TOC 8.5.41 at Fleet Acft; 1 TC 26.5.41 for 31 B&GS; 6 RD 28.1.43; SOC 27.4.43 for spares
P6565/2000	TOC 1.7.41 at 8 RD and cv to TT; 2 TC 28.7.41 for 7 B&GS; SR 21.3.44; SOC 16.2.45 for WAC [1289 hrs]
P6566/1976	TOC 22.4.41 at 8 RD; 2 TC 14.8.41 for 7 B&GS; SR 16.11.42; SOC 11.1.43 for spares
P6567/1867	TOC 24.3.41 at Fleet Acft; 1 TC 25.4.41 for 1 B&GS; swung by gust while taxying and hit Anson 7622, Jarvis, 1.8.42; 9 RD 10.10.42; 6 RD 13.11.42; SOC 26.2.44 for spares
P6568/1920	TOC 5.4.41 at Acft Repair; 2 TC 12.5.41 for 5 B&GS; bellylanded with engine failure 8m NE of Dafoe, 20.7.42; undercarriage leg jammed; crashlanded, Dafoe, 29.6.42; SOC 11.1.43 for spares
P6569/1806	TOC 7.1.41 at Fleet Acft; 2 TC for 3 B&GS; swung on landing into mud and tipped up, MacDonald, 5.4.41. Engine failed on approach; hit ground and caught fire, MacDonald, Man., 27.6.41; DBF; Sgt W.G. Walker and LAC L. Fenner killed; SOC 14.8.41
P6599/1832	TOC 8.1.41 at Fleet Acft; 2 TC 12.3.41 for 3 B&GS; SR 17.4.43; SOC 16.2.45 for WAC [645 hrs]
P6620	TOC 29.1.41 at 31 SFTS; Fleet Acft 29.4.41; taxied into R7447 on runway, Kingston, 15.4.41; 1 TC 19.3.42 for 31 SFTS; 9 RD 4.9.42 for turret fitment; 2 TC 5.12.42 for 3 B&GS; SR 16.5.44; SOC 16.2.45 for WAC [984 hrs]
P6633/2120	TOC 9.1.42 at Fleet Acft; 9 RD 9.4.42 for turret fitment by CCF; 3 TC 26.8.42 for 9 B&GS; engine caught fire; bellylanded 2m SE of Luceville, Que., 22.5.43; 9 RD 2.3.44; SOC 23.5.44 for spares
P6639/2118	TOC 9.1.42 at Fleet Acft; 124 Ferry Sqn Rockliffe; bellylanded with engine trouble 1m E of St. Edward Labinière, 10.2.42; 9 RD 9.4.42; SOC 29.5.44
P6663/2053	TOC 12.8.41 at 8 RD; 8 RD 15.1.43; 124 Ferry Sqn. Engine cut on ferry flight to 2 TC ; hit trees and bellylanded 1m E of Ogaki, Ont., 7.4.43; SOC 3.5.43 for spares
P6665/2121	TOC 9.1.42 at Fleet Acft; 9 RD 13.4.42 for turret fitment by CCF; 3 TC 26.9.42 for 9 B&GS; engine cut after take-off for Mont Joli; crashlanded, St.Flavie, Que., 8.1.43; engine cut after take-off; bellylanded, Mont Joli, 9.11.44; SR 9.4.45; sold 17.6.46 to WAC [1312 hrs]
P6670	TOC 23.10.40 at Fleet Acft; 1 TC 12.11.40 for 31 SFTS; 6 RD 18.9.41; 9 RD 25.4.42 for turret fitment by CCF; 2 TC 9.11.42 for 3 B&GS; engine cut on take-off; bellylanded 1½m W of
	MacDonald, 18.12.43; SR 24.4.44; SOC 16.2.45 for WAC [946 hrs]
P6672	TOC 23.10.40 at Fleet Acft; 1 TC 2.11.40 for 31 SFTS. Crashed, Howe Island, Kingston, Ont., 21.12.40; Fleet Acft 29.4.41; SOC 9.8.41 on transfer to RNZAF
P6673/A125	TOC 13.1.41 at Toronto for TTS St.Thomas; allotted GI airframe A125; later to RNZAF as INST42
P6684/2129	TOC 10.3.42 at Fleet Acft; 9 RD 18.4.42 for turret fitment by CCF; hydraulics failed; undercarriage collapsed on landing, St.John, Que., 30.6.42; 3 TC 7.7.42 for 9 B&GS; undercarriage leg collapsed after landing, Mont Joli, 25.1.44. Engine seized and caught fire in circuit; bellylanded, Mont Joli, 18.11.44; PO J.G.R. Vanasse injured; SOC 6.3.45
P6689/1974	TOC 22.4.41 at 8 RD; 2 TC 10.7.41 for 7 B&GS; 4 TC 4.10.41 for 2 B&GS; bellylanded in error, Mossbank, 19.9.42; Central Acft 17.4.43; 3 TC SR 16.7.43; SOC 4.11.44 for WAC [584 hrs]
P6691/2133	TOC 22.1.42 at 4 RD; 9 RD 25.4.42 for turret fitment by CCF; 3 TC 22.9.42 for 9 B&GS; bellylanded after engine failure 13m SW of Mont Joli, 9.9.43; SR 9.4.45; sold 17.6.46 to WAC [1703 hrs]
P6692/2060	TOC 21.8.41 at Acft Repair; fitted with dual control; 4 TC 2.10.41 for 8 B&GS; engine cut; bellylanded 8m N of Cardston, 4.8.42; Acft Repair 11.8.42; Central Acft 28.1.43; 3 TC SR 20.5.43; SOC 4.11.44 for WAC [5 hrs]
P6724	TOC 6.11.40 at Fleet Acft; 1 TC 22.11.40 for 31 SFTS; 6 RD 13.8.41; CCF 8.12.41 for turret fitment; 3 TC 20.9.42 for 9 B&GS; collided with Nomad 3504 after gunnery exercise 4m SW of Mont Joli, 27.3.43; landed safely; hit by R7416 while parked, Mont Joli, 7.8.43. Engine failed after take-off; dived into ground ½m E of Mont Joli, 1.10.43; to 9 RD 7.10.43 for salvage; SOC 9.12.43
P6726/2144M	TOC 23.9.40 at 1 TTS St.Thomas as GI airframe A099; SOC 14.2.45
P6730	TOC 5.11.40 at Fleet Acft; 1 TC 28.11.40 for 31 SFTS; held off too high on night landing, Kingston, 18.4.41. Brakes failed; ran down slope and hit hangar, Kingston, Ont., 24.8.41; 6 RD 3.9.41; cv to GI airframe A141 20.10.41; SOC 24.10.44 for spares
P6731	TOC 23.10.40 at Fleet Acft; 1 TC 12.11.40 for 31 SFTS; 6 RD 13.8.41; 9 RD 21.7.42 for turret fitment by CCF; 3 TC 8.10.42 for 9 B&GS; SR 9.4.45; sold 17.6.46 to WAC [1265 hrs]
P6732	TOC 8.5.41 at Fleet Acft; 1 TC 2.6.41 for 31 SFTS; hit by R7360 at night, Kingston, 25.8.41; 6 RD 5.9.41; 9 RD 1.8.42 for turret fitment by CCF; 2 TC 4.11.43 for 3 B&GS; SR 16.5.44; SOC 16.2.45 for WAC [789 hrs]
P6734	TOC 5.11.40 at Fleet Acft; 1 TC 28.11.40 for 31 SFTS; 6 RD 18.9.41; 9 RD 3.12.41 for turret fitment by CCF; 3 TC 22.9.42 for 9 B&GS; taxied into 1627, Mont Joli, 26.6.43; engine cut; bellylanded 4m E of Priceville, Que., 11.1.45; SR 9.4.45; sold 17.6.46 to WAC [1578 hrs]
P6737/2123	TOC 9.1.42 at Fleet Acft; 3 TC 24.2.42 for 9 B&GS; 9 RD 13.4.42; SOC 29.5.44
P6750/2119	TOC 9.1.42 at Fleet Acft; 9 RD 13.4.42 for turret fitment by CCF; 3 TC 28.8.42 for 9 B&GS. Stalled off turn on approach and dived into ground, Mont Joli, 24.1.43; F/Sgt W.B. Oborn RNZAF seriously injured; 9 RD for spares recovery; SOC 7.4.43
P6760/2001	TOC 8.7.41 at 8 RD; 2 TC 30.7.41 for 3 B&GS; SR 24.4.44; SOC 16.2.45 for WAC [795 hrs]
R3922/1744	TOC 16.11.40 at Fleet Acft; 1 TC 9.12.40 for 4 B&GS; 9 RD 10.10.42 for turret fitment but not

carried out; 6 RD 13.11.42; Fairchild 13.4.43 for cv to Battle II but cancelled; 3 TC SR 24.8.43 and cv TT; 3 TC for 10 B&GS 11.11.43; SR 24.8.44; sold 17.6.46 to WAC [1033 hrs]

R3923/1770 TOC 16.11.40 at Acft Repair; 2 TC 5.3.41 for 3 B&GS as TT; 2 TC SR 21.3.44; SOC 16.2.45 for WAC [1477 hrs]

R3926/1777 TOC 16.12.40 at Acft Repair; 4 TC 14.1.41 for 2 B&GS; ran into 1768 taxying, Mossbank, 22.4.41; 8 RD 21.11.42; 9 RD 24.3.43 for turret fitment; apparently not carried out; 3 TC SR 24.7.44; SOC 6.11.44 for WAC [682 hrs]

R3930/1751 TOC 16.11.40 at Fleet Acft; 1 TC 9.12.40 for 4 B&GS; 9 RD 26.9.42 for turret fitment by CCF; 3 TC SR 25.3.43; SOC for WAC 7.3.45 [548 hrs]

R3932/1823 TOC 8.1.41 at Fleet Acft; 1 TC 27.1.41 for 4 B&GS; cv TT; 3 TC 4.2.42 for 9 B&GS; swung on landing and tipped up, Mont Joli, 29.5.42. Engine cut; forcelanded while target-towing in St.Lawrence River off No.1 Control Tower, 3.7.42; salvaged but BER; SOC 9.12.42

R3933/1775 TOC 26.11.40 at Acft Repair; 4 TC 14.1.41 for 2 B&GS; 8 RD 10.7.43; 9 RD 13.11.43; SOC 6.11.44 for WAC [938 hrs]

R3935/1701 TOC 23.9.40 at Trenton; 4 TC 1.11.40 for 2 B&GS; engine cut; forcelanded 15m NW of Mossbank, 21.6.41; tipped up in forced landing in fog 8m NW of Mossbank 5.7.41. Undercarriage leg jammed and collapsed on landing, Mossbank, 10.8.42; SR 13.10.42; SOC 11.1.43 for spares

R3937/1745 TOC 16.11.40 at Fleet Acft; 1 TC 9.12.40 for 4 B&GS; 6 RD 2.2.43; SOC 23.3.44 for spares

R3940/1732 TOC 5.11.40 at MacDonald Bros; 4 TC 2.12.40 for 2 B&GS; SR 9.1.42; tyre burst on take-off; swung and wing hit ground, Mossbank, 6.6.42; 9 RD 19.1.43 for turret fitment; Central Acft 28.4.43; SOC 24.2.44 for spares

R3941/1836 TOC 27.12.40 at Fleet Acft; 2 TC 24.3.41 for 3 B&GS; hit by 1837 while parked, MacDonald, 4.4.41; cv TT 22.4.43; 2 TC SR 21.3.44; SOC 16.2.45 for WAC [1223 hrs]

R3942/1711 TOC 26.9.40; 4 TC 3.11.40 for 2 B&GS; Central Acft 3.5.43; SR at 1 TC 26.10.43; SOC 13.2.45 for WAC [857 hrs]

R3943/1793 TOC 8.1.41 at Fleet Acft; 1 TC for 4 B&GS; GI airframe A253 allotted but not taken up 9.1.43; 6 RD 15.3.43; SOC 11.3.43 for spares

R3946/1728 TOC 5.11.40 at MacDonald Bros; 1 TC 2.12.40 for 2 B&GS; SR 13.10.42; 8 RD 14.5.43; Central Acft 22.7.43; SOC 12.4.44 for spares

R3947/1923 TOC 7.4.41 at Acft Repair; 2 TC 13.5.41; to 5 B&GS 15.5.41; bellylanded with engine failure 9m S of Dafoe, 4.3.42; SR 26.1.43; SOC 16.2.45 for WAC [488 hrs]

R3950/1899 TOC 7.4.41 at 8 RD and cv to TT; 2 TC for 7 B&GS 27.6.41; SR 16.11.42; 2 TC 7.12.42; SR 21.3.44; SOC 16.2.45 for WAC [968 hrs]

R3952/1845 TOC 6.3.41 at Acft Repairs; 2 TC 1.4.41 for 3 B&GS; lost power on take-off and hit fence, MacDonald, 23.6.41; brakes failed; ran into 1978, MacDonald, 27.9.41; SR 4.4.44; SOC 16.2.45 for WAC [6655 hrs]

R3953/1929 TOC 7.4.41 at Acft Repair; 2 TC 8.5.41; to 5 B&GS 13.5.41; engine cut; hit boulder on landing 2½m E of Dafoe, 4.12.41; SOC 11.1.43 for spares

R3955/1828 TOC 8.1.41 at Fleet Acft; 1 TC 7.2.41 for 31 B&GS; overshot flapless landing, Picton, 29.12.41; tyre burst on landing at night; swung and distorted wing, Picton 13.3.42; Fleet Acft 10.4.42; 9 RD 24.6.42 for turret fitment by CCF; 3 TC 1.10.42 for 9 B&GS; engine failed; bellylanded, Mont Joli, 10.12.44; 1 AC SR 9.4.45; sold 17.6.46 to WAC [1023 hrs]

R3958 TOC 3.1.41 at Fleet Acft; 1 TC 23.1.41 for 31 SFTS; overshot landing, Kingston, 21.2.41; 6 RD 9.8.41; 1 TC 1.11.41; 9 RD 4.9.42 for turret fitment by CCF; 3 TC SR 1.6.43; SOC 4.11.44 for WAC [660 hrs]

R3959 TOC 23.10.40 at Fleet Acft; 1 TC 17.12.40 for 31 SFTS; 6 RD 13.8.41; 9 RD 1.9.42 for turret fitment by CCF; 2 TC 20.12.42 for 3 B&GS. Elevator control failed; crashlanded, MacDonald, 27.3.43; cv to GI airframe A296 28.5.43; 8 RD 10.5.44; SOC 31.5.44 for spares

R3960 TOC 12.11.40 at Fleet Acft; 1 TC 9.12.40 for 31 SFTS; 6 RD 18.9.41; 9 RD 10.9.42 for turret fitment by CCF; 2 TC 20.12.42 for 3 B&GS. Engine cut; crashlanded 12m NE of Portage la Prairie, Que., 23.5.43; 8 RD 20.7.43; SOC 3.8.43 for spares

R3961 TOC 26.5.41 at 6 RD; 1 TC 10.6.41 for 31 B&GS; 9 RD 4.9.42 for turret fitment by CCF; 2 TC 9.11.42 for 3 B&GS; SR 21.3.44; SOC 16.2.45 for WAC [891 hrs]

R3962 TOC 21.1.41 at De Havilland; 1 TC 21.2.41 for 31 SFTS; 6 RD 9.9.41; 3 TC 20.12.41 for 9 B&GS; 9 RD 14.6.43; SOC 4.11.44 for WAC [1291 hrs]

R3963 TOC 21.1.41 at 31 SFTS; undercarriage jammed partly down; damaged on landing, Kingston, 26.5.41; 6 RD 11.9.41; 1 TC 1.11.41 for 31 B&GS; 9 RD 15.10.42 for turret fitment by CCF; 3 TC SR 1.6.43; SOC 4.11.44 for WAC [346 hrs]

R3964 TOC 21.1.41 at De Havilland; 1 TC 19.2.41 for 31 SFTS; 6 RD 9.8.41 and cv to TT; 4 TC 21.10.41 for 8 B&GS; SR 18.11.42; Central Acft 10.6.43; 9 RD 7.1.44; 3 TC 17.7.44 for 9 B&GS; SR 9.4.45; sold 17.6.46 to WAC [861 hrs]

R3965 TOC 29.11.40 at De Havilland; 1 TC 27.2.41 for 31 SFTS; engine cut; bellylanded, Amhurst Island, 4m W of Stelle, Ont., 10.2.42; 6 RD 3.3.42 and cv to TT; 3 TC 11.5.42 for 9 B&GS. Aircraft shuddered on take-off; abandoned take-off and swung into ditch, Mont Joli, 26.10.42; to 9 RD for spares recovery and SOC 6.2.43

R3966 TOC 21.1.41 at De Havilland; 1 TC 19.2.41 for 31 SFTS; brakes failed; ran into packing case, Kingston, 30.3.41; 6 RD 3.9.41; 9 RD 22.9.42 for turret fitment by CCF; 2 TC SR 6.4.43; 2 TC 21.9.43 for 3 B&GS; SR 11.5.44; SOC 16.2.45 for WAC [502 hrs]

R3967 TOC 29.11.40 at De Havilland; 1 TC 27.2.41 for 31 SFTS; 6 RD 9.9.41; 9 RD 20.9.42 for turret fitment by CCF; 2 TC 27.1.43 for 3 B&GS; SR 21.3.44; SOC 16.2.45 for WAC [515 hrs]

R3968/1882 TOC 7.4.41 at 8 RD; 2 TC 14.5.41; to 5 B&GS 19.5.41. Engine lost power; undercarriage hit boulder in forced landing and swung; tailplane torn off, Dilke, 8m SW of Dafoe, Sask., 5.8.42; SOC 11.12.42

R3969 TOC 21.1.41 at De Havilland; 1 TC 19.2.41 for 31 SFTS; taxied into Yale 3429, Kingston, 2.3.41; pilot overcome by fumes; bellylanded, Kingston, 23.5.41. Flew into lake, Seeley's Bay, Ont., 9.6.41; cause not known; ALA W. McCulloch killed; wreck to Kingston for examination; SOC 8.11.41 [150 hrs]

R3970/1838 TOC 11.2.41 at MacDonald Bros; 2 TC 10.5.41; to 5 B&GS 15.5.41; hit haystack low flying near Dafoe, 4.7.41; SR 16.11.42; 8 RD 16.2.43; Central Acft 8.5.43; cv TT; 3 TC SR 23.8.43; 3 TC 11.11.43 for 10 B&GS; hydraulic system blew up; bellylanded on approach, MacDonald, 20.1.44; sold 17.6.46 to WAC [951 hrs]

R3971/1819 TOC 7.1.41 at Fleet Acft; 1 TC 29.1.41 for 1 B&GS; engine cut; hit bump in forced landing and ran into fence, Jarvis 4.3.41; CCF 1.7.41 for experimental purposes; 6 RD 27.8.41; SOC

The effects of being hit by the propeller of another aircraft while taxying at Kingston. In this case, the rear cockpit was fortunately unoccupied. (M Langman via R Sturtivant)

R3990   8.12.41 for spares
TOC 21.1.41 at De Havilland as TT; 1 TC 22.2.41 for 31 SFTS; bellylanded in error, Kingston, 11.5.41; 6 RD 9.8.41; 3 TC 13.4.42 for 9 B&GS; cv to standard; landed with undercarriage unlocked, Mont Joli, 23.3.43; 9 RD 8.7.43 and reverted to TT; 3 TC 3.8.44 for 9 B&GS; SR 9.4.45; sold 17.6.46 to WAC [1091 hrs]

R3991   TOC 21.1.41 at De Havilland; 1 TC 22.2.41 for 31 SFTS; 6 RD 9.8.41; 4 TC 6.10.41; SR 18.11.42; Central Acft 3.6.43; 3 TC SR 1.2.44; SOC 7.3.45 for WAC [576 hrs]

R3992   TOC 17.4.41 at 6 RD; 1 TC 6.5.41 for 31 B&GS; 6 RD 14.12.42; SOC 1.5.44 for spares

R3993   TOC 10.4.41 at 6 RD; 1 TC 25.4.41 for 31 B&GS; engine cut on ferry flight; forcelanded 3m NW of Picton, 14.11.42; 6 RD 21.11.42; SOC 1.5.44 for spares

R3994   TOC 9.12.40 at Fleet Acft; 1 TC 31.12.40 for 31 SFTS; skidded into R7404 taxying on icy surface, Kingston, 18.2.41; 6 RD 9.9.41; 9 RD 1.10.42 for turret fitment by CCF; 3 TC 1.2.43 for 9 B&GS; SR 9.4.45; sold 17.6.46 to WAC [996 hrs]

R3995   TOC 18.4.41 at Fleet Acft as TT; 1 TC 5.5.41 for 31 SFTS; 6 RD 9.8.41; 1 TC 21.10.41; 9 RD 18.8.42 for cv to standard; 3 TC SR 22.2.44; sold 17.6.46 to WAC [487 hrs]

R3996   TOC 18.4.41 at Fleet Acft; 1 TC 5.5.41 for 31 SFTS. Engine failed; caught fire in forced landing 2m N of Shannonville, Ont., 2.6.41; DBF; SOC 19.9.41 [120 hrs]

R3997   TOC 18.4.41 at Fleet Acft as TT; 1 TC 5.5.41 for 31 SFTS; 6 RD 9.8.41; 1 TC 21.10.41; 3 TC 13.4.42 for 9 B&GS; 9 RD 31.5.43 and reverted to standard; SOC 4.11.44 for WAC [661 hrs]

R3998   TOC 10.4.41 at 6 RD; 1 TC 25.4.41 for 31

B&GS; engine cut after take-off from Picton; crashlanded, Woodrows Corners, 24.2.42; 6 RD 13.3.42; Central Acft 23.6.42; 9 RD 1.2.43; SOC 4.11.44 for WAC

R3999/1784   TOC 27.12.40 at De Havilland; 2 TC 9.2.41 for 3 B&GS; engine cut; bellylanded 1m N of MacDonald, 3.3.43; 8 RD 3.7.43; SOC 26.7.43 for spares

R4000   TOC 30.9.40 at 31 SFTS; engine cut; bellylanded, Kingston, 26.5.41; 4 TC 21.10.41 for 8 B&GS. Control lost; spun into ground near Magrath, 10m SW of Lethbridge, Alta., 19.8.42; Sgt L.R. Low, LAC G.G. Morin, LAC R.B. Sandman killed; to 10 RD for spares recovery and SOC 2.3.43

R4001/1999   TOC 26.7.41 at 6 RD; 1 TC 26.7.41 for 6 B&GS; 9 RD 18.8.42 for turret fitment by CCF; 3 TC 20.12.42 for 9 B&GS. Engine cut due to fuel mismanagement; bellylanded 2m E of Mont Joli, 26.6.43; 9 RD 5.7.43; SOC 19.11.43 for spares

R4005/1756   TOC 27.11.40 at MacDonald Bros; 4 TC 8.2.41 for 2 B&GS as TT; engine overheated after take-off; bellylanded, Mossbank, 1.10.42; 9 RD 22.12.43; 3 TC SR 26.7.44; SOC 4.11.44 for WAC [980 hrs]

R4007/1880   TOC 7.4.41 at 8 RD and cv to TT; 2 TC 14.5.41; to 5 B&GS 19.5.41; SR 26.1.43; 9 RD 25.3.43 for turret fitment by CCF; 3 TC SR 15.1.44; sold 17.6.46 to WAC [377 hrs]

R4010/1846   TOC 6.3.41 at Acft Repairs; 2 TC 5.4.41 for 3 B&GS; Central Acft 15.4.43; 1 TC SR 21.9.43; SOC 22.6.45 for WAC [844 hrs]

R4011/1786   TOC 27.12.40 at De Havilland; 2 TC 29.3.41 for 3 B&GS; engine gauge showed loss of oil pressure; bellylanded in field 10m N of MacDonald, 10.11.42; 9 RD 13.3.43; SOC 6.11.44 for WAC [459 hrs]

R4013   TOC 23.10.40 at Fleet Acft; 1 TC 26.12.40 for 31

Individual identity numbers were prominently displayed on No.1 SFTS aircraft. (M Langman via R Sturtivant)

SFTS; bellylanded, Kingston, 22.1.41; 6 RD 3.9.41; 3 TC 11.12.41 for 9 B&GS; 9 RD 8.7.43; SOC 4.11.44 for WAC [682 hrs]

R4014 TOC 6.11.40 at Fleet Acft; 1 TC 9.12.40 for 31 SFTS. Bellylanded in bad weather on navex 4m N of Peterborough, Ont., 11.3.41; to Fleet Acft 29.4.41 and SOC 22.11.41 for spares

R4015 TOC 8.11.40 at Fleet Acft; 1 TC 26.12.40 for 31 SFTS; 6 RD 27.8.41; 9 RD 7.1.43; SOC 4.11.44 for WAC [251 hrs]

R4016 TOC 29.10.40 at De Havilland; 1 TC 4.3.41 for 31 SFTS; cv to TT; 9 RD18.8.42 for turret fitment by CCF; 3 TC 5.12.42 for 9 B&GS; taxied into R7438, Mont Joli, 2.11.43; SR 22.1.44; issued to 9 B&GS 20.11.44; SR 8.4.45; sold 17.6.46 to WAC [1255 hrs]

R4017 TOC 3.12.40 at De Havilland; 1 TC 27.2.41 for 31 SFTS; bellylanded in error, Kingston, 8.7.41; 6 RD 9.8.41; 1 TC 1.11.41; 9 RD 1.8.42 for turret fitment by CCF; 3 TC 9.11.42 for 9 B&GS. Brakes failed taxying; rolled into ditch, Mont Joli, 2.8.44; 9 RD 14.8.44; not repaired and SOC 29.8.44

R4018 TOC 6.11.40 at Fleet Acft; 1 TC 22.11.40 for 31 SFTS; 6 RD 13.8.41; 9 RD 27.11.42 for turret fitment by CCF; 3 TC SR 6.5.43; sold 17.6.46 to WAC [357 hrs]

R4035/1783 TOC 27.12.40 at De Havilland; 1 TC 16.4.41 for 1 B&GS; overshot landing into fence, Jarvis, 9.10.41; 9 RD 28.9.42; 6 RD 13.11.42; SOC 24.3.44 for spares

R4036/1739 TOC 6.12.40 at Fleet Acft; 1 TC 14.1.41 for 1 B&GS; brakes failed, rolled into watch office, Jarvis, 15.3.41; 9 RD 28.9.42; 6 RD 13.11.42; 9 RD 9.2.43 for turret fitment by CCF; 3 TC SR 7.9.43; SOC 7.3.45 for WAC [427 hrs]

R4037 TOC 23.10.40 at Fleet Acft; 1 TC 26.12.40 for 31 SFTS; stalled on landing, Picton, 16.4.41; 6 RD 7.7.41 and cv to TT; 4 TC 21.10.41 for 8 B&GS; ground-looped in high wind and undercarriage collapsed, Lethbridge, 15.12.41; MacKenzie Air Services 28.1.42; Central Acft 28.1.43; 6 RD 22.6.43; 1 TC SR 21.9.43; SOC 13.2.45 for WAC [367 hrs]

R4038/1785 TOC 27.12.40 at De Havilland; 2 TC 17.2.41 for 3 B&GS; hit by 1837 while parked, MacDonald, 7.11.42; Central Acft 15.4.43; 1 TC SR 21.9.43; SOC 13.2.45 for WAC

R4039 TOC 21.1.41 at De Havilland; 1 TC 29.3.41 for 31 SFTS; undercarriage collapsed in heavy landing, Kingston, 9.5.41; 6 RD 10.9.41; 1 TC 1.11.41 for 31 B&GS; 6 RD 21.1.43; SOC 1.3.44 for spares

R4040/1788 TOC 27.12.40 at De Havilland; 2 TC 17.2.41 for 3 B&GS; SR 4.4.44; SOC 16.2.45 for WAC [732 hrs]

R4041 TOC 3.10.40 at 31 SFTS; 6 RD 13.8.41; cv to GI airframe A165 by 18.7.42; SOC 30.11.44

R4042 TOC 12.11.40 at Fleet Acft; 1 TC 20.12.40 for 31 SFTS; 6 RD 9.9.41; 9 RD 9.11.42 for turret fitment by CCF; 2 TC SR 25.3.43; issued to 3 B&GS 20.10.43. Caught fire after take-off; bellylanded 1m E of MacDonald, 4.12.43; 8 RD 6.12.43; SOC 14.12.43

R4043 TOC 5.11.40 at Fleet Acft; 1 TC 26.12.40 for 31 SFTS; 6 RD 13.8.41; 9 RD 19.8.42 for turret fitment by CCF; 3 TC SR 28.4.43; SOC 4.11.44 for WAC

R4044/1740 TOC 6.12.40 at Fleet Acft; 1 TC 20.1.41 for 4 B&GS; engine cut on take-off; bellylanded, Fingal, 5.4.42; 6 RD 29.1.43; SOC 24.3.44 for spares

R4045/1822   TOC 8.1.41 at Fleet Acft; 1 TC 27.1.41 for 4 B&GS; cv to TT; 3 TC for 9 B&GS; 4.2.42; swung off runway into snowdrift and damaged, Mont Joli, 30.3.42; ran into snow on landing and tipped up, Mont Joli, 13.1.43; engine cut on take-off; crashlanded 1½m NE of Mont Joli, 16.3.43; conv back to crew trainer by 1.6.43; 9 RD 8.7.43; 3 TC 17.6.44 for 9 B&GS; 1 AC SR 9.4.45; sold 17.6.46 [1110 hrs]

R4046   TOC 12.11.40 at Fleet Acft; 1 TC 9.12.40 for 31 SFTS; 6 RD 13.8.41; cv to GI airframe A164 18.7.42; SOC 14.2.45

R4047/1835   TOC 27.12.40 at Fleet Acft; 2 TC 12.3.41 for 3 B&GS; cv to TT by 22.4.43; 2 TC SR 21.3.44; SOC 16.2.45 for WAC [1045 hrs]

R4048/1792   TOC 8.1.41 at Fleet Acft; 1 TC 18.1.41 for 1 B&GS; cv to TT by 17.4.42; 3 TC SR 9.4.43; sold 17.6.46 to WAC [1505 hrs]

R4050   TOC 21.1.41 at De Havilland as TT; 1 TC 21.2.41 for 31 SFTS; 6 RD 9.8.41; 4 TC 21.10.41 for 8 B&GS; tyre burst on take-off; ground-looped, Lethbridge, 31.5.42; 4 TC SR 18.11.42; SOC 11.1.43 for spares

R4051   TOC 23.10.41 at Fleet Acft;1 TC 2.11.40 for 31 SFTS; 6 RD 13.8.41; 9 RD 9.11.42 for turret fitment; 3 TC 25.1.43 for 9 B&GS. Engine cut; crashlanded, St.Anaclet, 15m SW of Mont Joli, 24.9.44; 9 RD 28.9.44; SOC 27.10.44

R4052   TOC 2.10.40 at 31 SFTS; 6 RD 13.8.41; 9 RD 10.12.42 for turret fitment by CCF; 2 TC SR 25.3.43; issued to 3 B&GS 13.10.44; SR 5.6.45; SOC 9.7.46 for WAC [1753 hrs]

R4053   TOC 12.11.40 at Fleet Acft; 1 TC 9.12.40 for 31 SFTS; undercarriage leg collapsed on landing, Kingston, 2.6.41; later hit by R7462; Fleet Acft 11.6.41; 4 TC 3.11.41; SR 18.11.42; Central Acft 3.6.43; 3 TC SR 7.2.44; SOC 4.11.44 for WAC [594 hrs]

R4054/1787   TOC 27.12.40 at De Havilland; 2 TC 19.2.41 for 3 B&GS; engine lost power; forcelanded, MacDonald, 21.7.42; SOC 21.5.43 for spares

R7360   TOC 18.1.41 at 31 SFTS; taxied into P6732 at night, Kingston, 25.8.41; 6 RD 10.9.41; 9 RD 5.4.42 for turret fitment by CCF; 2 TC 8.10.42 for 3 B&GS; tyre burst on landing; swung and tipped up, MacDonald, 15.7.43; SR 24.4.44; SOC 16.2.45 for WAC [1056 hrs]

R7365/2003   TOC 1.7.41 at 8 RD; 2 TC 30.7.41 for 7 B&GS; 6 RD 21.11.42; 9 RD 19.2.43 for turret fitment by CCF; 3 TC SR 7.9.43; SOC 7.3.45 for WAC [784 hrs]

R7370   TOC 21.1.41 at 31 SFTS; collided with R7404 while taxying at night, Kingston, 16.4.41; damaged, Kingston, 5.8.41; 6 RD 9.9.41; 9 RD 4.5.42 for turret fitment by CCF; 2 TC 9.11.42 for 3 B&GS; hydraulic line burst on take-off; bellylanded 2½m W of MacDonald, 16.7.43; SR 21.3.44; SOC 16.2.45 for WAC [574 hrs]

R7373   TOC 9.5.41 at Fleet Acft; 1 TC 2.6.41 for 31 SFTS; 6 RD 28.8.41; 9 RD 9.6.42 for turret fitment by CCF; 3 TC 1.10.42 for 9 B&GS; collided with R7471 taxying, Mont Joli, 19.11.42; hit fence in forced landing after engine failure 1½m E of Mont Joli, 5.2.43; collided with R7373 taxying, Mont Joli, 1.11.43; SR 9.4.45; sold 17.6.46 to WAC [1211 hrs]

R7374   TOC 17.4.41 at Ottawa Car Co; 1 TC 8.5.41 for 31 SFTS; brakes failed; ran into bowser, Kingston, 2.6.41; 6 RD 9.8.41; 1 TC 10.10.41 for CTS Picton; 3 TC 8.12.41 for CTS Rockliffe; taxied into Goblin NR335, Rockliffe, 12.1.42; 9 RD 2.7.42 for turret fitment by CCF; 3 TC 27.1.43 for 9 B&GS. Engine lost power; bellylanded 2m W of Mont Joli, 21.7.44; 9 RD 1.8.44 and SOC 29.8.44

R7384   TOC 18.1.41 at 31 SFTS; 6 RD 9.9.41; 9 RD 28.6.42 for turret fitment by CCF; 2 TC 20.12.42 for 3 B&GS; 124 Ferry Sqn; damaged in heavy landing, Kenora, Ont., 3.2.43; 8 RD 13.3.43; 2 TC 20.8.43 for 3 B&GS; SR 21.3.44; selected for display purposes; 10 RD 10.7.50; Rockliffe 3.3.64; 25.2.69 transferred to and now preserved at National Aviation Museum, Rockliffe.

R7403   TOC 31.10.40 at Fleet Acft; 1 TC 23.11.40 for 31 SFTS; 6 RD 12.12.41; 3 TC 3.2.42; 9 RD 2.7.42 for turret fitment by CCF; 3 TC 22.9.42 for 9 B&GS; SR 22.1.44; sold 17.6.46 to WAC [1275 hrs]

R7404   TOC 23.10.40 at Fleet Acft; 1 TC 1.11.40 for 31 SFTS; hit by R3994 while parked, Kingston, 18.2.41; wing hit ground on night landing, Kingston, 5.4.41; collided with R7370 while taxying at night, Kingston, 16.4.41; 6 RD 9.8.41; 3 TC 31.12.41 for CTS Rockliffe; 9 RD 2.7.42 for turret fitment by CCF; 2 TC 10.10.42 for 3 B&GS; engine caught fire; bellylanded 15m E of MacDonald, 28.4.43. Developed glycol leak on take-off which blinded pilot; engine seized; bellylanded in field 2m NW of MacDonald, 11.8.43; cv to GI airframe A319 2.10.43; SOC 7.2.44 for spares

R7405   TOC 6.11.40 at Fleet Acft; 1 TC 19.11.40 for 31 SFTS; 6 RD 18.9.41; CCF 8.12.41 for turret fitment; 3 TC 1.10.42 for 9 B&GS; 9 RD 17.10.44; 3 TC SR 14.11.44; SOC 7.3.45 for WAC [1329 hrs]

R7408   TOC 6.11.40 at Fleet Acft; 1 TC 19.11.40 for 31 SFTS; engine cut on take-off; crashlanded, Kingston, 25.1.41; 6 RD 15.9.41; 9 RD 13.8.42 for turret fitment by CCF; 2 TC 22.10.42 for 3 B&GS; taxied into Lysander V9589, MacDonald, 10.3.44; SR 24.4.44; SOC 16.2.45 for WAC [756 hrs]

R7412   TOC 17.4.41 at Ottawa Car Ltd; 1 TC 13.5.41 for 31 B&GS; fitted with dual control; bellylanded in error, Picton, 11.5.42; 6 RD 2.2.43; SOC 1.5.44 for spares

R7413   TOC 23.10.40 at Fleet Acft; 1 TC 2.11.40 for 31 SFTS; undercarriage leg collapsed on landing, Kingston, 28.4.41; 6 RD 9.8.41; taxied into Harvard 2850, Picton, 7.11.41; 3 TC 8.12.41 for CTS Rockliffe; 9 RD 22.8.42 for turret fitment by CCF; 2 TC 9.11.42 for 3 B&GS; SR 3.4.43; issued to 3 B&GS 16.4.43; SR 16.5.44; SOC 16.2.45 for WAC [679 hrs]

R7414   TOC 5.11.40 at Fleet Acft; 1 TC 23.11.40 at 31 SFTS; landed with undercarriage unlocked, Norman Rogers Apt, 11.1.41; engine cut on take-off, Kingston, 14.3.41; 6 RD 7.7.41; CCF 8.12.41 for turret fitment; 2 TC 2.11.42 for 3 B&GS. Hydraulics blew out; bellylanded on approach, MacDonald, 20.1.44; DBR; to 8 RD 22.1.44 for spares recovery; SOC 4.2.44

R7415   TOC 6.11.40 at Fleet Acft; 1 TC 22.11.40 for 31 SFTS; 6 RD 9.8.41; 9 RD 9.6.42 for turret fitment by CCF; 2 TC 10.10.42 for 3 B&GS; SR 21.3.44; SOC 16.2.45 for WAC [394 hrs]

R7416   TOC 5.11.40 at Fleet Acft; 1 TC 23.11.40 for 31 SFTS; 6 RD 24.9.41; 9 RD 1.5.42 for turret fitment by CCF; 3 TC 14.8.42 for 9 B&GS; brakes failed while parked; rolled into Nomad 3500, Mont Joli, 20.7.43; taxied into P6724, Mont Joli, 7.8.43; collided with R7373 taxying, Mont Joli, 1.11.43; SR 9.4.45; sold 17.6.46 to WAC [1067 hrs]

R7417   TOC 23.10.40 at Fleet Acft; 1 TC 19.11.40 for 31 SFTS; hit R7417 after landing, Kingston, 3.4.41; 6 RD 10.9.41; 9 RD 11.6.42 for turret fitment by CCF; 3 TC 27.1.43 for 9 B&GS; engine cut; bellylanded ½m SW of Mont Joli, 19.1.45; SR

R7418 9.4.45; sold 17.6.46 to WAC [1181 hrs]
TOC 12.11.40 at Fleet Acft; 1 TC 28.11.40 for 31 SFTS. Crashed while lost 5m E of Watertown, NY, 21.12.40; SOC 26.2.41 [28 hrs]

R7419 TOC 15.1.41 at 1 TC for 31 SFTS. DBR in forced landing in snowstorm 8m N of Picton, Ont., 11.3.41; SOC 5.6.41

R7420 TOC 21.1.41 at 1 TC for 31 SFTS; 6 RD 3.12.41; 9 RD 10.6.42 for turret fitment by CCF; 2 TC 22.10.42 for 3 B&GS; taxied into 1723 on runway, MacDonald, 11.8.43; SR 21.3.44; SOC 16.2.45 for WAC [210 hrs]

R7421 TOC 12.11.40 at Fleet Acft; 1 TC 3.12.40 for 31 SFTS; engine overheated; bellylanded in field 1½m S of Odessa, Ont., 25.5.41; 6 RD 7.7.41; 1 TC 6.9.41 for CTS Picton; 3 TC 8.12.41 for CTS Rockliffe; taxied off strip into snow and tipped up, Rockliffe, 21.2.42; taxied into Lockheed 10A 1527, Rockliffe, 15.4.42; 9 RD 2.7.42 for turret fitment by CCF; 2 TC 10.10.42 for 3 B&GS; SR 5.5.43; issued to 3 B&GS 5.6.43; SR 21.3.44; SOC 16.2.45 for WAC [725 hrs]

R7422 TOC 5.11.40 at Fleet Acft; 1 TC 9.12.40 for 31 SFTS; overshot landing and bogged down; hit by R7417, Kingston, 3.4.41; 6 RD 7.7.41; 1 TC 6.9.41 for CTS Picton; undercarriage jammed; bellylanded, Picton, 16.10.41; 3 TC 8.12.41 for CTS Rockliffe; taxied into Norsemen 2479 and 2477, Rockliffe, 29.1.42; engine lost power; bellylanded, Pendleton airfield, 13.2.42; 9 RD 2.7.42 for turret fitment by CCF; 2 TC 18.2.43 for 3 B&GS; engine cut; bellylanded 12m SSW of MacDonald, 21.1.44; SR 21.3.44; SOC 16.2.45 for WAC [584 hrs]

R7423 TOC 3.12.40 at De Havilland; 1 TC 24.1.41 for 31 SFTS; undercarriage collapsed in night landing, Kingston, 19.5.41; Fleet Acft 3.6.41; 2 TC SR 18.10.41; SOC 11.1.43 for spares [272 hrs]

R7424 TOC 6.12.40 at De Havilland; 1 TC 15.5.41 for 31 SFTS; 6 RD 28.8.41; CCF 4.12.41 for turret fitment; 1 TC 8.6.42; 3 TC 1.9.42 for 9 B&GS; tipped up by gust in snow, Mont Joli, 21.4.43; engine cut; bellylanded 6m W of Mont Joli, 8.6.43; 9 RD 1.3.44; SOC 23.5.44 for spares

R7425 TOC 15.1.41 at 31 SFTS; 6 RD 24.9.41; 9 RD 28.5.42 for turret fitment by CCF; 3 TC 1.9.42 for 9 B&GS; undercarriage leg jammed; crashlanded, Mont Joli, 30.3.44; SR 9.4.45; sold 17.6.46 to WAC [1254 hrs]

R7426 TOC 21.1.41 at De Havilland; 1 TC 12.2.41 for 31 SFTS; 6 RD 28.8.41; 9 RD 16.6.42 for turret fitment by CCF; 2 TC 10.10.42 for 3 B&GS; SR 21.3.44; SOC 16.2.45 for WAC [542 hrs]

R7427 TOC 21.1.41 at De Havilland; 1 TC 12.2.41 for 31 SFTS; 6 RD 12.9.41; engine cut on ferry flight; forcelanded, Chatham, Ont., 24.12.42; 3 TC 7.8.43 for 9 B&GS; swung on landing and tipped up, Mont Joli, 22.1.45; SR 6.4.45; sold 17.6.46 to WAC [891 hrs]

R7428 TOC 3.12.40 at De Havilland; 1 TC 21.1.41 for 3 B&GS; 6 RD 8.10.41; 2 TC 12.3.42 for 3 B&GS; SR 24.4.44; SOC 16.2.45 for WAC [368 hrs]

R7429 TOC 3.1.41 at Fleet Acft; 1 TC 23.1.41 for 31 SFTS; undercarriage leg collapsed on landing, Kingston, 6.5.41; bellylanded in error, Kingston, 25.5.41; bellylanded in error, Kingston, 21.6.41; 6 RD 28.8.41; 9 RD 20.3.42 for turret fitment by CCF; 3 TC 5.8.42 for 9 B&GS. Hit by 2131 on taxiway, Mont Joli, 12.4.43; SOC 1.5.43

R7430 TOC 12.11.40 at Fleet Acft; 1 TC 3.12.40 for 31 SFTS; 6 RD 28.8.41; 9 RD 1.5.42 for turret fitment by CCF; 3 TC 17.9.42; SR 9.4.45; sold 17.6.46 to WAC [1693 hrs]

R7431 TOC 6.12.40 at De Havilland; 1 TC 15.5.41 for 31 SFTS; 6 RD 27.9.41; 9 RD 15.5.42 for turret fitment by CCF; 3 TC 3.9.42 for 9 B&GS; taxied into K7608, Mont Joli, 13.1.43; hit by 1319 while parked, Mont Joli, 9.4.43; SR 9.4.45; sold 17.6.46 to WAC [1321 hrs]

R7432 TOC 6.12.40 at De Havilland; 1 TC 12.2.41 for 31 SFTS; undercarriage jammed; bellylanded, Kingston, 22.2.41; bellylanded in error, Kingston, 2.6.41; engine failed during practice forced landing; hit obstruction 4m N of Sandhurst, Ont., 13.7.41; 6 RD 12.9.41; 3 TC 3.2.42; 9 RD 22.8.42 for turret fitment by CCF; 6 RD 8.3.42; Central Acft 17.6.42; 124 Ferry Sqn; taxied into tractor in bad visibility, Kapuskasing, 24.2.43; SOC 23.2.44

R7433 TOC 6.12.40 at De Havilland; 1 TC 12.2.41 for 31 SFTS; flew into ground on approach at night, Kingston, 19.7.41; Fleet Acft 7.8.41; 3 TC 16.12.41; 9 RD 9.11.42 for turret fitment by CCF; 9 RD 27.2.43; SOC 4.11.44 for WAC

R7434 TOC 12.11.40 at Fleet Acft; 1 TC 3.12.40 for 31 SFTS; 6 RD 24.9.41; 9 RD 28.3.42 for turret fitment by CCF; 3 TC 7.7.42 for 9 B&GS. Engine cut; damaged in heavy landing, Mont Joli, PQ, 10.4.44; SOC 8.6.44

R7435 TOC 12.11.40 at Fleet Acft; 1 TC 9.12.40 for 31 SFTS; engine cut on take-off, Kingston, 5.1.41; 6 RD 18.9.41; 9 RD 1.5.42 for turret fitment by CCF; 3 TC 28.8.42 for 9 B&GS. Engine failed; damaged in forced landing 8m SW of Mont Joli, 28.6.44; not repaired and SOC 29.8.44 for spares

R7436 TOC 27.12.40 at Fleet Acft; allotted to 1 TC 23.12.41 for 31 SFTS; 6 RD 18.9.41; 9 RD 25.4.42 for turret fitment by CCF; 3 TC 5.8.42 for 9 B&GS. Engine cut on take-off; bellylanded in ploughed field 1½m W of Mont Joli, 3.11.44; 9 RD 16.11.44; SOC 29.11.44

R7437 TOC 6.12.40 at De Havilland; 1 TC 1.2.41 for 31 SFTS; hit by R7467 taxying, Kingston, 5.4.41; 6 RD 10.6.41; 3 TC 3.2.42; 9 RD 22.8.42 for turret fitment by CCF; 3 TC 7.11.42 for 9 B&GS; SR 16.3.43; sold 17.6.46 to WAC [1279 hrs]

R7438 TOC 29.11.40 at De Havilland; 1 TC 24.1.41 for 31 SFTS; 6 RD 9.8.41; 9 RD 15.5.42 for turret fitment by CCF; 3 TC 22.9.42 for 9 B&GS; hit by R4016 while parked, Mont Joli, 22.11.43; swung by wind after landing into snowbank and tipped up, Mont Joli, 4.2.44; SR 9.4.45; sold 17.6.46 to WAC [1396 hrs]

R7439 TOC 29.11.40 at De Havilland; 1 TC 2.1.41 for 31 SFTS; 6 RD 29.8.41; 9 RD 21.7.42 for turret fitment by CCF; Fairchild 21.11.42 for fitment of Wright Cyclone G3B engine as Battle II; 3 TC 14.4.43; SR 1.3.44; 9 RD 24.4.44 for spares

R7440 TOC 12.11.40 at Fleet Acft; 1 TC 28.11.40 for 31 SFTS; 6 RD 13.8.41; CCF 8.12.41 for turret fitment; 6 RD 3.10.42; 3 TC 3.10.42 for 9 B&GS; SR 9.4.45; sold 17.6.46 to WAC [308 hrs]

R7441 TOC 9.12.40 at Fleet Acft; 1 TC 31.12.40 for 31 SFTS; overshot night landing into ditch, Kingston, 24.1.41; caught fire in air; forcelanded, Kingston, 4.6.41; 6 RD 9.8.41; CCF 8.12.41 for turret fitment; 3 TC 7.8.42 for 9 B&GS. Engine caught fire; bellylanded 1m E of Matane, Que., 18.11.44; SOC 6.3.45

R7442 TOC 6.12.40 at De Havilland; 1 TC 12.2.41 for 31 SFTS. Engine lost power in icing conditions on take-off; hit obstruction in forced landing, Jarvis, Ont., 14.3.41; to 6 RD for salvage; SOC 11.11.41

R7443 TOC 6.12.40 at De Havilland; 1 TC 12.2.41 for 31 SFTS; 6 RD 10.9.41; 9 RD 27.4.42 for turret fitment by CCF; 3 TC 17.9.42 for 9 B&GS; collided with 2109 5m SSW of Mont Joli, 19.6.43; landed safely; SR 9.4.45; sold 17.6.46 to WAC [1643 hrs]

R7444	TOC 12.11.40 at Fleet Acft; 1 TC 3.12.40 for 31 SFTS; 6 RD 9.8.41; 9 RD 24.3.43; SOC 4.11.44 for WAC [481 hrs]
R7445	TOC 6.12.40 at De Havilland; 1 TC 7.2.41 for 31 SFTS; hit by R7448 on runway at night, Kingston, 2.4.41; bellylanded in error, Kingston, 8.5.41; 6 RD 9.9.41; 9 RD 15.5.42 for turret fitment by CCF; 3 TC 17.9.42 for 9 B&GS; SR 9.4.45; sold 17.6.46 to WAC [1204 hrs]
R7446	TOC 21.1.41 at 31 SFTS; 6 RD 15.9.41; 9 RD 6.7.42 for turret fitment by CCF; 2 TC 20.12.42 for 3 B&GS; SR 21.3.44; SOC 16.2.45 for WAC [200 hrs]
R7447	TOC 6.12.40 at De Havilland; 1 TC 1.2.41 for 31 SFTS; hit by P6620 on runway, Kingston, 15.4.41; 6 RD 18.9.41; CCF 8.12.41 for turret fitment; 3 TC 7.8.42 for 9 B&GS; SR 9.4.45; sold 17.6.46 to WAC [1552 hrs]
R7448	TOC 6.12.40 at De Havilland; 1 TC 7.2.41 for 31 SFTS; taxied into R7445 at night, Kingston, 2.4.41; 6 RD 7.7.41; CCF 8.12.41 for turret fitment; 2 TC 23.11.42 for 3 B&GS; SR 21.3.44; SOC 16.2.45 for WAC [405 hrs]
R7461	TOC 6.12.40 at De Havilland; 1 TC 1.2.41 for 31 SFTS. Engine caught fire; undershot flare path, hit tree and lost wing, Kingston, 13.4.41; DBF; LAC J.A. Reardon killed; SOC 11.7.41
R7462	TOC 21.1.41 at 31 SFTS; skidded on ice into Finch 4735, Kingston, 29.3.41; collided with crashed 4053 on landing, Kingston, 3.6.41; Fleet Acft 11.6.41; 1 TC 9.3.42 for 31 B&GS; 6 RD 28.1.43; SOC 1.5.44 for spares
R7463	TOC 29.1.41 at 31 SFTS; 6 RD 9.9.41; CCF 8.12.41 for turret fitment; 3 TC 7.8.42 for 9 B&GS; bellylanded with glycol leak 8m W of Mont Joli, 6.3.44. Engine lost power; crashlanded, St. Luce, 3½m SW of Mont Joli, 11.12.44; SOC 15.2.45
R7464	TOC 6.12.40 at De Havilland; 1 TC 7.2.41 for 31 SFTS; 6 RD 28.8.41; 9 RD 16.6.42 for turret fitment by CCF; 3 TC 26.9.42 for 9 B&GS; sold 17.6.46 to WAC [1458 hrs]
R7465	TOC 21.1.41 at 31 SFTS; 6 RD 15.9.41; 9 RD 9.6.42 for turret fitment by CCF; 3 TC 22.9.42 for 9 B&GS; SR 22.6.44; sold 17.6.46 to WAC [777 hrs]
R7466	TOC 21.1.41 at 31 SFTS; 6 RD 10.9.41; 3 TC 31.12.41 for CTS Rockliffe; 9 RD 2.7.42 for turret fitment by CCF; 2 TC 20.12.42 for 3 B&GS; engine cut; crashlanded 3m ENE of MacDonald, 24.11.43; SR 24.4.44; SOC 16.2.45 for WAC [937 hrs]
R7467	TOC 21.1.41 at 31 SFTS; brakes failed; ran into R7437, Kingston, 5.4.41; 6 RD 11.9.41; 9 RD 12.4.42 for turret fitment by CCF; 3 TC 7.7.42 for 9 B&GS; SR 9.4.45; sold 17.6.46 to WAC [1250 hrs]
R7468	TOC 15.1.41 at 31 SFTS; brakes failed on overshot landing, Kingston, 26.4.41; 6 RD 9.8.41; 9 RD 24.6.42; SOC 7.3.45 for WAC [489 hrs]
R7469	TOC 15.1.41 at 31 SFTS; bellylanded in error, Kingston, 27.3.41; undercarriage raised in error after landing, Kingston, 24.4.41; 6 RD 18.9.41; CCF 8.12.41 for turret fitment; 2 TC 2.11.42 for 3 B&GS; SR 16.5.44; SOC 16.2.45 for WAC [629 hrs]
R7470	TOC 29.3.41 at Fleet Acft; 1 TC 16.4.41 for 31 SFTS coded 36; fitted with dual control; 6 RD 18.9.41; 3 TC 19.5.42 for 9 B&GS; SR 6.4.45; sold 17.6.46 to WAC [973 hrs]
R7471	TOC 29.3.41 at Fleet Acft; 1 TC 16.4.41 for 31 SFTS; 6 RD 15.9.41; 9 RD 28.6.42 for turret fitment by CCF; 3 TC 26.9.42 for 9 B&GS; collided with R7373 while taxying, Mont Joli, 19.11.42. DBR in forced landing with glycol leak 4m E of Mont Joli, 12.5.43; SOC 26.8.43 for spares
R7473	TOC 29.1.41 at 31 SFTS; damaged in heavy landing at night, Kingston, 5.5.41; 3 TC 8.12.41 for CTS Rockliffe; undercarriage leg collapsed taxying, Rockliffe, 26.1.42; 9 RD 2.7.42 for turret fitment by CCF; 2 TC 6.10.42 for 3 B&GS; to GI airframe A318 15.9.43; 8 RD 10.5.44; SOC 31.5.44 for spares
R7474	TOC 21.1.41 at 31 SFTS. Control lost; hit tree recovering from spin 1m N of Belleville, Ont., 14.7.41; LAC B.E. Fellows killed; SOC 16.9.41
R7475	TOC 29.1.41 at 31 SFTS; 6 RD 12.9.41; 3 TC 31.12.41 for CTS Rockliffe; 9 RD 2.7.42 for turret fitment by CCF; 2 TC 18.2.43 for 3 B&GS; SR 16.5.44; SOC 16.2.45 for WAC [389 hrs]
R7476	TOC 21.1.41 at 31 SFTS; undercarriage leg collapsed in heavy landing, Kingston, 17.6.41; undercarriage leg collapsed in heavy landing at night, Kingston, 26.6.41; 6 RD 3.9.41; 9 RD 28.6.42 for turret fitment by CCF; 2 TC 1.2.43 for 3 B&GS. Engine failed; bellylanded 12m N of MacDonald, 10.9.43; SOC 6.10.43
R7479	TOC 8.5.41 at Fleet Acft; 1 TC for 31 SFTS; 6 RD 8.10.41; 3 TC 31.12.41 for CTS Rockliffe; 9 RD 2.7.42 for turret fitment by CCF; 3 TC 9.11.42 for 9 B&GS; SR 16.3.43; issued to 9 B&GS 19.6.43; SR 9.4.45; sold 17.6.46 to WAC [1287 hrs]
R7480	TOC 1.7.41 at 6 RD for 31 SFTS; 6 RD 24.2.43; SOC 24.3.44 for spares
AR625/1704	TOC 23.9.40 at Trenton; 4 TC 25.10.40 for 2 B&GS; landed with undercarriage unlocked, Mossbank, 27.11.40; engine cut; bellylanded, Mossbank, Sask., 28.2.41; 3 B&GS; SR 13.10.42; 9 RD 19.1.43 and turret fitted; Central Acft 28.4.43; SOC 15.2.44

The Battles in the above tables are listed under their RAF serials. The equivalent RCAF serials are listed below for ease of reference.

1301	P2155	1654	P2369	1727	K9408	1800	L5536	1873	K9459
1302	P2171	1655	L5384	1728	R3946	1801	N2127	1874	K9190
1303	P2172	1656	L5177	1729	N2020	1802	K9341	1875	L5589
1304	P2173	1657	L5475	1730	L5032	1803	L5316	1876	P2325
1305	P2185	1658	L5410	1731	N2085	1804	L5557	1877	L5398
1306	P2186	1659	L5489	1732	R3940	1805	N2189	1878	K9214
1307	P2187	1660	L5167	1733	N2087	1806	P6569	1879	K9474
1308	P2196	1661	L5149	1734	K9456	1807	L5555	1880	R4007
1309	P2197	1662	P5245	1735	K9250	1808	L5318	1881	L4964
1310	P2198	1663	L5161	1736	P6539	1809	K7640	1882	R3968
1311	P2233	1664	L5408	1737	K9265	1810	N2241	1883	P6543
1312	P2235	1665	P2361	1738	K7660	1811	L5194	1884	L5092
1313	P2236	1666	L5473	1739	R4036	1812	N2029	1885	P5236
1314	P2238	1667	L5470	1740	R4044	1813	L4938	1886	L5314
1315	P2240	1668	L5405	1741	L5298	1814	P6492	1887	P6542
1316	P2241	1669	L5175	1742	P6556	1815	K9255	1888	P2257
1317	P2234	1670	L5147	1743	K9312	1816	K9479	1889	P6547
1318	P2237	1671	L5618	1744	R3922	1817	L5449	1890	L4953
1319	P2239	1672	L5621	1745	R3937	1818	L5492	1891	N2237
1320	P2242	1673	L5606	1746	L5007	1819	R3971	1892	L5220
1601	L5371	1674	L5607	1747	L4942	1820	N2147	1893	P6535
1602	N2239	1675	L5612	1748	N2099	1821	K9465	1894	K9332
1603	N2246	1676	L5614	1749	K9423	1822	R4045	1895	K9413
1604	N2158	1677	L5615	1750	P2156	1823	R3932	1896	L5237
1605	N2227	1678	L5616	1751	R3930	1824	K9212	1897	L5076
1606	N2156	1679	L5477	1752	L5355	1825	L5222	1898	N2248
1607	N2230	1680	L5169	1753	K9311	1826	L5245	1899	R3950
1608	L5341	1681	L5319	1754	K9407	1827	K9378	1900	P2302
1609	L5345	1682	L5620	1755	L4940	1828	R3955	1901	K9431
1610	L5346	1683	L5144	1756	R4005	1829	L5317	1902	L5081
1611	L5370	1684	L5181	1757	L4947	1830	L5043	1903	K9451
1612	L5373	1685	L5321	1758	L5002	1831	L5550	1904	L5269
1613	L5377	1686	L5605	1759	K9274	1832	P6599	1905	L5080
1614	L5340	1687	L5171	1760	P5250	1833	L5008	1906	L5304
1615	L5344	1688	L5484	1761	L4960	1834	P6494	1907	K9210
1616	L5372	1689	L5329	1762	K9405	1835	R4047	1908	K9455
1617	L5347	1690	L5622	1763	K7703	1836	R3941	1909	P2188
1618	L5342	1691	L5179	1764	P5293	1837	L5187	1910	L5273
1619	L5366	1692	L5483	1765	L4955	1838	R3970	1911	P5287
1620	L5364	1693	L5619	1766	L5386	1839	N2181	1912	P6504
1621	P2164	1694	L5627	1767	K9248	1840	P6552	1913	L5045
1622	L5145	1695	L5643	1768	K9316	1841	K9344	1914	L5521
1623	L5162	1696	L5645	1769	K9258	1842	K9182	1915	P6554
1624	P2170	1697	L5646	1770	R3923	1843	L5451	1916	P6507
1625	L5146	1698	L5647	1771	K9281	1844	N2106	1917	K7652
1626	L5157	1699	L5648	1772	K9453	1845	R3952	1918	P5274
1627	L5159	1700	L5649	1773	K9321	1846	R4010	1919	L5284
1628	L5148	1701	R3935	1774	L5016	1847	L5042	1920	P6568
1629	L5155	1702	L5479	1775	R3933	1848	K9466	1921	L5281
1630	L5153	1703	K9191	1776	K7587	1849	L5429	1922	L5453
1631	L5180	1704	AR625	1777	R3926	1850	L5426	1923	R3947
1632	P5241	1705	K9475	1778	P2259	1851	P2309	1924	N2083
1633	L5376	1706	L5109	1779	P6538	1852	L5567	1925	P6523
1634	L5154	1707	K9304	1780	N2162	1853	P6530	1926	P6545
1635	L5150	1708	K7695	1781	L5120	1854	P6559	1927	N2049
1636	L5166	1709	P6557	1782	K9454	1855	P6553	1928	P6500
1637	L5164	1710	P6544	1783	R4035	1856	N2103	1929	R3953
1638	L5481	1711	R3942	1784	R3999	1857	P6540	1930	L5379
1639	L5480	1712	P6502	1785	R4038	1858	L5537	1931	L5570
1640	L5485	1713	L5102	1786	R4011	1859	L5068	1932	L5336
1641	L5486	1714	K9376	1787	R4054	1860	L5353	1933	K9268
1642	L5388	1715	K9292	1788	R4040	1861	P2308	1934	P2312
1643	L5414	1716	K9326	1789	K9439	1862	L5575	1935	L5021
1644	L5411	1717	P6546	1790	L5490	1863	L5532	1936	P2165
1645	L5472	1718	N2226	1791	K9284	1864	P5278	1937	P5252
1646	P2367	1719	P6496	1792	R4048	1865	L5592	1938	P5282
1647	P2368	1720	L5020	1793	R3943	1866	L5504	1939	L5389
1648	L5613	1721	P5292	1794	L5104	1867	P6567	1940	P5280
1649	L5601	1722	K9299	1795	L5365	1868	K9365	1941	L5586
1650	L5608	1723	K9355	1796	L5518	1869	P2320	1942	L5420
1651	L5611	1724	L5378	1797	N2040	1870	K9351	1943	L5132
1652	P5228	1725	L5369	1798	L5106	1871	N2183	1944	L4994
1653	P2366	1726	P6497	1799	L5193	1872	K9211	1945	P6505

1946 P2329	1987 L4968	2028 L4969	2068 L5337	2108 P5237
1947 K9449	1988 L5445	2029 L5204	2069 K9350	2109 K9382
1948 K9401	1989 K9309	2030 L5189	2070 K9401	2110 L5095
1949 P2318	1990 L5064	2031 N2160	2071 P6486	2111 L4986
1950 P5279	1991 L5534	2032 L5211	2072 K7606	2112 L5053
1951 N2172	1992 L5119	2033 P5276	2073 L5198	2113 N2125
1952 P6563	1993 L5116	2034 L5535	2074 K7602	2114 P2303
1953 P6485	1994 N2041	2035 N2187	2075 L5501	2115 P2301
1954 L5271	1995 N2036	2036 K9213	2076 K9457	2116 P2319
1955 L5264	1996 L5033	2037 N2082	2077 L5404	2117 K9178
1956 L5380	1997 L5272	2038 P6490	2078 K9414	2118 P6639
1957 P6524	1998 P2306	2039 K9358	2079 L5040	2119 P6750
1958 P5270	1999 R4001	2040 P6527	2080 P5285	2120 P6633
1959 P6526	2000 P6565	2041 L5100	2081 K9187	2121 P6665
1960 P6550	2001 P6760	2042 K9203	2082 N2249	2122 K9215
1961 L5469	2002 K9300	2043 P6525	2083 K9231	2123 P6737
1962 L5118	2003 R7365	2044 L5496	2084 L5195	2124 N2257
1963 P5271	2004 L5055	2045 P5294	2085 L4961	2125 L4988
1964 P6508	2005 L5259	2046 L5121	2086 L5588	2126 N2242
1965 P6537	2006 L5399	2047 L5394	2087 N2047	2127 K9303
1966 L5421	2007 P6534	2048 K9317	2088 N2046	2128 K7634
1967 L5458	2008 L5209	2049 L5400	2089 K9425	2129 P6684
1968 L5448	2009 K9272	2050 N2023	2090 L4984	2130 K9298
1969 P6480	2010 K9379	2051 N2035	2091 K9427	2131 N2052
1970 L5101	2011 L5062	2052 N2190	2092 K9307	2132 K7633
1971 N2186	2012 L5392	2053 P6663	2093 P6488	2133 P6691
1972 K9275	2013 P5291	2054 K9288	2094 K9424	2134 L5463
1973 L5359	2014 L5562	2055 L5206	2095 L5441	2135 L5290
1974 P6689	2015 K9436	2056 L4957	2096 L4935	2136 L5139
1975 P5284	2016 K7559	2057 K9395	2097 L5349	2137 L5468
1976 P6566	2017 L4962	2058 P2199	2098 L5216	2138 L5131
1977 P5272	2018 L5542	2059 P5290	2099 L5111	2139 L5306
1978 K9217	2019 K9461	2060 P6692	2100 K9204	2140 L5130
1979 P6558	2020 L5263	2061 L5406	2101 K9229	A086 K7596
1980 P6548	2021 L5201	2062 L5126	2102 K9458	A087 K7636
1981 P2331	2022 L5207	2063 K9421	2103 K9253	A088 L5089
1982 L4937	2023 P2262	2064 L5026	2104 L5296	A099 P6726
1983 L5218	2024 L5135	2065 L5456	2105 L4990	A104 P2270
1984 P6498	2025 N2094	2066 N2056	2106 K9403	A125 P6673
1985 L5495	2026 L5219	2067 P5233	2107 L5424	A133 L5127
1986 L5203	2027 L5030			

Battles lined up at Evan's Head. (Jim Cowan via David Vincent)

Royal Australian Air Force

K7575   1 AD 12.9.42; 2 BGS 19.10.42; ANA Parafield for anti-corrosion treatment 4.8.43; 3 AOS 12.7.44; 5 CRD 6.11.44; SOC 14.12.45.

K7600   1 AP 2.1.42; 3 BGS 29.1.42; 1 AGS 12.12.43; damaged in forced landing near Yallourn, Vic., after engine failure, 27.1.44; 1 CRD 30.1.44; SOC 14.2.44.

K7607   2 AD 15.7.42; ANA 18.7.42; 2 AD 30.10.42; 1 BGS 30.11.42; 1 AOS 13.12.43; 1 CRD 23.3.44; SOC 6.2.45.

K7613   1 AP 24.5.41; 2 BGS 29.9.41; forced landing, struck fence, 20.12.41; collided with parked grader, 22.3.42; ANA Parafield 27.7.42; 2 BGS 1.9.43; 3 AOS 13.12.43. Damaged in forced landing near Landsborough, Vic., after engine failure, 28.2.44; SOC 25.4.44.

K7619   1 AD 5.4.42; 2 BGS 5.10.42; forcelanded with glycol leak, 15.12.42; 3 AOS 13.12.43; SOC 14.9.44.

K7622   1 AP 21.11.41; 3 BGS 13.2.42. Attempted wheels-up landing after engine failure; both mainplanes damaged, 15.7.42; SOC 6.8.42.

K7638   1 AP 24.5.41; 3 BGS 29.1.42; 1 AOS 12.12.43; 1 CRD 4.3.44; SOC 29.12.44.

K7643   1 AD 5.4.42; 1 AP 30.3.43; 2 BGS 9.5.43; 3 AOS 13.12.43; SOC at 5 CRD 14.9.44.

K7649   1 AP 16.8.41; 3 BGS 29.1.42; bellylanded after engine failure, 12.6.42; taxied into Oxford BG459, 31.8.43; 1 AGS 12.12.43; 1 CRD 11.3.44; SOC 29.12.44.

K7659   1 AD 15.7.42; 3 BGS 11.9.42; 1 AGS 12.12.43; 1 CRD 11.3.44; SOC 29.12 44

K7672   1 AP 8.3.43; 2 BGS 3.5.43; 3 AOS 13.12.43; SOC at 5 CRD 14.9.44.

K7676   1 AD 14.8.42; 1 BGS 4.10.43; 1 AOS 18.12.43; 1 CRD 22.3.44; SOC 29.12.44.

K7687   1 AP 12.9.41; 3 BGS 29.1.42; forced landing due to fumes in cockpit from hydraulic leak, 27.12.42; forced landing, 27.12.43; 1 AGS 12.12.43; 1 CRD 14.3.44; SOC 29.12.44.

K7705   1 AP for instructional purposes 29.8.41; 1 Engineering School 26.9.41, became Instructional Airframe No. 2; SOC 17.10.45.

K7710   1 AP 27.6.41; 1 AD 20.8.41; 2 BGS 8.9.41; 3 AOS 13.12.43; 6 SFTS for salvage; SOC 14.12.44.

K9177   Received 3.3.43; ANA Mascot 5.3.43; 2 AP 6.4.44; 5 AD store 9.5.44; SOC 27.11.45.

K9206   1 AP 24.5.41; 1 AD 9.7.41; 2 BGS 28.7.41; tailwheel collapsed, 2.11.41; damaged 10.6.41; 1 AD 13.7.42; 2 BGS 24.8.42; tipped on to nose, 2.10.42; 3 AOS 13.12.43; SOC at 5 CRD 14.9.44.

K9219   1 AP 5.12.41; 3 BGS 13.2.42; damaged 24.5.42; Crashed 2 miles west of West Sale after engine failure resulting in fire; crew (Sgt R. Rosevear, LAC H.H. Shortbridge, LAC F. Sinclair) baled out with only slight injuries; aircraft destroyed by fire, 22.10.42. SOC 5.11.42.

K9227   2 AD; ANA 14.5.42; 2 AD 28.6.42; 3 BGS 18.7.42; 1 AGS 12.12.43; 1 CRD 1.4.44; SOC 29.12.44.

K9228   1 AP 22.2.43; 2 BGS 22.3.43; 3 AOS 13.12.43; 1 CRD 1.3.44; SOC 29.12.44.

K9232   1 AP 5.12.41; 3 BGS 13.2.42; starboard oleo collapsed on landing, East Sale, 4.5.42; forced landing with wheels up, 22.5.42; 1 AGS 12.12.43; 1 CRD 11.3.44; SOC 29.12.44.

K9262   1 AP 12.4.43; 1 BGS 12.7.43; 1 AOS 13.12.43; 1 CRD 4.4.44; SOC 29.12.44.

K9282   1 AP 6.4.41; 1 AD 19.5.41; 2 BGS 7.6.41; damaged in heavy landing, Port Pirie, 15.5.42; forced landing after engine failure, 8.6.42; damaged 13.7.42; 1 AD 14.7.42; 2 BGS 24.8.42; port undercarriage collapsed in night landing, Port Pirie, 1.2.43; 3 AOS 13.12.43; 1 CRD 1.3.44; SOC 29.12.44.

K9290   1 AD 14.9.42; 2 BGS 29.10.42; 3 AOS 13.12.43; 1 CRD 28.2.44; SOC 29.12.44.

K9291   1 AD 29.3.42; 1 AP 30.3.43; 2 BGS 14.6.43; 3 AOS 13.12.43. Brakes failed and aircraft taxied into gun pit, Port Pirie, 15.12.43; SOC 13.1.44.

K9297   1 AP 24.5.41; 2 BGS 14.10.41; two rounds fired into port fuselage forward of tail, 23.11.41; hit by Battle L5551 while parked, Port Pirie, 27.12.41; became Instructional Airframe No. 3 2.10.42; SOC 22.9.43.

K9322   1 AP 6.4.41; 1 AD 7.6.41; 1 CF 15.6.41; forcelanded at Ballarat after engine failure, 15.8.41; 1 AD 24.8.41; 2 BGS 8.9.41; 3 AOS 13.12.43; SOC 14.9.44.

K9324   Received 3.12.40; 1 BGS; two forced landings after engine failure on 24.3.41 and 25.3.41; became Instructional Airframe No. 13 14.9.44; sold by CDC to All Souls School for £5.0.0.

K9346   1 AP 20.12.40; 1 AD 21.2.41; 1 BGS 24.3.41; forcelanded after engine failure, 24.3.41; taxying accident, 21.2.42; forcelanded after engine failure, 9.3.42; trainee fired several rounds through port fuselage and tailplane, 17.5.42; 1 AOS 13.12.43; 1 CRD 11.4.44; SOC 29.12.44.

K9362   1 AD 17.9.42; 3 BGS 11.11.42; crashed at No. 4 Air-to-Ground Firing Range, Walla Wullock, after flames seen coming from engine; crew (Sgt R.P. Stevens, LAC C.T. Epps, LAC D.C.R. Fisher) all killed; aircraft destroyed by fire 7.6.43; SOC 15.7.43.

K9368   1 AP 24.5.41; 1 AD 21.8.41; 2 BGS 8.9.41; 3 AOS 13.12.43; 1 CRD 28.2.44; SOC 29.12.44.

K9371   1 AP 1.6.42; 1 AD 9.7.42; 3 BGS 20.7.42; 1 AGS 12.12.43; 1 CRD 11.3.44; SOC 29.12.44.

K9375   1 AP 1.6.42; 1 AD 9.7.42; 3 BGS 9.9.42; forcelanded after engine caught fire; aircraft destroyed by fire, 16.9.42; SOC 2.10.42.

K9380   1 AP 24.5.41; 1 AD 9.7.41; 2 BGS 21.7.41. Mid-air collision with Battle L5654; crew (Sgt R.H. Johns, LAC L. Grant, LAC J.D. Gardiner, LAC R.D. Griffiths) all killed, 9.9.43; 6 SFTS Salvage Section 9.9.43; SOC 14.9.44.

K9388   1 AP 1.3.43; 2 BGS 15.4.43; 3 AOS 13.12.43; 1 CRD 22.3.44; SOC 29.12.44.

K9393   1 AP 9.8.41; 1 AD 20.9.41; 2 BGS 29.9.41; forcelanded after engine failure, 27.1.42; ANA Parafield 12.4.43; 2 BGS 29.11.43; forcelanded at Yarram, Vic., due to engine failure during ferry flight to 1 AGS 8.12.43; 1 AGS 20.12.43; 1 CRD 12.43; SOC 18.2.44.

K9411   Received 3.12.40; 1 AP 8.12.40; 1 BGS 6.1.41; 1 AOS 13.12.43; became Instructional Airframe No. 12, 8.9.44; Army Salvage Depot, Townsville, for sale by auction 8.8.46; sold to Townsville Grammar School for £5.0.0 18.3.47.

K9422   1 AP 9.8.41; 1 AD 21.8.41; 2 BGS 8.9.41; 3 AOS 13.12.43; SOC at 5 CRD 14.9.44.

K9426   ANA Mascot 23.11.42; 2 AP 10.1.43; 2 BGS 18.1.43. 20-lb bomb dropped off after landing and exploded; aircraft destroyed by fire, crew and 2 ground crew injured, 19.1.43; 6 SFTS Salvage Section 29.11.43; SOC 8.12.43.

K9429   1 AD 2.11.42; 2 BGS 9.2.43; 3 AOS 13.12.43; 1 CRD 16.3.44; SOC 29.12.44.

K9435   Ansett 13.11.42; 2 AP 6.1.43; 2 BGS 11.1.43; 3 AOS 13.12.43; ANA Parafield 31.12.43; 1 CRD 18.5.44; SOC 29.12.44

K9442   1 AP 2.1.42; 3 BGS 29.1.42; forcelanded and hit fence after engine failure, 20.5.42; taxying accident on soft ground, 22.6.42; collided with tree during forced landing at Lett's Beach, Vic., after engine failure, 16.4.43; 1 AGS 12.12.43; 1 CRD 13.4.44; to Werribee Bombing Range for bombing trials 24.1.45.

K9443   1 AP 8.3.43; 2 BGS 20.4.43; 3 AOS 13.12.43; SOC 14.9.44.

K9444   1 AP 23.5.41; 1 AD 9.7.41; 2 BGS 4.8.41; 3 AOS 13.12.43; 6 SFTS 26.1.44; SOC 14.9.44.

K9447   1 AD 9.11.42; 1 AP 13.4.43; 2 BGS 11.6.43; 3 AOS 13.12.43; 1 CRD 13.3.44; SOC 29.12.44.

K9464   1 AP 6.4.41; 2 BGS 14.6.41; port undercarriage collapsed on landing, 10.8.41; one wheel emergency landing after port wheel failed to lower, 11.5.42; ANA Parafield 21.4.43; 6 SFTS Salvage Section; SOC 27.10.43.

K9468   1 AP 6.4.41; 1 AD 5.6.41; 1 CF 15.6.41; 2 BGS 18.8.41; ANA Parafield for anti-corrosion treatment 3.10.43; SOC 14.9.44.

K9478   1 AP 24.5.41; 1 AD 9.7.41; 2 BGS 4.8.41; 3 AOS 13.12.43; forcelanded in paddock near Stawell, Vic., short of fuel due to leaking standby fuel tank; aircraft ran into a ditch, 29.2.44; 1 CRD 1.3.44; SOC 29.12.44.

K9486   1 AP 5.9.41; 2 BGS 14.10.41; 1 AD 17.6.42; forcelanded after engine failure, 5.7.42; 2 BGS 6.7.42; 1 AD 13.7.42; 2 BGS 28.9.42; ANA Parafield for anti-corrosion treatment 27.8.43; 2 BGS 24.9.43; 3 AOS 13.12.43; SOC at 5 CRD 14.9.44.

L4941   1 AP 16.8.41; 1 AD 4.10.41; 1 BGS 11.10.41; engine failed on take-off; forcelanded on waste ground with no damage, 24.2.42; wheels up landing, 11.5.42; force-landed 6m S of Evans Head, NSW, after in-flight collision with Battle L5650, 7.6.43; 1 AOS 13.12.43; 2 AD 13.1.44; 1 CRD 27.3.44; SOC 29.12.44.

L4954   1 AP 6.4.41; 1 AD 9.7.41; 2 BGS 4.8.41; taxied into Battle L5105 after night landing, Port Pirie, 27.1.43; 3 AOS 13.12.43; 1 CRD 16.3.44; SOC 29.12.44.

L4958   1 AP 8.2.43; 2 BGS 22.3.43; landing accident, Port Pirie, SA, 23.11.43; 3 AOS 13.12.43; 6 SFTS 20.12.43; SOC 15.12.43.

L4970   1 AP 24.5.41; 1 AD 21.8.41; 2 BGS 22.9.41; 3 AOS 13.12.43; SOC at 5 CRD 14.9.44.

L4974   1 AD 5.4.42; 1 AP 22.3.43; 2 BGS 5.7.43; 3 AOS 13.12.43; 1 CRD 16.3.44; SOC 29.12.44.

L4975   1 AD 12.3.42; 3 BGS 5.5.42; forcelanded, Gifford Strip, 8.11.42; 1 AGS 12.12.43; 1 AD for towing modification 1.2.44; 1 CRD 18.3.44; SOC 29.12.44.

L4982   1 AD 12.9.42; IC amplifier trials 19.10.42; 2 BGS 5.11.42; ANA Parafield for anti-corrosive treatment 19.7.43; 1 EFTS Special Duty Flight 3.4.44; ANA Parafield 27.4.44; 5 AD store 3.5.44; 3 AOS store 17.7.44; 5 CRD 6.11.44; AGS 13.11.44; AGS Stored Reserve 16.4.45; 1 CRD 24.6.45; 1 Stores 27.9.46; DAP for disposal 26.11.47; action complete 8.2.49.

L4985   1 AD 29.3.42; 2 BGS 26.4.43; 3 AOS 13.12.43; 1 CRD 1.3.44; SOC 7.12.45.

L4998   1 AD 12.3.42; 3 BGS 7.4.42; skidded and bogged in trench while taxying, 13.5.42; 1 AGS 12.12.43; 1 CRD 11.3.44; SOC 29.12.44.

L4999   1 AD 5.8.42; 2 BGS 25.1.43; 3 AOS 13.12.43; 1 AD 1.2.44; 1 CRD 11.3.44; SOC 29.12.44.

L5005   1 AP 5.11.40; 1 AD 24.11.40; 1 BGS 29.11.40; 1 AOS 13.12.43; 2 CRD 18.1.44; 1 CRD 29.3.44; SOC 7.12.45.

L5006   Received 11.7.40; 1 AD 29.7.40; 1 AP 5.8.40; 1 AD 22.9.40; 1 BGS 14.10.40; 1 AOS 13.12.43; 1 CRD 16.3.44; SOC 29.12.44.

L5012   Received 11.7.40; 1 AD 29.7.40; 1 AP 5.8.40; 1 AD 9.9.40; 1 BGS 25.11.40; 1 AOS 13.12.43; 1 CRD 4.4.44; SOC 29.12.44.

L5013   1 AD 2.11.42; 2 BGS 9.4.43; 3 AOS 13.12.43; 1 CRD 22.3.44; SOC 29.12.44.

L5015   1 AP; 1 AD 6.6.42; 3 BGS 9.9.42; starboard tailplane struck by Battle L5257 during formation flying, 19.6.43; elevator damaged by gunfire during drogue shoot, 1.9.43; 1 AGS 12.12.43; 1 AD for towing modification 1.2.44; 1 CRD 4.4.44; 3 AOS store 23.8.44; 5 CRD 6.11.44; SOC 14.12.45.

L5017   1 AD 29.3.42; 1 AP 1.8.42; 1 AD 25.9.42; 2 BGS 5.11.42; 3 AOS 13.12.43; 1 CRD 16.3.44; SOC

L5018   29.12.44.
1 AD 2.11.42; 2 BGS 17.1.43; struck wing of Battle R3957 while taxying, Port Pirie, 8.2.43; 3 AOS 13.12.43; 1 CRD 11.4.44; SOC 29.12.44.

L5022   Received 11.7.40; 1 AD 29.7.40; 1 AP 4.8.40; 1 AD 22.9.40; 1 BGS 7.10.40; bellylanded when engine failed after take-off, Evans Head, 2.7.42; 1 AOS 13.12.43; 1 CRD 17.3.44; SOC 29.12.44.

L5023   1 AD 5.4.42; 1 AP 29.3.43; 2 BGS 3.5.43; 3 AOS 13.12.43; 1 CRD 28.2.44; SOC 29.12.44.

L5028   1 AP 2.1.42; 3 BGS 29.1.42; 1 AGS 12.12.43; 1 AD 1.2.44; 1 CRD 14.4.44; SOC 29.12.44.

L5029   1 AD 29.3.42; 1 AP 19.4.43; 1 BGS 5.7.43; 1 AOS 13.12.43; 3 CRD 9.4.44; SOC 14.9.44.

L5031   1 AP 2.1.42; 3 BGS 29.1.42; overshot emergency strip and hit tree stump, 27.9.42; SOC 21.10.42.

L5038   1 AP 16.5.41; 2 BGS 14.10.41; 3 AOS 13.12.43; 1 CRD 1.3.44; became Instructional Airframe No. 9; 182 ATC Sqn Tasmania; disposed of through CDC 4.7.46.

L5044   1 AP 6.4.41; 1 AD 19.5.41; 2 BGS 7.6.41; ANA Parafield for anti-corrosive treatment 27.8.43; 3 AOS store 13.7.44; 5 CRD 6.11.44; SOC 14.12.45.

L5046   Mascot; ANA for erection 28.6.42; 2 AD 16.11.42; 1 BGS 30.11.42; 1 AOS 13.12.43; 3 CRD 9.4.44; SOC 14.9.44.

L5049   1 AP; 1 AD 6.6.42; 3 BGS 26.8.42; struck Oxford HN273 while taxying after brake control cable broke, East Sale, 8.4.43; 1 AGS 12.12.43; AGS Stored Reserve 16.4.45; 1 CRD 25.5.45; 1 SD 27.9.46; DAP for write-off 26.11.47; action completed 8.2.49.

L5050   1 AP 9.5.41; 3 BGS 29.1.42; forced landing on one wheel at Gifford Strip; fuselage holed by tree stump, 5.10.42; 1 AD 1.12.42; Ansett 11.12.42; 1 AD 19.7.43; Ansett 27.7.43; 1 AD 3.8.43; Ansett 20.8.43; 1 AD 27.9.43; 2 BGS 25.10.43; 3 AOS 13.12.43; 1 AD for towing modification 15.1.44; 1 CRD 13.3.44; SOC 29.12.44.

L5052   1 AP 5.9.41; 2 BGS 14.10.41; struck wire fence at end of landing run, Port Pirie, 13.7.42; 1 AD 14.7.42; 2 BGS 24.8.42; ANA Parafield 16.11.43; SOC at 5 CRD 14.9.44.

L5061   1 AP 16.8.41; 3 BGS 13.2.42; damaged in wheels up landing after engine failure, 9.7.42; 1 AD 7.9.42; 1 BGS 14.12.42; fuselage damaged by gunfire, 2.5.43; 1 AOS 13.12.43; 3 CRD 9.4.44; SOC 14.9.44.

L5069   1 AD 12.9.42; 3 BGS 11.10.42; 1 AGS 12.12.43; 1 CRD 24.3.44; SOC 29.12.44.

L5070   1 AP 6.4.41; 1 AD 19.5.41; 2 BGS 31.5.41; forced landing after engine failure on flight to Port Pirie; no damage, 26.6.41. Caught fire after forced landing due to glycol leak and destroyed by fire, 1.4.43; 6 SFTS 18.4.43; SOC 4.5.43.

L5082   1 AD 22.8.42; 1 BGS 14.12.42; Engine cut on night take-off; bellylanded, Evans Head, 18.6.43; DBF; SOC 6.7.43.

L5087   1 AP 24.5.41; 2 BGS 14.10.41; 3 AOS 13.12.43; SOC at 5 CRD 14.9.44.

L5094   1 AP 5.11.40; 1 AD 19.11.40; 1 BGS 7.12.40; struck wheelbarrow while taxying 3.11.41; 1 AOS 13.12.43; collided with range hut while low flying; climbed to 400 ft then crashed; crew (Sgt W.W. Hopper, LAC G.H. Harrison, LAC D.F. Grimsley) all killed, 14.1.44; 3 CRD 5.2.44; SOC 5.2.44.

L5096   1 AP 5.11.40; 1 AD 16.12.40; 1 BGS 3.2.41; 1 AOS 13.12.43; 3 CRD 9.4.44; SOC 14.9.44.

L5105   1 AP 6.4.41; 1 AD 19.5.41; 2 BGS 7.6.41; forcelanded after engine failure, 11.5.42; taxied into Battle L4954 after night flying, Port Pirie, 27.1.43; damaged 10.2.43; 3 AOS 13.12.43; 1 CRD 1.3.44; SOC 29.12.44.

L5108   1 AP; 1 AD 8.8.42; 2 BGS 19.10.42; damaged 9.2.43; 3 AOS 13.12.43; 1 CRD 11.4.44; AGS 27.9.44; AGS Stored Reserve 16.4.45; 1 CRD 3.6.45; 1 SD 5.7.46; DAP for write-off 26.11.47; action completed 8.2.49.

L5117   1 AP 12.9.41; 1 BGS 4.10.41; struck obstruction on aerodrome, damaging two bomb doors on port wing,

L5122   9.10.41; taxying accident; damaged starboard inner bomb door, 27.1.42; while landing at night, hit parked aircraft, 22.2.42; 1 AOS 13.12.43; 1 CRD 11.4.44; SOC 29.12.44.
1 AD 13.8.42; 3 BGS 28.12.42; 1 AGS 12.12.43; AGS Stored Reserve 16.4.45; 1 CRD 24.5.45; 1 SD 27.9.46; to DAP for write-off 26.11.47; action complete 8.2.49.

L5124   1 AD 29.3.42; 3 BGS 1.9.42; 1 AGS 12.12.43; bellylanded due to burst hydraulic line 5m W of East Sale, 19.10.44; SOC 7.11.44; 1 CRD 15.11.44.

L5128   1 AD 5.4.42; 3 BGS 1.9.42; forcelanded after radiator burst on take-off, East Sale, 20.4.43; 1 AGS 12.12.43; SOC at AGS, fuselage needed as auxiliary test stand, 23.8.44.

L5129   Ansett for assembly 13.11.42; 2 AP 11.12.42; 3 BGS 16.12.42; forcelanded on range, 1.2.43; forcelanded after engine failure, 9.3.43; 1 AGS 12.12.43; 1 CRD 17.3.44; SOC 29.12.44.

L5134   Received 3.3.43; ANA Mascot 5.3.43; 2 AP 8.9.43; 1 AGS 13.2.44; 1 CRD 14.3.44; 3 AOS store 19.7.44; 5 CRD 6.11.44; SOC 14.12.45.

L5142   1 AP 6.4.41; became Instructional Airframe No.1 due to salt water corrosion 2.5.41; 1 ES 9.5.41.

L5143   Received 18.7.40; 1 AD 29.7.40; 1 AP 4.8.40; GRS by 9.9.40; CFS 9.9.40; 1 BGS 23.9.40; forcelanded after engine failure, 8.12.40; forcelanded after engine failure; both undercarriage legs torn off and starboard wing damaged, 25.10.41; ANA 28.11.41; 1 AD 29.6.42; 2 BGS 28.12.42; 3 AOS 13.12.43; 1 AD for towing modification 15.1.44; 1 CRD 11.4.44; SOC 29.12.44.

L5151   1 AP 29.5.40; 1 BGS 29.9.40; SOC 20.2.42.

L5152   1 AP 5.11.40; 1 AD 28.12.40; 1 BGS 30.12.40; 1 AOS 12.12.43; 36 ATC Sqn, Lismore, New South Wales, for instructional purposes 18.8.44; became Instructional Airframe No.11, 5.9.44.

L5156   1 AD 22.6.40; 1 AP 30.6.40; 1 AD 22.9.40; 1 BGS 20.10.40; collided with obstruction on aerodrome during landing, Evans Head, 24.4.42; 1 AOS 13.12.43; 1 CRD 3.5.44; SOC 29.12.44.

L5158   Received 18.7.40; 1 AD 29.7.40; 1 AP 4.8.40; loan to GRS 1.9.40; 1 BGS 9.9.40; 1 AOS 13.12.43; 3 CRD 31.3.44; SOC 14.9.44.

L5163   1 AD 9.7.40; 1 AP 22.7.40; 1 BGS 30.9.40; struck hut with wingtip, 25.3.42; struck post during forced landing after engine failure, damaged, 23.5.42; Clyde Engineering for repair 26.10.42; mainplanes at ANA Mascot 4.12.42; 2 AD 6.10.43; SOC 27.10.43.

L5170   Received 1.7.40; 1 AD 29.7.40; 1 AP 4.8.40; 1 BGS 28.10.40; overshot flare path during night landing and collided with Battle R3928, Evans Head, 12.6.42; engine failed on take-off and undercarriage collapsed, Evans Head, 28.10.42; 1 AOS 13.12.43; 1 CRD 13.4.44; SOC 29.12.44.

L5173   1 AP 6.4.41; 1 AD 19.5.41; 2 BGS 31.5.41; 3 AOS 13.12.43; SOC at 5 CRD 14.9.44.

L5202   Received 3.12.40; 1 AP 8.12.40; 1 AD 18.12.40; 1 BGS 23.12.40; 1 AOS 13.12.43; 1 CRD 28.7.44; SOC 29.12.44.

L5212   1 AP 16.8.41; 2 BGS 14.10.41; undercarriage jammed; bellylanded, Port Pirie, 20.7.42; starboard under-carriage leg failed to lock down and collapsed on landing, Port Pirie, 25.8.43; 3 AOS 13.12.43; 1 CRD 1.3.44; SOC 29.12.44.

L5215   1 AP 2.1.42; 3 BGS 29.1.42; tipped onto nose when attempting forced landing on boggy ground, 23.7.42; 1 AGS 12.12.43; 1 CRD 21.3.44; SOC 29.12.44.

L5217   1 AP 2.1.42; 3 BGS 13.2.42; 1 AGS 12.12.43; 1 CRD 4.3.44; SOC 29.12.44.

L5221   1 AD 17.9.42; 1 BGS 23.12.42; 1 AOS 13.12.43; 1 CRD 13.4.44; 3 AOS store 23.8.44; 5 CRD 6.11.44; SOC 14.12.45.

L5223   2 AD 11.1.43; 2 BGS 1.3.43; ANA Parafield for anti-corrosive treatment 23.6.43; School of Photography Canberra 25.3.44; 5 AD store 2.7.44; SOC 27.11.45.

L5244   1 AP 24.5.41; 1 AD 20.9.41; 2 BGS 29.9.41; fuselage

holed by single accidentally-fired shot, 8.11.41; struck flagpole on range, 21.7.43; ANA Parafield for anti-corrosive treatment 31.8.43; 2 BGS 12.10.43; 3 AOS 13.12.43; 1 AD for towing modification 1.2.44; 1 CRD 21.3.44; AGS 27.9.44; AGS Stored Reserve 16.4.45; 1 CRD 24.5.45; 1 SD 27.9.46; DAP for write-off 26.11.47; action completed 8.2.49.

L5251   2 AD 11.1.43; ANA Mascot 19.2.43; 2 AP 5.6.43; 1 BGS 21.6.43; 1 AOS 13.12.43; 1 CRD 1.4.44; 3 AOS store 3.8.44; 5 CRD 6.11.44; SOC 14.12.45.

L5257   ANA 27.4.42; 2 AD 10.7.42; 3 BGS 17.8.42; port wing tip struck tailplane of Battle L5015 during formation flight, 19.6.43; 1 AGS 12.12.43; 1 CRD 11.3.44; to Instructional Airframe No. 8, 10.8.44; sold by CDC for £15.0.0, 8.6.46.

L5258   1 AD 5.4.42; 1AP 1.8.42; 1 AD 1.10.42; 3 BGS 20.11.42; 1 AGS 12.12.43; 1 CRD 14.3.44; SOC 29.12.44.

L5262   1 AD 22.8.42; 1 AP 8.3.43; 2 BGS 20.4.43; 3 AOS 13.12.43; SOC at 5 CRD 14.9.44.

L5267   1 AP 6.4.41; 2 BGS 14.6.41; 3 AOS 13.12.43; 1 CRD 16.3.44; SOC 29.12.44.

L5274   1 AP 5.12.41; 3 BGS 13.2.42; 1 AGS 12.12.43; 1 CRD 4.3.44; SOC 29.12.44; to be used for incendiary bomb trials at Werribee Bombing Range.

L5278   1 AP 27.6.41; 1 AD 21.8.41; 2 BGS 22.9.41; force-landed after loss of power, 17.1.43; 3 AOS 13.12.43; SOC at 5 CRD 14.9.44.

L5291   1 AD 5.4.42; ANA Essendon 27.1.43; 22 RSU awaiting erection 16.8.43; 3 BGS 14.9.43; 1 AGS 12.12.43; erection to 1 AGS strength 17.2.44; AGS Stored Reserve 16.4.45; 1 CRD 3.6.45; 1 SD 27.9.46; to DAP for write-off, 26.11.47; action completed 8.2.49.

L5302   1 AD 5.4.42; 1 AP 5.4.43; 2 BGS 18.5.43; 3 AOS 13.12.43; 1 CRD 1.3.44; SOC 29.12.44.

L5305   1 AP 5.12.41; 3 BGS 29.1.42; 1 AGS 12.12.43; 1 CRD 14.3.44; SOC 29.12.44.

L5311   1 AP 1.3.43; 1 AD Ferry Flight 8.5.43; 2 BGS 9.5.43; 3 AOS 13.12.43; 1 CRD 22.3.44; AGS 27.9.44; AGS Stored Reserve 16.4.45; 1 CRD 22.5.45; 1 SD 27.9.46; to DAP for write-off 26.11.47; action completed 8.2.49.

L5313   1 AD 9.8.42; 3 BGS 31.10.42; 1 AGS 12.12.43; 1 CRD 1.4.44; SOC 29.12.44.

L5320   Received 18.7.40; 1 AD 29.7.40; 1 AP 4.8.40; 1 AD 15.9.40; 1 BGS 30.9.40; 1 AOS 13.12.43; 3 CRD 14.4.44; SOC 14.9.44.

L5322   Received 18.7.40; 1 AD 29.7.40; 1 AP 4.8.40; 1 AD 6.10.40; 1 BGS 14.10.40; landing accident, 24.11.40; propeller struck oil unit while taxying, 23.10.41; force-landed after throttle linkage broke, 9.8.42; collided with Battle R3939, 3.12.42; 1 AOS 13.12.43; 3 CRD 11.4.44; SOC 14.9.44.

L5326   1 AD 14.8.42; 2 BGS 28.12.42; ANA Parafield for anti-corrosive treatment 21.8.43; 2 BGS 16.11.43; 3 AOS 13.12.43; 1 AD 1.2.44; 1 CRD 17.4.44; SOC 7.12.45.

L5354   1 AP 24.5.41; 1 AD 9.7.41; 2 BGS 21.7.41; forcelanded after engine failure, 21.1.42; struck fence during forced landing after engine failure, 14.1.43; 3 AOS 13.12.43; SOC 14.9.44.

L5357   1 AP 5.12.41; 3 BGS 29.1.42; 1 AOS 12.12.43; 1 CRD 1.4.44; SOC 29.12.44.

L5358   1 AP 6.4.41; 2 BGS 7.6.41; 3 AOS 13.12.43; 1 CRD 1.3.44; SOC 29.12.44.

L5382   1 AD 9.7.40; 1 AP 22.7.40; 1 BGS 30.9.40; while landing struck wing tip of stationary Battle R3928, 25.3.42; bellylanded in swampy ground after engine failure, 18.8.43; 1 AOS 13.12.43; 1 CRD 11.4.44; 3 AOS store 19.7.44; 5 CRD 6.11.44; SOC 14.12.45.

L5385   Received 18.7.40; 1 AD 29.7.40; 1 AP 4.8.40; 1 BGS 14.10.40; forcelanded with overheating engine, 30.1.42; 1 AOS 13.12.43; 3 CRD 11.4.44; SOC 14.9.44.

L5387   1 AD 22.6.40; 1 AP 30.6.40; 1 BGS 14.10.40; SOC 20.2.42.

L5390   1 AD 29.7.40; 1 AP 4.8.40; 1 AD 22.9.40; 1 BGS 14.10.40; bellylanded, 20.11.40; forcelanded when

L5403   undercarriage would not lower, 19.2.41; oleos collapsed after hitting drain on landing, 21.6.41; ANA Archerfield 22.7.41; 3 AD 5.10.42; 1 AD 23.2.43; 2 BGS 5.7.43; 3 AOS 13.12.43; 6 CU 4.1.44; 14 ARD 28.4.44; SOC 14.9.44.

L5403   1 AD 29.7.40; 1 AP 4.8.40; loan to GRS 1.9.40; CFS 9.9.40; 1 BGS 23.9.40; 1 AOS 13.12.43; 3 CRD 9.4.44; SOC at 8 CRD 14.9.44.

L5407   1 AD 29.5.40; 1 BGS 29.9.40; 1 AOS 13.12.43; 3 CRD 9.4.44; SOC 14.9.44.

L5409   1 AD 22.6.40; 1 AP 30.6.40; 1 AD 15.9.40; 1 BGS 30.9.40; 1 AOS 12.12.43; 3 CRD 9.4.44; SOC 14.9.44.

L5417   1 AD 5.4.42; 2 BGS 25.1.43; damaged by own gunfire, 11.4.43; ANA Parafield 19.4.43; 2 BGS 28.6.43; 3 AOS 13.12.43; damaged during forced landing after engine cut in circuit, Port Pirie, 26.12.43; 6 SFTS Salvage, SOC 27.1.44.

L5425   1 AP 6.4.41; 1 AD 19.5.41; 2 BGS 7.6.41; forced landing after collision with marker's shelter when aircraft lost height in turn, 29.4.42; damaged 15.5.42; forcelanded due to fuel shortage, 23.8.42; 3 AOS 13.12.43; 5 CRD Mallala 10.2.44; SOC 14.9.44.

L5434   1 AP 9.5.41; 1 AD 9.7.41; 2 BGS 12.7.41; pilot's hood became detached in flight and struck tailplane, 24.9.41; damaged 22.9.42; ANA Parafield for repair 6.11.42; 2 BGS 2.6.43; 3 AOS 13.12.43; 1 AD for towing modification 20.1.44; 1 CRD 18.3.44; SOC 29.12.44.

L5435   1 AP 6.4.41; 1 AD 19.5.41; 2 BGS 31.5.41; forcelanded after engine failure, 23.1.42; 3 AOS 13.12.43; SOC at 5 CRD 14.9.44.

L5444   1 AP 24.11.40; 1 AD 20.12.40; forced landing, 27.1.41; 1 BGS 28.1.41; 1 AOS 13.12.43; 3 CRD 31.3.44; SOC at 3 CRD 14.9.44.

L5452   1 AD 2.11.42; 1 BGS 18.1.43; 1 AOS 13.12.43; 3 CRD 9.4.44; SOC 14.9.44.

L5471   1 AD 11.7.40; 1 AP 4.8.40; CFS 9.9.40; 1 BGS 9.12.40; 1 AOS 13.12.43; 3 AD 9.1.44; 3 CRD 29.2.44; SOC 14.9.44.

L5478   1 AP 24.5.41; 2 BGS 4.8.41; forcelanded with wheels up, 6.9.41; 3 AOS 13.12.43; SOC at 5 CRD 14.9.44.

L5488   1 AP 6.4.41; 1 AD 19.5.41; 2 BGS 31.5.41; Battle L5522 taxied into rudder and damaged it, 27.6.41; ANA Parafield for anti-corrosive treatment 31.8.43; SOC at 5 CRD 14.9.44.

L5522   1 AP 6.4.41; 2 BGS 2.6.41; taxied into rudder of Battle L5488, 27.6.41; undercarriage collapsed on landing, Port Pirie, 26.11.41; 3 AOS 13.12.43; landed with one wheel retracted, 2.1.44; 1 CRD 1.3.44; SOC 29.12.44.

L5527   1 AP 5.9.41; 3 BGS 29.1.42; 1 AGS 12.12.43; 1 CRD 17.3.44; SOC 29.12.44.

L5529   1 AP 6.4.41; 1 AD 22.6.41; 1 CF 27.7.41; 1 AD 14.8.41; 2 BGS 1.9.41. Undercarriage collapsed on landing, Port Pirie, 20.4.42; became Instructional Airframe No. 4 2.10.42; SOC 22.9.43.

L5533   1 AP 24.5.41; 1 AD 21.8.41; 2 BGS 22.9.41; ANA Parafield for anti-corrosive treatment 2.9.43; 2 BGS 1.11.43; 3 AOS 13.12.43; 1 CRD 1.3.44; 3 AOS store 3.8.44; 5 CRD 6.11.44; SOC 14.12.45.

L5551   1 AP 23.5.42; 1 AD 22.6.41; 1 CF 6.7.41; 1 AD 14.8.41; 2 BGS 1.9.41; collided with stationary Battle K9297 on ground, Port Pirie, 27.12.41; 3 AOS 13.12.43; SOC at 5 CRD 14.9.44.

L5594   1 AD 2.11.42; 1 BGS 14.12.42; struck fence during landing, Evans Head, 24.12.42; bellylanded after engine failure, 2.6.43; 1 AOS 13.12.43; 1 CRD 11.4.44; AGS 27.9.44; AGS Stored Reserve 16.4.45; 1 CRD 21.6.45; approved for destruction by fire 3.4.46; destroyed by fire 5.4.46.

L5595   1 AP 28.12.42; 2 BGS 14.8.43; 3 AOS 13.12.43; 1 CRD 1.3.44; AGS 27.9.44; AGS Stored Reserve 16.4.45; 1 CRD 28.6.45; approved for destruction by fire 3.4.46; destroyed by fire 5.4.46.

L5596   Received 3.3.43; ANA Mascot 5.3.43; 2 AP 8.11.43; 3 BGS 23.11.43; 1 AGS 12.12.43; 1 AD for towing modification 1.2.44; 1 CRD 16.3.44; SOC 29.12.44.

A Battle from No.2 Bombing & Gunnery School, Port Pirie, force-landed in South Australia, a not-infrequent occurrence.
(via D Vincent)

L5599   1 AD 4.7.40; 1 AP 7.7.40; 1 AD 29.9.40; 1 BGS 14.10.40; 2 BGS 7.7.41; damaged 13.7.42; wing hit Battle L5703 while taxying, Port Pirie, 27.1.43; 3 AOS 13.12.43; AGS 29.2.44; bellylanded due to glycol leak, 19.2.45; 1 CRD 12.3.45; SOC at a Technical Salvage Unit 4.4.45.

L5600   1 AD 4.7.40; 1 AP 7.7.40; 1 AD 29.9.40; 1 BGS 14.10.40; 2 BGS 7.7.41; forcelanded after engine failure, 8.10.41; struck trees after dropping drogue, 27.9.43; 1 AGS 20.12.43; AGS Stored Reserve 16.4.45; 1 CRD 22.5.45; 1 SD 27.9.46; DAP for write-off 4.6.46; action complete 8.2.49.

L5602   1 AD 9.7.40; 1 AP 22.7.40; 1 AD 29.9.40; 1 BGS 28.10.40; undercarriage collapsed while taxying, Evans Head, 2.7.42; 1 AGS 21.12.43; AGS Stored Reserve 22.5.45; 1 SD 27.9.46; DAP for write-off 26.11.47; action complete 8.2.49.

L5603   1 AD 9.7.40; 1 AP 22.7.40; 1 AD 22.9.40; 1 BGS 14.10.40; forcelanded after engine failure on ferry flight, 29.6.41; 2 BGS 7.7.41; 2 OTU 15.6.42; forcelanded after engine problems, 3.8.42; 1 AD 10.8.42; 3 BGS 9.11.42; Oxford X7113 hit drogue wire during air-to-air gunnery, 21.6.43. Struck sand hills during attempted forced landing on beach 6m SW of Woodside, Vic., after engine failure, 8.7.43; collected by 22 RSU 8.8.43; SOC 24.7.43.

L5604   1 AD 4.7.40; 1 AP 7.7.40; 1 AD 29.9.40. Crashed in Tregalong Valley, NSW, during ferry flight from Laverton to Evans Head for delivery to BGS; pilot abandoned aircraft after losing control, 1.10.40; SOC 22.11.40.

L5609   1 AD 4.7.40; 1 AP 7.7.40; 1 AD 29.9.40; 1 BGS 7.10.40. Badly damaged in forced landing after drogue dropping; crew (F/O E. Bradbury, LAC A. Thompson) injured, 30.3.41; SOC 22.4.41.

L5610   1 AD 4.7.40; 1 AP 7.7.40; 1 AD 22.9.40; 1 BGS 4.11.40; forced landing after engine failure during ferry flight to 2 BGS, 29.6.41; 2 BGS 12.7.41; 2 OTU 15.6.42; 2 BGS 31.10.42; 1 AGS 20.12.43; AGS Stored Reserve 22.5.45; 1 CRD 11.6.45; 1 SD 27.9.46; DAP for write-off 26.11.47; action completed 8.2.49.

L5617   1 AD 29.7.40; 1 AP 4.8.40; 1 AD 29.9.40; 1 BGS 6.10.40; 2 BGS 7.7.41; 2 OTU 15.6.42. DBR in forced landing, 30.7.42; CGS 3.8.42; SOC by AMSE 11.8.42.

L5626   1 AD 2.11.42; 2 BGS 10.2.43; 3 AOS 13.12.43; AGS 14.3.44; AGS Stored Reserve 22.5.45; 1 CRD 11.6.45; 1 SD 27.9.46; DAP for write-off 26.11.47; action completed 8.2.49.

L5629   Assembled at Ansett 13.11.42; 2 AP 21.3.43; 1 OTU 6.4.43. DBR when struck by Beaufort A9-240 on ground, 3.9.43; 7 AD 22.9.43; SOC 27.10.43.

L5633   1 AD 15.9.42; 2 BGS 29.10.42; forcelanded after engine seized at 3,500 ft, 28.12.42; forcelanded after engine failure on take-off, 16.3.43; 3 AOS 13.12.43; AGS 13.3.44; AGS Stored Reserve 16.4.45; 1 CRD 3.6.45; 1 SD 27.9.46; DAP for write-off 26.11.47; action completed 8.2.49.

L5636   1 AP 12.7.43; 1 OTU 26.8.43; AGS 10.1.44; 1 CRD 25.5.45; 1 SD 27.9.46; DAP for write-off 26.11.47; action completed 8.2.49.

L5639   1 AD 15.9.42; 3 BGS 31.10.42; 1 AGS 12.12.43; AAGS 26.6.44; AGS 27.11.44; AGS Stored Reserve 22.5.45; 1 CRD 8.6.45; DAP for write-off 26.11.47; action completed 8.2.49.

L5640   1 AD 9.8.42; 2 BGS 5.11.42. Aircraft turned on its back, spun and crashed; crew (Sgt L.J. Hampstead, LAC

L5644   A.P. Gilmore, LAC G.L. Dore) all killed, 20.5.43; 6 SFTS 22.5.43; SOC 4.6.43.

L5644   1 AP 16.10.40; 1 AD 3.11.40; 1 BGS 18.11.40; belly-landed after engine trouble, 3.6.42; 1 OTU 30.8.42. Fuselage broke aft of cockpit after aircraft forcelanded after engine failure, 1.9.42; 1 AD 23.9.42; SOC 5.10.42.

L5650   1 AP 1.10.40; 1 AD store 20.10.40; 1 BGS 29.11.40; forcelanded after engine overheated when dropping drogue, 28.12.41; forcelanded on beach after engine failure, 3.8.42. Crashed into swamp at Evans Head after in-flight collision with Battle L4941; crew (Sgt G.W. Finch, LAC C.L. Mooney) both killed, 8.6.43; SOC 23.6.43.

L5651   1 AP 1.10.40; 1 AD 13.10.40; 1 BGS 14.10.40; AGS 21.12.43; AGS Stored Reserve 22.5.45; 1 CRD 11.6.45; 1 SD 27.9.46; DAP for write-off 26.11.47; action completed 8.2.49.

L5652   1 AP 20.10.40; 1 AD 3.11.40; 1 BGS 18.11.40; force-landed after engine failure 30.3.42; ANA Mascot by 25.9.42; SOC 4.8.44; 2 CRD 11.8.44.

L5653   1 AP 1.10.40; 1 AD 13.10.40; 1 BGS 20.10.40; 1 OTU 31.8.42; forcelanded after partial engine failure, 20.10.42; Ansett, Essendon 1.11.42; 1 AD 16.3.43; Ansett 23.3.43; 1 AD 6.4.43; 2 BGS 25.4.43; force-landed after engine failure, 13.8.43. Dived into ground after taking off with lock still on starboard aileron; crew (Sgt R.A. Scott, AC1 K.L. Stephen) both killed, 9.9.43; SOC 20.8.43; 6 SFTS Salvage Section 13.9.43.

L5654   1 AP 19.9.40; 1 AD 2.7.41; 2 BGS 21.7.41. Collided in flight with Battle K9380; crew (Sgt G.N. Ninness, AC1 C.A. Venables) both killed, 9.9.43; 6 SFTS Salvage Section 9.9.43; SOC 14.9.43.

L5655   1 AP 1.10.40; 1 AD 13.10.40; 1 BGS 20.10.40; 1 OTU 19.4.42; AGS 24.1.44; CGS 22.6.44; 1 CRD for storage 3.7.45; 1 SD 27.9.46; DAP for write-off 26.11.47; action completed 8.2.49.

L5656   1 AP 16.10.40; 1 AD 3.11.40; 1 BGS 2.12.40; 1 AOS 13.12.43. Bellylanded on beach after engine failure, 25.1.44; 3 CRD 14.2.44; SOC 22.2.44.

L5657   1 AP 19.9.40; 1 AD 6.10.40; 1 BGS 14.10.40; CGS 24.8.42; AGS 8.1.45; bellylanded 1m W of West Sale, Vic., after loss of power, 27.4.45; 1 CRD 14.5.45; SOC 29.5.45.

L5658   1 AP 16.10.40; 1 AD 3.11.40; 1 BGS 2.12.40; 1 OTU 19.4.42; 1 AD for engine change 26.7.42; 1 OTU 17.8.42; AGS 10.1.44; AGS Stored Reserve 22.5.45; 1 CRD 11.6.45; 1 SD 27.9.46; DAP for write-off 26.11.47; action completed 8.2.49.

L5659   1 AP 16.10.40; 1 AD 3.11.40; 1 BGS 23.12.40; 1 OTU 19.4.42; 1 AD for engine change 18.7.42; 1 OTU 17.8.42; damaged in forced landing after engine failure on approach, East Sale, 28.1.43; 7 AD 6.2.43; SOC 15.9.43.

L5660   1 AP 19.9.40; 1 AD 6.10.40; 1 BGS 14.10.40; CGS 1.9.42; AGS 8.1.45. Bellylanded near Seaspray, Vic., after glycol leak blinded pilot, 1.2.45; 1 CRD 12.2.45; SOC 27.2.45.

L5665   Received 14.1.43; ANA Mascot 19.2.43; 2 AP 6.4.43; 2 BGS 12.4.43; 3 AOS 13.12.43; AGS 29.2.44; unserviceable due to corrosion 31.12.44; 1 CRD 22.1.45; SOC 30.1.45.

L5670   1 AD 17.11.42; 1 AP 5.4.43; 3 BGS 19.5.43; damaged 9.7.43; AGS 12.12.43; AGS Stored Reserve 22.5.45; 1 CRD 24.6.45; 1 SD 27.9.46; SOC action completed by DAP 8.2.49.

L5675   1 AD 14.10.42; 2 BGS 6.1.43; 3 BGS 22.5.43; crashed through boundary fence after engine lost power on take off, East Sale, 9.7.43; AGS 8.1.44; extensive corrosion identified 2.4.44; 1 CRD 2.6.44; SOC 14.6.44.

L5676   1 AP; 1 AD 9.7.42; 1 OTU 31.8.42; AGS 10.1.44; AGS Stored Reserve (corroded) 12.3.45; 1 CRD 11.6.45; SOC 7.12.45.

L5677   1 AD 7.9.43; 3 BGS for completion of erection then strength 20.10.43; AGS 8.12.43; AAGS 26.6.44; AGS

L5678   14.11.44; AGS Stored Reserve 22.5.45; 1 CRD 11.6.45; 1 SD 27.9.46; DAP for write-off 26.11.47; action completed 8.2.49.

L5678   1 AP; 1 AD 9.7.42; 1 OTU 28.9.42; AGS 10.1.44; struck stationary aircraft while taxying after return from target towing flight for 1 OTU, East Sale, 25.2.44; 1 CRD; SOC 29.7.45.

L5679   1 AP 9.8.41; 1 AD 21.8.41; starboard wing tip struck port wing tip of Battle P5275 causing minor damage, 6.9.41; 2 BGS 8.9.41; forcelanded when power lost after take-off, Port Pirie; crew (Sgt R.W. Charlier, Cpl G.H. Cherry) both slightly injured, 19.12.41; damaged 23.9.42; ANA Parafield for anti-corrosive treatment 17.6.43; AGS 10.3.44; AGS Stored Reserve 16.4.45; 1 CRD 22.5.45; 1 SD 27.9.46; DAP for write-off 26.11.47; action completed 8.2.49.

L5683   1 AP 5.11.40; 1 AD 12.1.41. Collided with Battle L5700 during ferry flight to 1 BGS and dived into sea; P/O Norris killed, 16.1.41; SOC 13.3.42.

L5684   1 AD 2.11.42; 2 BGS 11.3.43; 3 AOS 13.12.43; AGS 1.3.44; AGS Stored Reserve 22.4.45; 1 CRD 7.8.45; 1 SD 27.9.46; DAP for write-off 26.11.47; action completed 8.2.49.

L5687   1 AD 2.11.42; 2 BGS 1.3.43; overshot runway during forced landing after fuel pressure lost, Port Pirie, 25.4.43; 3 AOS 13.12.43; AGS 29.2.44; AGS Stored Reserve 12.3.45; 1 CRD 6.6.45; 1 SD 27.9.46; DAP for write-off 26.11.47; action completed 8.2.49.

L5689   1 AP 4.10.43; Armament School 10.1.44; AGS 3.2.44; 1 CRD with fuselage corrosion 13.11.44; SOC 10.2.45.

L5692   1 AP 5.11.40; 1 AD 9.1.41; 1 BGS 3.2.41; forcelanded after power loss on take-off, Evans Head, 28.5.42; 1 AOS 13.12.43; AGS Stored Reserve 16.4.45; 1 CRD 3.6.45; 1 SD 27.9.46; DAP for write-off 26.11.47; action completed 8.2.49.

L5693   1 AP 5.1.41; 1 AD 22.1.42; SHQ Williamtown 23.3.42; 100 Sqn 4.5.42; SHQ Richmond 13.8.42; 1 OTU 21.9.42; AGS 10.1.44; AGS Stored Reserve 22.5.45; 1 CRD 11.6.45; 1 SD 27.9.46; DAP for write-off 26.11.47; action completed 8.2.49.

L5694   1 AP 5.1.41; 1 AD 22.1.42; SHQ Bankstown 9.3.42; 1 AD 28.3.42; SHQ Bankstown 6.4.42; 2 AP 13.7.42; 1 BGS 5.10.42; 1 AOS 13.12.43; AGS 3.3.44; AGS Stored Reserve 22.5.45; 1 CRD 2.8.45; 1 SD 27.9.46; DAP for write-off 26.11.47; action completed 8.2.49.

L5695   1 AP 5.1.41; 1 AD 22.1.42; 3 BGS 5.5.42; AGS 12.12.43; Forcelanded after fire in the air and engine failure 4m N of Stradbroke, Vic., 20.2.44; 1 CRD 26.2.44; SOC 14.3.44.

L5697   1 AP 27.10.40; 1 AD 25.11.40; 1 BGS 30.12.40; 1 AOS 13.12.43; AGS 12.3.44; CGS 22.6.44; AGS 8.1.45; AGS Stored Reserve 22.5.45; 1 CRD 11.6.45; 1 SD 27.9.46; DAP for write-off 26.11.47; action completed 8.2.49.

L5700   1 AP 5.11.40; 1 AD 9.1.41. Collided with Battle L5683 on ferry flight and dived into sea; P/O Wright killed, LAC Macpherson escaped by parachute, 16.1.41; SOC 13.3.42.

L5701   1 AP 27.10.40; 1 AD 19.11.40; 1 BGS 16.12.40. force-landed on beach after engine failure, 25.3.42; 1 AOS 13.12.43; AGS 12.3.44; AGS Stored Reserve 22.5.45; 1 CRD 11.6.45; 1 SD 27.9.46; DAP for write-off 26.11.47; action completed 8.2.49.

L5702   1 AP 27.10.40; 1 AD 3.11.40; 1 BGS 3.2.41; ground-looped and undercarriage partly collapsed after heavy landing, Evans Head, 8.7.41; 1 OTU 19.4.42; AGS 10.1.44; AGS Stored Reserve; 1 CRD 24.5.45; 1 SD 27.9.46; DAP for write-off 26.11.47; action completed 8.2.49.

L5703   1 AP 9.8.41; 1 AD 16.8.41; 2 BGS 1.9.41; landing accident, 28.1.42; 2 OTU 15.6.42; forcelanded 8m from Hay Field, 29.7.42; 2 BGS 28.9.42; forcelanded after engine failure, 17.1.43; forcelanded with fuel starvation 4m W of Port Pirie, 25.5.43; 3 AOS 3.12.43; AGS 14.3.44; 1 CRD 22.5.45; 1 SD 27.9.46; DAP for write-

L5603, a target tug of No. 2 Bombing & Gunnery School, at Port Pirie. ((Bob Deaves via D Vincent)

off 26.11.47; action completed 8.2.49.

L5704   1 AP 27.10.40; 1 BGS 16.12.40; while waiting to take-off, wing tip damaged by Battle L5751 which was landing, 17.2.42; 1 OTU 20.4.42; forcelanded after engine failure, 6.10.42; 26 RSU 12.12.42; Ansett, Essendon 8.12.42; 1 AD 31.5.43; 2 BGS 15.7.43; 3 AOS 13.12.43; AGS 29.2.44; bellylanded after engine failure, 8.12.44; 1 CRD 31.12.44; SOC 23.1.45.

L5709   1 AD 9.8.42; 3 BGS 31.10.42; AGS 12.12.43; AGS Stored Reserve 22.5.45; 1 CRD 11.6.45; 1 SD 27.9.46; DAP for write-off 26.11.47; action completed 8.2.49.

L5710   2 AD 11.1.43; ANA Mascot 19.2.43; 2 AP 20.4.43; 2 BGS 29.4.43. Forcelanded after engine failure; caught fire and almost totally burnt out, 8.10.43; 6 SFTS Salvage Section 14.10.43; SOC 23.10.43.

L5721   1 AD 9.8.43; 3 BGS to complete erection then on strength 7.10.43; AGS 12.12.43; AGS Stored Reserve 22.5.45; 1 CRD 2.8.45; 1 SD 27.9.46; DAP for write-off 26.11.47; action completed 8.2.49.

L5723   1 AD 9.11.42; 1 AP 12.4.43; CGS 16.5.43; 1 CRD 3.7.45; 1 SD 27.9.46; DAP for write-off 26.11.47; action completed 8.2.49.

L5725   1 AP 16.5.41; 2 BGS 4.8.41; 2 OTU 15.6.42; 1 AD 27.7.42; 3 BGS 9.11.42; engine cut after dropping drogue; forcelanded and ran into creek, 9.7.43; AGS 12.12.43; 1 CRD 17.3.44; SOC 10.2.45.

L5727   1 AP 1.3.43; 1 OTU 21.3.43; AGS 10.1.44; AGS Stored Reserve 16.4.45; 1 CRD 28.6.45; 1 SD 27.9.46; DAP for write-off 26.11.47; action completed 8.2.49.

L5728   1 AD 2.11.42; 1 BGS 14.1.43; 1 AOS 13.12.43; AGS 3.3.44; airframe found to be badly corroded 24.5.44; 1 CRD 2.6.44; SOC 29.7.44.

L5734   1 AD 14.10.42; 1 AP 5.4.43; 3 BGS 19.5.43; AGS 12.12.43; CGS 22.6.44; 1 CRD 3.7.45; 1 SD 27.9.46; DAP for write-off 26.11.47; action completed 8.2.49.

L5735   1 AP 12.6.42; 1 AD 22.6.42; allotted to 4 BOTU USAAC but abandoned by USAAC at Geelong, 8.7.42; 1 AD 14.9.42; 2 BGS 11.11.42; taxied into three concrete blocks, 30.12.42; forcelanded due to probable glycol leak, 27.9.43; AGS 12.12.43; AGS Stored Reserve 22.5.45; 1 CRD 5.6.45; 1 SD 27.9.46; DAP for write-off 26.11.47; action completed 8.2.49.

L5736   1 AP 26.9.41; 2 BGS 20.10.41; 2 OTU 18.5.42; 1 AD 27.7.42; 3 BGS 9.11.42; 1 AD for drogue towing on naval co-op 25.5.43; 3 BGS 28.6.43; forcelanded after engine failure due to glycol leak, 20.10.43; AGS 12.12.43; 1 CRD 13.3.44; to be issued to 1 APU for incendiary bomb trials on Werribee Bombing Range 25.5.45; SOC 29.7.45.

L5738   2 AD 11.1.43; ANA Mascot 19.2.43; 2 AP 17.6.43; 1 OTU 21.6.43; AGS 10.1.44; AGS Stored Reserve 22.5.45; 1 CRD 11.6.45; 1 SD 27.9.46; DAP for write-off 26.11.47; action completed 8.2.49.

L5741   1 AD 2.11.42; 2 BGS 10.2.43; 3 AOS 13.12.43; force-landed after engine failure with undercarriage partially extended, 20.12.43; AGS 23.3.44; AGS Stored Reserve 16.4.45; 1 CRD 24.6.45; 1 SD 27.9.46; DAP for write-off 26.11.47; action completed 8.2.49.

L5751   1 AP 27.10.40; 1 AD 4.11.40; CFS 9.12.40; 1 BGS 6.1.41; while landing, touched wingtip of Battle L5704 which was waiting to take-off, 17.2.42; 1 OTU 19.4.42; forcelanded after engine cut, 25.6.42; AGS 10.1.44; AGS Stored Reserve 22.5.45; 1 CRD 26.6.45; 1 SD 27.9.46; DAP for write-off 26.11.47; action completed 8.2.49.

L5754   1 AD 25.5.42; 3 BGS 4.10.42; AGS 12.12.43; AAGS 26.6.44; AGS 14.11.44; AGS Stored Reserve 16.4.45; 1 CRD 24.6.45; 1 SD 27.9.46; DAP for write-off 26.11.47; action completed 8.2.49.

L5756   1 AP 8.12.40; 1 BGS 6.1.41; bellylanded in bushes after engine failed while climbing to stream drogue, 26.4.42; ANA Mascot 25.9.42; 2 AP 8.8.44; AGS 16.10.44; AGS Stored Reserve 22.5.45; 1 CRD 5.6.45; DAP for write-off 26.11.47; action completed 8.2.49.

L5757 1 AP 27.10.40; taxying accident 4.11.40; 1 AD 19.11.40; 1 BGS 23.12.40; 1 AOS 13.12.43; tipped on nose, Mascot, 10.3.44; not repaired; 2 CRD 9.11.44; SOC 5.12.44.

L5758 1 AP 9.8.41; 1 AD 21.8.41; 2 BGS 1.9.41; struck by Battle N2089 on ground, Port Pirie, 24.6.43; 3 AOS 14.2.44; AGS 29.2.44; AGS Stored Reserve 22.5.45; 1 CRD 11.6.45; 1 SD 27.9.46; DAP for write-off 26.11.47; action completed 8.2.49.

L5759 1 AP 16.5.41; 1 AD 29.7.41; 2 BGS 4.8.41; forcelanded with glycol fumes in cockpit, 21.8.41; hit by Wirraway A20-326 while parked, Port Pirie, 13.10.41. Spun into sea; crew (Sgt R.M. Plummer, LAC L.G. Price) missing, 13.8.42; SOC 10.9.42.

L5760 1 AP 9.8.41; tail struck Anson W2110 wingtip in mid-air, 15.8.41; 1 AD 21.8.41; 2 BGS 8.9.41; 1 AD 29.6.42; 2 BGS 3.8.42. Stall-turned and dived into ground; crew (Sgt S.R. Scholz, AC1 D. Thomson) both killed, 22.11.42; SOC 14.12.42.

L5763 1 AP 21.11.41; 1 OTU 20.12.41; AGS 10.1.44; taxying accident 26.2.44; AGS Stored Reserve 22.5.45; 1 CRD 25.5.45; 1 SD 27.9.46; DAP for write-off 26.11.47; action completed 8.2.49.

L5764 1 AP 5.12.41; 3 BGS 29.1.42; 22 Sqn via 2 AD 9.2.42; 2 AD 19.7.42; SHQ Richmond 12.9.42; 3 BGS 21.12.42; ran into creek after emergency landing, Seaspray, Vic., 12.5.43; AGS 12.12.43; AGS Stored Reserve 22.5.45; 1 CRD 5.6.45; 1 SD 27.9.46; DAP for write-off 26.11.47; action completed 8.2.49.

L5765 1 AP 21.11.41; 1 OTU 20.12.41. Overran runway at Mallacoota and ploughed through stump, 25.10.42; SOC 12.11.42; 1 AD 1.12.42.

L5770 1 AD 22.8.42; 1 AP 5.4.43; 2 BGS 3.5.43; 3 AOS 13.12.43; AGS 1.3.44; AGS Stored Reserve 22.5.45; 1 CRD 11.6.45; 1 SD 27.9.46; DAP for write-off 26.11.47; action completed 8.2.49.

L5772 1 AP 16.5.41; 2 BGS 21.7.41; port elevator damaged 9.8.41; struck tree while attempting forced landing, 26.4.43; 3 AOS 12.12.43; AGS 29.2.44; forcelanded with one wheel up 25 mls E of Lakes Entrance, Vic., with glycol leak; 13.4.45; AGS Stored Reserve 22.5.45; 1 CRD 28.5.45; SOC 7.12.45.

L5774 1 AP 16.5.41; 1 AD 9.7.41; 2 BGS 21.7.41; SHQ Pearce 3.9.42; 35 Sqn 28.9.42; 7 CU 10.11.43; AGS 9.10.44; AGS Stored Reserve 22.5.45; 1 CRD 11.6.45; 1 SD 27.9.46; DAP for write-off 26.11.47; action completed 8.2.49.

L5778 1 AP 24.3.41; 1 AD 3.5.41; 4 SFTS 26.5.41; HQ Pearce 3.8.41; 4 SFTS 17.8.41; 35 Sqn 9.2.43; 7 CU 10.11.43; starboard undercarriage collapsed on landing, Pearce, 28.2.44; AGS 24.9.44; AGS Stored Reserve 22.5.45; 1 CRD 5.6.45; 1 SD 27.9.46; DAP for write-off 26.11.47; action completed 8.2.49.

L5779 1 AP 24.3.41; 1 AD 3.5.41; 4 SFTS 26.5.41; forcelanded after hydraulic line burst, 5.1.42; SHQ Pearce 16.8.42; 35 Sqn 28.9.42; 7 CU 10.11.43; AGS 24.9.44; AGS Stored Reserve 22.5.45; 1 CRD 6.6.45; 1 SD 27.9.46; DAP for write-off 26.11.47; action completed 8.2.49.

L5781 1 AD 22.8.42; 2 BGS 16.3.43; 3 AOS 13.12.43; AGS 29.2.44; AGS Stored Reserve 22.5.45; 1 CRD 6.6.45; 1 SD 27.9.46; DAP for write-off 26.11.47; action completed 8.2.49.

L5785 1 AD ex USAAFIA Geelong 12.6.42; 1 AD ex 1 AP 22.6.42; 1 OTU 21.9.42; AGS 10.1.44; AGS Stored Reserve 22.5.45; 1 CRD 6.6.45; 1 SD 27.9.46; DAP for write-off 26.11.47; action completed 8.2.49.

L5789 1 AD 25.5.42; 1 AD via SHQ Laverton 27.7.42; 3 BGS 4.10.42; AGS 12.12.43; drogue cable struck civilians while aircraft low flying along beach, 27.12.43; taxied into fuel tanker, 15.3.44; AGS Stored Reserve 22.5.45;

1 CRD 22.5.45; 1 SD 27.9.46; DAP for write-off 26.11.47; action completed 8.2.49.

L5790 1 AP 24.3.41; 1 AD 9.6.41; 22 Sqn 20.7.41; 2 AD 14.7.42; SHQ Richmond 19.9.42; 1 BGS 21.9.42; 1 AOS 13.12.43; AGS 6.3.44; AGS Stored Reserve 22.5.45; 1 CRD 24.6.45; 1 SD 27.9.46; DAP for write-off 26.11.47; action completed 8.2.49.

L5791 1 AP 24.3.41; 1 AD 9.6.41; 1 CU 29.6.41; 12 Sqn Darwin 14.7.41; 3 BGS 22.3.43; AGS 12.12.43; 1 AD for use as sample 1.2.44; AGS 29.8.44; AGS Stored Reserve 22.5.45; 1 SD 27.9.46; DAP for write-off 26.11.47; action completed 8.2.49.

L5792 1 AP 4.10.43; AGS 26.1.44; AGS Stored Reserve 22.5.45; 1 CRD 11.6.45; 1 SD 27.9.46; DAP for write-off 26.11.47; action completed 8.2.49.

L5794 1 AP 24.3.41; 1 AD 5.6.41; 24 Sqn 26.7.41; forcelanded after engine failure, 7.6.42; 3 AD 30.8.42; 1 OTU 6.6.43; 1 BGS 10.9.43; 1 AOS 13.12.43; AGS Stored Reserve 22.5.45; 1 CRD 21.6.45; 1 SD 27.9.46; DAP for write-off 26.11.47; action completed 8.2.49.

L5797 1 AP; 1 AD 17.8.42; struck fence on take-off but flew on; became lost, then forcelanded after engine failure, 1.10.42; 2 BGS 19.10.42; forcelanded with overheating engine, 19.1.43; AGS 7.12.43; 1 AGS 20.12.43; undercarriage collapsed after forced landing, Sale, Vic., 28.3.44. AGS reserve 22.5.45; 1 CRD 11.6.45; Stores Depot 27.9.46; DAP for disposal 26.11.47; action completed 8.2.49.

N2027 Received 3.12.40; 1 AP 8.12.40; 1 AD 16.12.40; 1 BGS 18.12.40; engine caught fire over range during gunnery exercise, 16.8.43; 1 AOS 13.12.43; 3 CRD 3.3.44; SOC 14.9.44.

N2038 1 AD 2.11.42; 2 BGS 9.2.43; 3 AOS 13.12.43; 1 CRD 28.2.44; 3 AOS store 12.7.44; 5 CRD 6.11.44; SOC 14.12.45.

N2039 1 AP 27.6.41; 2 BGS 29.9.41; port tailplane damaged during firing exercise, 18.1.41; forcelanded with ignition problem, 20.3.42; 3 AOS 13.12.43; 1 CRD 22.3.44; SOC 29.12.44.

N2045 1 AD 2.11.42; 2 BGS 16.2.43; 3 AOS 13.12.43; 6 SFTS 6.1.44; SOC at 5 CRD 14.9.44.

N2053 1 AD 8.2.43; 1 BGS 1.3.43; 1 AOS 13.12.43; 3 CRD 3.4.44; 1 AOS 10.4.44; 1 CRD 31.7.44; SOC 6.2.45.

N2054 1 AD 2.11.42; 2 BGS 18.2.43; 3 AOS 13.12.43; 6 SFTS Salvage 30.1.44; SOC at 5 CRD 14.9.44.

N2063 1 AD 13.8.42; 2 BGS 1.3.43; 3 AOS 13.12.43; 1 CRD 28.2.44; SOC 29.12.44.

N2064 1 AD 17.9.42; 1 BGS 23.11.42; badly damaged when undercarriage collapsed in ground loop after landing, Evans Head, 6.1.43; ANA Mascot 19.4.43; 2 AD 6.10.43; SOC 27.10.43.

N2065 1 AD 9.9.42; 3 BGS 11.10.42; forcelanded after engine failure, 12.4.43; gun accidentally fired by gunner when in stowed position, 29.8.43; AGS 12.12.43; 1 CRD 1.4.44; SOC 7.12.45.

N2066 1 AP 12.12.41; 3 BGS 29.1.42; AGS 12.12.43; 1 CRD 11.3.44; SOC 29.12.44.

N2089 1 AD 2.11.42; 2 BGS 5.4.43; hit Battle L5758 when brakes failed while taxying, Port Pirie, 23.6.43; 3 AOS 13.12.43; 1 CRD 28.2.44; SOC 29.12.44.

N2090 1 AD via 1 AP 4.10.42; 1 AP 15.3.43; 1 BGS 12.5.43; 1 AOS 13.12.43; 3 CRD 9.4.44; SOC 14.9.44.

N2091 1 AP 21.11.41; 1 BGS 14.1.42; shots fired into fuselage when trainee tried to stow gun with drum still attached 21.7.43; 1 AOS 13.12.43; 2 AD 13.1.44; CFS 16.6.44; became Instructional Airframe No. 10 1.9.44; SOC 8.11.44.

N2092 1 AD 5.4.42; 1 AP 12.4.43; 2 BGS 6.9.43; 3 AOS 13.12.43; 1 CRD 1.3.44; forcelanded at Mallala after engine failure on ferry flight to 3 AOS store, 15.7.44; 5 CRD for engine change; 3 AOS 28.9.44; 5 CRD 6.11.44; SOC 29.12.44.

N2096 1 AD via 1 AP 25.5.42; 3 BGS 14.9.42; bellylanded in ploughed field after engine failed on take-off, East Sale, 27.1.43; AGS 12.12.43; 1 CRD 4.3.44; SOC 29.12.44.

N2107   1 AD 14.10.42; 1 BGS 11.1.43; 1 AOS 13.12.43; 3 CRD 3.4.44; 1 AOS 10.4.44; 1 CRD 24.2.44; SOC 29.12.44.

N2124   1 AD 12.9.42; 2 BGS 19.10.42; 3 AOS 13.12.43; 1 CRD 22.3.44; SOC 29.12.44.

N2163   1 AP 6.4.41; 1 AD 19.5.41; 2 BGS 7.6.41; ANA Parafield 2.4.43; 5 AD 14.4.44; 3 AOS 7.7.44; 5 CRD 6.11.44; SOC 14.12.45.

N2166   1 AD 1.11.42; 1 AP 5.4.43; 2 BGS ex 2 AP 28.6.43; 3 AOS 13.12.43; 1 CRD 22.3.44; 3 AOS store 3.8.44; 5 CRD 6.11.44; SOC 14.12.45.

N2170   1 AP 11.1.43; 2 BGS 9.3.43; ANA Parafield for anti-corrosion treatment 27.7.43; 5 AD store 28.5.44; SOC 2.11.44; 2 CRD 14.11.44.

N2176   1 AD 12.3.42; 3 BGS 5.5.42; AGS 12.12.43; 1 CRD 14.3.44; SOC 29.12.44.

N2179   1 AP 12.9.41; 1 BGS 14.1.42; 1 AOS 13.12.43; 3 CRD 3.4.44; 1 AOS 10.4.44; 1 CRD 22.4.44; SOC 29.12.44.

N2182   1 AD 5.4.42; 1 AP 8.3.43; 2 BGS 20.4.43; 3 AOS 13.12.43; 1 CRD 1.3.44; SOC 29.12.44.

N2188   1 AP 27.6.41; 1 AD 20.8.41; 2 BGS 8.9.41; forcelanded in sea, 31.8.42; salvaged; forcelanded on swampy ground in 8-ft scrub due to glycol leak, 7.5.43; SOC 1.6.43; recovered from swamp and being rebuilt at Port Adelaide.

N2223   1 AD 2.11.42; 3 BGS 20.11.42; AGS 12.12.43; AGS Stored Reserve 16.4.45; 1 CRD 5.6.45; 1 SD 27.9.46; DAP for write-off 26.11.47; action completed 8.2.49.

N2225   1 AD 22.8.42; 2 BGS 6.1.43; 3 AOS 13.12.43; SOC at 5 CRD 14.9.44.

N2228   Received 15.12.42; ANA Mascot 18.12.42; 2 AP 13.3.43; 1 OTU 17.3.43; 3 BGS 29.3.43; AGS 12.12.43; 1 CRD 17.3.44; SOC 29.12.44.

N2229   ANA; 2 AP 8.12.42; 3 BGS 11.12.42; AGS 2.12.43; 1 CRD 24.3.44; SOC 29.12.44.

N2233   1 AP 6.4.41; 1 AD 19.5.41; 2 BGS 31.5.41; taxied into truck on runway, Port Pirie, 12.12.41; 3 AOS 13.12.43; 1 CRD 1.3.44; SOC 29.12.44.

N2236   1 AP 6.4.41; 1 AD 19.5.41; 2 BGS 7.6.41; forcelanded after engine failure, 18.2.42; 1 AD 17.6.42; 2 BGS 13.7.42; 3 AOS 13.12.43; 1 CRD 1.3.44; SOC 29.12.44.

N2240   ANA Mascot 23.11.42; 2 BGS via 2 AP 28.1.43; 3 AOS 13.12.43; 1 CRD 16.3.44; SOC 29.12.44.

N2244   1 AD 11.7.40; 1 AP 29.7.40; 1 BGS 7.10.40; hit tree during air-to-ground gunnery practice, 22.9.42; 1 AOS 13.12.43; 1 CRD 22.3.44; SOC 29.12.44.

N2247   1 AD 22.6.40; 1 AP 30.6.40; 1 BGS 7.10.40; 1 AOS 13.12.43; 3 CRD 9.4.44; SOC 14.9.44.

N2250   1 AD 12.3.42; 3 BGS 7.4.42; AGS 12.12.43; 1 CRD 24.3.44; SOC 29.12.44.

N2251   1 AD 9.8.42; 3 BGS 14.10.42; AGS 12.12.43; AGS Stored Reserve 16.4.45; 1 CRD 3.6.45; 1 SD 27.9.46; DAP for write-off 26.11.47; action completed 8.2.49.

N2255   1 AP 5.11.40; 1 AD 19.11.40; 1 BGS 23.12.40; crash-landed after damaging undercarriage on take-off, Evans Head, 29.9.41; ANA 23.10.41; 3 AD 5.10.42; SOC 5.5.43.

N2256   1 AP 5.12.41; 3 BGS 13.2.42; struck pyrotechnics hut while landing, East Sale, 18.10.42; AGS 12.12.43; 1 CRD 11.3.44; SOC 7.12.45.

P2157   1 AD 8.10.42; 1 BGS 14.12.42; 1 AOS 13.12.43; 3 CRD 31.3.44; SOC 14.9.44.

P2166   1 AP 29.5.40; CFS via 1 AD 15.9.40; 1 BGS 23.9.40; port oleo collapsed on landing, Evans Head, 19.12.41. Bellylanded on beach after engine failure; aircraft partially submerged, 19.5.42; SOC 6.8.42.

P2167   1 AP 3.5.40; CFS via 1 AD 15.9.40; 1 BGS 23.9.40; forcelanded after engine failure during bombing practice, Evans Head, 1.12.40; 1 AOS 13.12.43; 2 AD 13.1.44; 1 CRD 29.4.44; SOC 29.12.44.

P2168   1 AP 29.5.40; 1 AD 20.10.40; 1 BGS 25.11.40; force-landed in marshy ground, 12.12.40; ANA 7.7.41; 3 AD 5.10.42; SOC 5.5.43.

P2169   1 AP 3.5.40; loan to GRS 1.9.40; CFS 9.9.40; 1 BGS

23.9.40; bellylanded on airfield after starboard undercarriage would not extend, Evans Head, 12.1.41; forcelanded after engine failure, 27.9.41; taxied into truck, 13.2.42. Tail smashed when hit by Battle L5117 which was landing at night, Evans Head, 22.2.42; SOC 25.3.42.

P2245   1 AP 16.8.41; forcelanded after engine failure, 4.10.41; 2 BGS 20.10.41; 3 AOS 13.12.43; SOC at 5 CRD 14.9.44.

P2263   1 AP; 1 AD 4.10.42; 3 BGS 30.11.42. Hit high tension wires during forced landing after engine failure 10m from East Sale; crashed and DBF; crew (F/Sgt J.S. Alexander killed, LAC K.C. Toose, LAC J.R.H. Stapleton injured), 17.11.43; 1 CRD 12.12.43; SOC 12.43.

P2264   1 AD 5.4.42; 1 AP 15.3.43; 1 BGS 6.5.43; 1 CRD 1.4.44; 1 AOS store 12.7.44; 5 CRD 6.11.44; SOC 14.12.45.

P2276   1 AD 18.9.42; 1 BGS 23.11.42; 1 AOS 13.12.43. Crashed on beach at Disaster Bay, near Eden, NSW, during ferry flight from Evans Head, to Werribee, (1 CRD) 23.3.44; salvaged and SOC 21.8.44.

P2300   1 AP 6.4.41; 1 AD 2.7.41; 2 BGS 26.7.41; 1 AD for engine change 29.6.42; 2 BGS 3.8.42; forcelanded after engine failure 25.8.43; 3 AOS 13.12.43; 1 CRD 28.2.44; SOC 29.12.44.

P2305   1 AP 16.5.41; 1 AD 21.8.41; 2 BGS 8.9.41; 3 AOS 13.12.43; 5 CRD 24.2.44; SOC 14.9.44.

P2317   1 AP 22.3.43; 2 BGS 20.4.43; 3 AOS 13.12.43; 6 CU 4.1.44; 14 ARD 27.4.44; SOC at 8 CRD 14.9.44.

P2322   1 AD 29.3.42; 1 AP 5.4.43; 1 BGS 31.5.43; 1 AOS 13.12.43; 1 CRD 23.3.44; 3 AOS store 19.7.44; 5 CRD 6.11.44; SOC 14.12.45.

P2354   1 AP 12.4.43; 2 BGS 14.6.43; 3 AOS 13.12.43; 1 CRD 11.4.44; SOC 29.12.44.

P2363   1 AP 22.2.43; 2 BGS 22.3.43; 3 AOS 13.12.43; 1 CRD 28.2.44; 3 AOS store 12.7.44; 5 CRD 6.11.44; SOC 14.12.45.

P2364   1 AD 22.6.40; 1 AP 30.6.40; loan to GRS 2.9.40; CFS 9.9.40; 1 BGS 23.9.40; 1 AOS 13.12.43; 3 CRD 4.3.44; SOC 14.9.44.

P2365   1 AD 11.7.40; 1 AP 4.8.40; 1 BGS 7.10.40; 1 AOS 13.12.43; 2 AD 13.1.44; 1 CRD 23.3.44; SOC 29.12.44.

P5234   1 AP 21.12.41; 3 BGS 29.1.42; AGS 3.1.44; 1 CRD 24.3.44. Badly damaged in forced landing on Evans Head Range; crew (Sgt W.J. Hunter, LAC L.J. Watter, LAC D.B. Webb) severely injured, 24.10.44; SOC 29.12.44.

P5239   1 AD 3.5.40; 1 BGS 29.9.40. Written-off in forced landing, 24.10.41; SOC 5.12.41.

P5240   1 AP 9.5.41; 1 AD 9.7.41; 2 BGS 21.7.41; ANA Parafield 27.7.42; 2 BGS via 1 EFTS 29.7.43; 3 AOS 13.12.43; 1 CRD 1.3.44; 3 AOS store 10.7.44; 5 CRD 6.11.44; SOC 14.12.45

P5242   1 AD 29.5.40; CFS via 1 AP 15.9.40; 1 BGS 23.9.40; forcelanded after engine failure 21.10.40; SOC 12.10.43.

P5243   1 AP 29.5.40; 1 AD 15.9.40; 1 BGS 7.10.40; 1 AOS 13.12.43; 1 CRD 4.4.44; SOC 29.12.44.

P5247   1 AP 3.5.40; CFS 9.9.40; 1 BGS 23.9.40; hit boundary fence on landing, Evans Head, 6.7.41; 1 AOS 13.12.43; 3 CRD 31.3.44; SOC 14.9.44.

P5249   1 AD 29.5.40; 1 BGS 7.10.40; forcelanded on beach after glycol line burst, 5.3.42; landed with starboard wheel retracted, 4.5.43; 3 CRD 9.4.44; SOC 25.8.44.

P5273   1 AP 16.8.41; 1 BGS 13.9.41; landed with wheels partially down, Evans Head, 6.8.42; 1 AOS 13.12.43; 3 CRD 9.4.44; SOC 14.9.44

P5275   1 AP 24.5.41; 1 AD 9.7.41; 2 BGS 28.7.41; port wing tip struck starboard wing tip of Battle L5679, 6.9.41; 3 AOS 13.12.43; SOC at 5 CRD 14.9.44.

P5281   1 AP 27.6.41; 1 AD 21.8.41; 2 BGS 8.9.41; 3 AOS 13.12.43; 1 CRD 13.3.44; SOC 29.12.44.

P5289 1 AP 3.12.40; 1 AD 20.12.40; 1 BGS 6.1.41; 1 AOS 13.12.43; 3 CRD 10.4.44; SOC 14.9.44.

P6481 1 AP 6.4.41; 1 AD 7.6.41; 1 CF 22.6.41; 2 BGS 23.8.41; forcelanded after engine failure after take-off from Port Pirie; aircraft ran through fence and undercarriage collapsed, damaging mainplane, 15.4.42; ANA Parafield 22.2.43; 6 CU 28.1.44; 14 ARD 29.4.44; SOC at 8 CRD 14.9.44.

P6483 1 AP 24.5.41; 1 AD 11.8.41; 1 BGS 13.9.41; 1 AOS 13.12.43; 1 CRD 16.3.44; SOC 29.12.44.

P6484 1 AP 24.5.41; 2 BGS 4.8.41; during parachute dropping exercise, parachute opened while still attached to bomb rack, damaging rib of port mainplane, 11.11.41; starboard undercarriage failed to lower fully and wing struck ground on landing, damaging wing tip, aileron and flap, 8.12.41; forcelanded after hydraulics failed, 27.1.42; 3 AOS 13.12.43; SOC 14.9.44.

P6489 1 AP 6.4.41; 1 AD 2.7.41; 2 BGS 28.7.41; 3 AOS 13.12.43; SOC at 5 CRD 14.9.44.

P6493 1 AP 27.6.41; 1 AD 20.8.41; 2 BGS 1.9.41; ANA Parafield for anti-corrosive treatment 8.10.43; dismantled 22.10.43; SOC at 5 CRD 14.9.44.

P6499 1 AP 27.6.41; 1 AD 14.8.41; 2 BGS 22.9.41; forcelanded after engine failure, 8.10.41; forcelanded after engine failure on take-off, 4.6.42; 3 AOS 13.12.43; 1 CRD 1.3.44; SOC 29.12.44.

P6503 1 AP 24.5.41; 1 AD 21.8.41; 2 BGS 8.9.41; bullet hole in tailplane, 18.12.41; 3 AOS 13.12.43; 1 CRD 16.3.44; SOC 29.12.44.

P6509 1 AP 24.5.41; 2 BGS 4.8.41; forcelanded after engine failure, 19.11.41; struck rudder of Battle P6536 while taxying, 27.11.41; 3 AOS 13.12.43; 1 CRD 1.3.44; SOC 29.12.44.

P6531 1 AP 24.5.41; 1 AD 4.7.41; 2 BGS 28.7.41; gunner fired through tailplane, 1.8.41; ANA Parafield for anti-corrosion treatment 23.10.43; SOC at 5 CRD 14.9.44.

P6536 1 AP 27.6.41; 1 AD by 14.9.41; 2 BGS 22.9.41; rudder struck by taxying Battle P6509, 27.11.41; 3 AOS 13.12.43; SOC at 5 CRD 14.9.44.

P6602 1 AP 24.5.41; 2 BGS 14.10.41; ANA Parafield for anti-corrosion treatment 23.10.43; SOC at 5 CRD 14.9.44.

P6622 1 AD 8.10.42; 1 BGS 14.12.42; fitted with dual controls 22.10.43; 1 AOS 13.12.43; 1 CRD 8.5.44; SOC 29.12.44.

P6631 1 AD 19.2.42; 3 BGS 1.10.42; starboard undercarriage accidentally retracted on ground, 13.2.43; forcelanded after engine failure, 25.9.43; 1 AGS 12.12.43; AGS Stored Reserve 22.5.45; 1 CRD 11.6.45; 1 AD 27.9.46; DAP for disposal 26.11.47; action completed 8.2.49.

P6642 1 AP 12.12.41; 3 BGS 9.2.42; forcelanded after engine failure, 28.5.42; 1 AGS 12.12.43; AGS stored Reserve 22.5.45; 1 AD 27.9.46; DAP for disposal 26.11.47; action completed 8.2.49.

P6664 Mascot by 30.4.42; 2 AD 28.6.42; 1 BGS 6.7.42; dual control fitted 12.10.43; 1 AOS 13.12.43; 1 CRD 11.4.44; SOC 29.12.44.

P6677 1 AD 19.2.42; 3 BGS 7.4.42; undercarriage collapsed during forced landing practice, 15.12.42; forcelanded after engine failure, 10.2.43; 1 OTU 28.10.43; 1 AGS 10.1.44; AGS Stored Reserve 16.4.45; 1 CRD 22.5.45; DAP for disposal 26.11.47; action completed 8.2.49.

P6720 1 AD 12.3.42; 3 BGS 8.6.42; 1 AGS 12.12.43; AGS Stored Reserve 16.4.45; 1 CRD 24.5.45; 1 SD 1.10.46; DAP for disposal 26.11.47; action completed 8.2.49.

P6729 1 AD 13.3.42; 3 BGS 15.6.42; 1 BGS 1.11.43; 3 BGS 4.12.43; 1 AGS 12.12.43; AGS Stored Reserve 22.5.45; 1 CRD 21.6.45; destroyed by fire 5.4.46.

P6762 1 AP 5.12.41; 3 BGS 13.2.42; wheels-up landing, 18.6.42; CFS 27.11.42; 3 BGS 7.1.43; 1 AGS 12.12.43; 1 CRD for SOC 22.5.45.

R3924 1 AP 24.11.40; 1 AD 16.12.40; 1 BGS 23.12.40; struck building with port wing while taxying, 16.1.41; SOC 3.7.42.

R3925 Received 20.12.40; 1 AP 22.12.40; 1 AD 4.2.41; 1 BGS 25.2.41; collided with Battle R3939 while taxying, Evans Head, 23.9.43; 1 AOS 13.12.43; 3 CRD 3.4.44; 1 AOS 10.4.44; 1 CRD 22.4.44; SOC 29.12.44.

R3927 Received 3.12.40; 1 AP 8.12.40; 1 AD 13.12.40; 1 BGS 16.12.40; port undercarriage failed to lower; landed on one wheel, Evans Head, 27.12.40; 1 AOS 13.12.43; 1 CRD 14.3.44; SOC 29.12.44.

R3928 Received 3.12.40; 1 AP 8.12.40; 1 AD 13.12.40; 1 BGS 23.12.40; forcelanded after engine blow-back, 11.10.41; damaged wing tip after ground collision with Battle L5382, Evans Head, 25.3.42; propeller hit car while taxying, 30.4.42; 1 AD for engine change 12.6.42; hit by Battle L5170 which overshot flare path after night landing, 12.6.42; 1 BGS 13.7.42; 1 AOS 13.12.43; 3 CRD 31.3.44; SOC 15.4.44.

R3929 Received 20.12.40; 1 AP 22.12.40; 1 AD 12.1.41; 1 BGS 3.3.41; 1 AOS 13.12.43; 3 CRD 3.4.44; 1 AOS 10.4.44; 1 CRD 22.4.44; SOC 29.12.44.

R3931 1 AP 19.1.41; 1 AD 3.2.41; 1 BGS 12.2.41; 1 AOS 13.12.43; 3 CRD 11.4.44; SOC 14.9.44.

R3934 1 AP 24.11.40; 1 AD 12.12.40; 1 BGS 23.12.40; damaged 13.6.42; 1 AOS 13.12.43; 1 CRD 13.4.44; SOC 29.12.44.

R3936 Received 3.12.40; 1 AP 8.12.40; 1 AD 20.12.40; 1 BGS 6.1.41. Turned, flicked onto back and dived into ground; crew (P/O D.E. Allan, LAC A.J. Powell, LAC H.J. Pope) all killed, 18.1.41; SOC and scrapped 30.1.41.

R3939 1 AP 24.11.40; 1 AD 12.12.40; 1 BGS 23.12.40; forcelanded after engine trouble 1.10.41; forcelanded after engine failure, Evans Head, 8.4.42; collided with Battle L5322, 3.12.42; struck by Battle R3925 on ground, 23.9.43; 1 AOS 13.12.43; 2 AD 13.1.44; 2 CRD 6.5.44; SOC 29.12.44.

R3944 Received 3.12.40; 1 AP 8.12.40; 1 AD 9.1.41; 1 BGS 20.1.41; 1 AOS 13.12.43; 1 CRD 14.2.44; 3 AOS store 19.7.44; 5 CRD 6.11.44; SOC 14.12.45.

R3948 1 AP 6.4.41; 1 AD 2.7.41; 2 BGS 21.7.41; port undercarriage collapsed on landing, Port Pirie, 13.8.41; forced landing after engine failure, 2.2.42; 3 AOS 13.12.43; 1 CRD 28.2.44; SOC 29.12.44.

R3949 1 AP 24.5.41; 1 BGS 13.9.41; 1 AOS 13.12.43; 3 CRD 3.4.44; 1 AOS 10.4.44; 1 CRD 24.4.44; SOC 29.12.44.

R3951 1 AP 24.5.41; 2 BGS 4.8.41; wing tip struck petrol tank while taxying, 7.10.41; forcelanded after engine failure, 29.1.42; ANA Parafield for anti-corrosive treatment 25.6.43; 5 AD 1.5.44; 2 CRD 15.11.44; SOC 2.11.44.

R3954 1 AP 16.8.41; 1 BGS 14.1.42; wheels-up landing, 7.9.42; 1 AOS 13.12.43; 3 CRD 9.4.44; SOC 14.9.44.

R3956 1 AP 6.4.41; 1 AD 2.7.41; 2 BGS 21.7.41; wheels-up landing, 9.5.43; 3 AOS 13.12.43; SOC 14.9.44.

R3957 1 AP 6.4.41; 1 AD 9.7.41; 2 BGS 4.8.41; wing struck by Battle L5018 on ground, 9.2.43; 3 AOS 13.12.43; SOC 14.9.44.

R4002 1 AP 9.5.41; 2 BGS 14.10.41; rudder struck by Battle R7380 while parked, 27.11.41; ANA Parafield 27.7.42; 2 BGS 8.4.43; 3 AOS 13.12.43; SOC at 3 CRD 20.3.44.

R4006 1 AP 19.1.41; 1 AD 3.2.41; crashed at Moss Vale, NSW, on flight to 1 BGS; F/Lt H.W. Ross killed, 11.2.41; SOC 26.2.41; wreckage re-located early 1995.

R4008 1 AP 19.1.41; 1 AD 4.2.41; 1 BGS 25.2.41; crashed on airfield due to defective undercarriage, Evans Head, 26.10.43; 1 AOS 13.12.43; 3 AD 12.1.44; 3 CRD 9.2.44; SOC 14.9.44.

R4009 1 AP 19.1.41; 1 AD 3.2.41; 1 BGS 25.2.41. Crashlanded on beach 3m N of Evans Head after elevator control rod burned through, 17.2.43; SOC 8.3.43.

R4012 1 AP 19.1.41; 1 AD 21.2.41; 1 AP 10.3.41; 1 AD 27.3.41; 1 BGS 31.3.41; 1 AOS 13.12.43; 3 CRD 9.4.44; SOC 14.9.44.

R4019 1 AP 6.4.41; 1 AD 9.7.41; 2 BGS 28.7.41; trainee holed cockpit and cut control tube during firing exercise, 22.7.41; 1 AD 16.8.41; 2 BGS 20.10.41; collided with refueller on tarmac, Port Pirie, 23.7.42; 3 AOS 13.12.43; SOC 14.9.44.

Battles dispersed at Port Pirie with a mixture of camouflaged and striped examples. (A Turner via D Vincent)

R4049   Received 20.12.40; 1 AP 22.12.40; 1 AD 12.1.41; 1 BGS 20.1.41; 1 AOS 13.12.43; 1 CRD 16.3.44; SOC 29.12.44.

R7377   1 AD 8.10.42; 2 BGS 10.3.43; 3 AOS 13.12.43; 1 CRD 28.2.44; forcelanded 10.7.44; 3 AOS 28.9.44; 5 CRD 6.11.44; SOC 14.12.45.

R7380   1 AP 12.9.41; 2 BGS 20.10.41; struck rudder of Battle R4002 on ground, 27.11.41; 3 AOS 13.12.43; 1 CRD 28.2.44; 3 AOS store 19.7.44; 5 CRD 6.11.44; SOC 14.12.45.

R7385   2 AD 15.7.42; ANA Mascot 15.7.42; 2 AD 19.10.42; 1 BGS 9.11.42; fitted dual control 12.10.43; 1 AOS 13.12.43; 3 CRD 31.3.44; SOC 14.9.44.

V1201   1 AP 23.5.41; 1 AD 9.7.41; 2 BGS 21.7.41; 2 OTU 18.5.42; 2 BGS 12.10.42; 1 AGS 20.12.43; taxied into Battle P6642, Evans Head, 30.3.44; starboard wing damaged in taxying accident; AGS Stored Reserve 22.5.45; 1 CRD 25.5.45; 1 SD 27.9.46; DAP for disposal 26.11.47; action completed 8.2.49.

V1202   2 AP; ANA 7.12.43; AGS 15.5.44; AGS Stored Reserve 22.5.45; 1 CRD 3.6.45; 1 SD 1.10.46; DAP for disposal 26.11.47; action completed 8.2.49.

V1203   1 AP 23.5.41; 1 AD 9.7.41; 2 BGS 28.7.41; 2 OTU 15.6.42; 1 AD 10.8.42; 3 BGS 9.11.42; 1 AGS 12.12.43; AGS Stored Reserve 22.5.45; 1 CRD 3.6.45; 1 SD 1.10.46; DAP for disposal 26.11.47; action completed 8.2.49.

V1206   Received 3.12.40; 1 AP 8.12.40; 1 BGS 6.1.41; 1 AD for engine change 12.6.42; 1 BGS 13.7.42; 1 OTU 31.8.42; 1 AGS 24.1.44; AGS Stored Reserve 22.5.45; 1 CRD 2.8.45; 1 SD 27.9.46; DAP for disposal 26.11.47; action completed 8.2.49.

V1207   Received 3.12.40; 1 AP 8.12.40; 1 BGS 6.1.41; 2 OTU 7.9.42; 2 BGS 28.9.42; ground-looped while taxying, damaged wing tip, Port Pirie, 7.12.42; ANA Parafield 25.1.43; 3 BGS 3.12.43; 1 AGS 12.12.43; AGS Stored Reserve 22.5.45; 1 CRD 3.6.45; 1 SD 27.9.46; DAP for disposal 26.11.47; action completed 8.2.49.

V1208   Received 3.12.40; 1 AP 8.12.40; 1 AD 9.1.41; 1 BGS 3.2.41; starboard oleo collapsed on landing, Evans Head, 25.2.42; 1 OTU 19.4.42; 1 AGS 12.1.44; AGS Stored Reserve 16.4.45; 1 CRD 24.5.45; 1 SD 27.9.46; DAP for disposal 26.11.47; action completed 8.2.49.

V1209   Received 3.12.40; 1 AP 8.12.40; 1 BGS 6.1.41; 1 AGS 13.12.43; AGS Stored Reserve 22.5.45; 1 CRD 2.8.45; destroyed by fire 5.4.46.

V1210   Received 14.9.42; ANA Mascot 13.11.42; 2 AP 22.12.42; 1 BGS 11.1.43; 1 AOS 13.12.43; AGS 3.3.44; AGS Stored Reserve 22.5.45; 1 CRD 3.6.45; 1 SD 27.9.46; DAP for disposal 26.11.47; action completed 8.2.49.

V1219   1 AD 14.9.42; 1 BGS 18.1.43; 1 AOS 13.12.43; AGS 6.3.44. Dived into ground near Seaspray Safety Range after smoke seen coming from engine; almost totally destroyed; crew (Sgt M.J. Fahey killed, W/O G.F. Maley uninjured), 18.8.44; SOC 12.9.44.

V1221   1 AP 8.2.43; 2 BGS 9.3.43; 3 BGS 22.5.43; 1 AGS 12.12.43; AGS Stored Reserve 22.5.45; 1 CRD 28.6.45; 1 SD 27.9.46; DAP for disposal 26.11.47; action completed 8.2.49.

V1227   Received 14.1.43; ANA Mascot 19.2.43; 2 AP 19.3.43; 2 BGS 22.3.43; 1 AGS 20.12.43; AGS Stored Reserve 22.5.45; 1 CRD 25.5.45; 1 SD 27.9.46; DAP for disposal 26.11.47; action completed 8.2.49.

V1232   1 AD 25.5.42; 24 Sqn 10.7.42; Townsville SHQ 31.8.42; 1 BGS 12.11.42. Dived into ground 1m NE of Evans Head while towing drogue; crew (P/O M.A. Tait, LAC N.J.H. Campbell) both killed, 10.2.43; SOC 1.3.43.

V1233   1 AP 15.3.43; 3 CF 6.4.43; bellylanded after engine failure after take-off, Mascot, 9.4.43; ANA Mascot 17.4.43; 2 AD 6.10.43; SOC 27.10.43.

V1235   1 AP 5.1.41; 1 AD 22.1.42; SHQ Bankstown 9.3.42; 2 AP 13.7.42; to tow De Havilland EG-1 glider to Special Duties and Performance Flight, Laverton 5.10.42; PT Flight 1 AD 8.10.42; port wing tip and flap bent, 15.12.43; 2 AD to tow gliders allotted to 2 AOS 30.10.43; found unsuitable for glider towing 6.11.43; 3 BGS 26.11.43; 1 AGS 21.12.43; AGS Stored Reserve 22.5.45; 1 CRD 3.6.45; 1 SD 27.9.46; DAP for disposal 26.11.47; action completed 8.2.49.

End of the line for Battles in the Port Pirie boneyard. (Bill Penglase via D Vincent)

V1237   1 AD 9.9.42; 3 BGS 11.11.42; forcelanded, Kilmany, Vic., 4.1.43; 1 AGS 12.12.43; wheels-up landing, 30.12.43; AGS Stored Reserve 22.5.45; 1 CRD 21.6.45; 1 SD 27.9.46; DAP for disposal 26.11.47; action completed 8.2.49.

V1238   1 AD 2.11.42; 2 BGS 1.3.43; 3 BGS 22.5.43; 1 AGS 12.12.43; wheels-up forced landing, 29.12.43; AGS Stored Reserve 16.4.45; 1 CRD 24.6.45; 1 SD 27.9.46; DAP for disposal 26.11.47; action completed 8.2.49.

V1241   1 AD 14.9.42; 3 BGS 11.11.42; forcelanded and hit trees after oil leak partially blinded pilot's view, 2.3.43; Ansett 19.3.43; 1 AD 18.10.43; 2 BGS 22.11.43; 1 AGS 20.12.43; AGS Stored Reserve 16.4.45; 1 CRD 21.6.45; destroyed by fire 5.4.46.

V1242   1 AD 10.9.42; 3 BGS 11.11.42; taxied into stationary Oxford BH739, 4.9.43; engine removed 5.4.44; 1 CRD 15.5.44; SOC 10.2.45.

V1243   1 AP 22.2.43; 1 OTU 21.3.43; 1 AGS 10.1.44; AGS Stored Reserve 22.5.45; 1 CRD 24.6.45; 1 SD 27.9.46; DAP for disposal 26.11.47; action completed 8.2.49.

V1250   1 AD 15.7.42; 3 BGS 11.11.42; forcelanded after engine failure, 21.3.43; 1 AGS 12.12.43; AGS Stored Reserve 22.5.45; 1 CRD 2.8.45; destroyed by fire 5.4.46.

V1270   1 AP 26.4.43; 1 OTU 1.7.43; 1 AGS 12.1.44; AGS Stored Reserve 22.5.45; 1 CRD 24.6.45; 1 SD 27.9.46; DAP for disposal 26.11.47; action completed 8.2.49.

V1271   1 AP 12.4.43; 3 BGS 19.5.43; 1 AD 1.9.43; 3 BGS 21.9.43; forcelanded after engine failure, 27.10.43; 1 AGS 12.12.43; CRD 13.3.44; SOC 14.7.44; Werribee Bombing Range, Vic., 24.1.45.

V1277   ANA Mascot 13.11.42; 2 AP 14.12.42; 1 BGS 21.12.42; 1 AGS 13.12.43; AGS Stored Reserve 22.5.45; 1 CRD 24.6.45; 1 SD 27.9.46; DAP for disposal 26.11.47; action completed 8.2.49.

Battles of No. 42 Air School, Port Elizabeth. (P Jarrett collection)

South African Air Force

This table lists 182 Battle aircraft, 179 of which were for the SAAF and three of which were for the Rhodesian Air Training Group. The 182 aircraft consisted of 123 Battles, 54 Battle T.T. target tugs and five Battle (T) trainers. Many of the Battles were adapted for target towing after arrival in South Africa.

The columns are as follows: a: SAAF serial; b: date shipped; c: RAF serial; d: Units; e: strike-off date. + indicates those aircraft SOC as a result of accidents or enemy action. Surviving records do not permit a complete listing of units.

a	b	c	d	e	a	b	c	d	e
901	25.4.39	K9402	11	19.6.40+	922	2.7.40	L5506	11/15/71 Flt/43 AS	30.7.45
902	1.6.40	L5165	11/15	11.6.41+	923	2.7.40	P5246	11	25.3.41+
903	6.6.40	L5024	11	11.6.41+	924	2.7.40	L5374	11	14.12.42
904	6.6.40	L5487	11/15/71 Flt/AAS/65 AS	30.11.44	925	2.7.40	P6596	11/15/44 AS/41 AS	30.7.45
905	1.6.40	L5168	11/15	8.8.41+	926	19.7.40	R3938	2 SFTS/11	12.7.41
906	1.6.40	L5172	11	2.4.41+	927	19.7.40	R3945	11	22.11.40+
907	1.6.40	L5178	11	31.3.41+	928	5.2.41	P2179	42 AS	2.43
908	6.6.40	L5088	11	4.11.40+	929	5.2.41	L5525	11/10/42 AS/10/45 AS	30.8.44
909	6.6.40	L5093	11	10.4.41+	930	5.2.41	L5103	42 AS/43 AS	30.12.43+
910	6.6.40	L5097	11	16.11.43	931	5.2.41	R4004	42 AS/43 AS	2.8.44
911	6.6.40	L5090	11	12.9.40+	932	5.2.41	L5014	42 AS	2.43
912	6.6.40	L5375	11	9.9.40+	933	5.2.41	R4003	42 AS	12.43
913	6.6.40	L5098	11	12.9.40+	934	5.2.41	P6560	42 AS	19.5.43
914	19.6.40	L5174	11/15	21.6.41+	935	5.2.41	L5059	42 AS/71 Flt/ 41 AS/65-66 AS	2.8.44
915	19.6.40	L5074	11/68 AS	14.6.43					
916	19.6.40	L5078	11	16.11.40+	936	5.2.41	P2307	42 AS/43 AS/45 AS	2.8.44
917	19.6.40	R7359	11	13.12.40+	937	5.2.41	K9471	42 AS	2.8.44
918	19.6.40	L5176	11	5.12.40+	938	5.2.41	N2126	42 AS	2.43
919	19.6.40	N2161	11	9.5.41+	939	16.2.41	L5077	42 AS	30.8.44
920	19.6.40	N2165	2 SFTS/11/15/ 44 AS/68 AS/THQ CF	19.6.46	940	16.2.41	L5549	42 AS	1.43
					941	16.2.41	P6561	42 AS/65-66 AS	30.9 44
921	19.6.40	R7358	2 SFTS/CFS/71 Flt/ 44 AS/43 AS	30.7.45	942	16.2.41	N2030	42 AS	11.4.44
					943	16.2.41	P6491	42 AS	10.2.42+

a	b	e	c	d
944	28.2.41	L5545	42 AS/65-66 AS	2.8.44
945	28.2.41	R7478	42 AS/41 AS/44 AS	2.8.44
946	28.2.41	L5240	42 AS/43 AS/45 AS	30.8.44
947	28.2.41	L5058	42 AS	2.8.44
948	9.3.41	L5464	41 AS/43 AS	2.8.44
949	10.3.41	L4991	41 AS/68 AS/69 AS as GI	22.6.44
950	29.3.41	P2177	41 AS/43 AS	2.8.44
951	29.3.41	P6501	41 AS	7.5.42+
952	29.3.41	L5123	41 AS	19.5.43
953	29.3.41	L5339	15/41 AS/43 AS	2.8.44
954	29.3.41	L5160	41 AS/68 AS/69 AS	22.6.44
955	29.3.41	P6555	41 AS	30.7.45
956	11.5.41	L5367	41 AS	2.8.44
957	11.5.41	L5548	41 AS/43 AS	2.8.44
958	11.5.41	L5191	41 AS	2.8.44
959	11.5.41	L5125	41 AS	2.8.44
960	11.5.41	L5579	41 AS/61/23 AS	30.7.45
961	11.5.41	L5494	41 AS/43 AS	2.8.44
962	5.41	K9181	41 AS	15.11.41+
963	5.41	L5363	41 AS/43/10/44 AS/43 AS	30.8.44
964	6.41		42 AS/43 AS	2.8.44
965	6.41		41 AS	2.8.44
966	6.41		41 AS	2.8.44
967	6.41		41 AS	2.8.44
968	15.6.41	K9400	42 AS	30.7.45
969	15.6.41	K9269	42 AS	12.42
970	30.9.41	L5210	41 AS/42 AS/68 AS	2.8.44
971	6.41	K7697	41 AS/43 AS/45 AS	2.8.44
972	6.41	L5307	41 AS	2.8.44
973	6.41		42 AS/43 AS	2.8.44
974	6.41		42 AS/43 AS/43/10/11 OTU	2.8.44
975	24.7.41	L5268	42 AS	2.43
976	7.41		42 AS	.47
977	7.41		42 AS/65-66 AS	30.8.44
978	9.7.41	L5285	42 AS/65-66 AS	30.8.44
979	7.41		41 AS/43 AS	30.8.44
980	11.7.41	L5034	41 AS/23 AS/61	2.12.43
981	9.7.41	K9392	41 AS/65-66 AS	2.8.44
982	7.41		42 AS/43 AS	2.8.44
983	11.7.41	L5199	41 AS/65-66 AS	2.8.44
984	9.41		41 AS/65-66 AS	2.8.44
985	9.41		41 AS	2.8.44
986	15.7.41	L5224	41 AS	20.11.42+
987	9.41		41 AS/68 AS/69 AS as IS314	21.4.44
988	29.6.41	P6549	42 AS/43 AS	30.8.44
989	29.6.41	N2051	41 AS/42 AS/43 AS	31.8.43
990	11.7.41	N2050	41 AS/43 AS	30.9.43
991	7.41		41 AS/44 AS/43 AS	2.8.44
992	7.41		42 AS	1.43
993	11.7.41	N2043	42 AS/65-66 AS	2.8.44
994	8.41		41 AS/43 AS/45 AS	11.4.44
995	8.41		41 AS/43 AS/45 AS	2.8.44
996	8.41		41 AS/43 AS	2.8.44
997	8.41		41 AS/43 AS/45 AS	2.8.44
998	10.9.41	K9246	7 AD	25.10.43
999	9.41		41 AS	2.8.44
1000	1.42		44 AS	2.8.44
1001	16.1.42	L5729	44 AS	2.8.44
1002	30.9.41	L5666	44 AS	4.8.42+
1003	29.1.42	K9410	42 AS/43 AS/45 AS	2.8.44
1004	1.42		42 AS	2.8.44
1005	29.1.42	K9385	3 AD	30.7.45
1006	29.1.42	K9296	3 AD	11.11.43
1007	1.42		3 AD	2.8.44
1008	30.1.42	L5060	41 AS	2.8.44
1009	2.42		41 AS/43 AS	2.8.44
1010	15.2.42	L5795	65-66 AS	30.8.44
1011	18.1.42	V1278	44 AS	2.8.44
1012	7.10.41	V1245	41 AS	2.8.44
1013	1.42		43 AS	2.8.44
1014	1.42		43 AS	30.8.44
1015	1.42		7 AD	2.8.44
1016	15.4.42	K9415	3 AD	12.8.43
1017	2.42		43 AS	30.8.44
1018	2.42		41 AS	2.8.44
1019	2.42		41 AS/44 AS	2.8.44
1020	2.42		45 AS	2.8.44
1021	2.42		43 AS/44 AS	2.8.44
1022	2.42		44 AS	2.8.44
1023	2.42		41 AS	2.8.44
1024	2.42		43 AS/44 AS	11.4.44
1025	2.42		42 AS	2.8.44
1026	2.42		42 AS	2.43
1027	2.42		45 AS	2.8.44
1028	2.42		41 AS/43 AS	2.8.44
1029	2.42		41 AS	2.8.44
1030	2.42		43 AS	30.8.44
1031	2.42		7 AD	2.43
1032	2.42		CFAD/11 OTU	2.8.44
1033	2.42		42 AS/65-66 AS	2.8.44
1034	20.3.42	R7402	43 AS	30.8.44
1035	3.42		41 AS/42 AS	30.8.44
1036	3.42		44 AS	2.8.44
1037	3.42		43 AS	30.8.44
1038	3.42		44 AS	2.8.44
1039	3.42		44 AS	2.8.44
1040	3.42		44 AS	4.12.43
1041	28.9.42	L4981	41 AS	2.8.44
1042	30.6.42	L5674	44 AS	2.8.44
1043	6.42		45 AS	2.8.44
1044	30.6.42	L5744	65-66 AS	2.8.44
1045	6.42		45 AS	2.8.44
1046	30.6.42	L5673	CFADPE/11 OTU	2.8.44
1047	30.6.42	V1215	65-66 AS	2.8.44
1048	30.6.42	L5664	45 AS	2.8.44
1049	6.42		7 AD	12.42
1050	6.42		7 AD	2.8.44
1051	16.7.42	L5777	CFADCT/66 AS/11 OTU	2.8.44
1052	7.42		7 AD	2.8.44
1053	7.42		7 AD	2.8.44
1054	7.42		CFAD/10	11.2.43+
1055	19.7.42	L5747	CFAD/65-66 AS	2.8.44
1056	7.42		10	2.8.44
1057	7.42		45 AS	2.8.44
1058	7.42	L5726	41 AS/44 AS	2.8.44
1059	7.42		41 AS	2.8.44
1060	29.7.42	L5752	65-66 AS	2.8.44
1061	6.42		45 AS/10/11 OTU	2.8.44
1062	6.42	L5661	7 AD	2.8.44
1063	6.42		11 OTU	30.8.44
1064	10.7.42	K9286		
1065	18.8.42	L5743	CFAD/10/66 AS	2.8.44
1066	9.42		65-66 AS/42 AS	2.8.44
1067	9.42		44 AS	2.8.44
1068	9.42		44 AS	2.8.44
1069	9.42		7 AD	2.8.44
1070	28.11.42	L5782	3 AD	11.11.43
1071	11.42		3 AD	23.3.45
1072	28.11.42	L5719	3 AD	23.3.45
1073	28.11.42	V1246	3 AD	12.8.43
1074	1.43		7 AD	2.8.44
1075	1.43		44 AS	2.8.44
1076	1.43		Lost at sea*	
1077	1.43		Lost at sea*	
1078	1.43		Lost at sea*	
1079	3.43		7 AD	2.8.44
1080	3.43		7 AD	19.8.44+
1081	3.43		7 AD	2.8.44
1082	3.43			2.8.44

*These were L5748, N2104 and V1266

Due to lack of surviving records, the following RAF serials cannot be matched up to the SAAF serials.

Serial	Date shipped	Serial	Date shipped
K7599	28.2.42	L5762	13.4.43
K7670	30.6.42	L5766	31.12.42
K9233	2.3.42	L5780	28.2.42
K9308	15.6.41	L5784	28.2.42
K9320	29.1.42	L5786	2.12.42
K9386	11.7.41	L5787	28.2.42
K9394	16.7.42	L5788	28.2.42
K9432	6.4.43	N2062	16.7.42
K9446	24.7.41	N2097	2.12.42
K9460	15.6.41	N2168	11.7.41
L4945	2.3.42	N2234	29.1.42
L5085	29.1.42	P2174	9.41
L5086	2.3.42	P2178	10.9.41
L5114	15.6.41	P2181	2.3.42
L5136	29.1.42	P2321	11.7.41
L5138	2.3.42	P2323	2.3.43
L5183	28.2.42	P5230	24.7.41
L5213	15.7.41	P5251	15.7.41
L5276	15.7.41	P6487	9.7.41
L5309	6.4.43	P6506	11.7.41
L5381	.43	P6529	15.6.41
L5395	28.2.41	P6533	11.7.41
L5415	12.2.41	P6761	31.12.42
L5543	16.3.42	V1213	19.7.42
L5576	28.2.42	V1214	19.7.42
L5630	31.12.42	V1216	2.3.42
L5634	28.11.42	V1217	21.3.42
L5638	31.12.42	V1218	21.3.42
L5669	19.7.42	V1220	2.3.42
L5685	29.5.42	V1224	21.3.42
L5708	28.2.42	V1225	23.6.41
L5718	19.7.42	V1230	28.2.42
L5730	29.7.42	V1231	31.12.43
L5731	29.5.42	V1248	21.3.42
L5739	21.5.41	V1269	21.5.41
L5740	18.8.42	V1272	16.1 42
L5745	20.3.42	V1273	13.4.43
L5749	29.5.42	V1274	31.12.42
L5753	21.5.41	V1280	29.7.42

Write-offs

930 43 AS. Lost power on take-off due to glycol leak and crashlanded, Port Alfred, 30.12.43

943 42 AS. Engine cut after take-off due to glycol leak; forcelanded on beach near Port Elizabeth, 10.2.42

951 41 AS. Overshot drogue during gunnery exercise; turned steeply, stalled and spun into ground near East London, 7.5.42; Lt W.H. Sutton, LAC P.V.James, LAC T.R. Middelman killed

962 41 AS. Engine cut; ditched off East London, 15.11.41

986 41 AS. Damaged elevators while low flying; swung into ground off turn, 20.11.42; Lt R.H. Johnson, 2/Lt R.M. Fraser killed

1002 44 AS. Undercarriage leg jammed up; stalled on approach anrd hit trees, Grahamstown, 4.8.42; 2/Lt C.M.J. van Rensburg killed

1054 10 Sqn. Engine cut; crashlanded, Cloverwood, and broke in two, 11.2.43

1080 2 AD. Crashed on landing, Alexandersfontein, 19.8.44; DBR

SAAF Codes

The following code letter/numbers are known to have been carried on Battles at various times.

41 AS: 949 (B31); 951 (B37); 952 (B32); 955 (B36); 962 (A45); 963 (B38); 986 (A32); 987 (A27); 990 (9);

42 AS: 928 (A3); 930 (B4); 931 (A1); 932 (B3); 933 (B1); 934 (A4); 936 (A9); 937 (A7); 939 (A5); 940 (B2); 941 (A18); 942 (A6); 943 (A10); 944 (A19); 946 (B5); 947 (A8); 964 (A13); 968 (B10); 969 (B13); 973 (B9); 974 (A16); 975 (A17); 977 (B11); 978 (A12); 982 (A14); 988 (A11); 989 (B7); 992 (B12); 993 (A15)

43 AS: 921 (BA); 948 (BB); 950 (BE); 953 (BH); 957 (BJ); 959 (BK); 961 (BL); 963 (BC); 964 (BD); 979 (BM); 982 (BN); 988 (BO); 991 (BX); 996 (BG); 1009 (BP); 1013 (BQ); 1014 (BR); 1017 (BS); 1028 (BT); 1030 (BU); 1034 (BV); 1037 (BW)

44 AS: 1036 (97)

45 AS: 1003 (D9); 1027 (T7)

A Battle Trainer of the South African Air Force. (via Dave Becker)

ROLL OF HONOUR

ROYAL AIR FORCE

Name	Unit	Date	Name	Unit	Date
Adams, Sgt P.E.F.	150 Sqn	7.6.40	Bileanski, FO PAF	300 Sqn	29.10.40
Ainsworth, AC1 R.T.	12 Sqn	14.5.40	Blackwell, PO E.W.	1 AAS	28.10.40
Alderson, Sgt K.	12 Sqn	14.5.40	Bligh, LAC P.I.	103 Sqn	10.6.40
Allan, Sgt P.A.	218 Sqn	11.8.39	Blom, FO W.M.	150 Sqn	27.7.40
Anderson, PO C.C.R.	88 Sqn	26.5.40	Blowfield, PO P.H.	12 Sqn	14.6.40
Anderson, PO J.R.	52 Sqn	18.10.39	Blyskal, Sgt F.	12 OTU	26.11.40
Anning, Sgt W.J.	105 Sqn	12.5.40	Boddam-Whetham, PO A.J.T.	1 FTS	25.10.41
Arnoux, Capt J.R.C. FFAF	10 B&GS	29.9.41	Boddington, Sgt J.P.	12 Sqn	8.6.40
Atkinson, Sgt G.	105 Sqn	14.5.40	Bond, LAC	7 AGS	31.8.41
Bailey, AC1 A.	218 Sqn	20.4.40	Boon, PO J.	150 Sqn	14.5.40
Ballantyne, Sgt J.	88 Sqn	12.6.40	Bowen, Sgt D.J.	150 Sqn	14.5.40
Barker, F/Sgt G.T.	150 Sqn	14.5.40	Boyle, LAC W.D.	142 Sqn	19.5.40
Barker, AC2 R.E.	7 B&GS	27.7.40	Brams, Sgt G.C.	103 Sqn	3.8.40
Barnett, PO M.E.F.	12 OTU	8.4.40	Branton, Sgt J.R.	226 Sqn	7.4.40
Barringer, AC2 M.A.	7 B&GS	27.7.40	Brooke, PO D.S.	2 B&GS	16.2.41
Barwell, PO G.F.A.	63 Sqn	3.11.39	Brookes, Sgt J.	142 Sqn	14.5.40
Bazalgette, PO F.S.	218 Sqn	12.5.40	Brooks, ALA	1 FTS	25.10.41
Beale, PO R.C.	150 Sqn	13.6.40	Bull, AC1 L.R.	98 Sqn	9.12.39
Beames, Sgt F.E.	88 Sqn	14.5.40	Burt, LAC C.S.	12 Sqn	8.6.40
Beer, Sgt E.J.	106 Sqn	13.1.39	Butler, Sgt A.W.	226 Sqn	11.12.37
Belcher, Sgt E.J.	12 Sqn	19.5.40	Butler, Sgt R.W.	88 Sqn	26.5.40
Bennett, AC2 H.B.	13 OTU	10.6.40	Buttery, PO R.T.L.	218 Sqn	14.5.40
Bevan, Sgt H.C.	12 Sqn	7.6.40	Bylinski, PO PAF	4 AOS	14.7.41

Name	Unit	Date	Name	Unit	Date
Calder, Sgt R.C.	88 Sqn	11.6.40	Findley, Sgt D.C.	103 Sqn	27.3.40
Callaghan, Sgt J.B.	226 Sqn	13.6.40	Finlayson, PO W.D. NZ	12 OTU	24.5.40
Calvert, PO J.L.	150 Sqn	19.9.39	Fisher, PO A.V. NZ	12 OTU	6.8.40
Cameron, FO D.A.	226 Sqn	10.5.40	Flisher, Sgt L.C.	218 Sqn	12.5.40
Campbell-Irons, PO I.	150 Sqn	12.5.40	Footner, Sgt K.D.	12 Sqn	12.5.40
Cann, LAC(G)	150 Sqn	27.7.40	Fortune, Sgt T.	150 Sqn	14.5.40
Carter, Cpl D.B.	150 Sqn	13.6.40	Foster, LAC A.J.E.	12 FTS	21.4.41
Cartwright, Sgt G.A.	105 Sqn	14.5.40	Franklin, Sgt W.H.J. (G)	150 Sqn	27.7.40
Chalmers, FO A.	13 OTU	10.6.40	Froggatt LAC T.	9 B&GS	31.5.41
Chapman, Sgt E.W.J.	88 Sqn	29.5.40	Garland, FO D.E.	12 Sqn	12.5.40
Clark, Cpl R.S.	226 Sqn	14.5.40	Gay, AC1 K.V.	150 Sqn	30.9.39
Cole, Sgt W.F.L.	150 Sqn	30.9.39	Gebicki, FO PAF	300 Sqn	13.10.40
Colman, S/L C.H.A.	RAE	1.10.40	Gegg, LAC J.H.K.	88 Sqn	14.5.40
Conner, AC2 B.	35 Sqn	29.10.39	Gillam, PO J.D.W.	88 Sqn	11.6.40
Cook, LA H.E.	7 FTS	9.1.40	Goebel, Sgt PAF	300 Sqn	29.10.40
Cooper, PO G.L.	35 Sqn	5.5.39	Gould, Sgt (G)	150 Sqn	27.7.40
Cooper, PO W.A.	103 Sqn	9.9.40	Grant, LAC D.L.	12 Sqn	14.6.40
Corelli, FO F.M.C.	150 Sqn	30.9.39	Grant, LAC L.O.	150 Sqn	8.6.40
Cotterell, Sgt N.C.	12 Sqn	13.6.40	Gray, Sgt T.	12 Sqn	12.5.40
Coughtrey, Cpl F.	105 Sqn	31.3.40	Gregory, AC1 K.G.	218 Sqn	11.5.40
Coull, AC2 A.W.A.	12 OTU	24.5.40	Gulley, PO A.R.	150 Sqn	13.6.40
Craig, PO H.J.	1 FTS	27.3.41	Hall, LAC (G)	150 Sqn	27.7.40
Crane, FO J.F.R.	218 Sqn	14.5.40	Hamilton, PO K.P.	9 AOS	24.11.39
Cranston, Sgt J.F.	9 B&GS	31.5.41	Hanna, Sgt R.	12 OTU	29.7.40
Craven, Sgt D.J.	12 OTU	11.6.40	Harrison, Sgt R.L.	98 Sqn	7.11.39
Cumins, LAC O.	9 B&GS	31.5.41	Hatton, LAC H.	105 Sqn	14.5.40
Dabrowski, PO T.	9 B&GS	25.10.40	Hayward, Sgt E.G.	103 Sqn	26.5.40
Davidson, Sgt E.	218 Sqn	20.4.40	Herriot, Sgt N.B.	218 Sqn	14.5.40
Davies, LAC L.D.	218 Sqn	12.5.40	Hettle, Sgt R.M.	142 Sqn	28.7.40
Davies, LAC P.K.	226 Sqn	7.4.40	Hibberd, Sgt S.D.	226 Sqn	14.5.40
De La Rue, F/Lt T.P.	1 FTS	25.1.41	Hibbert, Sgt E.	88 Sqn	23.5.40
De Sanoual-Servier, S/Lt	103 Sqn	9.9.40	Hinson, Sgt F.	98 Sqn	9.12.39
Dean, PO A.A.	9 AOS	24.11.39	Hinton, PO I.P.	103 Sqn	27.3.40
Devoto, FO D.	150 Sqn	31.3.40	Hislop, LAC J.	12 Sqn	14.6.40
Dindorf, Sgt K.	7 AOS	20.4.41	Horner, F/Sgt J.B.	218 Sqn	12.5.40
Dingle, FO K.H.	4 FPP	12.5.40	Hubbard, AC1 W.F.	103 Sqn	26.5.40
Dockrill, Sgt C.J.E.	218 Sqn	11.5.40	Hudson, Sgt G.H.	12 OTU	3.6.40
Dormer, Sgt F.F.	218 Sqn	11.5.40	Hull, PO J.E.	207 Sqn	19.9.39
Drabble, FO K.J.	103 Sqn	10.5.40	Hunt, Lt H.G. RN	1 FTS	17.5.41
Drcka, LAC Cz	4 AOS	13.7.41	Hurst, PO T.	105 Sqn	12.5.40
Drinkwater, Sgt F.	103 Sqn	9.9.40	Hytkag, LAC Cz	4 AOS	14.7.41
Duffy, Sgt P.P.	142 Sqn	4.8.40	Ignaszal, PO A.	12 OTU	26.11.40
Duncan Sgt T.S.	142 Sqn	23.8.40	Ing, Sgt H.G.	88 Sqn	20.6.39
Dundera, LAC Cz	4 AOS	13.7.41	Ing, FO J.	150 Sqn	14.5.40
Dunn, F/Sgt W.A.	226 Sqn	14.5.40	Ingram, Sgt N.J.	150 Sqn	12.5.40
Edgar, FO A.M.	105 Sqn	26.3.40	Ingram, AC2 W.	106 Sqn	13.1.39
Edwards, AC1 C.A.	88 Sqn	29.5.40	James, PO A.C.	SD Flt	28.4.41
Edwards, F/Lt R.H.	142 Sqn	26.9.42	Jennings, Sgt C.M.	218 Sqn	11.5.40
Eggington, Sgt A.W.	88 Sqn	20.9.39	John, AC1 D.J.	88 Sqn	20.9.39
Egierski, Sgt PAF	300 Sqn	13.10.40	Johnson, Sgt A.G.	12 Sqn	14.5.40
Elliott, AC2	7 AOS	20.4.41	Jones, Cpl A.E.	105 Sqn	26.3.40
Ellis, PO J.	63 Sqn	25.11.38	Jones, Sgt T.	142 Sqn	19.5.40
Emery, Sgt G.H.	12 Sqn	14.6.40	Jooris, Sgt R.A.	12 OTU	12.9.40
Evans, AC1 E.	9 B&GS	25.10.40	Kendall, ALA G.J.B.	1 FTS	27.3.41
Everett, Sgt W.S.	88 Sqn	20.9.39	Keogh, AC1 R.A.W.	52 Sqn	18.10.39
Everitt, Sgt M.V.	12 OTU	24.7.40	Kerridge, F/Lt B.R.	226 Sqn	10.5.40
Evitt, FO H.G.	88 Sqn	29.5.40	Kilbuern, Sgt R.	12 FTS	21.4.41
Farrell, FO P.A.L.	142 Sqn	8.4.40	Killinski, PO J. PAF	301 Sqn	25.9.40
Fengler, PO D.	301 Sqn	8.8.40	Kinane, FO W.	218 Sqn	11.8.39
Ferrin, LAC J.L.	12 Sqn	12.5.40	Kirby, Sgt R.A.P.	88 Sqn	11.5.40
Field, Sgt F.	12 Sqn	7.6.40	Kirdy, PO M.J.A.	142 Sqn	28.7.40
Figg, LAC H.R.	150 Sqn	12.5.40	Kitching, PO	7 AGS	22.6.41

Name	Unit	Date	Name	Unit	Date
Krzysztoszek, Sgt J. PAF	1 OTU	11.7.42	Radford, AC1 E.A.W.	88 Sqn	20.9.39
Lamble, LAC P.J.	103 Sqn	10.5.40	Radley, Sgt T.J.	12 Sqn	1.8.40
Lamont, AC1 R.R.	12 OTU	24.5.40	Randle, AC1 J.T.S.	207 Sqn	23.3.39
Langton, AC1 L.M.	142 Sqn	10.5.40	Raper, Sgt L.A.	142 Sqn	8.4.40
Laws, PO F.S.	142 Sqn	10.5.40	Rea, FO K.M.	226 Sqn	14.6.40
Leonard, AC1 D.L.	12 OTU	3.6.40	Reynolds, LAC L.R.	12 Sqn	12.5.40
Levitt, Sgt W.E.	1 AAS	13.10.39	Rhind, FO G.A.C.	35 Sqn	29.10.39
Lewis, LAC P.A.	88 Sqn	7.6.40	Richardson, AC1	7 AOS	20.4.41
Little, Cpl H.F.	226 Sqn	14.5.40	Richardson, AC1 V.W.L.	218 Sqn	13.11.39
Livingston, Sgt A.	226 Sqn	20.5.40	Ridley, PO F.H.	105 Sqn	14.5.40
Long, Sgt B.A.	12 Sqn	1.8.40	Robb, Sgt W.	12 OTU	29.7.40
Long, Sgt H.E.M.	12 OTU	12.9.40	Roberts, AC1 I.	218 Sqn	11.8.39
Longcluse, Sgt N.	142 Sqn	28.7.40	Roberts, AC1	63 Sqn	25.7.39
Looker, AC1 E.W.	35 Sqn	29.10.39	Robertson, FO D.K.	98 Sqn	7.11.39
Lown, LAC P.H.	12 OTU	11.6.40	Robertson, FO D.M.	1 AAS	28.10.40
Lowry, Sgt L.M.	142 Sqn	22.8.40	Robinson, AC1 W.	218 Sqn	14.5.40
MacDermott, F/Sgt J.B.	59 OTU	15.11.42	Rochowski, FO L. PAF	10 B&GS	29.9.41
Mace, F/Lt C.R.	105 Sqn	31.3.40	Rogers, F/Lt K.R.	142 Sqn	14.5.40
Mahon, AC2 W.	TTF	26.2.40	Rolls, PO P.C.	207 Sqn	13.12.38
Makarewicz, PO W.	12 OTU	26.11.40	Ross, AC1 A.S.	103 Sqn	12.5.40
Malcolm, AC2 K.	207 Sqn	19.9.39	Ross, Sgt W.G.	88 Sqn	14.5.40
Malcolm, Sgt P.	38 MU	16.12.40	Rozmiarek, LAC E.	17 OTU	23.9.40
Mallard, Sgt J.W.	103 Sqn	3.8.40	Russell, F/Sgt J.A.	226 Sqn	11.6.40
Marland, Sgt F.	12 Sqn	12.5.40	Saunders, FO J.R.	150 Sqn	30.9.39
Marrows, Sgt E.	226 Sqn	11.6.40	Sedgwick, Sgt A.F.	226 Sqn	14.5.40
Marsalek, LAC Cz	4 AOS	14.7.41	Sewell, AC1 H.B.	103 Sqn	12.5.40
Marsh, AC1 J.L.	150 Sqn	19.9.39	Sharp, AC2 A.	5 B&GS	1.10.40
Martin, AC1 S.	150 Sqn	14.5.40	Sharpe, Cpl (G)	150 Sqn	27.7.40
Masters, Sgt H.E.	142 Sqn	4.8.40	Sharpe, AC2 J.A.	103 Sqn	27.3.40
McElligot, PO J.J.	12 Sqn	19.5.40	Shelton-Jones, Sgt C.	12 Sqn	14.5.40
McKrill, LAC	12 Sqn	7.6.40	Shennan, PO P.	15 Sqn	5.4.39
McLoughlin, Sgt G.P.	226 Sqn	11.6.40	Sheperd, AC2 R.	7 B&GS	4.3.41
Millar, AC2 M.B.	226 Sqn	14.5.40	Shepherd, Sgt A.J.	63 Sqn	25.7.39
Miller, Sgt R.F.	142 Sqn	10.5.40	Shepherd, PO G.C.	207 Sqn	23.3.39
Mitchell, Sgt L.G.	12 OTU	12.9.40	Sherriff, Sgt A.A.	63 Sqn	25.7.39
Morawa, Sgt PAF	300 Sqn	13.10.40	Shuttleworth, PO R.O.	12 OTU	2.8.40
Morgan, Sgt A.C.	105 Sqn	14.5.40	Sigley, PO P.N. NZ	12 OTU	24.5.40
Morgan-Dean, FO G.B.	103 Sqn	12.5.40	Skidmore, PO B.M.	88 Sqn	11.5.40
Morris, Sgt P.F.	226 Sqn	22.10.40	Skowron, Sgt H. PAF	10 B&GS	18.7.41
Mortimer, Mid O.G. RN	12 OTU	24.7.40	Skryzpczak, LAC F. PAF	1 AAS	28.10.40
Morton, PO E.E.	103 Sqn	12.5.40	Smith, AC1 B.B.C.	13 OTU	10.6.40
Moseley, Sgt V.H.	226 Sqn	14.5.40	Smith, Sgt T.D.	103 Sqn	10.5.40
Moss, FO B.E.	12 Sqn	1.8.40	Sokolowski, PO G. PAF	12 OTU	1.10.40
Naylor, Sgt C.L.	7 AGS	31.8.41	Sokulski, FO J. PAF	10 B&GS	29.9.41
Nolan, AC1 W.J.	150 Sqn	14.5.40	Staunch, AC2 J.	7 B&GS	4.3.41
Norman, Sgt F.C.T.	207 Sqn	23.3.39	Stephens, A/Sgt G.M.	12 OTU	24.5.40
Nugent, LAC R.H.	142 Sqn	14.5.40	Stewart, ALA D. RN	1 FTS	28.10.41
Odstreilek, Sgt O. Cz	12 OTU	30.9.40	Stewart, AC1 F. (G)	150 Sqn	27.7.40
Osmala, Sgt S.	5 B&GS	1.10.40	Sullivan, AC2	7 AGS	31.8.41
Owens, Sgt T.	TTF	26.2.40	Swann, F/Sgt G.T.	7 AGS	22.6.41
Page, F/Sgt D.A.	88 Sqn	20.9.39	Sweeney, AC2 J.	35 Sqn	5.5.39
Parker, F/Lt E.R.	150 Sqn	10.5.40	Szmajdowicz, Sgt PAF	300 Sqn	29.10.40
Parsons, AC1 W.L.	88 Sqn	11.5.40	Taylor, LAC A.J.	218 Sqn	14.5.40
Pearce, Sgt E.A.	142 Sqn	23.8.40	Taylor, AC1 W.F.	150 Sqn	31.3.40
Percival, Sgt F.J.	226 Sqn	14.5.40	Thomas, FO B.K.	12 FTS	18.5.41
Pettit, Sgt H.E.	105 Sqn	26.3.40	Thomas, FO C.V.	103 Sqn	10.6.40
Pike, Sgt R.C.L.	218 Sqn	13.11.39	Thomas, AC1 D.L.	150 Sqn	30.9.39
Pitfield, F/Lt A.L.	88 Sqn	12.6.40	Thomson, PO B.P.	12 OTU	11.6.40
Pittar, Sgt W.D.F.	150 Sqn	8.6.40	Thomson, AC1 J.S.	105 Sqn	14.5.40
Posselt, PO A.F.	150 Sqn	14.5.40	Thomson, Sgt R.C.	12 OTU	29.7.40
Potter, AC1 J.	105 Sqn	14.5.40	Thynne, PO R.	218 Sqn	13.11.39
Puklo, PO J. PAF	7 B&GS	2.5.41	Tipple, PO H.G.	264 Sqn	16.12.39

Name	Unit	Date	Name	Unit	Date
Tock, Sgt G.	7 B&GS	4.3.41	Wheeler, FO H.T.	7 B&GS	27.7.40
Todd, Cpl H.	142 Sqn	14.5.40	Whelan, AC1 M.	88 Sqn	23.5.40
Tompkins, Sgt J.F.	35 Sqn	5.5.39	White, Sgt E.F.	12 Sqn	14.5.40
Tremeger, Sgt F.J.	142 Sqn	4.8.40	White, PO H.E.	105 Sqn	14.5.40
Trescothic, Sgt H.F.	142 Sqn	14.5.40	Whiteley, Sgt B.O.	12 FTS	27.4.40
Turner, Sgt J.D.	150 Sqn	14.5.40	Whittle, Sgt E.J.M.	88 Sqn	11.5.40
Turner, Sgt L.	226 Sqn	13.6.40	Wickham, PO A.E.	88 Sqn	23.5.40
Tutt, Sgt H.J.F.	150 Sqn	13.6.40	Wigham, A/Sgt E.	12 OTU	24.5.40
Tyson, ALA S.H. RN	1 FTS	11.11.41	Wilburn, Cpl C.E.	142 Sqn	8.4.40
Ustyanowski, Sgt W.	9 B&GS	25.10.40	Wilcox, Sgt R.J.	12 Sqn	14.6.40
Vano, AC2 N.V.	150 Sqn	14.5.40	Wilkes, AC2 F.J.	98 Sqn	7.11.39
Vaughan, FO E.R.D.	12 Sqn	14.5.40	Wilks, Sgt E.	88 Sqn	26.5.40
Vernon, FO J.E.	150 Sqn	7.6.40	Williams, AC2 E.J.	7 B&GS	2.5.41
Wall Sgt C.	150 Sqn	31.3.40	Williams, Sgt J.D.F.	150 Sqn	14.5.40
Wall, F/Lt R.N.	105 Sqn	14.5.40	Williams, Sgt R.J.W.	103 Sqn	6.8.39
Waterston, AC2 W.C.	218 Sqn	14.5.40	Williams, PO T.R.	207 Sqn	28.11.39
Weeks, F/Lt R.A.	150 Sqn	8.6.40	Wilson, Sgt G.A.	150 Sqn	7.6.40
Wells, Sgt	4 AOS	13.7.41	Wood, Sgt E.P.	12 OTU	24.7.40
Wells, LAC C.R.	105 Sqn	12.5.40	Woodmason, Sgt T.B.	150 Sqn	19.9.39
Wetherburn, LAC W.	10 B&GS	18.7.41			

ROYAL CANADIAN AIR FORCE

Name	Unit	Date	Name	Unit	Date
Aitkens, LAC E.T.	8 B&GS	4.12.42	McCulloch, ALA W.	31 SFTS	9.6.41
Astell, LAC E.W. RAF	9 B&GS	7.10.43	McKinstry, LAC K.	9 B&GS	7.10.43
Bail, LAC J.P.A.	5 B&GS	23.7.42	McLean, F/Sgt D.J. NZ	9 B&GS	27.7.43
Barber, LAC F.G.	1 B&GS	9.12.41	McNabb, LAC R.	1 B&GS	6.7.41
Bounds, FO E.J.	1 B&GS	9.12.41	McNally, AC2 J.H.	4 B&GS	8.12.40
Bourne, AC2 E.W.	4 B&GS	8.12.40	McNeill, Sgt H.J.M.	7 B&GS	18.9.42
Brochu, Sgt G.W.M.	9 B&GS	31.5.43	Mongomery, FO E.	Ferry Sqn	10.2.42
Buzik, AC2 J.P.	3 B&GS	11.7.42	Morin, LAC G.G.	8 B&GS	19.8.42
Coles LAC C.A.	5 B&GS	1.12.41	Moss, Sgt N.	3 B&GS	11.7.42
Corbett, PO H.K.	Trenton	14.10.39	Musto, LAC F.W.A.	7 B&GS	18.9.42
Cote, Sgt J.L.G.	5 B&GS	1.12.41	Naoum, Sgt E.	5 B&GS	23.3.42
Crothers, LAC R.K.	5 B&GS	1.12.41	Nickerson, LAC O.V.	5 B&GS	23.7.42
Dean, F/Sgt R.	9 B&GS	7.10.43	Off, LAC C.	3 B&GS	11.7.42
Duncan, LAC D.W.	7 B&GS	2.9.42	Oldstead, PO G.J.	Trenton	14.10.39
Dunn, Sgt E.H.	5 B&GS	23.7.42	Parker, LAC R.C.	5 B&GS	23.7.42
Fellows, LAC B.E.	31 SFTS	14.7.41	Pearson, Sgt W.J.	10 B&GS	31.12.43
Fenner, LAC L.	3 B&GS	27.6.41	Pigerham, LAC H.C.	31 B&GS	14.8.42
Gilmour, LAC W.	7 B&GS	18.9.42	Reardon, LAC J.A.	31 SFTS	13.4.41
Gray, LAC J.S.W.	1 B&GS	9.12.41	Reed, LAC A.C.	1 B&GS	18.8.42
Halamka, PO A.F.	9 B&GS	19.5.42	Revzen, AC2 H.	9 B&GS	27.7.43
Harris, LAC C.G.	5 B&GS	23.3.42	Rooke, Cpl C.J.	9 B&GS	19.5.42
Harris, LAC E.P.	5 B&GS	23.3.42	Sandman, LAC R.B.	8 B&GS	19.8.42
Hood, LAC D.F.	5 B&GS	23.3.42	Scanlon, AC2 D.M.	10 B&GS	31.12.43
Hood, FO L.A.	4 B&GS	8.12.40	Shaw, LAC I.J.	9 B&GS	19.5.42
Hower, LAC G.G.J.	5 B&GS	23.3.42	Stephen, PO M.1.	Camp Borden	2.9.40
Huntula, AC2 H.W.	10 B&GS	31.12.43	Taggart, LAC C.	1 B&GS	6.7.41
Jones, LAC D.N.	31 B&GS	14.8.42	Trueman, LAC S.G.	9 B&GS	7.10.43
Kempton-Werchie, Sgt B.NZ	31 B&GS	14.8.42	Walker, Sgt W.G.	3 B&GS	27.6.41
Kirkby, LAC W.M.	1 B&GS	18.8.42	Ward, LAC R.A.	5 B&GS	23.7.42
Lambert, LAC K.A.	7 B&GS	2.9.42	Weal, LAC K.G.	9 B&GS	19.5.42
Low, Sgt L.R.	8 B&GS	19.8.42	Whitehead, Sgt J.W.	1 B&GS	18.8.42
Lowe, Sgt C.P.A.	7 B&GS	2.9.42	Williams, Sgt E.L.	8 B&GS	4.12.42

ROYAL AUSTRALIAN AIR FORCE

Name	Unit	Date	Name	Unit	Date
Alexander, F/Sgt J.S.	3 B&GS	17.11.43	Johns, Sgt R.A.	2 B&GS	9.9.43
Allan, PO D.E.	1 B&GS	18.1.41	Mooney, LAC C.L.	1 B&GS	8.6.43
Campbell, LAC N.H.J.	1 B&GS	10.2.43	Ninness, Sgt G.N.	2 B&GS	9.9.43
Dore, LAC G.L.	2 B&GS	20.5.43	Norris, PO	1 AD	16.1.41
Epps, LAC C.T.	3 B&GS	7.6.43	Plummer, Sgt R.M.	2 B&GS	13.8.42
Fahey, Sgt M.J.	AGS	18.8.44	Pope, LAC H.J.	1 B&GS	18.1.41
Finch, Sgt G.W.	1 B&GS	8.6.43	Powell, LAC A.J.	1 B&GS	18.1.41
Fisher, LAC D.C.	3 B&GS	7.6.43	Price, LAC L.G.	2 B&GS	13.8.42
Gardiner, LAC J.D.	2 B&GS	9.9.43	Ross, F/Lt	1 AD	11.2.41
Gilmore, LAC A.P.	2 B&GS	20.5.43	Scholz, Sgt S.R.	2 B&GS	22.11.42
Grant, LAC L.	2 B&GS	9.9.43	Scott, Sgt	2 B&GS	9.9.43
Griffiths, LAC R.D.	2 B&GS	9.9.43	Stephen, AC1	2 B&GS	9.9.43
Grimsley, LAC D.F.	1 AOS	14.1.44	Stevens, Sgt R.P.	3 B&GS	7.6.43
Hampstead, Sgt L.J.	2 B&GS	20.5.43	Tait, PO M.A.	1 B&GS	10.2.43
Harrison, LAC G.H.	1 AOS	14.1.44	Thomson, AC1 D.	2 B&GS	22.11.42
Hopper, Sgt W.W.	1 AOS	14.1.44	Venables, AC1 L.A.	2 B&GS	9.9.43
			Wright, PO	1 AD	16.1.41

SOUTH AFRICAN AIR FORCE

Name	Unit	Date	Name	Unit	Date
Adams, Sgt E.	11 Sqn	12.9.40	MacDonald, Lt M.	11 Sqn	13.12.40
Armstrong, Lt E.G.	11 Sqn	12.9.40	Marais, F/Sgt P.C.	11 Sqn	13.12.40
Ferreira, Lt M.G.T.	11 Sqn	10.4.41	Middelman, LAC T.R.	41 AS	7.5.42
Fraser, 2/Lt R.M.	41 AS	20.11.42	Schrooder, F/Sgt A.	11 Sqn	13.12.40
Grant, Sgt R.	11 Sqn	10.4.41	Steyn, Lt E.J.	15 Sqn	11.6.41
James, LAC P.V.	41 AS	7.5.42	Sutton, Lt W.H.	41 AS	7.5.42
Johnson, Lt R.H.	41 AS	20.11.42	van Rensburg, 2/Lt C.M.J.	44 AS	4.8.42
Kelly, Sgt F.W.	15 Sqn	11.6.41			

BELGIAN AIR FORCE

Name	Unit	Date
de Caters, Capt Jacques	5eme Esc	8.12.38
Delvigne, Adj	5eme Esc	11.5.40
Glorie, Capt	5eme Esc	11.5.40
Moens, Sgt	5eme Esc	11.5.40
Timmermans, Adj	9eme Esc	11.5.40

ROYAL HELLENIC AIR FORCE

Name	Unit	Date
Arnides, Sgt F	33 Mira	15.11.40
Papas, 2Lt A	33 Mira	15.11.40
Pitsikas, Major D	33 Mira	15.11.40
Stathakis, L/Col D	33 Mira	11.3.41

Codes

As individual identification, Battles began to carry code letters soon after entering service. Initially, aircraft also carried the squadron number but during the Munich crisis of October 1938, these were removed and pairs of letters substituted. Where still in use by the unit, the individual letters were retained. The codes applied were:
No.12 - QE; No.15 - EF; No.35 - WT; No.40 - OX; No.52 - MB; No.63 - JO, later ON; No.88 - HY, later QF; No.103 - GV; No.105 - MT; No.142 - KB; No.150 - DG; No.185 - ZM; No.207 - NJ; No.218 - SV; No.226 - KP. On the outbreak of war, these were changed to the following:

No.12 - PH; No.15 - LS; No.35 - TL; No.40 - BL; No.52 - none; No.63 - UB; No.88 - RH; No.103 - PM; No.105 - GB; No.142 - QT; No.150 - JN; No.185 - VO; No.207 -EM; No.218 - HA; No.226 - MQ. In addition, No.300 used BH, No.301 - GR; No.304 - NZ.

Listed below are known code letters used on Battles. No central record was kept of the allocations of individual code letters which were selected by the squadron or station. Where aircraft were replaced, the letters were re-allotted. On occasions, the letter was changed while the aircraft was still with the squadron.

K7559	63-A	K9301	EF-L/15 Sqn	K5451	PH-C/12 Sqn
K7560	63-M	K9308	OX-S/40 Sqn	L5491	PH-Z/12 Sqn
K7576	105-D	K9311	EF-O/15 Sqn	L5499	BH-Y/300 Sqn
K7578	105-F	K9322	RH-K/88 Sqn	L5520	PH-N/12 Sqn
K7594	226-C	K9324	HA-B/218 Sqn	L5535	GR-Q/301 Sqn
K7596	226-C	K9325	HA-D/218 Sqn	L5538	PH-R/12 Sqn
K7597	226-D	K9330	MQ-W/226 Sqn	L5540	JN-C/150 Sqn
K7602	52-B	K9353	HA-J/218 Sqn	L5544	RH-K/88 Sqn
K7606	52-N	K9358	EF-V/15 Sqn	L5546	PH-U/12 Sqn
K7607	52-L/J	K9368	PH-F/12 Sqn	L5555	GR-H/301 Sqn
K7612	52-U	K9372	GV-K/103 Sqn	L5558	RH-J,C/88 Sqn
K7612	A/16 ERFTS	K9377	QE-F/12 Sqn	L5559	RH-B/88 Sqn
K7613	B/16 ERFTS	K9423	NE-G/63 Sqn	L5571	RH-D/88 Sqn
K7620	226-H	K9471	WT-M/35 Sqn	L5572	RH-R/88 Sqn
K7622	105-Q	K9471	PM-N/103 Sqn	L5574	RH-Q/88 Sqn
K7622	122/22 ERFTS	K9483	DG-O/150 Sqn	L5580	PH-X/12 Sqn
K7624	226-B	L4944	PH-R/12 Sqn	L5590	RH-G/88 Sqn
K7627	98/1 SFTS	L4949	JN-C/E/150 Sqn	L5594	RH-J/88 Sqn
K7649	63-B	L4949	PH-V/12 Sqn	L5596	RH-A/88 Sqn
K7650	63-M	L4950	PH-V/12 Sqn	L5597	PH-U/12 Sqn
K7654	218-O	L4951	GB-C/105 Sqn	L5664	JQ-O/2 AACU
K7655	218-F	L4952	PH-X/12 Sqn	L5671	C/1 OTU
K7658	218-J	L4958	ON-R/63 Sqn	L5707	MF-X/55 OTU
K7660	218-L	L4996	MQ-L/226 Sqn	L5784	11/10 AGS
K7663	218-N	L5010	103-C	N2147	BH-Q/300 Sqn
K7664	218-O	L5038	103-H	M2150	PH-Y/12 Sqn
K7665	218-P	L5127	PH-K/12 Sqn	N2157	103-R
K7666	218-Q	L5137	S/3 BGS	N2162	PH-Q/12 Sqn
K7709	35-O	L5149	RH-Y/88 Sqn	N2163	103-T
K7712	207-C	L5188	PH-O/12 Sqn	N2231	PH-X/12 Sqn
K9176	35-G	L5190	PH-P/12 Sqn	N2241	BH-G/300 Sqn
K9180	35-X	L5216	RH-M/88 Sqn	P2199	RH-N/88 Sqn
K9182	MQ-J/226 Sqn	L5227	PH-J/12 Sqn	P2204	PH-K/12 Sqn
K9183	MQ-R/226 Sqn	L5241	PG-G/12 Sqn	P2243	PH-U/12 Sqn
K9191	GB-W/105 Sqn	L5285	RH-M/88 Sqn	P2261	RH-F/88 Sqn
K9200	207-Z	L5317	BH-T/300 Sqn	P2265	MQ-B/226 Sqn
K9227	15-E	L5324	PH-A/12 Sqn	P2306	103-D
K9228	15-F	L5328	PH-A/12 Sqn	P2307	103-K
K9223	15-J	L5330	RH-O/88 Sqn	P2308	103-G
K9244	RH-C/88 Sqn	L5336	103-F	P2320	103-B
K9248	RH-L/88 Sqn	L5356	BH-R/300 Sqn	P2322	PH-J/12 Sqn
K9261	103-A	L5361	RH-H/88 Sqn	P2354	MQ-H/226 Sqn
K9263	103-B	L5383	PH-F/12 Sqn	P2354	RH-L/88 Sqn
K9264	103-L	L5393	RH-P/88 Sqn	P6555	GR-G/301 Sqn
K9267	103-E	L5395	103-P	P6569	GR-D/301 Sqn
K9268	103-N	L5398	PH-G/12 Sqn	P6597	PH-V/12 Sqn
K9269	103-F	L5415	PH-O/12 Sqn	P6678	NZ-X/304 Sqn
K9271	103-G	L5420	PH-N/12 Sqn	P6723	NZ-Y/304 Sqn
K9273	SV-R/218 Sqn	L5427	BH-K/300 Sqn	R7365	12/1 SFTS
K9273	HA-R/218 Sqn	L5431	103-E	V1204	MF-X/59 OTU
K8282	RH-P/88 Sqn	L5439	PH-N/12 Sqn		

ABBREVIATIONS

AA	Anti-aircraft		GI	Ground instructional (airframe)
AACU	Anti-aircraft Co-operation Unit		GO	Gas-operated
AAGS	Air Armament and Gas School		Gp	Group
AAS	Air Armament School		GP	General Purpose
AASF	Advanced Air Striking Force		GRS	General Reconnaissance School
AAEE	Aeroplane and Armament Experimental		HAD	Home Aircraft Depot
	Establishment		HE	High Explosive
AC	Air Command (RCAF)		HF/DF	High Frequency Direction Finding
AD	Aircraft Depot		HQ	Headquarters
AES	Air Engineering School		IOM	Isle of Man
AGS	Air Gunners School		IOW	Isle of Wight
AI	Air Interception		JATS	Joint Air Training Scheme
ALG	Advanced landing ground		LAM	Long Aerial Mine
AMDP	Air Member for Development and Production		LC	Low Capacity
AMSE	Air Member for Supply and Equipment		LG	Landing ground
ANA	Australian National Airways		Mk	Mark
AOC	Air Officer Commanding		MU	Maintenance Unit
AOS	Air Observers School		Navex	Navigation Exercise
AP	Aircraft Park		NCO	Non-Commissioned Officer
APC	Armament Practice Camp		NFT	No further trace
APU	Aircraft Performance Unit (RAAF)		OAFU	Observers Advanced Flying Unit
ARD	Aircraft Repair Depot		OTU	Operational Training Unit
AS	Anti-Submarine		PATP	Packed Aircraft Transit Pool
AS	Air School (SAAF)		(P)FTS	Polish Flying Training School
AS	Armstrong Siddeley		PoW	Prisoner of War
ASP	Air Stores Park		PRU	Photographic Reconnaissance Unit
ATA	Air Transport Auxiliary		PV	Private Venture
ATC	Air Training Corps		RAAF	Royal Australian Air Force
ATC	Air Traffic Control (RAAF)		RAE	Royal Aircraft Establishment
ATS	Armament Training Station		RAF	Royal Air Force
BAFF	British Air Forces in France		RATG	Rhodesia Air Training Group
BEF	British Expeditionary Force		RCAF	Royal Canadian Air Force
BER	Beyond Economical Repair		RD	Repair Depot (RCAF)
BGS	Bombing and Gunnery School		RFT Flt	Refresher Flying Training Flight
CAONBGS	Combined Air Observer, Navigation, Bombing		RHAF	Royal Hellenic Air Force
	and Gunnery School		RL	Royal Laboratory
CAS	Chief of the Air Staff		RNZAF	Royal New Zealand Air Force
CCF	Canadian Car & Foundry		R-R	Rolls-Royce
CinC	Commander-in-Chief		ROS	Repaired on site
CDC	Commonwealth Disposals Commission		RD	Radio School
CF	Communications Flight		RSU	Repair and Servicing Unit
C&F Flt	Communications & Ferry Flight		SAAF	South African Air Force
CFS	Central Flying School		SAC	School of Army Co-operation
CGS	Central Gunnery School		SofAE	School of Aeronautical Engineering
CO	Commanding Officer		SAP	Semi-Armour-Piercing
CRD	Civilian Repair Depot		SD	Special Duties
CRD	Controller of Research & Development		SD	Stores Depot
CTS	Conversion Training Squadron (RCAF)		SF	Station Flight
CU	Communications Unit (RAAF)		SF	Servicing Flight
DAP	Department of Aircraft Production (RAAF)		SFTS	Service Flying Training School
DBF	Destroyed by fire		S&H	Short Bros. & Harland
DBR	Damaged beyond Repair		SHQ	Station Headquarters
D/F	Direction Finding		SNC	School of Naval Co-operation
DFC	Distinguished Flying Cross		SOC	Struck off Charge
DFM	Distinguished Flying Medal		Sqn	Squadron
DTD	Director of Technical Development		SofTT	School of Technical Training
EAC	Eastern Air Command (RCAF)		SR	Stored Reserve (RCAF)
ED	Equipment Depot		SRAF	Southern Rhodesian Air Force
EFTS	Elementary Flying Training School		TC	Training Command (RCAF)
EGM	Empire Gallantry Medal		T&DE	Test & Development Establishment (RCAF)
EO	Embarkation Officer		T&D Flt	Test & Development Flight (RCAF)
ERFTS	Elementary and Reserve Flying Training		TFU	Telecommunications Flying Unit
	School		THQ CF	Training Headquarters Communications Flight
ETA	Estimated time of arrival		TOC	Taken on Charge
EWS	Electrical and Wireless School		TT	Target Towing
Exp	Experimental		TTF	Target Towing Flight
FA	Flying accident		TTS	Technical Training School
FAA	Fleet Air Arm		UK	United Kingdom
FIS	Flying Instructors School		USAAC	United States Army Air Corps
Flt	Flight		USAAF	United States Army Air Forces
FP	Ferry Pool		USAAFIA	United States Air Forces in Australia
FPP	Ferry Pilot Pool		VR	Volunteer Reserve
FS	Ferry Squadron		WAC	War Assets Corporation
FTS	Flying Training School		WS	Wireless School
GHQ	General Headquarters		W/T	Wireless Telegraphy

Acknowledgements

The compilation of this monograph has necessitated reference to many and varied records. Most of these were accessed at the Public Record Office, The Royal Air Force Museum, the Ministry of Defence Air Historical Branch and the Imperial War Museum and the staffs of these institutions are thanked for their assistance.

Special thanks go to Jim Halley for the great help and encouragement which he gave to the project; his skill at searching out obscure information is second to none. Ray Sturtivant also gave significant help when it was needed.

Over half of all Battles built were sent overseas, most of them for use in the Empire Air Training Scheme and much information was needed from abroad. Assistance was freely and generously given by fellow researchers in Canada, Australia and South Africa.

In Canada the National Aviation Museum made the RCAF Battle aircraft record cards available. These were copied and sent to the UK by Lt Cdr Bob Murray RCN (Ret) and Steve Payne - all 740 of them. Very full information was admirably extracted from the RAAF records by Joe Barr. The SAAF had destroyed their aircraft record cards for the war period but much valuable information was provided by Ken Smy and Dave Becker. For Greece, Andrew Stamatopoulos unearthed some elusive information.

All of these gentlemen made a valuable contribution to this study.

Photographic coverage has been kindly provided mainly from the collections of Philip Jarrett, Bruce Robertson, David Howley, Ray Sturtivant, Dave Vincent, Dennis Thompson, Peter Green and Jennifer Gradidge.

The excellent cover painting is an original specially painted for this book by Alan Vernon showing Battles attacking German pontoon bridges over the Meuse on 14 May 1940, for which we are very grateful.

Colour side views were provided by David Howley.

Index

AIR-BRITAIN - THE INTERNATIONAL ASSOCIATION OF AVIATION HISTORIANS - FOUNDED 1948

For fifty years, Air-Britain has recorded aviation events as they have happened, because today's events are tomorrow's history. In addition, considerable research into the past has been undertaken to provide historians with the background to aviation history. Over 16,000 members have contributed to our aims and efforts in that time and many have become accepted authorities in their own fields.

Every month, *AIR-BRITAIN NEWS* covers the current civil and military scene.

Quarterly, each member receives *AIR-BRITAIN DIGEST* which is a fully-illustrated journal containing articles on various subjects, both past and present.

For those interested in military aviation history, there is the quarterly *AEROMILITARIA* which is designed to delve more deeply into the background of, mainly, British and Commonwealth military aviation than is possible in commercial publications and whose format permits it to be used as components of a filing system which suits the readers' requirements. Also published quarterly is *ARCHIVE*, produced in a similar format to *AEROMILITARIA* but covering civil aviation history in depth on a world-wide basis. Both magazines are well-illustrated by photographs and drawings.

In addition to these regular publications, there are monographs covering type histories, both military and civil, airline fleets, Royal Air Force registers, squadron histories and the civil registers of a large number of countries. Although our publications are available to non-members, prices are considerably lower for members who have priority over non-members when availability is limited. Normally, the accumulated price discounts for which members qualify when buying monographs far exceed the annual subscription rates.

A large team of aviation experts is available to answer members' queries on most aspects of aviation. If you have made a study of any particular subject, you may be able to expand your knowledge by joining those with similar interests. Also available to members are libraries of colour slides and photographs which supply slides and prints at prices considerably lower than those charged by commercial firms.

There are local branches of the Association in Blackpool, Bournemouth, Central Scotland, Exeter, Gwent, Heston, London, Luton, Manchester, Merseyside, North-East England, Rugby, Sheffield, Southampton, South-West Essex, Stansted, W. Cornwall and West Midlands. Overseas in France and the Netherlands.

If you would like to receive samples of Air-Britain magazines, please write to the following address enclosing 50p and stating your particular interests. If you would like only a brochure, please send a stamped self-addressed envelope to the same address (preferably 230 mm by 160 mm or over)

Air-Britain Membership Enquiries (Mil), 1 Rose Cottages, 179 Penn Road, Hazlemere, High Wycombe, Bucks., HP15 7NE

MILITARY AVIATION PUBLICATIONS

Royal Air Force Aircraft series: (prices are for members/non-members and are post-free). Others are currently out of stock.

J1-J9999	(£8.00/£12.00)	K1000-K9999	(see The K File below)	L1000-N9999	(£12.00/£18.00)
P1000-R9999	(£11.00/£14.00)	T1000-V9999	(£12.00/£15.00)	BA100-BZ999	(£6.00/£9.00)
DA100-DZ999	(£5.00/£7.50)	EA100-EZ999	(£5.00/£7.50)	FA100-FZ999	(£5.00/£7.50)
HA100-HZ999	(£6.00/£9.00)	JA100-JZ999	(£6.00/£9.00)	KA100-KZ999	(£6.00/£9.00)
LA100-LZ999	(£7.00/£10.50)	MA199-MZ999	(£8.00/£12.00)	NA100-NZ999	(£8.00/£12.00)
PA100-RZ999	(£10.00/£15.00)	SA100-VZ999	(£6.00/£9.00)		

Type Histories

The Halifax File	(£6.00/£9.00)*	The Lancaster File	(£8.00/£12.00)*	The Washington File	(£2.00/£3.00)*
The Whitley File	(£4.50/£6.75)*	The Typhoon File	(£4.00/£6.00)*	The Stirling File	(£6.00/£9.00)*
The Anson File	(£15.00/£22.50)	The Harvard File	(£7.00/£10.50)	The Hampden File	(£11.00/£16.50)
The Hornet File	(£9.00/£13.50)	The Beaufort File	(£10.00/£15.00)	The Camel File	(£13.00/£19.00)
The Norman-Thompson File (£13.50/£17.00)		The Defiant File	(£12.50/£16.00)	The S E 5 File	(£16.00/£20.00)
		The Hoverfly File	(£16.00/£19.50)		

Hardbacks

The Squadrons of the Royal Air Force and Commonwealth (£15.00/£22.50)
The Squadrons of the Fleet Air Arm (£24.00/£36.00)
Fleet Air Arm Aircraft 1939 - 1945 (£24.00/£36.00)
Royal Navy Shipboard Aircraft Developments 1912 - 1931 (£15.00/£22.50)
Royal Navy Aircraft Serials and Units 1911 - 1919 (£15.00/£22.50)
Central American and Caribbean Air Forces (£12.50/£18.75)
The British Aircraft Specifications File (£20.00/£30.00)
The K File - The Royal Air Force of the 1930s (£23.00/£30.00)
Royal Air Force Flying Training and Support Units (£20.00/£25.99)

Individual Squadron Histories

With Courage and Faith - The History of No.18 Squadron, Royal Air Force (£5.00/£7.50)
Scorpions Sting - The History of No.84 Squadron, Royal Air Force (£11.00/£16.50)
Rise from the East - The History of No.247 Squadron, Royal Air Force (£13.00/£16.50)
United in Effort - The History of No.53 Squadron, Royal Air Force (15.00/£19.00)

The above are available from Air-Britain Sales Department, 5 Bradley Road, Upper Norwood, London SE19 3NT
Access, Visa, Mastercard accepted